XView Programming Manual

The X Window System

The books in the X Window System Series are based in part on the original MIT X Window System documentation, but are far more comprehensive, easy to use, and are loaded with examples, tutorials and helpful hints. Over 20 major computer vendors recommend or license volumes in the series. In short, these are the definitive guides to the X Window System.

Volume 0:
X Protocol Reference Manual

A complete programmer's reference to the X Network Protocol, the language of communication between the X server and the X clients. 498 pages. $30.00.

Volumes 1 and 2:
Xlib Programming Manual
Xlib Reference Manual

Revised for Release 4. Complete guide and reference to programming with the X library (Xlib), the lowest level of programming interface to X. 672 and 792 pages. $60.00 for the set, or $34.95 each.

Volume 3:
X Window System User's Guide

Revised and enlarged for X11 Release 4. Describes window system concepts and the most common client applications available for X11. Includes complete explanation of the new window manager, *twm*, and a chapter on Motif. For experienced users, later chapters explain customizing the X environment. Useful with either Release 3 or Release 4. 749 pages. $30.00.

Volumes 4 and 5:
X Toolkit Intrinsics Programming Manual
X Toolkit Intrinsics Reference Manual

Complete guides to programming with the X Toolkit. The *Programming Manual* provides concepts and examples for using widgets and for the more complex task of writing new widgets. The *Reference Manual* provides reference pages for Xt functions, and Xt and Athena widgets. 582 and 545 pages. $55.00 for the set, or $30.00 each.

Volume 7:
XView Programming Manual

XView is an easy-to-use toolkit that is not just for Sun developers. It is available on MIT's R4 tape and System V Release 4, as well as being a part of Sun's Open Windows package. This manual provides complete information on XView, from concepts to creating applications to reference pages. 566 pages. $30.00.

The X Window System in a Nutshell

For the experienced X programmer, contains essential information from other volumes of the series in a boiled-down, quick reference format that makes it easy to find the answers needed most often. 380 pages. $24.95.

For orders or a free catalog of all our books, please contact us.

O'Reilly & Associates, Inc.

Creators and Publishers of Nutshell Handbooks
632 Petaluma Avenue, Sebastopol, CA 95472
email: uunet!ora!nuts · 1-800-338-6887 · 1-707-829-0515 · FAX 1-707-829-0104

Volume Seven

XView Programming Manual

---

for Version 11 of the X Window System

by Dan Heller

O'Reilly & Associates, Inc.

Revision and Printing History

January 1990: First Printing
April 1990:   Second Printing. Minor revisions.
July 1990:   Second Edition. Reflects Version 2 of the XView Toolkit.

Small Print

ISBN 0-937175-52-8

Table of Contents

Figures

Examples

Tables

Preface

Preface

Preface

XView (**X** Window-System-based **V**isual/**I**ntegrated **E**nvironment for **W**orkstations) is a user-interface toolkit to support interactive, graphics-based applications running under the X Window System. This toolkit, developed by Sun Microsystems, Inc., is derived from earlier toolkits for the SunView™ windowing system. With over 2000 SunView applications in the workstation market, there are many programmers already familiar with SunView application programmer's interface (API). XView makes it possible for SunView applications to enter the up and coming X marketplace.

XView has many advantages for programmers developing new applications in X, such as a mature and proven API based on the development experience of SunView programmers. It features an object-oriented style interface that is straightforward and simple to learn.

Like any X toolkit, XView provides a set of prebuilt, user-interface objects such as canvases, scrollbars, menus and control panels. The appearance and functionality of these objects follow the OPEN LOOK Graphical User Interface (GUI) specification. Jointly developed by Sun Microsystems and AT&T as the graphical user interface standard for System V Release 4, OPEN LOOK provides users with a simple, consistent and efficient interface for performing tasks within an application.

XView is based upon Xlib, the lowest level of the X Window System available to the programmer. While developing XView user interfaces does not require Xlib programming experience, there are good reasons for learning more about Xlib, especially if your application renders graphics.

Please Read This Section!

This manual provides a basic introduction to developing applications using the XView Toolkit. You do not need any knowledge of SunView, and prior experience with the X Window System is helpful, but also not required. Nonetheless, like any complex system, a programmer needs to know a lot to program effectively in XView.

For each functional area in XView, there are chapters that present the basic concepts and suggest some common ways to implement and use a particular function. Also addressed are some snags to watch out for when implementing certain combinations of functions. Care was taken to keep the content of the chapters brief and to the point. Simple and straightforward functions are not discussed in depth. The appendices provide a reference summary of XView, along with longer sample programs.

If you can't figure out how to accomplish a task because it is not documented here, don't despair—that does not mean it cannot be done. Some features in XView are not addressed in this book—especially the more advanced ones. You are encouraged to experiment with the toolkit and discover new ways of using XView.

At this writing, XView is still under development. There are more features to add, more bugs to fix and further design changes to improve existing functionality. We have described the XView Toolkit as accurately as possible, but consult the release notes that accompany your distribution for recent changes. Future editions of this book will incorporate these changes.

How to Use This Manual

The chapters in the book are designed to be read sequentially. However, this is not a strong requirement. Reading ahead probably won't affect your understanding of the material, although later chapters might reference earlier material.

The following paragraphs briefly describe contents of this book:

Chapter 1, *XView and the X Window System*, provides a conceptual overview of the X Window System, the role of the XView Toolkit and the OPEN LOOK graphical user interface. It provides a general introduction to basic X terminology, but it does not go into great detail about X.

Chapter 2, *The XView Programmer's Model*, provides an overview of XView as an object-oriented programming system. The programmer creates and modifies objects that implement the OPEN LOOK interface. This chapter also discusses windows as objects that receive events. It introduces callback functions as the method of registering application-specific event handlers.

Chapter 3, *Creating XView Applications*, begins from the application developer's point of view and explains the basic elements of an XView application. It describes what is involved in initializing XView and creating XView objects such as frames and subwindows.

Chapter 4, *Frames*, explains how to create window frames. There are two basic types of frames: base frames and command frames. Each application has at least one base frame that manages subwindows, panels and other objects. It presents the routines used to create and manage frames.

Chapter 5, *Canvases and Openwin*, presents canvases as the most basic type of subwindow or window pane. It presents the canvas model, which permits a drawing surface larger than what is visible in the canvas subwindow.

Chapter 6, *Handling Input*, explains how events are handled by X, the Notifier and XView objects.

Chapter 7, *Panels*, explains a variety of OPEN LOOK controls that are implemented as items on a control panel. It demonstrates how to create and use contain buttons, check boxes, choices, lists, messages, toggles, text items and sliders. A set of panel attributes controls the behavior in common with all panel items. There are also item-specific attributes.

Chapter 8, *Text Subwindows*, describes how to create a text subwindow and how to use its text editing features.

Chapter 9, *TTY Subwindows*, describes the tty subwindow that performs terminal emulation functions.

Chapter 10, *Scrollbars*, covers the creation and use of scrollbars. A scrollbar is a window attached to another window, such as a canvas or text subwindow or a panel. The scrollbar package only manages the scrollbar; the application must gauge the impact of scrolling on its windows.

Chapter 11, *Menus*, explains how to implement various sorts of pop-up menus.

Chapter 12, *Notices*, explains how pop-up windows serve as notices or dialog boxes.

Chapter 14, *Cursors*, shows various OPEN LOOK pointers and demonstrates their use.

Chapter 13, *Icons*, describes the use of bitmap images as application icons. When an application is closed, or iconified, the application is represented on the screen as an icon.

Chapter 15, *Nonvisual Objects*, describes objects that do not contain windows: Server, Screen and Fullscreen.

Chapter 16, *Fonts*, describes how to load and use fonts from the X server.

Chapter 17, *Resources*, describes the implications of X resources for an XView application. Resources allow individual users to control and customize their environment.

Chapter 18, *The Selection Service*, discusses how XView applications communicate with other applications, including window managers and applications that are not OPEN LOOK compliant. It shows how XView provides for selection and for other functions, as stated by the *Inter-Client Communication Conventions Manual*.

Chapter 19, *The Notifier*, describes the Notifier and advanced event handling. It describes the relationship of the Notifier and X to the host operating system.

Chapter 20, *Color*, discusses issues concerning color in windows and other XView objects.

Chapter 21, *Help and Error Handling*, discusses error handling and Help in XView packages.

Chapter 22, *XView Internals*, discusses the internals to the XView packages and introduces the concepts involved in writing your own packages.

Appendix A, *Attribute Summary*, provides alphabetically arranged descriptions of all attributes.

Appendix B, *Summary of Procedures and Macros*, provides alphabetically arranged descriptions of all procedures and macros.

Appendix C, *Data Types*, lists the data types defined by XView.

Appendix D, *Event Codes*, lists the event codes in numerical order by value.

Appendix E, *Command Line Arguments*, lists the values and defaults for command-line arguments.

Appendix F, *OPEN LOOK User Interface Compliance*, discusses XView's compliance with the *OPEN LOOK GUI Functional Specification*.

Appendix F, *Example Programs*, presents nine supplementary programs.

Assumptions

Readers should be proficient in the C programming language, although examples are provided for infrequently used features of the language that are necessary or useful when programming with X. In addition, general familiarity with the principles of raster graphics is helpful. Finally, if you do not understand how to use Xlib routines to render graphics, then writing useful programs might be difficult, although you should be able to build OPEN LOOK user interfaces easily.

Font Conventions Used in this Manual

Italic is used for:

- UNIX® pathnames, filenames, program names, user command names, and options for user commands.

- New terms where they are introduced.

`Typewriter Font` is used for:

- Anything that would be typed verbatim into code, such as examples of source code and text on the screen.

- XView packages.*

- The contents of include files, such as structure types, structure members, symbols (defined constants and bit flags) and macros.

- XView and Xlib functions.

- Names of subroutines of the example programs.

Italic Typewriter Font is used for:

- Arguments to XView functions, since they could be typed in code as shown but are arbitrary.

---

*When referring to all members of a particular package, such as CANVAS, the notation CANVAS_* will be used. This should not be interpreted as a C-language pointer construct.

Helvetica Italics are used for:

- Titles of examples, figures and tables.

Boldface is used for:

- Chapter and section headings.

Related Documents

The C Programming Language by B. W. Kernighan and D. M. Ritchie

The following documents are included on the X11 source tape:

OPEN LOOK Graphical User Interface Functional Specification

OPEN LOOK Graphical User Interface Style Guide

The following books in the X Window System series from O'Reilly and Associates, Inc. are currently available:

Volume Zero — *X Protocol Reference Manual*
Volume One — *Xlib Programming Manual*
Volume Two — *Xlib Reference Manual*
Volume Three — *X Window System User's Guide*
Volume Four — *X Toolkit Intrinsics Programming Manual*
Volume Five — *X Toolkit Intrinsics Reference Manual*
Volume Six — *X Toolkit Widgets Reference Manual* (available summer 1990)
Quick Reference — *The X Window System in a Nutshell*

Requests For Comments

Please write to tell us about any flaws you find in this manual or how you think it could be improved, to help us provide you with the best documentation possible.

Our U.S. mail address, phone numbers and e-mail addresses are as follows:

O'Reilly and Associates, Inc.
632 Petaluma Avenue
Sebastopol, CA 95472
in USA 1-800-338-6887, in CA 1-800-533-6887,
international +1 707-829-0515

UUCP: uunet!ora!xview   Internet: xview@ora.UU.NET

Acknowledgements

I always wanted to do this—but for my first *record album!* : −)

This book was influenced by an amalgamation of several sources: *The SunView Programmer's Manual* for design and structure of the chapters, the people on the XView development team at Sun Microsystems for technical detail and the latest up-to-the-minute changes, and my personal experience in programming for narrative content. Chapter 1, *XView and the X Window System*, is based on Chapter 1 of Volume Four, *X Toolkit Intrinsics Programming Manual*, by Adrian Nye.

This book was created using SoftQuad's *sqtroff*™, a PostScript™ laser printer and a Sun 3/60 color workstation.

Special thanks to everyone at O'Reilly & Associates for their diligent efforts. In particular, Dale Dougherty, Daniel Gilly, Laurel Katz, Lenny Muellner, Chris Reilley, Ruth Terry, and Sue Willing. Many others pitched in for the final push to complete this book.

At Sun Microsystems, I'd like to thank Richard Probst who helped make this entire project possible, Tom Jacobs, for keeping everything in order and reading *all that e-mail*, Tony Hillman and the rest of the reviewing squad.

Also, Bart Schaefer, for taking care of Mush while I've been too busy. Mike Ilnicki for continuing to play racquetball with me. Penguin's frozen yogurt for nutrition. David Letterman for being on at the perfect time: dinner.

...and most of all, I'd like to thank Tim O'Reilly—the only one who could talk me, a cast-in-stone programmer, into trying my hand at technical writing. Thanks for the confidence in me.

1

XView and the X Window System

In This Chapter:

1
XView and the X Window System

The XView Toolkit allows a programmer to build the interface to an application without having to learn many of the details of the underlying windowing system. However, it is valuable to have some understanding of X before attempting to build applications under XView. This chapter introduces many of the most important concepts on which the X Window System is based and describes the computing environment for X applications. It also describes the role of the XView Toolkit in the X Window System.

For the most part, this chapter assumes that you are new to programming the X Window System. This chapter describes the basics of the X Window System—further details will be described as necessary later in the manual. However, this book does not repeat the detailed description of Xlib programming found in Volume One, *Xlib Programming Manual*. If you already have some experience programming the X Window System, you might wish to begin at Chapter 2, *The XView Programmer's Model*.

1.1 The X Window System

X controls a bit-mapped display in which every pixel (dot on the screen) is individually controllable. This allows drawing of pictures in addition to text. Until recently, individual control of screen pixels was widely available only on personal computers (PCs) and high-priced technical workstations, while more general-purpose machines were limited to output on text-only terminals. X brings the same world of graphic output to both PCs and more powerful machines. Figure 1-1 shows an X application in comparison with a traditional text terminal.

Like other windowing systems, X divides the screen into multiple input and output areas called windows, each of which can act as an independent *virtual terminal*. Using a terminal emulator, windows can run ordinary text-based applications. However, windows can also run applications designed to take advantage of the graphic power of the bitmapped display.

X takes user input from a *pointer*, which is usually a mouse but could just as well be a trackball or tablet. The pointer allows the user to point at certain graphics on the screen and use the buttons on the mouse to control a program without using the keyboard. This method of using programs is often easier to learn than traditional keyboard control, because it is more intuitive. Figure 1-2 shows a typical pointer being used to select a menu item.

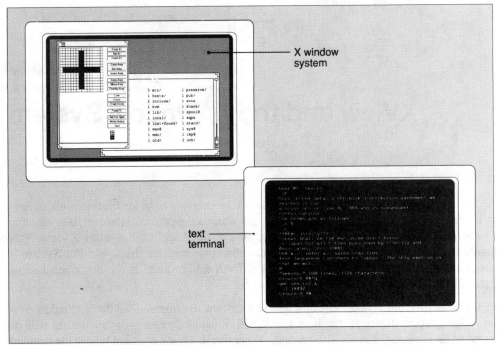

Figure 1-1. An X application and a traditional text terminal

Of course, X also handles keyboard input. The pointer is used to direct the input focus of the keyboard (often called the *keyboard focus*) from window to window with only one application at a time able to receive keyboard input.

In X, as in many other window systems, each application need not (and in fact usually does not) consist of only a single window. Any part of an application can have its own separate window, simplifying the management of input and output within the application code. Such *child* windows are only visible within the confines of their parent window. Each window has its own coordinate system where the origin is the upper-left corner of the window inside its border. In basic X, windows are rectangular and oriented along the same axes as the edges of the display. The application or the user can change the dimensions of windows.

Many of the above characteristics are also true of several other window systems. What has made X a standard is that X is based on a network protocol—a predefined set of requests and replies—instead of system-specific procedure calls. The *X Protocol* can be implemented for different computer architectures and operating systems, making X device-independent. Another advantage of a network-based windowing system is that programs can run on one architecture while displaying on another. Because of this unique design, the X Window System can make a network of different computers cooperate. For example, a computationally-intensive application might run on a supercomputer but take input from and display output on a workstation across a network.

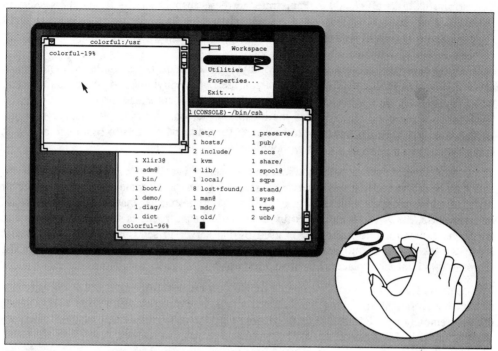

Figure 1-2. Selecting a menu item with the pointer

1.1.1 The Server and Client

To allow programs to be run on one machine and display on another, X was designed as a network protocol between two processes, one of which is an application program called a *client*, and the other, the *server*. The server is a resource server, controlling a user's resources (such as the display hardware, keyboard and pointer) and making these resources available to user applications. In other words, the X server isolates the device-specific code from the application.

The server performs the following tasks:

- Allows access to the display by multiple clients. The server can deny access from clients running on certain machines.

- Interprets network messages from clients and acts on them. These messages are known as requests. Some requests command the server to do two-dimensional drawing or move windows, while others ask the server for information.

- Passes user input to clients sending network messages known as events, which represent key or button presses, pointer motion and so forth. Events are generated asynchronously, and events from different devices might be intermingled. The server must de-multiplex the event stream and pass the appropriate events to each client.

- Maintains complex data structures, including windows and fonts, so that the server can perform its tasks efficiently. Clients refer to these abstractions by ID numbers. Server-maintained abstractions reduce the amount of data that has to be maintained by each client and the amount of data that has to be transferred over the network.

In X, the term *display* is often used as a synonym for server, as is the combined term *display server*. However, the terms *display* and *screen* are not synonymous. A screen is the actual piece of hardware on which the graphics are drawn. Both color and monochrome displays are supported. A server might control more than one screen. For example, one server might control a color screen and a monochrome screen for a user who wants to be able to debug an application on both types of screens without leaving his or her seat.

The communication path between a client and the server is called a *connection*. Several clients may be connected to a single server. Clients may run on the same machine as the server if that machine supports multitasking, or clients may run on other machines in the network. In either case, the X Protocol is used by the client to send requests to draw graphics or to query the server for information; it is used by the server to send user input or replies to requests back to the client. All communication from the client to the server and from the server to the client takes place using the X Protocol.*

It is common for a user to have programs running on several different hosts in the network, all invoked from and displaying their windows on a single screen (see Figure 1-3). Clients running remotely can be started from the remote machine or from the local machine using the network utilities *rlogin* or *rsh*.

This use of the network is known as *distributed processing*. The most important application of this concept is to provide graphic output for powerful systems that cannot have built-in graphics capabilities. However, distributed processing can also help solve the problem of unbalanced system loads. When one host machine is overloaded, the users running clients on that machine can arrange for programs to run on other hosts.

1.2 The Software Hierarchy

There are many different ways to write X applications because X is not restricted to a single language, operating system or user interface. The only requirement of an X application is that it generate and receive X Protocol messages.

Figure 1-4 shows the layering of software in an X application. Xlib is the lowest-level C language interface to X. The main task of Xlib is to translate C data structures and procedures into X Protocol events; it then sends them off and receives protocol packets in return that are unpacked into C data structures. Xlib provides full access to the capabilities of the X Protocol but does little to make programming easier. It handles the interface between an application and the network and includes some optimizations that encourage efficient network

---

*The X Protocol is independent of the networking hardware and runs on top of any network that provides point-to-point packet communication. TCP/IP and DECnet are the only networks currently supported. For more information about the X Protocol, see Volume Zero, *The X Protocol Reference Manual*.

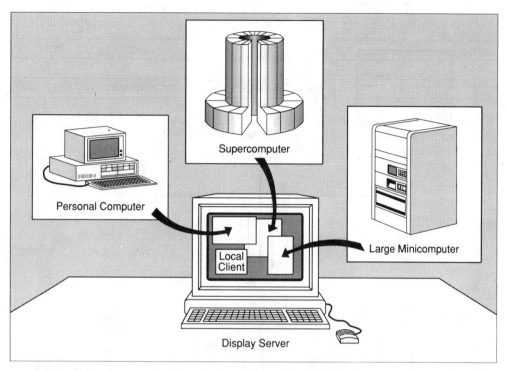

Figure 1-3. Applications can run on any system across the network

usage. The list of functions that Xlib performs is so extensive that if the programmer were responsible for handling all these pieces directly, application programs would be too large and prone to performance degradation and potential bugginess. For this reason, *toolkits* are used to modularize the more common functions that handle the user interface portion of an application.

XView is one of a half-dozen or so toolkits available for the X Window System. If you are familiar with other toolkits, you will recognize that the XView Toolkit is equivalent to the Xt Intrinsics and a widget set. Like the Intrinsics, XView is built upon Xlib. It is an object-oriented toolkit that provides reusable, configurable user interface components, equivalent to widgets.*

Toolkits handle many things for the programmer. They provide a framework for combining prebuilt user interface components with application-specific code. For example, if the application needs to prompt the user for a filename, a toolkit should provide a component (a *command frame*) that is functionally capable of displaying the query to the user and providing the user's response to the application.

---

*Widget sets are sometimes loosely referred to as toolkits. However, a toolkit comprises the functions of the Xt Intrinsics layer and one widget set (e.g., the Athena widget set). There are several different widget sets from various vendors that are designed to work with Xt. For more information on Xt Intrinsics-based toolkits, see Volume Four, *X Toolkit Intrinsics Programming Manual*.

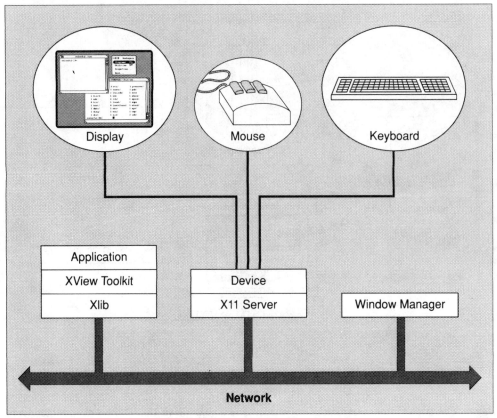

Figure 1-4. The software architecture of X applications

Any user interface component also needs to manage the interpretation of events delivered from the window system. When events are generated, the toolkit decides whether or not to propagate the event to the application or to use it for its own internal purposes. To continue the example, when the user types a filename in the command frame, events are generated in which the interface must decide whether that object should interpret the input or whether it should be sent to the application. A toolkit thus comprises a mechanism to dispatch events and a set of prebuilt interface objects that define the look and feel of an application.

Note that using a toolkit does not preclude calling Xlib directly to accomplish certain tasks such as drawing. In XView, graphics rendering is done most efficiently by using Xlib drawing routines, for instance.

1.3 Extensions to X

Another thing to know about X is that it is *extensible*. The code includes a defined mechanism for incorporating extensions, so that vendors are not forced to modify the existing system in incompatible ways when adding features. An extension requires an additional piece of software on the server side and an additional library at the same level as Xlib on the client side. After an initial query to see whether the server portion of the extension software is installed, these extensions are used just like Xlib routines and perform at the same level.

Among the extensions currently being developed are support for 2-D spline curves, for 3D graphics and for Display PostScript™. These extensions can be used in toolkit applications just like Xlib can.

1.4 The Window Manager

Because multiple applications can be running simultaneously, rules must exist for arbitrating conflicting demands for input. For example, does keyboard input automatically go to whichever window the pointer is in or must the user explicitly select a window for keyboard input?

Unlike most window systems, X itself makes no rules about this kind of thing. Instead, there is a special client called the *window manager* that manages the positions and sizes of the main windows of applications on a server's display. The window manager is just another client, but by convention, it is given special responsibility to mediate competing demands for the physical resources of a display including screen space, color resources and the keyboard. The window manager allows the user to move windows around on the screen, resize them and usually start new applications. The window manager also defines much of the visible behavior of the window system, such as whether windows are allowed to overlap or are tiled (side by side), and whether the keyboard focus simply follows the pointer from window to window or whether the user must click a pointer button in a window to change the keyboard focus (click-to-type).

Applications are required to give the window manager certain information that helps the window manager mediate competing demands for screen space or other resources. For example, an application specifies its preferred size and size increments. These are known as *window manager hints* because the window manager is not required to honor them. The XView Toolkit provides an easy way for applications to set the window manager hints.

The conventions for interaction with the window manager and with other clients have been standardized by the X Consortium as of July 1989 in a manual called the *Inter-Client Communications Conventions Manual* (ICCCM, for short). The ICCCM provides basic policy intentionally omitted from X itself, such as the rules for transferring data between applications (selections), transfer of keyboard focus, layout schemes, colormap installation and so on. As long as applications and window managers follow the conventions set out in the ICCCM, applications created with different toolkits will be able to coexist and work together on the same server. Toolkit applications should be immune to the effects of the change from earlier conventions.

1.5 Handling Events

The window that X provides is the connection between the XView application and the X server. The reason X windows are important to XView is that these windows are the input targets for the user's focus. They are the actual objects that get events from the user and pass the events through to the XView world.

An X *event* is a data structure sent by the server that describes something that just happened that is of interest to the application. The sources of events are the user's input, the window system, the operating system and the application programs. For example, the user's pressing a key on the keyboard or clicking a mouse button generates an event, and a window's being moved on the screen also generates events if it changes the visible portions of other applications. It is the server's job to distribute events to the various windows on the screen.

In XView, between the server and the application, there is an event dispatch mechanism called the Notifier, as shown in Figure 1-5.

After the set-up phase of the application, where you create XView objects such as buttons or scrollbars and determine how they will interact with your application code, you have several choices for input distribution. The simplest method is to hand off control of your application to XView. From then on, the XView Notifier automatically distributes events to the objects created by the application. These objects process many events internally so that your application does not need to get involved.

The key point is that your application is only told about events for which it specifically requested to be notified. By responding to these events, the application can perform its tasks. For example, if the user types the letter *A* in a window, X will pass the event to XView, which in turn can pass it to the application. An application's event handler can interpret this event and display the letter typed in the window. Finally, control returns to the top level so the next event can be read. This is a typical cycle of events that happens for each event generated by the user.

If the application created a scrollbar, then it would track certain events, such as when the scroll button is pressed. XView actually sends a request to the X server to create the X window that will become part of the scrollbar object. In the application's request, it can ask to be notified about or to ignore certain user events in the X window created.

The window system dictates which window gets an event. If the window currently has the keyboard focus and that window does not want to process the event, it has the option of throwing away the event or dropping it to the window below it. This is usually the parent of the window. For instance, if a panel item gets a keyboard press (the user typed an *A*) and if the panel item does not want to deal with the event, then the panel item might be configured so that the event is passed to the item's parent: the panel itself.

The Notifier does not just do input distribution; it also allows selection of different input sources. In addition to handling window system events, your application can also handle a number of interrupts that might be generated by the operating system. Your application can respond to signals, input on a file descriptor and interval timers. You could also pass events between clients in the same process, interpose on a Notifier client to change its behavior, and receive notification on the death of a child process which you have spawned. The use of

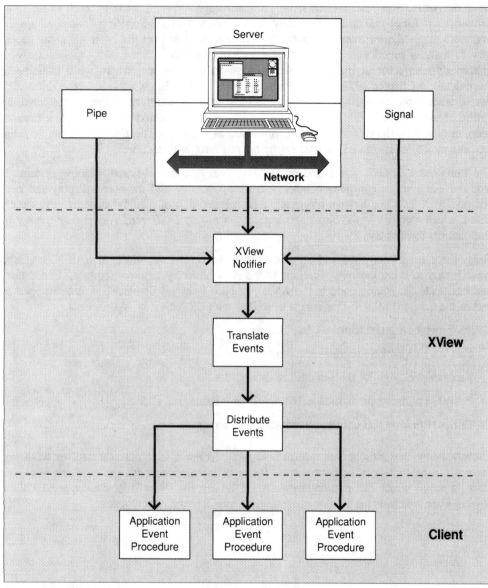

Figure 1-5. The Notifier exists between the server and the XView application

some of these input sources requires you to call the Notifier directly. The Notifier is covered again in the next two chapters as well as in Chapter 19, *The Notifier*.

1.6 Development of the XView Toolkit

Over the years, Sun Microsystems, Inc. has developed several toolkits, each more well-defined, more functional and aesthetically superior than the last. SunView 1 was perhaps the first well-accepted user interface toolkit Sun provided. It had all the basic elements necessary to make a functional user interface—including a well-defined API (application programmer's interface). It introduced the attribute-value interface, which we'll examine in more detail in Chapter 2, *The XView Programmer's Model*. It has very few procedure calls. For instance, you use a single function to create all user interface objects. You have the option of using default values, in which case the object is created with only a few lines of code, or of setting the values of specific attributes as required. These attributes can be set at the time the object is created, or later on, by using a different function.

The SunView 1 Toolkit was based on SunWindows™, a kernel-based window system. It required that a single computer control both the application and the user's display and keyboard. The X Window System represents a new generation of window systems. It is server-based, which means that the client application can run on a different system than the server that controls the display.

Today there are several thousand SunView applications, and one of the aims of XView is to make it easy to bring those applications to the X Window System marketplace. In addition, Sun has made the source code to the XView Toolkit freely available. It will be shipped as part of the standard MIT X distribution as well as with UNIX System V Release 4.

XView provides a set of windows that include:

- *Canvases* on which programs can draw.

- *Text subwindows* with built-in editing capabilities.

- *Panels* containing items such as buttons, choice items, and sliders.

- *TTY subwindows* that emulate character-based terminals.

These windows are arranged as *subwindows* within *frames*, which are themselves windows. Frames can be transitory or permanent. Transient interactions with the user can also take place in *menus* which can pop up anywhere on the screen. We will look more at all XView objects when we cover the XView programming model in the next chapter.

1.7 OPEN LOOK Graphical User Interface

An important feature of the XView Toolkit is that it implements the OPEN LOOK Graphical User Interface (GUI). The OPEN LOOK GUI aims to provide users with a simple, consistent and efficient interface. An example of an OPEN LOOK workspace is shown in Figure 1-6. OPEN LOOK is supported by Sun and AT&T as the graphical user interface standard for System V Release 4. Users and developers benefit from a standard because it ensures consistent behavior across a number of diverse applications. Programmers can concentrate on the design of the application without having to "invent" a user interface.

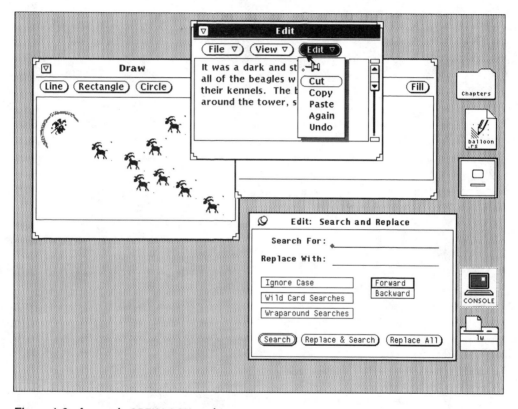

Figure 1-6. A sample OPEN LOOK workspace

A well-defined user interface should be generalized enough so that it can be implemented on any operating system, windowing system or graphics display. Because OPEN LOOK is not bound by any of these constraints, XView was built based entirely on specifications that could be mapped easily into the X Window System.

The visual design of OPEN LOOK is restrained. The design of each component in the user interface is simple and uncomplicated. The interface is based on a few simple concepts that result in a system that is easy to learn initially. And an XView application is relatively simple and easy to implement because many of the default values of interface components are adequate for most applications.

We will attempt to summarize the OPEN LOOK interface where appropriate in this document. However, the definitive document on OPEN LOOK for application programmers is the *OPEN LOOK Graphical User Interface Style Guide*. This book provides guidelines for developers on using the elements of the OPEN LOOK GUI in applications. Where appropriate, we will show examples, such as Figure 1-6, which are taken from the *OPEN LOOK GUI Specification Guide*.

2

The XView Programmer's Model

In This Chapter:

2
The XView Programmer's Model

XView is intended to simplify application development under the X Window System by providing the programmer with a set of predefined user interface components. These components implement the "look and feel" of the OPEN LOOK Graphical User Interface, developed by Sun Microsystems, Inc. and AT&T.

This chapter presents a model of XView for the programmer. It is important to understand this model before you begin writing XView applications. However, you might wish to skim the concepts presented in this chapter and proceed to Chapter 3, *Creating XView Applications*, to examine sample programs.

2.1 Object-oriented Programming

To the programmer, XView is an *object-oriented* toolkit. XView objects can be considered building blocks from which the user interface of the application is assembled. Each piece can be considered an *object* from a particular *package*. Each package provides a list of properties from which you can choose to configure the object. By selecting objects from the available packages, you can build the user interface for an application.

XView is based on several of the fundamental principles of object-oriented programming:

- Objects are represented in a class hierarchy.

- Objects are opaque data types.

- Objects have attributes which can be set via message passing functions.

- Objects may have callback procedures that are triggered by events. We will look at how these concepts are implemented in XView in the sections that follow.

2.1.1 Object Class Hierarchy

XView defines classes of objects in a tree hierarchy. For example, *frame* is a subclass of the more general class *window*, which in turn is a subclass of *drawable*. Drawable, like user interface object classes, is a subclass of the *Generic Object* class. Figure 2-1 shows the XView class hierarchy and the relationships between the classes. Each class has identifying features that make it unique from other classes or packages. In XView, a class is often called a *package*, meaning a set of related functional elements. However, there are XView packages that are not members of the object class hierarchy, such as the Notifier package.

Some objects are visual and others are not. Visual objects include windows, scrollbars, frames, panels and panel items, among others. Nonvisual objects are objects which have no appearance, per se, but they have information which aids in the display of visual objects. Examples of nonvisual objects include the server, screen and font objects. The screen, for example, provides information such as the type of color it can display or the default foreground and background colors that objects might inherit. The display can provide information about what fonts are available for objects that display text.

All objects, both visual and nonvisual, are a part of this object classing system. The system is extensible, so you can create new classes that might or might not be based on existing classes.

XView uses static subclassing and chained inheritance as part of its object-oriented model. All objects of a particular class inherit the properties of the parent class (also known as a superclass). The Generic Object XV_OBJECT contains certain basic properties that all objects share. For example, the same object can appear in many places on the screen to optimize storage. To keep a record of this, the Generic Object maintains a reference count of its instances. Since all objects have an owner, the parent of the object is stored in a field of the generic part of the object. As the needs of an object get more specific to a particular look or functionality, lower-level classes define properties to implement it.

Each class contains properties that are shared among all instances of that object. For example, *panels* are a part of the PANEL package, which has properties that describe, among other things, its layout (horizontal or vertical) or the spacing between items (buttons) in the panel. All panels share these properties, even though the state of the properties might differ for each instance of the object.

As mentioned earlier, XView uses subclassing so that each package can inherit the properties of its superclass. The PANEL package is subclassed from the WINDOW package, which has properties specific to all windows, such as window dimensions, location on the screen, border thickness, depth, visual and colormap information. The WINDOW package is subclassed from the root object XV_OBJECT, as are all objects, and the panel can access generic information such as the size and position of itself.

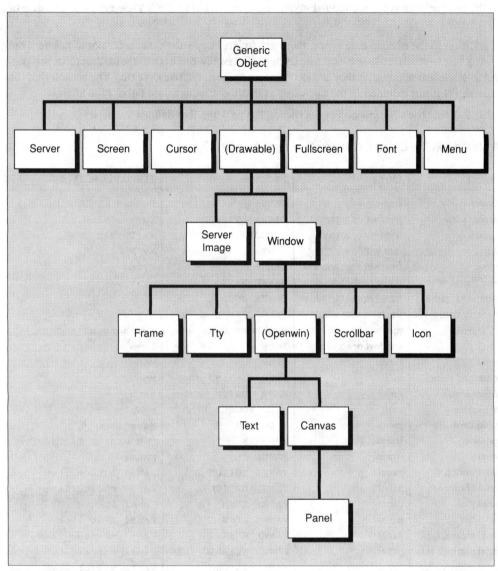

Figure 2-1. XView class hierarchy

2.1.2 Object Handles

When you create an object, the XView function returns a *handle* for the object. Later, when you wish to manipulate the object or inquire about its state, you pass its handle to the appropriate function. This reliance on object handles is a way of *information-hiding*. The handles are *opaque* in the sense that you cannot see through them to the actual data structure which represents the object.

Each object type has a corresponding type of handle. Since C does not have an opaque type, all the opaque data types mentioned above are typedef'd to the XView type Xv_opaque or Xv_object.

In addition to the opaque data types, there are several typedefs that refer not to pointers but to structures: Event, Rect and Rectlist. Generally pointers to these structures are passed to XView functions, so they are declared as Event *, Rect *, etc. The reason that the asterisk (*) is not included in the typedef is that the structures are publicly available.

Table 2-1 lists each XView object, its owner, the package that defines it, and its data type:

Table 2-1. XView Objects, Owners, Packages and Data Types

Object	Owner	Package	Handle Data Type
canvas	frame	CANVAS	Canvas
canvas view	window or screen	CANVAS_VIEW	Canvas_view
cursor	window or screen	CURSOR	Xv_Cursor
font	root window	FONT	Xv_Font
frame	frame or root window	FRAME	Frame
base frame	frame or root window	FRAME_BASE	
command frame	frame or root window	FRAME_CMD	
property frame	frame or root window	FRAME_PROPS	
fullscreen	root window	FULLSCREEN	Fullscreen
icon	window or screen	ICON	Icon
menu	server	MENU	Menu
command menu	null	MENU_COMMAND_MENU	Menu
choice menu	null	MENU_CHOICE_MENU	Menu
toggle menu	null	MENU_TOGGLE_ITEM	Menu
menu item	menu	MENUITEM	Menu_item
openwin	frame	OPENWIN	Openwin
panel	frame	PANEL	Panel
panel button	panel	PANEL_BUTTON	Panel_button_item
panel choice	panel	PANEL_CHOICE	Panel_choice_item
panel item	panel	PANEL_ITEM	Panel_item
panel list	panel	PANEL_LIST	Panel_list_item
panel message	panel	PANEL_MESSAGE	Panel_message_item
panel numeric text	panel	PANEL_NUMERIC_TEXT	Panel_numeric_text_item
panel slider	panel	PANEL_SLIDER	Panel_slider_item
panel text	panel	PANEL_TEXT	Panel_text_item
screen	null	SCREEN	Screen
scrollbar	panel or canvas	SCROLLBAR	Scrollbar
server	null	SERVER	Server
server image	screen	SERVER_IMAGE	Server_image
text subwindow	frame	TEXTSW	Textsw
tty	frame	TTY	Tty
window	frame	WINDOW	Xv_Window

2.2 Attribute-based Functions

A model such as that used by XView, which is based on complex and flexible objects, presents the problem of how the client is to manipulate the objects. The basic idea behind the XView interface is to provide a small number of functions, which take as arguments a large set of *attributes*. For a given call to create or modify an object, only a subset of the set of all applicable attributes will be of interest.

2.2.1 Creating and Manipulating Objects

There is a common set of functions that allows the programmer to manipulate any object by referencing the object handle. The functions are listed in Table 2-2:

Table 2-2. Generic Functions

Function	Role
xv_init()	Establishes the connection to the server, initializes the Notifier and the Defaults/Resource-Manager database, loads the Server Resource-Manager database, and reads the *˜/.Xdefaults* database and any passed attributes.
xv_create()	Creates an object.
xv_destroy()	Destroys an object.
xv_find()	Finds an object that meets certain criteria; or if the object doesn't exist, creates it.
xv_get()	Gets the value of an attribute.
xv_set()	Sets the value of an attribute.

Using these six routines, objects can be created and manipulated from all packages available in XView. When the programmer wants to create an instance of an object from a certain package, the routine xv_create() is used. For example:

```
Panel panel;
panel = xv_create(panel_parent, PANEL, NULL);
```

Here, an instance of a panel has been created from the PANEL package. All its attributes are set to the panel's *default* properties because no object-specific attributes have been specified. A handle to the new panel object is returned and stored in the variable panel. This handle is not a pointer and does not contain any useful information about the object itself.

The next section goes into detail about the use of xv_set() and xv_get(). Chapter 3, *Creating XView Applications*, discusses the use of xv_init(), xv_destroy() and xv_find().

2.2 Changing Object Attributes

The programmer uses the handle returned from the `xv_create()` function as a parameter to the functions `xv_get()` and `xv_set()` to get and set attributes of the object.

```
panel = xv_create(...)
xv_set(panel, PANEL_LAYOUT, PANEL_HORIZONTAL, NULL);
```

Here, the handle to the panel (`panel`) is used to change a `PANEL` package attribute, `PANEL_LAYOUT`, whose value is set to `PANEL_HORIZONTAL`. The attribute and value form an *attribute-value pair*. The functions `xv_create()`, `xv_destroy()`, `xv_find()`, `xv_set()` and, to some extent, `xv_get()` use attribute-value pairs. The functions can have any number of pairs associated with the function call. These *variable argument lists* are always terminated by a `NULL` pointer as the last argument in the list. Note that `NULL`, not the constant 0 (zero), should be used as the terminating argument.

The effect of this function call is to change the layout of the panel from the previous value, whatever it might be, to horizontal.

2.2.3 Types of Attributes

Attributes can be divided into three categories. Those that apply to all XView objects are termed *generic* attributes. Attributes that are supported by many, but not all objects, are termed *common* attributes. Attributes that are associated with a particular package or class of objects are called *specific* attributes.

XView uses naming conventions to simplify the identification of the task of an attribute. Those attributes that apply to a specific package have their name prefixed by the package name. The attributes have prefixes that indicate the type of object they apply to, i.e., CAN-VAS_*, CURSOR_*, FRAME_*, ICON_*, MENU_*, PANEL_*, SCROLLBAR_*, TEXTSW_*, TTY_*, etc.

Common and generic attributes apply to several different object types and are prefixed by XV_. For example, the generic attribute `XV_HEIGHT` applies to all objects since all objects must have a height. In contrast, attributes that apply only to windows are prefixed by WIN_. Attributes such as `WIN_HEIGHT` and `WIN_WIDTH` apply to all windows regardless of whether they happen to be panels or canvases.

The value part of an attribute-value pair can differ from attribute to attribute. The reason for this is that the attribute may describe a wide range of values. If the attribute describes the height or width of an object, the value associated with the attribute will be an integer. However, sometimes the attribute requires a variable-length list of values—this too must be `NULL`-terminated.

Look at the following code fragment that specifies an attribute-value list at the creation of a panel item:

```
Panel_item panel_item;
panel_item = xv_create(panel, PANEL_CYCLE,
    XV_WIDTH,                50,
    XV_HEIGHT,               25,
    PANEL_LABEL_X,           100,
    PANEL_LABEL_Y,           100,
    PANEL_LABEL_STRING,      "Open File"
    PANEL_CHOICE_STRINGS,    "Append to file",
                             "Overwrite contents",
                             NULL,
    NULL);
```

All the attributes except PANEL_CHOICE_STRINGS take a single value. The PANEL_CHOICE_STRINGS attribute takes a list of strings, and that list is NULL-terminated. The last NULL terminates the list of attribute-value pairs passed to the xv_create() function.

Don't worry for now what each of these attributes does. Simply notice the mixture of generic attributes (XV_WIDTH and XV_HEIGHT) and class-specific attributes (all the PANEL_* attributes). Because all packages are subclasses of the XV_OBJECT package, the XV_* attributes can be used with all xv_create() calls.

2.3 Internal Attribute-Value Lists

For a discussion of the way that XView handles attribute-value lists internally, see Chapter 22, *XView Internals*. The subject is important for those who wish to write XView extensions or utilize the advanced features of the error package, but programmers interested in general XView programming usage can skip that chapter.

2.4 Types of Objects

The following section describes on a conceptual level the different types of objects that XView offers. In many cases, figures taken from the *OPEN LOOK GUI Specification Guide* are used to show the appearance of the object. Details about the objects themselves, how to create them, their properties, their default values and so forth are discussed in later chapters that are specific to those object packages. A list of the objects that can be created include:

- Generic Objects
- Windows
- Frames
- Openwins
- Canvases
- Text Windows

- Menus
- Scrollbars

2.4.1 Generic Objects

The Generic Object is the root object of the class hierarchy. One never creates an instance of a Generic Object because, by itself, it has no function. Figure 2-2 shows the path taken when an object is created.

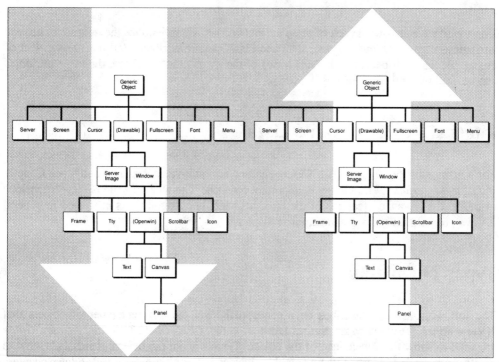

Figure 2-2. Object creation is top down; attribute setting is bottom up

First, the Generic Object is created; then the subclass of that object is created all the way down until the object class of the type of object desired is created. At that point, a complete instance of the object has been created with all the default properties of the classes set. If there were any attribute-value pairs specified in the xv_create() call, those attributes are set in reverse order—the attributes specific to the class of the instance of the object are set first, followed by its parent's class attributes and so on, until the generic attributes are set.

Consider the code below, which creates a panel:

```
extern xv_font font;
Panel panel;

panel = xv_create(frame, PANEL,
                  XV_Y,        5,
                  WIN_HEIGHT,  50,
                  PANEL_FONT,  font,
                  NULL);
```

When the panel is created, the first thing created is a generic object. Next a window instance is created, followed by a panel object. Each is created with the default properties of the object specific to each class.

Here, the reverse traversal takes place, and the attributes specified in the xv_create() call for each class are set to override the default properties inherited from the class. First, the panel package attributes are set. The panel's default font is controlled by the attribute PANEL_FONT; its assigned value, *font*, must be previously initialized. Then the window package attributes are set. The panel's window width is controlled by the attribute WIN_WIDTH which is not explicitly set, so its assigned value defaults to WIN_EXTEND_TO_EDGE. This value indicates that the width of the window should always be the width of its parent. The height of the window, however, is specified. So the window package sets the height to be 50 pixels.

Finally, the generic attributes are set. The panel's *x* and *y* location, indicating where it should be placed within its parent, is controlled by setting the XV_X and XV_Y attributes. The example sets the *y* position only; the *x* position is not set because the window package is told to extend the width of the panel to the edges of its parent. The parent in this case is the object frame (which is presumed to be from the FRAME package).

2.4.2 Window Objects

Many XView objects contain X windows in order to display themselves and receive events. Examples include frames, tty windows, scrollbars and icons.

The XView window class, like the Generic Object class, is a hidden class: a *window* object is never explicitly created. Rather, an object that is a subclass of the window class is created. This includes most visual objects with the exception of panel items.

Nonvisual objects are so named because they do not contain, or are not a subclass of, windows. Fonts, for example, are displayed in windows, or in a memory image or somewhere that contains a bitmap, but fonts do not contain or require windows to be used.

Some attributes of windows include depth (XV_DEPTH), the border width around their perimeter (WIN_BORDER_WIDTH) as well as foreground and background colors.

2.4.3 Frames and Subframes

There are two kinds of frames:

- *Base Frames*

- *Pop-up Frames*

With one exception, all frames are free-floating windows that contain subwindows that are bound by the frame and tiled (they do not overlap one another). Base frames reside on the root window and are not constrained by any other window, though all frames can overlap one another. The base frame is also known as the application's frame. (More than one base frame may be associated with an application.) Subframes are frames whose owner is a frame; they are controlled by the base frames of the application. For example, extraneous dialog boxes (subframes) will go away if the main application's base frame is *iconified* (closed). Figure 2-3 shows an example of a fully featured base frame from the *OPEN LOOK GUI Specification Guide*.

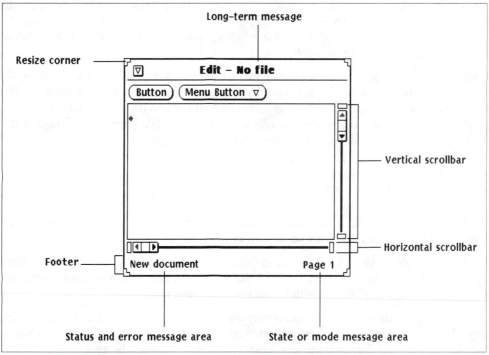

Figure 2-3. Fully-featured base frame (includes optional elements)

Chapter 4, *Frames*, goes into more detail about the elements of a frame and how to set attributes and override default values. It should be noted that many features of the frame are attributes of the window manager. Figure 2-3 assumes an OPEN LOOK-compliant window manager; if another window manager is used, base frames might not look the same. XView defines attributes that give hints to the window manager to provide such features as title bar information, resize corners and so on. If a non-OPEN LOOK window manager is used, there is no guarantee that these attributes will have any effect.

Pop-up frames are typically used to perform one or more transient functions. They are not intended to stay up after the set of functions has been completed, although they might remain up if the user or the application so chooses. This functionality can be handled by a pushpin at the upper-left corner of the frame. There are different kinds of pop-up frames:

Command Frames give operands and set parameters needed for a command. This is implemented as a subframe that contains a default panel.

Help Frames display help text for the object under the pointer. This is implemented as a text subwindow within a subframe.

Notices are special pop-up windows that are used to confirm requests, to display messages and conditions that must be brought to the user's attention and handled immediately. These require immediate attention and suspend the application by disallowing the focus from leaving the Notice.

Figure 2-4 shows a sample unpinned command frame from the *OPEN LOOK GUI Specification Guide*.

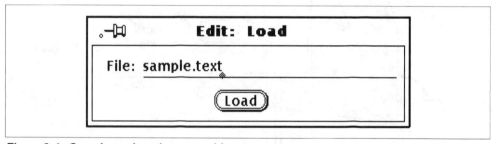

Figure 2-4. Sample unpinned command frame

The user may select the option, and the frame will be *dismissed* (be undisplayed). The pushpin at the upper-left corner is out of its hole. If the pushpin were in, the command frame would remain visible even after the user selects an action to take. Figure 2-5 shows a sample pinned help frame from the *OPEN LOOK GUI Specification Guide*.

Figure 2-6 shows a sample notice from the *OPEN LOOK GUI Specification Guide*.

The user can do nothing but choose either Save or Cancel. Choosing either one will cause the notice to be dismissed immediately.

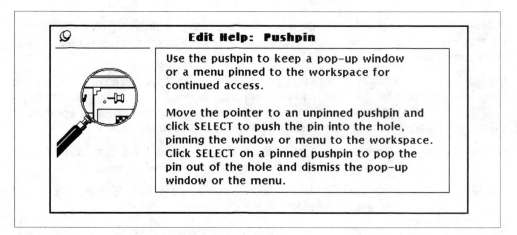

Figure 2-5. Sample help window

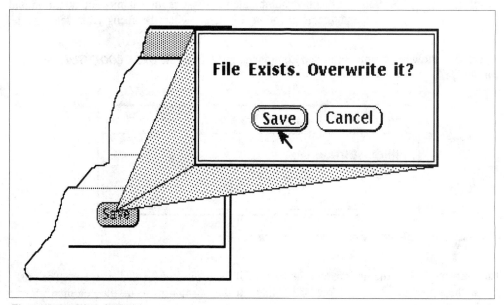

Figure 2-6. Sample notice

2.4.4 Subwindows

Subwindows differ from frames in several basic ways. They never exist independently; they are always owned and maintained by a frame or another window, and they may not themselves own frames. While frames can be moved freely around the screen, subwindows are constrained to fit within the borders of the frame to which they belong. Also, in contrast to frames, subwindows are *tiled*—they may not overlap each other within their frame. Within these constraints (which are enforced by a run-time *boundary manager*), subwindows may be moved and resized by either a program or a user.

Canvas subwindows and text subwindows are subclassed from the OPENWIN package, a hidden class which implements the notion of *splittable views* described by OPEN LOOK. Figure 2-7 shows an example of one canvas object providing separate views into one graphic image. Each view into the object has scrollbars attached. The scrollbars provide the ability to scroll independently from all the other views attached to the subwindow and to split the views again.

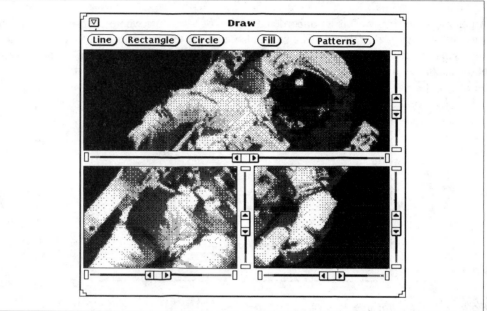

Figure 2-7. A window with multiple views

All the views, however, are still a part of the same OPENWIN object. Using the scrollbars, the user can split or join different views.

Canvas Subwindows

The canvas is the most basic type of subwindow. It provides a drawing surface—a place in which the result of Xlib graphics calls can be displayed. A canvas object can be configured to permit the application to draw on an area larger than the size of the visible window. The entire region representing the drawing surface is a window called the *paint window*. The visible portion of the paint window is the *view window*. It is the view window that appears in the canvas subwindow. In the previous figure, the paint window contains a picture of an astronaut. Multiple view windows each show a particular region of the paint canvas. The view windows are independent of each other. See Chapter 5, *Canvases and Openwin*, for a full discussion and illustration of the Canvas model.

Text Subwindows

Another basic window type is a text subwindow. It provides basic text editing capabilities using the OPEN LOOK text editing model.

Panels

A panel (or *control area*) is an unbordered region of a window where controls such as buttons and settings are displayed. The panel also controls the arrangement of its controls in a horizontal or vertical fashion. The panel shown in Figure 2-8 presents the typical positioning of the control area—the top of a base frame with a canvas subwindow under it.

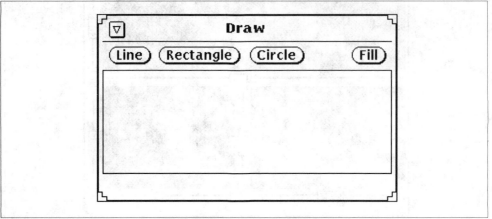

Figure 2-8. A control area above a subwindow

The panel shown in Figure 2-9 presents a control area that is to the right of a canvas subwindow.

Control areas within panes usually contain varied combinations of the following controls:

- Buttons
- Exclusive and nonexclusive choice lists
- Check boxes
- Sliders
- Gauges
- Text and numeric fields

A command frame (subframe) contains only a panel and no other subwindows. Figure 2-10 shows a control area in a command frame. It contains text fields, choice lists and buttons. See Chapter 7, *Panels*, for a discussion of panel items and the PANEL package.

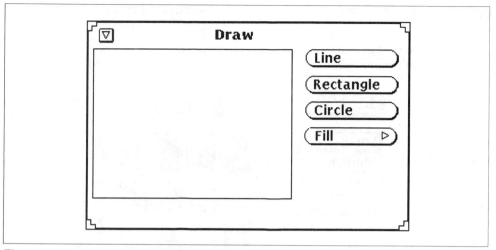

Figure 2-9. A control area to the right of a pane

```
┌──────────────────────────────────────────────┐
│  ⬡     Edit:  Search  and  Replace            │
│                                               │
│      Search For: ◆_____ │
│                                               │
│      Replace With:  _____ │
│                                               │
│   ┌─────────────────────┐  ┌───────────┐      │
│   │ Ignore Case         │  │ Forward   │      │
│   └─────────────────────┘  │ Backward  │      │
│   ┌─────────────────────┐  └───────────┘      │
│   │ Wild Card Searches  │                     │
│   └─────────────────────┘                     │
│   ┌─────────────────────┐                     │
│   │ Wraparound Searches │                     │
│   └─────────────────────┘                     │
│                                               │
│  (Search)  (Replace & Search)  (Replace All)  │
│                                               │
└──────────────────────────────────────────────┘
```

Figure 2-10. A control area in a command window

Menus

Menus are subclassed from the Generic Object. A menu by itself is a windowless object. Only when the menu is activated by the user is it bound to a window. This implementation avoids creating multiple X11 windows (one for each menu) since not all the menus will be displayed at once. XView has three types of menus:

1. Pop-up menus that are displayed when the user presses the menu button in a window.

2. Pullright menus that are displayed as a menu to the right of a menu.

3. Pulldown menus that are displayed below a menu button on a panel.

Figure 2-11 shows an example of a pop-up menu on the left; on the right, a pullright submenu is displayed.

Pushpins can be used in some menus, allowing them to be *pinned* so that the menu remains on the screen for repeated use.

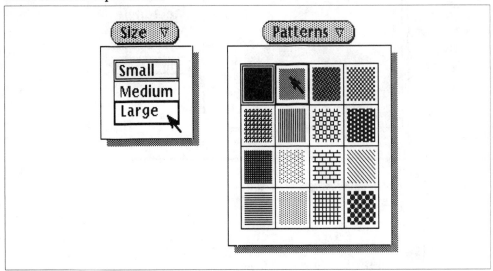

Figure 2-11. Example of a pop-up menu with a pullright submenu

Scrollbars

Scrollbars implement the OPEN LOOK metaphor of an elevator on a cable. These components are shown in Figure 2-12.

A scrollbar is an object that can exist independently or attach itself to various types of subwindows. The scrollbar is subclassed from the WINDOW class since it is a visual object. However, because its functionality is very tightly bound to other objects, the scrollbar is sometimes considered to be a property of those objects. OPENWIN subclasses (canvas and text-based packages) require scrollbars to provide splittable views, and scrollbars can be created automatically by such objects. Typically, it is your responsibility to pass a hint to the object that it should create the scrollbar using the appropriate attribute-value pair. Nevertheless, scrollbars can be manually attached or detached to OPENWIN objects, or they can be created independently of these objects for other purposes entirely.

The SCROLLBAR package manages only the scrollbar window. It does not control the window to which it is attached. When a scrolling action results from the user clicking on a portion of the scrollbar, the window to which the scrollbar is attached must modify its data (a view in most cases). It is not the scrollbar's responsibility to notify the window it is attached to. The scrollbar informs the object interested in its scrolling by use of callback routines that the owner of the scrollbar must install.

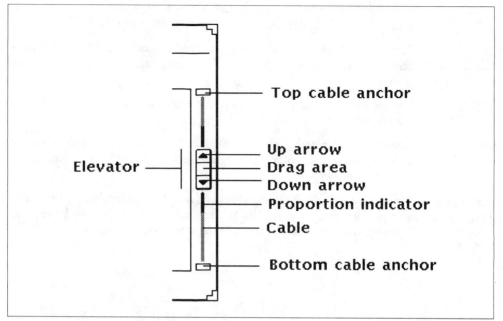

Figure 2-12. Vertical scrollbar components

Scrollbars can be oriented vertically or horizontally, but some packages might not allow a particular scrollbar orientation. Text subwindows, for example, contain vertical scrollbars by default but do not permit horizontal scrollbars.

Icons

An icon is a small image representing the application when the application's frame is in a closed, or iconified, state. The ICON package is very small. It is subclassed from the WINDOW package because it is a window that displays graphics and accepts input. The only attributes that you can set in the ICON package specify the image to display in the window and the geometry of the image. Other important attributes that an icon can have (such as width, height, label and font) are attributes of the generic class.

2.4.5 Nonvisual Objects

There are several nonvisual objects that cannot be represented on the screen but are subclassed from the Generic Object:

SERVER   This package interacts with the X server. The window-server is the program that does the drawing to the screen and receives the user's input. The server also maintains font information and user-configurable resources, which can be set for specific applications.

SCREEN	This object describes the visual and other characteristics of the physical screen. This object is separate from Xlib SCREEN object.
FONT	The font package allows the programmer to request fonts of varying attributes such as font *family* and *style*. Fonts can be accessed by name, size or scaling.
CURSOR	The cursor, or pointer, is a visual object indicating the mouse location on the screen.
CMS	Colormap segments (cms) are objects that are associated with windows which provide their color specifications. Cms objects may be shared by multiple windows.

These objects are closely tied with the X Window System, and they are manipulated by making requests to set or get attributes from X. While there are Xlib calls that can be used to acquire the same information, these packages simplify the work required to do so.

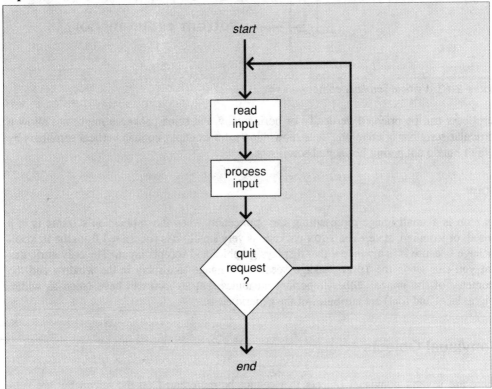

Figure 2-13. Flow of control in a conventional program

2.5 The Notifier Model

XView is a *notification-based* system. The Notifier acts as the controlling entity within a user process, reading input from the operating system and formatting it into higher-level *events*, which it distributes to the different XView objects.*

2.5.1 Callback Style of Programming

In the conventional style of interactive programming, the main control loop resides in the application. An editor, for example, will read a character, take some action based on the character, then read the next character and so on. When a character is received that represents the user's request to quit, the program exits. Figure 2-13 illustrates this approach.

Notification-based systems invert this straight line control structure. The main control loop resides in the Notifier, not the application. The Notifier reads events and *notifies*, or *calls out* to, various procedures which the application has previously registered with the Notifier. These procedures are called *notify procs* or *callback procs*. This control structure is shown in Figure 2-14.

2.5.2 Why a Notification-based System?

If you are not used to it, this callback style of programming takes some getting used to. Its big advantage is that it takes over the burden of managing a complex, event-driven environment. In XView, an application typically has many objects. In the absence of a centralized Notifier, each application must be responsible for detecting and dispatching events to all the objects in the process. With a centralized Notifier, each component of an application receives only the events the user has directed towards it.

2.5.3 Relationship Among the Notifier, Objects and the Application

It is not necessary for you to interact with the Notifier directly in your application. XView has a two-tiered scheme in which the packages that support the various objects—panels, canvases, scrollbars, etc.—interact with the Notifier directly, registering their own callback procedures. The application, in turn, registers its own callback procedures with the object.

Typically, when writing an XView application, you first create the various windows and other objects you need for your interface and register your callback procedures with the objects. Then you pass control to the Notifier. The work is done in the various callback procedures.

---

*XView events are in a form that you can easily use: an ASCII key has been pressed, a mouse button has been pressed or released, the mouse has moved, the mouse has entered or exited a window, etc. Events are described in detail in Chapter 6, *Handling Input*.

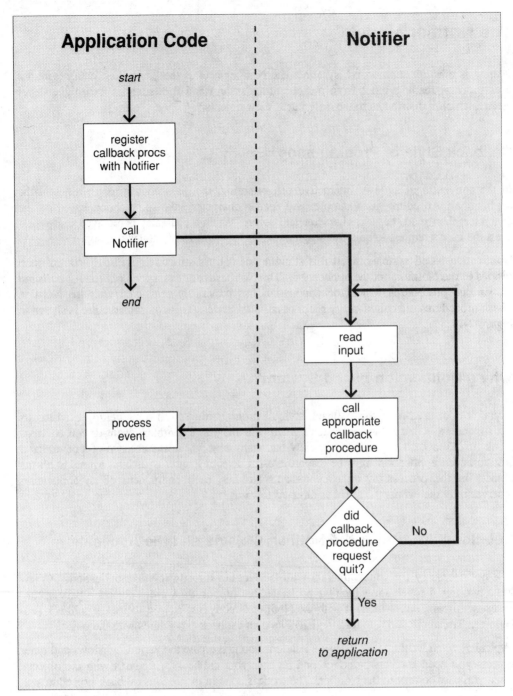

Figure 2-14. Flow of control in a Notifier-based program

Let's illustrate the relationship of the Notifier. Figure 2-15 illustrates how the Notifier receives X events from the X server, as well as operating system "events" such as signals or input on file descriptors. Event procedures are supplied by XView packages as well as the application itself.

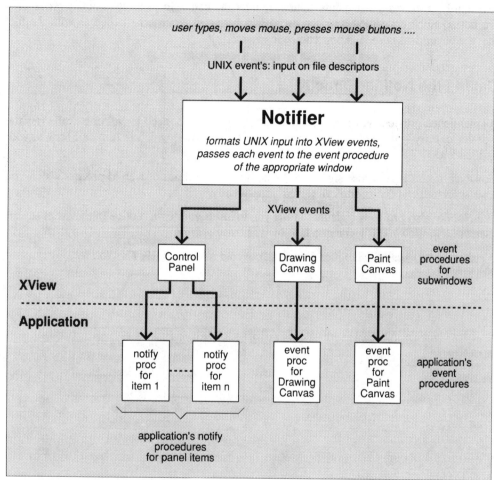

Figure 2-15. Flow of input events in an XView application

The main point of Figure 2-15 is to clarify the double-tiered callback scheme. How you register the callback procedures will be explained in Chapter 5, *Canvases and Openwin*, and Chapter 7, *Panels*.

One point worth mentioning is the distinction between the *event procedures* for the canvases and the *notify procedures* for the panel items. They are all callback procedures, but they have different purposes. The canvas's event procedure does not do much work—basically, it calls out to the application's event procedure each time an event is received. The application sees every event and is free to interpret the events however it likes.

The event procedure for panels, on the other hand, does quite a bit of processing. It determines which item should receive the event and places its own interpretation on events—the middle mouse button is ignored, and the left mouse button down over an item is interpreted as a tentative activation of the item, etc. It does not call back to the notify procedure for the item until it receives a left mouse button up over the item. So panel item notify procedures are not so much concerned with the event which caused them to be called as with the fact that the button was pushed, a new choice made, etc.

2.5.4 Calling the Notifier Directly

As mentioned previously, for many applications, you will not need to call or be called by the Notifier directly—the Notifier calls back to the subwindows, which in turn call back to your application.

However, if you need to use signals or be notified of the death of a child process which you have spawned, you do need to call the Notifier directly.

The Notifier also provides calls that allow you to insert your own routine in the event stream ahead of a window. This technique is known as *interposition*.

When and how to call the Notifier directly is covered in Chapter 19, *The Notifier*.

3

Creating XView Applications

In This Chapter:

3
Creating XView Applications

This chapter covers the XView programming interface. It describes the basic XView distribution and how you use it to compile and link XView applications. It also presents the proper structure for XView applications. The structure can be summarized as:

- Initialize XView using xv_init().

- Create a top-level window (FRAME) to manage subwindows.

- Add subwindows as children of the FRAME.

- Add objects to subwindows.

- Specify notification callbacks and select input events.

- Call xv_main_loop() to start the dispatching of events.

This chapter also discusses error recovery procedures.

3.1 Interface Overview

This section gives an overview of the XView programming interface. It covers reserved words and naming conventions in XView. It also includes a complete sample program, which we will look at more closely when describing the calling sequence for a program.

3.1.1 Compiling XView Programs

To compile an XView program, you must link with the XView library and the OPEN LOOK graphics library. These libraries comprise the entire XView Toolkit. XView is written for X11, of course, so you need to add the standard X library, which contains all the Xlib routines.

Thus, to compile a typical XView application whose source is *myprog.c*, you use the command:

```
% cc myprog.c -lxview -lolgx -lX11 -o myprog
```

3.1.2 XView Libraries

The XView library is made up of two other libraries: *libxvol.a* and *libxvin.a*. XView functions are found mostly in the library *libxvol.a*. These libraries include the code to create and manipulate high-level objects such as frames, panels, scrollbars and icons. These packages in turn call routines in *libxvin.a* to create and manipulate windows and interact with the Notifier. These libraries are both included in the library *libxview.a*. The XView libraries call routines in the Xlib library (*libX11.a*) that do the drawing on the screen.

The library specified by −lolgx is the OPEN LOOK graphics library. This library has routines that draw all the OPEN LOOK objects such as scrollbars and panel items. This library is not called from the client application; it is only called by the internals to XView.

Many of the images used by this library are gotten from special fonts that must be installed on your X11 server. The X11R4 server as well as the X/NeWS server has these fonts. However, if you are running on an X server that precedes X11R4, you may need to obtain these fonts separately and install them manually. Refer to the X documentation for information on installing new fonts.

3.1.3 Header Files

The basic definitions needed by an XView application (windows, frames, menus, icons and cursors) are obtained by including the header file *<xview/xview.h>*. All XView applications should have the line:

```
#include <xview/xview.h>
```

This header file includes many other header files that set up standard types. It also declares external functions and includes some system-specific header files that are required by all the XView header files. Once *<xview/xview.h>* has been included, other include files specific to the packages are included. Each object package has its own header file to declare object types, to provide definitions for frequently used macros and to make external definitions for routines that are specific to that object's package. Frequently these files include other files, which in turn may include other packages or system header files.

For instance, if your code uses the FRAME, PANEL and FONT packages, then these include files must be specified:

```
#include <xview/xview.h>
#include <xview/frame.h>
#include <xview/panel.h>
#include <xview/font.h>
```

However, investigation shows that some header files include other header files by default. For example, *<xview/xview.h>* includes *<xview/frame.h>*. Since there are "wrappers" inside the XView header files which prevent them from being included more than once, if the file has already been included and is inadvertently included again, the second and subsequent attempts to include it are discarded. Because of this, it is safe to include header files more than once.

3.1.4 Naming Conventions

All the examples throughout this manual follow a consistent method in the naming of data types, package names and even variable names. Because of the large number of packages and data types, you could easily confuse what a lexical string represents. Therefore, you are advised to follow certain criteria when naming variables and declaring data types that are not specific to XView. Whatever naming convention you choose, you should always try to be consistent.

Reserved Names

XView reserves names beginning with the object types, as well as certain other prefixes, for its own use. The prefixes in Table 3-1 should not be used by applications in lower, upper or mixed case.

Table 3-1. Reserved Prefixes

attr_	icon_	seln_
canvas_	menu_	server_
cursor_	notify_	server_image_
defaults_	panel_	termsw_
ei_	pixrect_	text_
es_	pr_	textsw_
ev_	pw_	tty_
event_	rect_	ttysw_
font_	rl_	win_
frame_	screen_	window_
fullscreen_	scroll_	wmgr_
generic_	scrollbar_	xv_

To help you choose what *not* to use for data types and other lexical tokens in your application, review Table 2-1, "XView Objects, Owners, Packages and Data Types."

3.1.5 Example of XView-style Programming

The flavor of the XView programming interface is illustrated by the code in Example 3-1. This program, *quit.c*, creates a frame containing a panel with one item: a button labeled Quit.

There are a few things to notice in the program. First, note the NULL that terminates the attribute lists in the xv_create() and xv_set() calls. The most common mistake in using attribute lists is to forget the final NULL. This will not be flagged by the compiler as an error. The results are actually unpredictable, but the most common result is that XView will generate a run-time error message and the program will exit.

Second, the object returned by the xv_create() for the PANEL_BUTTON is not stored into a variable. This is primarily because it is not needed by any other portion of the code. One of the most common programming inefficiencies is the use of global variables when they are not needed. If you are not going to reference an object created via xv_create(), you should not retain its handle. If you need its handle, but only temporarily, then it should be a local variable, not a global or static one. For example, the panel variable (type Panel) is used as a local variable.

Example 3-1. The quit.c program

```
/*
 * quit.c -- simple program to display a panel button that says "Quit".
 * Selecting the panel button exits the program.
 */
#include <xview/xview.h>
#include <xview/frame.h>
#include <xview/panel.h>

Frame frame;

main (argc, argv)
int argc;
char *argv[];
{
    Panel panel;
    void quit();

    xv_init (XV_INIT_ARGC_PTR_ARGV, &argc, argv, NULL);

    frame = (Frame)xv_create (NULL, FRAME,
        FRAME_LABEL,     argv[0],
        XV_WIDTH,        200,
        XV_HEIGHT,       100,
        NULL);

    panel = (Panel)xv_create (frame, PANEL, NULL);

    (void) xv_create (panel, PANEL_BUTTON,
            PANEL_LABEL_STRING,        "Quit",
            PANEL_NOTIFY_PROC,         quit,
            NULL);

    xv_main_loop (frame);
    exit(0);
}

void
```

Example 3-1. The quit.c program (continued)

```
quit()
{
    xv_destroy_safe(frame);
}
```

Figure 3-1 shows the output resulting from *quit.c.* In the sections that follow, we are going to look at how this program demonstrates the structure of XView programs.

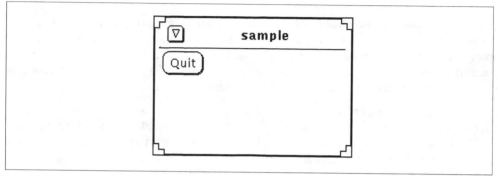

Figure 3-1. A frame containing a Quit button

3.2 Initializing XView

Initializing the XView system should be done as soon as possible in the application. The `xv_init()` function performs many tasks, including:

- Opening the connection to the server.
- Initializing the Notifier.
- Initializing the Resource Manager database.*

The form of `xv_init()` is:

```
Xv_Server
xv_init(attrs)
    <attribute-value list> attrs;
```

By default, `xv_init()` opens a connection to the server described by the `DISPLAY` environment variable. With the appropriate command-line options (discussed later), a different server may be specified. Also, given appropriate command-line attribute-value pairs, a particular server may be specified. No matter which server is ultimately used, `xv_init()` returns a handle to that server object.

---

*See Chapter 17, *Resources,* for more information about the resource database.

Creating XView
Applications

All subsequent XView objects that are created will use this server by default. This includes the physical screen(s) and resources. If you want your application to span multiple servers, you need to open a separate connection to those servers via the SERVER package. For further information on how to do this and other details of the SERVER package, see Chapter 15, *Non-visual Objects* for details.

3.2.1 Using xv_init()

Initialization should be done before the application attempts to parse its own command-line options. Since many programs tend to have command-line parameters, a program tends to report unknown parameters as illegal arguments. Because XView parameters can also be specified on the command line to the application, the program must be able to distinguish between the application's parameters and XView's parameters.

xv_init() accepts the attributes XV_INIT_ARGS and XV_INIT_ARGC_PTR_ARGV for purposes of parsing command-line arguments. These attributes both take two parameters as values: argc and argv. These are typically the same ones passed into main(). Using the XV_INIT_ARGC_PTR_ARGV attribute, the xv_init() function can be told to modify argc and argv by removing parameters that are XView-specific, like so:

```
xv_init(XV_INIT_ARGC_PTR_ARGV, &argc, argv, NULL);
```

When xv_init returns, argv contains only those parameters that are not specific to XView, and the application can now assume that all remaining arguments are specific to the application. So a hypothetical command line might look like this:

```
% program -display maui:0
```

The command line is first parsed by xv_init(), and in this case, all arguments are stripped from the argv variable, leaving just argv[0], whose value is program. argc is modified to have the value 1 (it was originally 3). The example command-line parameters change the default server to be the X server running on the machine named *maui*.

The macro XV_INIT_ARGS is similar:

```
xv_init(XV_INIT_ARGS, argc, argv, NULL);
```

Here, argc and argv are not modified at all and are returned unchanged by xv_init(). Therefore, the *value*, not the address, of argc is used. This method is less advantageous for initializing XView because it leaves the application with the responsibility of parsing XView command-line parameters later.

NOTE

Once XView has been initialized, subsequent calls to xv_init() are ignored, as are all parameters consisting of XV_INIT_ARGS or XV_INIT_ ARGC_PTR_ARGV.

A common error that users make is to enter bad command-line arguments. These arguments can be specific to XView or specific to the application, so XView handles the XView-specific argument and then expects the programmer to handle application-specific arguments.

Upon receiving a bad argument, XView prints an error message, indicating what XView-specific values are legal, and then calls exit(1). The function that provides this message is specified by the attribute XV_USAGE_PROC. In most cases, you want to leave this alone because it is *not* the way you handle application-specific arguments.

The attribute XV_ERROR_PROC is used to install an error recovery routine. See Chapter 21, *Help and Error Handling* for details about error handling.

3.3 Creating and Modifying Objects

After the system has been initialized, objects can be created and modified using xv_create(), xv_find(), xv_get(), and xv_set(). A closer look at xv_create() and xv_find() shows how these functions can be used to create new objects or find existing objects with particular attributes from various packages.

3.3.1 Using xv_create()

xv_create() is typically used as in Example 3-2:

Example 3-2. xv_create() creates XView objects

```
#include <xview/xview.h>

main(argc, argv)
char *argv[];
{
    Frame frame;

    xv_init(XV_INIT_ARGC_PTR_ARGV, &argc, argv, NULL);
    frame = (Frame)xv_create(NULL, FRAME, NULL);
    xv_main_loop(frame);
}
```

In Example 3-2, a frame is created from the FRAME package and no additional attribute-value pairs are specified. Therefore, all the default properties from the frame class are set into the instance of this new frame when it is created.

The form of xv_create() is:

```
Xv_object
xv_create(owner, package, attrs)
    Xv_object       owner;
    Xv_pkg          package;
    <attribute-value list> attrs
```

In most cases, owner is another XView object. As shown in the example, when the frame is created, it has no owner, per se. This means that the owner should default to a pre-specified owner that XView has in mind. Defaulting is not always possible, but for this base frame, the default owner is the root window of the current server. As a child of the root window, the frame is under the constraints that the window manager might impose upon it (the colormap, for example).

Objects must have an owner for several reasons. One reason is that the X server may not be running on the same machine as the application (client) program. Therefore, because XView is running on the client side, objects that are created by the application have to contact the server. There could be more than one server to contact if the application supports multiple displays or runs on several machines simultaneously. To do this, XView needs to know what server or screen a particular object is associated with.

Another reason is that certain attributes are inherited from the owner, such as color and event masks. It is up to the individual package to determine what it inherits from its owner.

When `owner` is NULL, the owner of the object being created is either defaulted to a predetermined owner, or the object is said to have *delayed binding*. That is, the object is not associated with any other object until it is displayed on the screen. A scrollbar that is created with a NULL owner will not be displayed until it is attached to an object, and this object becomes its owner. Most objects are required to have owners at the time of their creation. Frames, windows and fonts must have a valid (default) owner because they need to access the screen's default colors, available fonts and so on.

Table 3-2 shows the default owner if `owner` is NULL in the call to `xv_create`.

Table 3-2. Default Ownership of Objects

Object's Package	Owner	If Owner is NULL
FRAME	Another frame or the root window	The window manager of `xv_default_screen`
CANVAS, TEXT, PANEL	Frame	The window manager of `xv_default_screen`
CMS	Screen	`xv_default_screen`
Panel Items	Panel	NULL owner not allowed
MENU	Ignores its owner	Always use NULL
Menu Items	Menu	Allows delayed binding
CURSOR	Window, screen or anything that returns XV_ROOT	The window manager of `xv_default_screen`
ICON	Same as cursor	Same as cursor
SCROLLBAR	An openwin object	Allows delayed binding
SCROLLABLE_PANEL	Frame	NULL not allowed
SCREEN, FULLSCREEN	Server	`xv_default_server`
SERVER	Doesn't matter	Always use NULL
SERVER_IMAGE	Screen	`xv_default_screen`

The object that is returned from `xv_create()` is an opaque data type called `Xv_object`. The return value should be coerced into the type of the object being created.

Each time `xv_create()` is used, it creates a new and entirely different object. The type of object that is returned depends on the *package* specified.

```
Panel panel;
panel = (Panel)xv_create(frame, PANEL, NULL);
```

Here, a panel is created as a child of a frame. As in the previous example, there are no attribute-value pairs specified, so the panel is created with all the default values intrinsic to a generic panel object from the PANEL package. The panel is then installed inside the frame accordingly. Panel items can be installed inside the panel as:

```
Panel_item button;
button = (Panel_item)xv_create(panel, PANEL_BUTTON,
    PANEL_LABEL_STRING,   "Quit",
    PANEL_NOTIFY_PROC,    quit,
    NULL);
```

Here, `xv_create()` is used to create a panel item of type PANEL_BUTTON. This is a special type of object that is created inside of panels only. That is why the owner of the item is the panel created in the previous example. In the attribute-value list provided in this example, the label is set by specifying the PANEL_LABEL_STRING attribute and a string as the value portion of the pair. Similarly, the callback routine specified is the routine called `quit()`. Because the intent of panel buttons is to select them with the pointer, the callback routine is the function to call if the user presses the mouse button in the panel button item.

3.3.2 Using xv_find()

In all the examples so far, the routine `xv_create()` has been used to create new objects of different types or classes. However, it might not always be possible to know whether or not a particular object has been created. The best way to handle such cases is to use `xv_find()`. If the object has been created, `xv_find()` returns the handle to the pre-existing object; if not, `xv_find()` creates it. The definition of the routine follows:

```
Xv_opaque
xv_find (owner, package, attrs)
    Xv_object          owner;
    Xv_pkg             package;
    <attribute-value list>   attrs;
```

As you can see, the form of `xv_find()` is the same as `xv_create()`. Fonts are objects that usually only need to be created once and are then used throughout the application wherever necessary. For example, say the application needs to use the font named *fixed* (because it is usually available on any X server and is almost guaranteed to be found). Several places in the application need to use the font, but only one instance of the font needs to be created. To avoid multiple instances of the object, the following function call is made:

```
Xv_Font my_font;
my_font = xv_find(frame, FONT,
    FONT_NAME, "fixed",
    NULL);
```

This code segment demonstrates how xv_find() tries to find an existing font named *fixed* that has already been created by the application. If the application has not yet created this font, then xv_find() acts just like xv_create(), and a new font is created. This function is not intended to replace xv_create() at all. It is intended to be used in the case where only one instance of an object is desired and that one instance is shared throughout the application. While you could use xv_find() rather than xv_create() in the other examples shown so far, the problem arises if you need two copies of a particular instance of an object. For example, if you were going to create another PANEL using all the default values of the PANEL package, then xv_find() would return the previously created panel. Any new objects attached to that panel would also be attached to the other panel because they are, in fact, one and the same.

As shown, fonts are frequent users of the xv_find() function.*

3.3.3 Using xv_destroy()

The correct way for an XView application to exit is to destroy all objects created and call exit() with an appropriate exit status. The function xv_destroy() destroys an instance of an XView object. The function xv_destroy_safe() does the same thing but ensures that it is *safe* to do so.† In general, it is better to be safe than sorry. The definition of these routines are as follows:

```
int
xv_destroy_safe(object)
    Xv_opaque object;

int
xv_destroy(object)
    Xv_opaque object;
```

The return value from the routines is either XV_OK or XV_ERROR. Example 3-1 shows a base frame containing a panel subwindow with one panel button created inside it. The callback routine for the panel item, quit(), is intended to exit the application. Rather than actually calling exit(), a more elegant way to exit would be to destroy all the objects that have been created. If a text subwindow had its text modified since the last update, this would give the package an opportunity to prompt the user for an update. Or you might install a routine that interposes any request for destruction on a particular object (such as a frame).‡

The quit() routine looks like this:

```
void
quit()
{
    if (xv_destroy_safe(frame) == XV_OK)
        exit(0);
}
```

---

*Chapter 16, *Fonts*, describes how to create fonts using xv_find().
†Chapter 19, *The Notifier*, discusses the difference between a safe and an *immediate* destruction of an object.
‡Chapter 19, *The Notifier*, describes how to install destroy interpose functions.

Rather than calling `xv_destroy_safe()` on all objects, it is only called for the base frame. Because the base frame is the owner of all the other objects, `xv_destroy()` and `xv_destroy_safe()` descend into the objects' children and destroys all of them with the same call.

`xv_destroy()` may be called at any time without notice. It may result from actions the user takes with the window manager, from a separate process or from events sent by other applications.

3.3.4   Using xv_set() and xv_get()

As discussed in the previous chapter, attributes about objects can be set, reset and retrieved using the calls `xv_set()` and `xv_get()`. The definition of these routines are:

```
Xv_opaque
xv_set(object, attrs)
    Xv_object           object;
    <attribute-value list>   attrs;


Xv_opaque
xv_get(object, attr)
    Xv_object           object;
    Attr_attribute      attr;
```

`xv_set()` is just like `xv_create()` with respect to the attribute-value parameters. Use `xv_set()` to set or change the value of one or more attributes of an object that has already been created. The following code segment uses a single `xv_set()` call to change three attributes of a frame:

```
#include <xview/xview.h>

main()
{
    Frame frame;
    frame = xv_create(NULL, FRAME, NULL);
    ...
    xv_set(frame,
        FRAME_LABEL,        "XView Demo",
        FRAME_SHOW_LABEL,   TRUE,
        FRAME_NO_CONFIRM,   TRUE,
        NULL);
    ...
    xv_main_loop(frame);
}
```

`xv_get()` is different from `xv_set()` in that the `value` parameter is not passed to the function—instead, the value is returned from `xv_get()`:

```
Xv_Window root_win;
Frame frame;
Rect *rect;

/* create the base frame for the application */
frame = xv_create(NULL, FRAME, NULL);

/* get the root window of the base frame of the application */
```

```
root_win = (Xv_Window *) xv_get(frame, XV_ROOT);

/* get the dimensions (rectangle) of the root window */
rect = (Rect *) xv_get(root_win, XV_RECT);
```

Because `xv_get()` returns the value of the attribute specified, only one attribute of the object can be retrieved by an `xv_get()` call. The return value for the function is going to be an opaque data type, so it must be *typecast* into the type expected. However, note that the value `XV_ERROR` might be returned in the event that the object passed is not a valid object or if an attribute does not apply. In this case, the return value should be checked to see if it is `XV_ERROR`. One potential problem is that the value of `XV_ERROR` might happen to be the same as the expected return value. Fortunately, an error returned from `xv_get()` is unlikely in a properly debugged application.

In many packages, certain properties may be retrieved but not set. That is, you may use `xv_get()` for the property `FRAME_FOREGROUND_COLOR` to get the foreground color of a frame, but you may not use `xv_set()` to set the foreground color. In this case, `xv_set` returns `XV_ERROR`.* In the more likely event that the call was successful in setting attributes using `xv_set()`, then the value `XV_OK` will be returned.

3.4 xv_main_loop() and the Notifier

Once all the objects have been created, you are ready to have all the windows displayed and have event processing begin. At this point, the program calls `xv_main_loop()`. The job of `xv_main_loop()` is to start the Notifier. Once the Notifier has started, the program will begin to receive and process events such as `Expose`, `MapNotify`, `ConfigureNotify`, `KeyPress` and so on. The X server generates these events and sends them to the client. While it is up to the client to handle all events that the X server sends to it, the Notifier layer of XView handles much of this work automatically.

The Notifier's main job is to process these events and dispatch them to the client if it has registered a callback routine for that event type with the Notifier. Otherwise, the Notifier might ignore the event. Of course, XView attempts to provide reasonable default actions for all events that the application typically does not want to deal with. For example, a simple application that contains nothing but a command frame (which has nothing but a panel/control area) might not care to handle resize events if the user resizes the window. XView must handle this so it can resize the panel and/or reposition the panel items within it.

Those events that the application would be most interested in are things like `KeyPress` and `ButtonPress` events of various types. For events like these, the application should install callback routines for the Notifier to call if one of those events has taken place.

In the examples shown, the only callback routine installed is the one in the panel item, `quit()`. When selected, the Notifier notifies the application by calling the callback routine associated with the object in which the event took place. In this case, the Notifier calls the routine `quit()` and the application has control of the program again. As one might expect,

---

*The foreground color for a frame can be set only in `xv_create()`. Once the frame is created, the color cannot be changed. See Chapter 21, *Help and Error Handling* for details about error handling.

the Notifier has relinquished control of the program while the application's callback routine is being called. The Notifier does no more event processing at all until the callback routine has returned. However, the programmer can query events from within the callback routine if necessary.

If the code within the callback routine creates new objects or destroys existing objects, nothing will happen on the display until the callback routine is finished and returns control to the Notifier.

Just because the Notifier handles the delivery of events to the application, that does not mean that the application will be notified of all events that might occur. The application is only notified of the events that it has registered with the Notifier. Events that the client can register with the Notifier include CreateWindow, MapWindow, ConfigureWindow, Query-Font, GetInputFocus and so on. These are general X events, not XView-specific events. However, XView has a corresponding event definition for the purpose of registering events with the Notifier. Event registration is covered in detail in Chapter 19, *The Notifier*. Event types and specifications are discussed in Chapter 5, *Canvases and Openwin*, and Chapter 6, *Handling Input*.

When a frame is displayed on the screen, a MapNotify event is generated by the X server (since the frame is *mapped*, or displayed, to the screen). However, there has been no callback routine specified to handle the map event, so the Notifier passes it back to XView, which handles it internally. This default action, in fact, does nothing special; it simply allows the frame to be displayed. Further events are generated: expose events, visibility events (for the frames that are covered up by the new frame), enter and leave events when the user moves the mouse in and out of the frame, motion events and so on. If none of these events have an application-defined callback routine associated with them, the Notifier handles them.

Note that when objects such as frames or canvases are created, only the objects themselves and the associated attributes of those objects are created. What is *not* created are the objects' windows. These are not created until after xv_main_loop() is called. This is due to the fact that one of the events that is generated is the *realize* event—this indicates that an object has been realized to the screen and a window has been (or needs to be) generated. The objects' packages internally handle the creation of windows at the appropriate time. Since that does not occur until after the call to xv_main_loop(), there should be no attempts to render graphics into objects' windows before then.

4
Frames

In This Chapter:

4
Frames

A frame is a container for other windows. It manages the geometry and placement of *subwindows* that do not overlap and are fixed within the boundary of the frame. The OPEN LOOK specification refers to subwindows, or *panes*, as *tiled* windows because they do not overlap one another. Subwindow types include canvases, text subwindows, panels and scrollbars. These subwindows cannot exist without a parent frame to manage them.

Figure 4-1 shows an example of a screen that displays three frames, each one containing at least one subwindow. Note that frames do overlap. The File Manager frame has the keyboard focus, as indicated by the title bar having its foreground and background colors reversed. The setting of the keyboard focus is handled by the window manager, not the FRAME package. In this case, an OPEN LOOK window manager is using click-to-type to set the keyboard focus. This is demonstrated by the cursor's location within an unselected frame (the *Edit: File* frame).

The FRAME package provides the following capabilities:

- A communication path between the application and the window manager.

- A mechanism to receive input for the application.

- A visual container for user interface objects.

- A method to group windows with related functionality.

A frame depends upon the window manager for its *decorations* and many basic operations. The FRAME package does *not* manage headers (title bars), footers, resize corners or the colors of those objects. These are all strictly functions of the window manager. The application gives hints to the window manager about some of these attributes through the FRAME package (including not to display decorations at all if so desired), but results vary depending on which window manager the user is running. The examples in this book assume the user is running an OPEN LOOK window manager.

Frames do not manage events; this task is left up to the windows that the frame manages. That is, frames do not get mouse and keyboard events and propagate them to child windows. While frames are subclassed from the window package, the frame's window rarely sees any events at all, and if they do, these are not intended to be processed by the application programmer.

Frames

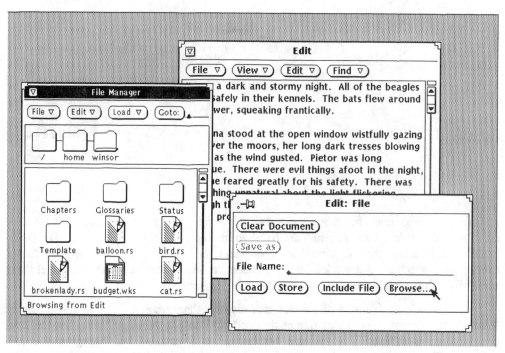

Figure 4-1. Three base frames

4.1 Types of Frames

Basically, two types of frames are available in XView: base frames and command frames. The main frame of the application is called the *base frame*. The base frame resides on the root window; its handle is passed to xv_main_loop() to begin application processing.

A special kind of frame, called a *command frame*, is created with a panel subwindow by default. Command frames are useful as help frames, property frames and such defined by OPEN LOOK. Programmatically, a command frame is no different from a frame with one subwindow that is a panel.

A base frame's *parent* is the root window, whereas a subframe's parent is another frame (either a base frame or a subframe). When a frame goes away (quit or close), all of its child windows, including subframes, also go away. For example, assume you create a command subframe to display application-specific help. When this command subframe is activated, it might display explanatory text along with an OK button to dismiss the help. If you close the base frame, the help subframe also closes.

XView allows for multiple frames that are not children of the base frame. For instance, you could create a help frame that is independent of the application's base frame. The parent of this frame is the root window of the display and not the base frame. The help frame will remain visible even if the base frame goes away. The term subframe defines a relationship among frames at creation time and a slight difference in functionality.

4.1.1 The Role of the Window Manager

It is important to understand what effect the window manager has in determining the appearance and behavior of an XView frame. As mentioned earlier, many attributes defined in the FRAME package are really hints to the window manager. The window manager is responsible for frame and window decoration, as well as the size and placement of windows on the screen (screen geometry). That is, it is the window manager's job to provide such decorations as title bars and to set attributes such as the color of decorations. It also handles resizing windows, moving windows, closing windows (iconifying) and so on. The application can ask the window manager to do things in a certain way, but the window manager is not obligated to act on these requests.

For your application and the window manager to communicate properly, the window manager must comply with the specifications in the *Inter-Client Communication Conventions Manual* (ICCCM).* Since the window manager is a client of the X server just as the application is a client, the two clients must follow specified conventions to communicate with one another. The FRAME package assumes it is communicating with an OPEN LOOK-compliant window manager. If not, some of the frame attributes might not work as described here.

For example, using an OPEN LOOK window manager, a command subframe is a pop-up window that has a pushpin in the upper-left corner. The state of the pushpin (unpinned or pinned) determines whether or not the window remains on the screen after the command has been executed. The pin objects are provided by the OPEN LOOK window manager. If XView applications are run with another window manager, they might not necessarily be pinnable.

4.2 Base Frames

Let's first create a base frame using the default attribute settings. To create a frame, use xv_create, specifying the owner of the frame and identifying the FRAME package. The program in Example 4-1 shows how to create a simple base frame:

Example 4-1. The simple_frame.c program

```
#include <xview/xview.h>

main()
{
    Frame frame;
    frame = (Frame)xv_create(NULL, FRAME, NULL);
    xv_main_loop(frame);
}
```

---

*The *Inter-Client Communication Conventions Manual* is reprinted as Appendix L of Volume Zero, *X Protocol Reference Manual*.

Note that the header file associated with the FRAME package, *<xview/frame.h>*, is included indirectly by *<xview/xview.h>*. (A separate inclusion has no harmful effect, however.)

The frame displayed by this program is shown in Figure 4-2.

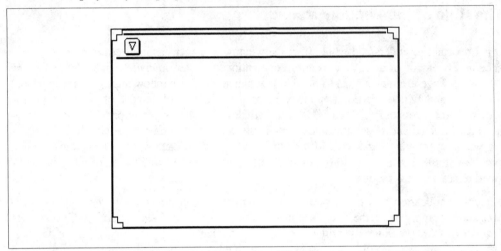

Figure 4-2. Simple base frame created without any FRAME attributes specified

4.2.1 XView Initialization and Base Frames

The first XView object to be created by an application is typically the base frame. However, xv_init() is always called first to get any command-line parameters, initialize the connection to the X server, set resources, and so on. The code segment in Example 4-2 shows how argc and argv can be used in conjunction with xv_init():

Example 4-2. Creating a base frame after calling xv_init()

```
main(argc, argv)
int argc;
char *argv[];
{
    Frame frame;
    ...
    xv_init(XV_INIT_ARGC_PTR_ARGV, &argc, argv, NULL);
    frame = (Frame)xv_create(NULL, FRAME, NULL);
    ...
    xv_main_loop(frame);
    exit(0);
}
```

In this sample code segment, the program expects no parameters that are specific to the program. Any parameters that the user supplies are expected to be specific to XView or X. When xv_init() is called with attribute XV_INIT_ARGC_PTR_ARGV, &argc and argv are passed as values; upon return, argv is stripped of the parameters that are X or XView-specific. The argc variable is also modified to reflect the number of parameters that remain after processing. If the user specified no other parameters, then `argc` should be 1 and `argv` should contain one element in its array of strings: the name of the program (since that is what `argv[0]` is). If there are any more parameters, then the application has the opportunity to look for application-specific parameters or to report unknown parameters as errors.

When the attribute `XV_INIT_ARGS` is used, the value of `argc` (not the address of `argc`) is passed, and neither variable is modified.

4.2.2 Headers and Footers

The OPEN LOOK window manager provides frames with headers and footers that display text. The header typically displays information such as the application name. The text is centered and its font is not alterable by the application. The header also has a Close button at the upper-left corner; selecting the button causes the frame to iconify—that is, the frame turns into a graphical image, or *icon*, and is displayed (probably) elsewhere on the screen. The application's *state* is now closed. This usually indicates that the program is idle.

The footer of a base frame shows text such as error messages, a page number, the date or other miscellaneous information. The footer is split in two parts: the left footer where text is left justified, and the right footer where the text is right justified.

Unless otherwise specified by giving the appropriate attribute-value pairs, the header of a base frame is displayed, but the footer is not. The header does contain the abbreviated menu button, but there is no default header label. Thus, to create a header with a label, the attribute `FRAME_LABEL` must have a string value.* This may be a constant string or a variable pointing to a string. When the frame is displayed, the string will be centered in the header. The header label can be turned off by setting the `FRAME_SHOW_HEADER` attribute to `FALSE`. In this case, even if the header label is set, the header (including the Close button) will not be displayed at all. If `FRAME_SHOW_HEADER` is later set to `TRUE`, then the label will be displayed again (see Figure 4-3).

The code segment in Example 4-3 sets `FRAME_SHOW_HEADER` to `FALSE` at creation but sets it to `TRUE` in a separate call. The header displays the name of the program.

Example 4-3. Setting separate values for a frame header

```
...
Frame frame;
frame = (Frame)xv_create(NULL, FRAME,
    FRAME_LABEL, argv[0],
    FRAME_SHOW_HEADER, FALSE, NULL);
...
xv_set(frame, FRAME_SHOW_HEADER, TRUE, NULL);
...
```

Footers in base frames are not displayed by default, so setting either the left or right footer messages also requires the boolean `FRAME_SHOW_FOOTER` to be set to `TRUE`. Note that setting the footer on and off resizes the total size of the base frame, and while it does not cause

---

*`FRAME_LABEL` is defined to be `XV_LABEL` in *<xview/frame.h>*.

Frames

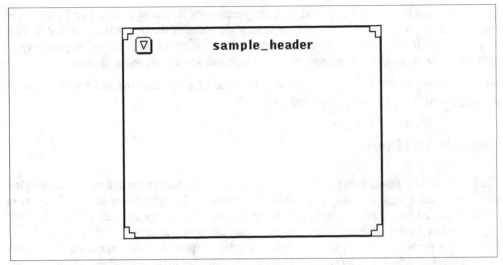

Figure 4-3. A sample header label display in a frame

any subwindows to be resized, it is rather distracting to change the frame frequently (or at all). Therefore, you should decide ahead of time whether you are going to use footers and set them to be on or off at the time the frame is created. If the footer is no longer needed, set the left or the right footer string to the null string—*not* the constant NULL. That is, use " ". Figure 4-4 shows what is displayed when the code in Example 4-4 is run:

Example 4-4. Creating a footer

```
    . . .
    Frame frame;
    frame = (Frame)xv_create(NULL, FRAME,
        FRAME_LABEL,         "hdrs_n_footers",
        FRAME_SHOW_FOOTER,   TRUE,
        FRAME_LEFT_FOOTER,   "left side",
        FRAME_RIGHT_FOOTER,  "right side",
        NULL);
    . . .
```

4.2.3 Closed Base Frames

Base frames are distinct from other types of frames because they can be closed, or *iconified*. When the frame is closed, an icon replaces the entire base frame, including all subwindows and control areas.* If any subframes are associated with the base frame, then they are taken down for as long as the application is closed. Using the appropriate attribute-value pairs, it is possible to set the image and size of the icon. By default, no icon is associated with a base frame and the size of the area occupied by an icon is 64x64. See Chapter 13, *Icons*, for more

_____
*Only base frames have icons associated with them.

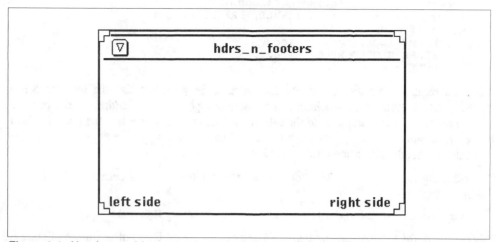

Figure 4-4. Headers and footers on base frame

information on creating icons used by frames. The bounding box (or Rect) of the icon is independent of the size of the icon, so the bounding box should be set explicitly if its value is anything other than the default.

The frame's dimensions when closed and the icon it uses may be set using xv_create() or by using xv_set() after the frame has been created. Figure 4-5 shows what any application or base frame looks like when it is closed, providing that the application uses the base frame with default values. The figure also shows a graphical icon used by an application.

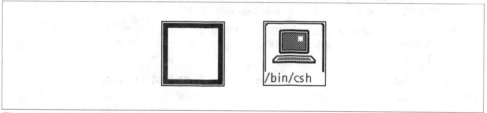

Figure 4-5. Default icon and application icon

To set the icon for the base frame, the icon must already have been created. However, assuming one is available, the icon can be set in the base frame using the FRAME_ICON attribute-value pair. Because the icon might not be the default size (64x64), it is usually a good idea to set the size of the frame when it is in the closed state. To do this, set the attribute FRAME_CLOSED_RECT to be a pointer to a variable of type Rect * (pointer to a Rect). (Rect is an XView data type defined in <xview/rect.h>.)

The best way to handle it is to use xv_set() after the call to xv_create():

```
    . . .
    extern Icon icon;
    Frame       frame;
    Rect        rect;
    . . .
    rect.r_width = (int)xv_get(icon, XV_WIDTH);
```

Frames

```
rect.r_height = (int)xv_get(icon, XV_HEIGHT);
frame = (Frame)xv_create(NULL, FRAME, NULL);
xv_set(frame,
    FRAME_ICON,          icon,
    FRAME_CLOSED_RECT,   &rect,
    NULL);
```

This code segment sets the size of the icon area to be whatever size the icon is. Since FRAME_CLOSED_RECT takes a pointer to a variable of type Rect, the address of the variable is given as the value parameter to the call to xv_set(). Also note that the other fields of the rect variable, (r_top, r_left) are not used because FRAME_CLOSED_RECT only uses the width and height dimensions from the variable.

The following call can be made to determine whether the frame is currently closed from within the application:

```
is_closed = (Boolean) xv_get(frame, FRAME_CLOSED);
```

This call is useful for applications that are graphics-intensive. If a complex piece of code is about to be executed, the application could check to see if the frame is open to display the graphics.

4.2.4 Quit Confirmation

OPEN LOOK specifies that a notice is generally not needed to confirm a "quit" action unless data will be lost. The base frame, which usually handles this type of action through the window manager, can be set to ask for confirmation. The attribute FRAME_NO_CONFIRM, which defaults to TRUE, can be set to FALSE to force confirmation:

```
frame = (Frame)xv_create(NULL, FRAME,
    FRAME_NO_CONFIRM, FALSE,
    NULL);
```

When the attribute FRAME_NO_CONFIRM is set to FALSE and the user initiates a "quit" action, a notice dialog box will appear to request confirmation.

4.3 Command Frames

Command frames are normally subframes in that they are most often created as children of base frames. Most of the time, they are pop-up frames that serve one function and then go away. Instead of having a Close button in the frame's header, the command frame might have a pushpin. The pushpin governs whether the frame remains up after the user performs the functions that the pop-up frame provides. When a command frame is created, a default panel is also created automatically. The panel on a command frame can be used to hold the panel items, such as buttons or sliders, that the user interacts with. When command frames are created, a panel is also created. xv_get() can be used on command frames to get the default panel and to avoid creating a new one.

Example 4-5 shows a simple program that creates a pop-up frame as a child of the base frame. Figure 4-6 displays the output of this program.

Example 4-5. Creating a subframe

```
/*
 * subframe.c -- display a subframe from a base frame.
 */
#include <xview/xview.h>
main(argc, argv)
int argc;
char *argv[];
{
    Frame frame, subframe;

    xv_init(XV_INIT_ARGC_PTR_ARGV, &argc, argv, NULL);

    frame = (Frame)xv_create(NULL, FRAME,
        XV_WIDTH,       100,
        XV_HEIGHT,      100,
        FRAME_LABEL,    "Base Frame",
        NULL);

    subframe = (Frame)xv_create(frame, FRAME_CMD,
        XV_WIDTH,       100,
        XV_HEIGHT,      100,
        FRAME_LABEL,    "Popup",
        NULL);

    xv_set(subframe, XV_SHOW, TRUE, NULL);

    xv_main_loop(frame);
}
```

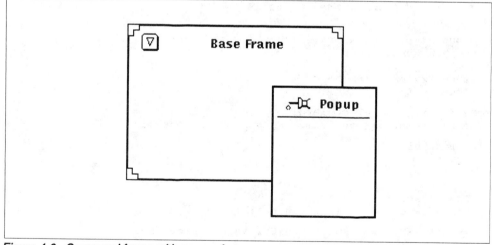

Figure 4-6. Command frame with pop-up frame

4.3.1 Manually Displaying Frames

The attribute XV_SHOW sets whether a window (or frame, in this case) will be displayed. If it is set to FALSE, the frame will not be seen. Base frames are always displayed because xv_main_loop sets the XV_SHOW attribute to TRUE. Pop-up frames are not displayed unless the XV_SHOW attribute is set by the application. An application might create many pop-up dialog boxes initially and then determine the appropriate time to actually display them. A callback routine invoked by some action (e.g., panel button selection) from the base frame might be used to display the pop-up frame.

4.3.2 The Pushpin

On a command frame, the pushpin at the upper-right corner is unpinned by default. It can be pinned by setting the attribute FRAME_CMD_PUSHPIN_IN to TRUE. This attribute can also be queried using xv_get(), which will return TRUE if the pushpin is in and FALSE if it is not.

A simple example can demonstrate how some of the frame attributes interact. The program in Example 4-6 builds a base frame with a panel button that says, "Hello." If selected, a command frame pops up. The new frame has a panel button that says, "Push Me," and if pushed, "Hello World" is printed to *stdout*. If the command frame's pushpin is out, once the Push Me button is selected, the frame is taken down. To get the frame up again, the user must select Hello again. However, if the pin is in, then the frame remains up for repeated use. Selecting Hello while the frame is already up causes the command frame to be raised to the top of the window tree. This is useful in case the command frame gets obscured by other windows.

Example 4-6. Using several frame attributes

```
/*
 * popup.c -- popup a frame and allow the user to interact with
 * the new popup frame.
 */
#include <xview/xview.h>
#include <xview/panel.h>

Frame frame;      /* top level application base-frame */
Frame subframe;   /* subframe (FRAME_CMD) is a child of frame */

main(argc, argv)
int argc;
char *argv[];
{
    Panel panel;
    int show_cmd_frame(), pushed();

    xv_init(XV_INIT_ARGC_PTR_ARGV, &argc, argv, NULL);

    /* Create base frame */
    frame = (Frame)xv_create(NULL, FRAME,
        FRAME_LABEL, argv[0],
        NULL);

    /* Install a panel and a panel button */
    panel = (Panel)xv_create(frame, PANEL, NULL);
```

Example 4-6. Using several frame attributes (continued)

```
    (void) xv_create(panel, PANEL_BUTTON,
        PANEL_LABEL_STRING, "Hello",
        PANEL_NOTIFY_PROC,  show_cmd_frame,
        NULL);

    /* Create the command frame -- not displayed until XV_SHOW is set */
    subframe = (Frame)xv_create(frame, FRAME_CMD,
        FRAME_LABEL,        "Popup",
        NULL);

    /* Command frames have panels already created by default -- get it */
    panel = (Panel)xv_get(subframe, FRAME_CMD_PANEL);
    (void) xv_create(panel, PANEL_BUTTON,
        PANEL_LABEL_STRING,  "Push Me",
        PANEL_NOTIFY_PROC,   pushed,
        NULL);

    xv_main_loop(frame);
}

/* Called when base frame's button is pushed -- show/raise subframe */
show_cmd_frame(item, event)
Frame item;
Event *event;
{
    xv_set(subframe, XV_SHOW, TRUE, NULL);
}

/* Called when command frame's button is pushed */
pushed(item,event)
Panel_item  item;
Event   *event;
{
    printf("Hello world.\n");

    /* Check to see if the pushpin is in -- if not, close frame */
    if ((int)xv_get(subframe, FRAME_CMD_PUSHPIN_IN) == FALSE)
        xv_set(subframe, XV_SHOW, FALSE, NULL);
}
```

Several things are noteworthy in this sample program. First, there is only one `Panel` variable (called `panel`). It is used to store the handle to the panel created by the base frame. It does not matter that this variable is also used to store the return value of the call to:

```
    xv_create(frame, PANEL, NULL)
```

because its use is temporary. This demonstrates that the programmer need not maintain handles to objects that are never referenced. A common programming efficiency error is to declare many variables that reference objects created via `xv_create()` and then never to use them. The panel is needed, but only long enough to use it as the *owner* of the panel button that is created. Once ownership is established, the handle to that panel is no longer needed. Therefore, the variable is reused in the call that gets the *already created panel* from the subframe. This call is as follows:

```
    panel = (Panel)xv_get(subframe, FRAME_CMD_PANEL)
```

The handles to the buttons are never needed, so the return values of those creation calls are ignored. On the other hand, it is always prudent to check for return values in case of error—had the panel creation returned a NULL handle, then the buttons should not be created. The sample programs do not demonstrate this type of error checking in order to keep the examples simple and readable.

4.3.3 The FRAME_DONE_PROC Procedure

If the pushpin is pushed in by the user, the application has no knowledge of this action. However, if the user pulls the pin out, then the application calls the command frame's FRAME_DONE_PROC routine. By default, the routine takes down the subframe. The programmer can override this by setting FRAME_DONE_PROC to another routine. This is only needed if you want to check that the frame can be dismissed. Suppose that the purpose of the subframe is to query for a filename. If the filename was not given, you might want to display a notice indicating the fact and allow the user to type in a filename. In this case, the FRAME_DONE_PROC is responsible for doing the necessary checking and deciding on whether to display a notice or to take the frame down.

When you install your own FRAME_DONE_PROC routine, XView will *not* take down the frame regardless of what your code does. If you want the frame to go down, set it down.

The parameter passed to your routine is a handle to the subframe itself (see Example 4-7):

Example 4-7. The subframe.c program

```
#include <xview/xview.h>
#include <xview/frame.h>

/*
 * subframe.c -- create a base frame that has an associated subframe.
 * Pull the pin out of the subframe and its FRAME_DONE_PROC procedure
 * gets called.
 */
main(argc, argv)
int argc;
char *argv[];
{
    Frame frame, subframe;
    int done_proc();

    xv_init(XV_INIT_ARGC_PTR_ARGV, &argc, argv, NULL);

    frame = (Frame)xv_create(NULL, FRAME, NULL);

    subframe = (Frame)xv_create(frame, FRAME_CMD,
        FRAME_DONE_PROC, done_proc,
        XV_SHOW,         TRUE,
        NULL);
    xv_main_loop(frame);
}

/*
 * when the pushpin is pulled out, this routine is called
 */
done_proc(subframe)
Frame subframe;
{
```

Example 4-7. The subframe.c program (continued)

```
    /* we have the choice of vetoing or granting the user's
     * request to dismiss the frame -- if we choose to dismiss
     * the frame, we must do it manually.  Like so:
     */
    xv_set(subframe, XV_SHOW, FALSE, NULL);
    /* otherwise, we should push the pin back in */
}
```

The call to `xv_set(XV_SHOW, FALSE)` is safe because no action is taken at all if this was not the result of the pin being pulled out. The frame will not go down (i.e., the `xv_set()` is a no-op) if the pin is in or is already out. This gives the programmer the flexibility of using the same function (something like `done_proc()`) in other places throughout the application. For example, it could be used in a callback routine for a panel button.

If the subframe must be taken down regardless of whether the pin is in or out, the application should forcefully remove the pin using:

```
    xv_set(subframe, FRAME_CMD_PUSHPIN_IN, FALSE, NULL);
```

Forcefully removing the pin in this fashion does not result in the frame's done procedure getting called. This routine is only called when the pin has been removed as a result of an action that the user has taken and when the application has no knowledge of this action.

4.3.4 Showing Resize Corners

It should also be noted that the command frame has no resize corners as the base frame does. This is the default behavior for command frames, but the attribute `FRAME_SHOW_RESIZE_CORNER` can be set to `TRUE` to force the resize corners to be shown. This allows the user to resize command frames the same as base frames. Base frames have resize corners by default, but they can be turned off at creation time or at any time *before the frame is mapped to the screen*. After the frame has been displayed, the resize corners may not be turned off.

4.4 Miscellaneous Attributes

The attributes discussed in this section are attributes that are also used by the `FRAME` package to communicate with the window manager. You will get unpredictable results if the window manager does not understand these attributes, if the user is not running an OPEN LOOK window manager or if there is no window manager running at all.

Frames

4.4.1 Busy Frames

When running the Push Me application, you might notice a delay between the time that the Hello button is pressed and the time that the subframe is displayed. If a delay might confuse the user about what might be happening, you can provide visual feedback that the application is at work. You can set the FRAME_BUSY attribute for the frame that issues the request that might cause the delay. In Example 4-7, we set the XV_SHOW attribute in the base frame. Thus, show_cmd_frame() might have looked like the following code fragment:

```
show_cmd_frame(subframe,event)

Frame subframe;
Event *event;
{
    xv_set(baseframe, FRAME_BUSY, TRUE, NULL);
    xv_set(subframe, XV_SHOW, TRUE, NULL);
    xv_set(baseframe, FRAME_BUSY, FALSE, NULL);
}
```

The effect of this action is that the base frame's header will be grayed out and the cursor will change to a timeout cursor. When the subframe has been displayed, the base frame's appearance is resumed and the cursor restored. If excessively long delays are expected, then this method might not be adequate—all other buttons and events are suspended until the callback routine has returned control to the Notifier.

Note that FRAME_BUSY only grays the title bar and sets the busy cursor for the frame passed to xv_set(). If your application has many subframes and you wish each of them to become busy, you need to set this attribute for each frame.

4.4.2 Frame Sizes

The size of any type of frame can be set or queried using either of two convenience functions available from the FRAME package. They are frame_get_rect() and frame_set_rect(). Both use a Rect data type. The origin of the frame as well as its width and height can be set using frame_set_rect(). Of course, the frame must already be created in order to use this function. In the following code, the frame is set at 10,10 on the screen and the dimensions are set to 200 by 300:

```
Frame frame;
Rect rect;

rect.r_top = rect.r_left = 10;
rect.r_width = 200;
rect.r_height = 300;
...
frame = (Frame)xv_create(NULL, FRAME, NULL);

frame_set_rect(frame, &rect);
```

Conversely, the dimensions as well as the position of the frame can be gotten:

```
extern Frame frame;
extern Rect rect;
...
```

```
        frame_get_rect(frame, &rect);
        printf("frame is at %d, %d and is %d by %d\n",
            rect.r_left, rect.r_top, rect.r_width, rect.r_height);
```

4.4.3 Frame Colors

In frames, you can set several attributes pertaining to color. FRAME_FOREGROUND_COLOR
and FRAME_BACKGROUND_COLOR can be set to colors that correspond to the frame's foreground and background colors, respectively. These colors do not affect the frame's header
and footer, but they do affect the window in the frame. Setting these attributes can have little
effect unless the attribute FRAME_INHERIT_COLORS is also set. This attribute tells the
FRAME package to propagate the colors to the subwindows and subframes that the frame
owns. Therefore, if a panel is installed in a frame, the panel will inherit the colors specified
in the frame.

Example 4-8 shows a program that displays a frame with the appropriate foreground and
background colors set in the variables, fg and bg. The panel will inherit those colors from
the frame, so the panel will be brown and the panel button will be yellow.*

Example 4-8. Setting colors in a frame

```
#include <xview/xview.h>
#include <xview/panel.h>
#include <xview/cms.h>

main()
{
    Frame               frame;
    Panel               panel;
    Xv_singlecolor      fg, bg;

    fg.red = 250, fg.green = 230, fg.blue = 20;
    bg.red = 180, bg.green = 100, bg.blue = 20;

    frame = (Frame)xv_create(NULL, FRAME,
        FRAME_BACKGROUND_COLOR, &bg,
        FRAME_FOREGROUND_COLOR, &fg,
        FRAME_INHERIT_COLORS,   TRUE,
        NULL);

    panel = (Panel)xv_create(frame, PANEL, NULL);
    (void) xv_create(panel, PANEL_BUTTON,
        PANEL_LABEL_STRING,     "Push Me",
        NULL);

    xv_main_loop(frame);
}
```

One caveat to setting the colors in frames is that they can be set once and only once in the
call to xv_create(). Once the colors are set, they cannot be reset. One reason for this is
that the colors cannot be propagated to the child objects in the object tree.

---

*This depends on your colormap setting and the type of display you have.

Note that only the frame and subordinate objects have the colors specified. The window manager controls the colors of the title bar and other decorations.

4.4.4 Child Windows

The very purpose of frames is to manage subwindows such as panels and canvases. Basically, parenting responsibilities are handled transparently by XView and do not require intervention by the programmer. When creating a new object (such as a panel), you simply specify the frame as the panel's parent or owner.

There are several attributes that can obtain subwindows and subframes from the frame. FRAME_NTH_SUBWINDOW and FRAME_NTH_SUBFRAME are attributes that can be used with xv_get(). Assuming the application has created a subframe, the following code fragment will return the first subframe created:

```
Frame subframe;

subframe = xv_get(frame, FRAME_NTH_SUBFRAME, 1);
```

Similarly, if a frame creates a panel and then a canvas, you can get the canvas (because it was the second one created) by using the call:

```
Canvas canvas;

canvas = xv_get(frame, FRAME_NTH_SUBWINDOW, 2);
```

If you attempt to get a subwindow or subframe index but it does not exist, xv_get() will return NULL.

Laying out subwindows in frames is somewhat automatic, but more explicit layouts can be accomplished by using the macro defined in *<xview/frame.h>* called frame_fit_all(). This macro loops on xv_get() to get each FRAME_NTH_SUBWINDOW and call window_fit() to make sure that all the subwindows fit in the frame (if possible). window_fit() also serves as a hint for the frame to give it permission to resize any of its subwindows whenever a resize event occurs. For example, say a frame contains a canvas subwindow, but that subwindow's dimensions are set via XV_WIDTH and XV_HEIGHT. If the user uses the window manager to resize the frame, the frame may or may not resize the canvas depending on whether or not it was given permission to do so via either of the calls to window_fit(), window_fit_height() or window_fit_width(). See Chapter 5, *Canvases and Openwin*, for more information on window_fit().

4.5 Destroying Frames

When the application wants to exit, the user typically initiates the action via the frame menu. A call to `xv_destroy()` destroys the object as well as all objects descended from it. Therefore, all the objects created by an application can be destroyed simply by destroying the base frame, assuming that the base frame is the owner of all those objects. Subframes of the base frame are included, as are icons and panels and so forth. There are exceptions to this (such as server images or fonts), but those exceptions are covered later in chapters specific to those objects.

The following code segment demonstrates how to destroy a base frame. When the routine `quit()` is called, which calls `xv_destroy_safe()` on the base frame, it destroys all the objects in the frame's tree, including panels and panel items.

```
{
    ...
    xv_main_loop(frame);
    puts("The program is now done.");
    exit(0);
}
quit()
{
    xv_destroy_safe(frame);
}
```

What is significant about this segment is that there is code following the call to `xv_main_loop()` so that the routine will return when no more frames are left to display. The FRAME package keeps track of all the frames in the application. Each time a frame is created or destroyed, the FRAME package updates its internal count of the number of existing frames. This includes frames that are not displayed or frames that are iconified. When the last frame is destroyed, the Notifier stops and `xv_main_loop()` returns. (Note that the FRAME package has its own destruction procedures.) Most applications simply exit as shown in the code fragment above. However, if desired, more frames can be created and the Notifier can be restarted. For example, the following code shows how the same base frame may be created five times, assuming that the program does not exit in some manner.

```
Frame   frame;
int     i;

for (i = 0; i < 5; i++) {
    frame = (Frame)xv_create(NULL, FRAME, NULL);
    ...
    xv_main_loop(frame);
}
```

For this to work, there must be a call to `xv_destroy()` for each frame in the application. Granted, this example is rather silly, but consider an application driven by timer interrupts or by network traffic listening for a particular request. Here, there may be no frames displayed until the timer goes off or until the network protocol is initiated. Once this happens, the application that requires user input will create the base frames and enter `xv_main_loop()`. When the user is done and has destroyed all the frames, `xv_main_loop()` returns and the application can continue waiting for alarm timeouts or listening for network traffic.

Frames

4.6 Frame Package Summary

Table 4-1 lists the attributes in the FRAME package; the procedures and macros are listed below. This information is described fully in Appendices A and B.

```
frame_get_rect()
frame_set_rect()
```

Table 4-1. Frame Attributes

Frame	Base Frame	Command Frame
FRAME_BACKGROUND_COLOR	FRAME_CLOSED	FRAME_CMD_PANEL
FRAME_BUSY	FRAME_CLOSED_RECT	FRAME_CMD_PUSHPIN_IN
FRAME_FOREGROUND_COLOR	FRAME_ICON	FRAME_DEFAULT_DONE_PROC
FRAME_INHERIT_COLORS	FRAME_NO_CONFIRM	FRAME_DONE_PROC
FRAME_LEFT_FOOTER		
FRAME_NTH_SUBFRAME		
FRAME_NTH_SUBWINDOW		
FRAME_RIGHT_FOOTER		
FRAME_SHOW_FOOTER		
FRAME_SHOW_HEADER		
FRAME_SHOW_LABEL		
FRAME_SHOW_RESIZE_CORNER		
XV_LABEL		

5

Canvases and Openwin

In This Chapter:

5
Canvases and Openwin

Perhaps the most important object in the XView Toolkit is a *canvas*—the area in which an application displays graphics and handles input. The canvas object is similar to that of a painter's canvas. The artist's painting is drawn onto the canvas and the canvas is mounted in a frame. The canvas may be larger than the frame, but the person looking at the canvas only sees what is within the boundaries of the frame. If the canvas is larger than what is viewable, the painting can be moved around making different portions of the canvas visible.

An XView canvas object allows the user to view a graphic image that is too large for the window or even the display screen. The viewable portion of the graphic image is part of the *viewport* or *view window* of the image. Many different views of the image can use the same canvas object. While each view maintains its own idea of what it is displaying, the canvas object manages all the view windows as well as the graphic image that all views share. The ability for the canvas to maintain different views of the graphic image is a property that is inherited from the canvas's superclass, the OPENWIN package. These properties provide for *splitting* and *scrolling* views. You cannot create a canvas object with multiple views; views are split and joined generally by the user via the attached scrollbars. It is possible to pro-grammatically split and scroll views, but OPEN LOOK's interface specification indicates that scrollbars provide the ability to split views. When a view is split, each new view may be further split into two more views, and so on. All the views are still a part of the same canvas object.

The OPENWIN package is an example of a *hidden* class. You cannot instantiate an openwin object independently from canvas or text subwindows. Chapter 8, *Text Subwindows*, contains information about text subwindows. The canvas object is different from the text object in that it maintains an image that can be manipulated by the user. The openwin object, and thus the canvas object, are broken down into three parts: the *main subwindow*, the *view window* and the *paint window*.

Each view displays a portion of a corresponding paint window. The paint window need not be the size of the corresponding view or the canvas subwindow. Figure 5-1 shows an example of one canvas object providing separate views into one graphic image. What each view displays is independent of what the other views display. A view may even display a portion of an image that is currently displayed in another view.

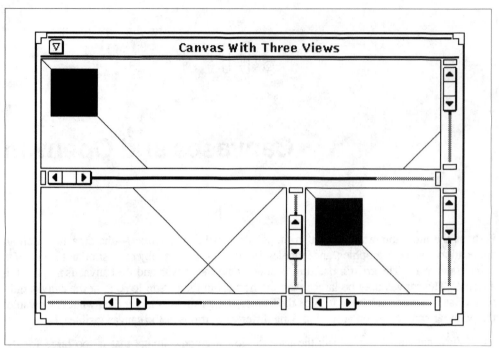

Figure 5-1. A canvas subwindow with multiple views

5.1 Canvas Model

The components of a canvas subwindow and their relationships can be seen in Figure 5-2.

To summarize, three types of windows are involved with the canvas object:

Canvas Subwindow   Owned by a frame and manages one or more views. The canvas is subclassed from the OPENWIN package so all Openwin attributes must be set to the instance of the canvas object.

View Window   Represents the visible portion of the paint window—whenever the paint window associated with a view window changes, it is reflected in the view window. If there is more than one view window, the views are tiled. Vertical and/or horizontal scrollbars can be attached to the view subwindow to allow the user to modify which portion of the paint window is displayed for that particular view. The size of the view window can vary among all the views. Only views can be split. No graphics or user events take place in this window.

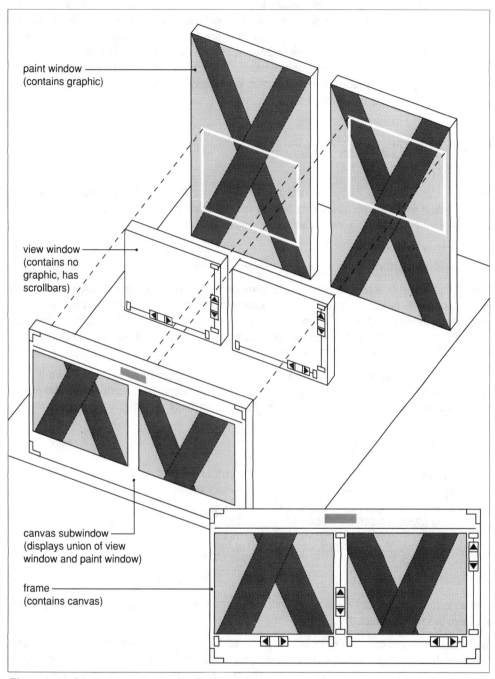

paint window
(contains graphic)

view window
(contains no
graphic, has
scrollbars)

canvas subwindow
(displays union of view
window and paint window)

frame
(contains canvas)

Figure 5-2. Canvases, views and paint windows

Paint Window   Graphics and events (mouse/keyboard) take place in the paint win-
                    dow. There is one paint window per view window. All paint win-
                    dows in the canvas are the same size regardless of the size of the

canvas or of the corresponding view windows. When a view is split, the old view reduces in size and a new view is created. With the new view, a new paint window is created that is identical to the paint window from the old view. This includes the same visual, width, height, depth and graphic image. However, callback functions and event masks are not inherited and must be manually installed in all new paint windows.

5.2 Creating a Canvas

The CANVAS package is defined in the header file *<xview/canvas.h>* so programs that use canvases must include this file. This header file includes the OPENWIN package automatically. Like all objects in XView, a canvas is created with xv_create():

```
Canvas canvas;

canvas = (Canvas)xv_create(owner, CANVAS, attrs);
```

Here, xv_create() returns a handle to a new canvas subwindow. The owner of a canvas must be a FRAME object. All three subwindows of the canvas are created at this point: the canvas subwindow, the view window and the paint window. By using this syntax, the attributes of the canvas default to those set for the CANVAS package plus any attributes that may be inherited from the owner of the canvas.

Colors are usually something that are inherited from the parent frame. The following code fragment shows that the foreground and background colors can be inherited from the parent frame if the frame sets the FRAME_INHERIT_COLORS attribute to TRUE:

```
Frame            frame;
Canvas           canvas;
Xv_singlecolor fg, bg;

fg.red = 250, fg.green = 230, fg.blue = 20;
bg.red = 180, bg.green = 100, bg.blue = 20;

frame = (Frame)xv_create(NULL, FRAME,
    FRAME_INHERIT_COLORS,    TRUE,
    FRAME_FOREGROUND_COLOR,  &fg,
    FRAME_BACKGROUND_COLOR,  &bg,
    NULL);

canvas = (Canvas)xv_create(frame, CANVAS, NULL);
```

Even though a default canvas was created, its foreground and background colors are inherited from the frame object.

The windows in the canvas object inherit many of their attributes from the canvas's parent, screen or display (depending on the window property). However, some attributes are set or reset explicitly. For example, the attribute CANVAS_RETAINED, which controls whether the server should retain windows, is turned on.* Toggling this attribute causes the canvas to cycle through all of the paint windows and change their WIN_RETAINED attribute. Also, the

---

*CANVAS_RETAINED does not affect the view windows, which are not retained.

window has its `BitGravity` set to `NorthWestGravity` by default. This value is set by the attribute `CANVAS_FIXED_IMAGE`. If `TRUE`, then the `BitGravity` property on the paint window is set to `NorthWestGravity`. If `FALSE`, `BitGravity` is set to `ForgetGravity`. This is discussed in more detail in Section 5.3, "The Repaint Procedure."

The width and height of the paint window and the view window default to the size of the canvas when it is realized. Unless otherwise specified, those sizes are governed by the object that is the owner of the canvas.

5.2.1 Drawing in a Canvas

The use of canvases implies that your application wants to display a graphic image that the user can either manipulate or generate. In conventional (not server-client based) windowing systems, when you request to create a window, you usually get a window back that you can draw into. This is not exactly true for X. Although you get a window back from the request, you are not guaranteed to be able to draw into it until it has been successfully mapped (displayed) on the screen. In the general case for XView, this does not happen until `xv_main_loop()` is called. Therefore, you should *not* do the following:

```
canvas = (Canvas)xv_create(frame, CANVAS, NULL);
win = (Window)xv_get(canvas_paint_window(canvas), XV_XID);

XDrawString(dpy, win, gc, x, y, "Hello World.", 11);
```

Instead, you should design your program such that your repaint routine knows exactly what the contents of the canvas should be so that it can reproduce the image. Here are two helpful hints for typical applications:

• *Use your repaint proc.*
  Never call any graphics routines before `xv_main_loop()` is called. Routines that draw anything into windows should be called directly or indirectly from your canvas repaint procedure or event handler.

• *Use internal data.*
  The repaint routine should be able to repaint a canvas window based on some sort of internal data. To maintain system performance, the data should be in core; it should *not* be on disk (in a file), from a network connection or from interaction with the user. If the data is received from those media, the data should already have been updated by the time the repaint routine is called.

To give you an idea of the issues involved here, we'll look at several common applications that typically use canvases.

Draw Programs

Draw programs are usually applications which maintain a *display list* of geometric shapes such as lines, circles, rectangles and so on. The user generates these shapes using the mouse or keyboard. The canvas's WIN_EVENT_PROC procedure handles mouse and keyboard input from the user, and the user interface generally describes the shape that is currently being drawn.

When the user initiates mouse clicks, drags or keyboard actions, the event handler picks up these events and is fully expected to modify the canvas window accordingly (e.g., by "rubber banding" the object). Upon receipt of the appropriate event (button release, perhaps), the event handler adds the new geometric item to the display list.

In order to reconstruct what the canvas should be displaying, the repaint routine references the updated display list. Obviously, the display list should contain enough information in it to be able to tell the repaint routine what colors to use, line thickness and so on.

Paint Programs

Paint programs are *pixel based*, meaning that the image that the user manipulates is typically a bitmap (monochrome) or a color pixmap. In this case, the pixmap is used as the internal data. If the user uses a *brush* to modify the image, the modification to the canvas window is handled in the event procedure as above, but the image that the user is editing is also updated so that when the repaint routine is called, it can use a function such as XCopyArea() to copy the portion of the image onto the canvas window. This is also a case where the event handler may draw directly onto the window.

If the program starts up and already has an image to work with (e.g., the user requests to load a previously saved image that was stored into the file), *do not render the image onto the paint window before* xv_main_loop() *is called.* Eventually, the repaint procedure will be called and the image should be rendered at that time.

Text-based Programs

If you want to display text, as in desktop publishing packages, or if you just want a simple program that displays a window with text, then the same thing applies as with the previous examples: render the text in the repaint routine based on internal data (e.g., a text string or set of strings). Again, the data must contain enough information to allow your repaint routine to repaint the text as it was intended (e.g., font type, style, size, color).

Event-handling routines that accept keyboard input may render the new text directly to the canvas window, but the text entered should also be saved internally for the benefit of the repaint routine.

Visualization Programs

It is common to have an application that displays the time, network traffic, CPU usage, file system integrity or the current Dow Jones Industrial Averages. Such applications get their data from a variety of sources such as the system clock, UNIX sockets, the file system or the output of another application that has been forked. In the past, such applications might have been written where the repaint routine accesses the information. This model does not apply in a networked windowing system because of its asynchronous nature; the window system and the application may not be in sync. A program should have a separate method for retrieving data apart from the repaint procedure. See the program *animate.c* in Chapter 19, *The Notifier*, for an example.

In many of these cases (with the possible exception of the *meters*), if the application is well designed, the repaint routines and the event handlers may be calling the same internal routines which render graphics. Therefore, when writing functions that draw into a canvas, you should consider the generic case where the function could be called from a repaint routine, event handler or anywhere else. The program *canvas_event.c* (shown in Example 5-3) calls the repaint routine directly from the event handler.

Rendering Graphics

The preferred form of rendering graphics from an XView application is to use Xlib graphics calls. Volume One, *Xlib Programming Manual*, has a complete discussion of Xlib graphics programming. Throughout this book, you will find examples of drawing into canvases using Xlib graphics routines. Appendix F, *Example Programs*, has several longer programs that demonstrate Xlib graphics. The XView graphics model, which is available, is almost identical to the SunView model for graphics and is provided for backwards compatibility with SunView. Because XView graphics calls are wrappers to the underlying Xlib calls, these functions are not recommended for graphics-intensive applications or for use by programmers who are not already familiar with SunView.

5.3 The Repaint Procedure

It is always the responsibility of the application to repaint its canvas at any time. Even though there may be a retained canvas that the X server maintains, there is no guarantee that there will be enough memory for the server to maintain it. For this reason, all canvases should install a routine to handle repainting.

To install a repaint procedure, use the attribute CANVAS_REPAINT_PROC and specify a callback function as its value:

```
extern void my_repaint_proc();
...
canvas = (Canvas)xv_create(frame, CANVAS,
    ...
    CANVAS_REPAINT_PROC,    my_repaint_proc(),
    ...
    NULL);
```

The repaint routine installed is called any time all or a portion of the canvas needs to be re-displayed. This always happens when the canvas is mapped on the screen for the first time (causing an Expose event). If the canvas is *not* retained, the repaint procedure is called when:

- The canvas is resized.

- The canvas has been moved in front of obscuring windows.

- The user uses the scrollbar to render a different part of the paint window visible.

If the canvas *is* retained and has not changed size, the server refreshes the window without calling the repaint routine. This includes all exposures except for those that are the result of a resize of the window or the initial mapping of the canvas onto the screen. However, if the canvas is not retained, the repaint routine is called in all of these cases.

The repaint callback routine will be called once for each view the canvas is maintaining. If the canvas has been split several times, then the repaint routine will get called for each view that needs repainting. One of the parameters to the callback routine is a variable that describes the region that has been exposed or needs repainting. When a window is initially displayed on the screen, the exposed region is the entire canvas. However, this area may not be a contiguous area of the window. For example, as shown in Figure 5-3, if a window that is partially obscured by two windows is brought forward, two separate areas are exposed.

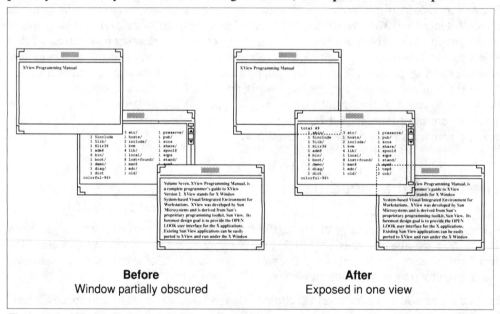

Before
Window partially obscured

After
Exposed in one view

Figure 5-3. Window before and after an Expose event

The attribute WIN_COLLAPSE_EXPOSURES governs how many times the repaint routine is called. By default, XView collapses Expose (and GraphicsExpose) X events destined for the same window; that is, XView waits for the exposure count member to reach zero. After all exposure X events have arrived (when count == 0), XView generates a WIN_REPAINT event and calls the repaint procedure. This `WIN_REPAINT` represents all the areas in the window that have been damaged (it can be a disjoint set of rectangles). The X event associated with the `WIN_REPAINT` event (accessed through the `event_xevent()` macro) represents a bounding rectangle of all the damaged areas in the window (basically the union of all the damaged areas in the window).

However, sometimes the application wants to monitor the incoming `Expose` (and `GraphicsExpose`) X events, monitoring piece by piece the count member in the `Expose` X event itself. This can be done by setting `WIN_COLLAPSE_EXPOSURES` to `FALSE`. As exposures come into a window with this attribute set to `FALSE`, they will be immediately sent to the client's repaint procedure. The client will thus receive several `WIN_REPAINT` events, all for the same window. The area of exposure is set to each region as it is exposed.

By default, the repaint routine is called once per window exposed. However, there may be situations where there are more windows exposed in the same canvas object. For example, in Figure 5-4, two view windows have been exposed as a result of bringing the window to the top of the window stack. In this case, the repaint routine will be called twice—once for the paint window of each view exposed. Only one area of each view window is exposed, so the value of the `WIN_COLLAPSE_EXPOSURES` attribute does not apply.

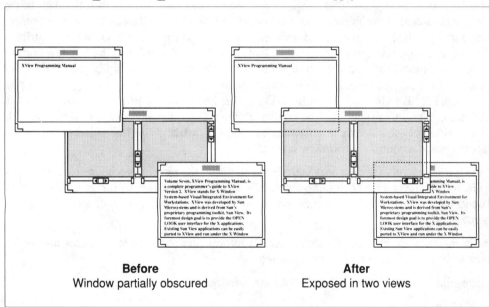

Before
Window partially obscured

After
Exposed in two views

Figure 5-4. Window with two views before and after an Expose event

If at any time you need to get the entire viewable area of the canvas, or more specifically, of an arbitrary paint window within the canvas, you can use the attribute `CANVAS_VIEW-ABLE_RECT`:

```
Rect *rect;
Xv_Window pw = canvas_paint_window(canvas);

rect = (Rect *)xv_get(canvas, CANVAS_VIEWABLE_RECT, pw);
```

The `rect` pointer returned points to an internal data structure that describes the viewable area of the paint window specified. This structure changes for each call, so if the value is to be retained, it should be copied.

Before the repaint routine is called, the window can be cleared in one of two ways. If `CANVAS_AUTO_CLEAR` is set to `TRUE`, then the paint window being repainted is automatically cleared. `CANVAS_AUTO_CLEAR` is really defined as `OPENWIN_AUTO_CLEAR` since this is a property of the `OPENWIN` package. Automatically clearing the window happens any time the window needs repainting. This means that the exposed area represents the entire window. If this attribute is set to `FALSE` (the default), the repaint routine should prepare to clear all, or portions of, the window that needs to be repainted. The contents of the window in the exposed areas is undefined. If you are going to repaint those areas opaquely (that is, leave no transparent portions), then you do not need to clear the area. However, if any transparent portion of the area will be repainted (e.g., if your `gc.function` is set to `GXxor`), you should clear the window first by using `XClearArea()` or `XClearWindow()`.

Alternatively, the window may be cleared automatically by the Xlib internals if the window has actually changed size. The `BitGravity` attribute for the window controls whether the data in the window is cleared or just moved around to different locations of the window according to its new size. If `BitGravity` is set to `ForgetGravity`, then the data in the window is discarded, resulting in the window getting cleared and the canvas's repaint procedure getting called. As mentioned before, this value can be set by setting the attribute `CANVAS_FIXED_IMAGE` to `FALSE`. But to have more direct control over the `BitGravity` of the window, the window attribute `WIN_BIT_GRAVITY` may be set to any of the legal values provided by Xlib (`ForgetGravity`, `NorthGravity`, `NorthWestGravity` and so on). Section 4.3.3, "Bit Gravity," in Volume One, *Xlib Programming Manual*, discusses this in full detail. Note: this should not be confused with `WIN_WINDOW_GRAVITY` which controls the reposition of subwindows when a parent window is resized. This task is left to the `FRAME` package, since it controls subwindow layout.

If the attribute `CANVAS_CMS_REPAINT` is set to `TRUE`, the repaint procedure is called automatically whenever a new colormap segment is set on the canvas or the foreground and background colors of the canvas are changed using `WIN_FOREGROUND_COLOR` and `WIN_BACK-GROUND_COLOR`.

The parameters to the repaint routine provide information about which window and which areas within the window need to be repainted.

The repaint procedure takes one of two different forms:

```
        void
        repaint_proc(canvas, paint_window, repaint_area)
            Canvas        canvas;
            Xv_Window     paint_window
            Rectlist      *repaint_area;
or:
        void
        repaint_proc(canvas, paint_window, dpy, xwin, area)
            Canvas        canvas;
            Xv_Window     paint_window
            Display       *dpy;
```

```
Window        xwin;
Xv_xrectlist *area;
```

The routine takes the first or second form depending on the value of the attribute `CANVAS_X_PAINT_WINDOW`. If `FALSE`, the first, simpler form of the repaint procedure is called. If `TRUE`, the repaint routine gets passed the parameters shown in the second form. The second method is more useful since it saves you from writing code for extracting the `Display` and the `XID` of the paint window.

In both forms, the first two parameters are rather obvious—the `paint_window` is the paint window associated with the canvas that needs repainting (not the view window). The `paint_window` contains an X window whose `XID` can be gotten by using `xv_get()`:

```
Window xwin = (Window)xv_get(paint_window, XV_XID);
```

xwin is set to the actual X window referenced by the paint window. This is the way to obtain the XID from the paint window because the first form of the repaint procedure (when `CANVAS_X_PAINT_WINDOW` is `FALSE`) does not provide a handle for you.

In the first form of the repaint procedure, the only other parameter is the `repaint_area`. This is a linked list of rectangular areas in the paint window that have been exposed and need to be repainted. The `Rectlist` type is a linked list of `Rect`'s as shown in *<xview/rect.h>*. The declaration for the `Rect` type is:

```
typedef struct rect {
    coord r_left, r_top;
    short r_width, r_height;
} Rect;
```

The type `coord` is #define'd as type `short`. The `Rectlist` is declared in *<xview/rectlist.h>* as:

```
typedef struct  rectnode {
    struct rectnode *rn_next;   /* Pointer to next rectnode */
    struct rect       rn_rect;
} Rectnode;
typedef struct rectlist {
    coord              rl_x, rl_y; /* Offset to apply to each rect
                                    * in list including bound */
    struct rectnode *rl_head;   /* Pointer to first rectnode */
    struct rectnode *rl_tail;   /* Pointer to last rectnode */
    struct rect       rl_bound;  /* Describes bounding rect of
                                    * all rects in list */
} Rectlist;
```

The `repaint_area` parameter is of type `Rectlist`, so the application has several ways it can approach repainting the window. It could just ignore the parameter and repaint the entire window, or it could repaint the entire area described by the `rl_bound` field of the `rectlist` structure or it could loop through all the `Rectnode`'s and repaint those areas individually. Deciding which method to choose should be based on how complicated the redrawing is.

When `CANVAS_X_PAINT_WINDOW` is set to `FALSE`, the internal clipping for the paint window is set to be the same region or regions described by the repaint parameter of the repaint routine. In most cases, this means that `OPENWIN_AUTO_CLEAR` will only clear those areas— not the entire window.* The default behavior may be overridden by setting

---

*For those using the SunView-compatible drawing routines such as `pw_vector()`, rendering is clipped to the area or areas described by `repaint_area`.

WIN_NO_CLIPPING to TRUE for the *canvas*. Setting this attribute cycles through all the paint windows in the canvas and sets the window property WIN_NO_CLIPPING. Having the clipping on the window turned off means that OPENWIN_AUTO_CLEAR will cause the entire window to be cleared.*

By setting the attribute CANVAS_X_PAINT_WINDOW to TRUE, the repaint routine gets passed the extra X-specific parameters as shown in the second form of the repaint procedure. These extra parameters include handles to the Display and the X window of the paint_window.

Example 5-1 shows how a repaint procedure might be used.

Example 5-1. The line.c program

```
/*
 * line.c -- demonstrates installing a repaint routine in a canvas.
 * The routine is called whenever the canvas needs to be repainted.
 * This usually occurs when the canvas is exposed or resized.
 */
#include <X11/Xlib.h>
#include <xview/xview.h>
#include <xview/canvas.h>
#include <xview/xv_xrect.h>
main(argc, argv)
int argc;
char *argv[];
{
    Frame   frame;
    void    canvas_repaint_proc();

    xv_init(XV_INIT_ARGC_PTR_ARGV, &argc, argv, NULL);

    frame = (Frame)xv_create(NULL, FRAME, NULL);

    (void) xv_create(frame, CANVAS,
        CANVAS_REPAINT_PROC,    canvas_repaint_proc,
        CANVAS_X_PAINT_WINDOW,  TRUE,
        NULL);

    xv_main_loop(frame);
}
/*
 * repaint routine draws a line from the top left to the bottom right
 * corners of the window
 */
void
canvas_repaint_proc(canvas, paint_window, dpy, xwin, xrects)
Canvas          canvas;         /* unused */
Xv_Window       paint_window;   /* unused */
Display         *dpy;
Window          xwin;
Xv_xrectlist *xrects;           /* unused */
{
    GC gc;
    int width, height;
```

---

*This also affects the SunView-compatible routines—pw_vector() will not be clipped.

Example 5-1. The line.c program (continued)

```
    gc = DefaultGC(dpy, DefaultScreen(dpy));
    width = (int)xv_get(paint_window, XV_WIDTH);
    height = (int)xv_get(paint_window, XV_HEIGHT);

    XDrawLine(dpy, xwin, gc, 0, 0, width, height);
}
```

Because the program uses Xlib calls (and thus, the repaint routine is being passed different parameters), the header files *<X11/Xlib.h>* and *<xview/xv_xrect.h>* must be added at the top of the program. The parameters display and xwin are handles to the X Display and the X Window, respectively. The GC (graphics context) is taken from the default GC of the screen.

The xrects parameter represents the exposed, or "damaged," region of the paint window. When the canvas is first displayed, this region will be the entire paint window (or the portion that is viewable by the view window). But in cases where another window that has partially obscured it moves away, perhaps only a portion of the paint window will need repainting. Therefore, the xrects variable can aid in setting the clip rectangles in the GC, as shown in Example 5-2.

Example 5-2. Repainting objects within a damaged region

```
/* canvas_repaint_proc()
 *
 * Draws onto the canvas using Xlib drawing functions.
 *
 * Uses the current clipping rectangle to:
 *   1. Restrict graphics output by setting the
 *      clip_mask in the graphics context.
 *   2. Do "smart repainting" by only painting the objects
 *      that lie within the damaged region (not being done
 *      in this example).
 */
void
repaint_proc(canvas, paint_window, display, xid, xrects)
    Canvas canvas;
    Xv_Window paint_window;
    Display *display;
    Window xwin;
    Xv_xrectlist *xrects;
{
    extern GC gc;
    int width, height;

    width = (int)xv_get(paint_window, XV_WIDTH);
    height = (int)xv_get(paint_window, XV_HEIGHT);

    /*
     * Set clip rects, if any
     */
    if (xrects)
        XSetClipRectangles(display, gc, 0, 0, xrects->rect_array,
            xrects->count, Unsorted);
    else {
        XGCValues gc_val;
```

Example 5-2. Repainting objects within a damaged region (continued)

```
        gc_val.clip_mask = None;
        XChangeGC(display, gc, GCClipMask, &gc_val);
    }

    XDrawLine(display, xwin, gc, 0, 0, width, height);
}
```

Because this routine sets the clip mask of the GC, we want to be sure that we *do not use the default* GC of the screen as we did in Figure 5-1, or it will interfere with other programs (such as the window manager). The GC shown here is declared as `extern`, assuming that the application has created it somewhere else using `XCreateGC()`.

5.4 Controlling Canvas Sizes

The size of the canvas subwindow is usually determined by the frame window. Thus, the canvas changes as the user resizes the frame. Applications largely concern themselves with the size of the paint window.* The paint window does not affect the size of the viewable canvas, but the viewable portion of the paint window is important.

Although the width and height of the canvas subwindow can be set explicitly, unless done so, the default size of the subwindow and the paint window is determined by the parent frame. If the frame resizes, the canvas object resizes proportionally according to how the frame chooses to resize the canvas. If several other windows (canvases, panels, whatever) are in the frame, the frame might choose to lay out and size those subwindows differently (according to available and required space from other windows). The canvas window itself, as well as all window objects, can be sized using `XV_WIDTH` and `XV_HEIGHT`. Managing the size of the paint windows under the canvas is dealt with later in this chapter.

5.4.1 Automatic Canvas Sizing

The paint window's size may fluctuate with that of the canvas subwindow's size. The attributes `CANVAS_AUTO_EXPAND` and `CANVAS_AUTO_SHRINK` maintain the relation of the canvas subwindow and paint window in the event of any kind of window resizing. Both of these attributes default to `TRUE`, allowing the paint window to always correspond to the size of the canvas subwindow. If the canvas subwindow becomes larger, the paint window size changes to that size. If the frame changes size, the canvas subwindow changes size and so does the paint window. This happens regardless of how many view windows there are. The size of view windows does not affect the size of the paint window.

Specifically, if `CANVAS_AUTO_EXPAND` is `TRUE`, then the width and height of the paint window cannot be less than that of the canvas subwindow. Setting `CANVAS_AUTO_EXPAND` allows the paint window to grow bigger as the user stretches the window. If a resize of the

---

*There may be more than one paint window to a canvas, but all paint windows in a canvas are the same size, so it's a moot point.

subwindow occurs such that the size of the paint window is less than the size of the canvas subwindow, the paint window is expanded to be at least that size. Conversely, if the canvas subwindow's size shrinks, then the paint canvas size does not change because its size is already greater than or equal to the size of the canvas subwindow—no expansion is necessary.

If CANVAS_AUTO_SHRINK is TRUE, the canvas object checks that width and height of the paint window are not greater than that of the canvas subwindow. Setting CANVAS_AUTO_SHRINK forces the paint window to grow smaller as the size of the canvas subwindow gets smaller. If the user resizes the frame such that the canvas subwindow is smaller than the size of the paint window, then the paint window is reduced to the size of the new subwindow.

You can also set a minimum width and height for the canvas using the attributes CANVAS_MIN_PAINT_WIDTH and CANVAS_MIN_PAINT_HEIGHT.

5.4.2 Explicit Canvas Sizing

The attributes CANVAS_WIDTH and CANVAS_HEIGHT can be set to establish the size of the *paint window*. Automatic sizing should be turned off. Otherwise, as soon as the canvas window is realized, the paint window may be automatically resized to the new dimensions. This all depends on whether either or both of the auto-expand or auto-shrink attributes are set. The following code fragment shows that one can be set and the other unset for specific needs:

```
Canvas canvas;

canvas = (Canvas)xv_create(frame, CANVAS,
    CANVAS_AUTO_SHRINK,   FALSE,
    CANVAS_AUTO_EXPAND,   TRUE,
    CANVAS_WIDTH,         100,
    CANVAS_HEIGHT,        200,
    NULL);
```

With these settings, the paint window will initially be set to 100 by 200. If the subwindow is realized at a larger size, the canvas will be expanded to the new dimensions. That is, if the frame in which the canvas resides is larger, it may affect the initial size of the paint window. However, if the canvas is realized or resized at smaller dimensions, the canvas will retain its original size. In short, these settings will force the paint window to grow to the maximum size that the window will ever be—it will never shrink. In typical usage, you would set the auto-expand and auto-shrink attributes to FALSE and explicitly set CANVAS_WIDTH and CANVAS_HEIGHT. Alternatively, you would not initialize the width and height and set both CANVAS_AUTO_EXPAND and CANVAS_AUTO_SHRINK to TRUE. A draw program might allow the paint window to be sized automatically, since the display list of geometric objects is the underlying feature of the program. However, a paint program would set explicit width and height attributes of the graphic, disallowing any resizing of that graphic.

The following code fragment creates a canvas with a fixed-size paint window that is not affected by resizing:

```
Canvas canvas;

canvas = (Canvas)xv_create(frame, CANVAS,
    CANVAS_AUTO_SHRINK,    FALSE,
    CANVAS_AUTO_EXPAND,    FALSE,
    CANVAS_WIDTH,          1000,
    CANVAS_HEIGHT,         1000,
    NULL);
```

This call sets the initial size of the paint window to 1000 by 1000 pixels. The origin of the paint window's coordinate system is the upper-left corner (0,0) and the lower-right corner (CANVAS_WIDTH-1, CANVAS_HEIGHT-1). Note that we did not set the size of the canvas subwindow. Instead, we allowed it to be determined by the frame size. The size of the paint window remains constant regardless of how the frame and canvas subwindow is resized. If the frame or the canvas subwindow resizes, the subwindow merely changes its view of the underlying paint window, which remains constant.

In the following code fragment, we set the size of the canvas subwindow, using generic attributes:

```
Canvas canvas;

canvas = (Canvas)xv_create(frame, CANVAS,
    CANVAS_AUTO_SHRINK,    FALSE,
    CANVAS_AUTO_EXPAND,    FALSE,
    CANVAS_WIDTH,          1000,
    CANVAS_HEIGHT,         1000,
    XV_WIDTH,              200,
    XV_HEIGHT,             100,
    NULL);
```

Here, a canvas subwindow is created that is 200 pixels wide and 100 pixels high. All other attributes about this canvas object are the same as the previous example: the paint window is going to be 1000x1000 in width and height. The problem with this canvas is that the user has no way to view different parts of the paint window. To handle that, scrollbars should be attached to the canvas to provide scrolling. See Section 5.5, "Scrolling Canvases."

5.4.3 Tracking Changes in the Canvas Size

In the event that the canvas has been resized, the program has the opportunity to track this event by installing a callback routine. This routine is installed, using CANVAS_ RESIZE_PROC. The client's resize procedure is called whenever the width or height of the canvas changes. Its form is:

```
void
sample_resize_proc(canvas, width, height)
    Canvas canvas;
    int    width;
    int    height;
```

The parameters to the resize procedure are the canvas and the new width and height of the canvas. Unlike the repaint routine, the resize procedure is not called for each view in the canvas. It is just called for the canvas window itself. The resize procedure should never repaint any of the canvas's paint windows. If any new area is to be painted, the repaint procedure will be called separately for each view. The width and height of the new views are available within the repaint routine.

5.5 Scrolling Canvases

Many applications need to view and manipulate a large object through a smaller viewing window. To facilitate this, packages that are subclassed from the openwin class may have scrollbars attached to their subwindows.

The following code fragment creates a canvas that can be scrolled in both directions:

```
Canvas      canvas;
Scrollbar  h_scrollbar, v_scrollbar;

canvas = (Canvas)xv_create(frame, CANVAS,
    CANVAS_AUTO_EXPAND,  FALSE,
    CANVAS_AUTO_SHRINK,  FALSE,
    CANVAS_WIDTH,        1000,
    CANVAS_HEIGHT,       1000,
    NULL);

h_scrollbar = (Scrollbar)xv_create(canvas, SCROLLBAR,
    SCROLLBAR_DIRECTION, SCROLLBAR_HORIZONTAL,
    NULL);

v_scrollbar = (Scrollbar)xv_create(canvas, SCROLLBAR,
    SCROLLBAR_DIRECTION, SCROLLBAR_VERTICAL,
    NULL);
```

Because the SCROLLBAR package is being used here, the header file *<xview/scrollbar.h>* must be included. Chapter 10, *Scrollbars*, discusses scrollbars more completely and also gives further examples of how to scroll canvases.

The owner of the scrollbars is the canvas so that the scrollbars are automatically attached to the canvas's view. If the user scrolls the canvas, your canvas's repaint procedure will be called provided that the canvas's WIN_RETAINED attribute is set to FALSE. This is important because setting WIN_RETAINED to TRUE assumes that you are not interested in handling repainting for scrolling. In other words, as long as the user does not do anything that changes the contents of the image, you do not need to be informed when the user scrolls the image. If you want to be informed of scrolling, set WIN_RETAINED to FALSE and your repaint routine will be called with the *exposed area* parameter describing the new area that just scrolled into view.* If there are many views in the canvas, the paint window associated with the view that scrolled is in the second parameter to the repaint function: the paint_window.

---

*The exposed area passed to the repaint procedure is of type Xv_xrectlist if CANVAS_X_PAINT_WINDOW is set to TRUE or Rectlist if CANVAS_X_PAINT_WINDOW is set to FALSE.

5.6 Splitting Canvas Views

There are two methods by which the application may split the views of a canvas (or any openwin-classed object). The first method is for the user to use the scrollbars to split views. This method is more common and complies with the OPEN LOOK specification. The alternate method is for the application to make calls to `xv_set()` with attribute-value pairs that tell where and how a view should be split.

Whenever views are split, the following attributes are propagated from the split paint window to the new paint window:

- `WIN_BACKGROUND_COLOR`
- `WIN_FOREGROUND_COLOR`
- `WIN_CMS`
- `WIN_CMS_DATA`
- `WIN_CMS_NAME`
- `WIN_COLUMN_GAP`
- `WIN_COLUMN_WIDTH`
- `WIN_CURSOR`
- `WIN_EVENT_PROC`
- `WIN_ROW_GAP`
- `WIN_ROW_HEIGHT`
- `WIN_X_EVENT_MASK`

5.6.1 Splitting Views Using Scrollbars

To set up the canvas so that the user can split it using scrollbars, the canvas should have scrollbars attached as shown in the previous example with the additional attribute `SCROLLBAR_SPLITTABLE` set to TRUE:

```
h_scrollbar = (Scrollbar)xv_create(canvas, SCROLLBAR,
    SCROLLBAR_DIRECTION,    SCROLLBAR_HORIZONTAL,
    SCROLLBAR_SPLITTABLE,   TRUE,
    NULL);

v_scrollbar = (Scrollbar)xv_create(canvas, SCROLLBAR,
    SCROLLBAR_DIRECTION,    SCROLLBAR_VERTICAL,
    SCROLLBAR_SPLITTABLE,   TRUE,
    NULL);
```

With this attribute set, the scrollbars have the ability to split view windows in two. The user splits the view by selecting the *cable anchors* at the endpoints of the scrollbars and dragging them towards the center of the scrollbar. A pop-up menu provided with the scrollbars also provides this functionality. The entire view will be split at the point the mouse button is released, provided there is enough room for a new view at that point. Each view can scroll its own underlying paint window independently of other views.

5.6.2 Splitting Views Using xv_set()

Splitting a view by setting attribute-value pairs in the view is a less common method since the scrollbar already provides this functionality. However, there is a programmatic interface for splitting views whether or not those views have scrollbars attached to them.

The attribute OPENWIN_SPLIT is followed by a list of attribute-value pairs that indicate specifically how a view is to be split. Only attributes that are prefixed with OPENWIN_SPLIT may be used in this NULL-terminated list. Other attributes are ignored. The following demonstrates how an arbitrary view window can be split into two parts:

```
Xv_Window view;
view = (Xv_Window)xv_get(canvas, CANVAS_NTH_VIEW, 0);

xv_set(canvas,
    OPENWIN_SPLIT,
        OPENWIN_SPLIT_VIEW,         view,
        OPENWIN_SPLIT_DIRECTION,    OPENWIN_SPLIT_HORIZONTAL,
        NULL,
    NULL);
```

This very simple example shows that the first *view window* in the canvas will be split horizontally. The place in which the split takes place is, by default, the position of the scrollbar in the view. Assuming the code fragment above, the window is split so that the new view is the same width as the original view but the height is split at the position of the scrollbar. The original view is the remaining height and is on top of the new view.

5.6.3 Getting View Windows

If a canvas has been split several times resulting in multiple view and paint windows, it is possible to get a handle to a particular view or paint window. This can be done either at the time the view was split or by using xv_get().

Getting the Newest View

If you want to be notified when the user splits or joins views, you can specify the attributes OPENWIN_SPLIT_INIT_PROC for when the user *splits* a view, and OPENWIN_SPLIT_DESTROY_PROC when the user *joins* a view. These attributes are set in the canvas (or any openwin object). Set these functions by using xv_create() or xv_set() in the following manner:

```
extern void init_split(), join_view();

xv_create(frame, CANVAS,
    ...
    OPENWIN_SPLIT,
        OPENWIN_SPLIT_INIT_PROC,     init_proc,
        OPENWIN_SPLIT_DESTROY_PROC, join_view,
    NULL,
    ...
NULL);
```

Write the split and join functions, which take the following parameters:

```
void
init_split(origview, newview, pos)
    Xv_Window origview, newview;
    int pos;

void
join_view(view)
    Xv_Window view;
```

The `origview` and the `newview` parameters in the first function represent the view that was originally split and the new resulting view, respectively. These are *not* the paint windows; they are the views themselves. To get a handle to the associated paint window from these views, you can use:

```
Xv_Window paint_window;
```

```
paint_window = (Xv_Window)xv_get(view, CANVAS_VIEW_PAINT_WINDOW);
```

Example 6-1 in Chapter 6, *Handling Input* shows how to handle input in different views.

Getting Arbitrary Views

For each view in an OPENWIN object, you can get either the view window or the paint window by choosing either the CANVAS_NTH_PAINT_WINDOW or the OPENWIN_NTH_VIEW attribute and an integer value for the view window. The first window is 0 and the last window is *n*-1, where *n* is the number of view windows. For instance, to get the second paint window in the canvas, you can use:

```
xv_get(canvas, CANVAS_NTH_PAINT_WINDOW, 1, NULL);
```

You can get the number of available views by calling:

```
int nviews = (int)xv_get(canvas, OPENWIN_NVIEWS);
```

Remember that the number of views corresponds directly to the number of paint windows. Each paint window can be accessed in order, using a simple loop like the following:

```
Xv_Window window;
Canvas     canvas;
int        i = 0;

while (window = (Xv_Window)xv_get(canvas, CANVAS_NTH_PAINT_WINDOW, i)) {
    draw_into_window(window);
    i++;
}
```

The call to xv_get() returns NULL if you try to get a window number that does not exist (XView does the error checking). Thus, the loop terminates when xv_get() returns NULL. The value of i represents the number of views in the canvas subwindow.

XView provides a pair of macros that facilitate looping through a set of views in a canvas: CANVAS_EACH_PAINT_WINDOW and CANVAS_END_EACH. The previous loop could be written as:

```
Xv_Window window;
Canvas     canvas;

CANVAS_EACH_PAINT_WINDOW(canvas, window)
    draw_into_window(window);
CANVAS_END_EACH
```

Because the paint windows are different from the view windows, another, slightly different method is used for getting view windows.

```
Xv_Window view;
Canvas     canvas;
int        i = 0;

while (window = (Xv_Window)xv_get(canvas, OPENWIN_NTH_VIEW, i)) {
    /* process window */
    i++;
}
```

There is also a macro that loops through all the views in the canvas:

```
Xv_Window view;
Canvas     canvas;

OPENWIN_EACH_VIEW(canvas, view)
    ...
OPENWIN_END_EACH
```

You can get the paint window associated with a view by using the attribute CANVAS_VIEW_PAINT_WINDOW:

```
Xv_Window view;
Xv_Window paint_window;

paint_window = (Xv_Window)xv_get(view, CANVAS_VIEW_PAINT_WINDOW);
```

This is useful in situations where you are given the view window and need to get the paint window associated with it. For example, the routines called when views are *split* or *joined* are passed handles to view windows. When a view is split, you will need to get the paint window associated with the new view to install event or repaint callbacks.

5.7 Handling Input in the Canvas Package

This section discusses, to a limited degree, the method for handling and specifying events in a canvas. For a detailed discussion of the types of events used and the proper method for handling them, see Chapter 6, *Handling Input*.

5.7.1 Default Events

By default, the CANVAS package enables the following events for its window and paint windows: LOC_WINENTER, LOC_WINEXIT, LOC_MOVE and the three mouse buttons MS_LEFT, MS_MIDDLE and MS_RIGHT. Other events may be added to the window event mask by using xv_set() and passing the appropriate parameters. The following shows how to add keyboard ASCII events:

```
xv_set(canvas_paint_window(canvas),
    WIN_CONSUME_EVENT, WIN_ASCII_EVENTS,
    NULL);
```

An application that needs to track mouse motion while the mouse button is down would enable LOC_DRAG by calling:

```
xv_set(canvas_paint_window(canvas),
    WIN_CONSUME_EVENT, LOC_DRAG,
    NULL);
```

5.7.2 Notification of Events

In addition to specifying which events the application needs to know about, the program should also install an event callback routine that is called when one of the specified events takes place. The callback routine for event handling is installed using WIN_EVENT_PROC. Included are samples that demonstrate how to handle events appropriately using a combination of repaint and event callback routines. However, for a complete discussion of events, you should consult Chapter 6, *Handling Input*, and Chapter 19, *The Notifier*.

The sample program *canvas_event.c* (see Example 5-3), first creates a base frame, then a canvas with the attribute CANVAS_X_PAINT_WINDOW set to TRUE because its repaint procedure (repaint_proc) uses Xlib routines to clear the window and draw text strings in the canvas.

Next we specify the events that the application should handle when they occur on the paint_window. We are going to listen for keyboard events, pointer motion events and pointer button events. We have not assigned any responses to these events yet; we have just registered them for this window with XView so that the application will be called back if they occur.

We then set the paint window's event handling procedure to be event_proc. This is the routine that will decide what to do when the events occur. XView is then started up by calling xv_main_loop(), in which event processing starts.

The event_proc is called by the Notifier whenever a registered event takes place in any view that has an event handling procedure set. The event_proc looks at the type of event it has received and determines the appropriate message to display in the paint window. There is a different message for each type of events that we have registered. There are three message buffers, one each for keyboard events, pointer motion events and pointer button events. After the message buffers are updated, the repaint procedure is called to display them. Note that we are reusing the repaint_proc, instead of writing more code just to display the messages. See Section 5.2.1, "Drawing in a Canvas."

If the event we have received is of no interest to us, then we return. It is important to do this because the events WIN_REPAINT and WIN_RESIZE are delivered regardless of the events we have registered with the Notifier. These two events will eventually result in the Notifier calling the repaint procedure anyway, so it is not necessary to call it redundantly from here. See Chapter 6, *Handling Input*, for details about this.

In *canvas_event.c*, the repaint_proc simply clears the paint window and then displays the three messages in it, at a fixed position and using the default font. In the case of a pure repaint callback (from the Notifier, not the event_proc), the messages will just repeat the last event's messages.

Example 5-3. The canvas_event.c program

```
/*
 *  canvas_event.c
 *  Demonstrates how to get keyboard and mouse events in an canvas
 *  window.  Looks for keyboards, pointer movement and button
 *  events and displays the info in the canvas.
 */
#include <X11/Xlib.h>
#include <xview/xview.h>
#include <xview/canvas.h>
#include <xview/xv_xrect.h>

void    event_proc(), repaint_proc();
char    kbd_msg[128], ptr_msg[128], but_msg[128];

/*
 * main()
 *      Create a canvas specifying a repaint procedure.
 *      Get the paint window for the canvas and set the input
 *      mask and the event procedure.
 */
main(argc, argv)
int argc;
char *argv[];
{
    Frame       frame;
    Canvas      canvas;

    /* Initialize XView */
    xv_init(XV_INIT_ARGC_PTR_ARGV, &argc, argv, NULL);

    /* Create windows -- base frame and canvas. */
    frame = (Frame)xv_create(NULL, FRAME, NULL);

    canvas = (Canvas)xv_create(frame, CANVAS,
        XV_WIDTH,               300,
```

Example 5-3. The canvas_event.c program (continued)

```
        XV_HEIGHT,                 110,
        CANVAS_X_PAINT_WINDOW,     TRUE,
        CANVAS_REPAINT_PROC,       repaint_proc,
        NULL);
    window_fit(frame);

    /* Set input mask */
    xv_set(canvas_paint_window(canvas),
        WIN_EVENT_PROC,            event_proc,
        WIN_CONSUME_EVENTS,
            KBD_DONE, KBD_USE, LOC_DRAG, LOC_MOVE, LOC_WINENTER,
            LOC_WINEXIT, WIN_ASCII_EVENTS, WIN_MOUSE_BUTTONS,
            NULL,
        NULL);

    /* Initial messages */
    strcpy(kbd_msg, "Keyboard: key press events");
    strcpy(ptr_msg, "Pointer: pointer movement events");
    strcpy(but_msg, "Button: button press events");

    /* Start event loop */
    xv_main_loop(frame);
}

/*
 * event_proc()
 *      Called when an event is received in the canvas window.
 *      Updates the keyboard, pointer and button message strings
 *      and then calls repaint_proc() to paint them to the window.
 */
void
event_proc(window, event)
Xv_Window window;
Event     *event;
{
    if (event_is_ascii(event))
        sprintf(kbd_msg, "Keyboard: key '%c' %d pressed at %d,%d",
                event_action(event), event_action(event),
                event_x(event), event_y(event));
    else
        switch (event_action(event)) {
            case KBD_USE:
                sprintf(kbd_msg, "Keyboard: got keyboard focus");
                break;
            case KBD_DONE:
                sprintf(kbd_msg, "Keyboard: lost keyboard focus");
                break;
            case LOC_MOVE:
                sprintf(ptr_msg, "Pointer: moved to %d,%d",
                    event_x(event), event_y(event));
                break;
            case LOC_DRAG:
                sprintf(ptr_msg, "Pointer: dragged to %d,%d",
                    event_x(event), event_y(event));
                break;
            case LOC_WINENTER:
                sprintf(ptr_msg, "Pointer: entered window at %d,%d",
```

Example 5-3. The canvas_event.c program (continued)

```
                        event_x(event), event_y(event));
                break;
            case LOC_WINEXIT:
                sprintf(ptr_msg, "Pointer: exited window at %d,%d",
                    event_x(event), event_y(event));
                break;
            case ACTION_SELECT:
            case MS_LEFT:
                sprintf(but_msg, "Button: Select (Left) at %d,%d",
                    event_x(event), event_y(event));
                break;
            case ACTION_ADJUST:
            case MS_MIDDLE:
                sprintf(but_msg, "Button: Adjust (Middle) at %d,%d",
                    event_x(event), event_y(event));
                break;
            case ACTION_MENU:
            case MS_RIGHT:
                sprintf(but_msg, "Button: Menu (Right) at %d,%d",
                    event_x(event), event_y(event));
                break;
            default:
                return;
        }

    /* call repaint proc directly to update messages */
    repaint_proc((Canvas)NULL, window,
        (Display *)xv_get(window, XV_DISPLAY),
        xv_get(window, XV_XID), (Xv_xrectlist *) NULL);
}

/*
 * repaint_proc()
 *      Called to repaint the canvas in response to damage events
 *      and the initial painting of the canvas window.
 *      Displays the keyboard, pointer and button message strings
 *      after erasing the previous messages.
 */
void
repaint_proc(canvas, paint_window, dpy, xwin, xrects)
Canvas          canvas;         /* Ignored */
Xv_Window       paint_window;   /* Ignored */
Display         *dpy;
Window          xwin;
Xv_xrectlist *xrects;           /* Ignored */
{
    GC gc = DefaultGC(dpy, DefaultScreen(dpy));

    XClearWindow(dpy, xwin);
    XDrawString(dpy, xwin, gc, 25, 25, kbd_msg, strlen(kbd_msg));
    XDrawString(dpy, xwin, gc, 25, 50, ptr_msg, strlen(ptr_msg));
    XDrawString(dpy, xwin, gc, 25, 75, but_msg, strlen(but_msg));
}
```

The result produced by Example 5-3 is shown in Figure 5-5.

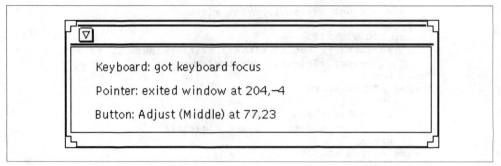

Figure 5-5. A window created with canvas_event.c

5.8 Canvas and Openwin Package Summaries

This section lists the attributes, procedures and macros for the CANVAS and OPENWIN packages. This information is described fully in Appendices A and B.

Table 5-1. Canvas Attributes, Procedures and Macros

Attributes	Procedures and Macros
CANVAS_AUTO_EXPAND	canvas_paint_window()
CANVAS_AUTO_SHRINK	canvas_repaint_proc()
CANVAS_FIXED_IMAGE	canvas_resize_proc()
CANVAS_HEIGHT	CANVAS_EACH_PAINT_WINDOW
CANVAS_MIN_PAINT_HEIGHT	CANVAS_END_EACH
CANVAS_MIN_PAINT_WIDTH	
CANVAS_NO_CLIPPING	
CANVAS_NTH_PAINT_WINDOW	
CANVAS_PAINT_CANVAS_WINDOW	
CANVAS_PAINTWINDOW_ATTRS	
CANVAS_REPAINT_PROC	
CANVAS_RESIZE_PROC	
CANVAS_RETAINED	
CANVAS_VIEW_CANVAS_WINDOW	
CANVAS_VIEW_PAINT_WINDOW	
CANVAS_VIEWABLE_RECT	
CANVAS_WIDTH	
CANVAS_X_PAINT_WINDOW	

Table 5-2. Openwin Attributes, Procedures and Macros

Attributes	Procedures and Macros
`OPENWIN_ADJUST_FOR_HORIZONTAL_SCROLLBAR`	`OPENWIN_EACH_VIEW()`
`OPENWIN_ADJUST_FOR_VERTICAL_SCROLLBAR`	`OPENWIN_END_EACH()`
`OPENWIN_AUTO_CLEAR`	
`OPENWIN_HORIZONTAL_SCROLLBAR`	
`OPENWIN_NO_MARGIN`	
`OPENWIN_NTH_VIEW`	
`OPENWIN_NVIEWS`	
`OPENWIN_SELECTED_VIEW`	
`OPENWIN_SHOW_BORDERS`	
`OPENWIN_SPLIT`	
`OPENWIN_SPLIT_DESTROY_PROC`	
`OPENWIN_SPLIT_DIRECTION`	
`OPENWIN_SPLIT_INIT_PROC`	
`OPENWIN_SPLIT_POSITION`	
`OPENWIN_SPLIT_VIEW`	
`OPENWIN_SPLIT_VIEW_START`	
`OPENWIN_VERTICAL_SCROLLBAR`	
`OPENWIN_VIEW_ATTRS`	
`OPENWIN_VIEW_CLASS`	

6

Handling Input

In This Chapter:

6
Handling Input

In discussing canvases in the previous chapter, we showed how to do some basic event handling in the canvas's paint window. This chapter goes into detail about the content of such events, the breakdown of the Event data structure that describes the event, the different types of input events that can be handled and the specifics about what gets passed to the program's event handling callback routine. Chapter 19, *The Notifier*, should be reviewed for an in-depth discussion of how to handle events on a somewhat more advanced level. Chapter 19 addresses the event types themselves, how to register which events you want to be notified of and how to interpret the events you receive.

This chapter discusses the following:

- The design of event handling.

- The breakdown of the Event data structure.

- Registering an event handler and the events you are interested in.

- Interpreting the events your event handler received.

- Sending messages to other windows or clients.

- Explicit reading of events from the server.

6.1 Introduction to Events in XView

Events are generated from several sources, including standard devices such as the keyboard and mouse, special input devices such as graphics tablets, and the window system itself. XView does not directly receive events from the hardware devices; the X server is responsible for managing these events and communicating them to the XView application. The Notifier receives all X events on behalf of the client application and dispatches them to the appropriate callback procedures registered by XView objects.

Because the Notifier multiplexes the input stream between windows, each individual window operates under the illusion that it has the user's full attention. That is, it sees precisely those input events that the user has directed to it. Each window indicates which events it is prepared to handle using *input masks*. An event callback procedure processes the events when they occur. Many windows have default event handlers that are installed internally by certain XView packages. Panels, for example, have a default event notification procedure that is used to identify which panel item received the input. Text subwindows capture events to allow typing and monitor text selection generated by using the mouse. However, some events may result in separate callback procedures being notified as well—repaint and resize events, for example, may have separate callback routines installed.

Applications can send messages to separate windows within the same application or to other applications running under separate processes. The X function `XSendEvent()` sends client-specified X events to other windows. `XClientMessageEvent` is one such event that can be sent. XView provides the function `xv_send_message()` as an interface for sending client messages in this manner.

The X Window System has a full set of events that can be sent to client applications by the server. It is highly recommended that you review Chapter 8, *Events*, in Volume One, *Xlib Programming Manual*, for specifics on the nature of these events.

6.2 Classes of Events

Events are grouped into the following classes:

- Semantic Events

- ASCII Events

- Locator Button Events

- Locator Motion Events

- Function Key Events

- Repaint and Resize Events

- Client Messages

Each of these event types are discussed in Section 6.3, "Registering Events," and Section 6.7, "Interpreting Client Messages." There are separate issues to consider in both cases. However, *semantic* event codes are common to both. We will first address event IDs and semantic events and then move directly on to event registration. After we discuss how to register the events you are interested in, we will discuss how your event handling routine can interpret the events it receives.

Event IDs

Event IDs are integer values that have been assigned somewhat, but not completely, arbitrarily to events that may be generated in X.* Some event IDs represent keyboard events, function key events, window resize and repaint events and so on. Although both X and XView understand the same events, there is no correlation between the event ID and Xlib's event codes. Thus, keyboard event IDs are *not* key symbols as defined by X's `KeySym` or `XKey-Event.keycode` fields.

Event IDs are helpful when debugging applications; you can stop in event-handling routines and print the value of a particular event ID to identify the specific event type. One helpful hint is that the ASCII event IDs correspond to the ASCII codes generated. That is, if the user presses the *x* key, then the event ID is *x*.

Semantic Events

Also called *action* events, semantic events are used to describe the *meaning* of an event using semantic phrases, so to speak, rather than using the literal event code represented by an event *ID*. That is, the definition of the *macro* describes the value of the event as well as its meaning. When someone presses a key marked HELP on the keyboard, the event ID may represent a large, cryptic numeral such as 65034. However, the semantic code associated with the key event would be `ACTION_HELP`.

There are also cases where the keyboard has been remapped by some applications for other purposes. For example, in OPEN LOOK, the SELECT button defaults to the leftmost physical mouse button, also known as button **one**. Normally this button is activated using the index finger for a right-handed person. A left-handed person who places the mouse on the left may remap the semantics of the leftmost and rightmost buttons (assuming a multibutton mouse). This allows the left-handed user to also use his index finger to activate the SELECT button.

We recommend that you use semantic actions when referring to events for consistency with other applications as well as consistency with different computers.

6.3 Registering Events

Typically, when you specify which events a particular window is interested in, you also specify an event handler for that window. You register an event handler with an XView *window*, not the object with which the window is associated. Specifically, to register an event handler for canvases and panels, you use the *paint window* as in:

---

*This concept is carried over from SunView and is foreign to X.

```
Xv_Window  window;
Canvas     canvas;
int        win;

window = (Xv_Window)xv_get(canvas, CANVAS_NTH_PAINT_WINDOW, win);
```

For text subwindows, you use the *view window*:

```
Xv_Window  window;
Textsw     textsw;
int        win_no;

window = (Xv_Window)xv_get(textsw, OPENWIN_NTH_VIEW, win_no);
```

Once you have obtained the window, you can install the event handler using the WIN_EVENT_PROC attribute:

```
xv_set(window,
    WIN_EVENT_PROC,       sample_event_proc,
    WIN_CONSUME_EVENTS, WIN_ASCII_EVENTS, WIN_MOUSE_BUTTONS, NULL,
    NULL);
```

The window is of type Xv_Window. The event handler is a function that is called whenever any of the registered events occur in the specified windows. Details about this routine and how to interpret the events delivered to it are discussed later in this chapter, starting with Section 6.4, "The Event Handler."

This section discusses specifically how to register and unregister the events in which you are interested for a particular window. There are several ways to describe events you wish to register. You can specify action (semantic) events, literal events or event *classes* defined by XView (as shown in the example), or you can use X event masks (familiar to Xlib programmers). Which method you choose for registering events does not affect the function of the event handler; it maintains its function of receiving and understanding events.

6.3.1 Specifying X Event Masks

The simplest and most direct method for people familiar with Xlib programming is to use X event masks.* To register or unregister events using X masks, you can use:

```
WIN_CONSUME_X_EVENT_MASK
WIN_IGNORE_X_EVENT_MASK
```

The value for these attributes is a mask made up of any of the event masks defined in *<X11/X.h>*. Do not confuse event masks with actual event types.

WIN_CONSUME_X_EVENTS appends the specified event mask to the existing event mask for the object. However, to set the event mask explicitly to the specified mask, use WIN_EVENT_MASK. To clear the event mask completely, use:

```
xv_set(window, WIN_X_EVENT_MASK, NoEventMask, NULL);
```

---

*See Volume One, *Xlib Programming Manual*, for a complete discussion on event masks and their implications.

The following code segment demonstrates how a canvas would register interest in the keyboard and mouse buttons:

```
xv_set(window,
    WIN_CONSUME_X_EVENT_MASK, ButtonPressMask | KeyPressMask,
    NULL);
```

Notice that we did not specify `ButtonReleaseMask` or `KeyReleaseMask`. Thus, the event handler is going to receive the down-events only.

When you specify event masks with the attribute `WIN_IGNORE_X_EVENT_MASK`, then those events are not delivered to your event handler. You cannot use this attribute to unregister all events and expect that to unregister your event handler. You must set the `WIN_EVENT_PROC` to `NULL` to do that. It is perfectly legal to have no events registered with a window.

6.3.2 Specifying XView Events

XView events (or event *types*) are simply alternate ways to specify events when you register them or interpret them. When using these event types to register events, you are not adding any more functionality than using the Xlib event registration scheme in the previous section. However, XView event types may make it easier to identify more precisely which events you are interested in being notified of.

The header files *<xview/win_input.h>* and *<xview/win_event.h>* have several data types, and most XView event definitions allow you to register events with windows or the Notifier. There are two methods available to do this: using the `Inputmask` data structure or specifying XView event codes directly.

Although the `Inputmask` method tends to be less elegant than using XView event types, it is necessary in order to use `xv_input_readevent()` and other advanced-usage functions. See Section 6.8, "Reading Input Directly," for details about how the `Inputmask` structure is used.

The attribute `WIN_CONSUME_EVENTS` is used to register events via XView event types. The value for this attribute is a `NULL`-terminated list of the XView events defined in the header files mentioned above. Let's re-examine the example used in the previous section:

```
xv_set(window,
    WIN_EVENT_PROC,      sample_event_proc,
    WIN_CONSUME_EVENTS, WIN_ASCII_EVENTS, WIN_MOUSE_BUTTONS, NULL,
    NULL);
```

The values `WIN_ASCII_EVENTS` and `WIN_MOUSE_BUTTONS` encompass all the ASCII codes from 0 to 127, inclusive, and the mouse button events. The events specified are added to the existing input mask for the window. This does not override what the window had previously; the event mask specified is *appended* to the input mask for that window. To set an explicit event mask, the value `WIN_NO_EVENTS` should be specified first in the list.

```
xv_set(window,
    WIN_EVENT_PROC,          sample_event_proc,
    WIN_CONSUME_EVENTS,
        WIN_NO_EVENTS, WIN_ASCII_EVENTS, WIN_MOUSE_BUTTONS, NULL,
    NULL);
```

All events are cleared at the point in which WIN_NO_EVENTS is given in the list. If it is given in the middle of the list, then the events specified previous to that point are forgotten. If it is the only attribute in the list, then the event mask for the window is cleared. Note that this does not mean that your event handler will receive no events. There are certain events that are sent to your window, and thus to your event handler, whether you want them or not. This is addressed later in this chapter.

You can specify which events to ignore in the same way:

```
xv_set(window,
    WIN_IGNORE_EVENTS,
        WIN_UP_ASCII_EVENTS, LOC_WINENTER, LOC_WINEXIT,
        NULL,
    NULL);
```

Here we are telling the window to ignore the events caused by *releasing* the ASCII keys on the keyboard as well as window-enter and window-exit events. As with WIN_X_ EVENT_MASK, you cannot use WIN_IGNORE_EVENTS to unregister all the events and expect the event handler to be unregistered. It is perfectly legal to have a window that has no events registered with it.

While these attributes take a NULL-terminated list, you can use WIN_CONSUME_EVENT or WIN_IGNORE_EVENT to consume or ignore *one* event. Using these attributes, it is not necessary to specify a list of events.

Mouse Events

The mouse (or *locator*) resides at an (x,y) coordinate position in pixels; this position is transformed by XView to the coordinate space of the window receiving an event. You can request mouse motion events by specifying LOC_MOVE or LOC_DRAG. A LOC_MOVE event is reported when the mouse moves, regardless of the state of the locator buttons. If you only want to know about locator motion when a button is down, then enable LOC_DRAG instead of LOC_MOVE. This will greatly reduce the number of motion events that your application has to process. If you have both specified, you will only receive one event or the other; you will never receive one followed by the other.

Even if you do not request move or drag events, you may still monitor when the mouse moves in and out of windows by specifying LOC_WINENTER and LOC_WINEXIT. In the case of LOC_WINENTER, the window installs its colormap into the server, and, for LOC_WINEXIT, the window's colormap is uninstalled. If you have registered the colormap notify event (WIN_COLORMAP_NOTIFY), then you will receive the appropriate events when you enter and leave a window.

Each button that is associated with the mouse is assigned an event code; the *i-th* button is assigned the code BUT(i). Thus, the event codes MS_LEFT, MS_MIDDLE and MS_RIGHT correspond to BUT(1), BUT(2) and BUT(3). These are actual key codes, not semantic codes.

Keyboard Events

In order to be notified of keyboard events, you must specify any one of several XView event types depending on which event you want. Unlike the X event mask `KeyPressMask`, which generates events for all keys on the keyboard, including function keys, XView allows you to be more specific about which keyboard events you are interested in while not having to specify explicit keys.

The following list contains input event descriptors that may be used:

WIN_ASCII_EVENTS	Enable ASCII keycodes—these are events that fall between 0 and 127 in the ASCII character set. Using this attribute specifies up-events as well as down-events.
WIN_UP_ASCII_EVENTS	This is used mostly by WIN_IGNORE_EVENTS to turn off receiving the release event that usually follows a key press.
WIN_TOP_KEYS	This enables notification when any of the function keys on the *top* of the keyboard are specified. This is highly keyboard dependent. XView provides for up to 15 keys in this location. Keys that are labeled differently might produce different key codes.
WIN_LEFT_KEYS	This enables notification when any of the function keys on the *left* side of the keyboard are specified. There are also action events associated with each key on the left side of the keyboard. Again, XView provides for 15 keys and your mileage may vary.
WIN_RIGHT_KEYS	This enables notification when any of the function keys on the *right* of the keyboard are used. Typically, these include the arrow keys for cursor movement in some applications (like text editors).
WIN_META_EVENTS	This enables notification when the *meta* key(s) goes down.
WIN_UP_META_EVENTS	To be used with WIN_IGNORE_EVENT to ignore key releases.
WIN_UP_EVENTS	This is a general facility for ignoring all release events from mouse buttons and keyboard keys.

The XView event types `KBD_USE` and `KBD_DONE` can be specified to notify you when your window obtains the keyboard focus. OPEN LOOK specifies the click-to-type method for keyboard focus, so you may not get keyboard focus just because the mouse entered a window. The user can specify how keyboard focus should work without letting the application know about it. When a window gets keyboard focus and the window's event mask has `KBD_USE` set, then the window's event procedure is called.

Resize and Repaint Events

When the size of a window is changed (either by the user or programmatically), a WIN_RESIZE event is generated to give the client a chance to adjust any relevant internal state to the new window size. You should *not* repaint the window when receiving a resize event. You will receive a separate WIN_REPAINT event when a portion of the window needs to be repainted.

If you are using a canvas subwindow, you will not need to track resize and repaint events directly. The CANVAS package receives these events, computes the new window dimensions or the precise area requiring repainting and calls your resize or repaint procedures directly. See Chapter 5, *Canvases and Openwin*, for more details.

NOTE

You will get WIN_REPAINT and WIN_RESIZE events sent to your event handler routine no matter what. These events cannot be prevented from being delivered to your event handler. However, we recommend that you install repaint and resize handling routines using CANVAS_REPAINT_PROC and CANVAS_RESIZE_PROC rather than acting on these events from the event handler.

As pointed out in Chapter 5, *Canvases and Openwin*, there may be a WIN_REPAINT event generated for each region of a window that gets exposed. However, you can set whether or not all those exposure events are collapsed into one expose event specifying a region that covers the entire exposed area. The attribute WIN_COLLAPSE_EXPOSURES can be set to TRUE (the default) or FALSE to prevent multiple expose events.

You get graphics exposure events (WIN_GRAPHICS_EXPOSE) whenever you draw into a window using a GC whose graphics_exposures field is set to True. The same is true for WIN_NO_EVENTS. These events are not selected via WIN_CONSUME_EVENTS and cannot be ignored using this method. The only way to avoid receiving these events is by setting the graphics_exposures field in the GC to False. How you choose to deal with it is specific to your application.

Client Messages

Client messages are events that cannot be ignored by your event handler. Typically, these are messages that are used to implement a predefined protocol between your application and other applications that are familiar with the protocol. Because client messages cannot be ignored, we do not address the issue of client messages in this section. Read Section 6.7, "Interpreting Client Messages," for more information on how to interpret these events.

Miscellaneous Events

Consuming any one of the following events causes all of them to be consumed.

- `WIN_CIRCULATE_NOTIFY`

- `WIN_DESTROY_NOTIFY`

- `WIN_GRAVITY_NOTIFY`

- `WIN_MAP_NOTIFY`

- `WIN_REPARENT_NOTIFY`

- `WIN_RESIZE`

- `WIN_UNMAP_NOTIFY`

Alternatively you could just select `WIN_STRUCTURE_NOTIFY` which selects all of the above events.

If you select `WIN_CREATE_NOTIFY` on a parent object, you will receive this event whenever a child window of the parent object is created. You will also receive any of the above listed events on the subwindows whenever `WIN_CREATE_NOTIFY` or alternatively, `WIN_SUB-STRUCTURE_NOTIFY` is consumed on the parent.

Consuming any one of the following events causes all of them to be consumed, as specified in the X Protocol.

- `WIN_CIRCULATE_REQUEST`

- `WIN_CONFIGURE_REQUEST`

- `WIN_MAP_REQUEST`

Alternatively you could just select `WIN_SUBSTRUCTURE_REDIRECT` which selects all of the above events. A window manager is really the only client that should ever be interested in any of these.

6.4 The Event Handler

When one of the events in which you have expressed interest occurs, your event handler is called. The form of this routine is:

```
void
sample_event_proc(window, event, arg)
    Xv_Window   window;
    Event       *event;
    Notify_arg  arg;
```

The arguments to the routine are the window the event occurred in, a pointer to a data structure describing information about the event itself, and an optional argument supplied by the XView package responsible for the function being called.*

---

*This parameter is currently unused by XView packages but is available for new XView packages, extensions to them or with advanced Notifier usage. See Section 19.6.2, "Posting with an Argument."

6.5 The Event Structure

Events that are generated are passed to event handling procedures by the Notifier as `Event` pointers (type `Event *`). This structure is declared in *<xview/win_input.h>*:

```
typedef struct    inputevent {
        short           ie_code;              /* input code */
        short           ie_flags;
        short           ie_shiftmask;         /* input code shift state */
        short           ie_locx, ie_locy;  /* mouse position */
        struct timeval  ie_time;              /* time of event */
        short           action;               /* keymapped ie_code */
        Xv_object       ie_win;               /* window receiving event */
        char            *ie_string;           /* keycode binding string */
        XEvent          *ie_xevent;           /* actual XEvent struct */
} Event;
```

The `Event` data structure contains all the information about the event. The fields are broken down as follows:

`ie_code`	Actual XView event ID, as defined in *<xview/win_event.h>* and *<xview/win_input.h>*.* Event codes can take on any value in the range 0 through 65535. The values are useful when debugging.
`ie_flags`	Indicates whether the event was an up- or down-event, if applicable. A down-event occurs when a mouse button or keyboard key goes down. There must be a corresponding up-event, although the client may choose to ignore up-events.
`ie_shiftmask`	If a Shift key, Control key and/or mouse button was down when the event occurred, this mask will have the appropriate bits set.
`ie_locx, ie_locy`	*x,y* coordinates of the position of the locator (mouse) relative to the window in which the event occurred.
`ie_time`	The time of the event.
`action`	Semantic code representing predefined actions specific to the window manager or OPEN LOOK.
`ie_win`	Window in which the event took place.
`ie_string`	String in which a keycode (found in `ie_code`) is bound using `XRebindKeysym()`.
`ie_xevent`	The actual event structure generated by X. This event structure arrives untouched by XView for events generated by the server.

<xview/panel.h> also has a couple of event definitions, but they are not widely used. See Chapter 7, *Panels*, for details.

6.6 Determining the Event

In the `Event` structure, there is a pointer to the `XEvent` structure that was delivered by the X server as a direct result of the event that it describes. This section discusses how to interpret the event based on information in the `Event` structure only; it does not address the `XEvent` structure.

The header files *<xview/win_input.h>* and *<xview/win_event.h>* contain many macros that should be used rather than referencing fields in the `Event` data structure. If the structure is modified in the future, then the macros will be modified to support the changes and your code will not have to change. For example, to get the window in which the event took place, you should not use (assume *event* is of type `Event *`):

```
window = event->ie_win;
```

Instead you should use:

```
window = event_window(event);
```

To determine the actual event ID, you could use:

```
event_id(event)
```

This macro returns the actual event ID that took place, such as `MS_LEFT` to indicate the left mouse button. However, as discussed earlier, we recommend that you use the semantic action events provided by the macro:

```
event_action(event)
```

In the case where the user selected the left mouse button, `event_action` would return `ACTION_SELECT`. The two values do not map to the same thing; consider the case where left-handed users have remapped the mouse settings. On the other hand, if there is no action associated with an event, `event_action()` is set to `event_id()`. For example, consider when the letter *a* is pressed or when the `Expose` event is generated.

Event States

When a mouse button or keyboard event occurs, the event may be the result of a button or key being released or pressed. The way to determine this state from a particular event is to use one of these two macros:

```
event_is_up(event)
event_is_down(event)
```

Modifier Keys

Modifier keys include the left and right Shift keys, the Control key, and the Meta key. The locations of these keys on the user's keyboard are dependent on the make and model of your keyboard. The functions of modifier keys are to modify particular keyboard or mouse states. For example, the Shift key, when modifying the *a* key, results in the *A* key.

Unless you have explicitly requested to be notified of *modifier* key events, you will not be informed when their state changes (e.g., when a user presses or releases one of the keys). You probably do not need to know this anyway. Instead, you only need to know the state of the key at the time you are evaluating another event. In this case, you can use any of the following macros:

```
event_shift_is_down(event)
event_ctrl_is_down(event)
event_meta_is_down(event)
```

6.6.1 Keyboard Events

When XView translates keyboard events into `Event` codes, it does translation of the key depending on the state of the modifier keys. For example, when the user types Shift-A, intending to type a capital-A, then the event ID (that is, `event->ie_code`) is *A*. You do not need to use `event_shift_is_down` to translate the key to the upper case.*

The following macro is used to determine if a key event is within the ISO character set:

```
event_is_iso(event)
    Event *event;
```

You can use the following macro to determine if an event is an ASCII key:

```
event_is_ascii(event)
    Event *event;
```

This result does not tell you if you have a *printable* character. Depending on the font you are using, you may not be able to print anything with this event code. However, you can use any of the macros in *<ctype.h>* to determine whether the character is printable, a control character, a digit, a punctuation mark and so on. Remember, this works because you are using the *already-translated* version of the event code.

The macro `event_string()` can be used to determine the string value associated with the event ID. This value is the result of a call to `XLookupString()`. For normal ASCII event codes, `event_string()` will return a string value of the same key. However, the key (ASCII or not) could be rebound to a string using `XRebindKeysym()`:

---

*This is in contrast to the value of `XKeyEvent.keycode` used by Xlib.

```
Display *dpy = (Display *)xv_get(frame, XV_DISPLAY);
char *newstring = "Nine";

XRebindKeysym(dpy, XK_9, 0, 0, newstring, strlen(newstring));
```

Here, the *9* key is rebound to generate the string "Nine" whenever it is pressed. The following macro determines whether or not a string is associated with the event:

```
event_is_string(event)
```

In the event callback, the following code could be used:

```
...
if (event_is_string(event))
    printf("string = %s\n", event_string(event));
...
```

Function keys differ from keyboard to keyboard, and the default key mappings for your server are configurable (at the time you build your server). However, XView has provisions for keyboards that are sectioned off into four sets of fifteen function keys: left, top, right and bottom keys. To determine which set of keys a particular event is associated with, you can use the following macros:

```
event_is_key_left(event)
event_is_key_right(event)
event_is_key_top(event)
event_is_key_bottom(event)
```

To determine which function set a particular function key belongs to, use:

```
KEY_TOP(key)
KEY_LEFT(key)
KEY_RIGHT(key)
KEY_BOTTOM(key)
```

Here, you do not pass the event, you pass the event *ID*. Thus, to test to see if a particular event were the fifth function key in the top row of keys, you would use:

```
if (event_is_key_top(event) && event_id(event) == KEY_TOP(5))
    /* process the fifth top-function key. */
```

Notice that we are using `event_id()` rather than `event_action()`. The reason for this is that some function keys are mapped to particular semantic actions, and we want to be sure the user hits the *fifth* function key on the top row. Had we used `event_action()` instead, the equality test may have failed.

Mouse Events

XView supports a locator device (a mouse) with up to ten buttons on it. This device may generate various different types of events, such as:

Motion events   These events are generated whenever the mouse moves.

Drag events   These events result in mouse movement when any of the mouse buttons are down.

Button events   These events are generated whenever the state of a mouse button changes (e.g., when a button goes up or down).

The following macros determine the state of particular buttons for a three-button mouse (the most common type).

```
event_is_button(event)
event_left_is_down(event)
event_middle_is_down(event)
event_right_is_down(event)
event_button_is_down(event)
```

Note that none of these indicates an exclusive button state; that is, if event_right_is_down returns TRUE, that does not exclude the left button from being down, too.

You can determine which mouse button is changing state in the same way you determine a function key position, by passing the *ID* of the event to:

```
BUT(i)
```

To determine whether the second mouse button was down, you could use:

```
if (event_is_down(event) && event_id(event) == BUT(2))
    /* process button-2 event handling */
```

Again, we recommend that rather than determining the state of a particular mouse button, you use the semantic codes:

```
if (event_is_down(event) && event_action(event) == ACTION_ADJUST)
    /* process "adjust" event handling */
```

Keyboard Focus

One way for the application to direct keyboard focus automatically to a particular window is to use win_set_kbd_focus(). The calling parameters are the window and the XID of the window that is supposed to get the focus. For example, if a window gets an event LOC_WINENTER, you can grab the keyboard focus automatically:

```
my_event_proc(window, event)
Xv_Window    window;
Event        *event;
{
    switch (event_id(event)) {
        . . .
        case LOC_WINENTER :
            win_set_kbd_focus(window, xv_get(window, XV_XID));
            break;
        . . .
    }
}
```

win_set_kbd_focus() generates a KBD_USE event for the window that is getting the focus and a WIN_KBD_DONE event for the window that lost its focus. The window that lost its focus must have WIN_KBD_DONE specified in its event mask to be notified.

Another way to grab keyboard focus for a window is to grab *all* the input for that window. This can be accomplished in various ways, including the use of the FULLSCREEN package described in Chapter 15, *Nonvisual Objects*. However, perhaps a much more convenient method is to use the WIN_GRAB_ALL_INPUT attribute. Setting this attribute to TRUE causes a grab that forces all input to be directed to that window. Setting it to FALSE releases the grab.

This is useful when you want to display a dialog box with panel items and confirmation or cancel buttons that the user must respond to before interacting with any other portion of the application. In this case, you should set the grab on the paint window of a panel. Be sure to reset this attribute once it is no longer needed. Also, be careful that you code the segment of the program that uses the grab carefully, or you might generate a grab you cannot get out of.

6.7 Interpreting Client Messages

Client messages may be delivered to your event handler for two reasons.

First, OPEN LOOK has a mechanism known as *drag and drop* that allows the user to move or copy text selections to other windows. In this scenario, the user selects text in a text subwindow and then uses the SELECT button to *drag* it to another location and *drop* it into a new window. Similarly, for cut and paste operations, a client message is sent to the recipient window informing it that data is waiting in the *shelf* selection.

For these cases, the Notifier interposes your event handler and replaces the client message event with an action event (described later). From the event handler's point of view, the action describes the type of drop and drag action taken or cut and paste operations.

Second, your event handler may receive client messages if the event was sent by another source using XSendEvent() or xv_send_message(). This implies that the sender of the message has loaded some arbitrary information into client-message format and sent it to you directly. In this case, the sender assumes you know how to interpret the information in the message.

Let's consider the OPEN LOOK use of client messages first.

6.7.1 Drag and Drop

A drag and drop operation occurs when the user grabs the text selection using the SELECT mouse button, drags it somewhere (perhaps another window or application) and then drops it onto that window. The window onto which the selection has been dropped receives an event (XClientMessage) informing it that data intended for that window is available in the primary selection. The destination window can use the contents of the selection as input data and the selection should be deleted from the original window. Thus, the selection appears to have *moved*.

In this scenario, the receiving window's event handler is called with the `event_action(event)` set to `ACTION_DRAG_MOVE` and the client application decodes the event accordingly.

Rather than moving the text selection, the user may wish to *copy* it to another window. In this case, the same scenario applies as described above, except that the user has the Control key down at the time the selection was grabbed. After dragging, and when the button is released, the event handler is called with `event_action(event)` set to `ACTION_DRAG_COPY` and, again, the client application decodes the event accordingly.

Due to changes in the implementation, the current method for decoding these events is not well-established. For the time being, however, the convenience function, `xv_decode_drop()` may be used to decode a drop event by reading the event and storing the data into an application-provided buffer.

```
int
xv_decode_drop(event, buf, size)
    Event *event;
    char *buf;
    int size;
```

The function decodes an `ACTION_DRAG_LOAD` or `ACTION_DRAG_COPY` event into the text being dragged. The text associated with `ACTION_DRAG_LOAD` corresponds with the name of a file being dragged. This applies only to the OPEN LOOK *file manager* application. At most, `size` bytes, including the NULL string-terminator, are placed in `buf`. If more data is available, it is discarded. However, the function returns the actual number of bytes that were available to help determine if data was actually lost. A buffer length of size `SELN_BUFSIZE` (defined in *<xview/seln.h>*) should be sufficient.

The value −1 is returned if `xv_decode_drop()` is unable to obtain a selection.

Drag and Load

OPEN LOOK's *file manager* application displays a graphical layout of files and directories on the file system. The user can select and drag an icon representing a file or directory and drop it onto a window of another application in the same way that text can be selected and dragged. However, when using the file manager, the intent is to have the application act on that file as input. A mail program, for example, might be able to load a file as a mail folder, or a graphics application might interpret that file as if it had page description commands (such as PostScript™). Thus, the application *loads* the file.

In this case, *file manager*, or any other application that might want to provide similar functionality, would send the action event `ACTION_DRAG_LOAD`. When your event handler receives this action event, it gets the filename from the primary selection and attempts to open that file and process it. It should be sure to do proper error checking on parsing the given file, since the user is not restricted as to which file s/he drops on your window.

CAUTION

The filename specified may not be accessible because the *file manager* application may be running on a different machine than the application that received the event. Also, the primary selection may have changed since the drop message was received. Thus, this interface may change in the future.

6.7.2 Sending and Reading Client Messages

`xv_send_message()` is used to send client messages to other windows. This is the way the file manager and the text subwindow implement their drag and drop features. When the user performs the correct sequence of events, the applications load the primary selection with the appropriate text and then call `xv_send_message()` to deliver the event. As described in the previous section, the Notifier handles this case automatically. However, for other uses (specific to the application's needs), regular client messages can still be exchanged using the same function, `xv_send_message()`.

The form for this function is:

```
Xv_private int
xv_send_message(window, addressee, msg_type, format, data, len)
    Xv_object       window;
    Xv_opaque       addressee;
    char            *msg_type;
    int             format;
    Xv_opaque       *data;
    int             len;
```

The function sends the message encoded in `data` to the `addressee` window. If the `addressee` parameter is an X window, then the message is sent to that window. Otherwise, the `addressee` may be either `PointerWindow` or `InputFocus` to correspond to the window under which the pointer happens to be lying or the window which happens to have the current focus. This depends on whether the user has click-to-type or focus-follows-mouse mode in the window manager.

The `window` parameter is an XView window/object from which the event is being sent. This is only used to extract the `Display *`. The `format` may be 8, 16 or 32. The value 8 is typically used to represent string values. `len` is the `strlen()` of the `data`.

The actual `XEvent` that is generated is `XClientMessageEvent`. When the Notifier detects the event, before passing it onto your event handler, it checks to see if the message content represents a drag and drop operation. If so, then the event action is set to the appropriate action. The `XEvent` structure's `ie_xevent` field remains unchanged.

If the client message is not a drag and drop operation, then you are responsible for deciphering the message. Clearly, this is something you have to be expecting, or there is no way to tell what to do with the information. Thus, you can create your own protocol between clients. You can determine the content of the message using `xv_get()` and the attributes:

```
WIN_CLIENT_MESSAGE_DATA
WIN_CLIENT_MESSAGE_TYPE
WIN_CLIENT_MESSAGE_FORMAT
```

These attributes map directly to the XClientMessageEvent data structure in *<X11/Xlib.h>*. Therefore, you could reference the appropriate fields in the ie_xevent pointer from the Event structure passed to the callback function. Using the type, format and data of the client message, you can read the message content. See Volume One, *Xlib Programming Manual*, for more information about unwrapping a client message.

6.8 Reading Input Directly

You can read input *immediately* using xv_input_readevent(). This function, which returns the window associated with the event read, takes the form:

```
Xv_object
xv_input_readevent(window, event, block, type, im)
    Xv_object       window;
    Event           *event;
    int             block, type;
    Inputmask       *im;
```

The window parameter identifies the window you want to read the events from. If NULL, XNextEvent() is called and the function returns the window that received the next event. In this case, you should probably have a server grab for the window from which you are reading the event. Otherwise, you will have to propagate the received event to the appropriate window later.

The event parameter is a pointer to an Event type that is filled in when the function returns. The block parameter indicates whether or not the function should wait if there are no events pending to be read. If block is FALSE and there are no events, the function returns immediately without having read an event.

The type parameter tells whether to use the input mask already set in the window or whether to use the input mask specified by the im parameter. The Inputmask is declared in *<xview/win_input.h>*:

```
typedef   struct inputmask {
    short      im_flags;
    char       im_keycode[IM_MASKSIZE];
} Inputmask;
```

The structure consists of an input code array and flags that indicate which user actions belong in the input queue. The following macro should be used to initialize the mask:

```
event_init(im)
```

The following macros are used to manipulate XView event codes in an Inputmask:

```
win_setinputcodebit(im, code)
win_unsetinputcodebit(im, code)
```

Here, `code` is an XView code as described earlier. The `flags` field may be set to any of the following bits:

IM_NEGEVENT   Send input negative events (release, or "up," events), too. This includes all keyboard keys and mouse buttons.

IM_ASCII   Enable ASCII codes 0 through 127—equivalent to `WIN_ASCII_EVENTS`.

IM_META   Enable META codes 128 through 255—equivalent to `WIN_META_EVENTS`.

IM_NEGASCII   Enable release, or "up," ASCII codes 0 through 127—this is more specific than IM_NEGEVENT above. It is primarily used to unset the code bits once ASCII bits have been set.

IM_NEGMETA   Enable release, or "up," META codes 128 through 255—used to unset these code bits.

IM_TOP   Enable TOP function keys.

IM_NEGTOP   Enable release events for TOP function keys.

With these macros, we set the `Inputmask` that is passed to `xv_read_inputevent()`. As it turns out, this method can also be used to set the input mask for regular windows. This is not the recommended method for providing the input mask, but it can be done by specifying the attribute `WIN_INPUT_MASK`:

```
Inputmask im;

win_setinputcodebit(im, WIN_MOUSE_BUTTONS);
win_setinputcodebit(im, WIN_ASCII_EVENTS);
im.im_flags &~ IN_NEGEVENTS;

xv_set(window, WIN_INPUT_MASK, &im, NULL);
```

Similarly, you can get the input mask in the same way:

```
Inputmask *im;

im = (Inputmask *)xv_get(window, WIN_INPUT_MASK);
```

6.9 Sample Program

This section provides a sample program that demonstrates most of what has been discussed in this chapter. In Example 6-1, the canvas window where the events occur may be split into several views. Each new view handles its own events and therefore handles its own graphic rendering into its paint window.

The intent is for the user to split the views several times and move the mouse between the views. Each view prints the events it receives in its own window at the upper-right corner. New views created from a split view may not be positioned correctly to see the text describing the events. It is not possible to scroll individual views programmatically to arbitrary locations, so the user must do so manually.

Pay careful attention to which window receives events so as to get a feeling for how the keyboard focus is handled. In some cases, the keyboard focus does not follow the mouse—a particular view may continue to receive keyboard focus even though the mouse is no longer in that subwindow. Usually, selecting the SELECT mouse button forces the focus to be directed to that view window.

Example 6-1. The canvas_input.c program

```
/*
 * canvas_input.c --
 * Display a canvas whose views may be split repeatedly.  The event
 * handler is installed for each view, so events are displayed in
 * each paint window.
 */
#include <xview/xview.h>
#include <xview/canvas.h>
#include <xview/scrollbar.h>
#include <xview/xv_xrect.h>

Canvas   canvas;
Frame    frame;
char     msg[128];
void     init_split(), my_event_proc(), my_repaint_proc();

main(argc,argv)
int      argc;
char     *argv[];
{
    /*
     * Initialize, create base frame (with footers) and create canvas.
     */
    xv_init(XV_INIT_ARGS, argc, argv, NULL);
    frame = (Frame)xv_create(NULL,FRAME,
        FRAME_LABEL,             "Split View Windows.",
        FRAME_SHOW_FOOTER,       TRUE,
        NULL);
    canvas = (Canvas)xv_create(frame,CANVAS,
        CANVAS_X_PAINT_WINDOW,   TRUE,
        OPENWIN_SPLIT,
            OPENWIN_SPLIT_INIT_PROC,     init_split,
            NULL,
        CANVAS_REPAINT_PROC,     my_repaint_proc,
        NULL);

    (void) xv_create(canvas, SCROLLBAR,
        SCROLLBAR_SPLITTABLE,    TRUE,
        SCROLLBAR_DIRECTION,     SCROLLBAR_VERTICAL,
        NULL);
    (void) xv_create(canvas, SCROLLBAR,
        SCROLLBAR_SPLITTABLE,    TRUE,
        SCROLLBAR_DIRECTION,     SCROLLBAR_HORIZONTAL,
        NULL);

    /*
     * Set input mask
     */
    xv_set(canvas_paint_window(canvas),
        WIN_CONSUME_EVENTS,
```

Example 6-1. The canvas_input.c program (continued)

```
            WIN_NO_EVENTS,
            WIN_ASCII_EVENTS, KBD_USE, KBD_DONE,
            LOC_DRAG, LOC_WINENTER, LOC_WINEXIT, WIN_MOUSE_BUTTONS,
            NULL,
        WIN_EVENT_PROC, my_event_proc,
        NULL);

    xv_main_loop(frame);
}

/*
 * when a viewport is split, this routine is called.
 */
void
init_split(splitview, newview, pos)
Xv_Window splitview, newview;
int pos;
{
    Xv_Window    view;
    int          i = 0;

    /*
     * Determine view # from the new view and set its scrollbar to 0,0
     */
    OPENWIN_EACH_VIEW(canvas, view)
        if (view == splitview) {
            /* identify the view # of the view the user just split. */
            sprintf(msg, "Split view #%d", i+1);
            xv_set(frame, FRAME_LEFT_FOOTER, msg, NULL);
        } else if (view == newview) {
            xv_set(xv_get(canvas, OPENWIN_VERTICAL_SCROLLBAR, view),
                SCROLLBAR_VIEW_START, 0,
                NULL);
            xv_set(xv_get(canvas, OPENWIN_HORIZONTAL_SCROLLBAR, view),
                SCROLLBAR_VIEW_START, 0,
                NULL);
        }
        i++;
    OPENWIN_END_EACH
    sprintf(msg, "Total views: %d", i);
    xv_set(frame, FRAME_RIGHT_FOOTER, msg, NULL);
}

/*
 * Called when an event is received in an arbitrary paint window.
 */
void
my_event_proc(window, event, arg)
Xv_Window       window;
Event           *event;
Notify_arg      arg;
{
    register char *p = msg;

    *p = 0;

    /* test to see if a function key has been hit */
    if (event_is_key_left(event))
```

Example 6-1. The canvas_input.c program (continued)

```
            sprintf(p, "(L%d) ", event_id(event) - KEY_LEFTFIRST + 1);
        else if (event_is_key_top(event))
            sprintf(p, "(T%d) ", event_id(event) - KEY_TOPFIRST + 1);
        else if (event_is_key_right(event))
            sprintf(p, "(R%d) ", event_id(event) - KEY_RIGHTFIRST + 1);
        else if (event_id(event) == KEY_BOTTOMLEFT)
            strcpy(p, "bottom left ");
        else if (event_id(event) == KEY_BOTTOMRIGHT)
            strcpy(p, "bottom right ");
        p += strlen(p);

        if (event_is_ascii(event)) {
            /*
             * note that shift modifier is reflected in the event code by
             * virtue of the char printed is upper/lower case.
             */
            sprintf(p, "Keyboard: key '%c' (%d) %s at %d,%d",
                event_action(event), event_action(event),
                event_is_down(event)? "pressed" : "released",
                event_x(event), event_y(event));
        } else switch (event_action(event)) {
            case ACTION_CLOSE :
                xv_set(frame, FRAME_CLOSED, TRUE, NULL);
                break;
            case ACTION_OPEN :
                strcpy(p, "frame opened up");
                break;
            case ACTION_HELP :
                strcpy(p, "Help (action ignored)");
                break;
            case ACTION_SELECT :
                sprintf(p, "Button: Select (Left) %s at %d,%d",
                    event_is_down(event)? "pressed" : "released",
                    event_x(event), event_y(event));
                break;
            case ACTION_ADJUST :
                sprintf(p, "Button: Adjust (Middle) %s at %d,%d",
                    event_is_down(event)? "pressed" : "released",
                    event_x(event), event_y(event));
                break;
            case ACTION_MENU :
                sprintf(p, "Button: Menu (Right) %s at %d,%d",
                    event_is_down(event)? "pressed" : "released",
                    event_x(event), event_y(event));
                break;
            case SHIFT_RIGHT :
                sprintf(p, "Keyboard: right shift %s",
                    event_is_down(event)? "pressed" : "released");
                break;
            case SHIFT_LEFT :
                sprintf(p, "Keyboard: left shift %s",
                    event_is_down(event)? "pressed" : "released");
                break;
            case SHIFT_LEFTCTRL : case SHIFT_RIGHTCTRL :
                sprintf(p, "Keyboard: control key %s",
                    event_is_down(event)? "pressed" : "released");
```

Example 6-1. The canvas_input.c program (continued)

```
                    break;
            case SHIFT_META :
                sprintf(p, "Keyboard: meta key %s",
                    event_is_down(event)? "pressed" : "released");
                break;
            case SHIFT_ALT :
                sprintf(p, "Keyboard: alt key %s",
                    event_is_down(event)? "pressed" : "released");
                break;
            case KBD_USE:
                sprintf(p, "Keyboard: got keyboard focus");
                break;
            case KBD_DONE:
                sprintf(p, "Keyboard: lost keyboard focus");
                break;
            case LOC_MOVE:
                sprintf(p, "Pointer: moved to %d,%d",
                        event_x(event),event_y(event));
                break;
            case LOC_DRAG:
                sprintf(p, "Pointer: dragged to %d,%d",
                        event_x(event), event_y(event));
                break;
            case LOC_WINENTER:
                win_set_kbd_focus(window, xv_get(window, XV_XID));
                sprintf(p, "Pointer: entered window at %d,%d",
                        event_x(event), event_y(event));
                break;
            case LOC_WINEXIT:
                sprintf(p, "Pointer: exited window at %d,%d",
                        event_x(event), event_y(event));
                break;
            case WIN_RESIZE :
            case WIN_REPAINT :
                return;
            default :
                /* There are too many ACTION events to trap -- ignore the
                 * ones we're not interested in.
                 */
                return;
        }

    my_repaint_proc(canvas, window,
        xv_get(canvas, XV_DISPLAY), xv_get(window, XV_XID), NULL);
}
/*
 * my_repaint_proc()
 *      Called to repaint the canvas in response to damage events
 *      and the initial painting of the canvas window.
 *      Displays the keyboard, pointer and button message strings
 *      after erasing the previous messages.
 */
void
my_repaint_proc(canvas, pw, dpy, xwin, xrects)
Canvas          canvas;
Xv_Window       pw;
```

Example 6-1. The canvas_input.c program (continued)

```
Display         *dpy;
Window          xwin;
Xv_xrectlist    *xrects;
{
    char        win_num[16];
    Xv_Window   w;
    int         i = 0;
    GC          gc = DefaultGC(dpy, DefaultScreen(dpy));

    /*
     * Determine which paint window we're writing in.
     */
    CANVAS_EACH_PAINT_WINDOW(canvas, w)
        if (w == pw)
            break;
        i++;
    CANVAS_END_EACH
    sprintf(win_num, "(Window #%d) ", i+1);

    XClearWindow(dpy, xwin);
    XDrawString(dpy, xwin, gc, 25, 25, win_num, strlen(win_num));
    XDrawString(dpy, xwin, gc, 25, 45, msg, strlen(msg));
}
```

This sample program initializes XView and creates a frame. It then creates a canvas with two scrollbars attached to it. Chapter 5, *Canvases and Openwin*, addresses how to attach scrollbars to a canvas. The canvas installs a callback routine that will be called when its views are split. This routine installs the existing event masks and callback routine in the new view's paint window. Remember, that is necessary because new windows need to be initialized by the application.

The callback routine my_event_proc() handles all events for all the windows in the program. It determines which event has taken place and constructs a descriptive message identifying the event. It then calls the repaint routine to display the message in the window in which the event occurred. Note that the repaint callback routine may be called by the application—it is not a function reserved for the window system to call exclusively. In this case, the graphics is limited to calling XDrawString() to display text.

6.10 Extensions for Events

In X11, it is possible to create extensions to the server that may generate their own set of events, depending on the way your X11 server has been configured.* For example, in X11 Release 4, the *Shape* extension was added, allowing you to display windows of arbitrary shape in addition to the usual rectangular windows. Not all X11 servers support all known extensions, and there is a further limitation: all window managers may not be able to handle a

---

*Server extensions should not be confused with XView extensions discussed in Chapter 22, *XView Internals*.

given extension like the Shape extension. Therefore, this chapter is only intended for those who are well-aware of how server extensions work and are using them in their applications.

The only thing that XView is concerned about with respect to extensions is the delivery of events that have an event type outside of the normal range defined by the X Protocol; in other words, events that are defined by the server extension. Thus, the attribute SERVER_EXTEN-SION_PROC is used to specify a function to be called when such an extension event occurs. Unlike other event handlers, you do not register an extension procedure with a window, you register it with the server object itself:

```
extern void proc();
xv_set(XV_SERVER_FROM_WINDOW(frame),
    SERVER_EXTENSION_PROC, proc,
    NULL);
```

Note the use of XV_SERVER_FROM_WINDOW. This macro returns the Xv_Server object associated with an XView object. The object can be any one that contains a window (so most panel items are excluded). In this case, it happens to be a frame. Be aware that if your application is using multiple servers, you should use an object associated with the server that contains the extension.

The proc function is called whenever there is an event associated with the server extension. The form of the procedure is:

```
void
ext_event_proc(dpy, event, object)
    Display *dpy;
    XEvent  *event;
    Xv_object object;
```

The display and event types are strictly X11 types defined in <X11/Xlib.h>. The object is an XView object that is associated with the event, if available. If it is impossible to determine the object, the value is NULL.

7

Panels

In This Chapter:

7
Panels

The PANEL package implements the OPEN LOOK *control area*. Panels are used in many different contexts—property sheets, notices, and menus all use panels in their implementation. The main function of a panel is to manage a variety of *panel items*. Figure 7-1 shows examples of panel items from the *OPEN LOOK GUI*. Because some panel items may not contain windows that handle their own events, the PANEL package is responsible for propagating events to the appropriate panel item. This chapter addresses issues specific to panels, the management of panel items and the distribution of events to those items. We look at basic issues common to all panel items before introducing each of the eight different panel item packages. Finally, we look at several advanced topics regarding panel usage.

The PANEL package is subclassed from the WINDOW package. In typical usage, you create a panel and set certain panel-specific attributes.

Panels set up and manage their own event handling masks and routines for themselves and their panel items. The application does not set event masks or install an event callback routine unless it needs to track events above and beyond what the PANEL package does by default (typical applications will not need to do this). Even so, this is probably better accomplished via interposing functions discussed in Chapter 19, *The Notifier*.

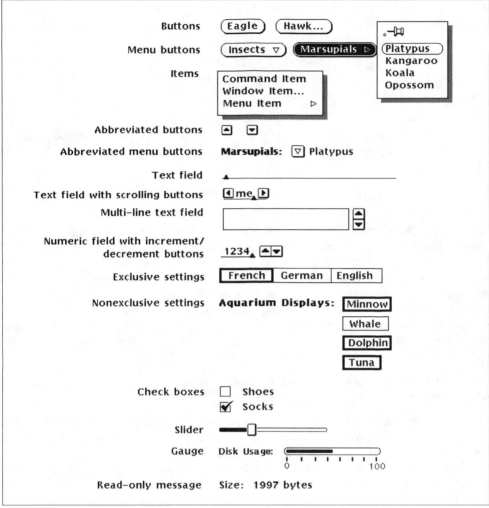

Figure 7-1. Controls in an OPEN LOOK GUI implementation*

The PANEL package handles all the repainting and resizing events automatically. Panels are not used to display graphics, so there is no need to capture repaint events. Rather than deal with other events specifically, callback routines are not installed on panels, but set for each panel item. Because of the varying types of panel items, each item's callback function may be invoked by a different action from the user. While clicking on a panel button is all that is necessary to activate the button's callback routine, a text panel item might be configured to call its notification callback routine upon the user pressing the RETURN key.

Since panel items express interest in different events, it is the responsibility of the PANEL package to track all events within the panel's window and dispatch events to the proper panel item depending on its type. In some cases, if an event happens over a certain panel item and

---

*XView does not support multiline text items. Also, the scrolling list item is supported but not shown here.

that item is not interested in that event, the event may be sent to another panel item. For example, what happens if a key is pressed over a panel button? Because the panel button has no interest in the event, the panel will send the event to a text panel item, if one exists elsewhere in the panel.

Section 7.14, "Advanced Panel Usage," describes panel event handling and repainting.

7.1 Creating a Panel

Creating a panel is achieved by calling xv_create() and specifying the PANEL package and a NULL-terminated list of attribute-value pairs. A panel must be created as a child of the frame. All programs that use panels or panel items must include *<xview/panel.h>*. Because panels are uninteresting without panel items, Example 7-1 shows how to create a simple frame, a panel and a panel button. Selecting the panel button causes the program to exit. This is the same *quit.c* program as shown in Chapter 3, *Creating XView Applications*.

Example 7-1. The quit.c program

```
/*
 * quit.c -- simple program to display a panel button that says "Quit".
 * Selecting the panel button exits the program.
 */
#include <xview/xview.h>
#include <xview/frame.h>
#include <xview/panel.h>

Frame frame;

main (argc, argv)
int argc;
char *argv[];
{
    Panel panel;
    void quit();

    xv_init (XV_INIT_ARGC_PTR_ARGV, &argc, argv, NULL);

    frame = (Frame)xv_create (NULL, FRAME,
        FRAME_LABEL,    argv[0],
        XV_WIDTH,       200,
        XV_HEIGHT,      100,
        NULL);

    panel = (Panel)xv_create (frame, PANEL, NULL);

    (void) xv_create (panel, PANEL_BUTTON,
            PANEL_LABEL_STRING,     "Quit",
            PANEL_NOTIFY_PROC,      quit,
            NULL);

    xv_main_loop (frame);
    exit(0);
}

void
quit()
```

Example 7-1. The quit.c program (continued)

```
{
    xv_destroy_safe(frame);
}
```

Fonts and Panels

OPEN LOOK is somewhat restrictive about the use of fonts within panels. Many panel items cannot have their fonts changed at all. Of those that can, none can have their fonts set individually.* However, if a font is set in the panel itself, it is then inherited by the panel items whose fonts can be changed. This guarantees the consistency of fonts in panels.

7.1.1 Scrollable Panels

Scrollable panels are not OPEN LOOK-compliant, but are provided for historical reasons. They are basically just like panels, except that typically not all panel items are in view. A vertical scrollbar attached to the panel allows the user to navigate to the panel items desired. Again, because this type of interface is not OPEN LOOK-compliant, you are discouraged from using this package.

In order to deal with the complications involved with attaching a scrollbar to a panel, the scrollable panel package is subclassed from the CANVAS package and thus, the OPENWIN package. Scrollable panels are created the same way panels are, but the package name to use is SCROLLABLE_PANEL. The scrollable panel package does not create the scrollbars, however. You must create them separately:

```
Scrollable_panel sp;
Scrollbar sb;

sp = xv_create(frame, SCROLLABLE_PANEL, NULL);
sb = xv_create(sp, SCROLLBAR, NULL);
```

The principle difference between canvases and scrollable panels is the management of events and the existence of panel items. In canvases, the programmer installs callback routines for events and for repaint and resize routines. An input mask is set for notification of certain events that the application is interested in. However, like normal panels, the scrollable panel does this automatically. Other than this, scrollable panels may take the same attributes as normal panels.

---

*The exact list of panel items varies and may change. Currently, it includes the text used in the value of panel text items.

7.2 Creating Panel Items

Panel items are created using `xv_create()` as usual:

```
Panel_item
xv_create(panel, item_type, attrs)
    Panel panel;
    <item type>              item_type;
    <attribute-value list> attrs;
```

The value of `item_type` must be a panel item from one of the panel item packages:

- `PANEL_BUTTON`
- `PANEL_CHOICE`
- `PANEL_LIST`
- `PANEL_MESSAGE`
- `PANEL_NUMERIC_TEXT`
- `PANEL_SLIDER`
- `PANEL_GAUGE`
- `PANEL_TEXT`

The items in this list represent the items found in Figure 7-1. Each item's type can be retrieved by calling:

```
Panel_item_type type;
type = (Panel_item_type)xv_get(panel_item, PANEL_ITEM_CLASS);
```

`Panel_item_type` is an enumerated type found in *<xview/panel.h>* and contains the following types:

- `PANEL_BUTTON_ITEM`
- `PANEL_CHOICE_ITEM`
- `PANEL_LIST_ITEM`
- `PANEL_MESSAGE_ITEM`
- `PANEL_NUMERIC_TEXT_ITEM`
- `PANEL_SLIDER_ITEM`
- `PANEL_GAUGE_ITEM`
- `PANEL_TEXT_ITEM`
- `PANEL_TOGGLE_ITEM`

Some of these panel items have values that are displayed separately. For example, the choice item displays either vertically or horizontally, next to each choice's label.

As panel items are created, they are added to a stack of panel items. The first panel item in a panel is considered at the bottom of the stack. When more items are added, they are added on top of the stack. The first item on the panel is said to be at the bottom, while the last item added is at the top. The order in which items lie on the panel has no effect on the display of the items. If items overlap, the last item to repaint itself will appear to be at the top of the stack despite its order on the panel. This behavior is described by the term *Z-order*, because in addition to the (*x, y*) coordinates of the panel items, there is a virtual *z* coordinate associated with panel items that has no effect on the graphical representation of the object.

Most panel items are drawn using Xlib calls directly onto the panel window. These panel items have no windows associated with them. Because there are no windows associated with panel items, panel items should be careful not to overlap one another, because one item will not *clip* the one under it. For event processing, when a button event occurs in a panel, the panel loops through the items in its stack (according to its Z-order) and if the event occurs in the panel item, then that item is notified of the event, even though it is entirely possible that another panel item may share the same space. For this reason, it is important that panel items are *tiled* and do not intersect partially or completely.

Note that this is *not* the case for Xt Intrinsics-based toolkits, whose items may be window-based. It is not unusual to do this sort of thing in some toolkits, but you should avoid doing it in XView. If you need to place more than one item at the same location, you should probably have one item's XV_SHOW attribute set to FALSE while the other's is TRUE. Toggle the attribute's values in each of the panel items.

7.3 Panel Layout

A panel lays out panel items in rows and columns. The width and height of the rows and columns may be set by panel and window attributes and/or by the sizes of the panel items themselves.

Whenever panel items are created, they are added to the adjacent panel in either a row-first or a column-first order. As each new item is added, it is placed at the next position depending on the value of the panel's PANEL_LAYOUT attribute. The default value, PANEL_HORIZONTAL, lays out panel items horizontally until the items have reached the edge of the panel. A new row is then started and the next item is placed at the left edge of the panel. Setting the value of PANEL_LAYOUT to PANEL_VERTICAL causes items to be laid out by column first; when the height of the panel is reached, the next column is started.

Use the attributes PANEL_NEXT_ROW and PANEL_NEXT_COL to explicitly specify the row or column gap for the next item only. The value −1 uses the value of WIN_ROW_GAP and WIN_COL_GAP (see Section 7.3.2, "General Positioning of Items").

Since different panel items have different sizes, the grid is not rigidly adhered to and the position of items may fluctuate within a row. However, it is possible to force items to line up to specific rows and columns, as will be shown later.

The gap between items as they are laid out vertically and horizontally can be set by the attributes PANEL_ITEM_X_GAP and PANEL_ITEM_Y_GAP. The default gap is 10 pixels in the horizontal direction and 5 pixels in the vertical direction.

Figure 7-2 shows how panels items are laid out as they are created.

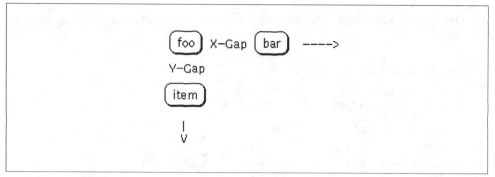

Figure 7-2. Layout of panel items

7.3.1 Explicit Item Positioning

To position panel items explicitly, the attributes XV_X and XV_Y are used. These specify absolute positioning relative to the panel. The attributes PANEL_ITEM_X and PANEL_ITEM_Y are specific to panels. These values reflect the coordinates of the last item created. Therefore, they are both get-only attributes. The following code fragment shows how both are used:

```
panel = (Panel)xv_create(frame, PANEL, NULL);

xv_create(panel, PANEL_BUTTON,
    XV_X,                 50,
    XV_Y,                 75,
    PANEL_LABEL_STRING, "Quit",
    NULL);

printf("The last item in the panel was at %d %d.\n",
    xv_get(panel, PANEL_ITEM_X), xv_get(panel, PANEL_ITEM_Y));
```

This code segment would print:

```
The last item in the panel was at 50 75.
```

When positioning panel items, if the position of the new panel item extends beyond the edges of the panel in the positive direction, the size of the panel increases to include the item. This happens regardless of whether the panel's size was set explicitly at the time it was created.*

7.3.2 General Positioning of Items

Two functions that are available for general positioning of panel items within windows are xv_row() and xv_col(). These functions use the values of WIN_ROW_GAP and WIN_COLUMN_GAP of the panel. While these attributes control the spacing between panel items, the distance between items and the edge of the panel is set to a constant 4 pixels.

---

*Setting an item to negative coordinates does not increase the size of the panel—only if the item is wide enough or high enough to stretch into the panel window will any of it be visible.

Consider the following code fragment that positions items within regimented rows and columns:

```
int          rows, cols;
extern char *names[3][5];

frame = (Frame)xv_create(NULL, FRAME, NULL);
panel = (Panel)xv_create(frame, PANEL,
    WIN_ROW_GAP,         70,
    WIN_COLUMN_GAP,      20,
    NULL);

for (rows = 0; rows < 3; rows++)
    for (cols = 0; cols < 5; cols++)
        (void) xv_create(panel, PANEL_BUTTON,
            XV_X,                xv_col(panel, cols),
            XV_Y,                xv_row(panel, rows),
            PANEL_LABEL_STRING,  names[rows][cols],
            PANEL_NOTIFY_PROC,   (rows+cols==0)? quit : selected,
            PANEL_CLIENT_DATA,   frame,
            NULL);
```

This code displays a panel with a 70-pixel distance between the upper-left corners of the panel items. Thus, each panel item must be greater than 70 pixels wide or they will overlap one another. This contrasts with PANEL_ITEM_X_GAP and PANEL_ITEM_Y_GAP, which specify the gap between the right and left sides of adjacent panel items. Note that this does not affect the distance between the edge of the panel and the items along the perimeter; that distance remains constant at 4 pixels.

The xv_col() and xv_row() method of explicit panel item placement does not take into account the sizes of the panel items. If not enough space is given between the rows and columns (WIN_COLUMN_GAP, WIN_ROW_GAP), then items will lie on top of one another.

7.3.3 Layout of Panel Items with Values

For panel items with values, special attributes should be used instead of the XV_X and XV_Y attributes mentioned above. These panel items display their values by printing a separate piece of the item apart from the panel item's label, as shown in Figure 7-3. Text items, for example, display their values as text strings adjacent to the text item's label.

Text Item Label: Value

Figure 7-3. Layout of panel item with value

It is possible to position the text item's label and text string (value) independently of one another. This is accomplished by using the following four attributes:

*   PANEL_LABEL_X
*   PANEL_LABEL_Y

- PANEL_VALUE_X
- PANEL_VALUE_Y

Setting PANEL_ITEM_X and PANEL_ITEM_Y position the *label* portion of the panel item to the coordinates specified. Similarly, setting PANEL_VALUE_X and PANEL_VALUE_Y position the value portion of the panel item. Each X/Y attribute pair should be used together; otherwise, if one is set, the other's value is changed to a default value. If PANEL_VALUE_X is set to 100 and PANEL_LABEL_X is not specified, the label's position and, thus, *the whole panel item* is moved so that the value portion is aligned with its *x* coordinate at 100.

It is important *not* to use XV_X and XV_Y when using the label and value positioning attributes.

7.3.4 Sizing Panels

The size of a panel, by default, extends to the bottom and right edges of the frame in which it is placed (assuming there are no other subwindows in the frame). Alternatively, the panel's dimensions can be set explicitly using XV_WIDTH and XV_HEIGHT. If it is important to maintain the layout of the panel items in a panel, then the dimensions should be set explicitly.

More often than not, you want the panel to be just the minimum height and width required to encompass all of its items. You can set the minimum height and width using the macros window_fit_height() or window_fit_width(), respectively. You can set both in a single call to window_fit(). These macros are called after all the items have been created.

The attributes PANEL_EXTRA_PAINT_WIDTH and PANEL_EXTRA_PAINT_HEIGHT specify the increment by which a panel will grow in the *x* and *y* directions, respectively.

7.4 Panel Item Values

Many panel items are associated with a specific value. A text item has a *string* value, a text-number item has an integer value, a list item has a list-choice value, a choice item has a current-choice value, and so on.* To set a value, use:

```
xv_set(item, PANEL_VALUE, value, NULL)
```

Of course, the type of value is dependent on the type of panel item whose value is being set. Consider the following examples:

```
/* Set the text field in the text item to print "Hello World" */
xv_set(text_item, PANEL_VALUE, "Hello world.", NULL);

/* Set the numeric value of the number-text item to be 10 */
xv_set(text_num_item, PANEL_VALUE, 10, NULL);
```

---

*For details about the value type of a panel item, see the corresponding sections on specific panel items (Sections 7.7 through 7.13).

```
/* Set the current choice in choice_item to be the fifth choice */
xv_set(choice_item, PANEL_VALUE, 5, NULL);
```

NOTE

The values for string-valued attributes are dynamically allocated when they are
created or set. The value you specify is *copied* into the newly allocated space. If
a previous value was present, the panel item frees its old data first.*

Panel item values are retrieved in a similar way:

```
xv_get(item, PANEL_VALUE);
```

Since the `xv_get()` routines are used to retrieve attributes of all types, you should coerce
the value returned into the type appropriate to the attribute being retrieved:

```
int val;
val = (int)xv_get(num_text_item, PANEL_VALUE);
printf("The int-value in the num_text_item is: '%d'\n", val);
```

To get the image for a choice item's current choice (assuming the choice item is a
`Server_image` choice):

```
Server_image image;
image = (Server_image)xv_get(item, PANEL_CHOICE_IMAGE,
                             xv_get(item, PANEL_VALUE));
```

NOTE

`xv_get()` does not dynamically allocate storage for the values it returns. If the
value returned is a pointer, it points directly into the panel's private data. It
should be considered *read-only*—do not change the contents of the pointer; it is
your responsibility to copy the information pointed to.

For choice items whose `PANEL_CHOOSE_NONE` value is `TRUE`, a `PANEL_VALUE` of -1 may be
set or returned, indicating that no choices are set for that item.

---

*This contrasts with menu items. See Chapter 11, *Menus*.

7.5 Iterating Over a Panel's Items

You can iterate over each item in a panel with the two attributes `PANEL_FIRST_ITEM` and `PANEL_NEXT_ITEM`. A pair of macros, `PANEL_EACH_ITEM()` and `PANEL_END_EACH` are also provided for this purpose. For example, to destroy each item in a panel:

```
Panel_item item;

PANEL_EACH_ITEM(browser, item)
    xv_destroy(item);
PANEL_END_EACH
```

A semicolon is not required after `PANEL_END_EACH`.

7.6 Panel Item Classes

Eight types of panel items are presented here:

- Panel Buttons
- Checkboxes
- Exclusive and Nonexclusive Choices
- Abbreviated Choices
- Scrolling Lists
- Message Items
- Sliders
- Text and Numbered Text Items

Items are made up of one or more displayable components. One component shared by all item types is the *label*. An item label is either a string or a graphic image.

The user interacts with items through various methods ranging from mouse button selection to keyboard input. This interaction typically results in a *callback* function being called for the panel item. The callback functions also vary on a per-item basis. Each item type is described in the following sections.

7.7 Button Items

A button item allows the user to invoke a command or bring up a menu. Examples of various buttons are listed in Figure 7-4. The button's label identifies the name of the command or menu. A button label that ends in three dots (. . .) indicates that a pop-up menu will be displayed when the button is selected.

A button requires a label specified by the attribute `PANEL_LABEL_STRING` or `PANEL_LABEL_IMAGE`. OPEN LOOK describes which font is used for the button label—it cannot be changed or emboldened.

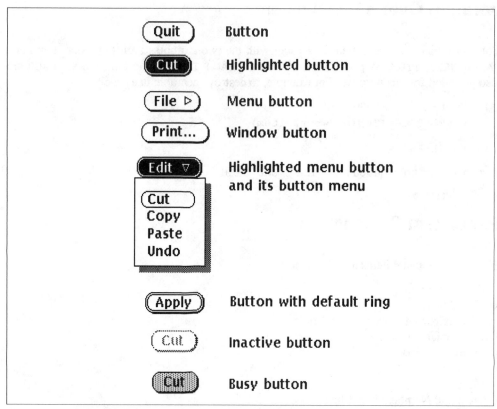

Figure 7-4. Visual feedback for button controls

7.7.1 Button Selection

The user invokes a panel button by clicking the SELECT mouse button on it. When this happens, the button's notify procedure is called. The notify procedure is installed by specifying PANEL_NOTIFY_PROC, as in the following example:

```
xv_create(panel, PANEL_BUTTON,
    PANEL_NOTIFY_PROC,    quit_proc,
    PANEL_LABEL_STRING,   "Quit",
    NULL);
```

When the button is selected, the notify procedure is called. The form of the notify procedure for a button is:

```
void
button_notify_proc(item, event)
    Panel_item  item;
    Event       *event
```

The function does not return a value, but if the action that the button had intended to take fails, then you should set the item's PANEL_NOTIFY_STATUS to XV_ERROR. For example, if the button was labeled "save" but the actual save operation failed, you should set the status accordingly. It is set to XV_OK by default.

7.7.2 Menu Buttons

It is often useful to attach a menu to a button. The menu may provide alternate values or functions for the button to invoke. Since the menu is a separate entity (e.g., it is not created when the button is created—you have to create it on your own), the menu may have callback routines associated with it and its menu items. Therefore, if the menu is used to make a selection, then the menu item's notify procedure is called and the panel button's notify procedure is *not* called.* However, if the button is selected without bringing up the menu, *both* callback routines are called—the button's callback is called *first*, followed by the default menu item's callback routine.

Menu buttons contain a triangle pointing in the direction in which the menu will be displayed.

The *btn_menu.c* program demonstrates how a menu can be attached to a panel button. This program is shown in Example 7-2:

Example 7-2. The btn_menu.c program

```
/*
 * btn_menu.c -- display a panel that has an OPEN LOOK menu button.
 * The choices displayed are Yes, No and Quit.  If Quit is selected
 * in the menu, the program exits.
 */
#include <xview/xview.h>
#include <xview/panel.h>
#include <xview/openmenu.h>

main(argc, argv)
int argc;
char *argv[];
{
    Frame       frame;
    Panel       panel;
    Menu        menu;
    int         selected();
    void        menu_proc();

    xv_init(XV_INIT_ARGC_PTR_ARGV, &argc, argv, NULL);

    frame = (Frame)xv_create(NULL, FRAME, NULL);
    panel = (Panel)xv_create(frame, PANEL, NULL);

    /* Create the menu _before_ the panel button */
    menu = (Menu)xv_create(NULL, MENU,
        MENU_NOTIFY_PROC,       menu_proc,
        MENU_STRINGS,           "Yes", "No", "Quit", NULL,
        NULL);
    (void) xv_create(panel, PANEL_BUTTON,
        PANEL_LABEL_STRING,     "Y/N/Q",
        PANEL_NOTIFY_PROC,      selected,
        PANEL_ITEM_MENU,        menu, /* attach menu to button */
        NULL);
    window_fit(panel);
```

---

*Chapter 11, *Menus*, should be read for details about menus and menu items.

Example 7-2. The btn_menu.c program (continued)

```
    window_fit(frame);
    xv_main_loop(frame);
}

int
selected(item, event)
Panel_item item;
Event *event;
{
    printf("%s selected...\n", xv_get(item, PANEL_LABEL_STRING));
    return XV_OK;
}

void
menu_proc(menu, menu_item)
Menu menu;
Menu_item menu_item;
{
    printf("Menu Item: %s\n", xv_get(menu_item, MENU_STRING));
    if (!strcmp((char *)xv_get(menu_item, MENU_STRING), "Quit"))
        exit(0);
}
```

The output produced by this program is shown in Figure 7-5.

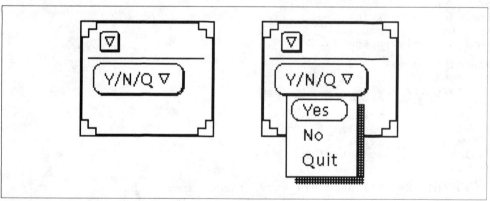

Figure 7-5. Sample menu button (unselected and selected)

Normally, when the user selects a panel button that has a menu attached to it, the menu's
default menu item callback routine is called first, even though the menu has not been popped
up. Following that, the panel button's notify procedure is called, provided one has been
installed. Thus, unless you want to be notified twice when the button is selected, you should
probably rely on the callback routines of the menu items to perform the work behind the
menu button.

When the button is in a panel owned by a *command frame** and the button is selected, the
command   frame   is   dismissed.   Internally,   if   the   value   of   the   button's

---

*See Chapter 4, *Frames*, for details on command panels.

PANEL_NOTIFY_STATUS is XV_OK after the button's callback routine returns, the frame is dismissed. This is the default action XView imposes.

You can prevent the frame from being dismissed by setting the button's PANEL_NOTIFY_STATUS to XV_ERROR. However, if the menu is already up and not pinned in, bringing up the panel button's menu again and selecting an item will dismiss that first menu. You can prevent this by setting MENU_NOTIFY_STATUS on the menu item to XV_ERROR. This is one reason for having a button item callback routine separate from the menu item's callback routines.

Destroying Menu Buttons

Destroying menu buttons is typically no different from destroying most other panel items: all data associated with the button is destroyed, including the button's menu. The exception is client data that you may have attached to the item. If you used PANEL_CLIENT_DATA or XV_KEY_DATA to attach information to the item, it is your responsibility to free the data yourself.*

If you do not wish to destroy the extra data, then you should do nothing special. However, this is not the case for the menu attached to the item. XView automatically destroys the menu associated with the button unless there are other references to the menu. For each button or any other XView object that references the menu in question, the menu's XV_REF_COUNT is incremented. Thus, if five buttons reference the same menu, then destroying one button will not destroy the menu, but it will decrement the reference count by one. If the destruction of the panel item would decrement the reference count to 0, then the menu itself is destroyed. Therefore, if you wish to prevent the menu from being destroyed, you can forcefully increment the reference count by at least one more than what it is. That way, no matter how many times the menu is used, it will always be set to a value greater than zero, and it will never be destroyed by destroying panel items that use it. Of course, you can always call xv_destroy() on the menu explicitly when you want to destroy the menu once and for all.

You can use the attributes XV_INCREMENT_REF_COUNT and XV_DECREMENT_REF_COUNT on any item.

```
xv_set(menu, XV_INCREMENT_REF_COUNT, NULL);
```

This is not recommended except when you need to circumvent the normal functionality of XView.

---

*You may have specified a routine via XV_KEY_DATA_REMOVE_PROC to free XV_KEY_DATA automatically. In this case, you are not responsible for freeing this data automatically. See Section 7.16, "Attaching Data to Panel Items."

7.8 Choice Items

Choice items provide a list of different choices to the user in which one or more choices may be selected. There are variations of choice items which implement different OPEN LOOK objects such as:

- Exclusive and Nonexclusive Choices (or Settings)
- Abbreviated Choice Items
- Checkboxes

Behind the flexibility of presentation lies a uniform structure consisting of a label, a list of choices and an indication of which choice or set of choices is currently selected. The choices can be displayed as either text strings (PANEL_CHOICE_STRINGS) or server images (PANEL_CHOICE_IMAGES). For a choice item to be displayed, at the very least, either a choice or a label must be set in the item. The number of items in a list is returned by xv_get() passing the PANEL_NCHOICES attribute. This is true for toggle items as well.

7.8.1 Display and Layout of Item Choices

The attribute PANEL_DISPLAY_LEVEL determines which of an item's choices are actually displayed. The display level may be set to:

PANEL_ALL   The default. All choices are shown.

PANEL_CURRENT   Only the current choice is shown. This setting is used to imple-
                    ment the *abbreviated choice item.*

PANEL_NONE   No choices are shown.

When the display level of a choice item is set to PANEL_NONE, an *abbreviated menu button* is created because the current value is not displayed. You still have to create your own menu for this item.

The choices are laid out either horizontally or vertically next to the label depending on the value of the item's value for PANEL_LAYOUT. By default, this value is inherited from the parent panel. If you want an explicit layout pattern for the choice item only, you should specify it explicitly by setting the PANEL_LAYOUT attribute for the *panel item*, not the panel.

Sometimes, the number of choices in a choice list can get long and the menu for the item may look aesthetically bad or not fit on the screen. You can specify that choices appear in row and column layout by specifying either the number of rows or the number of columns with the attributes PANEL_CHOICE_NROWS and PANEL_CHOICE_NCOLS. If both are specified, the last one specified takes precedence.

7.8.2 Parallel Lists

Parallel lists are lists of values for particular attributes that correspond to each choice in the panel item. An example of a parallel list is PANEL_CHOICE_XS and PANEL_CHOICE_YS. These two attributes take as values a NULL-terminated list of coordinates to specify explicit placement of the choices when they are displayed (assuming PANEL_ALL is the display format). These attributes are used to display choices in adjacent rows and columns, as in the following example:

```
xv_create(panel, PANEL_CHOICE,
    PANEL_CHOICE_STRINGS,    "One", "Two", "Three",
                            "Four", "Five", "Six", NULL,
    PANEL_CHOICE_XS,        10, 70, 130, NULL,
    PANEL_CHOICE_YS,        90, 120, NULL,
    PANEL_VALUE,            2,
    PANEL_NOTIFY_PROC,      notify_proc,
    NULL);
```

The item has three choices: the strings "One", "Two" and "Three." We have specified explicit positioning of the choice items using the PANEL_CHOICE_XS and PANEL_CHOICE_YS attributes. These attributes take precedence over PANEL_LAYOUT, so that layout is ignored if specified. Note that the list PANEL_CHOICE_YS has only one element. When any of the parallel lists are abbreviated in this way, the last element given will be used for the remainder of the choices. So, in the example above:

```
90, NULL
```

serves as shorthand for:

```
90, 90, 90, NULL
```

All the choices will appear at y coordinate 90, while the x coordinates for the choices will be 10, 70 and 130, respectively.

You cannot specify that a choice appear at $x = 0$ or $y = 0$ by using the attributes PANEL_CHOICE_XS or PANEL_CHOICE_YS. Since these attributes take NULL-terminated lists as values, the zero would be interpreted as the terminator for the list. You may achieve the desired effect by setting the positions individually. The attributes PANEL_CHOICE_X or PANEL_CHOICE_Y take as values the number of the choice followed by the desired position. The following example demonstrates setting the position of choice items:

```
Panel_item    choice;
int           i;
extern char *strings[];

choice = (Panel_item)xv_create(panel, PANEL_CHOICE,
    PANEL_CHOOSE_ONE,       FALSE,
    NULL);
for (i = 0; i < sizeof(strings) / sizeof(char *); i++)
    xv_set(choice,
        PANEL_CHOICE_STRING, i, strings[i],
        PANEL_CHOICE_X,      i, i*20,
        PANEL_CHOICE_Y,      i, i*20,
        NULL);
```

After the choice item is created, the *x* and *y* positions of the choices are set individually in a loop.

7.8.3 Exclusive and Nonexclusive Choices

When a default choice item is created, its type is an exclusive choice item allowing the user to select only one choice from the list. The value of the panel item is the currently selected item. In the following example, we create several choice items as exclusive settings:

```
xv_create(panel, PANEL_CHOICE,
    PANEL_LABEL_STRING,     "Choices",
    PANEL_CHOICE_STRINGS,   "One", "Two", "Three", "Four", NULL,
    PANEL_NOTIFY_PROC,      selected,
    PANEL_VALUE,            3,
    NULL);
```

This code fragment produces the panel item shown in Figure 7-6.

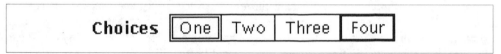

Figure 7-6. Sample panel with exclusive choices

Figure 7-6 represents a panel item that has four choices, the third of which is *set*. If the user makes another choice, the value of the item, and therefore the value of PANEL_VALUE, changes to the ordinal number of the choice.

To reset the value of the choice item so that no choice is selected, use:

```
xv_set(choice_item, PANEL_CHOOSE_NONE, TRUE, NULL);
```

This attribute may be used on choice items whos PANEL_CHOOSE_ONE attribute is set to TRUE. Otherwise, PANEL_CHOOSE_NONE has no effect.

The choice item can be made nonexclusive (allowing more than one of the choices to be selected) when the macro PANEL_TOGGLE is set to FALSE. This macro affects the panel item in two ways. More than one choice may be set in the visual feedback, and the value of the item is set as a mask indicating the choices selected. In the following example, the choice items in the previous example are shown as nonexclusive settings:

```
xv_create(panel, PANEL_TOGGLE,
    PANEL_LABEL_STRING,     "Choices",
    PANEL_CHOICE_STRINGS,   "One", "Two", "Three", "Four", NULL,
    PANEL_NOTIFY_PROC,      selected,
    PANEL_VALUE,            5,
    NULL);
```

This code fragment would produce the panel item shown in Figure 7-7.

Figure 7-7 represents a panel item that has two choices set, the first and the third. The reason for this is that the panel's value is set to 5, which is a mask that represents the first and third bits. For example, 5 in binary is ... 00101.* In the binary representation, the first and third

---

*The value for nonexclusive choice items is stored as an unsigned int.

Figure 7-7. Sample panel with nonexclusive choices

bits from the right are 1's. This means that the first and third choices are selected. This is how the value is interpreted on calls to `xv_set()` or `xv_create()`, and this is what is returned for calls to `xv_get()`.

7.8.4 Checkbox Choices

Checkboxes can be displayed instead of the default for choices by using `PANEL_CHECK_BOX`. The following example demonstrates checkboxes:

```
xv_create(panel, PANEL_CHECK_BOX,
    PANEL_LAYOUT,           PANEL_VERTICAL,
    PANEL_CHOOSE_ONE,       FALSE,
    PANEL_LABEL_STRING,     "Choices",
    PANEL_CHOICE_STRINGS,   "One", "Two", "Three", "Four", NULL,
    PANEL_NOTIFY_PROC,      selected,
    PANEL_VALUE,            5,
    NULL);
```

The only difference from previous examples is that the panel item is marked using checkboxes for selected choices and empty boxes for nonselected choices. The panel items created by this code are shown in Figure 7-8.

Figure 7-8. Sample panel with checkbox

All of the items can be selected in the same way and their values can be set identically.

7.8.5 Abbreviated Choices

Abbreviated choices are similar to choice items. However, only the current value is displayed. A menu is used to display all the choices. To implement abbreviated choice items, specify the macro `PANEL_CHOICE_STACK`. The following example demonstrates creating abbreviated choice items:

```
xv_create(panel, PANEL_CHOICE_STACK,
    PANEL_LAYOUT,           PANEL_VERTICAL,
    PANEL_LABEL_STRING,     "Choices",
    PANEL_CHOICE_STRINGS,   "One", "Two", "Three", "Four", NULL,
    PANEL_NOTIFY_PROC,      selected,
    PANEL_VALUE,            1,
    NULL);
```

The panel item created by this code is shown in Figure 7-9.

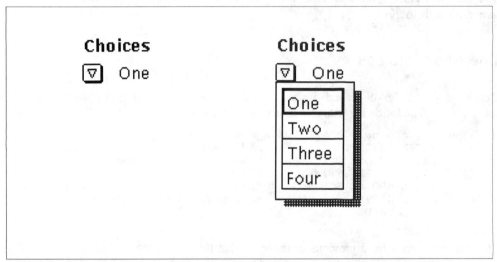

Figure 7-9. Sample panel with abbreviated choice (unselected and selected)

Here, since only the current selection is visible, the only way to make other choices in the item is to bring up a menu. The value of the panel item is similar.

Choice Selection and Notification

The user can make a selection from a choice item by selecting the desired choice directly with the SELECT mouse button.

The procedure specified via the attribute PANEL_NOTIFY_PROC will be called when any of its choices are selected. If a choice item's current selection or value changes as a result of a call to xv_set() from somewhere else, then the notify procedure is not called. The choice notify procedure is passed the item, the current value of the item, and the event that caused notification:

```
void
choice_notify_proc(item, value, event)
    Panel_item   item;
    int          value;
    Event        *event;
```

Like the button's notify procedure, the choice notify procedure is also a void function. If the function fails to perform its task, you should set the item's PANEL_NOTIFY_STATUS to XV_ERROR.

For exclusive choices, the value passed to the notify procedure is the ordinal number corresponding to the current choice (the choice that the user has just selected). The first choice has ordinal number zero. For nonexclusive choices, the value is a mask of the currently selected choices in the list (see the previous section).

The `event` is the event that caused the notify procedure to be called. For these types of choices, the event action will probably be `ACTION_SELECT`.

7.8.6 Abbreviated Menu Buttons

An abbreviated menu button is different from an abbreviated choice (stack) item in several ways. The menu button does not have its current value displayed and it cannot be turned on (e.g., `PANEL_DISPLAY_LEVEL` cannot be changed). These items may not take a list of choices and there is no callback procedure associated with it. The intended use of this object is that the programmer creates a separate menu and attaches it to the item using the `PANEL_ITEM_MENU` attribute.

Abbreviated menu items are created using the `PANEL_ABBREV_MENU_BUTTON` package.

```
Panel_item item;
extern Menu menu; /* created separately */

item = xv_create(panel, PANEL_ABBREV_MENU_BUTTON,
    PANEL_ITEM_MENU,   menu,
    NULL);
```

This is a simple item and does not utilize most panel attributes. You may set the item's color, label and position, but not much else. When the user selects the item with the MENU button, the menu is automatically popped up. The normal callback mechanisms for menus is the way to be notified when the user selects a menu item. See Chapter 11, *Menus*, for details.

7.9 Scrolling Lists

OPEN LOOK's specification for *scrolling lists* is implemented by the `PANEL_LIST` panel item. List items allow the user to make selections from a scrolling list of choices larger than can be displayed on the panel at one time. The selections can be exclusive or nonexclusive, like the choice items outlined in the previous section. The list is made up of strings or images and a scrollbar that functions like any scrollbar in XView, except that it cannot be split.* List items are laid out in rows only—one list entry per row. Below is a code fragment for creating a simple list:

```
xv_create(panel, PANEL_LIST,
    PANEL_LIST_STRINGS,     "One", "Two", "Three", NULL,
    NULL);
```

The list items produced by this code are shown in Figure 7-10.

---
*See Chapter 10, *Scrollbars*, for a further description of how scrollbars work.

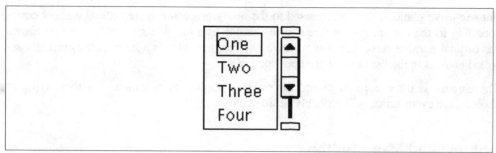

Figure 7-10. Sample panel with scrolling list

7.9.1 Displaying List Items

You can use either text strings or server images to display the choice to the user; you can even intermix them. You specify the choices either one at a time or in a group. To set only one choice, use PANEL_LIST_STRING or PANEL_LIST_GLYPH. When creating a new string or glyph entry, if the index into the list specified is larger than the total number of entries, then the new item is added to the end of the list. Use PANEL_LIST_STRINGS or PANEL_LIST_GLYPHS to set all the choices in a group. If no items exist in the list, the appropriate number of rows is created to fit all of the items. If the list already contains items, then the first *n* rows of items are replaced by the newly specified strings or glyphs (where *n* is the number of strings or glyphs specified).

The width of the list item can be set to explicit pixel values using PANEL_LIST_WIDTH. However, the minimum value for this attribute is 25. Alternatively, the number of rows that are displayed in the list item can be controlled through the value of the PANEL_LIST_DISPLAY_ROWS attribute. This value governs the height of the list item.

The height of each row in the list may be set using PANEL_LIST_ROW_HEIGHT. If the items in the list are glyphs, then the height of each row must be specified by at least the height of the tallest glyph in the list. This should be determined before the list of glyphs is set in the list item. Entries in the list can be either glyphs or strings; an entry containing both a string and a glyph will display both. The glyph on the left and the string on the right. Consider the program in Example 7-3.

Example 7-3. The list_glyphs.c program

```
/*
 * list_glyphs.c -- show a scrolling list with three items in it.
 * Each item is an icon (a pattern) and a string.
 */
#include <xview/xview.h>
#include <xview/panel.h>
#include <xview/svrimage.h>

#define gray1_width 16
#define gray1_height 16
static char gray1_bits[] = {
    0x55, 0x55, 0xaa, 0xaa, 0x55, 0x55, 0xaa, 0xaa, 0x55, 0x55,
    0xaa, 0xaa, 0x55, 0x55, 0xaa, 0xaa, 0x55, 0x55, 0xaa, 0xaa,
    0x55, 0x55, 0xaa, 0xaa, 0x55, 0x55, 0xaa, 0xaa, 0x55, 0x55,
```

Example 7-3. The list_glyphs.c program (continued)

```
    0xaa, 0xaa
};

#define gray2_width 16
#define gray2_height 16
static char gray2_bits[] = {
    0x11, 0x11, 0x00, 0x00, 0x44, 0x44, 0x00, 0x00, 0x11, 0x11,
    0x00, 0x00, 0x44, 0x44, 0x00, 0x00, 0x11, 0x11, 0x00, 0x00,
    0x44, 0x44, 0x00, 0x00, 0x11, 0x11, 0x00, 0x00, 0x44, 0x44,
    0x00, 0x00
};

#define gray3_width 16
#define gray3_height 16
static char gray3_bits[] = {
    0x22, 0x22, 0xee, 0xee, 0x33, 0x33, 0xee, 0xee, 0x22, 0x22,
    0xee, 0xee, 0x33, 0x33, 0xee, 0xee, 0x22, 0x22, 0xee, 0xee,
    0x33, 0x33, 0xee, 0xee, 0x22, 0x22, 0xee, 0xee, 0x33, 0x33,
    0xee, 0xee
};

main(argc, argv)
int     argc;
char    *argv[];
{
    Frame           frame;
    Panel           panel;
    Server_image gray1, gray2, gray3;
    extern void exit(), which_glyph();

    xv_init(XV_INIT_ARGS, argc, argv, NULL);

    gray1 = (Server_image)xv_create(NULL, SERVER_IMAGE,
        XV_WIDTH,               gray1_width,
        XV_HEIGHT,              gray1_height,
        SERVER_IMAGE_BITS,      gray1_bits,
        NULL);
    gray2 = (Server_image)xv_create(NULL, SERVER_IMAGE,
        XV_WIDTH,               gray2_width,
        XV_HEIGHT,              gray2_height,
        SERVER_IMAGE_BITS,      gray2_bits,
        NULL);
    gray3 = (Server_image)xv_create(NULL, SERVER_IMAGE,
        XV_WIDTH,               gray3_width,
        XV_HEIGHT,              gray3_height,
        SERVER_IMAGE_BITS,      gray3_bits,
        NULL);
    frame = (Frame)xv_create(NULL, FRAME, NULL);
    panel = (Panel)xv_create(frame, PANEL, NULL);

    (void) xv_create(panel, PANEL_BUTTON,
        PANEL_LABEL_STRING,     "quit",
        PANEL_NOTIFY_PROC,      exit,
        NULL);

    (void) xv_create(panel, PANEL_LIST,
        PANEL_LIST_ROW_HEIGHT,  16,
        PANEL_LIST_GLYPHS,      gray1, gray2, gray3, NULL,
        PANEL_LIST_STRINGS,     "Pattern1", "Pattern2", "Pattern3", NULL,
```

Example 7-3. The list_glyphs.c program (continued)

```
        PANEL_LIST_CLIENT_DATAS, 1, 2, 3,
        PANEL_NOTIFY_PROC,        which_glyph,
        NULL);

    window_fit(panel);
    window_fit(frame);

    xv_main_loop(frame);
}

void
which_glyph(item, string, client_data, op, event)
Panel_item      item; /* panel list item */
char            *string;
caddr_t         client_data;
Panel_list_op   op;
Event           *event;
{
    printf("item = %s (#%d), op = %d\n", string, client_data, op);
}
```

The output produced by *list_glyphs.c* is shown in Figure 7-11.

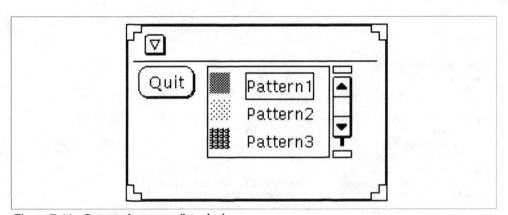

Figure 7-11. Output of program list_glyphs.c

The height of each row in the list is determined by the height of the font used by the string. If glyphs are used, this calculation is not done automatically, so the programmer is responsible for setting row height. In the example, all the glyphs in the list are the same height (16 pixels), so the calculation is easy: PANEL_LIST_ROW_HEIGHT is set to 16. If a glyph is assigned to a row whose height is not as high as the glyph, then a warning is printed and the glyph is ignored.

The use of the notify procedure is discussed later in Section 7.9.4, "List Notification."

7.9.2 Adding and Deleting List Entries

List entries are denoted by row number. The first entry is row 0. They are added and deleted from the list at run time. The attribute PANEL_LIST_DELETE value specifies the list item to delete. The string and/or image resources are deallocated and the list is updated appropriately.

When deleting multiple list items, you must delete them in descending order. When a row is deleted, the row numbers are adjusted to a sequential order. For example, to delete rows 1 through 5:

```
int row;
for (for = 4; rows > 0; rows--)
    xv_set(panel_list_item, PANEL_LIST_DELETE, row, NULL);
```

To add a list item, PANEL_LIST_INSERT is used in the same way. When adding a new list item in this manner, all the succeeding items are incremented and the list size grows by one. Space for a new item is created, and a new string or glyph may be added. These are all done at the time the attribute is evaluated, so they may be combined into one xv_set() call. You can move an item by deleting it from its old location and reassigning it to a new location. Look at the following code:

```
char *buf[128];

strcpy(buf, xv_get(list_item, PANEL_LIST_STRING, 4));

xv_set(list_item,
    PANEL_LIST_DELETE,    4,
    PANEL_LIST_INSERT,    8,
    PANEL_LIST_STRING,    8, buf,
    NULL);
```

The value for the string *must* be copied because as soon as the list item is deleted, the data is freed. When the new entry is created, the old entry number 8 is moved to 9, as are all succeeding items; the new list entry number 8 is set to the string described by buf.

The selected choice(s) can be set at list creation or later by using PANEL_LIST_SELECT. For example:

```
PANEL_LIST_SELECT, 3, TRUE,
```

will set choice 3 as selected. If the list item is nonexclusive, you can set more than one choice at one time. For example:

```
PANEL_LIST_SELECT, 3,  TRUE,
PANEL_LIST_SELECT, 13, TRUE,
PANEL_LIST_SELECT, 14, TRUE,
```

sets the 3rd, 13th and 14th entries as selected.

To determine if a list entry is selected, use:

```
xv_get(list_item, PANEL_LIST_SELECTED, i);
```

`xv_get()` returns TRUE if list entry *i* is selected.

7.9.3 List Selection

Items in the list are selected by using the SELECT mouse button while pointing at an item or by dragging the pointer over the list items. If the list attribute PANEL_CHOOSE_ONE has a value of TRUE, then only one list entry may be selected. Otherwise, more entries may be selected.

7.9.4 List Notification

The procedure specified via the attribute PANEL_NOTIFY_PROC is called when a list item is selected or deselected. List notify procedures are passed the list item, the string indicating the label of the item being acted upon, any client data associated with the list entry, and op, a parameter indicating the action being taken and the event which caused notification:

```
void
list_notify_proc(item, string, client_data, op, event)
    Panel_item          item; /* panel list item */
    char                *string;
    caddr_t             client_data;
    Panel_list_op       op;
    Event               *event;
```

`item` is the panel list item that contains the list entry that was acted upon. The `string` parameter is the label of the list item selected. If the string is an image and there is no string entry associated with the entry, the parameter is NULL. If the selected list entry contains both a string and an image, then the string is passed as the parameter.

`op` is either SELECT or DESELECT. If the user selects an item that is not currently selected, the notify procedure is called twice. The first time, it is called with the previously selected list item and the op is DESELECT. The next time the function is called, the op is SELECT. If the user selects an item that is already selected, the function is called once, passing the item selected (op is SELECT).

List Item Client Data

The `client_data` parameter is set to whatever client data is associated with the list item for that row number. *list_glyphs.c* uses the attribute PANEL_LIST_CLIENT_DATAS to assign a set of values to the list items. Each value could have been assigned to the list entries one by one using the attribute PANEL_LIST_CLIENT_DATA. This attribute takes two values: the first is the list entry to assign the data to, and the second is the data itself.

```
xv_create(panel, PANEL_LIST,
    ...
    PANEL_LIST_CLIENT_DATA, 0, "one",
    PANEL_LIST_CLIENT_DATA, 1, "two",
    PANEL_LIST_CLIENT_DATA, 2, "three",
    ...
    NULL);
```

You can still assign client data to the panel list item itself using PANEL_CLIENT_DATA as any other panel item. However, this data can only be retrieved using xv_get() from the panel list item itself, the first parameter in the callback function.

7.10 Message Items

Message items display a text or image message within a panel. The only visible component of a message item is the label itself. Message items are useful for annotations of all kinds, including titles, comments, descriptions, pictures and dynamic status messages. The message is often used to identify elements on the panel. A message has no value.

You may set or change the label for a message item via PANEL_LABEL_STRING or PANEL_LABEL_IMAGE. Message items, like buttons, are selectable and can have notify procedures. Panel message items are the only panel items whose font can be set to boldface. This is done using the attribute PANEL_LABEL_BOLD.

Since message buttons cannot be selected, their primary use is for display purposes only. In Example 7-4, two message items are used together to give a warning message. The other two panel button items are used for actual functionality.

Example 7-4. The stop_frame.c program

```
/*
 * stop_frame.c -- Use a server image as a panel message item.
 */
#include <xview/xview.h>
#include <xview/svrimage.h>
#include <xview/panel.h>

static short stop_bits[] = {
    0x3E00, 0x7F00, 0xFF80, 0xFF80, 0xFF80, 0xFF80, 0xFF80, 0x7F00,
    0x3E00, 0x0800, 0x0800, 0x0800, 0x0800, 0x0800, 0x7F00, 0x0000
};

main(argc, argv)
char *argv[];
{
    Frame frame;
    Panel panel;
    Server_image stopsign;

    xv_init();

    frame = (Frame)xv_create(NULL, FRAME,
        FRAME_SHOW_HEADER,  FALSE,
        NULL);
```

Example 7-4. The stop_frame.c program (continued)

```
    panel = (Panel)xv_create(frame, PANEL, NULL);

    stopsign = (Server_image)xv_create(NULL, SERVER_IMAGE,
        XV_WIDTH,            16,
        XV_HEIGHT,           16,
        SERVER_IMAGE_DEPTH,  1,
        SERVER_IMAGE_BITS,   stop_bits,
        NULL);

    (void) xv_create(panel, PANEL_MESSAGE,
        PANEL_LABEL_IMAGE,   stopsign,
        NULL);
    (void) xv_create(panel, PANEL_MESSAGE,
        PANEL_LABEL_STRING,
            "This action will cause unsaved edits to be lost.",
        NULL);
    (void)xv_create(panel, PANEL_BUTTON,
        PANEL_NEXT_ROW,      -1,
        XV_X,                110,
        PANEL_LABEL_STRING,  "Ok",
        NULL);
    (void)xv_create(panel, PANEL_BUTTON,
        PANEL_LABEL_STRING,  "Cancel",
        NULL);

    window_fit(panel);
    window_fit(frame);
    xv_main_loop(frame);
}
```

The output from this program is shown in Figure 7-12.

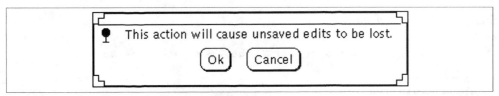

Figure 7-12. Sample panel with message item

7.11 Slider Items

Slider items allow the graphical representation and selection of a value within a range as shown in figure Figure 7-13. Sliders are appropriate for situations where it is desired to make fine adjustments over a continuous range of values. The user selects the slider bar and drags it to the value that s/he wishes. A slider has four displayable components: the label, the current value, the slider bar and the minimum and maximum allowable integral values (the range).

Sliders may be horizontal or vertical depending on the value of PANEL_DIRECTION. This attribute defaults to PANEL_HORIZONTAL, but may be set to a vertical orientation by using the value PANEL_VERTICAL. The attribute PANEL_SLIDER_END_BOXES sets whether the boxes at the endpoints of the slider are visible. This attribute defaults to FALSE. The PANEL_TICKS attribute takes a numeric value that indicates how many evenly spaced "tickmarks" are drawn next to the item. When PANEL_SHOW_VALUE is TRUE, the current value is shown after the label in an editable numeric text field. The minimum and maximum allowable values are set with PANEL_MIN_VALUE and PANEL_MAX_VALUE. The width of the slider bar corresponding to the current value is filled with black and can be adjusted using the PANEL_SLIDER_WIDTH attribute. When PANEL_SHOW_RANGE is TRUE, the minimum value of the slider PANEL_MIN_VALUE is shown to the left of the slider bar and the maximum value PANEL_MAX_VALUE is shown to the right of the slider bar.*

7.11.1 Slider Selection

Only the slider bar of a slider may be selected. When the SELECT button is pressed within the slider bar, the black area of the bar will advance or retreat with the position of the cursor. The slider value can also be changed via the numeric text field.

7.11.2 Slider Notification

Slider notify procedures are passed the item, the item's value at time of notification, and the event which caused notification:

```
void
slider_notify_proc(item, value, event)
    Panel_item  item;
    int         value;
    Event       *event;
```

The notification behavior of a slider is controlled by the value of PANEL_NOTIFY_LEVEL. It can be set to one of two values:

PANEL_DONE   The default. The notify procedure is called only when the SELECT button is released within the panel or when the user types in a new value for the slider's numeric text field.

---

*The top and bottom of the slider is used when the orientation is vertical.

PANEL_ALL   The notify procedure is called whenever the value of the slider is changed; this includes when the user selects, drags or releases the SELECT button in a slider. For each movement of the mouse while the SELECT button is down, the slider's notify procedure is called.

7.11.3 Slider Value

The value of a slider is an integer in the range PANEL_MIN_VALUE to PANEL_MAX_VALUE. You can retrieve or set a slider's value with the attribute PANEL_VALUE and the functions xv_set() or xv_get().

The following code fragment produces a slider with a label:

```
xv_create(panel, PANEL_SLIDER,
     PANEL_LABEL_STRING,    "Brightness: ",
     PANEL_VALUE,           75,
     PANEL_MIN_VALUE,       0,
     PANEL_MAX_VALUE,       100,
     PANEL_SLIDER_WIDTH,    300,
     PANEL_TICKS,           5,
     PANEL_NOTIFY_PROC,     brightness_proc,
     NULL);
```

The output from this program is displayed in Figure 7-13.

Figure 7-13. Sample panel with slider item

7.12 Gauges

Gauges are just like sliders, but they are "output only" items. That is, you set the value of the item and the display of the gauge changes just as it would for sliders. Also, there is no optional type-in field and there is no slider bar for the user to interactively change the value of the gauge. The gauge is intended to be used only as a feedback item.

To create a gauge, use the PANEL_GAUGE package. To set a gauge's width or height, use PANEL_GAUGE_WIDTH. This attribute sets the length of the object, whether it is vertically or horizontally oriented. As with the slider, the orientation is set by the attribute PANEL_DIRECTION.

7.13 Text Items and Numeric Text Items

A text panel item contains as its value a NULL-terminated string. Typically, it contains only printable ASCII characters with no newlines. When a panel receives keyboard input (regardless of where the pointer is as long as it is within the boundaries of the panel), the keyboard event is passed to the item with the keyboard focus. A caret is used to indicate the insertion point where new text is added. You can type in more text than fits on the text field. If this happens, a right arrow pointing to the left will appear on the left on the field, indicating that some text to the left of the displayed text is no longer visible. Similarly, if text is inserted causing text on the right to move out of the visible portion of the text item, then an arrow pointing to the right will appear to the right of the text.

Numeric text items are a special type of text item. They can include buttons to increment or decrement the value displayed in the field.

Text items use the attribute PANEL_LABEL_STRING as do most other panel items, to label the text item accordingly. The value of a text item is also a string, as shown by the following code:

```
xv_create(panel, PANEL_TEXT,
    PANEL_LABEL_STRING,  "Name:",
    PANEL_VALUE,         "Edward G. Robinson",
    NULL);
```

The output from this code fragment is shown in Figure 7-14.

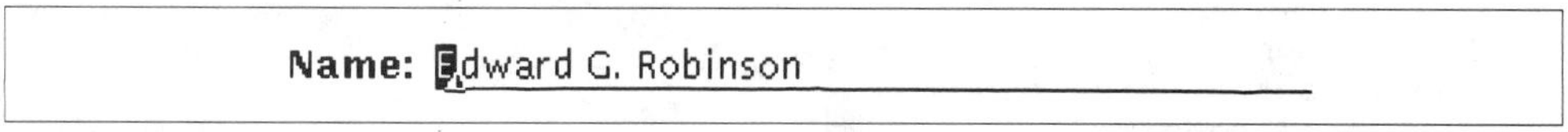

Name: Edward G. Robinson

Figure 7-14. Sample panel with text item

If PANEL_LAYOUT is set to PANEL_VERTICAL, the value is placed below the label. The default is PANEL_HORIZONTAL.

The number of characters of the text item's value that are displayed is set via PANEL_VALUE_DISPLAY_LENGTH. The maximum number of characters that can be typed into a text item (independently of how many are displayable) is set via the attribute PANEL_VALUE_STORED_LENGTH. When characters are entered beyond this length, and when PANEL_VALUE_STORED_LENGTH is greater than the display length, the value string is scrolled one character to the left so that the most recently entered character is always visible. As the string scrolls to the left, the leftmost characters move out of the visible display area. The presence of these temporarily hidden characters is indicated by a small left-pointing triangle.

It is sometimes desirable to have a protected field where the user can enter confidential information. The attribute PANEL_MASK_CHAR is provided for this purpose. When the user enters a character, the character specified as the value of PANEL_MASK_CHAR will be displayed in place of the character the user has typed. Setting PANEL_MASK_CHAR to an asterisk (*) would produce a string of asterisks instead of the characters typed. The value of the text is still the string the user types.

If you want to disable character echo entirely so that the caret does not advance and it is impossible to tell how many characters have been entered, use the space character as the mask. You can remove the mask and display the actual value string at any time by setting the mask to NULL.

7.13.1 The Current Text Item

A panel may have several text items, exactly one of which may be *current* at any given time. The current text item is the one to which keyboard input is directed and is indicated by a caret at the item's value. Selection of a text item (i.e., pressing and releasing the SELECT mouse button anywhere within the item's bounding box) causes that item to become the current text item.

You can find out which text item has the caret or give the caret to a specified text item, by means of the panel attribute PANEL_CARET_ITEM:

```
current_item = (Panel_item)xv_get(panel, PANEL_CARET_ITEM);
xv_set(panel, PANEL_CARET_ITEM, another_item, NULL);
```

You can set the current item to the next or previous text item in the panel by using the following two routines:

```
Panel_item
panel_advance_caret(panel)
    Panel panel;

Panel_item
panel_backup_caret(panel)
    Panel panel;
```

They return the text panel items that now have the caret. Advancing past the last text item places the caret at the first text item, while backing up past the first text item places the caret at the last text item.

7.13.2 Text Selection

You can use the *selection service* to select text within a text panel item. Chapter 18, *The Selection Service*, goes into detail about how to get the current selection from a text item. You can use the examples in that chapter to get the current selection from the selection's owner and set the text item's value to the text from the selection.

7.13.3 Text Notification

The notification behavior of text items is more complex than that of the other item types. You can control whether your notify procedure is called on each input character or only on selected characters.

When your notify procedure will be called is determined by the value of PANEL_NOTIFY_LEVEL. Possible values are given in Table 7-1:

Table 7-1. Text Item Notification Level

Notification Level	Level Causes Notify Procedure to be Called ...
PANEL_NONE	Never
PANEL_NON_PRINTABLE	On each non-printable input character
PANEL_SPECIFIED	If the input char is found in the string given for the attribute PANEL_NOTIFY_STRING
PANEL_ALL	On each input character

The default for PANEL_NOTIFY_LEVEL is PANEL_SPECIFIED, and the default for PANEL_NOTIFY_STRING is \n\r\t (i.e., notification on line-feed, carriage-return and tab).

The user's editing characters are treated specially. If you have asked for the character by including it in PANEL_NOTIFY_STRING, the PANEL package will call your notify procedure. After the notify procedure returns, the appropriate editing operation will be applied to the value string. (Note that the editing characters are never appended to the value string, regardless of the return value of the notify procedure.)

Characters other than the special characters described above are treated as follows. If the character typed by the user does *not* result in your notify procedure getting called, then the character, if printable, is appended to the value string. If it is not printable, it is ignored. If your notify procedure *is* called, what happens to the value string and whether the caret moves to another text item is determined by the notify procedure's return value. Table 7-2 shows the possible return values.

Table 7-2. Return Values for Text Item Notify Procedures

Value Returned	Action Caused
PANEL_INSERT	Character is appended to item's value
PANEL_NEXT	Caret moves to next text item
PANEL_PREVIOUS	Caret moves to previous text item
PANEL_NONE	Ignore the input character

If you do not specify your own notify procedure, the default procedure, panel_text_notify(), is called at the appropriate time as determined by the setting of PANEL_NOTIFY_LEVEL.

7.13.4 Writing Your Own Text Notify Procedure

By writing your own notify procedure, you can tailor the notification behavior of a given text item to support whatever the needs are for the application. At one extreme, you may want to process each character as the user types it in. For a different application, you may not care about the characters as they are typed in and may only want to look at the value of the string in response to some other button. A typical example is getting the value of a filename field when the user presses a **Load File** panel button.

The form of the text notification procedure is:

```
Panel_setting
panel_text_notify(item, event)
    Panel_item  item;
    Event       *event;
```

This procedure returns a panel setting enumeration which has the following side effects:

PANEL_NONE   Do not advance the caret to the next text item. The current text item and insertion point remain unchanged.

PANEL_NEXT   The caret moves to the *next* text item (defined by the text item that was created *after* the current text item). If there is no next text item, the first text item in the panel is used.

PANEL_PREVIOUS   The caret moves to the *previous* text item in the panel (defined by the text item that was created *before* the current text item). If there is no previous text item, the last text item in the panel is used.

PANEL_INSERT   The character which caused the notification procedure to be called is inserted into the text item's value at the location of the caret (insertion point).

The input character is referenced by `event_action(event)`. The code fragment below calls the notify procedure `name_proc` when the ESCAPE key, the RETURN key or the TAB key is typed by the user. If any of these three keys are typed, the caret moves to the next panel item. However, output is only generated when the ESCAPE key or the RETURN key is used; the TAB key simply advances the caret without taking an action.

```
...
name_item = (Panel_item)xv_create(panel, PANEL_TEXT,
    PANEL_LABEL_STRING,   "Enter Name Here:",
    PANEL_NOTIFY_LEVEL,   PANEL_SPECIFIED,
    PANEL_NOTIFY_STRING,  "\n\r\t\033",
    PANEL_NOTIFY_PROC,    name_proc,
    NULL);
...

Panel_setting
name_proc(item, event)
Panel_item  item;
Event       *event;
{
    switch (event_action(event)) {
        case '\n':
        case '\r' :
```

```
            case '\033': /* [Esc] */
                printf("Entered value: '%s'\n",
                    xv_get(item, PANEL_VALUE));
                /* FALL THRU */

            case '\t': /* [tab] just advance caret -- don't print */
                return (PANEL_NEXT);

            default:
                return (panel_text_notify(item, event));
    }
}
```

7.13.5 Text Value

You can set or get the value of a text item at any time via PANEL_VALUE. The following call
retrieves the value of name_item into name:

```
Panel_item name_item;
char name[NAME_ITEM_MAX_LENGTH];
        ...
strcpy(name, (char *)xv_get(name_item, PANEL_VALUE));
```

Note that name_item should have been created with a PANEL_VALUE_STORED_LENGTH not
greater than NAME_ITEM_MAX_LENGTH so the buffer name will not overflow.

7.14 Numeric Text Items

Numeric text items are virtually the same as panel text items except that the value displayed
is of type int. Also, convenience features (such as increment and decrement buttons) ease
the manipulation of the text string's numeric value, but there is little programmatic difference between the text item and the numeric text item. You can create a numeric text item using the PANEL_NUMERIC_TEXT package. You can also set the minimum and maximum
range for the numeric text field by using PANEL_MIN_VALUE and PANEL_MAX_VALUE, respectively.

7.15 Advanced Panel Usage

The following sections address some advanced topics dealing with panels. They cover
attaching data to panel items, repainting panels (installing a repaint procedure), and handling
events in panels and in panel items. Handling panel repainting and panel events are features
which are available but are not generally used by most applications. Attaching data to panel
items should be a practice closely followed for more efficient programs.

7.16 Attaching Data to Panel Items

Callback routines are called separately and independently from the application's main routine. If the callback routine needs data, there are two ways to make it available. One way is to store the data in global variables or data structures so the callback routine can reference the data or the data can be attached directly to panel items (whose handle has already been retrieved by the notification procedure).

In the spirit of good programming practice, it is wise to avoid creating global variables. The preferred method for making data available to callback routines is to *attach* the data to the panel items. A handle to the panel item is already made available to the callback function as the first parameter to the function. Two attributes can be used to attach data to panel items: XV_KEY_DATA or PANEL_CLIENT_DATA.*

Using XV_KEY_DATA requires a *key*, which must be some arbitrary, but unique, integer. An example of usage would be:

```
#define PANEL_ITEM_KEY    123
...
xv_create(panel, PANEL_BUTTON,
    PANEL_BUTTON_LABEL,    "Push Me",
    XV_KEY_DATA,           PANEL_ITEM_KEY,    "text",
    PANEL_NOTIFY_PROC,     my_notify_proc,
    ...
    NULL);
```

If this method is used, my_notify_proc() retrieves the data using xv_get():

```
char *data = (char *)xv_get(item, XV_KEY_DATA, PANEL_ITEM_KEY);
```

The common element in this case is the use of the constant PANEL_ITEM_KEY. A constant need not be used, but it is better than creating a global int variable to store the key. If that were the case, you might as well make the *data* portion that you wanted to attach to the panel item a global variable.

One advantage to using XV_KEY_DATA is that you can specify any number of keys and attach as many pieces of data to objects as you like.

An alternate method for attaching data to panel items is to use PANEL_CLIENT_DATA. This attribute is similar to XV_KEY_DATA in that the data is attached to the item, but in this case, you can only attach one piece of data to the panel item. You can, however, use *both* XV_KEY_DATA and PANEL_CLIENT_DATA on the same panel item. The advantage to using PANEL_CLIENT_DATA is that you do not have to keep track of a key. Since you can only attach one piece of data to a panel item, xv_get() returns only that data.

For a real example of this situation, let's modify the *quit.c* program (from the beginning of this chapter), which displays a frame, panel and a panel item labeled Quit. The modified pro-

---

*XV_KEY_DATA can be used with any XView object. Client data can as well, but the name to use varies with the object package, e.g., WIN_CLIENT_DATA is for windows, MENU_CLIENT_DATA is for menus, etc.

gram, *client_data.c*, is shown in Example 7-5. Selecting the panel button exits the program gracefully. The call to `xv_destroy_safe(frame)` causes the frame to be destroyed and thus, `xv_main_loop()` returns and the program exits.

Example 7-5. The client_data.c program

```
/*
 * client_data.c -- demonstrate the use of PANEL_CLIENT_DATA attached
 * to panel items.  Attach the base frame to the "Quit" panel item so
 * that the notify procedure can call xv_destroy_safe() on the frame.
 */
#include <xview/xview.h>
#include <xview/panel.h>

main(argc, argv)
int argc;
char *argv[];
{
    Frame   frame;
    Panel   panel;
    int     quit();

    xv_init(XV_INIT_ARGC_PTR_ARGV, &argc, argv, NULL);

    frame = (Frame)xv_create(XV_NULL, FRAME, NULL);
    panel = (Panel)xv_create(frame, PANEL, NULL);
    (void) xv_create(panel, PANEL_BUTTON,
        PANEL_LABEL_STRING,     "Quit",
        PANEL_NOTIFY_PROC,      quit,
        PANEL_CLIENT_DATA,      frame,
        NULL);

    xv_main_loop(frame);
    puts("The program is now done.");
    exit(0);
}

quit(item)
Panel_item item;
{
    Frame frame = (Frame)xv_get(item, PANEL_CLIENT_DATA);
    xv_destroy_safe(frame);
}
```

In this program, the `frame` object is not a global variable; it is a local, or *automatic*, variable. Since there is a close association between the panel button and the frame (meaning that the panel button is going to access the handle to the frame in the callback routine), we attach the frame to the panel button as *client data*. `PANEL_CLIENT_DATA` takes a generic address of type `caddr_t`. In the callback routine for the panel button, the first parameter to the callback function is the panel item that called the notification. From that handle, the frame is retrieved via `xv_get()`.

This worked because the frame was created via `xv_create()`. That is, the object was *allocated*. You cannot attach data that has not been allocated. Thus, the following code segment is not advised:

```
dummy_functon()          /* Wrong way */
{
    char *home = (char *)getenv("HOME");
    xv_set(panel_item, XV_KEY_DATA, HOME_KEY, home);
}
```

The reason for this is that getenv() returns a pointer to static data that is *overwritten on each call*. The next call that the application makes to getenv() will change the value for the panel item XV_KEY_DATA. Likewise, the following should not be used:

```
dummy_function()        /* Also wrong */
{
    char home[MAXPATHLEN], *ptr;
    if ((ptr = (char *)getenv("HOME")) != NULL) {
        (void) strcpy(home, ptr);
        xv_set(panel_item, XV_KEY_DATA, HOME_KEY, home);
    }
}
```

This does not work because as soon as dummy_function() returns, the value of home is lost because it is an automatic variable. The correct way to handle this is to make home either a static variable or a pointer whose storage is allocated via malloc().

The problem with home being static is that if dummy_function() is called more than once, the value of home will be overwritten on each call. So, the *best* way to handle this case is to allocate the data:

```
dummy_function()        /* Best way */
{
    extern char *malloc(), *getenv();
    char *home, *ptr;
    if ((ptr = getenv("HOME")) != NULL &&
        (home = malloc(strlen(ptr)+1))) {
        (void) strcpy(home, ptr);
        xv_set(panel_item, XV_KEY_DATA, HOME_KEY, home);
    }
}
```

Having allocated data for XV_KEY_DATA, we now assume the responsibility of freeing that data when the object is destroyed. Otherwise, the data is left free with no references to it. This is also known as creating a *core leak*. Because you don't always know when an object is being destroyed (destroying a panel may or may not cause a panel item to be destroyed), you can specify a function that explicitly frees the data pointed to by XV_KEY_DATA. To do this, use the attribute XV_KEY_DATA_REMOVE_PROC:

```
dummy_function()
{
    extern void free_data();
    extern char *malloc(), *getenv();
    char *home, *ptr;
    if ((ptr = getenv("HOME")) != NULL &&
        (home = malloc(strlen(ptr)+1))) {
        (void) strcpy(home, ptr);
        xv_set(panel_item,
            XV_KEY_DATA,              HOME_KEY, home,
            XV_KEY_DATA_REMOVE_PROC, free_data,
            NULL);
```

```
        }
    }
    void
    free_data(object, key, data)
    Xv_object object;
    int       key;
    caddr_t   data;
    {
        free(data);
    }
```

Whenever an object is freed, all the "key data" objects are scanned. If "remove procedures" are associated with them, they are called with the key data as the parameter. In this case, `free_data()` is called—it merely frees the data associated with that particular key.

If you need to assign a new key to the *same* key data of an object, the old key data is automatically freed by XView by calling the remove procedure (if it exists). If you wish to delete a key without having to assign a new key, then you can call:

```
    xv_set(object, XV_KEY_DATA_REMOVE, key, NULL);
```

7.17 Repainting Panels

Due to the differences between panels and canvases, the same methods should not be used for repainting and resizing them. OPEN LOOK describes control areas as unbordered regions of a window where application controls (panel items) are displayed. Typically, these areas are painted with a solid background color and the panel items are displayed using either or both of the foreground and background colors. These colors are inherited from the parent frame if the parent has FRAME_INHERIT_COLORS set to TRUE. But this appearance is not *required* by OPEN LOOK—you may, if you so choose, write a repaint routine that will paint the panel's window however you want: render another color, a pattern or an image of some sort.

7.17.1 Using PANEL_REPAINT_PROC

There are already facilities in the CANVAS package to handle repaint events. However, because the panel must repaint the panel items within it, the canvas repaint method does not work; it will paint over the panel items. Therefore, the PANEL package provides an alternative property for installing a repaint routine. This repaint routine is called before the panel items have been rendered again but otherwise conforms to all other qualities of the canvas repaint routine.

The following code fragment demonstrates how a repaint routine can be installed on a panel. This repaint routine draws a gray background on the panel behind any existing panel items.

Example 7-6. The panel_repaint.c program

```
/*
 * panel_repaint.c -- repaint a panel background without disturbing
 * the repainting of panel items.
 */
#include <xview/xview.h>
#include <xview/panel.h>
#include <xview/svrimage.h>
#include <X11/Xlib.h>
#include <X11/X.h>
#include <X11/bitmaps/gray1>

#define PANEL_GC_KEY    101  /* any arbitrary number */

main(argc, argv)
int argc;
char *argv[];
{
    Display      *display;
    Frame         frame;
    Panel         panel;
    int           quit();
    void          panel_repaint();
    XGCValues     gcvalues;
    Server_image  grey;

    Mask          gcmask = 0L;
    GC            gc;

    xv_init(XV_INIT_ARGC_PTR_ARGV, &argc, argv, NULL);

    frame = (Frame)xv_create(XV_NULL, FRAME, NULL);
    panel = (Panel)xv_create(frame, PANEL,
        PANEL_REPAINT_PROC,     panel_repaint,
        NULL);

    (void) xv_create(panel, PANEL_BUTTON,
        PANEL_LABEL_STRING,     "Quit",
        PANEL_NOTIFY_PROC,      quit,
        PANEL_CLIENT_DATA,      frame,
        NULL);

    window_fit(frame);

    grey = (Server_image)xv_create(NULL, SERVER_IMAGE,
        XV_WIDTH,               gray1_width,
        XV_HEIGHT,              gray1_height,
        SERVER_IMAGE_DEPTH,     1, /* clarify for completeness*/
        SERVER_IMAGE_BITS,      gray1_bits,
        NULL);

    display = (Display *)xv_get(panel, XV_DISPLAY);
    gcvalues.stipple = (Pixmap) xv_get(grey, XV_XID);
    gcvalues.fill_style = FillOpaqueStippled;
    gcvalues.plane_mask = 1L;
    gcvalues.graphics_exposures = False;
    gcvalues.foreground = BlackPixel(display, DefaultScreen(display));
    gcvalues.background = WhitePixel(display, DefaultScreen(display));
    gcmask = GCStipple | GCFillStyle | GCPlaneMask |
        GCGraphicsExposures | GCForeground | GCBackground;
    gc = XCreateGC(display, xv_get(panel, XV_XID), gcmask, &gcvalues);
```

Example 7-6. The panel_repaint.c program (continued)

```
    /* attach the GC to the panel for use by the repaint proc above */
    xv_set(panel, XV_KEY_DATA, PANEL_GC_KEY, gc, NULL);

    xv_main_loop(frame);
    exit(0);
}

/*
 * repaint procedure for the panel paints a gray pattern over the
 * entire panel.  Use the GC attached to the panel via XV_KEY_DATA.
 */
void
panel_repaint(panel, pw)
Panel panel;
Xv_Window pw;
{
    /* get the GC attached to the panel in main() */
    GC gc = (GC)xv_get(panel, XV_KEY_DATA, PANEL_GC_KEY);

    /* call XFillRectangle on the entire size of the panel window */
    XFillRectangle(xv_get(panel, XV_DISPLAY), xv_get(pw, XV_XID), gc,
        0, 0, xv_get(pw, XV_WIDTH), xv_get(pw, XV_HEIGHT));

}

quit(item)
Panel_item item;
{
    Frame frame = (Frame)xv_get(item, PANEL_CLIENT_DATA);
    xv_destroy_safe(frame);
}
```

The output produced by this program is shown in Figure 7-15.

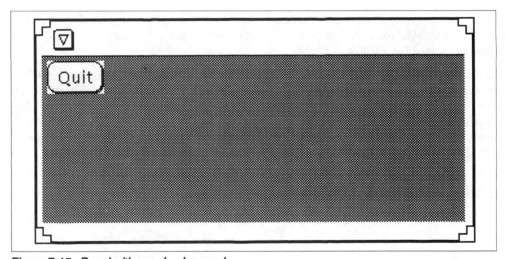

Figure 7-15. Panel with gray background

The PANEL package does not retain its paint windows by default, so the repaint routine may be called more frequently than one might expect. Therefore, when the panel is created, the attribute WIN_RETAINED may be set to TRUE; otherwise, the routine should try to be as computationally cheap as possible to maintain good performance. It is not recommended that you retain the panel's window unless you have provided a repaint routine that might utilize graphics expensively. Typically, you will set the background to a solid color, render a pattern or display an image.

If a panel item is added, deleted or moved, then the repaint routine is called regardless of whether or not the panel's window is retained.

7.17.2 Painting Panel Items

To repaint either an individual item or an entire panel, use:

```
panel_paint(panel_object, paint_behavior)
    Panel_item     panel_object;
    Panel_setting paint_behavior;
```

The panel_object may be a panel item or a panel itself. If it is a panel, the items within the panel are repainted one by one. The argument paint_behavior is either PANEL_CLEAR, which causes the rectangle occupied by the panel or item to be cleared prior to repainting, or PANEL_NO_CLEAR, which causes repainting to be done without any prior clearing. This setting will override the default paint behavior set in the panel item's PANEL_PAINT attribute.

7.18 Panel Event Handling

This section describes how the PANEL package handles events. If you require a behavior not provided by default, you can write your own event handling procedure for either an individual item or the panel as a whole.

The default event handling mechanism for panels processes events for all the panel items in a uniform way. A single routine reads the events, updates an internal state machine, and maps the event to an *action* to be taken by the item. Actions fall into two categories: *previewing* and *accepting*. The previewing action gives the user visual feedback indicating what will happen when the mouse button is released. The accepting action causes the item's value to be changed and/or its notify procedure to be called, with the event passed as the last argument.

The default event-to-action mapping is given in Table 7-3:

Table 7-3. Default Event to Action Mapping

Event	Action
Left button down or drag in w/left button down	Begin previewing
Drag with left button down	Update previewing
Drag out of item rectangle with left button down	Cancel preview
Left button up	Accept
Right button down	Display menu & accept user's selection
Keystroke	Accept keystroke if text item

What actually happens when an item is told to perform one of the above actions depends on the type of the item. For example, when asked to begin previewing, a button item inverts its label, a message item does nothing, a slider item redraws the shaded area of its slider bar, etc.

ASCII events and some `action` events (described in Chapter 6, *Handling Input*) are automatically redirected towards the item with keyboard focus. Since only one text item may receive keyboard events, if there is more than one text item in the panel, the one that is receiving events has a solid caret.* You may use `PANEL_CARET_ITEM` with `xv_set()` or `xv_get()` to set or get the text item that currently has the active caret.

Handling events by the application in panels is a task best avoided since the panel does this automatically. But there are certainly situations where the application might like to supervise or handle events itself. In such situations, there are several methods available for event handling. You can use:

- The usual `WIN_EVENT_PROC` method (described in Chapter 6, *Handling Input*, and Chapter 5, *Canvases and Openwin*)

- `PANEL_BACKGROUND_PROC`

- `PANEL_EVENT_PROC`

- `notify_interpose_event_func()`

For normal panels, each of these methods should be used on the panel itself. However, for the `SCROLLABLE_PANEL`, the event handler must be set on the panel's paint window(s) exactly as is done for canvases.

Each of these methods works somewhat differently from one another, but they all have one thing in common: they are notified when events happen in panels.

---

*Noncurrent text panel items have a gray caret to show the insertion point.

Panels

Using an Interpose Function

The Notifier's interpose functions may be installed on panels just as they are for any other window-based package. See Chapter 19, *The Notifier*, for details.

7.18.1 Using WIN_EVENT_PROC

The `WIN_EVENT` procedure is used exactly the same way as for canvases.

```
extern void my_event_proc();

panel = (Panel)xv_create(frame, PANEL, NULL);
xv_set(panel,
    WIN_EVENT_PROC,     my_event_proc,
    NULL);
```

The panel has already set up the correct event masks, so setting event masks explicitly is not recommended. The example above sets up `my_event_proc()` to receive events in the panel's window. This does not interfere with the normal event processing handled by the panel. Selecting panel items still takes place, but now `my_event_proc()` will also know about the occurrence of such events.

7.18.2 Using PANEL_BACKGROUND_PROC

The `PANEL_BACKGROUND_PROC` is similar to the `WIN_EVENT_PROC` except that the notification routine is only notified of events that do not happen in, or are redirected to, panel items. The application would want to know about events that are not sent to panel items:

```
extern void my_event_proc();

panel = (Panel)xv_create(frame, PANEL,
    PANEL_BACKGROUND_PROC,   my_event_proc,
    NULL);
```

Another difference between using `PANEL_BACKGROUND_PROC` and `WIN_EVENT_PROC` is that `PANEL_BACKGROUND_PROC` is installed in the *panel*, not the panel's subwindow as is the case for the `WIN_EVENT_PROC` method. Also, the calling parameters to the routine are different. The parameters to the routine for `PANEL_BACKGROUND_PROC` are:

```
void
my_event_proc(panel, event)
    Panel   panel;
    Event  *event;
```

The `panel` here is not the window of the panel but the panel object itself.

The `PANEL_BACKGROUND_PROC` does not, by default, get keyboard events passed to it. Therefore, rather than trying to set this mask explicitly in the panel's window, the attribute `PANEL_ACCEPT_KEYSTROKE` can be set to `TRUE`. With this attribute set, ASCII events and function-key events are passed to the routine, provided there are no panel items that accept keyboard input. If there are such items, those panel items will continue to get keyboard events regardless of the attribute `PANEL_ACCEPT_KEYSTROKE`. If you wish to get keyboard events instead of the panel items that consume those events, you should use an event interposing function discussed in Chapter 19, *The Notifier*.

7.18.3 Using PANEL_EVENT_PROC

Just as PANEL_BACKGROUND_PROC specifies a routine to handle events that happen outside of panel items, you can also get events that happen only *within* panel items using PANEL_EVENT_PROC. When this routine is installed in the panel, the default event procedure for all successively created items calls the installed event handler. If the PANEL_EVENT_PROC is later set to NULL, then the panel item's default event procedure is called.

```
xv_set(panel, PANEL_EVENT_PROC, my_event_proc, NULL);
```

Using this routine causes the default event handling for that item to be ignored in favor of the new event procedure. In other words, this routine *does* interfere with the normal event processing for panel items, and the panel item's callback routine is no longer automatically called by the PANEL package.

If the PANEL_EVENT_PROC routine for the panel item is not interested in the event, or if that routine intends for the panel item to process the event normally, it may call panel_default_handle_event(). The public routine takes the form:

```
Xv_public void
panel_default_handle_event(item, event)
    Panel_item    item;
    Event         *event;
```

Panel text items are an exception. Those items use a different default event handler called panel_text_handle_event(). However, panel_text_handle_event() is a static function within XView, so you cannot call it directly. The workaround is to get a handle to that function and save it.

```
old_event_proc = (void (*)())xv_get(text_item, PANEL_EVENT_PROC);
xv_set(text_item,
    PANEL_CLIENT_DATA,    old_event_proc_key,
    PANEL_EVENT_PROC,     my_event_proc,
    NULL);

...

my_event_proc(item, event)
Panel_item item;
Event *event;
{
    void (*func)() = (void (*)())xv_get(item, PANEL_CLIENT_DATA);
    /* do whatever you want to do */
    (func)(item, event);
}
```

PANEL_EVENT_CANCEL and PANEL_EVENT_DRAG_IN

There are two event codes especially for panel events: PANEL_EVENT_CANCEL and PANEL_EVENT_DRAG_IN. These two events are special because they track situations that are not always easy to track. Consider what happens when a panel button is selected. It is inverted, and as long as the pointer remains in the button, it should remain *highlighted* (inverted). But if the user drags the pointer out while the button is still down, the application needs to restore the button (turn highlighting off). In this case, the event PANEL_EVENT_CANCEL is sent to the routine installed as the PANEL_EVENT_PROC. Similarly, if the pointer is dragged into the window (with the button down), then the routine will receive the PANEL_EVENT_DRAG_IN event.

7.18.4 Event Handling Example

The program *item_move.c* (a longer program listed in Appendix F, *Example Programs*) demonstrates how events can be handled in panels. The program allows you to create, destroy and move around three different types of panel items. Two panels are displayed (see Figure 7-16). The control panel contains three panel items: a Quit button to exit the program, a text item to type in panel item names and a choice item providing the different item types that may be created. The other panel is where newly created panel items are placed. After items are created, you may move them around the panel using the ADJUST mouse button. Moving the item off the panel deletes the item.

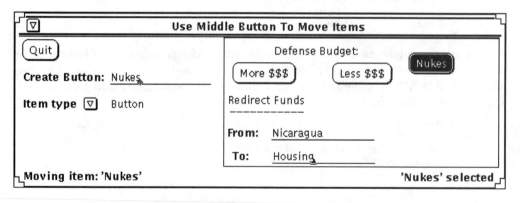

Figure 7-16. Output of item_move.c in use

item_move.c focuses on the use of WIN_EVENT_PROC to handle events within a panel. This does not interfere with the normal event processing for the panel; events continue to be dispatched to the panel items. Since the program is only interested in ADJUST button events that occur on panel items, it would seem appropriate to use PANEL_EVENT_PROC since it is designed to notify the routine only when panel items receive events. However, we chose not to use this method because when the mouse button is *dragged* around the frame to move the item, the dragging events may move outside of the button and the event callback would not be called.

Because panel items have no sense of Z-order (see Section 7.2, "Creating Panel Items"), care is taken to disallow panel items from being moved on top of one another.

7.19 Panel Package Summary

Table 7-4 lists the procedures and macros for the PANEL package; Table 7-5 lists the attributes. This information is fully described in Appendices A and B.

Table 7-4. Panel Procedures and Macros

Panel Procedures and Macros	
panel_advance_caret()	PANEL_EACH_ITEM()
panel_backup_caret()	PANEL_END_EACH()
panel_default_handle_event()	panel_paint()
PANEL_CHECK_BOX	panel_text_notify()
PANEL_CHOICE_STACK	PANEL_TOGGLE

Table 7-5. Panel Attributes

Panel Area	Panel Item	Panel List Item
PANEL_ACCEPT_KEYSTROKE	PANEL_ACCEPT_KEYSTROKE	PANEL_LIST_CHOOSE_NONE
PANEL_BACKGROUND_PROC	PANEL_EVENT_PROC	PANEL_LIST_CHOOSE_ONE
PANEL_CARET_ITEM	PANEL_INACTIVE	PANEL_LIST_CLIENT_DATA
PANEL_DEFAULT_ITEM	PANEL_ITEM_CLASS	PANEL_LIST_CLIENT_DATAS
PANEL_EVENT_PROC	PANEL_ITEM_COLOR	PANEL_LIST_DELETE
PANEL_EXTRA_PAINT_HEIGHT	PANEL_ITEM_RECT	PANEL_LIST_DISPLAY_ROWS
PANEL_EXTRA_PAINT_WIDTH	PANEL_LABEL_IMAGE	PANEL_LIST_FONT
PANEL_FIRST_ITEM	PANEL_LABEL_STRING	PANEL_LIST_FONTS
PANEL_ITEM_X	PANEL_LABEL_WIDTH	PANEL_LIST_GLYPH
PANEL_ITEM_X_GAP	PANEL_LABEL_X	PANEL_LIST_GLYPHS
PANEL_ITEM_Y	PANEL_LABEL_Y	PANEL_LIST_HEIGHT
PANEL_ITEM_Y_GAP	PANEL_LAYOUT	PANEL_LIST_INSERT
PANEL_LAYOUT	PANEL_NEXT_COL	PANEL_LIST_NROWS
PANEL_REPAINT_PROC	PANEL_NEXT_ITEM	PANEL_LIST_ROW_HEIGHT
	PANEL_NEXT_ROW	PANEL_LIST_SELECT
	PANEL_NOTIFY_PROC	PANEL_LIST_SELECTED
	PANEL_PAINT	PANEL_LIST_STRING
	PANEL_PARENT_PANEL	PANEL_LIST_STRINGS
	PANEL_READ_ONLY	PANEL_LIST_WIDTH
	PANEL_REPAINT_PROC	
	PANEL_VALUE_X	
	PANEL_VALUE_Y	
	XV_SHOW	

Panel Choice Item	Panel Slider Item	Panel Text Item
PANEL_CHOICE_FONT	PANEL_MAX_VALUE	PANEL_LABEL_WIDTH
PANEL_CHOICE_IMAGE	PANEL_MIN_VALUE	PANEL_MASK_CHAR
PANEL_CHOICE_IMAGES	PANEL_NOTIFY_LEVEL	PANEL_NOTIFY_LEVEL
PANEL_CHOICE_STRING	PANEL_SHOW_RANGE	PANEL_NOTIFY_STRING
PANEL_CHOICE_STRINGS	PANEL_SHOW_VALUE	PANEL_READ_ONLY
PANEL_CHOOSE_ONE	PANEL_SLIDER_WIDTH	PANEL_VALUE
PANEL_DEFAULT_VALUE	PANEL_VALUE	PANEL_VALUE_DISPLAY_LENGTH
PANEL_DISPLAY_LEVEL		PANEL_VALUE_STORED_LENGTH
PANEL_FEEDBACK		PANEL_VALUE_UNDERLINED
PANEL_TOGGLE_VALUE		
PANEL_VALUE		

Panel Button Item	Panel Message Item
PANEL_ITEM_MENU	PANEL_LABEL_BOLD

8

Text Subwindows

In This Chapter:

Panels

☞

8
Text Subwindows

This chapter describes the TEXTSW package, which allows a user or client to display and edit a sequence of ASCII characters. Figure 8-1 shows an example of a text subwindow. The text contains a vertical scrollbar but may not contain a horizontal scrollbar. The vertical scrollbar can be used to split views into several views (see Chapter 5, *Canvases and Openwin*). The font used by the text can be specified using the TEXTSW_FONT attribute, but only one font per text subwindow can be used, regardless of how many views there may be. See the program *textsw.font.c* in Appendix F, *Example Programs*, for an example about changing fonts in text subwindows.

The contents of a text subwindow are stored in a file or in memory on the client side, not on the X server. Whether the *source* of the text is stored on disk or in memory is transparent to the user. When the user types characters in the text subwindow, the source might be changed immediately or synchronized later depending on how the text subwindow is configured. The TEXTSW package provides basic text editing features such as inserting arbitrary text into a file. It also provides complex operations such as searching for and replacing a string of text.

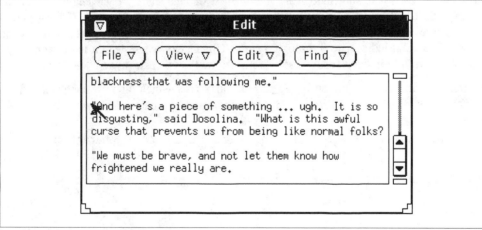

Figure 8-1. A sample text subwindow

8.1 Creating Text Subwindows

Applications need to include the file *<xview/textsw.h>* to use text subwindows. This header file is dependent upon the header file *<xview/sel_attrs.h>*, so it must be included first.* You create a text subwindow the same way you create any XView object, by calling xv_create() with the appropriate type parameters:

```
Textsw textsw;
textsw = (Textsw)xv_create(base_frame, TEXTSW, NULL);
```

8.2 Setting Text Subwindow Attributes

As for all XView objects, you can set attribute-value pairs to configure the text subwindow accordingly. Like the CANVAS package, the text subwindow object is subclassed from the OPENWIN package and can therefore be split into separate views. The package handles all of its own events and redisplaying of text, so none of these things is handled by the application.

Most text subwindow attributes are orthogonal; that is, attribute order does not effect the object. In a few cases, however, the attributes in a list might interact, so you must specify them in a particular order. Such cases are noted in the sections that follow. For example, you must pass TEXTSW_STATUS first in any call to xv_create() or xv_set() if you want to find the status after setting some other attribute in the same call.

8.3 Text Subwindow Contents

The contents of a text subwindow are a sequence of characters. Each character can be uniquely identified by its position in the sequence (type Textsw_index). Editing operations, such as inserting and deleting text, can cause the index of successive characters to change. The valid indices are 0 through *length* −1 inclusive, where *length* is the number of characters currently in the text subwindow, returned by the TEXTSW_LENGTH attribute.

The text subwindow has a notion of the current index after which the next character will be inserted. This is called the *insertion point* and is indicated by a caret, as shown in Figure 8-2.

```
The contents of a text subwindow are a sequence of characters.
Each character can be uniquely identified by its position
```

Figure 8-2. A caret marks the insertion point

---

*Later revisions of XView may not require this, but redundant inclusion of the file doesn't hurt.

8.4 Editing a Text Subwindow

A text subwindow can be edited by the user or by a client program. When you create a text subwindow, the user is normally allowed to edit it. By using the special attributes discussed in this section, the client program can edit the subwindow. These edits are then stored in */tmp/textProcess-id.Counter*.

The next five sections explain the functions and attributes that you will use to load, read, write, edit and finally save a text file.

8.4.1 Loading a File

You can load a file into a text subwindow by using `TEXTSW_FILE`, as in:

```
xv_set(textsw, TEXTSW_FILE, file_name, NULL);
```

Keep in mind that if the existing text has been edited, then these edits will be lost. To avoid such loss, first check whether there are any outstanding edits by calling:

```
int modified = (int)xv_get(textsw, TEXTSW_MODIFIED)
```

If there have been updates, you may choose to synchronize with the *source* if necessary. That is, if the existing text is part of a file, you can overwrite the existing changes before loading in a new file.

The above call to `xv_set()`, which loads the new file, positions the new text so that the first character displayed has the same index as the first character that was displayed in the previous file. This is probably not what you want. The code segment below shows how to load the file at a set position:

```
xv_set(textsw,
    TEXTSW_FILE,   file_name,
    TEXTSW_FIRST,  position,
    NULL);
```

The first character displayed has its index set by `position`. The order of these attributes matters. Because attributes are evaluated in the order given, reversing the order would first reposition the existing file, then load the new file. This would cause an unnecessary repaint. It would also mis-position the old file if it was shorter than `position`.

8.4.2 Checking the Status of the Text Subwindow

Both of the calls in the previous example blindly trust that the load of the new file was successful. This is, in general, a bad idea. The following code segment shows how to find out whether the load succeeded, and if not, why it failed:

```
Textsw_status status;

xv_set(textsw,
    TEXTSW_STATUS,    &status,
    TEXTSW_FILE,      file_name,
    TEXTSW_FIRST,     position,
    NULL);
```

NOTE

The TEXTSW_STATUS attribute and handle must appear in the attribute list *before* the operation whose status you want to determine.

The range of values for such a variable are enumerated in Table 8-1. Note that in the first column, each value begins with the prefix TEXTSW_STATUS_, which has been omitted from the table to improve readability.

Table 8-1. Range of Values for Status Variables

Value (TEXTSW_STATUS_ ...)	Description
OKAY	The operation encountered no problems.
BAD_ATTR	The attribute list contained an illegal or unrecognized attribute.
BAD_ATTR_VALUE	The attribute list contained an illegal value for an attribute, usually an out-of-range value for an enumeration.
CANNOT_ALLOCATE	A call to calloc(2) or malloc(2) failed.
CANNOT_OPEN_INPUT	The specified input file does not exist or cannot be accessed.
CANNOT_INSERT_FROM_FILE	The operation encountered a problem when trying to insert from file.
OUT_OF_MEMORY	The operation ran out of memory while editing in memory.
OTHER_ERROR	The operation encountered a problem not covered by any of the other error indications.

8.4.3 Writing to a Text Subwindow

To insert text into a text subwindow at the current insertion point, call:

```
Textsw_index
textsw_insert(textsw, buf, buf_len)
    Textsw  textsw;
    char    *buf;
    int     buf_len;
```

The return value is the number of characters actually inserted into the text subwindow. This number will equal `buf_len` unless either the text subwindow has had a memory allocation failure or the portion of text containing the insertion point is read only. The insertion point is moved forward by the number of characters inserted.

This routine does not do terminal-style interpretation of the input characters. Thus, editing characters (such as CTRL-H or DEL for character erase) are simply inserted into the text subwindow rather than performing edits to the existing contents of the text subwindow. To emulate a terminal, scan the characters to be inserted and invoke `textsw_edit()` where appropriate, as described in the next section.

Setting the Insertion Point

The attribute `TEXTSW_INSERTION_POINT` is used to interrogate and set the insertion point. For instance, the following call determines where the insertion point is:

```
Textsw_index point;

point = (Textsw_index)xv_get(textsw, TEXTSW_INSERTION_POINT);
```

Whereas the following call sets the insertion point to be just before the third character of the text:

```
xv_set(textsw, TEXTSW_INSERTION_POINT, 2, NULL);
```

To set the insertion point at the end of the text, set `TEXTSW_INSERTION_POINT` to the special index `TEXTSW_INFINITY`. This call does not ensure that the new insertion point will be visible in the text subwindow, even if `TEXTSW_INSERT_MAKES_VISIBLE` is `TRUE`. To guarantee that the caret will be visible afterwards, call `textsw_possibly_normalize()`, a procedure that is described later in this chapter.

8.4.4 Reading from a Text Subwindow

Many applications that incorporate text subwindows never need to read the contents of the text directly from the text subwindow. For instance, the text subwindow might display text for the user to view but not to edit.

Even when the user is allowed to edit text, some applications simply wait for the user to perform some action that indicates that all of the edits have been made. The application can then use either `textsw_save()` or `textsw_store_file()` to place the text in the file.

The text can then be read via the usual file input utilities, or the file itself can be passed off to another routine or program.

It is, however, useful to be able to directly examine the text in the text subwindow. You can do this using the TEXTSW_CONTENTS attribute. The code fragment below illustrates how to use TEXTSW_CONTENTS to get a span of characters from the text subwindow. It gets 1000 characters beginning at position 500 out of the text subwindow and places them into a NULL-terminated string.

```
#define TO_READ 1000

char          buf[TO_READ+1];
Textsw_index next_pos;

next_pos = (Textsw_index) xv_get(textsw, TEXTSW_CONTENTS, 500,
                                 buf, TO_READ);

if (next_pos != 500+TO_READ) {
    /* handle error case */
} else
    buf[TO_READ] = '\0';
```

8.4.5 Deleting Text

You can delete a contiguous span of characters from a text subwindow by calling:

```
Textsw_index
textsw_delete(textsw, first, last_plus_one)
    Textsw         textsw;
    Textsw_index   first, last_plus_one;
```

first specifies the first character of the span that will be deleted; last_plus_one specifies the first character *after* the span that will *not* be deleted. first should be less than or equal to last_plus_one. To delete to the end of the text, pass the special value TEXTSW_INFINITY for last_plus_one.

The return value is the number of characters deleted or:

```
last_plus_one - first
```

unless all or part of the specified span is read-only. In this case, only those characters that are not read-only will be deleted, and the return value will indicate how many such characters there were. If the insertion point is in the span being deleted, it will be left at first.

A side effect of calling textsw_delete() is that the deleted characters become the contents of the global Clipboard. To remove the characters from the text subwindow without affecting the Clipboard, call:

```
Textsw_index
textsw_erase(textsw, first, last_plus_one)
    Textsw         textsw;
    Textsw_index   first, last_plus_one;
```

Again, the return value is the number of characters removed, and last_plus_one can be TEXTSW_INFINITY.

Both of these procedures will return 0 if the operation fails.

8.4.6 Emulating an Editing Character

You can emulate the behavior of an editing character, such as CTRL-H, with `textsw_edit()`:

```
Textsw_index
textsw_edit(textsw, unit, count, direction)
    Textsw      textsw;
    unsigned  unit, count, direction;
```

Depending on the value of `unit`, this routine will erase either a character, a word or a line. Set `unit` to:

- `TEXTSW_UNIT_IS_CHAR` to erase individual characters.

- `TEXTSW_UNIT_IS_WORD` to erase the span of characters that make up a word (including any intervening white space or other nonword characters).

- `TEXTSW_UNIT_IS_LINE` to erase all characters in the line on one side of the insertion point.

If the `direction` parameter is 0, the operation will affect characters after the insertion point; otherwise, it will affect characters before the insertion point.

The `count` parameter determines the number of times the operation will be applied. Set it to 1 to do the edit once or to a value greater than 1 to do multiple edits in a single call. `textsw_edit()` returns the number of characters actually removed.

For example, suppose you want to interpret the function key F7 as meaning *delete word forward*. On receiving the event code for the F7 key, you would make the call:

```
textsw_edit(textsw, TEXTSW_UNIT_IS_WORD, 1, NULL);
```

8.4.7 Replacing Characters

While a span of characters can be replaced by calling `textsw_erase()` followed by `textsw_insert()`, character replacement is done most efficiently by calling:

```
Textsw_index
textsw_replace_bytes(textsw, first, last_plus_one, buf, buf_len)
    Textsw          textsw;
    Textsw_index  first, last_plus_one;
    char            *buf;
    int             buf_len;
```

The span of characters to be replaced is specified by `first` and `last_plus_one`, just as in the call to `textsw_erase()`. The new characters are specified by `buf` and `buf_len`, just as in the call to `textsw_insert()`. Once again, if `last_plus_one` is `TEXTSW_INFINITY`, the replace operation affects all characters from `first` to the end of the text. If the insertion point is in the span being replaced, it will be left at:

```
first + buf_len
```

The return value is the net number of bytes inserted. The number is negative if the original string is longer than the one that replaces it. If a problem occurs when an attempt is made to replace a span, it will return an error code of 0.

`textsw_replace_bytes()`, like `textsw_erase()`, does *not* put the characters it removes on the global Clipboard.

8.4.8 The Editing Log

All text subwindows allow the user to undo editing actions. The `TEXTSW` package keeps a running log of all the edits. If a file is associated with the text subwindow, this log is kept in a file in the */tmp* directory. This file can grow until the file system in which this directory resides runs out of space. To limit the size of the edit log and to avoid filling up all of */tmp*, the user can set the text wrap-around size with `TEXTSW_WRAPAROUND_SIZE`. If there is no associated file, the edit log is kept in memory, and the maximum size of the log is controlled by the attribute `TEXTSW_MEMORY_MAXIMUM`, which defaults to 20,000 bytes.

Unfortunately, once a memory-resident edit log has reached its maximum size, no more characters can be inserted into or removed from the text subwindow. In particular, since deletions as well as insertions are logged, space cannot be recovered by deleting characters.

It is important to understand how the edit log works, since you might want to use a text subwindow with no associated file to implement a temporary scratch area or error message log. If such a text subwindow is used for a long time, the default limit of 20,000 bytes might well be reached, and either the user or your code will be unable to insert any more characters, even though only a few characters might be visible in the text subwindow. Therefore, it is recommended to set `TEXTSW_MEMORY_MAXIMUM` to a much higher value, say 200,000.

8.4.9 Which File is Being Edited?

To find out the name of the file in the text subwindow, call:

```
int
textsw_append_file_name(textsw, name)
    Textsw    textsw;
    char     *name;
```

If the text subwindow is editing memory, then this routine will return a nonzero value. Otherwise, it will return 0 and append the name of the file to the end of `name`. The following code gets the name of the current file:

```
char name[BUFSIZ];

name[0] = '\0';
if (textsw_append_file_name(textsw, name) == 0)
    printf("File name is: %s\n", name);
```

Interactions with the File System

Suppose the current file is called *myfile*. If the user chooses 'Save Current File' from the subwindow's menu (or if the client code invokes `textsw_save()`), the following sequence of file operations occurs:

- *myfile* is copied to *myfile%*.

- The contents of *myfile%* are combined with information from the edit log file (*/tmp/TextProcess-id.Counter*) and written over *myfile*, thereby preserving all its permissions, etc.

- The edit log file is removed from */tmp*.

If *myfile* is a symbolic link to *../some_dir/otherfile*, then the backup file is created as *../some_dir/otherfile%*.

Keep in mind that the user can change the current directory by selecting 'Load File' or 'Set Directory' from the text subwindow menu. If *myfile* is a relative path name, then both the copy to *myfile%* and the save take place in the current directory.

8.5 Saving Edits in a Subwindow

To save any edits made to a file currently loaded into a text subwindow call:

```
unsigned
textsw_save(textsw, locx, locy)
    Textsw  textsw;
    int     locx, locy;
```

`locx` and `locy` are relative to the upper-left corner of the text subwindow and are used to position the upper-left corner of the alert should the save fail for some reason—usually they should be 0. The return value is 0 if and only if the save succeeded.

8.5.1 Storing Edits

The text subwindow might not contain a file, or the client might wish to place the edited version of the text (whether or not the original text came from a file) in some specific file. To store the contents of a text subwindow to a file, call:

```
unsigned
textsw_store_file(textsw, filename, locx, locy)
    Textsw  textsw;
    char    *filename;
    int     locx, locy;
```

Again, `locx` and `locy` are used to position the upper-left corner of the message box. The return value is 0 if and only if the store succeeded.

Text Subwindows

By default, this call changes the file that the text subwindow is editing, so that subsequent saves will save the edits to the new file. To override this policy, set the attribute TEXTSW_STORE_CHANGES_FILE to FALSE.

8.5.2 Discarding Edits

To discard the edits performed on the contents of a text subwindow, call:

```
void
textsw_reset(textsw, locx, locy)
    Textsw   textsw;
    int      locx, locy;
```

locx and locy are as above. Note that if the text subwindow contains a file that has not been edited, the effect of textsw_reset is to unload the file and replace it by memory provided by the TEXTSW package; thus, the user will see an absolutely empty text subwindow. Alternatively, if the text subwindow was already editing memory, then another, untouched, piece of primary memory will be provided and the edited piece will be deallocated.

8.6 Setting the Contents of a Text Subwindow

The rest of this chapter describes the other functions that are available for text subwindows. These features include setting the contents of a subwindow, setting the primary selection and dealing with multiple or split views.

You might want to set the initial contents of a text subwindow that your application uses. To set the initial contents of a text subwindow, use one of three attributes: TEXTSW_INSERT_FROM_FILE, TEXTSW_FILE_CONTENTS and TEXTSW_CONTENTS. Each attribute is illustrated in code fragments given below.

8.6.1 TEXTSW_FILE_CONTENTS

The attribute TEXTSW_FILE_CONTENTS allows a client to initialize the text subwindow contents from a file yet still edit the contents in memory. The user can return a text subwindow to its initial state after an editing session by choosing 'Undo All Edits' in the text menu.

The code fragment below shows how you would use this attribute:

```
extern char *filename;

xv_set(textsw,
    TEXTSW_FILE_CONTENTS, filename,
    TEXTSW_FIRST,         0,
    NULL);
```

When the client calls the undo routine and filename is not a null string, the memory used by the text subwindow is reinitialized with the contents of the file specified by filename.

When the client calls the undo routine and the `filename` is a null string, the memory used by the text subwindow is reinitialized with the previous contents of the text subwindow.

8.6.2 TEXTSW_CONTENTS

`TEXTSW_CONTENTS` lets you insert a text string from memory, instead of a file, into the text subwindow. The default for this attribute is `NULL`.

Using `xv_create()` with this attribute specifies the initial contents for a nonfile text subwindow.

Using `xv_set()` with this attribute sets the contents of a window, as in:

```
xv_set(textsw, TEXTSW_CONTENTS, "text", NULL);
```

If you use `xv_get()` with this attribute, you will need to provide additional parameters, as in:

```
xv_get(textsw, TEXTSW_CONTENTS, pos, buf, buf_len);
```

The return value is the next position to be read. The buffer array:

```
buf[0 ... buf_len-1]
```

is filled with the characters from `textsw` beginning at the index `pos` and is `NULL`-terminated only if there were too few characters to fill the buffer.

8.6.3 TEXTSW_INSERT_FROM_FILE

`TEXTSW_INSERT_FROM_FILE` allows a client to insert the contents of a file into a text subwindow at the current insertion point. It is the programming equivalent of a user choosing 'Include File' from the text menu.

The code below demonstrates this attribute:

```
Textsw          textsw;
Textsw_status   status;

xv_set(textsw,
    TEXTSW_STATUS,            &status,
    TEXTSW_INSERT_FROM_FILE, filename,
    NULL);
```

Three status values can be returned for this attribute when the argument `TEXTSW_STATUS` is passed in the same call to `xv_create()` or `xv_set()`:

```
TEXTSW_STATUS_OKAY
TEXTSW_STATUS_CANNOT_INSERT_FROM_FILE
TEXTSW_STATUS_OUT_OF_MEMORY
```

8.7 Positioning the Text Displayed in a Text Subwindow

Usually, more text is managed by the text subwindow than can be displayed all at once. As a result, it is often necessary to determine the indices of the characters that are being displayed and to control exactly which portion of the text is visible.

8.7.1 Screen Lines and File Lines

When there are long lines in the text, it is necessary to distinguish between two definitions of "line of text."

A *screen line* reflects what is actually displayed on the screen. A line begins with the left-most character in the subwindow and continues across until either a newline character or the right edge of the subwindow is encountered. A *file line*, on the other hand, can only be terminated by the newline character. It is defined as the span of characters starting after a newline character (or the beginning of the file) running through the next newline character (or the end of the file).

Whenever the right edge of the subwindow is encountered before the newline, if the following attribute-value pair were specified:

```
TEXTSW_LINE_BREAK_ACTION, TEXTSW_WRAP_AT_CHAR
```

then the next character and its successors would be displayed on the next lower screen line. In this case, there would be two screen lines, but only one file line. From the perspective of the display there are two lines; from the perspective of the file, only one. On the other hand, if the following attribute-value pair were specified:

```
TEXTSW_LINE_BREAK_ACTION, TEXTSW_WRAP_AT_WORD
```

then the entire word would be displayed on the next line.

Unless otherwise specified, all text subwindow attributes and procedures use the *file line* definition. Line indices have a zero-origin, like the character indices; that is, the first line has index 0, not 1.

8.7.2 Absolute Positioning

Two attributes are provided to allow you to specify which portion of the text is displayed in the text subwindow.

Setting the attribute `TEXTSW_FIRST` to a given index causes the first character of the line containing the index to become the first character displayed in the text subwindow. Thus, the following call causes the text to be positioned so that the first displayed character is the first character of the line that contains index 1000:

```
xv_set(textsw, TEXTSW_FIRST, 1000, NULL);
```

Since the text subwindow is subclassed from the OPENWIN package and can be split into several views, the previous code fragment would only cause the positioning of one view. To position all of the views in a text subwindow, use the attribute `TEXTSW_FOR_ALL_VIEWS`, as in the following call:

```
xv_set(textsw,
    TEXTSW_FOR_ALL_VIEWS,  TRUE,
    TEXTSW_FIRST,          1000,
    NULL);
```

Conversely, the following call retrieves the index of the first displayed character:

```
index = (Textsw_index)xv_get(textsw, TEXTSW_FIRST);
```

A related attribute, useful in similar situations, is `TEXTSW_FIRST_LINE`. When used in a call on `xv_set()` or `xv_get()`, the value is a file line index within the text.

You can determine the character index that corresponds to a given line index (both zero-origin) within the text by calling:

```
Textsw_index
textsw_index_for_file_line(textsw, line)
    Textsw  textsw;
    int     line;
```

The return value is the character index for the first character in the line, so character index 0 always corresponds to line index 0.

8.7.3 Relative Positioning

To move the text in a text subwindow up or down by a small number of lines, call the routine:

```
void
textsw_scroll_lines(textsw, count)
Textsw  textsw;
int     count;
```

A positive value for `count` causes the text to scroll up, while a negative value causes the text to scroll down.

When calling `textsw_scroll_lines()`, you might want to know how many screen lines are in the text subwindow. You can find this out by calling:

```
int
textsw_screen_line_count(textsw)
    Textsw  textsw;
```

8.7.4 Which File Lines are Visible?

Exactly which file lines are visible on the screen is determined by calling:

```
void
textsw_file_lines_visible(textsw, top, bottom)
    Textsw  textsw;
    int     *top, *bottom;
```

This routine fills in the addressed integers with the file line indices of the first and last file lines being displayed in the specified text subwindow.

Guaranteeing What Is Visible

To ensure that a particular line or character is visible, call:

```
void
textsw_possibly_normalize(textsw, position)
    Textsw        textsw;
    Textsw_index position;
```

The text subwindow must be displayed on the screen before this function will work.

If the character at the specified position is already visible, then this routine does nothing. If it is not visible, then it repositions the text so that it is visible and at the top of the subwindow.

If a particular character should always be at the top of the subwindow, then calling the following routine is more appropriate:

```
void
textsw_normalize_view(textsw, position)
    Textsw        textsw;
    Textsw_index position;
```

Ensuring that the Insertion Point is Visible

Most of the programmatic editing actions do not update the text subwindow to display the caret, even if TEXTSW_INSERT_MAKES_VISIBLE is set. If you want to ensure that the insertion point is visible, use:

```
textsw_possibly_normalize(textsw,
    (Textsw_index) xv_get(textsw, TEXTSW_INSERTION_POINT));
```

8.8 Finding and Matching a Pattern

A common operation performed on text is to find a span of characters that match some specification. The text subwindow provides several rudimentary pattern matching facilities. This section describes two functions that you can call in order to perform similar operations.

8.8.1 Matching a Span of Characters

To find the nearest span of characters that match a pattern, call:

```
int
textsw_find_bytes(textsw, first, last_plus_one, buf,
                  buf_len, flags)
```

```
Textsw          textsw;
Textsw_index *first, *last_plus_one;
char            *buf;
unsigned        buf_len;
unsigned        flags;
```

The pattern to match is specified by `buf` and `buf_len`. The matching operation looks for an exact and literal match—it is sensitive to case and does not recognize any kind of meta-character in the pattern. `first` specifies the position at which to start the search. If `flags` is 0, the search proceeds forward through the text; if `flags` is 1, the search proceeds backwards. The return value is –1 if the pattern cannot be found; otherwise it is some non-negative value, in which case the indices addressed by `first` and `last_plus_one` will have been updated to indicate the span of characters that match the pattern.

8.8.2 Matching a Specific Pattern

Another useful operation is to find delimited text. For example, you might want to find the starting and ending brace in a piece of code. To find a matching pattern, call:

```
int
textsw_match_bytes(textsw, first, last_plus_one,
                   start_sym, start_sym_len,
                   end_sym, end_sym_len, field_flag)
Textsw          textsw;
Textsw_index *first, *last_plus_one;
char            *start_sym, *end_sym;
int             start_sym_len, end_sym_len;
unsigned        field_flag;
```

`first` stores the starting position of the pattern that you want to search for. `last_plus_one` stores the cursor position of the end pattern. Its value is one position past the text. `start_sym` and `end_sym` store the beginning position and ending position of the pattern, respectively. `start_sym_len` and `end_sym_len` store the starting and ending pattern's length, respectively.

Use one of the following three field flag values to search for matches:

TEXTSW_DELIMITER_FORWARD	Begins from `first` and searches forward until it finds `start_sym` and matches it forward with `end_sym`.
TEXTSW_DELIMITER_BACKWARD	Begins from `first` and searches backward for `end_sym` and matches it backward with `start_sym`.
TEXTSW_DELIMITER_ENCLOSE	Begins from `first` and expands both directions to match `start_sym` and `end_sym` of the next level.

If no match is found, then `textsw_match_bytes()` will return a value of –1. If a match is found, then it will return the index of the first match.

The code fragment below can be used to find delimited text. Notice that the `field_flag` value is `TEXTSW_DELIMITER_FORWARD`.

```
Textsw_index      first, last_plus_one, pos;

first = (Textsw_index) xv_get(textsw, TEXTSW_INSERTION_POINT);
pos = textsw_match_bytes(textsw, &first, &last_plus_one,
                "/*", 2,
                "*/", 2, TEXTSW_DELIMITER_FORWARD);
if (pos > 0) {
    textsw_set_selection(textsw, first, last_plus_one, 1);
    xv_set(textsw, TEXTSW_INSERTION_POINT, last_plus_one, NULL);
} else
    (void) window_bell(textsw);
```

This code searches forward from `first` until it finds the starting /* and matches it forward
with the next */. If no match is found, a bell will ring in the text subwindow.

8.9 Marking Positions

Often a client wants to keep track of a particular character or group of characters that are in
the text subwindow. Given that arbitrary editing can occur in a text subwindow and that it is
very tedious to intercept and track all of the editing operations applied to a text subwindow, it
is often easier to simply place one or more marks at various positions in the text subwindow.
These marks are automatically updated by the text subwindow to account for user and client
edits. There is no limit to the number of marks you can add.

A new mark is created by calling:

```
Textsw_mark
textsw_add_mark(textsw, position, flags)
    Textsw          textsw;
    Textsw_index    position;
    unsigned        flags;
```

The `flags` argument is either TEXTSW_MARK_DEFAULTS or TEXTSW_MARK_
MOVE_AT_INSERT. The latter causes an insertion at the marked position to move the mark to
the end of the inserted text, whereas the former causes the mark to not move when text is
inserted at the mark's current position. As an example, suppose that the text managed by the
text subwindow consists of the two lines:

```
this is the first line
not this, which is the second
```

Assume a mark is set at position 5 (just before the *i* in *is* on the first line) with `flags` of
TEXTSW_MARK_MOVE_AT_INSERT.

If the user makes a selection just before the *is* (thereby placing the insertion point before the
i, at position 5) and types an *h*, making the text read:

```
this his the first line
not this, which is the second
```

the mark moves with the insertion point and they both end up at position 6.

However, if the flags had been TEXTSW_MARK_DEFAULTS, then the mark would remain at position 5 after the user typed the *h*, although the insertion point moved on to position 6.

Now, suppose instead that the user made a selection before the *this* on the first line, and typed *Kep*, making the text read:

```
Kepthis is the first line
not this, which is the second
```

In this case, no matter what flags the mark had been created with, it would end up at position 8, still just before the *i* in *is*.

If a mark is in the middle of a span of characters that is subsequently deleted, the mark moves to the beginning of the span. Going back to the original scenario, with the original text and the mark set at position 5, assume that the user deletes from the *h* in *this* through the *e* in *the* on the first line, resulting in the text:

```
te first line
not this, which is the second
```

When the user is done, the mark will be at position 1, just before the *e* in *te*.

The current position of a mark is determined by calling:

```
Textsw_index
textsw_find_mark(textsw, mark)
    Textsw        textsw;
    Textsw_mark   mark;
```

An existing mark is removed by calling:

```
void
textsw_remove_mark(textsw, mark)
    Textsw        textsw;
    Textsw_mark   mark;
```

Note that marks are dynamically allocated, and it is the client's responsibility to keep track of them and to remove them when they are no longer needed.

8.9.1 Getting a Text Selection

A user selects a portion of the contents of the text subwindow using a pointer. A text selection is indicated on the screen with reverse-video highlighting. An application needs to know which window has the current selection and what the contents of a text selection are. The TEXTSW package does not provide procedures to get this information. Instead, these functions are carried out by the Selection Service. For an example of how this is done, see Chapter 18, *The Selection Service*. Figure 8-3 shows a text selection:

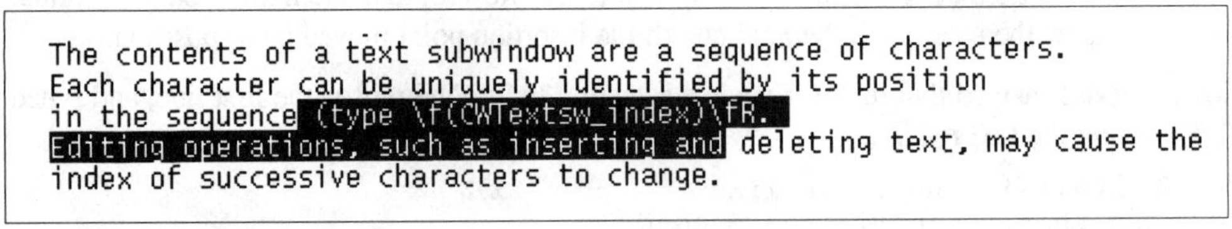

```
The contents of a text subwindow are a sequence of characters.
Each character can be uniquely identified by its position
in the sequence (type \f(CWTextsw_index)\fR.
Editing operations, such as inserting and deleting text, may cause the
index of successive characters to change.
```

Figure 8-3. A text selection

8.9.2 Setting the Primary Selection

Primary and secondary selections are maintained. The primary selection can be set by calling:

```
void
textsw_set_selection(textsw, first, last_plus_one, type)
    Textsw        textsw;
    Textsw_index  first, last_plus_one;
    unsigned      type;
```

A value of 1 for type means *primary selection*, while a value of 2 means *secondary selection* and a value of 17 is *pending delete*. Note that there is no requirement that all or part of the selection be visible; use `textsw_possibly_normalize()` to guarantee visibility (see Section 8.7.4, "Which File Lines are Visible?").

8.10 Dealing with Multiple Views

By splitting a text view, the user can create multiple views of the text being managed by the text subwindow. Although these additional views are usually transparent to the client code controlling the text subwindow, it might occasionally be necessary for a client to deal directly with all of the views. This is accomplished by using the following routines, with the knowledge that split views are simply extra text subwindows that happen to share the text of the original text subwindow.

```
Textsw
textsw_first(textsw)
    Textsw textsw;
```

Given an arbitrary view out of a set of multiple views, `textsw_first()` returns the first view (currently, this is the original text subwindow that the client created). To move through the other views of the set, call:

```
Textsw
textsw_next(textsw)
    Textsw textsw;
```

Given any view of the set, `textsw_next()` returns some other member of the set or NULL if there are none left to enumerate. The loop coded below is guaranteed to process all of the views in the set:

```
    for (textsw = textsw_first(any_split); textsw;
                 textsw = textsw_next(textsw)) {
        /* processing involving textsw */
    }
```

When you create a text subwindow, take into account that the user might split the window. If you try to do something like enlarge the window, you might run into problems.

8.11 Notifications from a Text Subwindow

The text subwindow notifies its client about interesting changes in the subwindow's or text's state by calling a notification procedure. It also calls this procedure in response to user actions. If the client does not provide an explicit notification procedure by using the attribute TEXTSW_NOTIFY_PROC, then the text subwindow provides a default procedure. The declaration for this procedure looks like:

```
void
notify_proc(textsw, avlist)
    Textsw       textsw;
    Attr_avlist  avlist;
```

avlist contains attributes that are the members of the Textsw_action enumeration.

Your notification procedure must be careful either to process all of the possible attributes or to pass through the attributes that it does not process to the standard notification procedure. This is important because among the attributes that can be in the *avlist* are those that cause the standard notification procedure to implement the possible *Front, Back, Open, Close* and *Quit* accelerators of the user interface.

Example 8-1 presents a client notify procedure for a text subwindow:

Example 8-1. Client notify procedure for a text subwindow
```
void (*default_textsw_notify)();

void
client_notify_proc(textsw, attributes)
Textsw          textsw;
Attr_avlist     attributes;
{
    int  pass_on   = FALSE;
    Attr_avlist    attrs;

    for (attrs = attributes; *attrs; attrs = attr_next(attrs)) {
        switch ((Textsw_action)(*attrs)) {
            case TEXTSW_ACTION_CAPS_LOCK:
                /* Swallow this attribute */
                ATTR_CONSUME(*attrs);
                break;
            case TEXTSW_ACTION_CHANGED_DIRECTORY:
                /* Monitor the attribute, don't swallow it */
                strcpy(current_directory, (char *)attrs[1]);
                pass_on = TRUE;
                break;
```

Text Subwindows

Example 8-1. Client notify procedure for a text subwindow (continued)

```
                default:
                    pass_on = TRUE;
                    break;
            }
        }
    if (pass_on)
        default_textsw_notify(textsw, attributes);
}
default_textsw_notify =
    (void (*) ()) xv_get(textsw, TEXTSW_NOTIFY_PROC);
xv_set(textsw, TEXTSW_NOTIFY_PROC, client_notify_proc, NULL);
```

The `Textsw_action` attributes that can be passed to your notify procedure are listed in Table 8-2. Note that in the first column, each attribute begins with the prefix `TEXTSW_ACTION_`, which has been omitted from the table to improve readability. Remember that the attributes constitute a special class that are passed to your text subwindow notification procedure. They are not attributes of the text subwindow in the usual sense and cannot be retrieved or modified using `xv_get()` or `xv_set()`.

Table 8-2. Textsw_action Attributes

Attribute (TEXTSW_ACTION_ ...)	Type	Description
CAPS_LOCK	Boolean	The user pressed the Caps Lock key to change the setting of the Caps Lock (it is initially 0, meaning off).
CHANGED_DIRECTORY	char *	The current working directory for the process has been changed to the directory named by the provided string value.
EDITED_FILE	char *	The file named by the provided string value has been edited. Appears once per session of edits (see below).
EDITED_MEMORY	none	Monitors whether an empty text subwindow has been edited.
FILE_IS_READONLY	char *	The file named by the provided string value does not have write permission.
LOADED_FILE	char *	The text subwindow is being used to view the file named by the provided string value.
TOOL_CLOSE	(no value)	The frame containing the text subwindow should become iconic.
TOOL_DESTROY	Event *	The tool containing the text subwindow should exit, without checking for a veto from other subwindows. The value is the user action that caused the destroy.

Table 8-2. Textsw_action Attributes (continued)

Attribute (`TEXTSW_ACTION_ ...`)	Type	Description
`TOOL_QUIT`	`Event *`	The tool containing the text subwindow should exit normally. The value is the user action that caused the exit.
`TOOL_MGR`	`Event *`	The tool containing the text subwindow should do the window manager operation associated with the provided event value.
`USING_MEMORY`	(no value)	The text subwindow is being used to edit a string stored in primary memory, not a file.

The attribute `TEXTSW_ACTION_EDITED_FILE` is a slight misnomer, as it is given to the notify procedure *after* the first edit to *any* text, whether or not it came from a file. This notification only happens once per session of edits, where notification of `TEXTSW_ACTION_LOADED_FILE` is considered to terminate the old session and start a new one.

NOTE

The attribute `TEXTSW_ACTION_LOADED_FILE` must be treated very carefully because the notify procedure gets called with this attribute in several situations: after a file is initially loaded, after any successful 'Save Current File' menu operation, after an 'Undo All Edits' menu operation and during successful calls to `textsw_reset()`, `textsw_save()` and `textsw_store()`.

The appropriate response by the procedure is to interpret these notifications as being equivalent to:

The text subwindow is displaying the file named by the provided string value; no edits have been performed on the file yet. In addition, any previously displayed or edited file has been either reset, saved or stored under another name.

8.12 Text Subwindow Package Summary

Table 8-3 lists the attributes, procedures and macros for the TEXTSW package. This information is described fully in Appendices A and B.

Table 8-3. Text Subwindow Attributes, Procedures and Macros

Attributes	Procedures and Macros
TEXTSW_AGAIN_RECORDING	textsw_add_mark()
TEXTSW_AUTO_INDENT	textsw_append_file_name()
TEXTSW_AUTO_SCROLL_BY	textsw_delete()
TEXTSW_BLINK_CARET	textsw_edit()
TEXTSW_BROWSING	textsw_erase()
TEXTSW_CHECKPOINT_FREQUENCY	textsw_file_lines_visible()
TEXTSW_CLIENT_DATA	textsw_find_bytes()
TEXTSW_CONFIRM_OVERWRITE	textsw_find_mark()
TEXTSW_CONTENTS	textsw_first()
TEXTSW_CONTROL_CHARS_USE_FONT	textsw_index_for_file_line()
TEXTSW_DISABLE_CD	textsw_insert()
TEXTSW_DISABLE_LOAD	textsw_match_bytes()
TEXTSW_EDIT_COUNT	textsw_next()
TEXTSW_FILE	textsw_normalize_view()
TEXTSW_FILE_CONTENTS	textsw_possibly_normalize()
TEXTSW_FIRST	textsw_remove_mark()
TEXTSW_FIRST_LINE	textsw_replace_bytes()
TEXTSW_HISTORY_LIMIT	textsw_reset()
TEXTSW_IGNORE_LIMIT	textsw_save()
TEXTSW_INSERT_FROM_FILE	textsw_screen_line_count()
TEXTSW_INSERT_MAKES_VISIBLE	textsw_scroll_lines()
TEXTSW_INSERTION_POINT	textsw_set_selection()
TEXTSW_LENGTH	textsw_store_file()
TEXTSW_LINE_BREAK_ACTION	
TEXTSW_LOWER_CONTEXT	
TEXTSW_MEMORY_MAXIMUM	
TEXTSW_MODIFIED	
TEXTSW_MULTI_CLICK_SPACE	
TEXTSW_MULTI_CLICK_TIMEOUT	
TEXTSW_NOTIFY_PROC	
TEXTSW_READ_ONLY	
TEXTSW_STATUS	
TEXTSW_STORE_CHANGES_FILE	
TEXTSW_SUBMENU_EDIT	
TEXTSW_SUBMENU_FILE	
TEXTSW_SUBMENU_FIND	
TEXTSW_SUBMENU_VIEW	
TEXTSW_UPPER_CONTEXT	

9

TTY Subwindows

In This Chapter:

TTY Subwindows

9
TTY Subwindows

The TTY (or *terminal emulator*) subwindow emulates a standard terminal, the principal difference being that the row and column dimensions of a tty subwindow can vary from that of a standard terminal. In a tty subwindow, you can run arbitrary programs, including a complete interactive shell. Or you can emulate terminal interface applications that use the *curses*(3X) terminal screen optimization package without actually running a separate process. The TTY subwindow accepts the standard ANSI escape sequences for doing ASCII screen manipulation, so you can use *termcap* or *termio* screen-handling routines. This chapter discusses the TTYSW package.

9.1 Creating a TTY Subwindow

Programs using tty subwindows must include the file *<xview/tty.h>*. Like all XView windows, you create a tty subwindow by calling xv_create() with the appropriate type parameter, as in:

```
Tty tty;
tty = xv_create(frame, TTY, NULL);
```

The default tty subwindow will fork a shell process and the user can use it interactively to enter commands. This program does not interact with the processing of the application in which the TTY subwindow resides; it is an entirely separate process. For example, if you want to start the tty subwindow with another program, say *man*, you can do so by specifying the name of the program to run via the TTY_ARGV attribute, as shown in Example 9-1:

Example 9-1. The sample_tty.c program

```
/*
 * sample_tty.c -- create a base frame with a tty subwindow.
 * This subwindow runs a UNIX command specified in an argument
 * vector as shown below.  The example does a "man cat".
 */
#include <xview/xview.h>
#include <xview/tty.h>

char *my_argv[] = { "man", "cat",  NULL };
```

TTY Subwindows

Example 9-1. The sample_tty.c program (continued)

```
main(argc, argv)
char *argv[];
{
    Tty tty;
    Frame frame;

    xv_init();
    frame = (Frame)xv_create(NULL, FRAME, NULL);
    tty = (Tty)xv_create(frame, TTY,
        WIN_ROWS,        24,
        WIN_COLUMNS,     80,
        TTY_ARGV,        my_argv,
        NULL);

    window_fit(frame);
    xv_main_loop(frame);
}
```

The output of Example 9-1 is shown in Figure 9-1.

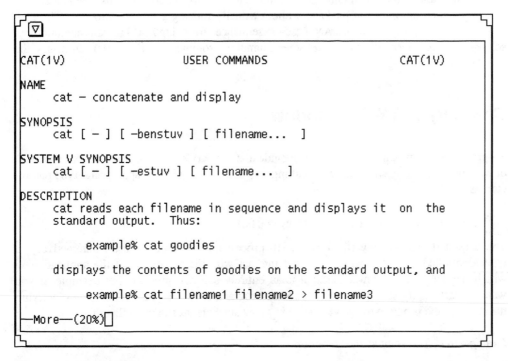

Figure 9-1. Output of sample_tty.c

Note that you can have only one tty subwindow per process.

9.2 Driving a TTY Subwindow

You can drive the terminal emulator programmatically. There are procedures both to send input to the terminal emulator (as if the user had typed it in the tty subwindow) and to send output (as if a program running in the tty subwindow had output it). You can send input to a tty subwindow programmatically with the function:

```
int
ttysw_input(tty, buf, len)
    Tty    tty;
    char *buf;
    int    len;
```

`ttysw_input()` appends the character sequence in `buf` that is `len` characters long onto `tty`'s input queue. It returns the number of characters accepted. The characters are treated as if they were typed from the keyboard in the tty subwindow. `ttysw_input()` provides a simple way for a window program to send input to a program running in its tty subwindow. You can send output to a tty subwindow programmatically with the function:

```
int
ttysw_output(tty, buf, len)
    Tty    tty;
    char *buf;
    int    len;
```

`ttysw_output()` runs the character sequence in `buf` that is `len` characters long through the terminal emulator of `tty`. It returns the number of characters accepted. The effect is similar to executing this:

```
echo character_sequence > /dev/ttyN
```

where `ttyN` is the pseudo-tty associated with the tty subwindow. `ttysw_output()` can be used to send ANSI escape sequences to the tty subwindow.

Note the differences between the input and output `TTY` routines. If an application is running in the tty subwindow, then the characters sent to the tty subwindow using `ttysw_input()` are sent to that program as its `stdin`. Characters sent to the tty subwindow using `ttysw_ouput()` are sent to the tty subwindow itself and have nothing to do with the application that might be running in the window.

The program in Example 9-2 creates a text subwindow in which the user can type input. There is a panel button called "Text to Tty" which, if selected, reads the data in the text subwindow and sends it to the tty subwindow using `ttysw_input()`.

Example 9-2. The textsw_to_ttysw.c program

```
/*
 * textsw_to_ttysw.c -- send text from a text subwindow to a
 * tty subwindow using ttysw_output()
 */
#include <stdio.h>
#include <xview/panel.h>
#include <xview/xview.h>
#include <xview/textsw.h>
#include <xview/tty.h>
```

Example 9-2. The textsw_to_ttysw.c program (continued)

```
Textsw   textsw;
Tty      ttysw;

main(argc,argv)
int      argc;
char     *argv[];
{
    Frame        frame;
    Panel        panel;
    void          text_to_tty(), exit();

    xv_init(XV_INIT_ARGC_PTR_ARGV, &argc, argv, NULL);

    frame = (Frame)xv_create(XV_NULL, FRAME,
        FRAME_LABEL, argv[0],
        NULL);
    panel = (Panel)xv_create(frame, PANEL,
        PANEL_LAYOUT, PANEL_VERTICAL,
        NULL);
    (void) xv_create(panel, PANEL_BUTTON,
        PANEL_LABEL_STRING,      "Quit",
        PANEL_NOTIFY_PROC,        exit,
        NULL);
    (void) xv_create(panel, PANEL_BUTTON,
        PANEL_LABEL_STRING,      "Text To Tty",
        PANEL_NOTIFY_PROC,        text_to_tty,
        NULL);
    window_fit(panel);

    textsw = (Textsw)xv_create(frame, TEXTSW,
        WIN_ROWS,        10,
        WIN_COLUMNS,     80,
        NULL);
    ttysw = (Tty)xv_create(frame, TTY,
        WIN_BELOW,       textsw,
        WIN_X,           0,
        TTY_ARGV,        TTY_ARGV_DO_NOT_FORK,
        NULL);

    window_fit(frame);
    xv_main_loop(frame);
}

/*
 * callback routine for the panel button -- read text from textsw
 * and send it to the ttysw using ttysw_output()
 */
void
text_to_tty(item, event)
Panel_item item;
Event *event;
{
    char buf[BUFSIZ];

    (void) xv_get(textsw, TEXTSW_CONTENTS, 0, buf, sizeof buf);
    ttysw_output(ttysw, buf, strlen(buf));
}
```

Figure 9-2 shows the output of Example 9-2.

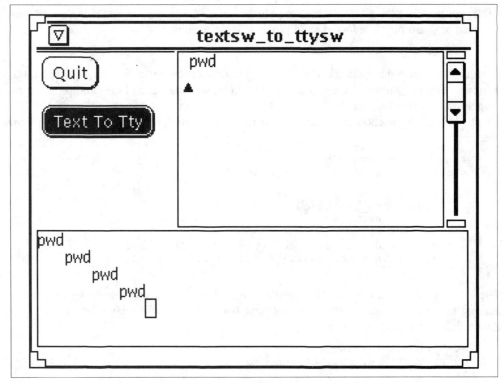

Figure 9-2. Output of textsw_to_ttysw.c

Using `ttysw_output()` shows that the text is simply output to the dummy terminal emulator described by `ttysw`. `ttysw_input()` is useful for sending data as input to a program running in the tty subwindow. For example, a window-based front end for a text editor could be written where all the common functions such as Save and Next Page can be programmed into panel buttons. Selecting one of those panel buttons would cause a constant string to be sent to the application to be processed as input. The *write filename* function in *vi* could have a button that uses `ttysw_input()` to send the string "w!\n" to the tty subwindow containing the program.

9.3 Monitoring the Program in the TTY Subwindow

When you use the `TTY_ARGV` attribute to pass the name of a program to run to the tty subwindow, the program runs as a forked child process. If the attribute:

```
TTY_QUIT_ON_CHILD_DEATH
```

is set to `TRUE`, then the application exits when the forked program exits. But, by default, this attribute is set to `FALSE`. You can use `TTY_PID` to monitor the state of the child process running in the tty window via the Notifier using `notify_interpose_wait3_func()`. The client's `wait3()` function gets called when the state of the process in the tty subwindow changes*:

```
#include <sys/wait.h>
static Notify_value      my_wait3();

    ...
    ttysw = xv_create(base_frame, TTY,
        TTY_ARGV,                  my_argv,
        NULL);
    child_pid = (int)xv_get(ttysw, TTY_PID);
    notify_interpose_wait3_func(ttysw, my_wait3, child_pid);
    ...
```

The `wait3()` function can then do something useful, such as destroying the tty window or starting up another process. The code fragment below detects when any of the tty subwindow's child processes has died.

```
static Notify_value
my_wait3(ttysw, pid, status, rusage)
Tty              ttysw;
int              pid;
union wait       *status;
struct rusage    *rusage;
{
    int    child_pid;

    notify_next_wait3_func(ttysw, pid, status, rusage);
    if (!(WIFSTOPPED(*status))) {
    /* rerun the program */
        xv_set(ttysw, TTY_ARGV, my_argv, NULL);
        child_pid = (int)xv_get(ttysw, TTY_PID);
        notify_interpose_wait3_func(ttysw, my_wait3, child_pid);
    }
    return NOTIFY_DONE;
}
```

You can set `TTY_PID` as well as get it, but if you set it, you are responsible for setting:

```
notify_interpose_wait3_func()
```

to catch the child's death. You are also responsible for directing the standard input and standard output of the child to the pseudo-tty.

---

*This includes when the program *stops* in addition to when it exits.

9.4 Talking Directly to the TTY Subwindow

Setting `TTY_ARGV` to `TTY_ARGV_DO_NOT_FORK` tells the system not to fork a child in the tty subwindow. In combination with `TTY_TTY_FD`, this allows the tool to use standard I/O routines to read and write to the tty subwindow by getting the file descriptor of the pseudo-tty associated with the tty subwindow. You can then use this to read and write to the pseudo-tty using standard UNIX I/O routines.

Example 9-3 uses a tty subwindow to create a pseudo *terminal* in which *curses* routines can be used. Five panel items are displayed. Along with the usual Quit button to exit the program, a Print button displays the text in the text panel item at the coordinates input in the X and Y numeric text items.

Example 9-3. The ttycurses.c program

```
/*
 * ttycurses.c -- An application that uses a tty subwindow that
 * emulates a tty so well, you can use curses(3X) routines in it.
 * This program does not handle resizes -- resizing the base frame
 * produces unpredictable results.  To handle resizing properly,
 * the application should install a resize event handler and
 * call endwin() followed by initscr() to reinitialize curses
 * to reflect the size of the window.
 *
 * cc ttycurses.c -lxview -lcurses -ltermlib
 */

#include <curses.h>
#undef WINDOW /* defined by curses.h -- needs to be undefined */
#include <xview/xview.h>
#include <xview/panel.h>
#include <xview/textsw.h>
#include <xview/tty.h>

/* panel items contain the x,y info for outputting text to the ttysw */
Panel_item      x, y, text;

main(argc,argv)
int      argc;
char      *argv[];
{
    Frame        frame;
    Panel        panel;
    Tty          ttysw;
    char         buf[16];
    void         output(), exit();

    xv_init(XV_INIT_ARGC_PTR_ARGV, &argc, argv, NULL);

    frame = xv_create(XV_NULL, FRAME,
        FRAME_LABEL,              argv[0],
        FRAME_SHOW_FOOTER,        TRUE,
        NULL);

    panel = (Frame)xv_create(frame, PANEL, NULL);
    (void) xv_create(panel, PANEL_BUTTON,
        PANEL_LABEL_STRING,              "Quit",
```

Example 9-3. The ttycurses.c program (continued)

```
            PANEL_NOTIFY_PROC,              exit,
            NULL);
        (void) xv_create(panel, PANEL_BUTTON,
            PANEL_LABEL_STRING,            "Print",
            PANEL_NOTIFY_PROC,             output,
            NULL);
    x = (Panel_item)xv_create(panel, PANEL_NUMERIC_TEXT,
        PANEL_LABEL_STRING,            "X:",
        PANEL_VALUE_DISPLAY_LENGTH,    3,
        NULL);
    y = (Panel_item)xv_create(panel, PANEL_NUMERIC_TEXT,
        PANEL_LABEL_STRING,            "Y:",
        PANEL_VALUE_DISPLAY_LENGTH,    3,
        NULL);
    text = (Panel_item)xv_create(panel, PANEL_TEXT,
        PANEL_LABEL_STRING,            "Text:",
        PANEL_VALUE_DISPLAY_LENGTH,    10,
        PANEL_VALUE,                   "X",
        NULL);
    window_fit(panel);

    ttysw = (Tty)xv_create(frame, TTY,
        WIN_BELOW,       panel,
        WIN_X,           0,
        TTY_ARGV,        TTY_ARGV_DO_NOT_FORK,
        NULL);
    window_fit(frame);

    dup2((int)xv_get(ttysw, TTY_TTY_FD), 0); /* dup2 closes 0 first */
    dup2((int)xv_get(ttysw, TTY_TTY_FD), 1); /* dup2 closes 1 first */

    /* initscr() initializes the curses package and determines
     * characteristics about the window as if it were a terminal.
     * The curses specific variables, LINES and COLS are now set
     * to the row and column sizes of the window.
     */

    initscr();

    xv_set(x, PANEL_MAX_VALUE, COLS-1, NULL);
    xv_set(y, PANEL_MAX_VALUE, LINES-1, NULL);
    sprintf(buf, "LINES: %d", LINES-1);
    xv_set(frame, FRAME_LEFT_FOOTER, buf, NULL);
    sprintf(buf, "COLS: %d", COLS-1);
    xv_set(frame, FRAME_RIGHT_FOOTER, buf, NULL);

    xv_main_loop(frame);
}
/*
 * callback routine for the <print> panel button.  Get the coordinates
 * and the text to print on the tty subwindow and use curses library
 * routines to render the text.
 */

void
output()
{
    int X = (int)xv_get(x, PANEL_VALUE);
    int Y = (int)xv_get(y, PANEL_VALUE);
```

Example 9-3. The ttycurses.c program (continued)

```
    char *Text = (char *)xv_get(text, PANEL_VALUE);
    mvaddstr(Y, X, Text);
    refresh();
}
```

9.5 Package Summary

Table 9-1 lists the attributes, procedures and macros for the TTYSW package. This information is described fully in Appendices A and B.

Table 9-1. TTY Subwindow Attributes, Procedures and Macros

Attributes	Procedures and Macros
TTY_ARGV	ttysw_input()
TTY_ARGV_DO_NOT_FORK	ttysw_output()
TTY_CONSOLE	
TTY_PAGE_MODE	
TTY_PID	
TTY_QUIT_ON_CHILD_DEATH	
TTY_TTY_FD	

10
Scrollbars

In This Chapter:

10
Scrollbars

Scrollbars are used to change what you view in a subwindow. For instance, in a text subwindow, scrollbars are used to scroll through a document. In a canvas subwindow, scrollbars can be used to see another portion of the paint window (which can be larger than the canvas subwindow). This chapter addresses specific functions of scrollbars themselves. These functions are applicable to any XView package that has scrollbars attached. If you are interested in how to utilize scrollbars for a particular package, you should consult the chapter that discusses that package.

OPEN LOOK describes scrollbars using the visual metaphor of an elevator riding on a cable, which is attached at both ends to anchors. Figure 10-1 shows a scrollbar from the *OPEN LOOK GUI Specification Guide*.

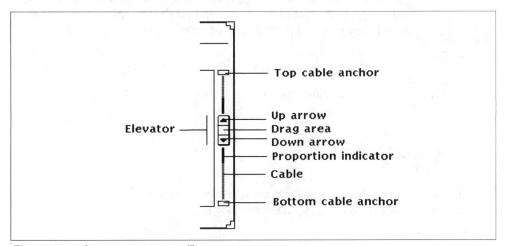

Figure 10-1. An OPEN LOOK scrollbar

The elevator contains directional arrows and a drag box. A subwindow can have vertical or horizontal scrollbars. Horizontal scrollbars are placed to the right of the subwindow while vertical scrollbars are placed at the bottom. OPEN LOOK defines precisely how scrollbars look and behave—the programmer or user cannot change it. All the programmer can control is the scrollbar's color, length and various other common and generic attributes.

One of the functions of the scrollbar is the ability to *split a view*. The OPENWIN package provides objects such as text subwindows and canvases that may be split into several views; the scrollbar provides the functional interface. Certain XView packages, such as text subwindows, automatically create their own scrollbars. Canvases, on the other hand, require the programmer to create scrollbars and attach scrollbars.

The scrollbar's look and feel is related to the size of the object it scrolls. Attributes are associated with each of the following terms:

Orientation   The orientation of a scrollbar indicates whether it is horizontal or vertical.

Object Length   The length of the object is registered with the scrollbar. The *proportional indicator* (the darkened part of the elevator cable) uses this value. For example, the object length for a text subwindow is the number of lines in the editing buffer.

Page Length   When the object length is larger than what the view window can contain, the overall area is broken up into *pages*. When the user selects the elevator cable, the scrollbar scrolls in page segments in the direction of the cursor (e.g., left, right, up or down) relative to the elevator.

Unit Length   When the user clicks on the elevator arrows, the scrollbar scrolls one *unit*. Units are measured in pixels, so arbitrary or abstract objects that are to be scrolled should be measured in terms of pixels so that scrolling seems consistent with the object. For example, a text subwindow sets its scrollbar's unit length to the size of the characters in the font. Unit scrolling results in the window moving line by line up or down.

View Length   The view length is the same size as the height or width of the subwindow the scrollbar is associated with depending on the scrollbar's orientation.

Figure 10-2 illustrates the terminology used above.

10.1 Creating Scrollbars

The definitions necessary to use scrollbars are found in the header file *<xview/scrollbar.h>*. The basic scrollbar is created using the following code fragment:

```
Scrollbar scrollbar;

scrollbar = (Scrollbar)xv_create(owner, SCROLLBAR, NULL);
```

The owner must be an object subclassed from the OPENWIN package or the FRAME package. The scrollbar inherits certain attributes from the parent while other attributes are initialized automatically. For example, if the owner of the scrollbar is a canvas, the scrollbar's color is inherited from the canvas, while the scrollbar's object length is set by the canvas explicitly; that is, you are not required to set it. This is usually desirable when creating objects that are used together.

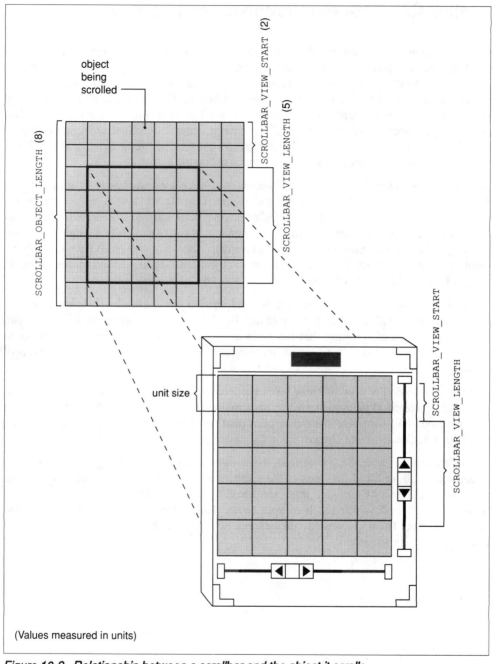

object
being
scrolled

SCROLLBAR_VIEW_START (2)

SCROLLBAR_VIEW_LENGTH (5)

SCROLLBAR_OBJECT_LENGTH (8)

SCROLLBAR_VIEW_START

SCROLLBAR_VIEW_LENGTH

unit size

(Values measured in units)

Figure 10-2. Relationship between a scrollbar and the object it scrolls

10.2 Relationship Between Scrollbars and Objects

Most scrollbar attributes describe the relationship between the scrollbar and the object such as a canvas or text subwindow that is affected by scrolling. The foremost is SCROLLBAR_PIXELS_PER_UNIT, which describes the number of pixels in a scrolling *unit*. For text subwindows, the unit is the text width and height. For canvases, it is one pixel (by default). If you were to build a canvas subwindow intended to browse a set of 64x64 bitmaps, then you would set this to 64. Scrolling actions occur in scrollbar units, so this would mean that the clicking on one of the elevator arrows causes a scrolling movement of 64 pixels at a time. Most scrollbar attribute values are based on the *unit* value.

The size of the object itself (a graphic image, text stream or whatever) is stored as the SCROLLBAR_OBJECT_LENGTH while the size of the viewable window is represented as the scrollbar's SCROLLBAR_VIEW_LENGTH. After having been scrolled, the scrollbar's current offset into the object is reflected in SCROLLBAR_VIEW_START. When *paging* is done (selecting the *cable* portion of the elevator), the amount scrolled is set by SCROLLBAR_PAGE_LENGTH. These values are in object units, so to get their values in pixels, multiply by the value of SCROLLBAR_PIXELS_PER_UNIT.

The scrollbar manages its own events, resizes and repaints automatically. It is not necessary to interpose event handlers for the scrollbar. By default, the event handling mechanism determines the type of scrolling that has been done and changes the appropriate attributes. All OPENWIN objects that support scrollbars also redisplay the window to show the results of scrolling.

Even though you do not need to know when the scrollbar is scrolled to manage the scrolling, you might be interested in knowing when the scrolling action occurs. XView objects such as text subwindows that manage their own data (text, in this case) handle this automatically. See Chapter 5, *Canvases and Openwin*, for discussion on scrolling canvases.

If a window that has a scrollbar is resized, the scrollbar is resized accordingly. If the window is sized too small for all of the parts of the scrollbar to be visible or usable, then those parts cannot be available. At the very least, the scrolling *arrows* must be visible. Figure 10-3 shows a text subwindow that has been split twice. Notice the scrollbars to the right of the text subwindows. The uppermost window cannot be split again because the minimum size of the scrollbar has been reached.

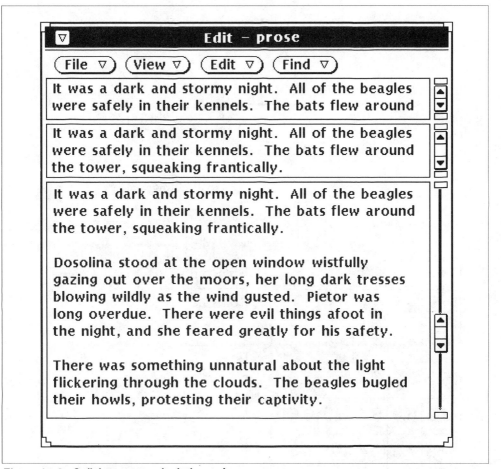

Figure 10-3. Splitting a text subwindow twice

10.3 An Example

Let's suppose that you want to display a list of icons that have dimensions of 64x64. You wish to display the icons in rows and columns in a canvas. Because there may be more icons than the canvas can display at once, you attach scrollbars to the canvas. When the user uses the scrollbars to view the icons, each scrolling action should scroll an entire icon or set of icons into view. *Paging* should scroll the next *page* of icons into view.

For demonstration purposes, rather than display actual icons, we present a grid where each *cell* in the grid represents an icon (see Figure 10-4).

Each cell is considered a *unit* to the scrollbars, so the number of pixels per scrollbar-unit must be set to the size of the cell. Thus, the attribute SCROLLBAR_PIXELS_PER_UNIT is set to 64 for each scrollbar (the width and height are the same). With this attribute set, when the user selects an arrow on the scrollbar, an entire cell is scrolled into view (depending on which arrow is selected).

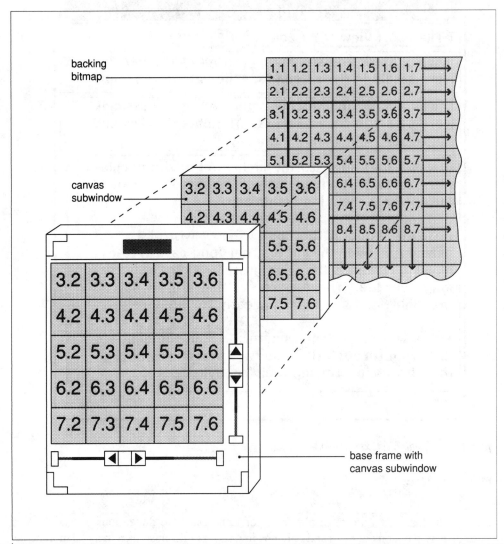

Figure 10-4. Model for scroll_cells.c

We set SCROLLBAR_PAGE_LENGTH to be the same as SCROLLBAR_VIEW_LENGTH to specify the paging size. When the user selects any part of the scrollbar cable, the view is paged and a new set of icons is scrolled into view (depending on which side of the elevator is selected). The page length could be set to one unit less than the view length, so that paging causes the last cell in the old block to be the first cell in the new block. Remember, the "lengths" mentioned here are given in *units*.

The setting of the scrollbar unit size also assures that the upper-left corner of a cell maps to the upper-left corner of the window so as not to display a portion of the cell. This guarantee cannot be made for the lower and right-hand edges of the window because we cannot control the resizing of the frame by the user.

In the program in Example 10-1, the variable `cell_map` is a `Pixmap` of depth 1. But, the depth is arbitrary—we use 1 because we know that the icons we are displaying are of depth 1. The canvas, on the other hand, may be any depth at all; color canvases have a depth greater than 1. Copying drawables of different depths onto one another is an X Protocol error, so we use `XCopyPlane()` to guarantee that the pixmap is rendered into the canvas correctly.

Example 10-1. The scroll_cells.c program

```
/*
 * scroll_cells.c -- scroll a bitmap of cells around in a canvas.
 * The cells are rectangular areas labeled with numbers which may
 * represent arbitrary data such as icon images.  The cell sizes are
 * defined to be 64 by 64 aligned in rows and columns.  This example
 * is used to demonstrate how to configure scrollbars to accommodate
 * arbitrary data within a window.
 */
#include <stdio.h>
#include <X11/X.h>
#include <X11/Xlib.h>    /* Using Xlib graphics */
#include <xview/xview.h>
#include <xview/canvas.h>
#include <xview/scrollbar.h>
#include <xview/font.h>
#include <xview/xv_xrect.h>

#define CELL_WIDTH          64
#define CELL_HEIGHT         64
#define CELLS_PER_HOR_PAGE  5 /* when paging w/scrollbar */
#define CELLS_PER_VER_PAGE  5 /* when paging w/scrollbar */
#define CELLS_PER_ROW       8
#define CELLS_PER_COL       16

Pixmap          cell_map;           /* pixmap copied onto canvas window */
Scrollbar       horiz_scrollbar;
Scrollbar       vert_scrollbar;
GC              gc;                  /* General usage GC */

main(argc, argv)
int argc;
char *argv[];
{
    Frame       frame;
    Canvas      canvas;
    void        repaint_proc();

    /* Initialize, create frame and canvas... */
    xv_init(XV_INIT_ARGC_PTR_ARGV, &argc, argv, NULL);

    frame = (Frame)xv_create(XV_NULL, FRAME,
        FRAME_LABEL,            argv[0],
        FRAME_SHOW_FOOTER,      TRUE,
        NULL);

    canvas = (Canvas)xv_create(frame, CANVAS,
        /* make subwindow the size of a "page" */
        XV_WIDTH,               CELL_WIDTH * CELLS_PER_HOR_PAGE,
        XV_HEIGHT,              CELL_HEIGHT * CELLS_PER_VER_PAGE,
        /* canvas is much larger than the window */
```

Example 10-1. The scroll_cells.c program (continued)

```
        CANVAS_WIDTH,            CELL_WIDTH * CELLS_PER_ROW + 1,
        CANVAS_HEIGHT,           CELL_HEIGHT * CELLS_PER_COL + 1,
        CANVAS_AUTO_EXPAND,      FALSE,
        CANVAS_AUTO_SHRINK,      FALSE,
        /* don't retain window -- we'll need
         * to repaint it all the time */
        CANVAS_RETAINED,         FALSE,
        /* we're using Xlib graphics calls in repaint_proc() */
        CANVAS_X_PAINT_WINDOW,   TRUE,
        CANVAS_REPAINT_PROC,     repaint_proc,
        /* we'll be repainting over exposed areas,
         * so don't bother clearing */
        OPENWIN_AUTO_CLEAR,      FALSE,
        NULL);

    /*
     * Create scrollbars attached to the canvas.  When user clicks
     * on cable, page by the page size (PAGE_LENGTH).  Scrolling
     * should move cell by cell, not by one pixel (PIXELS_PER_UNIT).
     */
    vert_scrollbar = xv_create(canvas, SCROLLBAR,
        SCROLLBAR_DIRECTION,          SCROLLBAR_VERTICAL,
        SCROLLBAR_PIXELS_PER_UNIT,    CELL_HEIGHT,
        SCROLLBAR_OBJECT_LENGTH,      CELLS_PER_COL,
        SCROLLBAR_PAGE_LENGTH,        CELLS_PER_VER_PAGE,
        SCROLLBAR_VIEW_LENGTH,        CELLS_PER_VER_PAGE,
        NULL);
    horiz_scrollbar = xv_create(canvas, SCROLLBAR,
        SCROLLBAR_DIRECTION,          SCROLLBAR_HORIZONTAL,
        SCROLLBAR_PIXELS_PER_UNIT,    CELL_WIDTH,
        SCROLLBAR_OBJECT_LENGTH,      CELLS_PER_ROW,
        SCROLLBAR_PAGE_LENGTH,        CELLS_PER_HOR_PAGE,
        SCROLLBAR_VIEW_LENGTH,        CELLS_PER_HOR_PAGE,
        NULL);

    /*
     * create pixmap and draw cells into it ... this is the abstraction.
     * The cell_map is copied into the window via XCopyPlane in the
     * repaint procedure.
     */
    {
        short           x, y, pt = 0;
        Xv_Font         font;
        XPoint          points[256]; /* keep Xlib calls to a minimum */
        XGCValues       gcvalues;
        Display *dpy = (Display *)xv_get(canvas, XV_DISPLAY);

        font = (Xv_Font)xv_find(frame, FONT,
            FONT_NAME,              "icon",
            NULL);
        cell_map = XCreatePixmap(dpy, DefaultRootWindow(dpy),
            CELLS_PER_ROW * CELL_WIDTH + 1,
            CELLS_PER_COL * CELL_HEIGHT + 1,
            1); /* We only need a 1-bit deep pixmap */

        /* Create the gc for the cell_map -- since it is 1-bit deep,
         * use 0 and 1 for fg/bg values.  Also, limit number of
```

Example 10-1. The scroll_cells.c program (continued)

```
             * events generated by setting graphics exposures to False.
             */
            gcvalues.graphics_exposures = False;
            gcvalues.background = 0;
            gcvalues.foreground = 1;
            if (font)
                gcvalues.font = (Font)xv_get(font, XV_XID);
            gc = XCreateGC(dpy, cell_map,
                GCFont|GCForeground|GCBackground|GCGraphicsExposures,
                &gcvalues);

            if (!font) {
                /* dot every other pixel */
                for (x = 0; x <= CELL_WIDTH * CELLS_PER_ROW; x += 2)
                    for (y = 0; y <= CELL_HEIGHT * CELLS_PER_COL; y += 2) {
                        if (x % CELL_WIDTH != 0 && y % CELL_HEIGHT != 0)
                            continue;
                        points[pt].x = x, points[pt].y = y;
                        if (++pt == sizeof points / sizeof points[0]) {
                            XDrawPoints(dpy, cell_map, gc, points, pt,
                                CoordModeOrigin);
                            pt = 0;
                        }
                    }
                if (pt != sizeof points) /* flush remaining points */
                    XDrawPoints(dpy, cell_map, gc,
                                points, pt, CoordModeOrigin);
            }
            /* Icon font not available.  Instead, label each cell
             * with a string describing the cell's coordinates.
             */
            for (x = 0; x < CELLS_PER_ROW; x++)
                for (y = 0; y < CELLS_PER_COL; y++) {
                    char buf[8];
                    if (!font) {
                        sprintf(buf, "%d,%d", x+1, y+1);
                        XDrawString(dpy, cell_map, gc,
                            x * CELL_WIDTH + 5, y * CELL_HEIGHT + 25,
                            buf, strlen(buf));
                    } else {
                        buf[0] = x + y * CELLS_PER_COL;
                        XDrawString(dpy, cell_map, gc,
                            x * CELL_WIDTH, y * CELL_HEIGHT, buf, 1);
                    }
                }
            /* we're now done with the cell_map, so free gc and create
             * a new one based on the window that will use it.  Otherwise,
             * the GC may not work because of different depths.
             */
            if (font)
                xv_destroy(gc);
            XFreeGC(dpy, gc);
            gcvalues.background = WhitePixel(dpy, DefaultScreen(dpy));
            gcvalues.foreground = BlackPixel(dpy, DefaultScreen(dpy));
            gcvalues.plane_mask = 1L;
            gc = XCreateGC(dpy, DefaultRootWindow(dpy),
```

Example 10-1. The scroll_cells.c program (continued)

```
                GCForeground|GCBackground|GCGraphicsExposures, &gcvalues);
    }

    /* shrink frame to minimal size and start notifier */
    window_fit(frame);
    xv_main_loop(frame);
}

/*
 * The repaint procedure is called whenever repainting is needed in
 * a paint window.  Since the canvas is not retained, this routine
 * is going to be called any time the user scrolls the canvas.  The
 * canvas will handle repainting the portion of the canvas that
 * was in view and has scrolled onto another viewable portion of
 * the window.  The xrects parameter will cover the new areas that
 * were not in view before and have just scrolled into view.  If
 * the window resizes or if the window is exposed by other windows
 * disappearing or cycling through the window tree, then the number
 * of xrects will be more than one and we'll have to copy the new
 * areas one by one.  Clipping isn't necessary since the areas to
 * be rendered are set by the xrects value.
 */
void
repaint_proc(canvas, paint_window, dpy, win, xrects)
Canvas          canvas;
Xv_Window       paint_window;
Display         *dpy;
Window          win;
Xv_xrectlist    *xrects;
{
    int x, y;

    x = (int)xv_get(horiz_scrollbar, SCROLLBAR_VIEW_START);
    y = (int)xv_get(vert_scrollbar, SCROLLBAR_VIEW_START);

    for (xrects->count--; xrects->count >= 0; xrects->count--) {
        printf("top-left cell = %d, %d -- %d,%d %d,%d\n", x+1, y+1,
            xrects->rect_array[xrects->count].x,
            xrects->rect_array[xrects->count].y,
            xrects->rect_array[xrects->count].width,
            xrects->rect_array[xrects->count].height);

        XCopyPlane(dpy, cell_map, win, gc,
            xrects->rect_array[xrects->count].x,
            xrects->rect_array[xrects->count].y,
            xrects->rect_array[xrects->count].width,
            xrects->rect_array[xrects->count].height,
            xrects->rect_array[xrects->count].x,
            xrects->rect_array[xrects->count].y, 1L);
    }
}
```

XView Programming Manual

10.4 Managing Your Own Scrollbar

A scrollbar may have *delayed binding*—that is, it may be created without an owner and attached to objects that were created separately.

In most cases, you would probably never need to create a scrollbar that was not part of a text subwindow or a canvas. These two packages handle all of the dirty work involved in managing and maintaining the types of attributes mentioned above. If you are using the CANVAS or TEXTSW packages, you do not need to worry about any of this. If you do try to create your own scrollbars and have them manage your own windows, you will probably find that you will have reinvented the wheel in the form of the CANVAS package.

If you are going to attempt this type of activity, you will need to follow these guidelines:

* Maintain the relationship between the object to be scrolled and the scrollbar itself. This includes using all the scrollbar attributes mentioned in Section 10.1, "Creating Scrollbars."

* Manage geometry (size, position and orientation) of the scrollbar. You must place the scrollbars in the appropriate places around the object you intend to scroll. Typically, the scrollbars should match the width and height of the object being scrolled.

* Install appropriate SCROLLBAR_NORMALIZE_PROC and SCROLLBAR_COMPUTE_SCROLL_PROC procedures to change the display of the scrolling object.

10.4.1 Monitoring When Scrollbar Events Occur

When events take place in the scrollbar, the scrollbar normally interprets these events as *scrolling events* and adjusts itself appropriately. Since scrollbars are attached to objects such as canvases and text subwindows, those objects are also notified of the scrolling event so they can control the display of the data within their associated windows. For example, a canvas may get a SCROLLBAR_REQUEST event indicating that the user has initiated a scrolling action and that the object associated with the scrollbar needs to change its display by the requested amount.

The object to which the scrollbar is attached is set in the scrollbar's SCROLLBAR_NOTIFY_CLIENT attribute.* The internals to the scrollbar attempt to get information from this client such as its size. For canvases, the *view* window is used. Since you normally query for user events on the canvas's *paint* window, this doesn't interfere with the scrollbar processing and also explains why your event handlers never see this event. For text subwindows, programmers normally do not concern themselves with events, so again, scrollbar processing is not affected.

---

*While this is a settable attribute, it is not recommended that you change the notify client for scrollbars for the current release.

If you are interested in managing the scrolling mechanisms of a scrollbar, or if all you need is to be notified of *when* the user invokes scrolling actions, you can install an event-interposing function on the scrollbar itself. This involves using the routine `notify_inter-pose_event_func()` discussed in Chapter 19, *The Notifier*. You can set one up in the following way:

```
Canvas        canvas;
Scrollbar     sb;
Notify_func monitor_scroll();
...
canvas = xv_create(frame, CANVAS, NULL);

sb = xv_create(canvas, SCROLLBAR, NULL);

notify_interpose_event_func(
    xv_get(sb, SCROLLBAR_NOTIFY_CLIENT), monitor_scroll, NOTIFY_SAFE);
...
```

When the user invokes any scrolling events in the scrollbar, the function `monitor_scroll` is called with the event type set to `SCROLLBAR_REQUEST`.

Example 10-2 demonstrates how this is done in an application. By default, a canvas is set up of size `1000x1000` and a scrollbar attached. When the user scrolls the canvas, the function `monotir_scroll()` is called, which prints information about how much the canvas scrolled.

Example 10-2. The scrollto.c program

```
/* scroll_to.c -- demonstrate how to monitor the scrolling
 * requests invoked by the user.  Requests can be monitored,
 * ignored or changed programmatically.  This program creates
 * a canvas window by default or a textsw with the -textsw
 * command line option.  Both contain a scrollbar.
 */
#include <stdio.h>
#include <xview/xview.h>
#include <xview/textsw.h>
#include <xview/canvas.h>
#include <xview/scrollbar.h>

main(argc, argv)
int argc;
char *argv[];
{
    Frame         frame;
    Textsw        textsw;
    Canvas        canvas;
    Scrollbar     sbar;
    Notify_value  monitor_scroll();

    (void) xv_init(XV_INIT_ARGC_PTR_ARGV, &argc, argv, NULL);

    frame = xv_create(NULL, FRAME, NULL);

    if (argc > 1 && !strcmp(argv[1], "-textsw")) {
        textsw = xv_create(frame, TEXTSW,
            TEXTSW_FILE_CONTENTS, "/etc/termcap",
            NULL);
        sbar = xv_get(textsw, TEXTSW_SCROLLBAR);
```

Example 10-2. The scrollto.c program (continued)

```
    } else {
        canvas = xv_create(frame, CANVAS,
            CANVAS_WIDTH, 1000,
            CANVAS_HEIGHT, 1000,
            CANVAS_AUTO_SHRINK, FALSE,
            CANVAS_AUTO_EXPAND, FALSE,
            NULL);
        sbar = xv_create(canvas, SCROLLBAR,
            SCROLLBAR_DIRECTION, SCROLLBAR_VERTICAL,
            SCROLLBAR_PIXELS_PER_UNIT, 10,
            NULL);
    }
    notify_interpose_event_func(xv_get(sbar, SCROLLBAR_NOTIFY_CLIENT),
        monitor_scroll, NOTIFY_SAFE);

    xv_main_loop(frame);
}

/*
 * To change the behavior of the scrolling of the canvas, do not pass
 * on the event via notify_next_event_func() when the event type is
 * SCROLLBAR_REQUEST.
 */
Notify_value
monitor_scroll(client, event, sbar, type)
Notify_client       client;
Event               *event;
Scrollbar           sbar;
Notify_event_type type;
{
    int     view_start, last_view_start, pixels_per, is_neg = 0, total;

    if (event_id(event) == SCROLLBAR_REQUEST) {
        view_start = (int)xv_get(sbar, SCROLLBAR_VIEW_START);
        last_view_start = (int)xv_get(sbar, SCROLLBAR_LAST_VIEW_START);
        pixels_per = (int)xv_get(sbar, SCROLLBAR_PIXELS_PER_UNIT);
        if ((total = view_start - last_view_start) < 0)
            total = -total, is_neg = 1;
        printf("scrolled from %d to %d: %d pixels (%d units) %s\n",
            last_view_start, view_start, pixels_per * total, total,
            is_neg? "up" : "down");
    }
    return notify_next_event_func(client, event, sbar, type);
}
```

If the command-line option −textsw is given, a text subwindow is used instead of a canvas.

The application can change the scrolling behavior by not calling notify_next_event_func(). It can choose to set the scrollbar to any position it desires via xv_set() and the appropriate attributes, or it can ignore the scroll request entirely. In any event, the function should return either NOTIFY_DONE or the return value of notify_next_event_func().

The parameters to `monitor_scroll()` include the `client` (the object set by `SCROLLBAR_NOTIFY_CLIENT`), the `event` (which is probably `SCROLLBAR_REQUEST`), the scrollbar itself, and an unused `type` parameter indicating whether this was called via `NOTIFY_SAFE` or `NOTIFY_IMMEDIATE`.

10.5 Scrollbar Package Summary

The procedures and macros in the `SCROLLBAR` package are listed below:

```
scrollbar_default_compute_scroll_proc()
scrollbar_paint()
```

Table 10-1 lists the attributes in the `SCROLLBAR` package. This information is described fully in Appendices A and B.

Table 10-1. Scrollbar Attributes

Scrollbar Attributes

SCROLLBAR_COMPUTE_SCROLL_PROC	SCROLLBAR_OBJECT_LENGTH
SCROLLBAR_DIRECTION	SCROLLBAR_PAGE_LENGTH
SCROLLBAR_LAST_VIEW_START	SCROLLBAR_PIXELS_PER_UNIT
SCROLLBAR_MENU	SCROLLBAR_SPLITTABLE
SCROLLBAR_NORMALIZE_PROC	SCROLLBAR_VIEW_LENGTH
SCROLLBAR_NOTIFY_CLIENT	SCROLLBAR_VIEW_START

11
Menus

In This Chapter:

11
Menus

Menus play an important role in an application's user interface. An OPEN LOOK menu may display text or graphics. Menus may be attached to most XView objects such as *menu buttons*, *scrollbars* or *text subwindows*, or they may exist independently from objects and be displayed on demand.

The user may cause a menu to be pinned up by selecting an optional *pushpin* in the pop-up menu. When this happens, the menu is taken down and a corresponding command frame is put up at the same location. Panel items in the pinup window correspond to the menu items in the menu. Once a menu has been pinned up, the user continues to interact with it just as if the menu were popped up each time. Menus that are used frequently are good candidates for having pushpins so the user does not have to repeat the sequence of redisplaying the menu to make selections.

OPEN LOOK requires that menus have titles. Menus or submenus that originate from *menu buttons* or *pullright* items do not need to have titles, since the name of the menu button or menu item acts as the title.

Fonts may not be specified in either menu items or menu titles; menu items follow the same constraints outlined for *panel buttons*. However, if text is not used, then menu items may contain graphic images, in which case, the font is of no concern. That is, you could specify a `Server_image` that has a string rendered in a particular font.

11.1 Menu Types

There are three different types of menus: *pop-up*, *pulldown* and *pullright* menus. The general term *pop-up menu* may describes all three types in certain contexts since menus are *popped up*. However, pulldown and pullright menus have distinct characteristics that make them unique.

11.1.1 Pop-up Menus

Pop-up menus are displayed when the user selects the MENU mouse button over XView objects such as *scrollbars* or *text subwindows*. An OPEN LOOK window manager also utilizes pop-up menus in the root window and from base frame title bars. XView objects handle the display of menus automatically. Applications may wish to track ACTION_MENU events in objects such as canvases and display their own pop-up menus. Figure 11-1, from the *OPEN LOOK GUI Specification Guide*, shows a *Window* menu-generated from the title bar of an OPEN LOOK base frame.

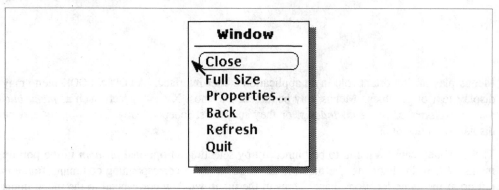

Figure 11-1. The Window menu

11.1.2 Pulldown Menus

Pulldown menus are attached to *menu buttons*. Menu buttons have a set of choices associated with them that the user can access only via the pulldown menu. When the user presses the MENU mouse button over a menu button, the choices are displayed in the form of a pulldown menu. If the menu button is selected using the SELECT button, the default menu item is selected. See Chapter 7, *Panels*, for details on creating menu buttons. Figure 11-2, from the *OPEN LOOK GUI Specification Guide*, shows sample pulldown menus activated from a menu button.

11.1.3 Pullright Menus

OPEN LOOK provides for items in the menu to have *pullright menus* associated with them. Also called *cascading menus*, these menus are activated from the user dragging the MENU mouse button to the right of a menu item that has an arrow pointing to the right. The cascading menu that results is a pop-up menu that can also have menu items with pullrights attached. Figure 11-3, from the *OPEN LOOK GUI Specification Guide*, shows a pullright menu originating from a menu item in a pulldown menu.

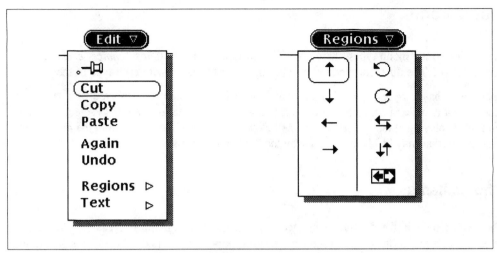

Figure 11-2. Menu buttons each with a pulldown menu

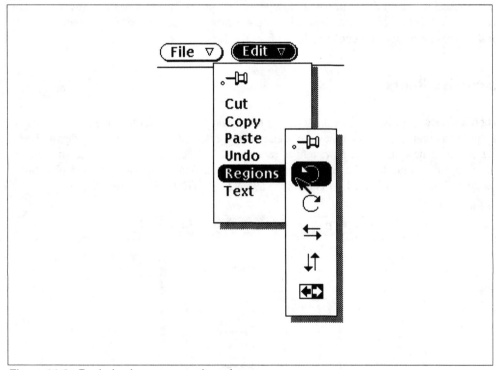

Figure 11-3. Pushpins in a menu and a submenu

11.2 Menu Items

In addition to the menu types, there are different types of menu items: *choice, exclusive* and *nonexclusive*. The different menu item types may be associated with each type of menu.

Each menu has a *default selection* associated with it. This item is displayed uniquely from other menu items and designates a default action to take if the user wants to select the menu without displaying it (see *pulldown menus* below). Typically, the first item in the menu is the default, but that may be changed either by the application or by the user.

11.2.1 Choice Items

The *choice* item is the default menu item type used when a menu is created. The default selection in a menu has a ring around it. When a pop-up menu is displayed, it is positioned so that the mouse is pointing at the default item. Choice menu items may have pullright menus associated with them, in which case there is a pullright arrow at the right side of the item. If the selection of a menu item brings up a dialog box (command frame), then the label for the menu item typically ends in ellipses (. . .).

11.2.2 Exclusive Items

When a choice item is selected, an action is taken and the menu forgets about it. Exclusive menu items retain the fact that they are selected even after the menu has popped down. If the user selects a new item, the new item is remembered. Because this is an exclusive menu, only one choice may be selected at a time. The *default* item is indicated by a double-lined box around the item. Figure 11-4 is from the *OPEN LOOK GUI Specification Guide*.

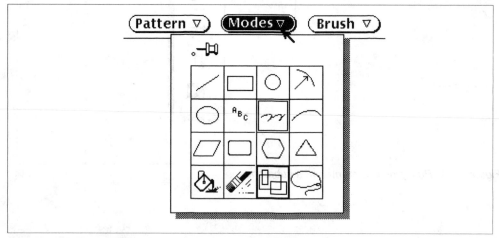

Figure 11-4. Exclusive settings on a menu

When exclusive settings are used on menus, the current choice has a bold border when the pointer is not on a menu choice. When the user drags the pointer onto other settings, the bold border follows the pointer. Exclusive choice menus may not have items with pullright menus.

11.2.3 Nonexclusive Items

Also called *toggle items*, menus that have toggle items support multiple choices from the menu to be selected at the same time. That is, the user may *toggle* whether a particular choice is selected. This action has no affect on the other menu items. Figure 11-5 shows an example of a menu that has items and a submenu that has nonexclusive settings.

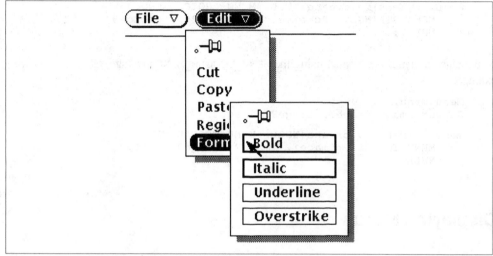

Figure 11-5. Nonexclusive settings on a submenu

In this figure, the chosen settings on the submenu are Bold and Italic. The choices not selected are Underline and Overstrike.

11.3 Creating Menus

The header file for the MENU package is *<xview/openmenu.h>*, but the file is already included by *<xview/xview.h>*. The basic menu is created using xv_create():

```
Menu menu;

menu = (Menu)xv_create(server, MENU, NULL);
```

Menus (and sometimes menu items) are discrete objects that may have *delayed binding*. That is, they may be created independently from any XView object and attached later using attributes specific to that object, such as the way that PANEL_ITEM_MENU can be used to attach an existing menu to a *menu button*). However, the association between menus and the items they are attached to does not imply "ownership."

The owner of a menu is a server object. By default, (if NULL is specified as the owner) the default server is used. Menus may be used only on the server specified; they may not be shared across different servers. Thus, the menu owner is only a concern for applications that spread across multiple servers. See Chapter 15, *Nonvisual Objects*, for details on opening a connection to different servers.

The *parent* of a menu, however, may be a pullright item from another menu. See the section on *Pullright Menus* later in this chapter.

Exclusive menus are created using the MENU_CHOICE_MENU package, as in the following example:

```
Menu menu;

menu = (Menu)xv_create(NULL, MENU_CHOICE_MENU,
    MENU_STRINGS,  "choice1", "choice2", "choice3", NULL,
    NULL);
```

Nonexclusive menus are created using the MENU_TOGGLE_MENU package, as in the following example:

```
Menu menu;
Server_image image1, image2, image3;

menu = (Menu)xv_create(NULL, MENU_TOGGLE_MENU,
    MENU_IMAGES,  image1, image2, image3, NULL,
    NULL);
```

11.4 Displaying Menus

Menus are displayed (popped up) using the function menu_show().* It displays the specified menu and immediately returns. The function takes the form:

```
void
menu_show(menu, window, event, NULL);
    Menu            menu;
    Xv_Window       window;
    Event           *event;
```

The menu is a menu created from xv_create() or a menu extracted from an existing XView object (such as a button menu). The X window associated with the menu calls XGrabPointer() to grab the server's mouse events. The pointer grab stays in effect until the user releases the MENU mouse button (e.g., the ACTION_MENU action with event_is_up() being TRUE). This is independent of the event that caused the menu to be displayed. Releasing the MENU button results in the user having either made a selection, *not* made a selection or pinned up the menu (provided that the menu has a pushpin).

---

*This function is called internally by other XView objects such as scrollbars, menu buttons and text subwindows to display menus associated with them.

The `window` attribute defines the window where the menu appears. The `event` parameter contains the event that caused the decision to display the menu. The most common use for it is to extract the *x,y* coordinate pair so as to remember the location of the pointer at the time the menu was displayed. This event structure can be retrieved later by calling:

```
Event *event = (Event *)xv_get(menu, MENU_FIRST_EVENT);
```

Similarly, when the user releases the MENU button, this event can be retrieved using the `MENU_LAST_EVENT` attribute.

The last parameter to `menu_show()` must be `NULL`. It actually represents a list of attribute-value pairs but is used internally by other XView packages that utilize menus.

Menus can also be created at run time by procedures that are called whenever a menu is needed. This is covered in Section 11.8.1, "Menu-generating Procedures."

The routine, `MENU_DONE_PROC` is called whenever a pop-up menu has been taken down (after a menu item has been selected), pinned up, or simply dismissed without a selection being made. Again, this overrides the default action of setting `XV_SHOW` to `FALSE`, so this responsibility lies with the `MENU_DONE_PROC` routine.

11.5 A Simple Program

Given the information provided so far, we can demonstrate how to pop up a menu. Example 11-1 shows how the canvas object tracks for pointer events and calls `menu_show()` when the `ACTION_MENU` event occurs.

Example 11-1. The simple_menu.c program

```
/*
 * simple_menu.c -
 * Demonstrate the use of an XView menu in a canvas subwindow.
 * A Menu is brought up with the MENU mouse button.  The choices
 * in the menu toggle the display of the scrollbar next to the canvas.
 */
#include <xview/xview.h>
#include <xview/canvas.h>
#include <xview/scrollbar.h>

#define SCROLLBAR_KEY     100
#define MENU_KEY          200

main(argc,argv)
int     argc;
char    *argv[];
{
    Frame       frame;
    Canvas      canvas;
    Scrollbar   scrollbar;
    Menu        menu;
    void        menu_notify_proc(), pw_event_proc();

    xv_init(XV_INIT_ARGC_PTR_ARGV, &argc, argv, NULL);
```

Example 11-1. The simple_menu.c program (continued)

```
    /*
     *   Create a frame, canvas and menu.
     *   A canvas receives input in its canvas_paint_window().
     */
    frame = (Frame)xv_create(NULL, FRAME,
        FRAME_LABEL,        argv[0],
        NULL);
    canvas = (Canvas)xv_create(frame, CANVAS,
        XV_WIDTH,           300,
        XV_HEIGHT,          200,
        NULL);
    scrollbar = (Scrollbar)xv_create(canvas, SCROLLBAR,
        SCROLLBAR_DIRECTION,    SCROLLBAR_VERTICAL,
        NULL);

    menu = (Menu)xv_create(NULL, MENU,
        MENU_TITLE_ITEM,        "Scrollbar",
        MENU_STRINGS,           "On", "Off", NULL,
        MENU_NOTIFY_PROC,       menu_notify_proc,
        XV_KEY_DATA,            SCROLLBAR_KEY, scrollbar,
        NULL);

    xv_set(canvas_paint_window(canvas),
        WIN_EVENT_PROC,         pw_event_proc,
        XV_KEY_DATA,            MENU_KEY, menu,
        NULL);

    window_fit(frame);
    window_main_loop(frame);
}
/*
 * menu_notify_proc - toggle the display of the scrollbar
 * based on which menu item was chosen.
 */
void
menu_notify_proc(menu, menu_item)
Menu menu;
Menu_item menu_item;
{
    char *menu_choice = (char *)xv_get(menu_item, MENU_STRING);
    int show_it = !strcmp(menu_choice, "On");

    xv_set(xv_get(menu, XV_KEY_DATA, SCROLLBAR_KEY),
        XV_SHOW,            show_it,
        NULL);
}
/*
 * Call menu_show() to display menu.
 */
void
pw_event_proc(canvas_pw, event)
Xv_Window       canvas_pw;
Event *event;
{
    if (event_action(event) == ACTION_MENU && event_is_down(event)) {
```

Example 11-1. The simple_menu.c program (continued)

```
        Menu menu = (Menu)xv_get(canvas_pw, XV_KEY_DATA, MENU_KEY);
        menu_show(menu, canvas_pw, event, NULL);
    }
}
```

In Example 11-1 above, *simple_menu.c* shows the simplest and most common method for creating and using pop-up menus. The menu, menu items and the callback routine are all created at the same time using the call:

```
menu = (Menu)xv_create(NULL, MENU,
     MENU_TITLE_ITEM,        "Scrollbar",
     MENU_STRINGS,           "On", "Off", NULL,
     MENU_NOTIFY_PROC,       menu_notify_proc,
     NULL);
```

Figure 11-6 shows the result of running *simple_menu.c* and selecting the menu.

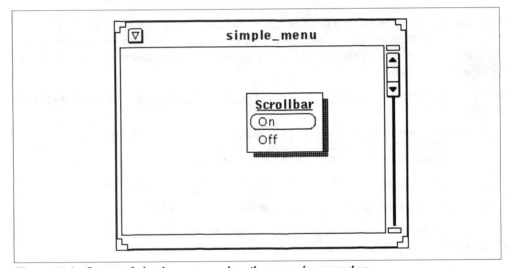

Figure 11-6. Output of simple_menu.c when the menu is popped up

Since this menu is not attached to a menu button panel item and is not a pullright menu of another menu item, a title bar is added using MENU_TITLE_ITEM. The attribute MENU_STRINGS takes a list of strings and creates a menu item for each string.

NOTE

The MENU package, in contrast to the PANEL package, does not save strings which you pass in as the menu item's label (string). You should either pass a constant string, as in the example above, or static storage that you have dynamically allocated (e.g., malloc()).

menu_notify_proc() is a routine that is called whenever any of the menu items are selected. The routine is passed a handle to the menu and the menu item selected. The canvas serves no other purpose than to capture events—the event callback routine for the canvas determines if the user generated the ACTION_MENU event and, if so, calls menu_show().

The use of XV_KEY_DATA is used to associate one object with another. In this case, we associate the scrollbar with the menu so when the menu callback routine is called, the scrollbar can be retrieved easily. The menu, on the other hand, is associated with the canvas's paint window since that window is going to get the event that pops up the menu.

The use of XV_KEY_DATA removes the need for the menu and the scrollbar to be global variables. It also clarifies the association between the objects that would otherwise not be as clear. Other examples of XV_KEY_DATA, including a complete discussion on usage, can be found in Chapter 7, *Panels*, and Chapter 3, *Creating XView Applications*.

11.6 Creating Menu Items

As noted, the use of MENU_STRINGS results in the creation of menu items *in-line*; that is, they are created automatically by the MENU package during the creation of the menu object. Other methods for creating menu items in-line include using the attributes, MENU_ITEM and MENU_ACTION_ITEM.*

MENU_ACTION_ITEM is used as a shortcut for separately specifying a label and a callback routine:

```
menu = (Menu)xv_create(NULL, MENU,
    MENU_ACTION_ITEM,  "item1",  callback1,
    MENU_ACTION_ITEM,  "item2",  callback2,
    ...
    NULL);
```

Two other methods for creating menu items are to:

- Use a separate call to xv_create() with the MENUITEM package.
- Provide a menu-generation routine.

The following subsections discuss the use of MENU_ITEM to create menu items in-line, MENUITEM to create separate menu items, and MENU_GEN_PROC to specify a routine that creates menus.

11.6.1 Using MENU_ITEM

Using the attribute MENU_ITEM indicates that a new menu item is to be created and appended to the existing menu. Use of this attribute means that the menu item is created in-line so a separate call to xv_create() is not necessary. The form of the value portion of the attribute is a NULL-terminated list of menu-item, attribute-value pairs:

---

*The attributes MENU_IMAGES and MENU_ACTION_IMAGE are just like MENU_STRINGS and MENU_ AC-TION_ITEM except that Server_images are used as labels rather than text.

```
            extern void on_notify_proc(), off_notify_proc();

      menu = (Menu)xv_create(NULL, MENU,
          MENU_TITLE_ITEM,        "Toggle",
          MENU_ITEM,
              MENU_STRING,        "On",
              MENU_NOTIFY_PROC, on_notify_proc,
              NULL,
          MENU_ITEM,
              MENU_STRING,        "Off",
              MENU_NOTIFY_PROC, off_notify_proc,
              NULL,
          NULL);
```

The code fragment shown above creates a menu with the same two menu items as shown in the previous example, except that the menu items are created more directly by the use of MENU_ITEM. Here we can specify item-specific attributes rather than accept all the defaults for the menu. In this case, we set a different notification routine for each menu item.*

If you have a Server_image to display rather than a string, you can replace MENU_STRING above with MENU_IMAGE and specify a Server_image rather than a string.

11.6.2 Using MENU_ACTION_ITEM

Rather than specifying menu item creation using a separate attribute-value list, the attribute MENU_ACTION_ITEM can be used as a shortcut, as shown in the example below:

```
      menu = (Menu)xv_create(NULL, MENU,
          MENU_TITLE_ITEM,        "Toggle",
          MENU_ACTION_ITEM,       "On",     on_notify_proc,
          MENU_ACTION_ITEM,       "Off",    off_notify_proc,
          NULL);
```

The attribute MENU_ACTION_IMAGE, with a Server_image as its value, may be used interchangeably with MENU_ACTION_STRING and its string value.

11.6.3 Using MENUITEM

The MENUITEM package allows you to create separate menu items using separate calls to xv_create(). The attributes used are menu item-specific attributes—the same as those that are used in the MENU_ITEM attribute above.

---

*Notification (callback) routines are discussed in Section 11.13, "Notification Procedures."

```
    Menu_item   on, off;

    on = (Menu_item)xv_create(NULL, MENUITEM,
        MENU_STRING,        "On",
        MENU_NOTIFY_PROC,   on_notify_proc,
        NULL);

    off = (Menu_item)xv_create(NULL, MENUITEM,
        MENU_STRING,        "Off",
        MENU_NOTIFY_PROC,   off_notify_proc,
        NULL);

    xv_set(menu,
        MENU_APPEND_ITEM,   on,
        MENU_APPEND_ITEM,   off,
        NULL);
```

These menu items are not created *in-line*; they are created independently using separate calls to xv_create(). They must therefore be added to the menu independently. In this case, they are added using MENU_APPEND_ITEM. (See the following section for more information.)

11.7 Adding Menu Items

There are several methods for adding separately created menu items to menus. For a list of menu item attributes, see the package summary at the end of this chapter. These attributes can be used when you are using xv_set() on a menu.

The code fragment below demonstrates the use of MENU_APPEND_ITEM. The menu items are created independently of the menu itself. They are added to the menu as they are created by using the attribute MENU_APPEND_ITEM:

```
    char        *names[] = { "One", "Two", "Three", "Four", "Five" };
    Menu        menu;
    Menu_item   mi;
    int         i;
    void        my_notify_proc();

    menu = (Menu)xv_create(NULL, MENU, NULL);

    for (i = 0; i < 5; i++) {
        mi = (Menu_item)xv_create(NULL, MENUITEM,
            MENU_STRING,        names[i],
            MENU_NOTIFY_PROC,   my_notify_proc,
            MENU_RELEASE,
            NULL);
        xv_set(menu, MENU_APPEND_ITEM, mi, NULL);
    }
```

This use of MENU_RELEASE is to indicate that the menu item is intended to be freed when the item's parent menu is destroyed. This attribute takes *no value*; specifying it is equivalent to specifying a TRUE value. Not specifying it implies FALSE. In-line menu items have this attribute set by default, but menu items that are not created in-line must set this attribute explicitly if you want them to be freed automatically. You do not want to set this attribute if you intend to use this menu item in more than one menu or if you want to reuse it later. See Section 11.15, "Destroying Menus," later in this chapter.

11.8 Pullright Menus

A pullright menu is simply another menu that is attached to a menu item. Note that for a menu item to contain a pullright menu, the menu must already have been created. This means that any menu group should be created from the bottom up. The attributes MENU_PULLRIGHT, MENU_PULLRIGHT_ITEM, and MENU_PULLRIGHT_IMAGE all allow a pullright menu to be attached to a menu item.

In the first case, MENU_PULLRIGHT can be assigned to a menu item to attach an existing menu to it, as shown below:

```
extern Server_image image1, image2, image3;
Menu image_menu, menu;
void image_notify_proc();

image_menu = (Menu)xv_create(NULL, MENU,
    MENU_IMAGES,        image1, image2, image3, NULL,
    MENU_NOTIFY_PROC,  image_notify_proc,
    NULL);

menu = (Menu)xv_create(NULL, MENU,
    MENU_ITEM,
        MENU_STRING,      "images",
        MENU_PULLRIGHT,  image_menu,
        NULL,
    NULL);
```

In the previous example, a menu of server images is created and is initialized to contain three images. Another menu is created that is initialized for one menu item, but that menu item has a pullright menu that is set to the menu_images menu.

The menu item created may also be initialized using the MENU_PULLRIGHT_ITEM attribute. This attribute takes two parameters as its *value*: a string and a menu. Therefore, the above code fragment could have been written:

```
menu = (Menu)xv_create(NULL, MENU,
    MENU_PULLRIGHT_ITEM, "images", image_menu,
    NULL);
```

Had the label for the pullright menu item been a Server_image rather than a string, the call would look like:

```
extern Server_image label_image;

menu = (Menu)xv_create(NULL, MENU,
    MENU_PULLRIGHT_IMAGE, label_image, image_menu,
    NULL);
```

In the code fragment below, we use another piece of code to demonstrate the same principle. This example demonstrates how a menu that represents font sizes may be set as the pullright menu for a list of fonts:

```
Menu       font_menu, size_menu;
Menu_item  mi;
int        i;
void       notify_font();
char       buf[4], *p;
```

```
. . .
size_menu = (Menu) xv_create(NULL, MENU,
    MENU_NOTIFY_PROC,    notify_size,
    NULL);

for (i = 8; i <= 20; i += 2) {
    sprintf(buf, "%d", i);
    p = strcpy(malloc(strlen(buf)+1), buf);
    mi = (Menu_item) xv_create(NULL, MENUITEM,
        MENU_STRING,       p,
        MENU_RELEASE,
        MENU_RELEASE_IMAGE,
        MENU_NOTIFY_PROC, notify_font,
        NULL);
    xv_set(size_menu, MENU_APPEND_ITEM, mi, NULL);
}

font_menu = (Menu) xv_create(NULL, MENU,
    MENU_TITLE_ITEM,       "Fonts",
    MENU_PULLRIGHT_ITEM, "courier",         size_menu,
    MENU_PULLRIGHT_ITEM, "boston",          size_menu,
    MENU_PULLRIGHT_ITEM, "times-roman",     size_menu,
    MENU_PULLRIGHT_ITEM, "lucidasans",      size_menu,
    MENU_PULLRIGHT_ITEM, "palatino-roman",  size_menu,
    NULL);
```

Each item in the main menu (font_menu) has a pullright menu (size_menu) associated with it. In the for loop where the string for the menu item is assigned, the data is allocated using malloc() and buf is copied into the allocated data using strcpy(). We cannot use buf directly, because unlike panel items, the menu item string is not copied by the MENU package—we must pass in allocated data. Because of this, we also specify the attribute MENU_RELEASE_IMAGE so that when the item is destroyed, the allocated data will be freed. Also note that because we used xv_create() to create the menu item, we specify MENU_RELEASE to indicate that the menu item should be freed when the parent menu is destroyed.

11.9 Menu-generating Procedures

In certain situations, the menu items for a particular menu cannot be known ahead of time. For example, a mail application allows users to write mail messages to files in a designated *folder directory*. If a menu is going to display the current folders in that directory, then the menu items should be updated any time a folder is created or deleted from that directory. But rather than updating the folder at the time the directory contents change, it would be better to scan the directory and use each filename in the directory as a menu item.

For such situations, it is necessary to defer the creation of the folder menu until it needs to be displayed. Therefore, you still create the pullright menu item so the user can select the item. But rather than specifying a pullright menu associated with the item, specify a routine that will generate the menu. When the menu needs to be displayed, the routine is called which returns a menu.

To do this, you specify the attribute MENU_GEN_PULLRIGHT when creating the menu item, as shown below:

```
Menu menu, gen_folder_menu();
void change_to_folder();

menu = (Menu)xv_create(NULL, MENU,
    MENU_TITLE_ITEM,        "Mail Folders",
    MENU_NOTIFY_PROC,       change_to_folder,
    MENU_STRINGS,           "/usr/spool/mail", "~/mbox", NULL,
    MENU_ITEM,
        MENU_STRING,        "~/Mail"
        MENU_GEN_PULLRIGHT, gen_folder_menu,
        NULL,
    NULL);
```

There is a shortcut attribute that allows you to specify both the menu item's string and the MENU_GEN_PULLRIGHT procedure in the same call. The attribute is MENU_GEN_PULLRIGHT_ITEM. It is used as follows:

```
MENU_GEN_PULLRIGHT_ITEM, "~/Mail", gen_folder_menu,
```

The menu-generating routine may do whatever is necessary to build a new menu, but you should be careful that the routine does not take too much processing time, since the user is waiting with the MENU button pressed for the menu to be displayed. Also remember that a pointer grab is going on, so the routine should avoid any interaction with the user (such as error dialog boxes).

The form of the menu-generating procedure is:

```
Menu
menu_gen_proc(menu_item, op)
    Menu_item menu_item;
    Menu_generate op;
```

This routine may be called *each time* the menu is needed. If the menu need only be created once, you can to return the same menu all the time.

The op parameter is one of the following enumerated types:

```
typedef enum {
    MENU_DISPLAY,
    MENU_DISPLAY_DONE,
    MENU_NOTIFY,
    MENU_NOTIFY_DONE
} Menu_generate;
```

op indicates the condition in which your routine has been called. The MENU_DISPLAY value indicates that the menu is going to be displayed while MENU_DISPLAY_DONE indicates that the menu has been displayed and dismissed. If the user makes a selection in the menu, the routine is called with MENU_NOTIFY before the menu's callback routine is called, then again with MENU_NOTIFY_DONE after the routine is called. If the user makes no selection, the latter two cases are not called. If they are called (the user did make a selection), then the latter two cases are called *after* MENU_DISPLAY_DONE is called.

Because you create your menus, you would think that you should destroy them as well. However, because of the unpredictable sequence of actions taken by the user, there is no way to determine when to free the menu. Therefore, you should never destroy menus at all. If the menu generating procedure is called multiple times for the same menu, just reconstruct the menu from the same menu handle that you have.

Furthermore, the menu-generating routine must always return the same menu that it passed to you. You cannot return other menus to display. If the new menu is going to contain a completely different set of menu items, you should destroy all the menu items before creating the new list. As it is the same with PANEL_LIST items, menu items are destroyed in *reverse* order.

The special case for this problem is: what if there is no menu to redisplay again? In this case, you are allowed to build a new menu and return a handle to it. The following code shows an example, testing to see if there already is a menu associated with a particular pullright menu item.

```
Menu
menu_gen_proc(menu_item, op)
Menu_item menu_item;
Menu_generate op;
{
    int i;
    Menu menu;

    ...
    switch (op) {
        ...
        case MENU_DISPLAY :
            if (menu = (Menu)xv_get(menu_item, MENU_PULLRIGHT)) {
                /* first destroy old menu items */
                for (i = (int)xv_get(menu, MENU_NITEMS); i > 0; i--) {
                    xv_set(menu, MENU_REMOVE, i, NULL);
                    xv_destroy(xv_get(menu, MENU_NTH_ITEM, i));
                }
            else
                menu = (Menu)xv_create(NULL, menu, NULL);
            /* now rebuild the menu items */
            ...
    }
    ...
}
```

In the above code fragment, we are removing the menu items sequentially in reverse order by using the MENU_REMOVE attribute. We start with the last item and move to item 1. The first item, remember, is the title item, if it exists. If you want to retain this item, stop at menu item 2.

The sample program *menu_dir2.c* in Appendix F, *Example Programs*, demonstrates how a menu-generating routine is used.

A debugging hint: if your menu-generating routine generates a run-time error, be careful when trying to debug the program under a debugger. The problem is that when you run the program in a debugger and the program generates a run-time error, the debugger will stop execution and wait for input. In the meantime, the server has a pointer grab so keyboard focus is directed to the menu's window which is not able to receive input.

At this point, there is no way to interact with any program on the console—you will have to go to another server, computer or terminal connected to your workstation and kill the debugger (this will terminate the program and release the pointer grab). You may think of more clever ways to handle this situation depending on your workstation configuration, but the point is that you should be aware of the extremely inconvenient side effects whenever you play with server grabs.

11.9.1 Parent Menus

Recall that the menu notification routines take two parameters: the menu that was popped up and the menu item that was selected. However, if the user chose an item from a long cascade of pullright menus, it may be necessary to determine the initial (root) menu of the cascade. To support this, the attribute MENU_PARENT is used to get the owner of a menu or menu item.

This attribute can only be used with xv_get(). When MENU_PARENT is used with a menu item, xv_get() returns the menu that owns the item.

```
Menu menu;

menu = xv_get(item, MENU_PARENT);
```

On the other hand, if xv_get() is passed a menu, the menu item returned is the pullright menu item that contains the specified menu.

```
Menu_item item;

item = xv_get(menu, MENU_PARENT);
```

If the item returned is NULL, the menu is the root menu.

The following code fragment shows how the entire menu cascade is traversed, starting from the leaf of the menu tree (the item the user selected).

```
Menu menu, item;

while (item = (Xv_opaque)xv_get(menu, MENU_PARENT))
    if ((Xv_pkg *)xv_get(item, XV_TYPE) != MENUITEM)
        break;
    else
        menu = item;
```

The above loop starts by getting the parent of an arbitrary menu. This menu could be the menu parameter in a menu item's callback routine. If the parent menu returned is NULL, then the menu is already the top level menu. Otherwise, get the type of the object returned. If the menu is a pullright menu, then the parent of the menu should be a MENUITEM (since its pullright is a menu). If it is not, then it could be a server object. Whatever it is, we have reached the top level of the menu cascade and should break out of the loop.

11.9.2 Using MENU_GEN_PROC

MENU_GEN_PROC specifies a function that is used to modify, add or delete menu items from the menu whose handle is passed to the procedure. You do not destroy the menu itself. If you do not know what the item will show as text or as an image at the time the menu is created or if there is other information that is not known, you can defer the creation of the menu item until the item is actually needed by specifying the item creation routine.

11.10 Using Toggle Menus

Toggle menus are menus with nonexclusive settings. The user can toggle menu items, turning them *on* or *off*. More than one menu item may be selected at a time. The only difference for creating these menu items is that MENU_TOGGLE_MENU is used as the *package* parameter to xv_create() and that menu items may not have pullright menus associated with them. Therefore, these are typically simple menus.

In the code below, we build a toggle menu that has three items in it. If the menu has been displayed and the user makes a selection, on or off, the notification routine is called no differently from any other menu notification procedure:

```
void toggle_bold(), toggle_size(), toggle_italic();
Menu menu;

menu = (Menu)xv_create(NULL, MENU_TOGGLE_MENU,
    MENU_TITLE_ITEM,     "Text Rendering",
    MENU_ACTION_ITEM,    "Bold Style",     toggle_bold,
    MENU_ACTION_ITEM,    "Large Font",     toggle_size,
    MENU_ACTION_ITEM,    "Italics",        toggle_italic,
    NULL);
```

In this case, we are specifying three different notify procedures for each menu item. Since each performs a completely separate function, the menu items need not call the same routine.

To determine exactly which menu items are selected, you must loop through all the items in the menu:

```
toggle_notify(menu, item)
Menu menu
Menu_item item;
{
    int i;

    for (i = (int)xv_get(font_menu, MENU_NITEMS); i > 0; i--)
        if (xv_get(xv_get(font_menu, MENU_NTH_ITEM, i),
                MENU_SELECTED)) {
            printf("item %d selected\n", i);
            /* do whatever other processing may need to be done */
        }
}
```

This loop starts at the last item and works towards the first. The first item starts at 1, not 0; the *0th* item is the menu's title item and cannot be retrieved.

11.11 Menu Layout

By default, pop-up menus place their items vertically. If there are too many items, a new column may be started in order to display the entire menu on the screen. You can specify the number of rows and columns for the menu by using the attributes MENU_NROWS and MENU_NCOLS.

Although specifying menu item layout is certainly legal and acceptable to OPEN LOOK, explicit menu item layout should be avoided for anything other than static menus. Dynamic menus will have problems maintaining menu item order, and if you use a pin-up menu, the command frame will almost certainly not match the appearance of the menu. To guarantee that your pin-up menu looks the same as the menu, specify your own pin-up procedure. (See the following section for more information.)

11.12 Making Pin-up Menus

As the programmer, you may give the user the option of pinning up a menu by providing the pushpin in the pop-up menu. To accomplish this, XView provides the attribute MENU_GEN_PIN_WINDOW. If specified, XView generates the pin window frame automatically by creating a command frame, a panel and a series of panel items that correspond to the menu items. This new frame is dynamic, so any changes to the menu are reflected in the pinup frame provided it is not currently being displayed. If the pinup frame is currently being displayed and the menu contents change, the pinned menu will not reflect the new changes. Whenever changing the contents of the menu, you should unpin the pinned up menu *before* changing menu items or attributes and then repin the menu.

This attribute takes two values as parameters. One is a base frame; the other is a string that acts as a title for the frame, as shown below:

```
Frame   frame;
Menu    menu;
void    func1(), func2();
...
/* Create base frame for the application */
frame = (Frame)xv_create(NULL, FRAME, NULL);
...
menu = (Menu)xv_create(NULL, MENU,
        /* the pinup menu subframe is a child of the base frame */
        MENU_GEN_PIN_WINDOW,    frame,  "title",
        MENU_ITEM,
            MENU_STRING,        "item1",
            MENU_NOTIFY_PROC,   func1,
            NULL,
        MENU_ITEM,
            MENU_STRING,        "item2",
            MENU_NOTIFY_PROC,   func2,
            NULL,
        NULL);
...
```

The new command frame is created as a subframe of the `frame` value. The title label for the menu and the frame is the *title* value. Note that you should not use `MENU_TITLE_ITEM` if you are using `MENU_GEN_PIN_WINDOW` as a menu item is automatically inserted at the top of the menu. If this item is removed, the pin will also be removed.

When the menu is displayed as a result of a call to `menu_show()`, a pushpin in the upper-left corner of the menu is displayed allowing the user to pin up the menu, that causes the menu to go away and the subframe to be displayed. You can get a handle to this subframe if you need it by calling:

```
Frame subframe = (Frame)xv_get(menu, MENU_PIN_WINDOW);
```

You can get a handle to the panel associated with that frame by calling:

```
Panel panel = (Panel)xv_get(frame, FRAME_CMD_PANEL);
```

If you choose to write your own pin window-generating procedures, there are several attributes that you might find helpful in implementing your routines:

MENU_PIN   This Boolean attribute indicates that the menu has a pushpin.

MENU_PIN_WINDOW   This attribute assigns the command frame you created to the menu's pin window. Once the pushpin is pushed in, the MENU package automatically sets the command frame's XV_SHOW attribute to TRUE, allowing the frame to be displayed.

MENU_PIN_PROC   This attribute provides the menu with a procedure that is called when the user pushes the pin in. You may override the default procedure that shows the `pin_window` of the menu by providing your own routine using this attribute. This routine overrides the default behavior of setting XV_SHOW on the command frame, so this responsibility lies in this routine.

MENU_DONE_PROC   This routine is called whenever a pop-up menu has been taken down after a menu item has been selected, pinned up or simply dismissed without a selection being made. Again, this overrides the default action of setting XV_SHOW to FALSE, so this responsibility lies with the MENU_DONE_PROC routine.

11.13 Notification Procedures

When a menu item is selected, a notification procedure is called to notify the host application that the user has made a selection. If the menu item does not have a notify procedure, the parent menu's notification procedure is called instead. If the menu does not have a notification procedure, no action is taken. Be sure that each menu item or its parent menu has a MENU_NOTIFY_PROC routine associated with it. Otherwise, choosing a menu item has no effect. If you wish to make a menu item *inactive*, you should set the attribute MENU_INACTIVE to TRUE.

The primary difference between the MENU package and the PANEL package with respect to the notification mechanism is that if a menu item has no notification procedure associated with it, the notify procedure of the parent menu is used. The PANEL package has no such feature. To differentiate between the notify procedure of a *menu* and the notify procedure of a *menu item*, the term *action procedure* is sometimes used to refer to the menu item's notify procedure. Thus, you may come across the term *action procedure* or the attribute MENU_ACTION_PROC outside of this manual.

However, because there is functionally no difference between the MENU_ACTION_PROC and the MENU_NOTIFY_PROC and since all other XView objects use notify procedures to register their callbacks, we are going to attempt to maintain consistency and avoid potential confusion with the terms by referring to both notify procedures commonly using MENU_NOTIFY_PROC.

The form of the callback routine is:

```
void
menu_notify_proc(menu, menu_item)
    Menu menu;
    Menu_item menu_item;
```

The program in Example 11-2 demonstrates several of the concepts introduced in the chapter so far. *xv_menu.c* creates a simple frame, a canvas and a pop-up menu. The menu is a *static* menu because all the menu items are created in-line with the menu-generating procedure. The menu itself has a notify procedure which is called if any of the menu items specified by MENU_STRINGS are selected. The result is to display the text of the selected item in the header of the frame. An additional menu item is specified that has a pullright menu that can be pinned up.

Example 11-2. The xv_menu.c program

```
/*
 * xv_menu.c -
 *      Demonstrate the use of an XView menu in a canvas subwindow.
 *      Menu is brought up with right mouse button and the selected
 *      choice is displayed in the canvas.  Allows menu to be pinned.
 */
#include <xview/xview.h>
#include <xview/canvas.h>

Frame       frame;

main(argc,argv)
int     argc;
char    *argv[];
{
    Canvas          canvas;
    Menu            menu;
    void            my_notify_proc(), my_event_proc();
    extern void exit();

    xv_init(XV_INIT_ARGC_PTR_ARGV, &argc, argv, NULL);

    frame = (Frame)xv_create(NULL, FRAME,
        FRAME_LABEL,    argv[0],
        NULL);
    canvas = (Canvas)xv_create(frame, CANVAS,
```

Example 11-2. The xv_menu.c program (continued)

```
            XV_WIDTH,        300,
            XV_HEIGHT,       200,
            NULL);
    menu = (Menu)xv_create(NULL, MENU,
            MENU_TITLE_ITEM,         "Junk",
            MENU_STRINGS,            "Yes", "No", "Maybe", NULL,
            MENU_NOTIFY_PROC,        my_notify_proc,
            MENU_ITEM,
                MENU_STRING,         "Save",
                MENU_NOTIFY_PROC,    my_notify_proc,
                MENU_PULLRIGHT,
                    xv_create(canvas, MENU,
                        MENU_GEN_PIN_WINDOW,        frame, "Save",
                        MENU_ITEM,
                            MENU_STRING,            "Update Changes",
                            MENU_NOTIFY_PROC,       my_notify_proc,
                            NULL,
                        NULL),
                NULL,
            MENU_ITEM,
                MENU_STRING,         "Quit",
                MENU_NOTIFY_PROC,    exit,
                NULL,
            NULL);

    xv_set(canvas_paint_window(canvas),
            WIN_CONSUME_EVENTS,      WIN_MOUSE_BUTTONS, NULL,
            WIN_EVENT_PROC,          my_event_proc,
            /* associate the menu to the canvas win for easy retrieval */
            WIN_CLIENT_DATA,         menu,
            NULL);

    window_fit(frame);
    window_main_loop(frame);
}
/*
 * my_notify_proc - Display menu selection in frame header.
 */
void
my_notify_proc(menu, menu_item)
Menu menu;
Menu_item menu_item;
{
    xv_set(frame,
        FRAME_LABEL,     xv_get(menu_item, MENU_STRING),
        NULL);
}
/*
 * Call menu_show() to display menu on right mouse button push.
 */
void
my_event_proc(window, event)
Xv_Window window;
Event *event;
{
```

Example 11-2. The xv_menu.c program (continued)

```
    if (event_action(event) == ACTION_MENU && event_is_down(event)) {
        Menu menu = (Menu)xv_get(window, WIN_CLIENT_DATA);
        menu_show(menu, window, event, NULL);
    }
}
```

The output of Example 11-2 is shown in Figure 11-7.

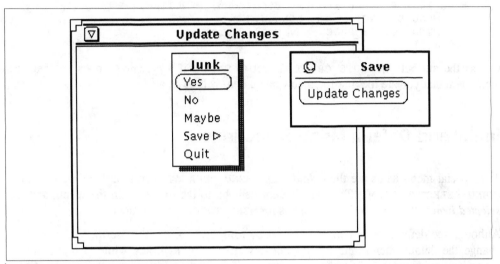

Figure 11-7. Output of xv_menu.c

11.14 Finding Menu Items

You can use xv_find() to locate menu items that match certain attribute-value pairs. The form of using xv_find() for menus is:

```
Menu_item item;

item = (Menu_item)xv_find(menu, MENU,
    <attribute-value list>,
    NULL);
```

xv_find() returns menu items, not menus. By default, when you search for items, each item in a menu is searched before descending into a menu item's pullright menu, should it exist. However, you can override this default behavior by specifying the attribute MENU_DESCEND_FIRST. During a menu search, if an item with a pullright is found, then this attribute indicates whether the search should continue through the pullright or to the next item in the current menu.

If a menu item or a menu item's pullright is a *generate* procedure, the generate procedure is called despite the fact that the menu or menu item will not be displayed. No matter how many attributes are given, `xv_find()` will return the first item found that matches all given attributes even though the item may have more attributes associated with it.

When specifying attribute-value pairs, you specify attributes in the same way as when you use `xv_create()`. For example, if you want to find a menu item with the string value of "fonts" and the callback routine of `my_notify_proc`, you would use:

```
menu_item = (Menu_item)xv_find(menu, MENUITEM,
    MENU_STRING,        "fonts,"
    MENU_NOTIFY_PROC,   my_notify_proc,
    NULL);
```

Unless the attribute `XV_AUTO_CREATE` is set to `FALSE`, if `xv_find()` does not find the menu item that you are looking for, a new menu item will be created.

11.15 Initial and Default Menu Selections

Two special menu items are the *default item* (`MENU_DEFAULT_ITEM`) and the *selected item* (`MENU_SELECTED_ITEM`). The default item defaults to the *first* item in the menu, and the *selected item* is the selected item (or items for `MENU_TOGGLE_MENU` menus).

Although the default menu item may be set by using `xv_set()`, the user may interactively change the default menu item by holding down the CONTROL key while also selecting a menu item with the MENU button. Therefore, if the user selects a menu item that has a pullright menu, *but the pullright menu is not activated,** when your notify procedure is called, you may choose to descend into the pullright menu and find the default menu item and call that item's callback routine.

11.16 Modifying Menu Dismissal

XView normally handles this process for you. That is, when a menu is up and the user makes a selection from the menu, the menu is dismissed if the pushpin (if visible) is out. However, you can modify its behavior if necessary by setting the value of `MENU_NOTIFY_STATUS`. If the user makes a selection and the default method of bringing down the menu is not desired (presumably, the selection was invalid), you can keep the menu from being dismissed by setting `MENU_NOTIFY_STATUS` to `XV_ERROR`. By default, the attribute is set to `XV_OK`, which indicates that the menu should be dismissed if the pushpin is out.

---

*This might happen if the user did not drag the mouse far enough to the right.

11.17 Destroying Menus

Destruction of menus is an important task because menus are frequently used and, if their resources are not freed adequately, you could find the size of your application growing rapidly until your system runs out of available memory. Therefore, proper cleanup of menu destruction is imperative. Menus are destroyed using `xv_destroy()`. In the case of *static menus*, nothing more is required than calling `xv_destroy()`. This is because the internals of XView automatically set attributes discussed in this section.

Be aware of several situations, such as when you:

- Allocate your own strings or server images as menu item labels.

- Create your own menu items using `xv_create(NULL, MENUITEM, ...)`.

- Generate your own pullright menus.

The destruction phase walks down each menu item in the menu and tests each menu item to see if it has the `MENU_RELEASE` attribute set. This is not a Boolean attribute—it has no value associated with it at all. If you specify the attribute, the attribute is set. If you do not specify it, then the attribute is not set. As noted, menu items that have been created in-line have `MENU_RELEASE` set already.

Menu items that you create yourself do not have `MENU_RELEASE` set by default. You also may or may not *want* it set. If you plan to reuse menu items—a need that is common—then you do not want to set this attribute. However, you must maintain a handle to the menu item or it is lost. If the attribute is set, then the menu item is freed, but no other data associated with the menu item is destroyed. Only the item itself is. If you have any allocated data associated with the menu item, then you either need to free it yourself or give a hint to XView to free it for you.

The following subsections discuss other data allocated for menu items. Remember that freeing menus and menu items is not done automatically; this only happens as a result of your calling `xv_destroy()`. So, if you decide to free menus or menu items, you should be sure to free pullright menus and/or client data yourself beforehand.

11.17.1 Freeing Allocated Strings

If you create a menu item with allocated data, you should *not* use them in a `MENU_STRINGS` list. Instead, you should create the menu items individually, as shown in Example 11-3.

Example 11-3. Creating individual menu items

```
char *str1;
if (str1 = malloc(strlen(buf)+1))
    strcpy(str1, buf);

menu = xv_create(NULL, MENU,
    MENU_ITEM,
        MENU_STRING,    str1,
```

Example 11-3. Creating individual menu items (continued)

```
            MENU_RELEASE_IMAGE,
            NULL,
    NULL);
```

The code in Example 11-3 shows a menu item that is created in-line because it is created using the MENU_ITEM attribute. However, because the string used as the menu item's label is allocated, we need to provide XView with a hint to release this data.

Similarly, if we used xv_create() to create a Server_image as the menu item's label, the MENU_RELEASE_IMAGE attribute suffices to free that data as well.

11.17.2 Freeing Pullright Menus

Even though a menu item has MENU_RELEASE set, if a pullright menu is associated with it, the menu will not be freed. In many cases, this is acceptable because many menu items may share the same pullright menu. If you are sure you do not need the menu anymore, then you should free it. Note that freeing the menu will attempt to free the menu items within it.

This is most commonly done in menu-generating routines installed as the MENU_GEN_PULLRIGHT attribute.

11.17.3 Menu Client Data

If a menu item is freed, you should be sure to free any client data that is associated with it. Client data may have been attached to the menu item using XV_KEY_DATA or MENU_CLIENT_DATA.

If you created menus for panel buttons, and you destroy the MENU button (or the panel associated with that button), then you are responsible for destroying the menu you created. The panel does not handle this for you. Destroying the menu attached to menu buttons is done the same way as it is for menus.

11.18 Example Program

The following brief descriptions are introductory notes about the programs *menu_dir.c* (listed here) and *menu_dir2.c* (listed in Appendix F, *Example Programs*). The comments in the programs as well as the code itself should be read for full details.

menu_dir.c demonstrates many of the features of the MENU package presented in this chapter. It displays a menu that contains all the files from the current directory. If a pathname is given on the command line, that directory is used. The entire menu hierarchy is built initially at start-up time, so directories that do not have extremely long paths should be specified.*

---

*Don't even think of specifying /.

For each directory found, a new menu is created and the directory is descended building items for the new menu. *menu_dir2.c* also builds cascading menus for directories, but instead of descending into the directory tree, a menu-generating routine is called only if the user tries to go into a pullright.

Example 11-4. The menu_dir.c program

```
/*
 * menu_dir.c -
 * Demonstrate the use of an XView menu in a canvas subwindow.
 * A menu is brought up with the MENU mouse button and displays
 * menu choices representing the files in the directory.  If a
 * directory entry is found, a new pullright item is created with
 * that subdir as the pullright menu's contents.  This implementation
 * creates the entire directory tree initially.  Do not attempt to
 * build a tree from /.  You will most likely run out of resources.
 *
 * argv[1] indicates which directory to start from.
 */
#include <xview/xview.h>
#include <xview/canvas.h>
#include <sys/stat.h>
#include <sys/dir.h>
#include <X11/Xos.h>
#ifndef MAXPATHLEN
#include <sys/param.h> /* probably sun/BSD specific */
#endif /* MAXPATHLEN */

Frame     frame;

/*
 * main -
 *      Create a frame, canvas and menu.
 *      A canvas receives input in its canvas_paint_window().
 *      Its callback procedure calls menu_show().
 */
main(argc,argv)
int     argc;
char    *argv[];
{
    Canvas      canvas;
    extern void exit();
    void        my_event_proc();
    Menu        menu;
    Menu_item   mi, add_path_to_menu();

    xv_init(XV_INIT_ARGC_PTR_ARGV, &argc, argv, NULL);

    frame = (Frame)xv_create(NULL, FRAME,
        FRAME_LABEL,             argv[1]? argv[1] : "cwd",
        FRAME_SHOW_FOOTER,       TRUE,
        NULL);
    canvas = (Canvas)xv_create(frame, CANVAS,
        FRAME_LABEL,    argv[0],
        XV_WIDTH,       400,
        XV_HEIGHT,      100,
        NULL);

    mi = add_path_to_menu(argc > 1? argv[1] : ".");
```

Example 11-4. The menu_dir.c program (continued)

```
    menu = (Menu)xv_get(mi, MENU_PULLRIGHT);

    /* associate the menu to the canvas win for easy retrieval */
    xv_set(canvas_paint_window(canvas),
        WIN_CONSUME_EVENTS,     WIN_MOUSE_BUTTONS, NULL,
        WIN_EVENT_PROC,         my_event_proc,
        WIN_CLIENT_DATA,        menu,
        NULL);

    window_fit(frame);
    window_main_loop(frame);
}

/*
 * my_action_proc - display the selected item in the frame footer.
 */
void
my_action_proc(menu, menu_item)
Menu        menu;
Menu_item           menu_item;
{
    xv_set(frame,
        FRAME_LEFT_FOOTER,      xv_get(menu_item, MENU_STRING),
        NULL);
}

/*
 * Call menu_show() to display menu on right mouse button push.
 */
void
my_event_proc(canvas, event)
Canvas   canvas;
Event *event;
{
    if ((event_id(event) == MS_RIGHT) && event_is_down(event)) {
        Menu menu = (Menu)xv_get(canvas, WIN_CLIENT_DATA);
        menu_show(menu, canvas, event, NULL);
    }
}

/*
 * return an allocated char * that points to the last item in a path.
 */
char *
getfilename(path)
char *path;
{
    char *p;

    if (p = rindex(path, '/'))
        p++;
    else
        p = path;
    return strcpy(malloc(strlen(p)+1), p);
}

/*
 * The path passed in is scanned via readdir().  For each file in the
 * path, a menu item is created and inserted into a new menu.  That
```

Example 11-4. The menu_dir.c program (continued)

```
 * new menu is made the PULLRIGHT_MENU of a newly created panel item
 * for the path item originally passed it.  Since this routine is
 * recursive, a new menu is created for each subdirectory under the
 * original path.
 */
Menu_item
add_path_to_menu(path)
char *path;
{
    DIR                 *dirp;
    struct direct       *dp;
    struct stat         s_buf;
    Menu_item           mi;
    Menu                next_menu;
    char                buf[MAXPATHLEN];

    /* don't add a folder to the list if user can't read it */
    if (stat(path, &s_buf) == -1 || !(s_buf.st_mode & S_IREAD))
        return NULL;
    if (s_buf.st_mode & S_IFDIR) {
        int cnt = 0;
        if (!(dirp = opendir(path)))
            /* don't bother adding to list if we can't scan it */
            return NULL;
        next_menu = (Menu)xv_create(XV_NULL, MENU, NULL);
        while (dp = readdir(dirp))
            if (strcmp(dp->d_name, ".") && strcmp(dp->d_name, "..")) {
                (void) sprintf(buf, "%s/%s", path, dp->d_name);
                if (!(mi = add_path_to_menu(buf)))
                    /* unreadable file or dir - deactivate item */
                    mi = xv_create(XV_NULL, MENUITEM,
                        MENU_STRING,            getfilename(dp->d_name),
                        MENU_RELEASE,
                        MENU_RELEASE_IMAGE,
                        MENU_INACTIVE,          TRUE,
                        NULL);
                xv_set(next_menu, MENU_APPEND_ITEM, mi, NULL);
                cnt++;
            }
        closedir(dirp);
        mi = xv_create(XV_NULL, MENUITEM,
            MENU_STRING,            getfilename(path),
            MENU_RELEASE,
            MENU_RELEASE_IMAGE,
            MENU_NOTIFY_PROC,   my_action_proc,
            NULL);
        if (!cnt) {
            xv_destroy(next_menu);
            /* An empty or unsearchable directory - deactivate item */
            xv_set(mi, MENU_INACTIVE, TRUE, NULL);
        } else {
            xv_set(next_menu, MENU_TITLE_ITEM, getfilename(path), NULL);
            xv_set(mi, MENU_PULLRIGHT, next_menu, NULL);
        }
        return mi;
    }
```

Example 11-4. The menu_dir.c program (continued)

```
    return (Menu_item)xv_create(NULL, MENUITEM,
        MENU_STRING,                getfilename(path),
        MENU_RELEASE,
        MENU_RELEASE_IMAGE,
        MENU_NOTIFY_PROC,           my_action_proc,
        NULL);
}
```

11.19 Menu Package Summary

Table 11-1 lists the attributes in the MENU package; the procedures and macros are listed below. This information is described fully in Appendices A and B.

```
menu_action_proc()
menu_return_item()
menu_return_value()
menu_show()
```

Table 11-1. Menu Attributes

Menu	Menu Item
MENU_ACTION_IMAGE	MENU_ACTION_IMAGE
MENU_ACTION_ITEM	MENU_ACTION_ITEM
MENU_APPEND_ITEM	MENU_ACTION_PROC
MENU_CLASS	MENU_FEEDBACK
MENU_COL_MAJOR	MENU_GEN_PROC
MENU_DEFAULT	MENU_GEN_PROC_IMAGE
MENU_DEFAULT_ITEM	MENU_GEN_PROC_ITEM
MENU_DESCEND_FIRST	MENU_GEN_PULLRIGHT
MENU_DONE_PROC	MENU_GEN_PULLRIGHT_IMAGE
MENU_FIRST_EVENT	MENU_GEN_PULLRIGHT_ITEM
MENU_GEN_PIN_WINDOW	MENU_IMAGE
MENU_GEN_PROC	MENU_IMAGE_ITEM
MENU_GEN_PULLRIGHT_IMAGE	MENU_INACTIVE
MENU_GEN_PULLRIGHT_ITEM	MENU_INVERT
MENU_IMAGE_ITEM	MENU_PULLRIGHT
MENU_IMAGES	MENU_PULLRIGHT_IMAGE
MENU_INSERT	MENU_PULLRIGHT_ITEM
MENU_INSERT_ITEM	MENU_RELEASE
MENU_ITEM	MENU_RELEASE_IMAGE
MENU_LAST_EVENT	MENU_SELECTED
MENU_NCOLS	MENU_STRING
MENU_NITEMS	MENU_STRING_ITEM
MENU_NOTIFY_PROC	MENU_TITLE
MENU_NROWS	MENU_TYPE

Table 11-1. Menu Attributes (continued)

Menu	Menu Item
MENU_NTH_ITEM	MENU_VALUE
MENU_PIN	
MENU_PIN_PROC	
MENU_PIN_WINDOW	
MENU_PULLRIGHT_IMAGE	
MENU_PULLRIGHT_ITEM	
MENU_REMOVE	
MENU_REMOVE_ITEM	
MENU_REPLACE	
MENU_REPLACE_ITEM	
MENU_STRINGS	
MENU_TITLE_IMAGE	
MENU_TITLE_ITEM	
MENU_TYPE	
MENU_VALID_RESULT	

Menus

12

Notices

In This Chapter:

Notices

12
Notices

A notice is a pop-up window that notifies the user of a problem or asks a question that requires an immediate response. The notice grabs the entire screen so no other windows or applications can receive input until the user responds to the notice. Figure 12-1 shows an example of a notice window from the *OPEN LOOK GUI Specification*.

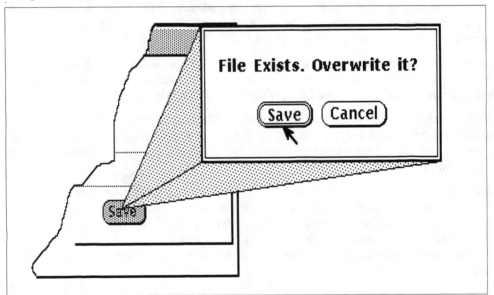

Figure 12-1. A sample notice window

Notices are implemented using the FULLSCREEN package to grab the keyboard and pointer events from the server. (The FULLSCREEN package is described in Chapter 15, *Nonvisual Objects*.) The notice window, which owns the fullscreen object, is a nonrectangular transient X window with the X-window attribute override_redirect* set. When the notice is

---

*override_redirect tells the window manager to not provide window decorations.

created, the notice window is immediately displayed. When the user responds to one of the available choices, the notice session ends.

12.1 Creating and Displaying Notices

To use the NOTICE package in applications, the header file *<xview/notice.h>* must be included. Notices are special XView objects because they are not created via xv_create(). Also, they cannot be modified using xv_set(). Notices are created using the special procedure notice_prompt():

```
int
notice_prompt(owner, event, attrs)
    Xv_Window    owner;
    Event        *event;
    attributes ...
```

When creating a notice, the owner must be a valid XView object that has a window associated with it. This can be a panel or a frame, but it is typically the window that causes the notice to be created. If the user tries to type in a read-only text subwindow, a notice might appear from that window informing the user of the error. The event might be NULL if you are not using NOTICE_TRIGGER (see Section 12.1.2, "Notice Triggers").

Because the notice window is not a part of any other XView package and it does not allow window-specific attributes, you cannot use any generic, common or window attributes to configure the notice window; you can only use NOTICE_* attributes.

Notice windows are explicitly specified by OPEN LOOK and cannot be modified. If you wish to create a notice-type interface that is not OPEN LOOK compliant (which is not recommended), you need to learn more about the fullscreen object described in Chapter 15, *Nonvisual Objects*.

Your application has control over the messages that are displayed in the notice window as well as the choices available to the user as responses. notice_prompt() creates a window, grabs the server, waits for the user to make a selection on one of the available button choices, then destroys the window. You never have a handle to the notice *object* itself—only the resulting choice made by the user. The result is the return value of the notice_prompt() function.

A very simple case of a notice prompt is demonstrated in Example 12-1:

Example 12-1. The simple_notice.c program

```
/*
 * simple_notice.c -- Demonstrate the use of notices.
 */
#include <xview/xview.h>
#include <xview/panel.h>
#include <xview/notice.h>

main(argc,argv)
int     argc;
char    *argv[];
```

Example 12-1. The simple_notice.c program (continued)

```
{
    Frame        frame;
    Panel        panel;
    Xv_opaque    my_notify_proc();

    /*
     * Initialize XView, create a frame, a panel and one panel button.
     */
    xv_init(XV_INIT_ARGS, argc, argv, NULL);

    frame = (Frame)xv_create(XV_NULL, FRAME, NULL);
    panel = (Panel)xv_create(frame, PANEL, NULL);
    xv_create(panel, PANEL_BUTTON,
        PANEL_LABEL_STRING,     "Quit",
        PANEL_NOTIFY_PROC,      my_notify_proc,
        NULL);

    /* make sure everything looks good */
    window_fit(panel);
    window_fit(frame);

    /* start window event processing */
    xv_main_loop(frame);
}
/*
 * my_notify_proc() -- called when the user selects the Quit button.
 *      The notice appears as a result of notice_prompt().  Here
 *      the user must chooses YES or NO to confirm or deny quitting.
 */
Xv_opaque
my_notify_proc(item, event)
Panel_item   item;
Event        *event;
{
    int              result;

    result = notice_prompt(panel, NULL,
        NOTICE_FOCUS_XY,          event_x(event), event_y(event),
        NOTICE_MESSAGE_STRINGS,   "Do you really want to quit?", NULL,
        NOTICE_BUTTON_YES,        "Yes",
        NOTICE_BUTTON_NO,         "No",
        NULL);

    if (result == NOTICE_YES)
        exit(0);
}
```

The program *simple_notice.c* contains a panel with a Quit button. When the user selects the Quit button, a notice pops up to prompt the user for confirmation. What the user sees is shown in Figure 12-2. If the user presses "Yes," the program exits.

The position from which the notice shadow emanates is described by the attribute NOTICE_FOCUS_XY. This value defaults to the current mouse position when the application calls notice_prompt(). As shown in *simple_notice.c*, the point from which the notice shadow emanates appears to be the same position as the location where the panel button was selected. Due to possible delays with the X server, by the time the notice_prompt() routine gets called, the location of the mouse may have moved from the place where the panel

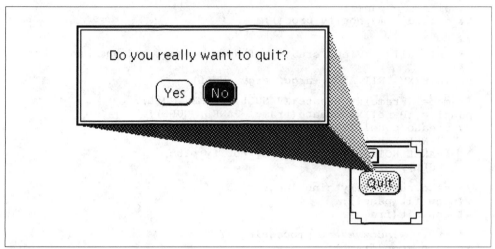

Figure 12-2. Output of simple_notice.c while the notice is up

button was selected. To be sure that the notice prompt appears to emanate from the original mouse-down location, we use the coordinates of the mouse position from the event structure. The values for NOTICE_FOCUS_XY are relative to the origin of the window passed as the first parameter to notice_prompt().

12.1.1 Response Choices and Values

Two responses are normally present whenever a notice appears: "Yes" and "No." These are defined for convenience in <xview/notice.h>:

```
#define NOTICE_YES   1
#define NOTICE_NO    0
```

These are the return values that notice_prompt() might return that correspond directly to the attributes NOTICE_BUTTON_YES and NOTICE_BUTTON_NO. As shown in simple_notice.c, these are the only two choices made available to the user.

These two choices are special in another way: they respond to *accelerator* keys. That is, the RETURN key can be used instead of selecting the NOTICE_BUTTON_YES button with the pointer, and the STOP key can be used instead of selecting NOTICE_BUTTON_NO.

Also, when these choices are used, the cursor is immediately bound to the button associated with NOTICE_BUTTON_YES because this is the *default* response to the notice. As a hint to the programmer, it is always desirable to word all questions so the default answer is "Yes."

It is quite common for the application to have more than one appropriate response to some kind of notice prompt. Suppose that your application is an editor of some kind. If the user selects the Quit button and there have been changes to the file that have not been accounted for, you might wish to inform the user and allow more than one response: quit, updating changes; quit, ignoring changes; or cancel the quit all together. To implement these new choices, use the NOTICE_BUTTON attribute to define the choices available:

```
result = notice_prompt(panel, NULL,
    NOTICE_MESSAGE_STRINGS,
        "There have been modifications since your last update",
        "Would you like to quit or continue editing?",
        NULL,
    NOTICE_BUTTON,      "Quit, Update changes",    101,
    NOTICE_BUTTON,      "Quit, Ignore changes",    102,
    NOTICE_BUTTON,      "Continue Editing",        103,
    NULL);
```

The NOTICE_BUTTON attribute takes two parameters: the button label* and the return value if that button is selected. In this case, the possible return values for the call to notice_prompt are 101, 102 and 103 (in addition to possible error return values). The application should make its decision on how to proceed based on the return value.

Because the NOTICE_BUTTON attribute is used, there is no default choice and no accelerators associated with the notice; the user must use the pointer to select one of the available choices.

12.1.2 Notice Triggers

If you want to assign accelerators to notice buttons, or if you find it necessary to give the user the choice of using mouse buttons or keyboard events to respond to a notice, you can identify *triggers* that cause the notice to return. The value returned in this case is NOTICE_TRIGGERED, and the event that caused the trigger will be in the Event * passed in the call to notice_prompt(). When triggers are not used, the Event * can be NULL.

Example 12-2 shows how one might use the NOTICE_TRIGGER to get a particular event:

Example 12-2. The trigger_notice.c program

```
/*
 * trigger_notice.c -- Demonstrate the use of triggers in notices.
 */
#include <xview/xview.h>
#include <xview/panel.h>
#include <xview/notice.h>

main(argc,argv)
int     argc;
char    *argv[];
{
    Frame       frame;
```

*The button can display text only; no graphic images can be displayed.

Example 12-2. The trigger_notice.c program (continued)

```
    Panel         panel;
    Xv_opaque     my_notify_proc();
    extern void exit();

    /*
     * Initialize XView, create a frame, a panel and one panel button.
     */
    xv_init(XV_INIT_ARGS, argc, argv, NULL);
    frame = (Frame)xv_create(XV_NULL, FRAME, NULL);
    panel = (Panel)xv_create(frame, PANEL, NULL);
    (void) xv_create(panel, PANEL_BUTTON,
        PANEL_LABEL_STRING,     "Quit",
        PANEL_NOTIFY_PROC,      exit,
        NULL);
    (void) xv_create(panel, PANEL_BUTTON,
        PANEL_LABEL_STRING,     "Move",
        PANEL_NOTIFY_PROC,      my_notify_proc,
        NULL);

    /* make sure everything looks good */
    window_fit(panel);
    window_fit(frame);

    /* start window event processing */
    xv_main_loop(frame);
}

/*
 * my_notify_proc() -- called when the user selects the "Move"
 * panel button.  Put up a notice_prompt to get new coordinates
 * to move the main window.
 */
Xv_opaque
my_notify_proc(item, event)
Panel_item  item;
Event       *event;
{
    int         result, x, y;
    Panel       panel = (Panel)xv_get(item, PANEL_PARENT_PANEL);
    Frame       frame = (Frame)xv_get(panel, XV_OWNER);

    x = event_x(event), y = event_y(event);
    printf("original click relative to panel: %d, %d\n", x, y);
    result = notice_prompt(panel, event,
        NOTICE_FOCUS_XY,            x, y,
        NOTICE_MESSAGE_STRINGS,
            "You may move the window to a new location specified by",
            "clicking the Left Mouse Button somewhere on the screen",
            "or cancel this operation by selecting
            NULL,
        NOTICE_BUTTON_YES,      "cancel",
        NOTICE_TRIGGER,         MS_LEFT,
        NOTICE_NO_BEEPING,      TRUE,
        NULL);

    if (result == NOTICE_TRIGGERED) {
        x = event_x(event) + (int)xv_get(frame, XV_X);
        y = event_y(event) + (int)xv_get(frame, XV_Y);
```

Example 12-2. The trigger_notice.c program (continued)

```
        printf("screen x,y: %d, %d\n", x, y);
        xv_set(frame, XV_X, x, XV_Y, y, NULL);
    }
}
```

When this program is run and the user selects the Move panel button, a notice is displayed instructing the user to select a new position for the application window. When the user selects a new location, the window frame moves to that position. Note that the window manager adds a title bar and other decorations around the frame; do not expect the upper-left corner of the frame to move to the new position. The real frame's origin is moved to the new position, and the frame's decorations are moved as well but not aligned to the same values (it will be somewhat higher).

When `notice_prompt()` returns, the `Event` structure that was passed to it contains the event that triggered the notice to return. The *x* and *y* coordinates in the `Event` structure are relative to the origin of the notice shadow. Thus, if you clicked at the point in which the shadow emanates from the screen, the `Event` structure's *x* and *y* coordinates will be 0,0.

To translate these coordinates to screen-specific coordinates, save the original event location and add to that the (*x*, *y*) coordinates returned when `notice_prompt()` returns as well as the current coordinates of the frame (main application).

Before leaving *trigger_notice.c*, we should mention the attribute NOTICE_NO_BEEPING that is used to prevent the notice from beeping when it is displayed. Beeping the screen is usually done when there is an error condition you wish to alert the user about. In this example, there is no error condition—it is a simple dialog with the user.

12.2 Another Example

In the previous example, we used many of the attributes covered in this section in addition to using some generic and common attributes for the panel items. Example 12-3 goes a little further to demonstrate how the NOTICE package works in conjunction with the rest of XView. It creates a frame, a panel with two panel buttons and a message item. Initially, only the Quit button and the Commit button are displayed. When the user selects either button, a notice pops up asking the user to confirm or cancel the proposed action. If the user confirms quitting the program, the program quits. Otherwise, the result, either Confirmed or Canceled, is displayed as the text of the message item.

Example 12-3. The notice.c program

```
/*
 * notice.c --
 * This application creates a frame, a panel, and 3 panel buttons.
 * A message button, a Quit button (to exit the program) and a
 * dummy "commit" button.  Extra data is attached to the panel
 * items by the use of XV_KEY_DATA.  The callback routine for the
 * Quit and Commit buttons is generalized enough that it can apply
 * to either button (or any arbitrary button) because it extracts
 * the expected "data" (via XV_KEY_DATA) from whatever panel
```

Example 12-3. The notice.c program (continued)

```
    * button might have called it.
    */
#include <xview/xview.h>
#include <xview/panel.h>
#include <xview/notice.h>

/*
 * assign "data" to panel items using XV_KEY_DATA ... attach the
 * message panel item, a prompt string specific for the panel
 * item's notice_prompt, and a callback function if the user
 * chooses "yes".
 */
#define MSG_ITEM         10 /* any arbitrary integer */
#define NOTICE_PROMPT    11
#define CALLBACK_FUNC    12

main(argc,argv)
int      argc;
char     *argv[];
{
    Frame        frame;
    Panel        panel;
    Panel_item   msg_item;
    Xv_opaque    my_notify_proc();
    extern int   exit();

    /*
     * Initialize XView, and create frame, panel and buttons.
     */
    xv_init(XV_INIT_ARGS, argc, argv, NULL);
    frame = (Frame)xv_create(XV_NULL, FRAME,
        FRAME_LABEL,                argv[0],
        NULL);
    panel = (Panel)xv_create(frame, PANEL,
        PANEL_LAYOUT,               PANEL_VERTICAL,
        NULL);
    msg_item = (Panel_item)xv_create(panel, PANEL_MESSAGE, NULL);
    (void) xv_create(panel, PANEL_BUTTON,
        PANEL_LABEL_STRING,         "Quit",
        PANEL_NOTIFY_PROC,          my_notify_proc,
        XV_KEY_DATA,                MSG_ITEM,        msg_item,
        /*
         * attach a prompt specific for this button used by
         * notice_prompt()
         */
        XV_KEY_DATA,                NOTICE_PROMPT,   "Really Quit?",
        /*
         * a callback function to call if the user answers "yes"
         * to prompt
         */
        XV_KEY_DATA,                CALLBACK_FUNC,   exit,
        NULL);
    /*
     * now that the Quit button is under the message item,
     * layout horizontally
     */
    xv_set(panel, PANEL_LAYOUT, PANEL_HORIZONTAL, NULL);
```

Example 12-3. The notice.c program (continued)

```
    (void) xv_create(panel, PANEL_BUTTON,
        PANEL_LABEL_STRING,      "Commit...",
        PANEL_NOTIFY_PROC,       my_notify_proc,
        XV_KEY_DATA,             MSG_ITEM,        msg_item,
        /*
         * attach a prompt specific for this button used by
         * notice_prompt()
         */
        XV_KEY_DATA,             NOTICE_PROMPT,   "Update all changes?",
        /*
         * Note there is no callback func here, but one could be
         * written
         */
        NULL);

    window_fit(panel);
    window_fit(frame);
    xv_main_loop(frame);
}

/*
 * my_notify_proc()
 * The notice appears as a result of notice_prompt().
 * The "key data" associated with the panel item is extracted via
 * xv_get().  The resulting choice is displayed in the panel
 * message item.
 */
Xv_opaque
my_notify_proc(item, event)
Panel_item   item;
Event        *event;
{
    int          result;
    int          (*func)();
    char         *prompt;
    Panel_item   msg_item;
    Panel        panel;

    func = (int(*)())xv_get(item, XV_KEY_DATA, CALLBACK_FUNC);
    prompt = (char *)xv_get(item, XV_KEY_DATA, NOTICE_PROMPT);
    msg_item = (Panel_item)xv_get(item, XV_KEY_DATA, MSG_ITEM);
    panel = (Panel)xv_get(item, PANEL_PARENT_PANEL);
    /*
     * Create the notice and get a response.
     */
    result = notice_prompt(panel, NULL,
        NOTICE_FOCUS_XY,          event_x(event), event_y(event),
        NOTICE_MESSAGE_STRINGS,
                prompt,
                "Press YES to confirm",
                "Press NO to cancel",
                NULL,
        NOTICE_BUTTON_YES,        "YES",
        NOTICE_BUTTON_NO,         "NO",
        NULL);

    switch(result) {
```

Notices

Example 12-3. The notice.c program (continued)

```
    case NOTICE_YES:
        xv_set(msg_item, PANEL_LABEL_STRING, "Confirmed", NULL);
        if (func)
            (*func)();
        break;
    case NOTICE_NO:
        xv_set(msg_item, PANEL_LABEL_STRING, "Cancelled", NULL);
        break;
    case NOTICE_FAILED:
        xv_set(msg_item, PANEL_LABEL_STRING, "unable to pop-up",
            NULL);
        break;
    default:
        xv_set(msg_item, PANEL_LABEL_STRING, "unknown choice",
            NULL);
    }
}
```

12.3 Notice Package Summary

Table 12-1 lists the attributes, procedures and macros for the NOTICE package. This information is described fully in Appendices A and B.

Table 12-1. Notice Attributes, Procedures and Macros

Attributes	Procedures and Macros
NOTICE_BUTTON	notice_prompt()
NOTICE_BUTTON_NO	
NOTICE_BUTTON_YES	
NOTICE_FOCUS_XY	
NOTICE_FONT	
NOTICE_MESSAGE_STRINGS	
NOTICE_MESSAGE_STRINGS_ARRAY_PTR	
NOTICE_NO_BEEPING	
NOTICE_TRIGGER	

13

Cursors

In This Chapter:

13
Cursors

A *cursor* is an image that tracks the mouse on the display. Each window has its own cursor which you can change. There are some cursors defined by OPEN LOOK that correspond to specific window manager operations such as resizing or dragging windows. For these cases, you cannot redefine a cursor. However, for windows in your application, you can assign any cursor image you like.

13.1 Creating Cursors

To use the CURSOR package, include the header file *<xview/cursor.h>*. It provides the necessary types and definitions for using the package. The cursor object's type is Xv_Cursor. In general, to create a cursor, create an image and a cursor using that image as the CURSOR_IMAGE data:

```
Server_image   svr_image;
Xv_Cursor      cursor;

cursor = (Xv_Cursor)xv_create(owner, CURSOR,
    CURSOR_IMAGE,   svr_image,
    NULL);
```

The owner of the cursor may be any XView object. The root window associated with the XView object is used internally by the CURSOR package. If NULL, then the root window of the default screen is used.

The cursor is then assigned to a window associated with an XView object such as a frame, canvas or panel:

```
xv_set(window, WIN_CURSOR, cursor, NULL);
```

It is illegal to assign a cursor to a window if the screens do not match. This is normally not a problem unless you are using multiple displays in your application. In this case, you should be sure to use an XView object that has a common display as the owner for the cursor. In the code line above, *window* should be the visible window to the application. For canvases and panels, this should be the *paint window*, not the canvas or panel object itself.* If you assign

---

*See Chapter 5, *Canvases and Openwin*, for more information about the paint window.

your own cursor to an openwin object (such as a canvas or panel) and the object has been split (either by the user *splitting views* or by the application), then the application is responsible for assigning the cursor to each new paint window.

13.1.1 simple_cursor.c

To introduce how to use the CURSOR package, we'll start with a short program that shows how to set the cursor for a canvas.

Example 13-1. The simple_cursor.c program

```
/*
 * simple_cursor.c -- create a cursor (looks like an hourglass) and
 * assign it to a canvas window.
 */
#include <xview/xview.h>
#include <xview/panel.h>
#include <xview/cursor.h>
#include <xview/svrimage.h>

/* data that describes the cursor's image -- see SERVER_IMAGE below */
short cursor_bits[] = {
/* Width=16, Height=16, Depth=1, */
    0x7FFE,0x4002,0x200C,0x1A38,0x0FF0,0x07E0,0x03C0,0x0180,
    0x0180,0x0240,0x0520,0x0810,0x1108,0x23C4,0x47E2,0x7FFE
};

main(argc, argv)
int argc;
char *argv[];
{
    Frame        frame;
    Canvas       canvas;
    Xv_Cursor    cursor;
    Server_image svr_image;

    xv_init(XV_INIT_ARGC_PTR_ARGV, &argc, argv, NULL);

    /*
     * create a server image to use as the cursor's image.
     */
    svr_image = (Server_image)xv_create(XV_NULL, SERVER_IMAGE,
        XV_WIDTH,              16,
        XV_HEIGHT,             16,
        SERVER_IMAGE_BITS,     cursor_bits,
        NULL);
    /*
     * create a cursor based on the image just created
     */
    cursor = (Xv_Cursor)xv_create(XV_NULL, CURSOR,
        CURSOR_IMAGE,          svr_image,
        NULL);

    /*
     * Create a base frame and a canvas
     */
    frame = (Frame)xv_create(XV_NULL, FRAME, NULL);
```

Example 13-1. The simple_cursor.c program (continued)

```
    canvas = (Canvas)xv_create(frame, CANVAS,
        XV_WIDTH,                   100,
        XV_HEIGHT,                  100,
        NULL);
    /*
     * set the cursor to the paint window for the canvas
     * Do not set it for the canvas itself.
     */
    xv_set(xv_get(canvas, CANVAS_NTH_PAINT_WINDOW, 0),
        WIN_CURSOR,                 cursor,
        NULL);

    window_fit(frame);
    window_main_loop(frame);
}
```

Beware that if a canvas (or any openwin object) is split, the new view (which has a corresponding paint window) does not inherit the cursor from the old view window.* Note that the server images used in cursors must be 1-bit deep. Cursors can have two colors associated with them by specifying foreground and background colors; you cannot specify server images whose depths are greater than 1. See Section 13.4, "Color Cursors."

13.2 Predefined Cursors

A number of predefined cursors are available in the CURSOR package for use as OPEN LOOK cursors. To use these cursors, you may specify the CURSOR_SRC_CHAR and CURSOR_MASK_CHAR attributes with certain predefined constants as values for these attributes. In *<xview/cursor.h>*, there are some OPEN LOOK cursor defines prefixed by OLC_. When using these attributes, you should not use the CURSOR_IMAGE attribute since you cannot use both simultaneously. Using the previous example, we can remove the SERVER_IMAGE references and modify the call to create the cursor:

```
    cursor = xv_create(NULL, CURSOR,
        CURSOR_SRC_CHAR,    OLC_BUSY_PTR,
        NULL);
```

Predefined cursors are really images from a prebuilt font. The *value* in the attribute-value pair is the character to use from that font—or rather, it is the index into the array of glyphs that the font contains. The glyph from the font is extracted and used as the image. You can use the attribute CURSOR_MASK_CHAR similarly. This image is used as the mask for the source image. If no mask is given, the same image used as the source is used as the mask.†

---

*Chapter 5, *Canvases and Openwin*, discusses splitting views.
†See XCreateGlyphCursor and XCreatePixmapCursor in Volume Two, *Xlib Reference Manual*.

13.3 The Hotspot and Cursor Location

The *hotspot* on a cursor is the location in which the cursor is located if the user generates an event like pressing a mouse button or typing at the keyboard, or if you were to query its position. For example, if a cursor is shaped like an arrow, the hotspot should be at the tip of the arrow. If the hotspot for a cursor were set to (0, 0) then the hotspot would be the upper-left corner of the image used. A cursor shaped like a bull's eye (16x16) might have its hotspot at (7, 7) to indicate that the focus for the cursor is in the middle.* You can find out what the current position of the cursor is by using the attribute WIN_MOUSE_XY, as in:

```
r = (Rect *)xv_get(window, WIN_MOUSE_XY);
```

The return value from xv_get() is a pointer to a Rect structure. The r_width and r_height fields of this structure are unused (0, 0), but the r_top and r_left fields indicate the position of the hotspot for the cursor with respect to the window, window. The program in Example 13-2 demonstrates how this is used, and it shows how to create your own pixmap for a cursor image.

Example 13-2. The hot_spot.c program

```
/*
 * hot_spot.c -- create a cursor and query its position on the
 * screen and in the panel's window.
 * Our own function, create_cursor(), attaches a new cursor to the
 * window parameter passed into the function.
 */
#include <X11/X.h>
#include <X11/Xlib.h>              /* for the xlib graphics */
#include <xview/xview.h>
#include <xview/panel.h>
#include <xview/cursor.h>
#include <xview/svrimage.h>

main(argc, argv)
int argc;
char *argv[];
{
    Frame        frame;
    Panel        panel;
    void         do_it();

    xv_init(XV_INIT_ARGC_PTR_ARGV, &argc, argv, NULL);

    /*
     * Create a base frame, a panel, and a panel button.
     */
    frame = (Frame)xv_create(XV_NULL, FRAME, NULL);
    panel = (Panel)xv_create(frame, PANEL, NULL);
    create_cursor(xv_get(panel, CANVAS_NTH_PAINT_WINDOW, 0));
    (void) xv_create(panel, PANEL_BUTTON,
        PANEL_LABEL_STRING,     "Push Me",
        PANEL_NOTIFY_PROC,      do_it,
        NULL);
```

---

*The value 7, 7 is used because the origin is at 0, 0—not 1, 1.

Example 13-2. The hot_spot.c program (continued)

```
    window_fit(panel);
    window_fit(frame);
    window_main_loop(frame);
}

/*
 * When user selects the panel button, the current mouse location is
 * printed relative to the panel's window and to the screen.
 * This location is governed by the hot spot on the cursor.
 */
void
do_it(item, event)
{
    Rect *r;
    Panel panel = (Panel)xv_get(item, PANEL_PARENT_PANEL);

    r = (Rect *)xv_get(xv_get(panel, XV_ROOT), WIN_MOUSE_XY);
    printf("Root window: %d %d\n", r->r_left, r->r_top);
    r = (Rect *)xv_get(xv_get(panel, CANVAS_NTH_PAINT_WINDOW, 0), WIN_MOUSE_XY);
    printf("Panel window: %d %d\n", r->r_left, r->r_top);
}

/*
 * create_cursor() creates a bull's eye cursor and assigns it
 * to the window (parameter).
 */
create_cursor(window)
Xv_Window window;
{
    Xv_Cursor       cursor;
    Server_image    image;
    Pixmap          pixmap;
    Display         *dpy = (Display *)xv_get(window, XV_DISPLAY);
    GC              gc;
    XGCValues       gcvalues;

    image = (Server_image)xv_create(XV_NULL, SERVER_IMAGE,
        XV_WIDTH,       16,
        XV_HEIGHT,      16,
        NULL);
    pixmap = (Pixmap)xv_get(image, XV_XID);
    /* Create GC with reversed foreground and background colors to
     * clear pixmap first.  Use 1 and 0 because pixmap is 1-bit deep.
     */
    gcvalues.foreground = 0;
    gcvalues.background = 1;
    gc = XCreateGC(dpy, pixmap, GCForeground|GCBackground, &gcvalues);
    XFillRectangle(dpy, pixmap, gc, 0, 0, 16, 16);
    /*
     * Reset foreground and background values for XDrawArc() routines.
     */
    gcvalues.foreground = 1;
    gcvalues.background = 0;
    XChangeGC(dpy, gc, GCForeground | GCBackground, &gcvalues);
    XDrawArc(dpy, pixmap, gc, 2, 2, 12, 12, 0, 360 * 64);
    XDrawArc(dpy, pixmap, gc, 6, 6, 4, 4, 0, 360 * 64);
```

Cursors

Example 13-2. The hot_spot.c program (continued)

```
    /* Create cursor and assign it to the window (parameter) */
    cursor = xv_create(XV_NULL, CURSOR,
        CURSOR_IMAGE,    image,
        CURSOR_XHOT,     7,
        CURSOR_YHOT,     7,
        NULL);
    xv_set(window, WIN_CURSOR, cursor, NULL);

    /* free the GC -- the cursor and the image must not be freed. */
    XFreeGC(dpy, gc);
}
```

When the program is running, each time the panel button is pushed, it prints the cursor's position relative to the panel's window and relative to the root window (absolute screen coordinates). You can move the base frame around on the screen to see how the root window coordinates change.

The routine `create_cursor()` creates a bull's eye cursor for the window passed as the parameter to the routine. The cursor image must be a `Server_image`, so we first create a server image, then get the `Pixmap` associated with it using the `XV_XID`, and lastly use Xlib graphics to draw two circles in the pixmap.

We need a GC, so we create one based on the pixmap obtained from the server image. The pixmap is one bit deep, so the foreground and background colors are set to 0, 1 (to clear the pixmap first), then to 1, 0 so as to draw the two circles. We then create the cursor using the server image and setting the hotspots accordingly. We free the `gc`, but the `Server_image` (which contains the pixmap) and the `cursor` must not be freed so the cursor can be maintained by the window.

If you would rather set the cursor for a window using raw Xlib calls such as `XCreate-PixmapCursor`, `XCreateGlyphCursor` or `XCreateFontCursor`, use the X window associated with the `Xv_Window` parameter. To get it, use:

```
    xv_get(window, XV_XID)
```

and assign an X `Cursor` object to that window.*

13.4 Color Cursors

You can define the foreground and background colors of a cursor independently of the window the cursor is assigned to. You may not have more than two colors per cursor because X does not support color images as cursor glyphs. Thus, to create or modify an existing cursor to have color, you need to specify foreground and background colors. Because of the use of color, the header file *<xview/cms.h>* must be included. The colors are of type `Xv_singlecolor` and should be initialized before use:

---

*See Volume One, *Xlib Programming Manual*.

```
#include <xview/cms.h>
. . .
Xv_singlecolor    fg, bg;

bg.red = 250, bg.green = 230, bg.blue = 30;
fg.red = 180, fg.green = 100, fg.blue = 20;

cursor = xv_create(NULL, CURSOR,
    CURSOR_IMAGE,                image,
    CURSOR_FOREGROUND_COLOR,    &fg,
    CURSOR_BACKGROUND_COLOR,    &bg,
    NULL);
```

13.5 Cursor Package Summary

Table 13-1 lists the attributes, procedures and macros for the CURSOR package. This information is described fully in Appendices A and B.

Table 13-1. Cursor Attributes, Procedures and Macros

Attributes	Procedures and Macros
CURSOR_BACKGROUND_COLOR	cursor_copy()
CURSOR_FOREGROUND_COLOR	
CURSOR_IMAGE	
CURSOR_SHOW_IMAGE	
CURSOR_X_HOT	
CURSOR_Y_HOT	

14
Icons

In This Chapter:

14
Icons

A user may *close* an application to save space on the display. The program is still running and it may even be active, but it is not receiving input from the user. In order to represent the application in its closed state, an *icon* is used. An icon is a small picture that represents the application, as shown in Figure 14-1 from the *OPEN LOOK GUI Specification Guide*.

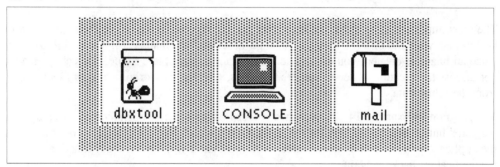

Figure 14-1. Three bordered default icons

The graphic image that icons use may be used for other purposes and, therefore, may be shared among other objects in the application. But the icon image should be designed to easily identify the application while in a closed state. Icons may also have text associated with them. Space is limited, so the text is usually the name of the application.

14.1 Creating and Destroying Icons

To use the ICON package, include the header file *<xview/icon.h>*. The form for creating an icon is:

```
Icon icon;

icon = (Icon)xv_create(owner, ICON, attributes, NULL);
```

The owner of an icon is a base frame, but it may be created with a NULL owner. Once an icon is assigned to a frame, the owner of the icon is changed to that frame. This is another example of *delayed binding*.

When destroying an icon, the server image associated with the icon is not destroyed—it is your responsibility to free the server image and the pixmap associated with the icon if needed.

14.2 The Icon's Image

The most important thing about the icon is its graphic representation, so you will also need to be familiar with the SERVER_IMAGE package described in Chapter 15, *Nonvisual Objects*. Once an image is created, you can create an icon and assign it to a frame. This chapter does not discuss the creation of server images for icons, whether they originate from filenames or from the actual data.

The program in Example 14-1 creates two server images—it uses *open.icon* as the image for the panel button and *closed.icon* for the application's icon.* Pressing the panel button causes the application to *close* to its iconic state. You must use a window manager function to open the application back up again.

Example 14-1. The icon_demo.c program

```
/*
 * icon_demo.c -- demonstrate how an icon is used.  Create a server
 * image and create an icon object with the image as the ICON_IMAGE.
 * Use the icon as the frame's icon.
 */
#include <xview/xview.h>
#include <xview/panel.h>
#include <xview/svrimage.h>
#include <xview/icon.h>

short open_bits[] =   {
#include "open.icon"
};

short closed_bits[] =   {
#include "closed.icon"
```

---

*The files *open.icon* and *closed.icon* are not included in this book due to their length and complexity. They are bitmap files represented in ASCII *hex* notation. The files are included with the XView distribution.

Example 14-1. The icon_demo.c program (continued)

```
};
main(argc, argv)
int     argc;
char    *argv[];
{
    Frame               frame;
    Panel               panel;
    Server_image        open_image, closed_image;
    Icon                icon;
    void                close_frame();

    xv_init(XV_INIT_ARGC_PTR_ARGV, &argc, argv, NULL);

    frame = (Frame)xv_create(XV_NULL, FRAME, NULL);
    panel = (Panel)xv_create(frame, PANEL, NULL);

    open_image = (Server_image)xv_create(NULL, SERVER_IMAGE,
        XV_WIDTH,               64,
        XV_HEIGHT,              64,
        SERVER_IMAGE_BITS,      open_bits,
        NULL);

    closed_image = (Server_image)xv_create(NULL, SERVER_IMAGE,
        XV_WIDTH,               64,
        XV_HEIGHT,              64,
        SERVER_IMAGE_BITS,      closed_bits,
        NULL);

    (void) xv_create(panel, PANEL_MESSAGE,
        PANEL_LABEL_IMAGE,      open_image,
        PANEL_NOTIFY_PROC,      close_frame,
        NULL);

    icon = (Icon)xv_create(frame, ICON,
        ICON_IMAGE,             closed_image,
        XV_X,                   100,
        XV_Y,                   100,
        NULL);
    xv_set(frame, FRAME_ICON, icon, NULL);

    window_fit(panel);
    window_fit(frame);
    xv_main_loop(frame);
}

void
close_frame(item, event)
Panel_item item;
Event *event;
{
    Frame frame = (Frame)xv_get(xv_get(item,
        PANEL_PARENT_PANEL), XV_OWNER);
    xv_set(frame, FRAME_CLOSED, TRUE, NULL);
}
```

The callback routine for the panel button, close_frame(), makes a call to an XView routine which sends window manager requests from the client to the window manager. In this case, we set the frame's FRAME_CLOSED attribute to TRUE to request that the window manager iconify the application associated with the frame parameter.*

The position of the image with respect to the icon is set using the attribute ICON_IMAGE_RECT, which takes as its value a pointer to a Rect structure. The r_top and r_left fields of the structure indicate the offset from the upper-left corner of the icon where the image is placed. The r_width and r_height fields describe the size of the image. If the icon is going to be a different size from the size of the icon's image, or if there is going to be text used with this icon, then the ICON_IMAGE_RECT attribute should be used. Section 14.2.1, "The Icon Text," has an example.

Color Icons

You can make color icons in several ways. You can create a color server image and use that as the ICON_IMAGE. You can set the foreground and background colors for a monochrome image (1-bit deep image) and change the colormap of the icon. For example:

```
Icon            icon;
unsigned long foregound_index, background_index;
Server_image  image; /* assume 1-bit deep monochrome image */

icon = (Icon)xv_create(frame, ICON,
    ICON_IMAGE,       image,
    WIN_CMS_NAME,     "colormap1",
    WIN_FOREGROUND,   foreground_index,
    WIN_BACKGROUND,   background_index,
    NULL);
```

The icon created assumes that the colormap named *colormap1* has been created. You may also use a Cms object and the WIN_CMS attribute (see Chapter 20, *Color*, for more information on colormap segments). The foreground and background colors are indices into the colormap. The image is rendered with the "on" bits in the foreground color and the "off" bits in the background color. Also see the program *xv_color.c* in Appendix F, *Example Programs*.

ICON_TRANSPARENT

If the ICON_TRANSPARENT attribute is set to TRUE (it's FALSE by default), the icon's background color is set to the background color of the root window. This may give the effect that the icon is transparent in the case where the root window is a solid color. However, be careful when the root window has a backing bitmap pattern or a different colormap from the icon.

---

*Window manager functions are discussed in Chapter 4, *Frames*.

ICON_MASK_IMAGE

The attribute ICON_MASK_IMAGE may be used to clip all drawing into the pixmap to the bits set in the Pixmap or Server_image specified here. Therefore, this image should be a 1-bit deep bitmap. The image used as the icon mask is usually a "shadow" of the icon's normal image. That is, it is the same image "filled in," resulting in a totally black 1-bit deep icon that has the same shape as the icon's image.

Example 14-1 can be modified to use this attribute by adding the following code:

```
image_mask = (Server_image)xv_create(NULL, SERVER_IMAGE,
    XV_WIDTH,            64,
    XV_HEIGHT,           64,
    XV_DEPTH,            1,
    SERVER_IMAGE_BITS,   closed_image_mask_bits,
    NULL);

icon = (Icon)xv_create(frame, ICON,
    ICON_IMAGE,         closed_image,
    ICON_MASK_IMAGE,    image_mask,
    XV_X,               100,
    XV_Y,               100,
    NULL);
```

When used in conjunction with the ICON_TRANSPARENT attribute, it may be possible to create an icon that appears to have a shape other than a square.

14.2.1 The Icon Text

Each icon can have text associated with it. This text is not part of the icon's image; it is rendered on top of the image after the image is rendered. To specify the text displayed in the icon, use the generic attribute ICON_LABEL.* By default, the text is displayed at the bottom of the icon area. This may overlap the icon's image. You can change the position in which the text is rendered by using the attribute ICON_LABEL_RECT. The value of the attribute describes a rectangular region in which the text will overwrite anything underneath it. If the text does not fit, it is clipped by this region. To keep the entire image on the icon and display the text without writing over the image, define your icon to be large enough to include both the image and the extents of the text without these regions overlapping. This might make your icon a nonstandard size, however. (The size of an icon is typically 64x64 pixels.)

The code fragment in Example 14-2 implements added sizes to compensate for text while preserving enough area to display the entire icon:

---

*ICON_LABEL is defined to be XV_LABEL in <xview/icon.h>.

Example 14-2. Redefining an icon's size to include its label

```
. . .
Rect            image_rect, label_rect;
Server_image image;
Icon            icon;
. . .
rect_construct(&image_rect, 0, 20, 64, 64);
rect_construct(&label_rect, 0, 0, 64, 20);
icon = xv_create(frame, ICON,
     XV_WIDTH,             64,
     XV_HEIGHT,            64 + 20,
     XV_LABEL,             "Sample",
     ICON_LABEL_RECT,      &label_rect,
     ICON_IMAGE,           image,
     ICON_IMAGE_RECT,      &image_rect,
     NULL);
xv_set(frame, FRAME_ICON, icon, NULL);
```

The first thing we do is construct the image and label area by using the rect_
construct() macro found in *<xview/rect.h>*. The image is positioned at 0, 20 and is a
size of 64x64. The text is positioned at the upper-left corner (0, 0), extends to the width of
the icon and is 20 pixels high. The size of the icon is 64, and the height of the text is 20, so
when we create the icon, we set the height of the icon object using XV_HEIGHT at 64+20.

14.2.2 ICON_TRANSPARENT_LABEL

The ICON_TRANSPARENT_LABEL attribute specifies a string that is drawn into the icon using
the foreground color only. Pixels other than those in the font set are not affected.

14.3 Icon Package Summary

There are no procedures or macros in the ICON package. The attributes for the ICON package
are listed below. This information is described fully in Appendix A, *Attribute Summary*.

```
ICON_IMAGE
ICON_IMAGE_RECT
ICON_LABEL_RECT
XV_LABEL
```

15

Nonvisual Objects

In This Chapter:

15
Nonvisual Objects

This chapter addresses nonvisual objects—objects that are not elements of the user interface. Nonvisual objects include the screen, the display, the X11 server and server images. The FULLSCREEN package is used to grab the X server, and an instance of it is considered a nonvisual object. Nonvisual objects are not viewed on the screen, but they have a place in the XView object hierarchy. Like all XView objects, they share many of the generic and common properties and can be manipulated using xv_create(), xv_set(), xv_get() or xv_find().

Nonvisual objects are typically used internally by XView and are seldom used directly in an application. Therefore, this chapter contains advanced material that may not be essential to all programmers.

15.1 The Display

There is no XView *Display* object. If you need the Display data structure as defined by X, you can get the value of the attribute XV_DISPLAY. This can be used on virtually any visible XView object except for panel items. For example, to get the display associated with the Frame, use:

```
Display *dpy;

dpy = (Display *)xv_get(frame, XV_DISPLAY);
```

The object does not have to be displayed or visible—just created. To do this, the header file *<X11/Xlib.h>* must be included for the declaration of the Display data structure. This structure contains a great deal of information that describes attributes of the workstation, the server being used, and more. See Volume One, *Xlib Programming Manual*, and Volume Two, *Xlib Reference Manual*, for more information.

15.2 The Screen Object

An Xv_Screen is associated with virtually all XView objects (similar to the Display pointer described in the previous section). To use the Xv_Screen object, you must include the file *<xview/screen.h>*. To get a handle on the current screen, use xv_get() on an object:

```
Xv_Screen xv_screen;

xv_screen = (Xv_Screen)xv_get(frame, XV_SCREEN);
```

The Xv_Screen object carries useful information such as the screen number of the root window, all the visuals, the colormap, the server and so on, that are associated with that screen.

The Xv_Screen object differs from the Screen data structure defined by Xlib and, in fact, has nothing to do with the X11 Screen data type (defined in *<X11/Xlib.h>*). That is, you cannot use the following call to xv_get() to get a corresponding Screen pointer.

```
xv_get(xv_screen, XV_XID)          /* Doesn't work */
```

There is no associated XID for the SCREEN package.

Because the X Screen type provides information not available from the Xv_Screen object, it may be useful to get the X Screen. Once the XView screen is obtained, the X Screen type can be gotten by using the SCREEN_NUMBER of the screen and the Display pointer associated with an arbitrary visual object. Example 15-1 demonstrates how to do this for a frame:

Example 15-1. Getting a pointer for a particular frame object (screen.c)

```
/*
 * screen.c -- get some simple info about the current screen:
 * width, height, depth.
 */
#include <xview/xview.h>
#include <xview/screen.h>

main(argc, argv)
int     argc;
char    *argv[];
{
    Frame               frame;
    Xv_Screen           screen;
    Display             *dpy;
    int                 screen_no;

    xv_init(XV_INIT_ARGC_PTR_ARGV, &argc, argv, NULL);

    frame = (Frame)xv_create(XV_NULL, FRAME, NULL);

    dpy = (Display *)xv_get(frame, XV_DISPLAY);
    printf("Server display = '%s'\n", dpy->vendor);
    screen = (Xv_Screen)xv_get(frame, XV_SCREEN);

    screen_no = (int)xv_get(screen, SCREEN_NUMBER);
    printf("Screen #%d: width: %d, height: %d, depth: %d\n",
        screen_no,
        DisplayWidth(dpy, screen_no),
        DisplayHeight(dpy, screen_no),
```

```
        DefaultDepth(dpy, screen_no));
}
```

As shown in Example 15-1 above, you can use any of the macros defined in *<X11/Xlib.h>* to get information about the default screen such as the width, height, depth and so on. From this information, you can get information about the physical frame buffer. These are Xlib-related issues not covered in this book.

15.2.1 Multiple Screens

Each X11 server supports multiple screens. Each screen can have different attributes such as colormaps, depth, size and so on. The screens can actually be different physical devices, although they are connected to the same physical computer. Each screen has its own root window as well, and since the root window is the parent for all base frames, XView can allow windows to exist on any screen.

The way we take advantage of this capability is to first establish a connection to the X11 server and then to get the root window of each screen. With a handle to the root window, we can use it as the parent to any frame we create.

Example 15-2 demonstrates how two frames can be created on two different screens attached to a single server. Note that this code relies on the fact that the server supports more than one screen.

```
/*
 * multiscreen.c -- display a base frame on two different screens
 * attached to the same X11 server.  In order for this program to
 * work, you must have two screens.
 */
#include <xview/xview.h>

main(argc,argv)
int     argc;
char    *argv[];
{
    Xv_Server   server;
    Xv_Screen   screen_0, screen_1;
    Xv_Window   root_0, root_1;
    Frame       frame_0, frame_1;

    server = xv_init(XV_INIT_ARGC_PTR_ARGV, &argc, argv, 0);

    screen_0 = (Xv_Screen) xv_get(server, SERVER_NTH_SCREEN, 0);
    root_0 = (Xv_Window) xv_get(screen_0, XV_ROOT);

    screen_1 = (Xv_Screen) xv_get(server, SERVER_NTH_SCREEN, 1);
    root_1 = (Xv_Window) xv_get(screen_1, XV_ROOT);

    frame_0 = (Frame) xv_create(root_0, FRAME,
        FRAME_LABEL,    "SCREEN 0",
        NULL);

    frame_1 = (Frame) xv_create(root_1, FRAME,
```

```
            FRAME_LABEL,      "SCREEN 1",
            NULL);
      win_insert(frame_1);
      xv_main_loop(frame_0);
}
```

The program implements the design discussed above: xv_init() opens a connection to the
server and returns a handle to the Xv_Server object (see the following section for details).
It also retrieves the Xv_Screen object as well as the root window for each screen. Next, a
base frame is created for each root window. However, since we are going to call
xv_main_loop() on frame_0, we need to insert frame_1 into the window tree. Otherwise, it will never be mapped to its screen, because xv_main_loop() only installs and maps
the window of the object passed to it.

15.3 The SERVER Package

The SERVER package may be used to initialize the connection with the X server running on
any workstation on the network. Once the connection has been made, the package allows
you to query the server for information. xv_init(), the routine that initializes the XView
Toolkit, opens a connection to the server and returns a handle to an Xv_Server object.
While more than one server can be created, xv_init() only establishes a connection to *one*
server. The server object returned by xv_init() is also the server pointed to by the external
global variable, xv_default_server. Programs that do not save the Xv_Server object
returned by xv_init() can reference this global variable instead.

Subsequent connections to other X11 servers must be made using separate calls to xv_cre-
ate(). Note that using separate screens is not the same as establishing a connection to other
servers—the same server can support multiple screens. See the previous section for ways to
access multiple screens in a server.

15.3.1 Creating a Server (Establishing a Connection)

When making any reference to Xv_Server objects, applications should include
<xview/server.h>. You can open a connection to any server by using xv_create():

```
      Server server;
      extern char *server_name;

      server = (Server)xv_create(NULL, SERVER,
          XV_NAME, server_name,
          NULL);
```

Because there is no owner for a server, the owner parameter is ignored and you may pass
NULL. The server described by server_name is assumed to have been initialized already. It
should be set to the standard format:

```
      hostname:display.screen
```

For example:

```
zipcode:0.1
```

connects the second screen on the first display to the host named *zipcode*. If the connection fails, NULL is returned.

Remember that the user can specify which display is the default by using the *-display* option:

```
% program_name -display zipcode:0
```

Remember that this command-line switch is parsed internally by XView when you call xv_init() in the following way:

```
xv_init(XV_INIT_ARGC_PTR_ARGV, &argc, argv, NULL);
```

If xv_init() has not been called by the time the first call to xv_create() is called, the call to xv_create() calls xv_init() internally. This means that if the program gets around to calling xv_init() after it has made any calls to xv_create(), it is a no-op. Likewise, xv_init() creates a server instance, so you cannot establish the *initial* server after calling xv_init().

15.3.2 Connecting to Multiple Servers

You can establish connections to other servers as well as the server opened by xv_init() by using xv_create() in the way shown above. The standard way for a user to specify a connection to a server is the **-display** switch; to allow the user to specify a connection to another server, you should provide an additional command-line option that you parse yourself.

The following code segment allows the user to specify an additional server by using the command-line switch **-display2**:

```
Xv_Server server1, server2 = NULL;

server1 = xv_init(XV_INIT_ARGC_PTR_ARGV, &argc, argv, NULL);

/* XView has parsed all the args it knows -- now look for ours */
while (*++argv) {
    if (!strcmp(*argv, "-display2")) {
        if (!*++argv) {
            fputs("Missing server name.\n", stderr);
            exit(1);
        }
        server2 = xv_create(NULL, SERVER, XV_NAME, *argv, NULL);
    }
}

if (server2 == NULL) {
    fputs("Must specify second server.\n", stderr);
    exit(1);
}
```

If you do this, a connection will be established for both servers.

15.3.3 Getting the Server

One way to get the server to which the application is connected is from the Xv_Screen
object described in the previous section:

```
server = (Server)xv_get(xv_get(frame, XV_SCREEN), SCREEN_SERVER);
```

With the server object, you can tell the server to synchronize with your application by calling:

```
Server server;
...
xv_set(server, SERVER_SYNC, TRUE, NULL);
```

If set to TRUE, the server will remain synchronized with your application until it is turned off
by setting the attribute to FALSE.

To synchronize once, but not have the server maintain its synchronous behavior, call:

```
Server server;

xv_set(server, SERVER_SYNC_AND_PROCESS_EVENTS, NULL);
```

Note that this attribute takes no value—you specify it and no other attributes. This attribute
makes sense only in xv_set().

15.4 Server Images

A server image is a graphic image stored on the X server. Images on the client side can be
stored as XImages or as memory *pixrects*.* The XView Server_image object is not equivalent to X Pixmaps, although pixmaps are part of the Server_image object. Even though
pixmaps are stored on the server, the XView object is a client-side object. Because it is an
XView object, you can query the dimensions of a Server_image by using XV_WIDTH or
XV_HEIGHT, which is something you cannot do with X11 Pixmaps.

15.4.1 Creating Server Images

Applications that wish to use the SERVER_IMAGE package should include <*xview/svrim-
age.h*>. Server_image objects contain graphic data that is used in icons, cursors, panel
buttons—in fact, just about everything in XView that contains graphics. The
Server_image object is created using xv_create() in the following manner:

```
#include <xview/svrimage.h>
...
Server_image image;
```

---

*The term *pixrect* is a data type brought over from SunView.

```
image = (Server_image)xv_create(owner, SERVER_IMAGE,
    attrs,
    NULL);
```

The owner in the call to `xv_create()` is an `Xv_Screen` object. The server that owns this screen owns the newly created image. If the owner is `NULL`, then the default screen is used. The dimensions of `Server_image` objects are 16 by 16 by 1, unless the attributes `XV_WIDTH`, `XV_HEIGHT` or `SERVER_IMAGE_DEPTH` are specified. The bitmap data for the server image may be set using either `SERVER_IMAGE_BITS` or `SERVER_IMAGE_X_BITS` depending on the format of the data. The data format choices are arrays of `short` or `char` types. X11 bitmap data is represented as array of chars, while Sun's pixrect library represents the data as an array of shorts.* The following code segment uses `SERVER_IMAGE_BITS` to produce a 1-bit deep image that looks like a trash can:

```
short image_bits[] = {
#include <images/trash.icon>
};

Server_image = (Server_image)xv_create(NULL, SERVER_IMAGE,
    XV_WIDTH,            32,
    XV_HEIGHT,           30,
    SERVER_IMAGE_BITS,   image_bits,
    NULL);
```

Here, the trash can icon was created with its bits stored in an array of `shorts`. To load an image stored as an array of `chars` (the format used by X11), use `SERVER_IMAGE_X_BITS`:

```
#include <X11/bitmaps/xlogo32>

xlogo_image = (Server_image)xv_create(NULL, SERVER_IMAGE,
    XV_HEIGHT,              xlogo32_width,
    XV_WIDTH,               xlogo32_height,
    SERVER_IMAGE_X_BITS,    xlogo32_bits,
    NULL);
```

In both of these cases, the file specified on the `#include` line must be accessible at the time the program is compiled. Once compiled, the data for the image is stored in the program and the file is no longer needed (e.g., the file may be deleted and the program still displays the image).

Rather than including the file containing the image's bitmap data, you could specify the actual file:

```
char *file = "/usr/include/X11/bitmaps/xlogo32";

server_image = (Server_image)xv_create(NULL, SERVER_IMAGE,
    SERVER_IMAGE_BITMAP_FILE,    file,
    NULL);
```

Be aware that this file must exist and be accessible by any person who runs this program at run time. If for some reason the file is not accessible, then an error is generated. And because the program may be run from any directory, a full pathname should be specified. As shown, the file points to a static string, but `file` could have a value that is changed by

---

*Many of Sun's existing applications should use `SERVER_IMAGE_BITS` when porting to XView. This attribute must be used in order to load bitmap data created by *iconedit*.

selecting from a list of bitmap filenames. In this case, the code fragment could use `xv_set()` to set the filename and thus, the `Server_image`'s data. Whenever `xv_set()` is used to change the data of the image like this, the values of `XV_WIDTH` and `XV_HEIGHT` are automatically updated.

Many XView objects require `Server_images` as values (such as `MENU_IMAGE_STRINGS` in the `MENU` package). If you have already created a pixmap and wish to attach it to a server image, you can use:

```
image = (Server_image)xv_set(NULL, SERVER_IMAGE,
    SERVER_IMAGE_PIXMAP,  pixmap,
    NULL);
```

The attribute `SERVER_IMAGE_PIXMAP` can also be used in `xv_get()` to return the `XID` of the pixmap associated with the `Server_image`.

Normally, a `Server_image` destroys its pixmap when a new pixmap is created using `SERVER_IMAGE_BITS`, `SERVER_IMAGE_X_BITS` or `SERVER_IMAGE_PIXMAP`. This default behavior can be turned off by setting the `SERVER_IMAGE_SAVE_PIXMAP` attribute to `TRUE`. Be sure to maintain a handle to the pixmap if you specify this attribute and destroy the `Server_image`.

If the depth of an image is unspecified, it defaults to 1. To create a color image, use `SERVER_IMAGE_DEPTH` to specify an alternate depth that can support color. You can also specify a colormap to use with this image by specifying `SERVER_IMAGE_COLORMAP`. This is used for multiplane color images and must be specified before the image bits are set. The colormap specified is assumed to have been created already including the `WIN_CMS_DATA` associated with the colormap name.

Example 15-2 demonstrates how to use a server image by creating a frame with a panel. On the panel is a button that uses a server image as the `PANEL_LABEL_IMAGE`. The bits used are the same as the *trash.icon* used above.

Example 15-2. The svrimage.c program

```
/*
 * svrimage.c -- demonstrate how a server image can be created and
 * used.  The "bits" used to create the image are taken arbitrarily
 * from <images/trash.icon>
 */
#include <xview/xview.h>
#include <xview/panel.h>
#include <xview/svrimage.h>
#include <X11/Xlib.h>

short image_bits[] =  {
    0x0000,0x0000, 0x0000,0x0000, 0x0000,0x0000, 0x0000,0x0000,
    0x0007,0xE000, 0x0004,0x2000, 0x03FF,0xFFC0, 0x0200,0x0040,
    0x02FF,0xFF40, 0x0080,0x0100, 0x00AA,0xAB00, 0x00AA,0xAB00,
    0x00AA,0xAB00, 0x00AA,0xAB00, 0x00AA,0xAB00, 0x00AA,0xAB00,
    0x00AA,0xAB00, 0x00AA,0xAB00, 0x00AA,0xAB00, 0x00AA,0xAB00,
    0x00AA,0xAB00, 0x00AA,0xAB00, 0x00AA,0xAB00, 0x00AA,0xAB00,
    0x00AA,0xAB00, 0x00AA,0xAB00, 0x00AA,0xAB00, 0x0091,0x1300,
    0x00C0,0x0200, 0x003F,0xFC00
};
```

Example 15-2. The svrimage.c program (continued)

```
main(argc, argv)
int      argc;
char     *argv[];
{
    Frame                   frame;
    Server_image            image;
    Panel                   panel;
    void                    exit();

    xv_init(XV_INIT_ARGC_PTR_ARGV, &argc, argv, NULL);

    image = (Server_image)xv_create(NULL, SERVER_IMAGE,
        XV_WIDTH,               32,
        XV_HEIGHT,              30,
        SERVER_IMAGE_BITS,      image_bits,
        NULL);

    frame = (Frame)xv_create(NULL, FRAME, NULL);
    panel = (Panel)xv_create(frame, PANEL, NULL);
    (void) xv_create(panel, PANEL_MESSAGE,
        PANEL_LABEL_IMAGE,      image,
        PANEL_NOTIFY_PROC,      exit,
        NULL);

    window_fit(panel);
    window_fit(frame);
    xv_main_loop(frame);
}
```

15.5 The FULLSCREEN Package

The FULLSCREEN package allows XView clients to grab the server for keyboard and/or pointer use either exclusively or nonexclusively with other applications. This package is used primarily to prompt the user for immediate feedback on a question or to notify the user of an error that needs attention. Typically, the user responds with a button press or a keyboard event. The NOTICE package uses the FULLSCREEN package extensively to implement its functionality. In most cases, you need nothing more than the NOTICE package and should rarely need to use the FULLSCREEN package. The need for this package arises if you choose to implement your own notice or perhaps a user interface item that is not OPEN LOOK-compliant. In either case, this is advanced usage and is beyond the scope of this book. Using the FULLSCREEN package can be very dangerous because it uses the X server's grabbing functions in Xlib. It is possible to get into a state from which you cannot get out except by killing the server remotely or rebooting your workstation. When using a debugger, be extremely careful that you do not set breakpoints within code when the server is in the middle of a grab of some kind. Whatever you do, *do not step through code that creates a* FULLSCREEN *instance*. If this is unavoidable, you should prepare for it by making sure that you have remote access to your workstation or by attaching a terminal to it so you can kill the debugger to free the server.

The flow of control for client code using the FULLSCREEN package is to create a fullscreen instance (grabbing the server), scan for a particular event and destroy the fullscreen instance (freeing the server).

Creating a fullscreen object (grabbing the server) involves xv_create() as usual:

```
Fullscreen fs;

fs = xv_create(owner, FULLSCREEN, NULL);
```

The owner in this case may be a visible XView object that has a window associated with it* and is currently displayed on the screen (e.g., XV_SHOW is TRUE). If owner is NULL, then the root window of the default screen is used as the owner.

Example 15-3 uses the FULLSCREEN package. A simple panel with two panel buttons is created. The Quit button quits the program, and the Fullscreen button calls the grab() routine that grabs the server using the FULLSCREEN package and waits for a button to be pressed. Once this happens, the routine frees the fullscreen object, thus releasing the server. In the default case, there is no event mask that the FULLSCREEN package has been instructed to allow to pass through to the client, so event types should be specified in the creation call. Similarly, since the call to xv_input_readevent() is used, a similar input mask should be set up.†

Example 15-3. The fullscreen.c program

```
/*
 * fullscreen.c
 * Demonstrate the fullscreen package.  Create a panel button that
 * creates a fullscreen instance, thus grabbing the X server.  User
 * presses a mouse button to release the server.
 */
#include <xview/xview.h>
#include <xview/panel.h>
#include <xview/fullscreen.h>

main(argc, argv)
char *argv[];
{
    Frame        frame;
    Panel        panel;
    void         exit(), grab();

    xv_init(XV_INIT_ARGC_PTR_ARGV, &argc, argv, NULL);

    frame = (Frame)xv_create(XV_NULL, FRAME, NULL);
    panel = (Panel)xv_create(frame, PANEL, NULL);
    (void) xv_create(panel, PANEL_BUTTON,
        PANEL_LABEL_STRING,    "Quit",
        PANEL_NOTIFY_PROC,     exit,
        NULL);
    (void) xv_create(panel, PANEL_BUTTON,
        PANEL_LABEL_STRING,    "Fullscreen",
        PANEL_NOTIFY_PROC,     grab,
        NULL);
```

---

*This does not include panel items.

†See Chapter 6, *Handling Input*, for more information about xv_input_readevent().

Example 15-3. The fullscreen.c program (continued)

```
        window_fit(panel);
        window_fit(frame);
        xv_main_loop(frame);
}
/*
 * Notify procedure for when the "Fullscreen" button is pushed.
 * Create a fullscreen instance, scan for a button event, then
 * destroy it.
 */
void
grab(item, event)
Panel_item item;
Event *event;
{
        Panel           panel = (Panel)xv_get(item, PANEL_PARENT_PANEL);
        Frame           frame = (Frame)xv_get(panel, XV_OWNER);
        Fullscreen      fs;
        Inputmask       im;

        /* set up an input mask for the call to xv_input_readevent(). */
        win_setinputcodebit(&im, MS_LEFT);
        win_setinputcodebit(&im, MS_MIDDLE);
        win_setinputcodebit(&im, MS_RIGHT);
        win_setinputcodebit(&im, LOC_MOVE);

        /*
         * Create a fullscreen object (initialize X server grab).
         * Specify which events should be allowed to pass through.
         * These events should match the input mask coded above.
         */
        fs = xv_create(panel, FULLSCREEN,
            WIN_CONSUME_EVENTS,
                WIN_MOUSE_BUTTONS, LOC_MOVE, NULL,
            NULL);

        /* Loop till user generates a button event */
        while (xv_input_readevent(panel, event, TRUE, TRUE, &im) != -1)
            if (event_is_button(event))
                break;

        /* Destroy the fullscreen (release the X server grab) */
        xv_destroy(fs);

        /* Report which button was pushed. */
        printf("event was button %d (%d, %d)\n",
            event_id(event) - BUT_FIRST+1,
            event_x(event) + (int)xv_get(frame, XV_X),
            event_y(event) + (int)xv_get(frame, XV_Y));
}
```

When this program is run and the user selects the Fullscreen panel item, the X server is grabbed and the user must select one of the mouse buttons to release it. To users, it may appear as though they can select another panel button. Although the panel window is the owner of the fullscreen object, events that occur while the server is grabbed by the fullscreen object are *not* propagated to XView objects under the pointer. In Example 15-3, if the user presses the button on top of a panel button while in fullscreen, the button-*down* event will trigger the call to `xv_input_readevent()` and break the loop. The corresponding but-ton-up event is not read yet and will get read by normal event processing after the call to `grab()` returns. If the button-up event happened over a panel button, then the panel button's notify routine will be called.

The event masks set by the FULLSCREEN package and by the `Inputmask` do not interfere with the event masks in any XView window.

Debugging and the FULLSCREEN Package

There are four global variables in the FULLSCREEN package that can be used to help debug XView programs that grab the server, keyboard or pointer. Note that these variables can only be used via the FULLSCREEN package. Here are the variables with their default values:

```
int fullscreendebug = 0;
int fullscreengrabserver = 1;
int fullscreengrabpointer = 1;
int fullscreengrabkbd = 1;
```

When `fullscreengrabserver` is set to 0 (in source code or in debugger), the X server will *not* be grabbed despite requests to grab it.

When `fullscreengrabpointer` is set to 0, the pointer will *not* be grabbed despite requests to grab it.

When `fullscreengrabkbd` is set to 0, the keyboard will *not* be grabbed despite requests to grab it.

When `fullscreendebug` is set to 1, no grabs of any kind are performed.

15.6 Nonvisual Package Summary

There are no nonvisual procedures or macros. Table 15-1 lists the attributes in the SCREEN, SERVER and SERVERIMAGE packages. Table 15-2 lists the attributes in the FULLSCREEN package. This information is described fully in Appendix A, *Attribute Summary*.

Table 15-1. Screen, Server and Server Image Attributes

Screen Attributes	Server Attributes	Server Image Attributes
SCREEN_NUMBER	SERVER_NTH_SCREEN	SERVER_IMAGE_BITS
SCREEN_SERVER	SERVER_SYNC	SERVER_IMAGE_COLORMAP
	SERVER_SYNC_AND_PROCESS_EVENTS	SERVER_IMAGE_DEPTH
	XV_NAME	XV_HEIGHT
		XV_WIDTH

Table 15-2. Fullscreen Attributes

Fullscreen Attributes

FULLSCREEN_ALLOW_EVENTS	FULLSCREEN_KEYBOARD_GRAB_PTR_MODE
FULLSCREEN_ALLOW_SYNC_EVENT	FULLSCREEN_INPUT_WINDOW
FULLSCREEN_COLORMAP_WINDOW	FULLSCREEN_OWNER_EVENTS
FULLSCREEN_CURSOR_WINDOW	FULLSCREEN_PAINT_WINDOW
FULLSCREEN_GRAB_KEYBOARD	FULLSCREEN_POINTER_GRAB_KBD_MODE
FULLSCREEN_GRAB_POINTER	FULLSCREEN_POINTER_GRAB_PTR_MODE
FULLSCREEN_GRAB_SERVER	FULLSCREEN_RECT
FULLSCREEN_KEYBOARD_GRAB_KBD_MODE	FULLSCREEN_SYNC

16

Fonts

In This Chapter:

Fonts

16
Fonts

In X, a large number of fonts are provided on the server. Deciding which font to use and then trying to specify fonts by name can be difficult since there are many different styles and sizes of fonts. Most fonts are used to render text strings, so the images, or *glyphs*, represent a character set defined mostly by the English language. However, a font may be built to support glyphs for other languages or to provide a set of glyphs that have nothing to do with a language. Fonts are stored on the server and are associated with the display of your workstation. The *font ID* is stored in the graphics context (GC), which is used by Xlib functions like `XDrawString()`. Using fonts to render text is perhaps the most common application. For example, the `Courier` font family displays the classic typewriter or constant-width character set. This text is set in Times-Roman, a proportionally spaced font. Often within a font family, there are different styles, such as **bold** or *italic*, and different point sizes.* For example, *Helvetica bold 14* refers to the Helvetica font family; bold is the style and 14 is the point size.

Not all server fonts have a variety of styles and sizes. These special-purpose fonts are generally specified by name only—there are no corresponding styles or families for these fonts.

When accessing fonts, you typically want to specify a font either by *name* or by the *family*, *style* and *size* or *scale* of the font. In addition, XView provides an interface for determining the dimensions (in pixels) of characters and strings rendered in a specified font.

OPEN LOOK uses predefined fonts for certain items such as panel buttons and other user interface elements. These items cannot be changed, but you can assign fonts to panel choices, text subwindows and other types of windows. We will address these issues later in this chapter.

---

*Note that point sizes on workstations are based on pixels, whereas point sizes for typesetters and printers are based on inches.

16.1 Creating Fonts

Applications that use the FONT package must include the header file, *<xview/font.h>*. In XView, when a font object is created, it loads the font from the X server. When we say, "create a font," we really mean, "load a font from the server and create an XView font object associated with that font."

While fonts can be created using xv_create(), it may not be necessary to create a new instance of a font. Fonts are typically cached on the server, and XView may already have a handle to a particular font. Therefore, you would obtain a handle to the font, if it already exists, rather than open another instance of the same font. xv_find() can be used to return the handle of an existing font. If the handle does not exist, xv_find() can create a new instance of the font. In general, if the attribute is set to False, xv_find() does *not* create a new object.

Both xv_find() and xv_create() will return an object of the type Xv_Font when using the FONT package. The form of the call is:

```
Xv_Font font;
font = (Xv_Font) xv_create(parent, FONT, attrs, NULL);
```

Or:

```
Xv_Font font;
font = (Xv_Font) xv_find(parent, FONT, attrs, NULL);
```

The *parent* of the font is usually the window in which the font is going to be used. Fonts may be used on any window or in memory pixmaps or Server_image, but these objects must have the same display associated with them as the font or you will get an X Protocol error. If the parent is NULL, the default server is used. Otherwise, the server as determined from the parent object is used. This is only an issue if your XView application is running on several servers at the same time.

Once a font object is created, it can be used to render text by assigning the font's XV_XID to the font field of a graphics context (GC) and then using any of the Xlib routines that use fonts such as XDrawString(). Example 16-1 lists *simple_font.c*, a program that builds a simple frame and canvas. The repaint routine for the canvas displays the string "Hello World" at the upper-left corner of the window.

Example 16-1. The simple_font.c program

```
/*
 * simple_font.c -- very simple program showing how to render text
 * using a font gotten from xv_find().  Hello World is printed in
 * the upper-left corner of a canvas window.
 */
#include <stdio.h>
#include <X11/X.h>
#include <X11/Xlib.h>    /* X.h and Xlib.h used for Xlib graphics */
#include <xview/xview.h>
#include <xview/canvas.h>
#include <xview/font.h>
#include <xview/xv_xrect.h>
```

Example 16-1. The simple_font.c program (continued)

```
#define GC_KEY  10 /* any arbitrary number -- used for XV_KEY_DATA */
main(argc, argv)
int       argc;
char      *argv[];
{
    Frame          frame;
    Canvas         canvas;
    XGCValues      gcvalues;
    Xv_Font        font;
    void           my_repaint_proc();
    Display        *dpy;
    GC             gc;

    xv_init(XV_INIT_ARGC_PTR_ARGV, &argc, argv, NULL);

    frame = (Frame)xv_create(XV_NULL, FRAME, NULL);

    canvas = (Canvas)xv_create(frame, CANVAS,
        XV_WIDTH,              400,
        XV_HEIGHT,             200,
        CANVAS_X_PAINT_WINDOW, TRUE,
        CANVAS_REPAINT_PROC,   my_repaint_proc,
        NULL);
    window_fit(frame);

    dpy = (Display *)xv_get(frame, XV_DISPLAY);
    font = (Xv_Font)xv_find(frame, FONT, FONT_NAME, "courier", NULL);
    if (!font) {
        fprintf(stderr, "%s: cannot use font: courier.\n", argv[0]);
        font = (Xv_Font)xv_get(frame, XV_FONT);
    }
    /* Create a GC to use with Xlib graphics -- set the fg/bg colors
     * and set the Font, which is the XV_XID of the XView font object.
     */
    gcvalues.font = (Font)xv_get(font, XV_XID);
    gcvalues.foreground = BlackPixel(dpy, DefaultScreen(dpy));
    gcvalues.background = WhitePixel(dpy, DefaultScreen(dpy));
    gcvalues.graphics_exposures = False;
    gc = XCreateGC(dpy, RootWindow(dpy, DefaultScreen(dpy)),
        GCForeground | GCBackground | GCFont | GCGraphicsExposures,
        &gcvalues);

    /* Assign the gc to the canvas object so we can use the same
     * gc each time we draw into the canvas.  Also avoids a global
     * variable to store the GC.
     */
    xv_set(canvas, XV_KEY_DATA, GC_KEY, gc, NULL);
    xv_main_loop(frame);
}
/*
 * Called every time the window needs repainting.
 */
void
my_repaint_proc(canvas, pw, dpy, xwin, xrects)
Canvas            canvas;
Xv_Window         pw;
```

Example 16-1. The simple_font.c program (continued)

```
Display          *dpy;
Window           xwin;
Xv_xrectlist     *xrects;
{
    GC gc = (GC)xv_get(canvas, XV_KEY_DATA, GC_KEY);

    XDrawString(dpy, xwin, gc, 10, 20,
        "Hello World", 11); /* 11 = strlen("Hello World") */
}
```

The program attempts to create the font named "courier."* If the font is not found, the frame's font is used as a backup. This font must exist, so there is no need to check for a failed return value.

Since the text is rendered using Xlib graphics, we need to use a GC that has the right attributes set: the foreground and background colors and a font. Because this GC is specifically used for the canvas window, we are going to *attach* the GC to the canvas by using the generic attribute XV_KEY_DATA. Using a unique key, GC_KEY (which can be any integer since no other keys have been assigned to the object yet), the GC is attached with the call:

```
    xv_set(canvas, XV_KEY_DATA, GC_KEY, gc, NULL);
```

Later, in my_repaint_proc(), the GC is retrieved:

```
    GC gc = (GC)xv_get(canvas, XV_KEY_DATA, GC_KEY);
```

This method of storing the GC by using XV_KEY_DATA avoids the need for a global variable.

When creating some fonts, it may take quite some time for the font to be found and completely loaded—especially large fonts, since they may be created at run time. Loading the font may result in the user having to wait longer than expected. It is recommended that the application provide visual feedback if the user must wait for some time. Do this by setting the FRAME_BUSY attribute to TRUE for the parent frame:

```
    xv_set(frame, FRAME_BUSY, TRUE, NULL);
    font = (Xv_Font) xv_find(frame, FONT,
        FONT_NAME,  "Courier-22",
        NULL);
    xv_set(frame, FRAME_BUSY, FALSE, NULL);
```

This code fragment attempts to create a 22-point size font. Note that not all servers can do so, either because of memory limitations or because the server cannot scale fonts at will. In this case, the font returned may be NULL.

---

*Font names are case-sensitive—courier and Courier are two different fonts.

16.1.1 Font Families and Styles

One way to create fonts is to specify a font family, style and size. The family of a font describes its basic characteristics. Figure 16-1 shows the Courier family in different styles and a range of point sizes.

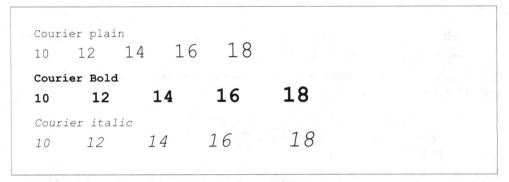

Figure 16-1. The Courier font in different styles and sizes

Some font families and styles known to XView are predefined in *<xview/font.h>*. To use a font other than the ones listed, you may specify any font family and style known by your X server. You may also specify fonts by *name* (see Section 16.1.4, "Fonts by Name"). The list of XView font families include:

- `FONT_FAMILY_DEFAULT`
- `FONT_FAMILY_DEFAULT_FIXEDWIDTH`
- `FONT_FAMILY_LUCIDA`
- `FONT_FAMILY_LUCIDA_FIXEDWIDTH`
- `FONT_FAMILY_ROMAN`
- `FONT_FAMILY_SERIF`
- `FONT_FAMILY_COUR`
- `FONT_FAMILY_OLGLYPH`*
- `FONT_FAMILY_OLCURSOR`*

The `FONT_FAMILY_DEFAULT` font is the default font for the server. This may be redefined depending on how the X server has been configured. The `FONT_FAMILY_DEFAULT_FIXEDWIDTH` font is guaranteed to be a fixed-width font, regardless of the kind of font used as the default font. All the characters in fixed-width fonts occupy the same amount of space. Other fonts are proportionally spaced; that is, each character occupies a different amount of space.

---

*The families `FONT_FAMILY_OLGLYPH` and `FONT_FAMILY_OLCURSOR` are used by the SCROLLBAR and CURSOR packages, respectively. They are not for general/public use.

The available styles are:

- `FONT_STYLE_DEFAULT`
- `FONT_STYLE_NORMAL`
- `FONT_STYLE_BOLD`
- `FONT_STYLE_ITALIC`
- `FONT_STYLE_BOLD_ITALIC`

The default style indicates the default for that particular font family—this style may be any of the other styles (normal, bold, italic or bold-italic).

The call to `xv_find()` in *simple_font.c* could have been written to specify the family and style of the font rather than the name of the font:

```
font = (Xv_Font)xv_find(frame, FONT,
    FONT_FAMILY,    FONT_FAMILY_COUR,
    FONT_STYLE,     FONT_STYLE_NORMAL,
    NULL);
```

Since normal is the default style of the font, this example renders the same font as in the earlier example. However, we could specify a different style:

```
font = (Xv_Font)xv_find(frame, FONT,
    FONT_FAMILY,    FONT_FAMILY_COUR,
    FONT_STYLE,     FONT_STYLE_BOLD,
    NULL);
```

This call returns a bold style of the Courier font. For most font families, you can specify a font family with any style, although some families may not support an italic or bold style of the font. Therefore, you should be prepared to handle a `NULL` return from the call to `xv_create()` or `xv_find()`:

```
if (!(font = (Xv_Font)xv_find(canvas, FONT,
    FONT_FAMILY,    FONT_FAMILY_FIXED,
    FONT_STYLE,     FONT_STYLE_ITALIC,
    NULL))) {
    /* Handle the case where the font fails. */
    font = (Xv_Font)xv_get(canvas, XV_FONT);
}
```

16.1.2 Font Sizes

Fonts can be specified in any size from one point on up, as long as there is enough memory in the server to support the font in that size. The server must also support scalable fonts. When a size is specified, provided the font is not already loaded, a new font is created at run time according to the family and style in the size specified, as below:

```
Xv_Font font;

font = (Xv_Font)xv_find(canvas, FONT,
    FONT_FAMILY,      FONT_FAMILY_ROMAN,
    FONT_STYLE,       FONT_STYLE_BOLD,
    FONT_SIZE,        36,
    NULL);
```

This code fragment attempts to find or create a font from the Times-Roman font family, in bold and in 36 point. The font may already exist in the server, or the font's family may exist but not the size. In the latter case, the server must attempt to scale the font to the specified size. If the font cannot be created because of memory limitations, the call to xv_find() will return NULL. Because a 36-point font takes a lot of memory, it might take a while to load this font.

16.1.3 Scaling Fonts

Bitmapped fonts are not scalable, but they are provided in so many sizes that they appear to be scalable to any size. On the other hand, some fonts are scalable because they are not stored as static bitmaps. However, in order to scale even these fonts, the server must support font scaling. Sun's *xnews* server is an example of such a server.

When fonts are created, four additional sizes of the font are created as well, if they fall within the constraints specified above. You can request a relative scale of a font with respect to other fonts within the same family. The relative scales are *small*, *medium*, *large* and *extra large*. These scales are represented by the attributes WIN_SCALE_SMALL, WIN_SCALE_MEDIUM, WIN_SCALE_LARGE and WIN_SCALE_EXTRALARGE.

These attributes are members of the enumerated type Window_rescale_state. They are WINDOW attributes because fonts can be scaled in proportion to their windows. For example, if your application is resized to a larger or smaller size, you may wish to reset the fonts for some windows according to different scaling sizes. By default, the sizes of the fonts corresponding to the scale is as follows:

Attribute	Font Size
WIN_SCALE_SMALL	10
WIN_SCALE_MEDIUM	12
WIN_SCALE_LARGE	14
WIN_SCALE_EXTRALARGE	19

If FONT_SIZE is not specified, then, when a font is requested, the size will correspond to the *medium* scale size. Specifying the font size overrides the request for a scaling factor. The code fragment below requests a font from the Lucida family with an italic style in large scale:

```
Xv_Font    font;

font = (Xv_Font)xv_find(canvas, FONT,
    FONT_FAMILY,      FONT_FAMILY_LUCIDA,
```

```
        FONT_STYLE,        FONT_STYLE_ITALIC,
        FONT_SCALE,        WIN_SCALE_LARGE,
        NULL);
```

If you have already created a font and wish to get it in a different scale, the attribute
FONT_RESCALE_OF is specified with two values: a font and a Window_ rescale_state.

```
    Xv_Font   font, small_font;

    font = (Xv_Font)xv_find(canvas, FONT,
        FONT_FAMILY,       FONT_FAMILY_LUCIDA,
        FONT_STYLE,        FONT_STYLE_BOLD,
        NULL);

    . . .

    small_font = (Xv_Font)xv_find(canvas, FONT,
        FONT_RESCALE_OF,    font, WIN_SCALE_SMALL,
        NULL);
```

When a font is created for the first time, it has at least four sizes corresponding to the scaling
factors mentioned above. Thus, when requesting a scaled version of an existing font, it is
very important to use xv_find() rather than xv_create(); this chances are that the font
exists for that scaling factor. Using xv_create() may create an unnecessary new version
of the font.

You can reset the sizes of fonts' scale factors by using the attribute FONT_SIZES_
FOR_SCALE. This attribute takes four *values* that correspond to each scaling factor:

```
    font = (Xv_Font)xv_find(canvas, FONT,
        FONT_FAMILY,          FONT_LUCIDA,
        FONT_STYLE,           FONT_STYLE_NORMAL,
        FONT_SIZES_FOR_SCALE, 12, 14, 16, 22,
        NULL);
```

In this example, the Lucida font is created so that the small, medium, large and extra-large
scaling sizes are 12, 14, 16 and 22, respectively. The font size returned is 14-point.

16.1.4 Fonts by Name

When specifying a font by name, the entire name of the font is given as it appears in the output of a program such as *xlsfonts* or by the Xlib call XListFonts().* These programs provide a complete list of all the fonts available to the server.

In Example 16-1 above, the program *simple_font.c* showed how to load a font using a given
name:

```
    font = (Xv_Font) xv_find(canvas, FONT, FONT_NAME, "Courier", NULL);
```

When specifying fonts by name, you cannot specify a family, style, scale or size; these attributes are ignored in favor of the font name. However, in some cases, you can specify style
and size attributes as part of the name of the font. For example, to create a Courier font, you
can specify the font named "Courier":

---

*See Volume Two, *Xlib Reference Manual*, for a description of XListFonts().

```
font = (Xv_Font) xv_find(canvas, FONT,
    FONT_NAME,      "Courier",
    NULL);
```

You can also specify a style along with the font family:

```
font = (Xv_Font) xv_find(canvas, FONT,
    FONT_NAME,      "Courier-boldoblique",
    NULL);
```

This creates a bold-italic, 16-point font from the Courier family. Of course, if you have chosen to use the family/style method of specifying fonts, then you can use xv_get() with the attribute FONT_NAME to get the name of the returned font. For example, if you created a font in the following manner:

```
Xv_Font     font;
font = (Xv_Font) xv_create(frame, FONT,
    FONT_FAMILY,    FONT_FAMILY_COUR,
    FONT_STYLE,     FONT_STYLE_BOLD_ITALIC,
    NULL);
```

you could retrieve the name of the font just created by calling:

```
char *name = (char *)xv_get(font, FONT_NAME);
```

This call would return the string "Courier-boldoblique".

16.2 Font Dimensions

Once a font is created, it can be used in applications using Xlib routines, as demonstrated in *simple_font.c* earlier in this chapter. In the program, text is rendered using the Xlib routine XDrawString(). This routine uses the font ID from the GC parameter. This ID is extracted from the font using xv_get() and XV_XID. You can also get a pointer to the font's XFontStruct structure by specifying the attribute FONT_INFO to xv_get(). This data structure is what describes the characteristics of the font such as width and height for each character. See Volume One, *Xlib Programming Manual*, for more information.

You can get information about the sizes of individual characters or the dimensions of entire strings of characters in a particular font using several methods. You can use the information in the XFontStruct data structure obtained from the font, or you can use Xlib routines such as XTextWidth() or XTextExtents(), or you can use xv_get() along with XView attributes such as FONT_CHAR_WIDTH, FONT_CHAR_HEIGHT, FONT_DEFAULT_CHAR_HEIGHT, FONT_DEFAULT_CHAR_WIDTH and FONT_STRING_DIMS.

The usage is as follows:

```
Xv_Font     font;
int         width, height;
```

The following code shows how to get the dimensions of a particular character in a font:

```
width  = (int)xv_get(font, FONT_CHAR_WIDTH, 'm');
height = (int)xv_get(font, FONT_CHAR_HEIGHT, 'm');
```

The calls to `xv_get()` return the width and height of the characters in pixels for that particular font. If you are using a fixed-width font, then each character will be the same width, so you can specify the default character width and height of the font. The following code shows how to get the dimensions of characters for a fixed-width font:

```
Xv_Font font;
int width, height;

width  = (int)xv_get(font, FONT_DEFAULT_CHAR_WIDTH);
height = (int)xv_get(font, FONT_DEFAULT_CHAR_HEIGHT);
```

If you use `FONT_DEFAULT_CHAR_WIDTH` (or height) on a variable-width font, you will get the *average* width of a character in that font.

To get the width and height dimensions of a complete string of text in a given font, use the `FONT_STRING_DIMS` attribute:

```
extern Xv_Font       font;
Font_string_dims  dims;

(void) xv_get(font, FONT_STRING_DIMS, "Hello World", &dims);
```

In this case, the call to `xv_get()` returns a pointer to the `dims` structure passed as the last argument. The return value may be ignored since the `dims` parameter will have the value filled in upon return of `xv_get()`. The `Font_string_dims` data structure is as follows:

```
typedef struct {
    int   width;
    int   height;
} Font_string_dims;
```

Thus, the `xv_get()` returns the dimensions of the string for the font specified. This would be equivalent to calling `XTextExtents()` in the manner below:

```
Font_string_dims dims;
extern char    *str;
int             len = strlen(str);
extern Xv_Font font;
XFontStruct    *font_info = (XFontStruct *)xv_get(font, FONT_INFO);
int             direction, ascent, descent;
XCharStruct     overall_return;

(void) XTextExtents(font_info, str, len,
          &direction, &ascent, &descent, &overall_return);

dims.width = overall_return.width;
dims.height = ascent + descent;
```

16.3 Font Package Summary

There are no procedures or macros in the FONT package. The attributes it contains are listed below. They are described fully in Appendix A, *Attribute Summary*.

```
FONT_CHAR_HEIGHT
FONT_CHAR_WIDTH
FONT_DEFAULT_CHAR_HEIGHT
FONT_DEFAULT_CHAR_WIDTH
FONT_FAMILY
FONT_RESCALE_OF
FONT_SCALE
FONT_SIZE
FONT_SIZES_FOR_SCALE
FONT_STRING_DIMS
FONT_STYLE
```

17

Resources

In This Chapter:

17
Resources

In the X Window System, the user can configure the interface according to options available in specific applications. The user accomplishes this through a *resource database* that resides in the X server. The X Protocol provides many ways to access the resource database, as well as many functions to aid in this task. You should consult Chapter 11, *Managing User Preferences*, in Volume One, *Xlib Programming Manual*, for a complete, in-depth discussion of X resource specification and management. Related programs include *xrdb*, and related functions can be found in Volume Two, *Xlib Reference Manual*.

XView provides many functions that allow the programmer to interact with the server to get or set resources specified by the user. Robust applications should account for user-definable defaults. That is, your programs should always consider the user's wishes for changing attribute values for things like fonts, colors and maybe even window sizes, as long as the values do not interfere with the normal running of the program. You should also provide the user with a list of resources that can be set, and you should test for them in your application.

17.1 Predefined Defaults

All of the packages in XView look for predefined defaults that the user can set in his/her resource environment. Table 17-1 outlines these defaults, their types and legal values. Note that the term *maxint* refers to the maximum value for an integer on your particular machine. These values tend to be rather large with respect to the intended values used by these resources. It is up to the user to use "reasonable" values.

Table 17-1. Resources and Default Values Understood by XView

Name	Type	Default	Legal Values
alarm.audible	boolean	True	True, False
alarm.visible	boolean	True	True, False
cmdtool.checkpointFrequency	integer	0	0, *<maxint>*
cmdtool.maxLogFileSize	integer	*<maxint>*	0, *<maxint>*
font.name	string	NULL	*fontname-size*
icon.font.name	string	NULL	*fontname-size*

Name	Type	Default	Legal Values
icon.pixmap	**string**	NULL	*pixmap filename*
icon.footer	**string**	NULL	*footer string*
icon.x	**integer**	0	—
icon.y	**integer**	0	—
keyboard.arrowKeys	**string**	Yes	Yes, No
keyboard.leftHanded	**string**	No	Yes, No
mouse.multiclick.space	**integer**		
notice.PopupJumpCursor	**boolean**	True	True, False
notice.beepCount	**integer**	1	—
openWindows.DragRightDistance	**integer**	100	0, <maxint>
openWindows.3DLook.color	**boolean**	True	True, False
openWindows.3DLook.monochrome	**boolean**	True	True, False
openWindows.multiClickTimeout	**integer**	4	1 through 10 (in sec/10)
openWindows.dragRightDistance	**integer**	5	—
openWindows.scrollbarPlacement	**string**	right	Left, Right
scrollbar.repeatDelay	**integer**	100	0, 999 (msec delay interval)
scrollbar.pageInterval	**integer**	100	0, 999 (msec delay interval)
scrollbar.lineInterval	**integer**	1	0, 999 (msec delay interval)
server.name	**string**	getenv(DISPLAY)	*hostnamedisplay*
term.boldStyle	**string**	Invert	xview.ICCCMCompliant@boolean@True@True, False None, OFFSET_X, OFFSET_Y, OFFSET_X_AND_Y, OFFSET_X_AND_XY, OFFSET_Y_AND_XY, OFFSET_X_AND_Y_AND_XY, OFFSET_XY, INVERT
term.enableEdit	**boolean**	True	True, False
term.inverseStyle	**string**	Enable	ENABLED, DISABLED, SAME_AS_BOLD
term.underlineStyle	**string**	Enable	ENABLED, DISABLED, SAME_AS_BOLD
text.againLimit	**integer**	1	0, 500
text.autoIndent	**boolean**	False	True, False
text.autoScrollBy	**integer**	1	0, 100
text.blinkcaret	**boolean**	True	True, False
text.checkpointFrequency	**integer**	0	0, <maxint>
text.confirmOverwrite	**boolean**	True	True, False
text.displayControlChars	**boolean**	False	True, False
text.enableScrollbar	**boolean**	True	True, False
text.extrasMenuFilename	**string**	*.text_extra_menu* (in /usr/lib)	*filename*
text.insertMakesCaretVisible	**string**	If_auto_scroll	If_auto_scroll, Always
text.lineBreak	**string**	Wrap_word	Clip, Wrap_char, Wrap_word

Name	Type	Default	Legal Values
text.margin.bottom	integer	0	–1, 50
text.margin.left	integer	8	0, 2000
text.margin.right	integer	0	0, 2000
text.margin.top	integer	2	–1, 50
text.maxDocumentSize	integer	20000	0, 0x80000000
text.retained	boolean	False	True, False
text.storeChangesFile	boolean	True	True, False
text.tabWidth	integer	8	0, 50
text.undoLimit	integer	50	0, 500
window.color.foreground	string	"0 0 0"	3 RGB values, 0-255
window.color.background	string	"255 255 255"	3 RGB values, 0-255
window.columns	integer	80	—
window.height	integer	34 rows	Greater than 0
window.header	string	NULL	*header string*
window.iconic	boolean	False	True, False
window.inheritcolor	integer	1	
window.mono.disableRetained	boolean	False	True, False
window.rows	integer	34	—
window.scale	string	Medium	Small, Medium, Large, Extra_Large
window.width	integer	80 columns	Greater than 0
window.x	integer	0	—
window.y	integer	0	—

XView provides many functions to get resource values from the database. Basically, values come in several types: `int`, `character` (strings), `boolean` (which can be specified using a number of string values; see below) and `enumerated` values.

Example 17-1 lists a simple application that introduces the use of one of the functions provided by the `defaults` package. The program *default_text.c* creates a frame with a text subwindow whose font is specified by the user's resource `textsw.font`.

Example 17-1. The default_text.c program

```
/*
 * default_text.c -- use the defaults package to get a font name from
 * the resource database to set the textsw's font.
 */
#include <xview/xview.h>
#include <xview/font.h>
#include <xview/defaults.h>
#include <xview/textsw.h>

main(argc, argv)
char *argv[];
{
    Frame       frame;
    Xv_Font     font;
```

Example 17-1. The default_text.c program (continued)

```
    char        *name;

    xv_init(XV_INIT_ARGC_PTR_ARGV, &argc, argv, NULL);

    frame = (Frame)xv_create(NULL, FRAME, NULL);

    name = defaults_get_string("textsw.font","Textsw.Font", "fixed"),
    font = xv_find(frame, FONT,
        FONT_NAME,      name,
        NULL);

    xv_create(frame, TEXTSW,
        XV_FONT,        font,
        WIN_COLUMNS,    80,
        WIN_ROWS,       10,
        NULL);

    window_fit(frame);
    xv_main_loop(frame);
}
```

default_text.c shows how an XView program queries the resource database for a string value associated with a name-class pair. `defaults_get_string()` gets the string value associated with `Textsw.Font`. If the resource database has this attribute, then the value is returned. If not, the default (`fixed`) is returned.

17.2 XView Resource Database Functions

The functions that XView provides are defined in *<xview/defaults.h>*. The following functions are provided by XView for setting and getting resource values to and from the database. Note that when setting resources *to* the database, the database on the *server* is updated—not the user's *defaults* database. Resources not updated to the user's defaults database are not retained for the next time the X server is started.

```
    void
    defaults_init_db()
```

This function is called automatically by `xv_init()`, so it need not be called by your application. `defaults_init_db()` calls `XrmInitialize()`.

```
    void
    defaults_load_db(filename)
        char *filename;
```

`defaults_load_db()` loads the database residing in the specified filename or the server database if filename is NULL. The database found in `filename` is loaded via `XrmGetFile-Database()` and is merged into the existing resource database via `XrmMerge-Databases()`.

```
    void
    defaults_store_db(filename)
        char *filename;
```

This function writes the database to the specified file via `XrmPutFileDatabase()`. This must be done in order to ensure that the database is accessible the next time the server is started.*

```
Bool
defaults_exists(name, class)
    char *name;
    char *class;
```

This function returns TRUE if the resource exists in the database via `XrmGetResource()`.

17.2.1 Boolean Resources

```
Bool
defaults_get_boolean(name, class, default_value)
    char *name, *class;
    int    default_value;

void
defaults_set_boolean(resource, value)
    char *resource;
    Bool  value;
```

`defaults_get_boolean()` looks up the name-class pair in the resource database and returns TRUE if the value is one of:
- `True`
- `Yes`
- `On`
- `Enabled`
- `Set`
- `Activated`
- `1`

It returns FALSE if the value is one of:
- `False`
- `No`
- `Off`
- `Disabled`
- `Reset`
- `Cleared`
- `Deactivated`
- `0`

If the value is none of the above, a warning message will be displayed and the default value will be returned. If the resource is not found, no error message is printed but the default value is still returned.

`defaults_set_boolean()` sets the resource to the value specified.

---

*The file *Xdefaults* in the user's home directory is a good candidate for *filename*.

17.2.2 Integer Resources

```
int
defaults_get_integer(name, class, default_value)
    char *name;
    char *class;
    int   default_value;

int
defaults_get_integer_check(name, class, default_value,
                           minimum, maximum)
    char *name;
    char *class;
    int   default_value;
    int   minimum;
    int   maximum;

void
defaults_set_integer(resource, value)
    char *resource;
    int   value;
```

defaults_get_integer() looks up the name-class pair in the resource database and returns the resulting integer value. If the database does not contain the resource, the default value is returned.

defaults_get_integer_check() looks up the name-class pair in the resource database and returns the resulting integer value. If the value in the database is not between the values minimum and maximum (inclusive), an error message is printed and the default value is returned. If the resource is not found, no error message is printed but the default value is returned.

defaults_set_integer() sets the resource to the value specified.

17.2.3 Character Resources

```
char
defaults_get_character(name, class, default_char)
    char *name;
    char *class;
    char  default_char;

void
defaults_set_character(resource, character)
    char *resource;
    char  character;
```

defaults_get_character() looks up the name-class pair in the resource database and returns the resulting character value. If the resource is not found, then the default character value is returned.

defaults_set_character() sets the resource to the character value.

17.2.4 String Resources

```
char *
defaults_get_string(name, class, default_str)
    char *name;
    char *class;
    char *default_str;
void
defaults_set_string(resource, string)
    char *resource;
    char *string;
```

`defaults_get_string()` returns the string value associated with the specified name-class pair in the resource database. If the resource is not found, the default string value is returned.

`defaults_set_character()` sets the resource to the specified string.

17.2.5 Enumerated Resources

Enumerated resources are those whose values are string values, but the legal values for the resource are restricted to a predefined list. For example, say you want to allow the user to specify the font scale for the font `lucidasans`. The legal `scale` values are: small, medium, large and extra large. You could use `defaults_get_string()` and determine, using `strcmp()`, whether the value returned is one of the legal scale values. Or you could use `defaults_get_enum()` and pass in a table describing the legal values. The *table* is an array of elements of the type:

```
typedef struct _default_pairs {
    char   *name; /* Name of pair */
    int     value; /* Value of pair */
} Defaults_pairs;
```

The *name* is a string, and the *value* is the returned value associated with the name. This value may be your own value and need not be sequential, but it must be an `int`.

```
int
defaults_get_enum(name, class, pairs)
    char           *name;
    char           *class;
    Defaults_pairs *pairs;
```

`defaults_get_enum()` looks up the value associated with name and class and scans the `pairs` table and returns the associated value. If no match is found, an error is generated and the value associated with the last entry is returned. `defaults_get_enum()` calls `defaults_get_string()` and determines the value returned by calling `defaults_lookup()` (below), passing the returned string as the name parameter.

```
int
defaults_lookup(name, pairs)
    char           *name;
    Defaults_pairs *pairs;
```

defaults_lookup() linearly scans the `pairs` array looking for name. The value associated with `name` is returned. The `pairs` array *must* contain a last element with a NULL name and a legal `value` associated with it. This value is returned if `name` does not match the `name` field of any of the elements in the `pairs` parameter.

Example 17-2 shows a program that implements the idea discussed earlier for allowing the user to specify a scale for a font.

Example 17-2. The default_size.c program

```c
/*
 * default_scale.c -- demonstrate the use of defaults_get_enum().
 * Specify a table of font scales and query the resource database
 * for legal values.  For example, you may have the following in
 * your .Xdefaults (which must be loaded into the resource database):
 *        font.scale: large
 */
#include <xview/xview.h>
#include <xview/font.h>
#include <xview/defaults.h>
#include <xview/textsw.h>

Defaults_pairs size_pairs[] = {
    "small",            WIN_SCALE_SMALL,
    "medium",           WIN_SCALE_MEDIUM,
    "large",            WIN_SCALE_LARGE,
    "extralarge",       WIN_SCALE_EXTRALARGE,
    /* the NULL entry is the default if Resource not found */
    NULL,               WIN_SCALE_MEDIUM,
};

main(argc, argv)
char *argv[];
{
    Frame       frame;
    Xv_Font     font;
    int         scale;

    xv_init(XV_INIT_ARGC_PTR_ARGV, &argc, argv, NULL);

    frame = (Frame)xv_create(NULL, FRAME, NULL);

    scale = defaults_get_enum("font.scale", "Font.Scale", size_pairs);
    /* get the default font for the frame, scaled to resource */
    font = xv_find(frame, FONT,
        FONT_RESCALE_OF,        xv_find(frame, FONT, NULL), scale,
        NULL);

    xv_create(frame, TEXTSW,
        XV_FONT,            font,
        WIN_COLUMNS,        80,
        WIN_ROWS,           10,
        NULL);

    window_fit(frame);
    xv_main_loop(frame);
}
```

In *default_size.c*, the `pairs` table describes an association between string constants and scaling factors. The resource database may specify the resource `font.scale` that describes a scaling factor. If the value in the resource is not one of the legal values included in the table, an error message is printed to inform the user that s/he has specified the resource incorrectly. In this case, or in the case where the resource is not specified, the default resource (associated with the `NULL` entry) is returned, namely, `WIN_SCALE_MEDIUM`.

NOTE

The `value` field in the `Defaults_pair` data structure is an `int`, so do not attempt to assign pointers, functions or attributes to this field. You can assign enumerated types since they are interpreted as `int`.

18

The Selection Service

In This Chapter:

18
The Selection Service

The X Window System provides several methods for separate applications to exchange information with one another. One of these methods is the use of the selection service. A *selection* transfers arbitrary information between two clients. An in-depth discussion of the selection mechanism that X provides is discussed in Volume One, *Xlib Programming Manual*. This chapter addresses XView's programmatic interface to the selection service provided by the X server.

While XView provides all the functions for applications to set and get selections of various sorts, OPEN LOOK applications must follow the conventions outlined in the *OPEN LOOK GUI Specification Guide*. All XView packages that have interactive text entry support the ability to make selections and to get selections from the server. Figure 18-1, from the *OPEN LOOK GUI Specification Guide*, shows one way to select text.

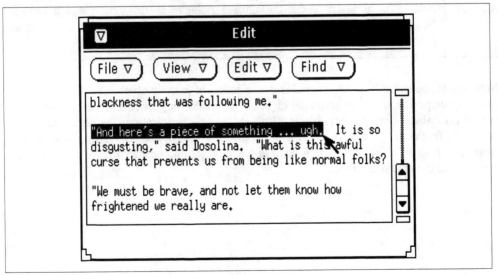

Figure 18-1. Dragging the pointer to select text

In OPEN LOOK, you select objects in basically the same way that you select windows or icons—using the SELECT and ADJUST mouse buttons. OPEN LOOK describes three functions that operate on selected objects: CUT, COPY and PASTE. These are *core functions* that are accessed from the keyboard.* CUT, COPY and PASTE operations use the *clipboard* to keep track of selected objects. The clipboard temporarily stores items selected via the selection service; it does not store selected windows or icons since these are not considered selectable objects by the selection service. Table 18-1 summarizes text selection for the OPEN LOOK GUI.

Table 18-1. Selecting Text

Action	Off Selection	On Selection
Click SELECT	Insert point is set at the pointer location.	When SELECT is released, insert point is set at pointer location and selection is cleared.
Drag SELECT	Text is highlighted as pointer is dragged (wipe-through selection).	Text move pointer is displayed. When you release SELECT, text is moved to pointer location if that location is outside the highlighted area.
Click ADJUST	Extends the highlighting to the pointer location extending either the beginning or the end of the current selection.	Moves the end of the highlighting to the pointer location. Beginning of selection is preserved.
Drag ADJUST	Adjusts an existing selection as the pointer is dragged (wipe-through). Beginning of selection is anchored at insert point.	Adjusts an existing selection as pointer is dragged (wipe-through). Beginning of selection is anchored at insert point.

Note that although OPEN LOOK specifies the selection of graphic objects, no XView objects currently support selection of graphical objects. A possible implementation is to have a canvas object, which has graphic objects displayed in it, set selections based on the event sequences outlined in Table 18-1. A *draw* application might consider a drawn geometric shape as a graphic object, whereas a *paint* application might consider the pixels in an arbitrary area as the graphical object.

---

*The function keys that are bound to these functions vary from keyboard to keyboard depending on the make and model of the computer.

18.1 The XView Selection Model

The XView selection model is based upon the requestor/owner model of peer-to-peer communications. The *owner* has the data representing the value of its selection, and the *requestor* receives it.

In the X environment, *all* data transferred between an owner and a requestor must transfer via the server. An X client cannot assume that another client can open the same files or even communicate directly. Such assumptions might result in an application that does not work in all network configurations or across heterogeneous computer architectures.

X makes provisions for selections and therefore generates certain events such as `Property-Notify` when a selection is acquired. For XView to implement its selection service, XView tracks all events that might be generated from selections. Because of this, you cannot use any of the selection mechanisms provided by Xlib. If you do, you will generate events that you will not be able to receive and that XView will be confused about.

The XView selection library deals with four discrete *ranks* under the general term *selection*. Those ranks are: primary, secondary, shelf and caret. Most familiar is the *primary* selection, which is normally indicated on the screen by inverting (*highlighting*) its contents. Selections made while a function key is held down (usually indicated with an underscore under the selection) are considered *secondary* selections.* These selections are used when the primary selection must be left undisturbed. The *shelf* (or *clipboard*) selection is used by the CUT and COPY operations to load the selection, while the PASTE operation retrieves the selection. Finally, the *caret* (the insertion point for interactive text objects) is also treated as a selection even though it has no contents.

When a user interface element, such as a text subwindow, wants to allow the user to make a selection, it must have a selection *client*. Through this client, the text subwindow can acquire a selection rank (primary, secondary, etc) and provide it with data (text). An application can have many such clients, but there is typically one client per XView object. Each selection rank is associated with each client—a separate client need not be created just to utilize other selection ranks. However, only one client can be the holder of a particular selection rank at any one time. If a client wishes to acquire the selection, the current selection *holder* must *yield* the selection to the new requestor. The client becomes the new holder of the selection and might provide any data it chooses.

---

*Which function key depends on your particular computer. By default the L6 function key should work for Sun Workstations or the F6 key for other computers.

Selection Services

18.2 Using the Selection Service

It is not necessary to create a selection service client just to query the holder of a selection or to get its contents. Since this is the most common usage, most of this chapter is dedicated to explaining this level of functionality. Creating a selection is typically used internally by packages in the XView library or by applications that wish to create their own objects that need to communicate via the selection service. Doing this is generally very intricate and complicated and is beyond the scope of this manual.

Nevertheless, to understand how to create a selection service client, it is best to learn how to request information from an existing client. Once you understand what to expect from a selection, you can understand how to create a client that provides information from other requests. Therefore, the bulk of the chapter addresses the process of querying for selections already provided by XView packages or other X-based applications.

OPEN LOOK assigns to function keys the special functions COPY, CUT and PASTE. The function keys generate and correspond to the XView events ACTION_CUT, ACTION_COPY and ACTION_PASTE. An OPEN LOOK application checks the state of these keys and modifies the selection rank accordingly. Note that it is the responsibility of the XView application (more specifically, each XView package) to set the state of the server's selection rank according to the state of some function keys. Unless you are writing your own XView package (a topic that this book does not address), you need not concern yourself about it.

Even though XView packages might query for the state of function keys, this does not interfere with normal event processing. All events that your application has registered to receive are not affected by the selection service. Note, however, that while the selection service might react to the state of these function keys, any action you take as a result of these keys might result in a *dual action* and might confuse the user. For example, if your application is coded to change the font of a text subwindow in the event of an L8-up event, you will not only get that event, but the selection service also gets it and will PASTE the contents of the shelf selection.

Whenever using the selection service either as a client or to query the selection from another client, application code must include the header file *<xview/seln.h>*. This file includes the files *<xview/sel_svc.h>* and *<xview/sel_attrs.h>*, which provide external declarations of available functions and data types.

18.3 Getting the Current Selection

Determining the current selection involves two steps: determining the holder of the current selection and getting the actual selection data from the holder. To determine who is holding the selection of a specified rank:

```
Seln_holder
selection_inquire(server, rank)
    Xv_Server server;
    Seln_rank rank;
```

The returned `holder` is used in other selection routines that allow you to access selection data for that rank. For example, the call `selection_ask()` asks for the data held by the holder of the selection. The form of the call is:

```
Seln_request *
selection_ask(server, holder, attrs)
    Xv_Server       server;
    Seln_holder     *holder;
    <attribute-value list>  attrs
```

The `holder` in this case is the address of the holder returned from the call to `selection_inquire()`.

The *server* is important to all the selection service routines because it identifies the X server in which the selection is associated. Because X applications can communicate with more than one server, specifying different servers can result in getting different selections.

The `Seln_rank` specifies which selection type you want. Its value corresponds with the four selection ranks outlined in the beginning of the chapter. However, there are six legal values in this enumerated data type:

SELN_UNKNOWN
: This is an error value, not a value you would use as a parameter or a legal or known rank.

SELN_CARET
: The caret selection is used with text subwindows and text panel items. It is usually used to describe where the insertion point is within the corresponding text stream of the object so there is no *data* associated with the caret selection. This selection type is not very widely used.

SELN_PRIMARY
: The primary selection is the most widely used and is usually the default type in most user interfaces and applications.

SELN_SECONDARY
: As noted earlier, the secondary selection is only used if the primary selection must not be removed or lost—or if it must remain clearly visible (visually selected) on the screen.

SELN_SHELF
: The selection buffers are stored in files. Clients of the selection service do not access these files; the selection service just uses them as temporary storage for data. As noted, this is not a good place to hold selections.

SELN_UNSPECIFIED   When this rank is used, either the primary or the secondary
                     selection is used depending on the state of the appropriate function
                     keys. This is usually passed as the rank parameter to
                     selection_inquire().

selection_ask() returns a pointer to a Seln_request data structure. The function goes
out and asks the server for the selection associated with the rank described in the holder
parameter. All the information about the selection is held in this data structure. The
attribute-value list following the holder parameter describes the attributes of the selection
you are interested in.

Before we go on, let's show an example program that illustrates what we have covered so far.
The simple program in Example 18-1 has a panel button that prints the current primary
selection to the standard output. The selection can be held by any client on the server.

Example 18-1. The simple_seln.c program

```
/*
 * simple_seln.c -- print the primary selection by pressing the panel
 * button.  The selection may have originated from any window or
 * application on the server.
 */
#include <stdio.h>
#include <xview/xview.h>
#include <xview/panel.h>
#include <xview/server.h>
#include <xview/seln.h>

Xv_Server server;

main(argc, argv)
char *argv[];
{
    Frame        frame;
    Panel        panel;
    void         exit();
    int          print_seln();

    xv_init(XV_INIT_ARGC_PTR_ARGV, &argc, argv, NULL);

    frame = (Frame) xv_create(NULL, FRAME,
        FRAME_LABEL,              argv[0],
        NULL);
    panel = (Panel)xv_create(frame, PANEL,
        WIN_WIDTH,                WIN_EXTEND_TO_EDGE,
        NULL);
    (void) xv_create(panel, PANEL_BUTTON,
        PANEL_LABEL_STRING,       "Quit",
        PANEL_NOTIFY_PROC,        exit,
        NULL);
    (void) xv_create(panel, PANEL_BUTTON,
        PANEL_LABEL_STRING,       "Print Selection",
        PANEL_NOTIFY_PROC,        print_seln,
        NULL);
    window_fit(panel);
    window_fit(frame);

    server = (Xv_Server)xv_get(xv_get(frame, XV_SCREEN), SCREEN_SERVER);
```

Example 18-1. The simple_seln.c program (continued)

```
    xv_main_loop(frame);
}

/*
 * Get the selection using selection_ask().  Note that if the
 * selection is bigger than about 2K, the whole selection will
 * not be gotten with one call, thus this method of getting
 * the selection may not be sufficient for all situations.
 */
int
print_seln(item, event)
Panel_item item;
Event *event;
{
    Seln_holder         holder;
    Seln_request        *response;
    char                text[BUFSIZ];

    /* get the holder of the primary selection */
    holder = selection_inquire(server, SELN_PRIMARY);
    response = selection_ask(server, &holder,
        SELN_REQ_CONTENTS_ASCII, NULL,
        NULL);

    strcpy(text, response->data + sizeof (SELN_REQ_CONTENTS_ASCII));
    printf("---selection---\n%s\n---end seln---0, text);

    return XV_OK;
}
```

selection_ask() does not return until it has contacted the server and gotten a response back from it. This implies that if the server does not respond, the application *blocks* until either a time-out occurs or the selection is received. The attribute-value pair that is passed (SELN_REQ_CONTENTS_ASCII, NULL) indicates that we are interested in the ASCII contents of the selection. Whether the selection is successful or not, a pointer to a Seln_request structure is returned. If there was an error, the status field of the structure will indicate so. If it succeeded, then the selection contents will be in the data field of the structure. All this is clarified in the next section.

18.3.1 The Seln_request Structure

The Seln_request data structure returned from selection_ask() contains information about the selection requested. The pointer returned points to static data that is overwritten on each call. Thus, if you need to save any of this data, it should be copied. The Seln_request structure is defined as follows:

Selection Services

```
typedef struct {
    Seln_replier_data    *replier;
    Seln_requester        requester;
    char                 *addressee;
    Seln_rank             rank;
    Seln_result           status;
    unsigned              buf_size;
    char                  data[SELN_BUFSIZE];
} Seln_request;
```

If there is no selection or if the selection fails in any way, the status field in the data structure is set to one of the values in the enumerated type Seln_result. If status is set to
SELN_FAILED, then the data field should not be examined as it will not contain any reli-
able values.

On the other hand, if selection_ask() returns successfully, the same attributes that were
passed into the function are copied into the data byte array along with the new values (see
Figure 18-2).

```
Seln_request  *request;

...

request = selection_ask(server, &holder,
    SELN_REQ_FIRST,           NULL,
    SELN_REQ_LAST,            NULL,
    SELN_REQ_CONTENTS_ASCII, NULL,
    NULL);
```

Figure 18-2 shows what is returned assuming that the selection contained the string
"Now is the time for all ...." The data field contains all the attributes passed in to
selection_ask(), but the attributes and the values are all aligned to 4-byte boundaries.
This includes the *string* returned from the selection. If the selection string is not a multiple of
4, then it is NULL-padded. The NULL-terminating byte of the string is required—if the last
character of the string aligns to a 4-byte boundary, the NULL-terminator pushes it into the
next 4-byte block and three more NULLs are required to align to the next boundary.

The value of buf_size is the number of bytes in the data array that is used by attribute-
value pairs including the text selection and alignment padding. The attributes
SELN_REQ_FIRST and SELN_REQ_LAST return the first and last indices into the object in
which the selection resides.*

To further demonstrate the use of the selection service, we will examine another program (see
Example 18-2) that is a little more intricate but that still follows the same principles outlined
in the first program. The new program, *text_seln.c*, also helps explain some of the new concepts introduced in this section.

text_seln.c contains a text subwindow in which selections can be made. A panel button that
prints the current primary selection is also provided. If the selection is made in the text

---

*Currently, the text subwindow is the only XView object that responds to these requests—panel text items do not.

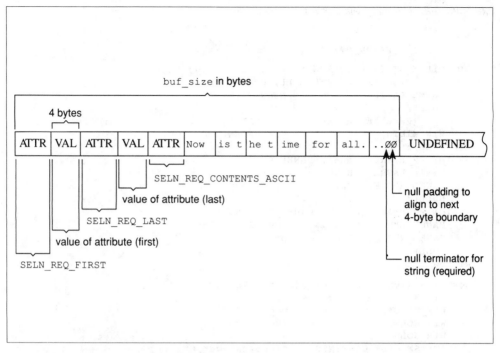

Figure 18-2. Byte stream after selection_ask() returns the current text selection

subwindow provided, information is printed about the relationship between the selected text and the rest of the subwindow. The program makes more extensive use of the `selection_ask()` function.

Example 18-2. The text_seln.c program

```
/*
 * text_seln.c -- print the primary selection from the server.  If the
 * selection is in a text subwindow, also print information about
 * the line number(s) the selection spans and the indexes of
 * the bytes within the textsw's buffer.
 */
#include <stdio.h>
#include <xview/xview.h>
#include <xview/textsw.h>
#include <xview/panel.h>
#include <xview/server.h>
#include <xview/seln.h>

Xv_Server       server;
Textsw          textsw;

char *get_selection();

main(argc, argv)
char *argv[];
{
    Frame       frame;
    Panel       panel;
```

Example 18-2. The text_seln.c program (continued)

```
    void         exit();
    int          print_seln();

    xv_init(XV_INIT_ARGC_PTR_ARGV, &argc, argv, NULL);
    frame = (Frame)xv_create(NULL, FRAME,
        FRAME_LABEL,              argv[0],
        NULL);
    panel = (Panel)xv_create(frame, PANEL,
        WIN_WIDTH,                WIN_EXTEND_TO_EDGE,
        NULL);
    (void) xv_create(panel, PANEL_BUTTON,
        PANEL_LABEL_STRING,       "Quit",
        PANEL_NOTIFY_PROC,        exit,
        NULL);
    (void) xv_create(panel, PANEL_BUTTON,
        PANEL_LABEL_STRING,       "Get Selection",
        PANEL_NOTIFY_PROC,        print_seln,
        NULL);
    window_fit(panel);

    textsw = (Textsw)xv_create(frame, TEXTSW,
        WIN_X,                    0,
        WIN_BELOW,                panel,
        WIN_ROWS,                 10,
        WIN_COLUMNS,              80,
        TEXTSW_FILE_CONTENTS,     "/etc/passwd",
        NULL);
    window_fit(frame);

    server = (Xv_Server)xv_get(xv_get(frame, XV_SCREEN), SCREEN_SERVER);

    xv_main_loop(frame);
}

int
print_seln()
{
    char *text = get_selection();

    if (text)
        printf("---selection---\n%s\n---end seln---0, text);

    return XV_OK;
}

/*
 * Get the selection using selection_ask().  Note that if the
 * selection is bigger than about 2K, the whole selection will
 * not be gotten with one call, thus this method of getting the
 * selection may not be sufficient.
 */
char *
get_selection()
{
    long             sel_lin_num, lines_selected;
    Textsw_index     first, last;
    Seln_holder      holder;
    Seln_result      result;
    int              len;
```

Example 18-2. The text_seln.c program (continued)

```
Seln_request          *response;
static char           selection_buf[BUFSIZ];
register char         *ptr;

/* get the holder of the primary selection */
holder = selection_inquire(server, SELN_PRIMARY);

/* If the selection occurs in the text subwindow, print lots of
 * info about the selection.
 */
if (seln_holder_same_client(&holder, textsw)) {
    /* ask for information from the selection service */
    response = selection_ask(server, &holder,
        /* get index of the first and last chars in the textsw */
        SELN_REQ_FIRST,              NULL,
        SELN_REQ_LAST,               NULL,
        /* get the actual selection bytes */
        SELN_REQ_CONTENTS_ASCII,     NULL,
        /* Now fool the textsw to think entire lines are selected */
        SELN_REQ_FAKE_LEVEL,         SELN_LEVEL_LINE,
        /* Get the line numbers of beginning and ending of the
         * selection */
        SELN_REQ_FIRST_UNIT,         NULL,
        SELN_REQ_LAST_UNIT,          NULL,
        NULL);
    /* set the ptr to beginning of data -- SELN_REQ_FIRST */
    ptr = response->data;
    /* "first" is data succeeding SELN_REQ_FIRST -- skip attr */
    first = *(Textsw_index *)(ptr += sizeof(SELN_REQ_FIRST));
    ptr += sizeof(Textsw_index); /* skip over value of "first" */
    /* "last" is data succeeding SELN_REQ_LAST -- skip attr */
    last  = *(Textsw_index *)(ptr += sizeof(SELN_REQ_LAST));
    ptr += sizeof(Textsw_index); /* skip over value of "last" */

    /* advance pointer past SELN_REQ_CONTENTS_ASCII */
    ptr += sizeof(SELN_REQ_CONTENTS_ASCII);
    len = strlen(ptr); /* length of string in response */
    (void) strcpy(selection_buf, ptr);
    /*
     * advance pointer past length of string.  If the string length
     * isn't aligned to a 4-byte boundary, add the difference in
     * bytes -- then advance pointer passed "value".
     */
    if (len % 4)
        len = len + (4 - (len % 4));
    ptr += len + sizeof(Seln_attribute); /* skip over "value" */

    /* advance pointer past SELN_REQ_FAKE_LEVEL, SELN_LEVEL_LINE */
    ptr += sizeof(SELN_REQ_FAKE_LEVEL) + sizeof(SELN_LEVEL_LINE);

    sel_lin_num = *(long *)(ptr += sizeof(SELN_REQ_FIRST_UNIT));
    ptr += sizeof(long);
    lines_selected = *(long *)(ptr += sizeof(SELN_REQ_LAST_UNIT));
    ptr += sizeof(long);

    /* hack to workaround bug with SELN_REQ_LAST_UNIT always
     * returning -1.  Count the lines explicitly in the selection.
     */
```

Selection Services

Example 18-2. The text_seln.c program (continued)

```
        if (lines_selected < 0) {
            register char *p;
            lines_selected++;
            for (p = selection_buf; *p; p++)
                if (*p == '\n')
                    lines_selected++;
        }
        printf("index in textsw: %d-%d, line number(s) = %d-%d\n",
            first+1, last+1, sel_lin_num+1,
            sel_lin_num + lines_selected + 1);
    } else {
        /* the selection does not lie in our text subwindow */
        response = selection_ask(server, &holder,
            SELN_REQ_CONTENTS_ASCII, NULL,
            NULL);
        if (response->status != SELN_SUCCESS) {
            printf("selection_ask() returns %d\n", response->status);
            return NULL;
        }
        (void) strcpy(selection_buf,
            response->data + sizeof(SELN_REQ_CONTENTS_ASCII));
    }
    return selection_buf;
}
```

There are several points of interest here. In the function `get_selection()`, once the holder of the client has been obtained, it is tested to see if the holder is the text subwindow using `seln_holder_same_client()`. If so, `selection_ask()` is called requesting information specific to the text subwindow. If the text subwindow is not the holder of the selection, then `selection_ask()` is called requesting only the ASCII contents. If there is no selection, then the `status` field of the structure is set to `SELN_FAILED`.

In the case where the holder is the text subwindow, we ask it for the first and last indices of the selection relative to the beginning of the text stream. Note that we might not be able to request this information from any object. For example, if the selection were inside an *xterm*, then this information would not be available and the *xterm*'s selection client would not respond to such requests.

The next attribute (`SELN_REQ_CONTENTS_ASCII`) requests the ASCII contents of the selection actually made. Following that, the attribute-value pair:

```
SELN_REQ_FAKE_LEVEL, SELN_LEVEL_LINE
```

fools the text subwindow into thinking that the user selected an entire line of text (in OPEN LOOK, this would have meant a triple-click with the SELECT mouse button). Had this attribute-value pair been listed *before* the request for ASCII contents, the text returned by the request would have contained the entire line of text on which the selection occurred *regardless of whether the selection began at the beginning of the line*.

The reason we fake the text window into thinking the entire line has been selected is: the attributes SELN_REQ_FIRST_UNIT and SELN_REQ_LAST_UNIT request the line numbers that the selection spans. As the names of the attributes imply, the request is for the first and last *units* selected. Setting the SELN_REQ_FAKE_LEVEL attribute to SELN_LEVEL_LINE indicates that the unit type should be line. Note that we fake the fact that the selection unit is set to line just to get the start and end line numbers of the selection. If we wanted to actually set the level, we would have used SELN_REQ_SET_LEVEL.

After selection_ask() returns a pointer to a Seln_request structure, the values of the requested attributes are found in data, the byte stream. As demonstrated in Example 18-2 above, the way to retrieve these values is by moving a pointer along the array:

```
Seln_request  *response;
char          *ptr;
long          value;
. . .
response = selection_ask(server, &holder,
     ATTR1,       NULL,
     ATTR2,       NULL,
     . . .
     NULL);
. . .
/* set the ptr to beginning of data response -- first attribute */
ptr = response->data;
/* value is data succeeding first attribute -- skip over attr */
value = *(long *)(ptr += sizeof(Seln_attribute));
ptr += sizeof(long); /* skip over the size of the type of value */
```

There is no need to test the attributes as you scan data; they are the same attributes that you used in selection_ask() and they remain in the same order. The values you get back are almost always long.* The exception to this is the text string returned when SELN_REQ_CONTENTS_ASCII is specified. However, the text string is padded to a 4-byte boundary to make sure that the alignment is correct. *text_seln.c* demonstrates how this is done.

18.4 Using selection_query()

One problem with using selection_ask() is handling large selections. In this context, "large" means a text string that is long enough so that it, along with all its attributes and values, does not fit in the data byte-stream. Of course, the fewer attributes that are requested, the more text is returned from the selection.

In this case, the problem is that there is an upper limit to the number of bytes that can be retrieved from the selection. There is no guarantee that the user is not going to select a large number of bytes from some arbitrary application on the screen. However, there is another way to get the selection, regardless of how large it is, by using selection_query():

---

*Architectures whose int type does not equal its long type must be sure to compensate for this.

```
    Seln_result
    selection_query(server, holder, reader, context, attrs)
        Xv_Server       server;
        Seln_holder     *holder;
        Seln_result     (*reader)();
        char            *context;
        <attribute-value list> attrs
```

The primary feature of this routine is that you provide it with a pointer to a function that does the scanning of the `data` array in the `Seln_request` structure, as demonstrated earlier. Your `reader` function is called by `selection_query()`, and it gets the `Seln_request` structure as the sole parameter to your function. Your function takes the form of:

```
    Seln_result
    reader(request)
        Seln_request *request;
```

Your function should return `SELN_SUCCESS` provided that you encountered no problems with scanning `request->data`. `selection_query()` returns the same `Seln_result` that your `reader` function returns. Your `reader` function is called by `selection_query()` for each *chunk* of data in the selection.* The flowchart in Figure 18-3 shows the sequence of operations.

The program in Example 18-3 demonstrates the use of `selection_query()`. It is similar to *text_seln.c*, but this new program also provides for selections from one of three selection ranks. The user chooses the selection rank from the panel choice item. When the Get Selection button is pressed, the current selection from that selection rank is displayed.

The point of the program is to demonstrate the flow of control between `selection_query()` and the client-installed `reader` procedure. The text subwindow in the application loads the file */etc/termcap*. When a selection is made, `selection_query()` is called, which in turn calls the reader procedure. You can make an arbitrarily large selection to show how `read_proc` is called many times. Start by initializing the selection and then *scrolling* the window and *extending* the selection by using the ADJUST mouse button on later text. Select the Get Selection panel button and the output is directed to `stdout`. Because the selection size can be large, the output text is truncated to the first 20 characters of the selection.

Example 18-3. The long_seln.c program

```
/*
 * long_seln.c shows how to get an arbitrarily large selection by
 * providing a reading procedure to selection_query().  The panel
 * items allow the user to choose between 3 selection ranks.
 */
#include <xview/xview.h>
#include <xview/textsw.h>
#include <xview/panel.h>
#include <xview/seln.h>

extern char *malloc();
```

---

*A *chunk* is the largest text string that will fit in the `data` field of the `Seln_request` structure.

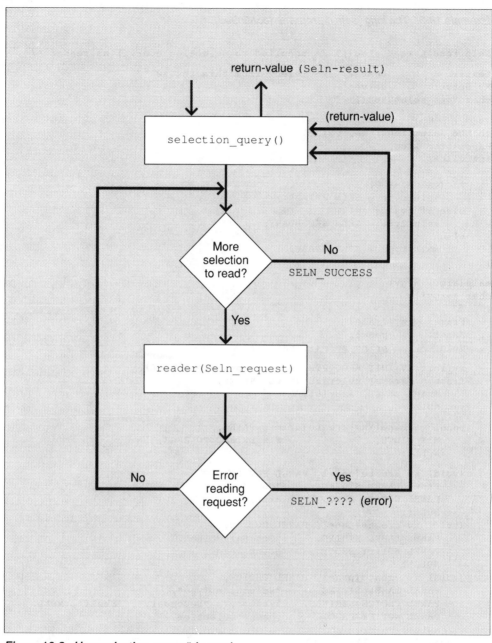

return-value (Seln-result)

(return-value)

selection_query()

More
selection
to read?

No

SELN_SUCCESS

Yes

reader(Seln_request)

No

Error
reading
request?

Yes

SELN_???? (error)

Figure 18-3. How selection_query() is used

Example 18-3. The long_seln.c program (continued)

```
Seln_rank seln_type = SELN_PRIMARY;

#define FIRST_BUFFER          0
#define NOT_FIRST_BUFFER        !FIRST_BUFFER

char *seln_bufs[3];      /* contents of each of the three selections */
```

Example 18-3. The long_seln.c program (continued)

```
Seln_result read_proc(); /* supplied to selection_query() as reader */

Textsw          textsw;  /* select from this textsw */
Xv_Server       server;
char *get_selection();

void
change_selection(item, value)
Panel_item item;
int value;
{
    if (value == 0)
        seln_type = SELN_PRIMARY;
    else if (value == 1)
        seln_type = SELN_SECONDARY;
    else
        seln_type = SELN_SHELF;
}

main(argc, argv)
char *argv[];
{
    Frame        frame;
    Panel        panel;
    void         print_seln(), exit();

    xv_init(XV_INIT_ARGC_PTR_ARGV, &argc, argv, NULL);
    frame = (Frame) xv_create(NULL, FRAME,
        FRAME_LABEL, argv[0],
        NULL);

    panel = (Panel)xv_create(frame, PANEL,
        WIN_WIDTH,              WIN_EXTEND_TO_EDGE,
        NULL);

    (void) xv_create(panel, PANEL_BUTTON,
        PANEL_LABEL_STRING,     "Quit",
        PANEL_NOTIFY_PROC,      exit,
        NULL);
    (void) xv_create(panel, PANEL_BUTTON,
        PANEL_LABEL_STRING,     "Get Selection",
        PANEL_NOTIFY_PROC,      print_seln,
        NULL);
    (void) xv_create(panel, PANEL_CHOICE,
        PANEL_LABEL_STRING,     "Selection Type",
        PANEL_CHOICE_STRINGS,   "Primary", "Secondary", "Shelf", NULL,
        PANEL_NOTIFY_PROC,      change_selection,
        NULL);
    window_fit(panel);

    textsw = (Textsw)xv_create(frame, TEXTSW,
        WIN_X,                  0,
        WIN_BELOW,              panel,
        WIN_ROWS,               10,
        WIN_COLUMNS,            80,
        TEXTSW_FILE_CONTENTS,   "/etc/termcap",
        NULL);
    window_fit(frame);
```

Example 18-3. The long_seln.c program (continued)

```
        server = (Xv_Server)xv_get(xv_get(frame, XV_SCREEN), SCREEN_SERVER);
        xv_main_loop(frame);
}

void
print_seln()
{
    char *text = get_selection();

    if (text)
        printf("---seln---\n%.*s [...]\n---end seln---0, 20, text);
}

/*
 * return the text selected in the current selection rank.  Use
 * selection_query() to guarantee that the entire selection is
 * retrieved.  selection_query() calls our installed routine,
 * read_proc() (see below).
 */
char *
get_selection()
{
    Seln_holder    holder;
    Seln_result    result;
    Seln_request   *response;
    char           context = FIRST_BUFFER;

    holder = selection_inquire(server, seln_type);
    printf("selection type = %s\n",
        seln_type == SELN_PRIMARY? "primary" :
        seln_type == SELN_SECONDARY? "secondary" : "shelf");

    /* result is based on the return value of read_proc() */
    result = selection_query(server, &holder, read_proc, &context,
        SELN_REQ_BYTESIZE,            NULL,
        SELN_REQ_CONTENTS_ASCII,      NULL,
        NULL);
    if (result == SELN_FAILED) {
        puts("couldn't get selection");
        return NULL;
    }

    return seln_bufs[seln_type];
}

/*
 * Called by selection_query for every buffer of information received.
 * Short messages (under about 2000 bytes) will fit into one buffer.
 * For larger messages, read_proc is called for each buffer in the
 * selection.  The context pointer passed to selection_query is
 * modified by read_proc so that we know if this is the first buffer
 * or not.
 */
Seln_result
read_proc(response)
Seln_request *response;
{
    char *reply;   /* pointer to the data in the response received */
    long seln_len; /* total number of bytes in the selection */
```

Example 18-3. The long_seln.c program (continued)

```
    static long seln_have_bytes;
        /* number of bytes of the selection
         * which have been read; cumulative over all calls for
         * the same selection (it is reset when the first
         * response of a selection is read)
         */

    printf("read_proc status: %s (%d)\n",
        response->status == SELN_FAILED? "failed" :
        response->status == SELN_SUCCESS? "succeeded" :
        response->status == SELN_CONTINUED? "continued" : "???",
        response->status);
    if (*response->requester.context == FIRST_BUFFER) {
        reply = response->data;

        /* read in the length of the selection -- first attribute.
         * advance "reply" passed attribute to point to actual data.
         */
        reply += sizeof(SELN_REQ_BYTESIZE);
        /* set seln_len to actual data now. (bytes selected) */
        seln_len = *(int *)reply;
        printf("selection size is %ld bytes\n", seln_len);
        /* advance "reply" to next attribute in list */
        reply += sizeof(long);

        /* create a buffer large enough to store entire selection */
        if (seln_bufs[seln_type] != NULL)
            free(seln_bufs[seln_type]);
        if (!(seln_bufs[seln_type] = malloc(seln_len + 1))) {
            puts("out of memory");
            return(SELN_FAILED);
        }
        seln_have_bytes = 0;

        /* move "reply" passed attribute so it points to contents */
        reply += sizeof(SELN_REQ_CONTENTS_ASCII);
        *response->requester.context = NOT_FIRST_BUFFER;
    } else {
        /* this is not the first buffer, so the contents of the
         * response is just more of the selection
         */
        reply = response->data;
    }

    /* copy data from received to the seln buffer allocated above */
    (void) strcpy(&seln_bufs[seln_type][seln_have_bytes], reply);
    seln_have_bytes += strlen(reply);

    return SELN_SUCCESS;
}
```

18.5 Selection Package Summary

Table 18-2 lists the procedures and macros in the SELECTION package; Table 18-3 lists the attributes in the SELECTION package. This information is described fully in Appendices A and B.

Table 18-2. Selection Procedures

Selection Procedures

selection_acquire()	selection_inform()
selection_ask()	selection_init_request()
selection_clear_functions()	selection_inquire()
selection_create()	selection_inquire_all()
selection_destroy()	selection_query()
selection_done()	selection_report_event()
selection_figure_response()	selection_request()
selection_hold_file()	selection_yield_all()

Table 18-3. Selection Attributes

Selection Attributes	Advanced Selection Attributes
SELN_REQ_BYTESIZE	SELN_REQ_COMMIT_PENDING_DELETE
SELN_REQ_CONTENTS_ASCII	SELN_REQ_CONTENTS_PIECES
SELN_REQ_DELETE	SELN_REQ_FAKE_LEVEL
SELN_REQ_END_REQUEST	SELN_REQ_FIRST
SELN_REQ_FILE_NAME	SELN_REQ_FIRST_UNIT
SELN_REQ_YIELD	SELN_REQ_LAST
	SELN_REQ_LAST_UNIT
	SELN_REQ_LEVEL
	SELN_REQ_RESTORE
	SELN_REQ_SET_LEVEL

Selection Services

19

The Notifier

In This Chapter:

19
The Notifier

In this chapter, we look at the Notifier in fuller detail, discussing its role in processing events for an XView application.

19.1 Basic Concepts

The Notifier maintains the flow of control in an application. To understand the basic concepts of the Notifier, we must distinguish between two different styles of input handling, *mainline* input and *event-driven* input, and consider how they affect where the flow of control resides within a program.

19.1.1 Mainline Input Handling

The traditional type of input handling of most text-based applications is mainline-based and input-driven. The flow of control resides in the main routine and the program *blocks* when it expects input. That is to say, no other portion of the program may be executed while the program is waiting for input. For example, in a mainline-driven application, a C programmer will use `fgets()` or `getchar()` to wait for characters that the user types. Based on the user's input, the program chooses an action to take. Sometimes, that action requires more input, so the application calls `getchar()` again. The program does not return to the main routine until the processing for the current input is done.

The tight control represented by this form of input handling is the easiest to program since you have control at all times over what to expect from the user and you can control the direction that the application takes. There is only one source of input—the keyboard—and the user can only respond to one interface element at a time. A user's responses are predictable in the sense that you know that the user is going to type *something*, even if you do not know what it is.

19.1.2 Event-driven Input Handling

Windowing systems are designed such that many sources of input are available to the user at any given time. In addition to the keyboard, there are other input devices, such as the mouse. Each keystroke and mouse movement causes an *event* that the application might consider. Further, there are other sources of events such as the window system itself and other processes. Another aspect of event-driven input handling is that you are not guaranteed to have any predictable sequence of events from the user. That is, a user can position the mouse on an object that receives text as input. Before the user is done typing, the user can move the mouse to another window and select a panel button of some sort. The application cannot (and should not) expect the user to type in window *A* first, then move to window *B* and select the button. A well-written program should expect input from any window to happen at any time.

19.2 Functions of the Notifier

The Notifier can do any of the following:

- Handle *software interrupts*—specifically, UNIX signals such as `SIGINT` or `SIGCONT`.

- Notice state changes in processes that your process has spawned (e.g., a child process that has died).

- Read and write through file descriptors (e.g., files, pipes and sockets).

- Receive notification of the expiration of timers so that you can regularly flash a caret or display animation.

- Extend, modify or monitor XView Notifier clients (e.g., noticing when a frame is opened, closed or about to be destroyed.)

- Use a non-notification-based control structure while running under XView (e.g., porting programs to XView).

The Notifier also has provisions, to a limited degree, to allow programs to run in the Notifier environment without inverting their control structure.

19.3 How the Notifier Works

Up until now, we have been saying that you should register an event handler for objects when they want to be notified of certain events such as mouse motion or selection or keyboard input. What you may not have been aware of is that you are indirectly registering these event handlers with the Notifier. When you specify *callbacks* or *notify procedures*, the XView object specified is said to be the *client* of the Notifier. Look at the following code:

```
extern void my_event_handler();

xv_set(canvas,
    CANVAS_PAINTWINDOW_ATTRS,
        WIN_CONSUME_X_EVENT_MASK,   ButtonPressMask | KeyPressMask,
        WIN_EVENT_PROC,             my_event_handler,
        NULL,
    NULL);
```

In the above code, each paint window of the canvas becomes a client of the Notifier.*

Generally stated, the Notifier detects events in which its clients have expressed an interest and dispatches these events to the proper clients in a predictable order. In the X Window System, events are delivered to the application by the X server. In XView, it is the Notifier that receives the events from the server and dispatches them to its clients. After the client's notify procedure processes the event, control is returned to the Notifier.

19.3.1 Restrictions

The Notifier imposes some restrictions on its clients. Designers should be aware of these restrictions when developing software to work in the Notifier environment. These restrictions exist so that the application and the Notifier do not interfere with each other. More precisely, since the Notifier is multiplexing access to user process resources, the application needs to respect this effort so as not to violate the sharing mechanism.

For example, a client should not call signal (3). The Notifier is catching signals on behalf of its clients. If a client sets up its own signal handler, then the Notifier will never notice the signal. The program should call notify_set_signal_func() instead of signal (3) (see Section 19.5, "Signal Handling").

System Calls to Avoid

Assuming an environment with multiple clients and an unknown Notifier usage pattern, you should not use any of the following system calls or C library routines:

signal (3)   The Notifier is catching signals on behalf of its clients. If you set up your own signal handler over the one that the Notifier has set up, then the Notifier will never notice the signal.

sigvec (2)   The same applies for sigvec (2) as for signal (3) above.

setitimer (2)   The Notifier is managing two of the process's interval timers on behalf of its many clients. If you access an interval timer directly, the Notifier could miss a timeout. Use notify_set_itimer_func() instead of setitimer (2).

---

*CANVAS_PAINTWINDOW_ATTRS tells the CANVAS package to register the input mask and callback routine for each of its paint windows.

Notifier

alarm (3)	Because `alarm` (3) sets the process's interval timer directly, the same applies here as for `setitimer` (2) above.
getitimer (2)	When using a Notifier-managed interval timer, you should call `notify_itimer_value ()` to get its current status. Otherwise, you can get inaccurate results.
wait3 (2)	The Notifier notices child process state changes on behalf of its clients. If you do your own `wait3` (2), then the Notifier may never notice the change in a child process or you may get a change of state for a child process in which you have no interest. Use `notify_set_wait3_func ()` instead of `wait3` (2).
wait (2)	The same applies for `wait` (2) as does for `wait3` (2) above.
ioctl (2) (. . . , FIONBIO, . . .)	This call sets the blocking status of a file descriptor. The Notifier needs to know the blocking status of a file descriptor in order to determine if there is activity on it. `fcntl` (2) has an analogous request that should be used instead of `ioctl` (2).
ioctl (2) (. . . , FIOASYNC, . . .)	This call controls a file descriptor's asynchronous IO (input/output) mode setting. The Notifier needs to know this mode in order to determine if there is activity on it. `fcntl` (2) has an analogous request that should be used instead of `ioctl` (2).
system (3)	In the SunOS, this function calls `signal` (3) and `wait` (2). Hence, you should avoid using this for the reasons mentioned above.

19.4 What is a Notifier Client?

A *client* of the Notifier is anything that has registered a callback routine with it. In XView, a client is an object such as a canvas or panel that you have created using `xv_create ()`. Typically, most of the event registration happens at the time such clients are created. However, to the Notifier, a client is nothing more than an ID that distinguishes it from all other Notifier clients. Thus, you could identify a client using a number such as "43" or the address of an object as in `&foo`. XView objects are commonly used as Notifier clients because `xv_create ()` returns a unique handle to an object that has been allocated dynamically.

The client ID which is of type `Notify_client` as declared in *<xview/notify.h>*.

```
Notify_func     func();
Frame           frame;

frame = (Frame)xv_create(NULL, FRAME, NULL);

notify_interpose_destroy_func(frame, func);
```

Up until the call to `notify_interpose_destroy_func()`, the `frame` may not have been registered as a client to the Notifier. Internally, the Notifier package looks up in its table of clients whether there is any other client using that identifier (the frame handle is the identifier). If so, the Notifier operation specified affects that client. Otherwise, a new client is allocated and the frame handle is also used as a handle to the new Notifier client.

The client can unregister the interposition by specifying `NOTIFY_FUNC_NULL` as the `func` parameter to the function. The same method is used to unregister all clients with the Notifier, not just interposers. If there are no more registrations involved with the client, the client is removed from the Notifier's list of clients.

Notifier clients are *not* XView objects for you to create or manipulate using `xv_create()` or `xv_set()`. In fact, the Notifier is completely independent of XView and can be used in applications that do not even use XView objects.

19.5 Signal Handling

Signals are UNIX software interrupts. The Notifier multiplexes access to the UNIX signal mechanism. A Notifier client may ask to be notified that a UNIX signal occurred either when it is received (asynchronously) and/or later during normal processing (synchronously).

Clients may define and register a signal event handler to respond to any UNIX signal desired. However, some of the signals that you might catch in a traditional UNIX program should be caught instead by the Notifier.

CAUTION

Clients of the Notifier should not directly catch any UNIX signals using `signal` (3) or `sigvec` (2). There are critical stages of event reading and dispatching that, if interrupted, could cause the program to jump to another location and interrupt the communication protocol between the X server and the application.

Exceptions to this are noted later in this section.

19.5.1 Signals to Avoid

Clients should not have to catch any of the following signals (even via `notify_set_ signal_func()` described below). If they are, you are probably utilizing the Notifier inappropriately. The Notifier catches these signals itself under a variety of circumstances and handles them appropriately.

SIGALRM   Caught by the Notifier's interval timer manager. Use `notify_set_ itimer_func()` instead.

SIGVTALRM The same applies for `SIGVTALRM` as for `SIGALRM` above.

SIGTERM   Caught by the Notifier so that it can tell its clients that the process is going away. Use `notify_set_destroy_func()` if that is why you are catching SIGTERM.

SIGCHLD   Caught by the Notifier so that it can do child process management. Use `notify_set_wait3_func()` instead.

SIGIO   Caught by the Notifier so that it can manage its file descriptors that are running in asynchronous IO mode. Use `notify_set_input_func()` or `notify_set_output_func()` if you want to know when there is activity on your file descriptor.

SIGURG   Caught by the Notifier so that it can dispatch exception activity on a file descriptor to its clients. Use `notify_set_exception_func()` if you are looking for out-of-band communications when using a socket.

The last two signals in the list are considered advanced topics and are not covered in this manual.

19.5.2 A Replacement for signal()

Instead of using `signal()` to catch signals delivered by UNIX, you should register a signal event handler by calling `notify_set_signal_func()`. This function allows you to call another function when a specified signal is generated. Its form is as follows:

```
Notify_func
notify_set_signal_func(client, signal_func, signal, when)
    Notify_client      client;
    Notify_func        signal_func;
    int                signal;
    Notify_signal_mode when;
```

`signal_func` is the function to call when the signal described by `sig` occurs.*

The **when** parameter is either `NOTIFY_SYNC` or `NOTIFY_ASYNC`. `NOTIFY_SYNC` causes notification during normal processing. In other words, the delivery of the signal is delayed to avoid interrupting Xlib Protocol communication between the X server and the application. When it is safe to do so, your `signal_func` function is called and you can display a notice, exit or jump to another place in the program. Typically, there is a very short time between signal delivery and notification to your callback routine. It is only a little slower than when you use `signal()`.

`NOTIFY_ASYNC` causes notification as soon as the signal is received. This mode mimics the UNIX `signal`(3) semantics.

---

*See <*signal.h*> for a list of signals and definitions.

CAUTION

When using asynchronous signals, your routine may set a variable, a condition or
a flag indicating that the signal was received, or it may change any internal state
to your program. Do *not* make any XView, Xlib or Notifier calls or call any
function that might manipulate any XView data structures. Also, do not call
`longjmp()` or `setjmp()`; they can cause a condition that can interfere with the
X11 Protocol.

`notify_set_signal_func()` returns a pointer to the function that was installed
before you set the new function. You should use this to reset the function if you want
to unregister your installed function.

When the specified signal occurs, your `signal_func` is called:

```
Notify_value
signal_func(client, sig, when)
    Notify_client       client;
    int                 sig;
    Notify_signal_mode  when;
```

The parameters to the signal handler are not the same as the ones given to a signal handler in
the call to `signal`(3). However, it is not advisable to use either one, except in unusual circumstances. As a general rule, you should use `notify_set_ signal_func()` for all
signal handling. If you want the signal *code* or *context* from the signal that was generated
(two parameters that are passed to a normal UNIX signal handler), you can use:

```
int
notify_get_signal_code()

struct sigcontext *
notify_get_signal_context()
```

These two functions take no parameters—they return the signal code and context (respectively) of the last signal generated. If you wish to save these values, you can copy them.

Using the Notifier, you can catch any signal except `SIGKILL` and `SIGSTOP`, which cannot be
caught by a UNIX application. Attempting to do so generates an error.

An example of common signal handling is shown below:

```
#include <xview/notify.h>

...

extern Notify_value sigint_func();

notify_set_signal_func(frame, sigint_func, SIGINT, NOTIFY_SYNC);
...
```

Notifier

```
Notify_value
sigint_func(client, sig, when)
Notify_client client;
int sig;
{
    puts("received interrupt -- exiting");
    xv_destroy_safe(frame);
    return NOTIFY_DONE;
}
```

The return value of your signal handler tells whether you handled the signal or ignored it.*

19.5.3 Timers

One specific type of signal is a *timer*. Timers can be set up to call a routine after the passage of a specified amount of time.† Such a routine may cause a caret to flash at regular intervals or allow a clock application to change the time display. The timer is handled differently from other signals in that multiple timers can be installed for various clients (say a flashing caret and a clock in the same application).

Because the Notifier handles timers, you should not make calls to such routines as `sleep()` or `setitimer()`. As pointed out above, you should not attempt to use `signal()` to catch `SIGALRM` or `SIGVTALRM` to trap timer signals. To set timers and be notified when they expire, use `notify_set_itimer_func()`. The form of the call is:

```
Notify_func
notify_set_itimer_func(client, timer_func, which, value, ovalue)
    Notify_client    client;
    Notify_func      timer_func;
    int              which;
    struct itimerval *value, *ovalue;
```

The parameter `which` indicates which type of timer you want to use. Its value is either `ITIMER_REAL` or `ITIMER_VIRTUAL`.

The `value` parameter is a pointer to an `itimerval` that indicates the initial timeout and an interval timeout. The interval timeout is what is used after the initial timeout times out. If the initial timeout is 0, then the timer is not called regardless of the value of the interval timer. The granularity of the timer is dependent on your hardware architecture and operating system. It is perhaps unwise to assume that you will be notified as frequently as 30 milliseconds or less. Some cases may have higher minimum limits—your mileage may vary.

The `ovalue` is also a pointer to an `itimerval` structure. If there was a previous timeout that has yet to expire, `itimerval` will have that time filled in. You may pass a `NULL` as `ovalue` if you are not interested in this value.

The `timer_func` parameter is the function to call when the timer expires. `notify_set_itimer_func()` returns the function that was previously set for this client (see `notify_set_signal_func` above). The form of the `timer_func` is:

---

*Currently, the return value is ignored.

†Event processing still takes place during this time segment.

```
        void
        timer_func(client, which)
            Notify_client client;
            int            which;
```

Example 19-1 demonstrates one possible use of `notify_set_itimer_func()`. The program displays an animation of several icons stored in the *icon* font. When animating, the next icon in a sequence is displayed using `XDrawString()` (since the icon is part of the font). The slider controls the rate at which the next icon is drawn. If the slider is set to 0, the animation stops. The slider is a panel item whose callback routine makes calls to `notify_set_itimer_func()` to set the timer to the new value or to turn it off by setting the function to `NOTIFY_FUNC_NULL`.

Example 19-1. The animate.c program

```
/*
 * animate.c -- use glyphs from the "icon" font distributed with XView
 * to do frame-by-frame animation.
 */
#include <stdio.h>
#include <ctype.h>
#include <X11/X.h>
#include <X11/Xlib.h>
#include <X11/Xos.h>                    /* for <sys/time.h> */
#include <xview/xview.h>
#include <xview/panel.h>
#include <xview/font.h>
#include <xview/notify.h>

Frame           frame;
Display         *dpy;
GC              gc;
Window          canvas_win;
Notify_value    animate();
struct itimerval timer;

#define ArraySize(x)   (sizeof(x)/sizeof(x[0]))
char *horses[] = { "N", "O", "P", "Q", "R" };
char *boys[] = { " 07", " 05", " 07", " 10" };
char *men[] = { "\\", "]", "Y", "Z", "[" };
char *eyes[] = {
    "2", "5", "4", "3", "4", "5",
    "2", "1", "0", "/", "0", "1"
};

int max_images = ArraySize(horses);
char **images = horses;
int cnt;

main(argc, argv)
int     argc;
char    *argv[];
{
    Panel       panel;
    Canvas      canvas;
    XGCValues   gcvalues;
    Xv_Font     _font;
    XFontStruct *font;
```

Example 19-1. The animate.c program (continued)

```
    void            adjust_speed(), change_glyph();
    extern void exit();

    xv_init(XV_INIT_ARGC_PTR_ARGV, &argc, argv, NULL);

    frame = (Frame)xv_create(XV_NULL, FRAME,
        FRAME_LABEL,               argv[0],
        FRAME_SHOW_FOOTER,         TRUE,
        NULL);

    panel = (Panel)xv_create(frame, PANEL,
        PANEL_LAYOUT,              PANEL_VERTICAL,
        NULL);
    xv_create(panel, PANEL_BUTTON,
        PANEL_LABEL_STRING,        "Quit",
        PANEL_NOTIFY_PROC,         exit,
        NULL);
    xv_create(panel, PANEL_SLIDER,
        PANEL_LABEL_STRING,        "Millisecs Between Frames",
        PANEL_VALUE,               0,
        PANEL_MAX_VALUE,           120,
        PANEL_NOTIFY_PROC,         adjust_speed,
        NULL);
    xv_create(panel, PANEL_CHOICE,
        PANEL_LABEL_STRING,        "Glyphs",
        PANEL_LAYOUT,              PANEL_HORIZONTAL,
        PANEL_DISPLAY_LEVEL,       PANEL_ALL,
        PANEL_CHOICE_STRINGS,      "Horse", "Man", "Boy", "Eye", NULL,
        PANEL_NOTIFY_PROC,         change_glyph,
        NULL);
    window_fit(panel);

    canvas = (Canvas)xv_create(frame, CANVAS,
        XV_WIDTH,                  64,
        XV_HEIGHT,                 64,
        CANVAS_X_PAINT_WINDOW,     TRUE,
        NULL);
    canvas_win = (Window)xv_get(canvas_paint_window(canvas), XV_XID);

    window_fit(frame);

    dpy = (Display *)xv_get(frame, XV_DISPLAY);
    _font = (Xv_Font)xv_find(frame, FONT,
        FONT_NAME,        "icon",
        NULL);
    font = (XFontStruct *)xv_get(_font, FONT_INFO);

    gcvalues.font = font->fid;
    gcvalues.foreground = BlackPixel(dpy, DefaultScreen(dpy));
    gcvalues.background = WhitePixel(dpy, DefaultScreen(dpy));
    gcvalues.graphics_exposures = False;
    gc = XCreateGC(dpy, RootWindow(dpy, DefaultScreen(dpy)),
        GCForeground | GCBackground | GCFont | GCGraphicsExposures,
        &gcvalues);

    xv_main_loop(frame);
}
void
change_glyph(item, value)
```

Example 19-1. The animate.c program (continued)

```
Panel_item item;
int value;
{
    cnt = 0;
    if (value == 0) {
        max_images = ArraySize(horses);
        images = horses;
    } else if (value == 1) {
        max_images = ArraySize(men);
        images = men;
    } else if (value == 2) {
        max_images = ArraySize(boys);
        images = boys;
    } else if (value == 3) {
        max_images = ArraySize(eyes);
        images = eyes;
    }
    XClearWindow(dpy, canvas_win);
}

/*ARGSUSED*/
Notify_value
animate()
{
    XDrawImageString(dpy, canvas_win, gc, 5, 40, images[cnt], 1);
    cnt = (cnt + 1) % max_images;

    return NOTIFY_DONE;
}

void
adjust_speed(item, value)
Panel_item item;
int value;
{
    if (value > 0) {
        timer.it_value.tv_usec = (value + 20) * 1000;
        timer.it_interval.tv_usec = (value + 20) * 1000;
        notify_set_itimer_func(frame, animate,
            ITIMER_REAL, &timer, NULL);
    } else
        /* turn it off */
        notify_set_itimer_func(frame, NOTIFY_FUNC_NULL,
            ITIMER_REAL, NULL, NULL);
}
```

Figure 19-1 shows one frame of an animated horse sequence produced by *animate.c*.

Notifier

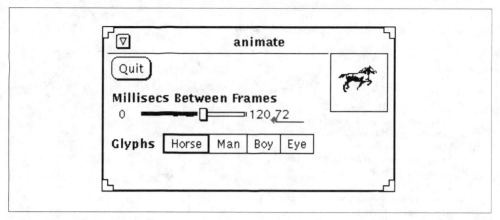

Figure 19-1. Output of animate.c

19.5.4 Handling SIGTERM

The SIGTERM signal is a software *terminate* signal. If you receive a SIGTERM signal, another process is telling your application to terminate. Rather than handling this signal with notify_set_signal_func(), you could use notify_set_destroy_func(). It takes the form:

```
Notify_func
notify_set_destroy_func(client, destroy_func)
    Notify_client  client;
    Notify_func    destroy_func;
```

Like the other Notifier functions, this one also returns the previously set function that was handling this signal. Note that it only interprets SIGTERM—it does not get called if the application chooses to kill itself by calling either exit() or xv_destroy() on the base frame or if the user selects the *quit* option from the title bar (provided by the OPEN LOOK window manager).

19.5.5 Handling SIGCHLD

Let's say that you want to fork a process to run another program. UNIX requires that you perform some housekeeping on that process. The minimum housekeeping required is to notice when that process dies and to reap it. Normally, the system call wait() is used to do this. By default, wait() will block until a spawned process has terminated. When wait() returns, it has information about the process that died. Rather than have the application sit and wait for a spawned (child) process to die, it should continue processing events and be notified automatically when the process dies.

To handle this, you can register a `wait3` event handler* that the Notifier will call whenever a child process changes state (dies) by calling the following:

```
Notify_func
notify_set_wait3_func(client, wait3_func, pid)
    static Notify_client client;
    Notify_func          wait3_func;
    int                  pid;
```

In the above call, the `pid` identifies the particular child process that the client wants to wait for. The `wait3_func` is the function to call when that child has died. Another reason that an application should use `notify_set_wait3_func()` is the semantics of the `wait3` (2) system call. `wait3` (2) will return with status about *any* process that has changed state. If two clients are managing different child processes, they should hear only about their own process. The Notifier keeps straight which client is managing which process.

Reaping Dead Processes

Many clients using child process control simply need to perform the required reaping after a child process dies. These clients can use the predefined `notify_default_wait3()` as their `wait3` event handler. This default handler does nothing but return—the fact that it handled the event is good enough for UNIX. The Notifier automatically removes a dead process's `wait3` event handler.

The code segment in Example 19-2 demonstrates how a *wait3* handler can be set up.

Example 19-2. Demonstrating a wait3 handler

```
#include <xview/notify.h>
#include <sys/wait.h>
#include <sys/time.h>
#include <sys/resource.h>

/* canvas created in another part of the program */
extern Canvas canvas;

/* declare our own wait3 handler */
Notify_value my_wait3_handler();

fork_it(argv)
char *argv[];
{
    int pid;

    /* here's the fork -- two processes are going to execute code
     * from this point down.
     */
    switch (pid = fork()) {
        case -1:
            perror("fork");
            return;
```

---

*The name *wait3 event* originates from the `wait3` (2) system call. There are other forms of *wait* including `wait()`, `wait2()` and `wait4()`. Since `wait4()` is not generally available, `wait3()` is the most efficient form of the *wait* functionality.

Notifier

Example 19-2. Demonstrating a wait3 handler (continued)

```
        case 0: /* this is the child of the fork -- the new process */
            /* execute the specified command */
            execvp(*argv, argv); /* execvp doesn't return unless failed */
            perror("execvp");
            _exit(0); /* don't call exit() -- man exec() for info */
        default: /* this is the parent -- the original process */
            /* Register a wait3 event handler */
            (void) notify_set_wait3_func(canvas, my_wait3_handler, pid);
    }
    /* parent returns -- child is happily processing away */
}

static Notify_value
my_wait3_handler(me, pid, status, rusage)
    Notify_client   me;
    int             pid;
    union wait      *status;
    struct rusage *rusage;
{
    if (WIFEXITED(*status)) {
        /* Child process exited with return code */
        printf("child exited with status %d\n", status->w_retcode);
        /* Tell the Notifier that you handled this event */
        return (NOTIFY_DONE);
    }
    /* Tell the Notifier that you ignored this event */
    return (NOTIFY_IGNORED);
}
```

Example 19-2 is a simple example for demonstration only. There are other things to consider for a complete and proper method for forking new processes. See Section 19.8, "Reading and Writing through File Descriptors," for a full example program that uses `notify_set_wait3_func()`.

19.6 Client Events

Client events are used by the application to communicate with clients of the Notifier. With this mechanism, you can have any portion of your application send an event to itself that the Notifier will dispatch to any of its clients that have expressed interest in that particular client event. These events can be considered *broadcast messages* for the entire application.

The process for the delivery of client events is similar to that of signals described above. However, because the entire process happens in the application, more control can be maintained by the Notifier. For example, optional parameters (extra information) may be passed to client message event handlers.

Client events are important and are frequently used by XView. They can also be used by the application, for instance, if it wants to notify all interested Notifier clients that input has been received from a pipe (see Section 19.8, "Reading and Writing through File Descriptors"). Once data has been read, the application can *post* it to the Notifier.

From the Notifier's point of view, client events are defined and generated by the application. Client events are not interpreted by the Notifier in any way; the Notifier does not *detect* client events, it just detects X events. However, when client events are *posted* to the Notifier, it dispatches these events to the receiving client's event handler.

19.6.1 Posting Client Events

A client event may be posted to the Notifier at any time. The poster of a client event may suggest to the Notifier when to deliver the event, but this is only a hint. The Notifier will see to it that it is delivered at an appropriate time (more on this below). The call to post a client event is:

```
typedef char * Notify_event;

Notify_error
notify_post_event(client, event, when_hint)
    Notify_client       client;
    Notify_event        event;
    Notify_event_type   when_hint;
```

The `client` handle from `notify_set_event_func()` is passed to `notify_post_event()`. `event` is defined and interpreted solely by the `client`. A return code of `NOTIFY_OK` indicates that the notification has been posted. Other values indicate an error condition. `NOTIFY_UNKNOWN_CLIENT` indicates that `client` is unknown to the Notifier. `NOTIFY_NO_CONDITION` indicates that `client` has no client event handler registered with the Notifier.

Usually it is during the call to `notify_post_event()` that the client event handler is called. Sometimes, however, the notification is queued up for later delivery. The Notifier chooses between these two possibilities by noting which kinds of client event handlers `client` has registered, whether it is safe and what the value of `when_hint` is. Here are the cases broken down by the kind of client event handlers `client` has registered:

Immediate only   If `when_hint` is `NOTIFY_SAFE` or `NOTIFY_IMMEDIATE`, the event is delivered immediately.

Safe only   If `when_hint` is `NOTIFY_SAFE` or `NOTIFY_IMMEDIATE`, the event is delivered when it is safe.

Both safe and immediate
        A client may have both an immediate client event handler as well as a safe client event handler. If `when_hint` is `NOTIFY_SAFE`, then the notification is delivered to the safe client event handler when it is safe. If `when_hint` is `NOTIFY_IMMEDIATE`, then the notification is delivered to the immediate client event handler right away. If the immediate client event handler returns `NOTIFY_IGNORED`, then the same notification will be delivered to the safe client event handler when it is safe.

Notifier

19.6.2 Posting with an Argument

XView posts a fixed field structure with each event. Sometimes additional data must be passed with an event. For instance, when the scrollbar posts an event to its owner to do a scroll, the scrollbar's handle is passed as an argument along with the event. `notify_post_event_and_arg()` provides this argument-passing mechanism (see below).

When posting a client event, there is the possibility of delivery being delayed. In the case of XView, the event being posted is a pointer to a structure. The Notifier avoids an invalid (dangling) pointer reference by copying the event if delivery is delayed. It calls routines the client supplies to copy the event information and later to free up the storage the copy uses. `notify_post_event_and_arg()` provides this storage management mechanism.

```
    Notify_error
    notify_post_event_and_arg(client, event, when_hint, arg,
                                    copy_func, release_func)
        Notify_client        client;
        Notify_event         event;
        Notify_event_type    when_hint;
        Notify_arg           arg;
        Notify_copy          copy_func;
        Notify_release       release_func;

    typedef caddr_t Notify_arg;

    typedef Notify_arg (*Notify_copy)();
    #define NOTIFY_COPY_NULL    ((Notify_copy)0)

    typedef void (*Notify_release)();
    #define NOTIFY_RELEASE_NULL   ((Notify_release)0)
```

`copy_func()` is called to copy `arg` (and, optionally, `event`) when `event` and `arg` need to be queued for later delivery. `release_func()` is called to release the storage allocated during the copy call when `event` and `arg` were no longer needed by the Notifier.

Any of `arg`, `copy_func()` or `release_func()` may be NULL. If `copy_func` is not NOTIFY_COPY_NULL and `arg` is NULL, then `copy_func()` is called anyway. This allows `event` the opportunity to be copied because `copy_func()` takes a pointer to `event`. The event pointed to may be replaced as a side affect of the copy call. The same applies to a NOTIFY_RELEASE_NULL release function with a NULL `arg` argument.

The `copy()` and `release()` routines are client-dependent, so you must write them yourself. Their calling sequences follow:

```
    Notify_arg
    copy_func(client, arg, event_ptr)
        Notify_client  client;
        Notify_arg     arg;
        Notify_event   *event_ptr;

    void
    release_func(client, arg, event)
        Notify_client  client;
        Notify_arg     arg;
        Notify_event   event;
```

19.6.3 Posting Destroy Events

When a destroy notification is set, the Notifier also sets up a synchronous signal condition for `SIGTERM` that will generate a `DESTROY_PROCESS_DEATH` destroy notification. Otherwise, a destroy function will not be called automatically by the Notifier. One or two (depending on whether the client can veto your notification) explicit calls to `notify_post_destroy()` need be made.

```
Notify_error
notify_post_destroy(client, status, when)
    Notify_client      client;
    Destroy_status     status;
    Notify_event_type  when;
```

`NOTIFY_INVAL` is returned if `status` or `when` is not defined. After notifying a client to destroy itself, all references to `client` are purged from the Notifier.

19.6.4 Delivery Time of Destroy Events

Unlike a client-event notification, the Notifier does not try to detect when it is safe to post a destroy notification. Thus, a destroy notification can come at any time. It is up to the good judgement of a caller of `notify_post_destroy()` or `notify_die()` (described in the Section 19.10, "Notifier Control") to make the call when a client is not likely to be in the middle of accessing its data structures.

If `status` is `DESTROY_CHECKING` and `when` is `NOTIFY_IMMEDIATE` then `notify_post_destroy()` may return `NOTIFY_DESTROY_VETOED` if the client does not want to go away. See Section 19.9.5, "Modifying a Frame's Destruction," for details on these values.

Often you want to tell a client to go away at a safe time. This implies that delivery of the destroy event will be delayed, in which case the return value of `notify_post_destroy()` cannot be `NOTIFY_DESTROY_VETOED` because the client has not been asked yet. To get around this problem, the Notifier will flush the destroy event of a checking/destroy pair of events if the checking phase is vetoed. Thus, a common idiom is:

```
(void) notify_post_destroy(client, DESTROY_CHECKING, NOTIFY_SAFE);
(void) notify_post_destroy(client, DESTROY_CLEANUP, NOTIFY_SAFE);
```

Notifier

19.7 Receiving Client Events

To register a client event handler call, use:

```
Notify_func
notify_set_event_func(client, event_func, when)
    Notify_client       client;
    Notify_func         event_func;
    Notify_event_type   when;

typedef enum notify_event_type {
    NOTIFY_SAFE        = 0,
    NOTIFY_IMMEDIATE   = 1,
} Notify_event_type;
```

The when parameter indicates whether the event handler will accept notifications only when it is safe (NOTIFY_SAFE) or at less restrictive times (NOTIFY_IMMEDIATE).

The calling sequence of a client event handler is:

```
Notify_value
event_func(client, event, arg, when)
    Notify_client       client;
    Notify_event        event;
    Notify_arg          arg;
    Notify_event_type   when;
```

The client is the one that called notify_set_event_func(). The event is passed through from notify_post_event(). The arg and event parameters are completely defined by the client. The types Notify_arg and Notify_event are of type caddr_t, a generic pointer type. The when parameter is the actual situation in which event is being delivered. It can have the value NOTIFY_SAFE or NOTIFY_IMMEDIATE and can be different from when_hint of notify_post_event().

The return value is either NOTIFY_DONE or NOTIFY_IGNORED.

19.8 Reading and Writing through File Descriptors

The Notifier is set up for testing whether or not there is input pending on file descriptors and whether file descriptors are available to accept data for writing. The file descriptors can represent files, pipes and sockets. System calls such as read() or write() can be used on any of these file descriptors.

In an event-driven system, the application cannot wait for data to be read. Instead it is better for the system to notify the application when data can be read. System calls such as read() will *block* if there is no input to be read. That is, read() waits until there is something to read before it returns. If your application is blocking on a read, then it cannot process events that the user may be generating, such as selecting a panel button. Rather than blocking on a call to read(), the Notifier can inform you when there is input ready on that file descriptor so that when you finally call read(), it returns immediately.

To handle this, the Notifier provides functions such as `notify_set_input_func()` and `notify_set_output_func()` to test whether a file descriptor has data to be read or is ready for writing. These functions inform you of the status of file descriptors, whether they are files, pipes or sockets.*

```
Notify_func
notify_set_input_func(client, input_func, fd)
    Notify_client   client;
    Notify_func     input_func;
    int             fd;
Notify_func
notify_set_output_func(client, output_func, fd)
    Notify_client   client;
    Notify_func     output_func;
    int             fd;
```

`input_func()` is called whenever the file descriptor (`fd`) has data to be read.† `output_func()` is called whenever the file descriptor (`fd`) is ready to receive data.

Generally, file descriptors open for writing are always ready to receive data, so this function may not be as widely used as the input function case. However, it is important if you are writing to a pipe where another process is probably on the other side of the pipe. Pipes have buffers which, when full, will not accept any more data on them until the process on the other side of the pipe reads the data written so far (thus emptying the buffer). If the process on the other side of the pipe is slow in reading the data you have written to it, then you may need to use `notify_set_output_func()` so that you can be notified when the pipe is ready to have more data written to it.

`input_func()` and `output_func()` take the following form:

```
Notify_value
func(client, fd)
    Notify_client   client;
    int             fd;
```

19.8.1 Reading Files

Our first example demonstrates how `notify_set_input_func()` can be used to read data from a file. The program is simple; it does not bother using any XView objects such as frames or canvases. Because of this, it makes use of `notify_start()`, which is covered in Section 19.10, "Notifier Control."

---

*`notify_set_exception_func()` is also available for determining if out-of-band data is available on a socket, but it is not covered in this manual.
†Exceptions to this are discussed in Section 19.8.1, "Reading Files."

Example 19-3. The notify_input.c program

```
/*
 * notify_input.c -- use notify_set_input_func to monitor the state of
 * a file.  The Notifier is running and checking the file descriptors
 * of the opened files associated with the command line args.  The
 * routine installed by notify_set_input_func() is called whenever
 * there is data to be read.  When there is no more data to be read
 * for that file, the input function is unregistered.  When all files
 * have been read, notify_start() returns and the program exits.
 */
#include <stdio.h>
#include <sys/ioctl.h>
#include <xview/notify.h>

main(argc, argv)
char *argv[];
{
    Notify_value    read_it();
    Notify_client   client = (Notify_client)10101; /* arbitrary */
    FILE            *fp;

    while (*++argv)
        if (!(fp = fopen(*argv, "r")))
            perror(*argv);
        else {
            (void) notify_set_input_func(client, read_it, fileno(fp));
            client++; /* next client is new/unique */
        }

    /* loops continuously */
    notify_start();
}

/*
 * read_it() is called whenever there is input to be read.  Actually,
 * it is called continuously, so check to see if there is input to be
 * read first.
 */
Notify_value
read_it(client, fd)
Notify_client   client;
int fd;
{
    char buf[BUFSIZ];
    int bytes, i;

    if (ioctl(fd, FIONREAD, &bytes) == -1 || bytes == 0)
        (void) notify_set_input_func(client, NOTIFY_FUNC_NULL, fd);
    else
        do
            if ((i = read(fd, buf, sizeof buf)) > 0)
                (void) write(1, buf, i);
        while (i > 0 && (bytes -= i) > 0);
    return NOTIFY_DONE;
}
```

The comments in this sample program describe what is going on up front. However, behind the scenes, there are interesting things happening.

The first thing to notice is that the clients used in the Notifier start at 10101 and, for each file on the command line, the client is incremented by one. Remember, the client is an arbitrary identifier and can be any unique value. Since there are no other clients of the Notifier, we know that 10101 is going to be unique.

The function `read_it()` is installed to read data from the files given on the command line. The first thing that `read_it()` does is check if there is data to be read. The `ioctl()` call returns the number of bytes to read in the `bytes` variable. If there is data to be read, then `read()` is used to read buffers (of size `BUFSIZ`) until it has read all the bytes pending. This continues until the program has read the entire file. Once this happens, the `ioctl()` call will return that there are no bytes to read. Normally, it would return -1 indicating that the end of file has been reached. However, the Notifier has modified the state of the file descriptor for internal purposes (to set nonblocking mode). When we have reached the end of the file, we unregister the client by calling `notify_set_input_func()` with a `notify_func` of `NOTIFY_FUNC_NULL`.

notify_input.c is not terribly interesting because you do not need to be notified of data to be read on a *file*; you can just open the file, read it till EOF and then close it. But if you know that the file is going to have data continuously added to it, you might want to be informed when there is new data to be read and then print it out.

This can be accomplished by not unregistering the input function with the Notifier when there is no data to be read. Unfortunately, your function is going to be called continuously whether there is new data to be read or not. This is true *only for file descriptors that represent files* and is not the case for pipes.

19.8.2 Reading and Writing on Pipes

A more interesting and likely problem occurs when an application has to execute another program, send data to it and read output from it all at the same time. The best way to handle such a situation is as follows:

- Setup a pipe for each stream (such as `stdin` and `stdout`). This is done using the `pipe()` system call.

- `fork()` a new process. The child will execute the program (using `execvp()`) and have its input and output redirected to the appropriate ends of the pipes (using `dup2()`).

- The parent registers *input* and *output* functions to read and write from the "other" ends of the pipes (using `notify_set_input_func()`). Also, the parent calls `notify_set_wait3_func()` (discussed earlier).

The example program that demonstrates this capability is a little longer, but it is still simple. It follows the steps outlined above and is the minimum needed to spawn a new process. Again, to keep the code short and simple, no XView objects are created. The existence of XView objects would not affect the program in any way.

The way to run this program is to specify a command on the command line of the program. For example:

```
% ntfy_pipe cat
```

Remember, there are *two* processes involved here: the parent process (ntfy_pipe) and the child process (cat). Both programs read from their respective stdin and write to their own stdout. However, because the child process (cat) was spawned off from the parent, we need to handle the IO (input/output) of the new process. After the call to fork(), its stdin and stdout must be redirected to the pipe that was set up before the fork. The parent, however, retains its IO—its stdin and stdout remain directed towards the window in which you typed the command.

Example 19-4. The ntfy_pipe.c program

```
/*
 * ntfy_pipe.c -- fork and set up a pipe to read the IO from the
 * forked process.  The program to run is specified on the command
 * line.  The functions notify_set_input_func() and
 * notify_set_output_func() are used to install functions which read
 * and write to the process' stdin and stdout.
 * The program does not use any XView code -- just the Notifier.
 */
#include <stdio.h>
#include <errno.h>
#include <signal.h>
#include <sys/time.h>
#include <sys/types.h>
#include <sys/wait.h>
#include <sys/resource.h>
#include <sys/ioctl.h>
#include <xview/notify.h>

Notify_client client1 = (Notify_client)10;
Notify_client client2 = (Notify_client)11;

int pipe_io[2][2]; /* see diagram */
/*
 *                    [0]                            [1]
 *     child reads:  |========= pipe_io[0] ========| <- parent writes
 *     pipe_io[0][0]                                   pipe_io[0][1]
 *
 *     parent reads: |========= pipe_io[1] ========| <- child writes
 *     pipe_io[1][0]                                   pipe_io[1][1]
 *
 * The parent process reads the output of the child process by reading
 * pipe_io[1][0] because the child is writing to pipe_io[1][1].
 * The child process gets its input from pipe_io[0][0] because the
 * parent writes to pipe_io[0][1].  Thus, one process is reading from
 * one end of the pipe while the other is writing at the other end.
 */
main(argc, argv)
char *argv[];
{
    Notify_value        read_it(), write_it(), sigchldcatcher();
    int                 i, pid;
    FILE                *fp;
```

Example 19-4. The ntfy_pipe.c program (continued)

```
    if (!*++argv)
        puts("specify a program [w/args]"), exit(1);

    pipe(pipe_io[0]); /* set up input pipe */
    pipe(pipe_io[1]); /* set up output pipe */
    switch (pid = fork()) {
        case -1:
            close(pipe_io[0][0]);
            close(pipe_io[0][1]);
            close(pipe_io[1][0]);
            close(pipe_io[1][1]);
            perror("fork failed");
            exit(1);
        case  0: /* child */
            /* redirect child's stdin (0), stdout (1) and stderr(2) */
            dup2(pipe_io[0][0], 0);
            dup2(pipe_io[1][1], 1);
            dup2(pipe_io[1][1], 2);
            for (i = getdtablesize(); i > 2; i--)
                (void) close(i);
            for (i = 0; i < NSIG; i++)
                (void) signal(i, SIG_DFL);
            execvp(*argv, argv);
            if (errno == ENOENT)
                printf("%s: command not found.\n", *argv);
            else
                perror(*argv);
            perror("execvp");
            _exit(-1);
        default: /* parent */
            close(pipe_io[0][0]); /* close unused portions of pipes */
            close(pipe_io[1][1]);
    }

    /* when the process outputs data, read it */
    notify_set_input_func(client1, read_it, pipe_io[1][0]);
    notify_set_wait3_func(client1, sigchldcatcher, pid);

    /* wait for user input -- then write data to pipe */
    notify_set_input_func(client2, write_it, 0);
    notify_set_wait3_func(client2, sigchldcatcher, pid);

    notify_start();
}
/*
 * callback routine for when there is data on the parent's stdin to
 * read.  Read it and then write the data to the child process via
 * the pipe.
 */
Notify_value
write_it(client, fd)
Notify_client    client;
int fd;
{
    char buf[BUFSIZ];
    int bytes, i;
```

Notifier

Example 19-4. The ntfy_pipe.c program (continued)

```
        /* only write to pipe (child's stdin) if user typed anything */
        if (ioctl(fd, FIONREAD, &bytes) == -1 || bytes == 0) {
            notify_set_input_func(client, NOTIFY_FUNC_NULL, pipe_io[0][1]);
            close(pipe_io[0][1]);
        } else
            while (bytes > 0) {
                if ((i = read(fd, buf, sizeof buf)) > 0) {
                    printf("[Sending %d bytes to pipe (fd=%d)]\n",
                        i, pipe_io[0][1]);
                    write(pipe_io[0][1], buf, i);
                } else if (i == -1)
                    break;
                bytes -= i;
            }
    return NOTIFY_DONE;
}

/*
 * callback routine for when there is data on the child's stdout to
 * read.  Read, then write the data to stdout (owned by the parent).
 */
Notify_value
read_it(client, fd)
Notify_client    client;
register int fd;
{
    char buf[BUFSIZ];
    int bytes, i;

    if (ioctl(fd, FIONREAD, &bytes) == 0)
        while (bytes > 0) {
            if ((i = read(fd, buf, sizeof buf)) > 0) {
                printf("[Reading %d bytes from pipe (fd=%d)]\n",
                    i, fd);
                (void) write(1, buf, i);
                bytes -= i;
            }
        }
    return NOTIFY_DONE;
}

/*
 * handle the death of the child.  If the process dies, the child
 * dies and generates a SIGCHLD signal.  Capture it and disable the
 * functions that talk to the pipes.
 */
Notify_value
sigchldcatcher(client, pid, status, rusage)
Notify_client client; /* the client noted in main() */
int pid; /* the pid that died */
union wait *status; /* the status of the process (unused here) */
struct rusage *rusage; /* resources used by this process (unused) */
{
    if (WIFEXITED(*status)) {
        printf("Process termined with status %d\n", status->w_retcode);
        /* unregister input func with appropriate file descriptor */
        notify_set_input_func(client, NOTIFY_FUNC_NULL,
```

Example 19-4. The ntfy_pipe.c program (continued)

```
            (client == client1)? pipe_io[1][0] : 0);
        return NOTIFY_DONE;
    }
    puts("SIGCHLD not handled");
    return NOTIFY_IGNORED;
}
```

Assuming that the program was run with `cat` (1) as described earlier, input to the child process comes from the function `write_it()`. That is, `write_it()` is the function that *writes* to the other side of the pipe that the child is reading from. This function was set up as the *input_func* for the *parent's* `stdin`. The function gets its input from whatever you type in the window in which you ran the program. It could have gotten its input from a text panel item or a selection using the selection service. It reads whatever data is sent through the pipe and ends up as the `stdin` for the child process.

Similarly, when the child process writes anything to its `stdout`, the data is redirected through the pipe. The parent reads from the other end of the pipe in `read_it()`. Whatever the parent reads is written to the parent's `stdout`, which is the user's tty window. It does this by calling `write(1, buf, i)`. This line of the program can easily be replaced by:

```
    textsw_insert(textsw, buf, i);
```

This shows how you can redirect the output (including `stderr` output) from a child process to a text subwindow.

The last thing to note about the program is its treatment of extraneous file descriptors and of signals handled by the child process after forking. When using `fork()`, the child process inherits all the file descriptors and signal handling set up by the parent.* This could seriously affect your program if the child process gets certain signals. In this case the best thing for the child to do is loop through all the signals that are dealt with by the parent and reset them to `SIG_DFL` using `signal` (3). Then it can close all file descriptors except for the child's `stdin` (0), `stdout` (1) and `stderr` (2) descriptors.

We use the `signal()` system call here because it is assumed that the child is not going to execute any of the XView code in the parent's program. Therefore, the child does not need to use the `notify_set_signal_func()` routine to unregister the signals. Releasing these signals in this way completely disassociates the program from the parent.

This very general program is used as an example, but it is useful in all applications that need to run external processes. The only modifications it needs are alternate sources for the input and output of the parent. `main()` could be replaced by a general function that simply gets an `argv` parameter containing the program to execute, including arguments.

The program could be modified to be used as a replacement for the `system` (3) call. Even if you do not expect to read the child's `stdout` or send data to its `stdin`, the child process still needs to be handled differently from `system` (3) because that function calls `wait()` and attempts to do its own signal handling.

---

*Unless the file descriptors were set to *close on exec* using: `ioctl(fd, FIOCLEX, 0)`.

Notifier

19.9 Interposition

The Notifier provides a mechanism called *interposition,* with which you can intercept control of the internal communications within XView. Interposition is a powerful way to both monitor and modify window behavior in ways that extend the functionality of a window object.

Interposition allows a client to intercept an event before it reaches the *base event handler.* The base event handler is the one set originally by a client. The client can call the base event handler before or after its own handling of the event or not at all.

There may be more than one interposer per Notifier client. As each interposer is added, it is inserted ahead of the last interposer installed. When an event arrives, the Notifier calls the function at the top of the interposer list for that client. An interposed routine may (indirectly) call the next function in the interposition sequence and receive its results.

Figure 19-2 illustrates the flow of control with interposition. Note that the interposer could have stopped the flow of control to the base event handler.

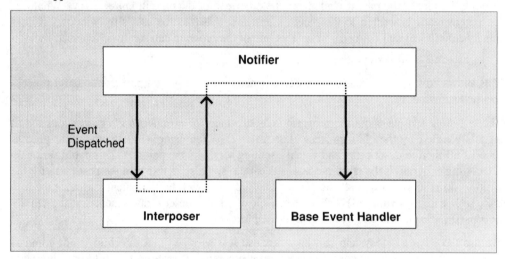

Figure 19-2. Flow of control in interposition

19.9.1 Uses of Interposition

Typically, it is application-level code that uses interposition. But, in general, any client's creator may want to use interposition. There are many reasons why an application might want to interpose a function in the call path to a client's event handler.

- An application may want to use the fact that a client has received a particular event as a trigger for some application-specific processing.

- An application may want to filter the events to a client, thus modifying the client's behavior.

- An application may want to extend the functionality of a client by handling events that the client is not programmed to handle.

XView window objects utilize the Notifier for much of their communication and cooperation. Thus, if an application wanted to monitor the user actions directed to a particular window, the application would use interposition to get into the flow of control.

19.9.2 Interface to Interposition

The Notifier supports interposition by keeping track of how interposition functions are ordered for each type of event for each client. Here is a typical example of interposition:

- An application creates a client. The client has set up its own client-event handler using `notify_set_event_func()`.

- The application tells the Notifier that it wants to interpose its function in front of the client's event handler by calling `notify_interpose_event_func()` (which uses the same calling sequence as `notify_set_event_func()`).

- When the application's interposed function is called it tells the Notifier to call the next function, i.e., the client's function, via a call to `notify_next_event_func()` (which uses the same calling sequence as that passed to the interposer function, not described here).

19.9.3 An Interposition Example

You can notice when a frame opens or closes by interposing in front of the frame's *client-event handler*. The client-event handler is an XView-specific event handler which is built on top of the Notifier's general client-event mechanism.* To register an interposer, the following routine is used:

```
Notify_error
notify_interpose_event_func(client, event_func, type)
    Notify_client      client;
    Notify_func        event_func;
    Notify_event_type  type;
```

The `client` must be the handle of the Notifier client in front of which you are interposing. In XView, this is the handle returned from `xv_create()`. The `type` is always `NOTIFY_SAFE` for XView clients.

Let's say that the application is displaying some animation and wants to do the necessary computation only when the frame is open. It can use interposition to notice when the frame opens or closes.

---

*The stream of events sent to a client-event handler is described in in Chapter 6, *Handling Input*.

In Example 19-5, note the call to `notify_next_event_func()`, which transfers control to the frame's client-event handler through the Notifier. `notify_next_event_func()` takes the same arguments as the interposer.

Example 19-5. Transferring control through the Notifier

```
#include <xview/xview.h>

main()
{
    Frame frame;
    Notify_value my_frame_interposer();

    /* Create the frame */
    frame = window_create(NULL, FRAME, NULL);  .

    /* Interpose in front of the frame's event handler */
    (void) notify_interpose_event_func(frame,
            my_frame_interposer, NOTIFY_SAFE);
    ...

    /* Show frame and start dispatching events */
    xv_main_loop(frame);
}

Notify_value
my_frame_interposer(frame, event, arg, type)
Frame               frame;
Event               *event;
Notify_arg          arg;
Notify_event_type   type;
{
    int closed_initial, closed_current;
    Notify_value value;

    /* Determine initial state of frame */
    closed_initial = (int) window_get(frame, FRAME_CLOSED);

    /* Let frame operate on the event */
    value = notify_next_event_func(frame, event, arg, type);

    /* Determine current state of frame */
    closed_current = (int) window_get(frame, FRAME_CLOSED);

    /* Change animation if states differ */
    if (closed_initial != closed_current) {
        if (closed_current) {
            /* Turn off animation because closed */
            (void) notify_set_itimer_func(me, my_animation,
                ITIMER_REAL, ITIMER_NULL, ITIMER_NULL);
        } else {
            /* Turn on animation because opened */
            (void) notify_set_itimer_func(me, my_animation,
                ITIMER_REAL, &NOTIFY_POLLING_ITIMER, ITIMER_NULL);
        }
    }
    return (value);
}
```

In Example 19-5, the base event handler is intended to handle the event (so that the frame gets closed/opened). If the interposed function replaces the base event handler and you do not want the base event handler to be called at all, your interposed procedure should not call `notify_next_event_func()`.

19.9.4 Interposing on Resize Events

Another use of interposition is to give your application more control over the layout of its subwindows. To do this, you set up an interpose event handler which checks if the event type is `WIN_RESIZE`. If so, rather than calling `notify_next_event_func()` to dispatch the event to the normal handler for resizing, you call your own resize routine:

```
Notify_value
my_frame_interposer(frame, event, arg, type)
Frame              frame;
Event              *event;
Notify_arg         arg;
Notify_event_type  type;
{
    Notify_value value;

    if (event_action(event) == WIN_RESIZE)
        value = resize(frame);
    else
        value = notify_next_event_func(frame, event, arg, type);

    return(value);
}
```

NOTE

A `WIN_RESIZE` event is *not* generated until the frame is resized. If you want your resize procedure to be called when the window first appears, you must do so yourself. This is different from a canvas with the `CANVAS_RESIZE` attribute set; its resize procedure is called the first time the canvas is displayed.

19.9.5 Modifying a Frame's Destruction

Suppose an application must detect when the user selects the "Quit" menu item in the frame menu in order to perform some application-specific confirmation. To accomplish this, the application should interpose a new function in front of the frame's *client-destroy event* handler using the following routine.

```
Notify_error
notify_interpose_destroy_func(client, destroy_func)
    Notify_client client;
    Notify_func   destroy_func;
```

Frame destruction may originate from several sources.

- The user may select the "Quit" menu item from the window manager's pulldown menu attached to the base frame.

- The application may be terminated by a software interrupt from the calling process.

- The connection to the server has been lost and the Notifier is informing the application that it is dying.

- `xv_destroy(frame)` was called from within the application.

Each of these scenarios results in a different method for the frame's destruction. When the frame is going to be destroyed, the process happens in two phases. First, the frame's destroy-interposer is called, informing it of the impending destruction. At this point, the interposer can *veto* the destruction or it can allow it to take place—at which time the Notifier proceeds to phase two, the actual frame destruction.

Destroy-event handlers use a status parameter to determine which phase of destruction the Notifier is in—whether the Notifier is requesting if it is feasible for the client to be terminated at present (phase one, DESTROY_CHECKING) or if it is making a request to terminate (phase two, DESTROY_CLEANUP or DESTROY_PROCESS_DEATH).

The destroy-interpose function takes the following form:

```
Notify_value
destroy_func(client, status)
    Notify_client client;
    Destroy_status status;

typedef enum destroy_status {
    DESTROY_PROCESS_DEATH,
    DESTROY_CHECKING,
    DESTROY_CLEANUP,
    DESTROY_SAVE_YOURSELF,
} Destroy_status;
```

If the `status` argument is DESTROY_CHECKING and the client cannot terminate at present, the destroy-event handler should call `notify_veto_destroy()`, indicating that termination would not be advisable at this time, and return normally. If the client can terminate at present, then the destroy handler should do nothing; a subsequent call will tell the client to actually destroy itself. This veto option is used, for example, to give a text subwindow the chance to ask the user to confirm the saving of any editing changes when quitting a tool.

If `status` is DESTROY_PROCESS_DEATH, then the client can count on the entire process dying and should do whatever it needs to do to clean up its outside entanglements, such as updating a file used by a text subwindow. Since the process is about to die, it need not free allocated memory which is implicitly freed by the process's termination.

Since the entire process is dying, you cannot display a notice or do any sort of prompting with the user to try to veto this request.

However, if `status` is DESTROY_CLEANUP then the client is asked to destroy itself and to be very tidy about cleaning up all the process internal resources that it is using, as well as its outside entanglements. This may be called on frames which are not the sole frames used by the application. If a frame is dismissed but the application is still running (e.g., dismissing a pinned up menu), then the frame should clean up—including freeing allocated memory.

The `status` is set to `DESTROY_SAVE_YOURSELF` when the window manager has sent a `WM_SAVE_YOURSELF` message to all the clients on the desktop. This means the user may have selected the "Save Workspace" option from an OPEN LOOK window manager's property sheet. Basically, this means that the application should save its current state in such a way that it could be resumed in the same state at a later time. For example, a text editing program would update the file being edited, a graphics program would output its image display to a file, or whatever.

Interposing a Client Destroy Handler

We present an example of interposing in front of the frame's client-destroy event handler. The following program displays a frame, a panel and a panel button labeled "Quit." When the user chooses the panel button or the frame's "Quit" menu selection, the interposer is called and indicates the fact that the frame is about to go away.

Example 19-6. The interpose.c program

```
/*
 * interpose.c -- shows how to use an interpose destroy function
 */
#include <xview/xview.h>
#include <xview/frame.h>
#include <xview/panel.h>
#include <xview/notice.h>

Frame frame;

Notify_value
destroy_func(client, status)
Notify_client client;
Destroy_status status;
{
    if (status == DESTROY_CHECKING) {
        int answer = notice_prompt(client, NULL,
            NOTICE_MESSAGE_STRINGS, "Really Quit?", NULL,
            NOTICE_BUTTON_YES,  "No",
            NOTICE_BUTTON_NO,   "Yes",
            NULL);
        if (answer == NOTICE_YES)
            notify_veto_destroy(client);
    } else if (status == DESTROY_CLEANUP) {
        puts("cleaning up");
        /* allow frame to be destroyed */
        return notify_next_destroy_func(client, status);
    } else if (status == DESTROY_SAVE_YOURSELF)
        puts("save yourself?");
    else
        puts("process death");
    return NOTIFY_DONE;
}

main (argc, argv)
int argc;
char *argv[];
{
    Panel panel;
```

Example 19-6. The interpose.c program (continued)

```
    int    quit();

    xv_init (XV_INIT_ARGC_PTR_ARGV, &argc, argv, NULL);

    frame = (Frame)xv_create (NULL, FRAME,
        FRAME_LABEL,        argv[0],
        XV_WIDTH,           200,
        XV_HEIGHT,          100,
        NULL);
    notify_interpose_destroy_func(frame, destroy_func);

    panel = (Panel)xv_create (frame, PANEL, NULL);
    (void) xv_create (panel, PANEL_BUTTON,
            PANEL_LABEL_STRING,         "Quit",
            PANEL_NOTIFY_PROC,          quit,
            NULL);
    xv_main_loop(frame);
}

int
quit()
{
    xv_destroy_safe(frame);
    return XV_OK;
}
```

The first time the interposer is called, the status is DESTROY_CHECKING. Here, we display a notice prompting the user to confirm the quit. We want the *default* action to be "No," so we make the NOTICE_YES button have the label "No" and the NOTICE_NO button have the label "Yes." This is because the notice's *default* button is the NOTICE_YES button.

If the user selects the default "No" choice, then notify_veto_client() is called, vetoing the destruction request. Otherwise, the routine returns and the destruction sequence continues as usual. The routine is then called again, notifying that it is being destroyed this time. It calls notify_next_destroy_func() to allow the process to continue. This is where any process cleaning up should take place.

19.10 Notifier Control

The Notifier is started automatically by calling xv_main_loop(). It takes a window object (typically the base frame of the application) and sets XV_SHOW to TRUE. Then it calls notify_start() and the Notifier is running. notify_start() continuously loops through the Notifier's processing loop waiting for events in which its clients have expressed interest. This continues until the application calls notify_stop() or there are no more clients registered. At this time, notify_start() returns and the application can continue.

When notify_start() is called, the Notifier takes over and none of the application code is executed unless it is directly or indirectly called by a *notify* or *callback* procedure. If the callback routine calls notify_stop(), when that callback function returns, notify_start() returns and, thus, xv_main_loop() returns. The Notifier can be stopped using this method despite the fact that there are still clients registered with the Notifier. At this point, the application may call `notify_start()` again, or it may attempt to do either *implicit* or *explicit* dispatching of events.

Explicit dispatching is done by calling `notify_dispatch()`. Here, the Notifier steps through one iteration of its normal control loop. This allows you to monitor events during the execution of a time-consuming or computationally complex portion of the program. Say your application generates a complex fractal image. The process is initiated from the selection of a panel button. Because the generation of fractals is very time consuming, you may wish to check every once in a while to see if the user has generated any events that need to be processed—like selecting a panel button labeled `Stop`. In this case, the callback procedure for the panel button should call `notify_stop()` and return. The Notifier returns to the top-level, `notify_start()` returns (and thus, `xv_main_loop()` returns) and your application begins to generate the fractal image. During each iteration of the loop (or more often, if necessary), `notify_dispatch()` is called to be sure to process any pending events that the user might have generated.

Implicit dispatching indicates that you are going to make calls to `read()` or `select()`—system calls which *block*. If `notify_do_dispatch()` is called, then events that the user generates (such as moving the mouse or selecting a panel button) will continue to be processed even though the `read()` has not yet returned.

Implicit and explicit dispatching may be used before or after the call to `xv_main_loop()` or `notify_start()`, but it is not permitted to call these functions while the Notifier is looping on its own (from within a call to `notify_start()`). Therefore, you should never attempt to do direct dispatching from within a callback routine or any function that has been called indirectly by the Notifier.

These two methods of dispatching make porting programs that do not use the Notifier much easier. Thus, building an XView interface on top of a typical mainline-based input-driven program is also much easier. Programs written from scratch should try to follow the event-driven input style of program design and try to avoid using implicit or explicit dispatching whenever possible.

19.10.1 Implicit Dispatching

Implicit dispatching is used whenever you wish to loop on a call that might block, such as `read` (2). Before calling `read()`, you should first call the function:

```
notify_do_dispatch();
```

This tells the Notifier that you are going to do implicit dispatching and that it should use its own version of `read()` rather than using the standard system call as the function. The two are equivalent with one exception—`read()` will return 0 on EOF rather than -1, as you might expect.

After `notify_do_dispatch()` has been called, you can either call `notify_dispatch()` directly (to process events you know to have been delivered already) or call `read()` (or both).

Notifier

The following example program demonstrates how this can be done. The program creates our usual frame, panel and "Quit" panel button, but instead of calling xv_main_loop(), we create a small loop which reads stdin waiting for typed input.

Example 19-7. The ntfy_do_dis.c program

```
/*
 * ntfy_do_dis.c -- show an example of implicit notifier dispatching
 * by calling notify_do_dispatch().  Create a frame, panel and "Quit"
 * button, and then loop on calls to read() from stdin.  Event
 * processing is still maintained because the Notifier uses its own
 * non-blocking read().
 */
#include <stdio.h>
#include <xview/xview.h>
#include <xview/frame.h>
#include <xview/panel.h>

Frame frame;

main (argc, argv)
int argc;
char *argv[];
{
    Panel panel;
    char  buf[BUFSIZ];
    int   n, quit();

    xv_init (XV_INIT_ARGC_PTR_ARGV, &argc, argv, NULL);

    frame = (Frame)xv_create (NULL, FRAME,
        FRAME_LABEL,     argv[0],
        XV_WIDTH,        200,
        XV_HEIGHT,       100,
        XV_SHOW,         TRUE,
        NULL);

    panel = (Panel)xv_create (frame, PANEL, NULL);

    (void) xv_create (panel, PANEL_BUTTON,
            PANEL_LABEL_STRING,      "Quit",
            PANEL_NOTIFY_PROC,       quit,
            NULL);

    /* Force the frame to be displayed by flushing the server */
    XFlush(xv_get(frame, XV_DISPLAY));

    /* tell the Notifier that it should use its own read() so that it
     * can also detect and dispatch events.  This allows us to loop
     * in this code segment and still process events.
     */
    notify_do_dispatch();

    puts("Frame being displayed -- type away.");
    while ((n = read(0, buf, sizeof buf)) >= 0)
        printf("read %d bytes\n", n);

    printf("read() returned %d\n", n);
}

int
quit()
```

Example 19-7. The ntfy_do_dis.c program (continued)

```
{
    xv_destroy_safe(frame);
    return XV_OK;
}
```

There are several things to note here. First, because `xv_main_loop()` is not called, we need to explicitly set the attribute `XV_SHOW` to `TRUE` for the base frame. Otherwise, it will never be displayed. Also, because of the nature of event dispatching, we must *flush* the connection between the X server and the application to make sure that the frame is displayed by the time the first `read()` call returns. If this is not done, the frame is not displayed until after the first `read()` returns.

19.10.2 Explicit Dispatching

Frequently, the programmer is plagued with the following problem: A great deal of processing has to be done to process something that the user has initiated. As mentioned before, the programmer might want to generate a fractal image or compute the value of *pi* when the user selects a panel button. Any time-consuming process that requires this type of functionality should utilize explicit dispatching. It seems like an easy solution to `fork()` and let the background process perform the operation, but this is frequently an expensive operation and should be avoided if explicit dispatching is sufficient. If forking is required, then Section 19.5.5, "Handling SIGCHLD," and Section 19.8.2, "Reading and Writing on Pipes," should be referenced.

The call `notify_dispatch()` does explicit event dispatching to service immediately an event that you know is waiting to be read and dispatched. Typically, this is called at particular locations within a control loop that is processing time-consuming tasks. It is assumed that this control loop does *not* call `read()` or `select()`. Rather, explicit dispatching is used within loops that might do heavy computation such as graphics processing or number crunching. This is necessary because while the computations are busy computing, the user might be attempting to interact with the application by selecting a panel button.

If `notify_dispatch()` is called frequently enough, then performance of the user interface may still be perceived as acceptable even though the program is very busy with its computations. Architecturally, such a program is designed in a similar way with *ntfy_do_dis.c* in Section 19.10.1, "Implicit Dispatching." That is, there is a central processing loop which is doing the main work of the program. In this case, `notify_do_dispatch()` is not called.

```
#include <xview/xview.h>
. . .
int finished;

main(argc, argv)
char *argv[];
{
    Display *dpy;
    Frame frame;

    . . .
```

Notifier

```
    xv_create(NULL, FRAME, NULL);

    ...

    dpy = (Display *)xv_get(frame, XV_DISPLAY);
    /* flush everything before starting loop */
    XFlush(dpy);
    while (!finished) {
        notify_dispatch();
        XFlush(dpy);
        /* compute PI to the next place */
        process_pi();
    }
}
```

Notice that after `notify_dispatch()`, `XFlush()` is called. It is imperative that this happen; otherwise, any Xlib calls (which result from many `xv_create()` or `xv_set()` calls) may not be displayed. You only need to call `XFlush()` once after one or more calls to a sequence of calls to `notify_dispatch()`. The rule of thumb is to flush the server whenever you want to see the latest display.

19.11 Error Codes

This section describes the basic error handling scheme used by the Notifier and lists the meaning of each of the possible error codes. Every call to the Notifier returns a value that indicates success or failure. On an error condition, `notify_errno` describes the failure. `notify_errno` is set by the Notifier as `errno` is set by UNIX system calls, i.e., `notify_errno` is set only when an error is detected during a call to the Notifier and is not reset to `NOTIFY_OK` on a successful call to the Notifier.

```
    enum notify_error {
        ... /* Listed below */
    };
    typedef enum notify_error Notify_error;

    extern Notify_error notify_errno;
```

Table 19-1 contains a complete list of error codes.

Table 19-1. Notifier Error Codes

Error Code	Description
NOTIFY_OK	The call was completed successfully.
NOTIFY_UNKNOWN_CLIENT	The `client` argument is not known by the Notifier. A `notify_set_*_func` call needs to be made in order for the Notifier to recognize it.

Table 19-1. Notifier Error Codes (continued)

Error Code	Description
NOTIFY_NO_CONDITION	A call was made to access the state of a condition but the condition was not set with the Notifier for the client in question. This can happen when a notify_get_*_func() type call is made before the equivalent notify_set_*_func(). Also, the Notifier automatically clears some conditions after they have occurred, e.g., when an interval timer expires.
NOTIFY_BAD_ITIMER	The which argument to an interval timer routine was not valid.
NOTIFY_BAD_SIGNAL	The signal argument to a signal routine was out of range.
NOTIFY_NOT_STARTED	A call to notify_stop() was made, but the Notifier was never started.
NOTIFY_DESTROY_VETOED	A client refused to be destroyed during a call to notify_die() or notify_post_destroy() when status was DESTROY_CHECKING.
NOTIFY_INTERNAL_ERROR	Some internal inconsistency in the Notifier itself has been detected.
NOTIFY_SRCH	The pid argument to a child process control routine was not valid.
NOTIFY_BADF	The fd argument to an input or output routine was not valid.
NOTIFY_NOMEM	The Notifier dynamically allocates memory from the heap. This error code is generated if the allocator could not get any more memory.
NOTIFY_INVAL	Some argument to a call to the Notifier contained an invalid argument.
NOTIFY_FUNC_LIMIT	An attempt to set an interposer function has encountered the limit of the number of interposers allowed for a single condition.

The routine notify_perror() acts like library call perror (3).

```
notify_perror(str)
     char *str;
```

notify_perror() prints the string str, followed by a colon and followed by a string that describes notify_errno to stderr.

Notifier

19.12 Issues

Here are some additional issues surrounding the Notifier:

- The layer over the UNIX signal mechanism is not complete. Signal blocking (`sigblock` (2)) can still be done safely in the flow of control of a client to protect critical portions of code as long as the previous signal mask is restored before returning to the Notifier. Signal pausing (`sigpause` (2)) is essentially done by the Notifier. Signal masking (`sigmask` (2)) can be accomplished via multiple `notify_set_signal_func()` calls. Setting up a process signal stack (`sigstack` (2)) can still be done. Setting the signal catcher mask and on-signal-stack flag (`sigvec` (2)) could be done by reaching around the Notifier, but this is not supported.

- Not all process resources are multiplexed (e.g., `rlimit` (2), `setjmp` (2), `umask` (2), `setquota` (2), and `setpriority` (2)); only ones that have to do with flow of control multiplexing. Thus, some level of cooperation and understanding needs to exist between packages in the single process.

- One might intercept `close` (2) and `dup` (2) calls so that the Notifier is not waiting on invalid or incorrect file descriptors if a client forgets to remove its conditions from the Notifier before making these calls.

- One might intercept `signal` (3) and `sigvec` (2) calls so that the Notifier does not get confused by programs that fail to use the Notifier to manage its signals.

- One might intercept `setitimer` (2) calls so that the Notifier does not get confused by programs that fail to use the Notifier to manage interval timers.

- One might intercept `ioctl`(2) calls so that the Notifier does not get fouled up by programs that use `FIONBIO` and `FIOASYNC` instead of the equivalent `fcntl` (2) calls.

- One might intercept `readv` (2) and `write` (2) just like `read` (2) and `select` (2) so that a program does not tie up the process.

- The Notifier is not a lightweight process mechanism that maintains a stack per thread of control. However, if such a mechanism becomes available, then the Notifier will still be valuable for its support of notification-based clients.

- Client events are disjoint from UNIX events. This is done to give complete freedom to clients as to how events are defined. One could imagine certain clients wanting to unify client and UNIX events. This could be done with a layer of software on top of the Notifier. A client could define events as pointers to structures that contain event codes and event specific arguments. The event codes would include the equivalents of UNIX event notifications. The event specific arguments would contain, for example, the file descriptor of an input-pending notification. When an input-pending notification from the Notifier was sent to a client, the client would turn around and post the equivalent client-event notification.

- One could imagine extending the Notifier to provide a record and replay mechanism that would drive an application. However, this is not supported by the current interface.

20

Color

In This Chapter:

20
Color

The X Window System has various ways of allocating, specifying and using colors. While all of these methods are available to applications without XView intervening, XView provides its own model for color specification that may be used as an alternative. It does not provide anything more than what is already available, but it may provide a simpler interface to request and specify colors. This model is especially useful when specifying colors for XView objects, such as panel buttons and scrollbars.

There is no overlap between XView's and Xlib's color usage. If you choose to use Xlib calls to create colormaps, to allocate color cells and so on, you can only attach the colormaps to actual X windows, not XView objects. For example, you would have to use XChange-WindowAttributes on the XV_XID of a canvas paint window.

This chapter does not directly discuss how to use colormaps and related Xlib color-specific functions. For a discussion of them, see Volume 1, *Xlib Programming Manual*, Chapter 7, *Color*. This chapter discusses only the XView color model.

Obviously, the user cannot view colors in an application without having a color display. But you cannot tell at the time your application is written whether the user's display is going to be able to support color. To do this, you can use the DisplayDepth() macro to determine whether the display can handle color:

```
Display *dpy = (Display *)xv_get(frame, XV_DISPLAY);
extern use_color;

if (DefaultDepth(dpy, DefaultScreen(dpy)) < 2)
    use_color = False;
```

20.1 XView Color Model

XView applications deal with color by using *colormap segments*. As a simple introduction, the following code fragment creates a colormap segment with the specified colors and returns a handle to it:

```
cms = (Cms)xv_create(NULL, CMS,
    CMS_SIZE,           4,
    CMS_NAMED_COLORS, "white", "red", "green", "blue", NULL,
    NULL);
```

Window-based objects (canvases, panels, textsw, etc.) use colormap segments to get their colors. These objects get a default colormap segment when they are created, but you can assign a new one using the WIN_CMS attribute:

```
canvas = (Canvas)xv_create(frame, CANVAS,
    WIN_CMS, cms,
    NULL);
```

Colormap segments must be applied to windows to assure that the window can access the color you are attempting to draw into. However, there is much to understand about colors, colormaps, colormap segments, visuals, servers and X11 to be able to use colors in an efficient and robust way. Unless done correctly, you may produce code that only works on specific machines or in specific environments.

What is a Colormap Segment?

A colormap segment (cms), is a subset of the available cells in a colormap on the X server. These are XView entities (i.e., not Xlib) that provide a veneer over the Xlib color mechanism. Colormap segments can be created as either *static* or *dynamic* and are derived from an underlying colormap of the same type.

Any object subclassed from the window object may allocate and use colormap segments. You can use Xlib routines to do all your color and colormap manipulation within canvas windows, pixmaps and other X-related objects, but you must use the colormap segment API for XView objects.

More than one XView object may reference the same colormap segment. However, a colormap segment does not keep track of the objects that are using it. The application is required to keep track of changes in colors and update its objects accordingly.

The internals to XView attempt to create colormap segments that are as small as possible so that numerous segments can share the same underlying colormap. If a colormap segment requires more colors than the current colormap has space for, a new colormap must be created.

20.1.1 Colormap Segment Types

You can create static or dynamic colormap segments. The type is set with the CMS_TYPE attribute. Its value can be either XV_STATIC_CMS or XV_DYNAMIC_CMS. A colormap segment's type cannot change, so the CMS_TYPE attribute is for xv_create() only.

The X11 Protocol specifies that the Visual type of a window must be declared at the time it is created. Therefore, XView objects that allocate colormap segments are required, at creation time, to specify the type of visual they propose to use. You can set the visual to be either static or dynamic by setting the attribute WIN_DYNAMIC_VISUAL to TRUE or FALSE respectively. The default visual is determined by the default visual of the screen.

Static Colormap Segments

Applications must always use static colormap segments unless they require read/write colors. Colors allocated from a static colormap segment are shared among *all* applications. In static colormaps segments, when a new color is asked for, the XView library will try to return the closest (or exact) matching color from the server (using XAllocColor()) if the default colormap on the server is StaticColor.

Whenever possible, a colormap segment is derived from the default colormap obtained from the screen in which the window resides (e.g., DefaultColormap()). Only when the colors on that colormap have been exhausted is a new colormap allocated. If XView needs to allocate a new colormap for a new cms, it does this internally. It is impossible for the application to specify a colormap for a colormap segment.

The cells in a static cms are initialized once and are read-only from then on. Static colormap segments, by sharing color cells across applications, use the shared hardware colormap resources more efficiently and reduce *flashing*. Flashing is a blinking effect you sometimes get when moving the cursor in and out of various windows on the screen. This is caused by the server popping different colormaps in and out as you move from one window to the next.

Dynamic Colormap Segments

When you ask for a dynamic cms, XView sends a request to the server to allocate read-write colors. When colors are requested from this cms, the color returned is the exact color; the closest match is not returned as it is with static colors.

20.2 Creating Colormap Segments

Applications that use color must include the file *<xview/cms.h>*. A cms can be created using the standard call to xv_create() with the package name CMS.

```
Cms cms;

cms = (Cms)xv_create(parent, CMS, attrs, NULL);
```

The *parent* of a colormap segment is the XView screen object with which the colormap is associated. If a parent is not specified, the default screen of the default server is used as the parent.

Cms Size

A cms may contain as many colors as you like as long as they fit within the largest colormap you can create. Having more than one colormap segment reference the same color value is perfectly legal and reasonable. Data is frequently shared among segments for optimal efficiency.

When creating a colormap segment, you must specify its size (i.e., the number of colors it has) using the CMS_SIZE attribute. If you don't set the size, it defaults to the macro, XV_DEFAULT_CMS_SIZE, which is 2. CMS_SIZE is a create- and get-only attribute; once a colormap is created, its size cannot be changed, although you can query a colormap's size using xv_get().

If all the colors in a colormap segment are not initialized, the uninitialized colors are undefined and should not be used. You can change colors within a dynamic cms at any time. Uninitialized colors of a static cms can be initialized using xv_set(), but once initialized, they may not be changed.

You might want to create a segment of a larger size than the number of colors you assign it because you may not have all the colors you know you'll need right away. For example, you create a colormap segment of size *n*, but initialize it with only *n-4* colors. When the rest of the colors are ready to be loaded into the segment, you do so at the location of the uninitialized colors, namely, at index *n-4*. The CMS_INDEX attribute is used to specify this location.

CAUTION

> All the colors in a static cms must be specified at the time of creation to avoid race conditions in the associated X11 colormap. Because static colormaps are shared with other applications, if you request *n* colors but do not initialize all of them, another application could request and initialize enough colors to fill up the colormap before you get a chance to set the rest of your colors.

When creating a cms or setting new colors, you may specify CMS_COLOR_COUNT to indicate the number of colors to load. Again, if you want to load these colors at a position other than the beginning of the segment, use CMS_INDEX. This is typically used only when you are creating a colormap segment and not initializing each color right away. Or, if you have already done this, you are adding more colors to a prebuilt colormap segment that hasn't had all of its colors initialized. Therefore, this is a create-only and set-only attribute.

20.2.1 Specifying Colors

You can specify actual colors by name or by RGB values. When using RGB values, you can use XView or Xlib data structures. In each case, we are going to create a colormap segment with the same four colors: white, red, green and blue.

Specifying Colors by Name

The attribute CMS_NAMED_COLORS takes as its value a NULL-terminated list of strings representing color names:

```
cms = (Cms)xv_create(parent, CMS,
    CMS_SIZE,          4,
    CMS_NAMED_COLORS, "white", "red", "green", "blue", NULL,
    NULL);
```

The colors specified by the names are converted into actual values using XParseColor()* and allocated into the colormap segment using XAllocColor() (for static colormaps) or XStoreColor() (for dynamic colormaps). The example shown probably works because the colors used are common colors found on most X servers' color databases. However, you should be careful when requesting named colors in this fashion because the database may not contain the color name you specify. If any of the colors requested fails, then no change to the cms is affected and xv_set() returns XV_ERROR. If a cms is being created via xv_create() and an error occurs, no cms is created and xv_create() returns NULL.

CMS_NAMED_COLORS cannot be used by xv_get().

Specifying Colors by RGB values

You can request colors more directly by specifying the actual red, green and blue (RGB) values using one of two attributes. CMS_COLORS takes as a value an array of Xv_singlecolor objects. This XView-defined type is declared as:

```
typedef struct xv_singlecolor {
    unsigned char red, green, blue;
} Xv_singlecolor;
```

---

*XParseColor() is an Xlib call that maps char * color names into RGB values.

We can use the following to produce a cms with the same colors:

```
static Xv_singlecolor colors[] = {
    { 255, 255, 255, }, /* white */
    { 255, 0, 0 },      /* red */
    { 0, 255 0, },      /* green */
    { 0, 0, 255 },      /* blue */
};
cms = xv_create(NULL, CMS,
    CMS_SIZE,     4,
    CMS_COLORS,   colors,
    NULL);
```

Alternatively, you can use the attribute CMS_X_COLORS to specify an array of XColor structures, defined in <X11/Xlib.h> as:

```
typedef struct {
    unsigned        long pixel;
    unsigned short  red, green, blue;
    char            flags;  /* do_red, do_green, do_blue */
    char            pad;
} XColor;
```

Here is a way to produce a colormap segment with the same colors but using an array of XColors:

```
static XColor colors[] = {
/* white */ { 0, 255<<8, 255<<8, 255<<8, DoRed|DoGreen|DoBlue, 0 },
/* red */   { 0, 255<<8,      0,      0, DoRed|DoGreen|DoBlue, 0 },
/* green */ { 0,      0, 255<<8,      0, DoRed|DoGreen|DoBlue, 0 },
/* blue */  { 0,      0,      0, 255<<8, DoRed|DoGreen|DoBlue, 0 },
};
cms = xv_create(NULL, CMS,
    CMS_SIZE,     4,
    CMS_X_COLORS, colors,
    NULL);
```

Note that the color values in the red, green and blue fields of the XColor data structure are left-shifted by 8. For more details on specifying colors with Xlib, see Volume 1, *Xlib Programming Manual*.

When storing colors, if the colormap segment type is static, XView uses XAllocColor(). If the colormap segment type is dynamic, XView uses XAllocColorCells() and XStoreColors() to allocate a dynamic colormap and store the requested colors in it.

After setting colors in a cms, the pixel values for the colors can be retrieved. These pixel values are indices into the colormap itself, not the colormap *segment*. See Section 20.3, "Color and Pixel Values."

The XView attributes to set colors can be used to get the colors from the cms as well. For example, to get the colors into an array of Xv_singlecolor, use:

```
Xv_singlecolor colors[SIZE];

xv_get(cms, CMS_COLORS, &colors);
```

The size of the colors array *must be the same size as the color segment* because xv_get() gets the entire colormap segment and stores the colors at the base of the array. You cannot get a partial list of colors from the cms. The same is true for getting the colors into an array of XColor:

```
XColor colors[SIZE];

xv_get(cms, CMS_X_COLORS, &colors);
```

In each case, xv_get() returns a pointer to the base of the array of data structures passed as the third argument. We choose to ignore it here because the array itself is sufficient.

20.2.2 Cms Name

Colormap segments can be named using CMS_NAME.* Windows can change between color-maps by setting their WIN_CMS_NAME to the names of allocated colormap segments. However, this old-style method of specifying colormap segments for windows is made obsolete by the attribute WIN_CMS, the recommended method for assigning colormap segments to windows.

If unnamed, a cms will get a unique name assigned to it. You can retrieve that name using xv_get() and CMS_NAME. WIN_CMS_NAME is also the only attribute for which you can use xv_find() for the CMS package.

20.3 Color and Pixel Values

By now, you know that a *color* is defined to be a set of red, green and blue (RGB) intensity values. For example, red is represented by a full intensity for the red value and no intensity for the green and blue values. Other shades are achieved by raising or lowering the intensities of one or more of the RGB values. A colormap is an array of RGB values; a *pixel* is an index into that array.

Logical vs. Real Indices

If a colormap segment of size n is created, its logical indices range from 0 to n-1. XView attributes that take color values (e.g., WIN_FOREGROUND_COLOR, PANEL_ITEM_COLOR, etc.) always deal with logical index values.

The *real* indices of a colormap segment are the actual indices into the hardware colormap. Each colormap segment maintains an internal table to translate from logical to real indices. Real index values (*pixels*) are used for setting the foreground and background colors in GCs used in Xlib calls.

---

*CMS_NAME is defined to be XV_NAME.

The index table from a colormap segment can be obtained using the attribute CMS_INDEX_TABLE.

```
unsigned long *colors;

colors = (unsigned long *)xv_get(cms, CMS_INDEX_TABLE);
```

Similarly, the pixel values from a *window-based object* can be obtained using the window attribute, WIN_X_COLOR_INDICES:

```
unsigned long *colors;

colors = (unsigned long *)xv_get(canvas, WIN_X_COLOR_INDICES);
```

Note the object passed to xv_get().

In both cases, the returned value is a pointer to an array of unsigned long types. For a colormap segment of size *n*, colors[0], colors[1], ... colors[0] contain the actual pixel values corresponding to the colors in the underlying X11 colormap. These pixel values can be used in calls to XSetForeground() or XSetBackground() to change GC values.

To get the real pixel value corresponding to a logical index value, you can use the CMS_PIXEL attribute:

```
Cms cms;
unsigned long red, blue;

cms = (Cms)xv_create(NULL, CMS,
    CMS_SIZE,           2,
    CMS_NAMED_COLORS,   "red", "blue", NULL,
    NULL);
red  = (unsigned long)xv_get(cms, CMS_PIXEL, 0);
blue = (unsigned long)xv_get(cms, CMS_PIXEL, 1);
```

CMS_PIXEL can only be used to get the value of pixels; you cannot use it to set cms color values.

As discussed earlier, the CMS_X_COLORS attribute can be used to get an array of XColor elements. This data structure has a pixel field that can be referenced to get the pixel values associated with colors.

20.3.1 Foreground and Background Colors

Foreground and background colors correspond to the last and first colors in a colormap segment. That is, the segment's *background* color corresponds to the logical index 0 in the cms, whereas the *foreground* color corresponds to the logical index *n*-1 (where *n* is the size of the cms).

Identifying the foreground and background colors on certain XView objects may not be as straightforward as it appears. For example, the background color of a canvas is the color the entire canvas is painted with when XClearArea() is called. The foreground color is a thin border color around the inside perimeter of each canvas view window. This is not necessarily the color in which graphics are rendered into the canvas using XCopyArea() or XDraw-String(). The color of the graphical images you see in a canvas is dependent on the foreground color set in the GC used by the Xlib routines.

The real pixel values for the foreground and background colors of a cms may be obtained directly using the attributes CMS_FOREGROUND_PIXEL and CMS_BACKGROUND_PIXEL.

```
Cms             cms;
unsigned long   fg, bg;

bg = (unsigned long)xv_get(cms, CMS_BACKGROUND_PIXEL);
fg = (unsigned long)xv_get(cms, CMS_FOREGROUND_PIXEL);
```

Colors of Frames and Control Objects

The FRAME package sets its foreground and background colors using the attributes FRAME_FOREGROUND_COLOR and FRAME_BACKGROUND_COLOR. This does not include frame's decorations since they are handled by the window manager (see Chapter 4, *Frames*). However, the attribute FRAME_INHERIT_COLORS, can be used to force subwindows of the frame to inherit its colors.

A *control object* in XView refers to panels, scrollbars, notices and menus. These packages cannot have their foreground and background modified programmatically in the same way as other window-based objects. This restriction applies to the 3D interface; the 2D interface may allow the foreground and background colors to be modified. However, OPEN LOOK states that the background of all control objects appear consistent; thus, a single *control color* is used. Panels, for example, ignore attempts to set the WIN_FOREGROUND_COLOR and WIN_BACKGROUND_COLOR attributes. Panel items, however, may have their colors set by setting PANEL_ITEM_COLOR to a logical index into the panel's cms. XView allows the user, not the programmer, to set the background color for control objects via the resource database. This is discussed in Section 20.5, "The Control Colormap Segment."

20.4 The color_logo.c Program

Using the basic principles discussed so far, we present Example 20-1 to demonstrate the creation and initialization of a colormap segment for an XView canvas. Pixel values are extracted from the colormap segment and set into a GC's foreground. Xlib calls are then used to render various items in the same four basic colors we've been using.

Example 20-1. The color_logo.c program

```
/* color_logo.c --
 *   This program demonstrates the combined use of the XView color
 *   model/API and Xlib graphics calls. The program uses XView to
 *   create and manage its colormap segment while doing its actual
 *   drawing using Xlib routines.
 *   The program draws the X logo in red, green and blue in a canvas.
 */
#include <xview/xview.h>
```

Example 20-1. The color_logo.c program (continued)

```
#include <xview/canvas.h>
#include <xview/cms.h>
#include <xview/xv_xrect.h>
#include <X11/bitmaps/xlogo64>

/* Color indices */
#define WHITE           0
#define RED             1
#define GREEN           2
#define BLUE            3
#define NUM_COLORS      4

GC gc;                          /* used for rendering logos */
unsigned long *pixel_table; /* pixel values for colors */
Pixmap        xlogo;            /* the xlogo */

/* Create a frame, canvas, and a colormap segment and assign the
 * cms to the canvas.  CMS_INDEX_TABLE returns the actual colormap
 * indices and are used to set the gc's foreground for XCopyPlane
 * calls.
 */
main(argc,argv)
int     argc;
char    *argv[];
{
    Frame           frame;
    XGCValues       gc_val;
    XGCValues       gcvalues;
    void            canvas_repaint_proc();
    Cms             cms;
    static Xv_singlecolor colors[] = {
        { 255, 255, 255 }, /* white */
        { 255,   0,   0 }, /* red */
        { 0,   255,   0 }, /* green */
        { 0,     0, 255 }, /* blue */
    };

    xv_init(XV_INIT_ARGC_PTR_ARGV, &argc, argv, NULL);

    cms = (Cms) xv_create(NULL, CMS,
        CMS_SIZE, 4,
        CMS_COLORS, colors,
        NULL);

    frame = (Frame)xv_create(XV_NULL, FRAME,
        FRAME_LABEL,    argv[0],
        XV_WIDTH,       448,
        XV_HEIGHT,      192,
        NULL);

    (void) xv_create(frame, CANVAS,
        CANVAS_X_PAINT_WINDOW,  TRUE,
        CANVAS_REPAINT_PROC,    canvas_repaint_proc,
        WIN_CMS,                cms,
        NULL);

    /* Get the actual indices into the colormap */
    pixel_table = (unsigned long *)xv_get(cms, CMS_INDEX_TABLE);

    /* create the xlogo -- get display/window from the frame obj */
```

Example 20-1. The color_logo.c program (continued)

```
    xlogo = XCreateBitmapFromData(
        xv_get(frame, XV_DISPLAY), xv_get(frame, XV_XID),
        xlogo64_bits, xlogo64_width, xlogo64_height);

    /* setup gc for rendering logos to screen */
    gcvalues.graphics_exposures = False;
    gcvalues.background = pixel_table[WHITE];
    gc = XCreateGC(xv_get(frame, XV_DISPLAY), xv_get(frame, XV_XID),
        GCBackground | GCGraphicsExposures, &gcvalues);

    xv_main_loop(frame);
}

/* Draws onto the canvas using Xlib drawing functions.
 * Draw the X logo into the window in three colors. In each case,
 * change the GC's foreground color to the pixel value specified.
 */
void
canvas_repaint_proc(canvas, pw, display, win, xrects)
    Canvas      canvas;     /* unused */
    Xv_Window   pw;         /* unused */
    Display     *display;
    Window      win;
    Xv_xrectlist *xrects; /* unused */
{
    /* Use XCopyPlane because the logo is a 1-bit deep pixmap. */
    XSetForeground(display, gc, pixel_table[RED]);
    XCopyPlane(display, xlogo, win, gc, 0, 0,
        xlogo64_width, xlogo64_height, 64, 64, 1);

    XSetForeground(display, gc, pixel_table[GREEN]);
    XCopyPlane(display, xlogo, win, gc, 0, 0,
        xlogo64_width, xlogo64_height, 192, 64, 1);

    XSetForeground(display, gc, pixel_table[BLUE]);
    XCopyPlane(display, xlogo, win, gc, 0, 0,
        xlogo64_width, xlogo64_height, 320, 64, 1);
}
```

Example 20-1 uses Xlib routines to draw into the canvas's paint window. Therefore, the GC's foreground color is set to an index from the colormap being used by that paint window. In order to get the correct color from the colormap, we need to get the color table for the window using the attribute CMS_COLOR_INDEX. The repaint routine draws the X logo in the specified colors.

20.5 The Control Colormap Segment

The management of colormap segments is a little different for control objects (panels, notices, menus, etc.) than it is for other XView objects. In order for XView to provide the same control colors for control objects, these objects must use a *control colormap segment*. This is just like a normal cms except that parts of it are reserved for the predefined colors.

Since OPEN LOOK suggests that the background of control objects in an application appear in a consistent color, XView sets that color to be that specified by the resource Open-Windows.WindowColor from the user's environment. This color is used as the background color, and along with a few others, they are set aside in the first few indices of the control colormap segment.

These *control* colors are used used to provide a 3D look for the control objects. Thus, the control colormap segment must be used for all control objects.

Aside from the added colors, there is little difference between a control cms and a normal cms. The cms may still request many colors and there is no limit to the choice of colors used in the new cms. However, these extra colors cannot be used as the background for control objects.

A control colormap segment is created by setting the boolean attribute CMS_CONTROL_CMS to TRUE in the call to xv_create(). The macro CMS_CONTROL_COLORS (defined in <*xview/cms.h*>) indicates how many predefined control colors there are, so the first CMS_CONTROL_COLORS indices in the cms are initialized by the XView library. If the application requires n other colors in this cms, it must explicitly ask that the segment be created with a size of:

    n + CMS_CONTROL_COLORS

In such a case, the application must refer to its own n colors using the index range:

    CMS_CONTROL_COLORS to CMS_CONTROL_COLORS + n−1

An application-defined colormap segment set on a control object (such as a panel) must be a control colormap segment so that the object can be pointed with the 3D look. If a non-control colormap segment is set on a control object, the object is painted with the 2D look.

```
#define WHITE       0
#define RED         1
#define GREEN       2
#define BLUE        3
#define NUM_COLORS  4

control_cms = xv_create(NULL, CMS,
    CMS_SIZE,          CMS_CONTROL_COLORS + NUM_COLORS,
    CMS_CONTROL_CMS,   TRUE,
    CMS_NAMED_COLORS,  "white", "red", "green", "blue", NULL,
    NULL);
```

We set the boolean attribute CMS_CONTROL_CMS to TRUE to indicate that we are creating a control cms. Notice that the size of the colormap segment is the number of colors *we* specified plus the number of control colors. This colormap segment contains both control colors and our colors; XView automatically allocates our colors after the control colors.

When we create the panel, we specify the new colormap segment as the panel's cms using the common window attribute, WIN_CMS:

```
panel = (Panel)xv_create(frame, PANEL,
    WIN_CMS, control_cms,
    NULL);
```

When we reference our own specified colors, we must offset those color values by CMS_CONTROL_COLORS:

```
/* assume a 1-bit deep 16x16 square pixmap */
extern Server_image chip;

xv_create(panel, PANEL_CHOICE,
    PANEL_LABEL_STRING, "Colors",
    PANEL_CHOICE_IMAGES, chip, chip, chip, chip, NULL,
    PANEL_CHOICE_COLOR, 0, WHITE + CMS_CONTROL_COLORS,
    PANEL_CHOICE_COLOR, 1, RED + CMS_CONTROL_COLORS,
    PANEL_CHOICE_COLOR, 2, GREEN + CMS_CONTROL_COLORS,
    PANEL_CHOICE_COLOR, 3, BLUE + CMS_CONTROL_COLORS,
    NULL);
```

Here, we create a choice item whose choices are colored "chips" in solid colors corresponding to the color names offset by the control colormap segment.

20.5.1 Coloring Panel Items

You can specify colors for panel items using PANEL_ITEM_COLOR. This attribute takes as a value an index into a colormap segment. The value −1 is reserved for the panel's foreground color, whatever that may be. It is also the default color of panel items unless you have specified otherwise with PANEL_ITEM_COLOR. Remember, if you're going to be using the 3D interface, then you must create the cms as a *control* cms. Example 20-2 briefly demonstrates how to create colored panel items.

Example 20-2. The color_panel.c program

```
/* color_panel.c --
 * This program demonstrates how to set panel items to different
 * colors using the XView API for color.
 */
#include <xview/xview.h>
#include <xview/panel.h>
#include <xview/cms.h>

/* Color indices */
#define WHITE          0
#define RED            1
#define GREEN          2
#define BLUE           3
#define NUM_COLORS     4
```

Example 20-2. The color_panel.c program (continued)

```
/* Create a frame, panel, and a colormap segment and assign the
 * cms to the panel.
 */
main(argc,argv)
int     argc;
char    *argv[];
{
    Frame           frame;
    Panel           panel;
    Cms             cms;
    extern void exit(), pressed();
    static Xv_singlecolor colors[] = {
        { 255, 255, 255 }, /* white */
        { 255,   0,   0 }, /* red */
        { 0,   255,   0 }, /* green */
        { 0,     0, 255 }, /* blue */
    };

    xv_init(XV_INIT_ARGC_PTR_ARGV, &argc, argv, NULL);

    cms = (Cms) xv_create(NULL, CMS,
        CMS_CONTROL_CMS,        TRUE,
        CMS_SIZE,               CMS_CONTROL_COLORS + 4,
        CMS_COLORS,             colors,
        NULL);

    frame = (Frame)xv_create(XV_NULL, FRAME,
        FRAME_LABEL,            argv[0],
        FRAME_SHOW_FOOTER,      TRUE,
        NULL);

    panel = xv_create(frame, PANEL,
        WIN_CMS,        cms,
        NULL);

    xv_create(panel, PANEL_BUTTON,
        PANEL_LABEL_STRING,     "Red",
        PANEL_ITEM_COLOR,       CMS_CONTROL_COLORS + RED,
        PANEL_NOTIFY_PROC,      pressed,
        NULL);
    xv_create(panel, PANEL_BUTTON,
        PANEL_LABEL_STRING,     "Green",
        PANEL_ITEM_COLOR,       CMS_CONTROL_COLORS + GREEN,
        PANEL_NOTIFY_PROC,      pressed,
        NULL);
    xv_create(panel, PANEL_BUTTON,
        PANEL_LABEL_STRING,     "Blue",
        PANEL_ITEM_COLOR,       CMS_CONTROL_COLORS + BLUE,
        PANEL_NOTIFY_PROC,      pressed,
        NULL);
    xv_create(panel, PANEL_BUTTON,
        PANEL_LABEL_STRING,     "Quit",
        PANEL_ITEM_COLOR,       CMS_CONTROL_COLORS + WHITE,
        PANEL_NOTIFY_PROC,      exit,
        NULL);

    window_fit(panel);
    window_fit(frame);
```

Example 20-2. The color_panel.c program (continued)

```
    xv_main_loop(frame);
}

void
pressed(item, event)
Panel_item item;
Event *event;
{
    char *name = (char *)xv_get(item, PANEL_LABEL_STRING);
    Frame frame = xv_get(xv_get(item, PANEL_PARENT_PANEL), XV_OWNER);

    xv_set(frame, FRAME_LEFT_FOOTER, name, NULL);
}
```

Notice how the color index for each panel item is offset by the number of colors in the control color item. If all the references to the CMS_CONTROL_COLORS and CMS_CONTROL_CMS attributes were removed, the result would be a 2D panel whose panel items are the same colors as their names.

20.6 Using xv_find() with colormap segments

xv_find() can be used to find a previously created colormap segment. Currently, the attribute CMS_NAME is the only attribute used by xv_find() to find a match.

```
    cms = (Cms)xv_find(screen, CMS,
        CMS_NAME, "palette",
        XV_AUTO_CREATE, FALSE,
        NULL);
```

This example returns a handle to a colormap segment whose name is "palette." XV_AUTO_CREATE is set to FALSE to prevent a new colormap segment from being created. If the colormap segment with that name is not found, then NULL is returned.

20.7 Canvases and Colormaps

When the colormap segment associated with a canvas is changed, the contents of the canvas must be repainted to reflect the new colors. If the boolean attribute CANVAS_CMS_REPAINT is set to TRUE, the library automatically calls the canvas's repaint procedure each time a new colormap segment is set on the canvas. The damage list passed to the routine contains the dimensions of the entire paint window.

Note that the application itself must track any changes in the contents of a colormap segment. CANVAS_CMS_REPAINT enables the library to generate a synthetic repaint event only when the actual colormap segment is switched.

For dynamic colormap segments, when a color changes, the pixel value remains the same but the *color* represented by the index into the colormap segment changes. Therefore, the repaint routine is not called and the window's appearance changes automatically. This method of colormap manipulation is commonly used to implement color animation.

20.8 Another Example

This final example demonstrates just about all of the features discussed in this chapter. It includes creating a colormap segment, initializing color, using foreground and background colors and setting colors on specific XView objects, including panel items.

In Example 20-3, the user selects objects (from the "Objects" item) to be colored by selecting one of the color tiles from the "Colors" choice item. The callback function for this panel item calls color_notify(), which sets the currently selected colors on the foreground or background of the selected objects. Whether to use foreground or background colors is dependent on the value of the "Fg/Bg" panel item; the items whose colors are affected are retrieved by getting the value of the "Objects" panel item. Since more than one object can be selected from this item, the value is a mask of the selected items. We loop through each bit in the mask identifying which objects should have their colors set.

Example 20-3. The color_objs.c program

```
/*
 * color_objs.c --
 *     This program demonstrates the use of color in XView. It allows
 *     the user to choose the foreground and background colors of the
 *     various objects in an interactive manner.
 */
#include <xview/xview.h>
#include <xview/svrimage.h>
#include <xview/textsw.h>
#include <xview/panel.h>
#include <xview/cms.h>
#include <xview/notice.h>

#define SELECT_TEXTSW            0
#define SELECT_TEXTSW_VIEW       1
#define SELECT_PANEL             2
#define SELECT_ICON              3

#define NUM_COLORS               8

/* Icon data */
static short icon_bits[] = {
#include "cardback.icon"
};

/* solid black square */
static short black_bits[] = {
    0xFFFF, 0xFFFF, 0xFFFF, 0xFFFF, 0xFFFF, 0xFFFF, 0xFFFF, 0xFFFF,
    0xFFFF, 0xFFFF, 0xFFFF, 0xFFFF, 0xFFFF, 0xFFFF, 0xFFFF, 0xFFFF
};

Panel_item      objects;
Textsw          textsw;
Panel           panel;
Icon            icon;
```

Example 20-3. The color_objs.c program (continued)

```
/*
 * main()
 *     Create a panel and panel items. The application uses panel items
 *     to choose a particular object and change its foreground and
 *     background colors in an interactive manner. Create a textsw.
 *     Create an icon. All the objects share the same colormap segment.
 */
main(argc,argv)
int      argc;
char     *argv[];
{
    Frame           frame;
    Panel_item      color_choices, panel_fg_bg;
    Cms             cms;
    int             i;
    Server_image    chip, icon_image;
    void            color_notify();
    extern void     exit();
    static Xv_singlecolor cms_colors[] = {
        { 255, 255, 255 }, /* white */
        { 255, 0, 0 },     /* red    */
        { 0, 255, 0 },     /* green  */
        { 0, 0, 255 },     /* blue   */
        { 255, 255, 0 },   /* yellow */
        { 188, 143, 143 }, /* brown  */
        { 220, 220, 220 }, /* gray   */
        { 0, 0, 0 },       /* black  */
    };

    xv_init(XV_INIT_ARGC_PTR_ARGV, &argc, argv, NULL);

    frame = (Frame)xv_create(NULL, FRAME,
        FRAME_LABEL,     argv[0],
        NULL);

    cms = (Cms)xv_create(NULL, CMS,
        CMS_NAME,            "palette",
        CMS_CONTROL_CMS,     TRUE,
        CMS_TYPE,            XV_STATIC_CMS,
        CMS_SIZE,            CMS_CONTROL_COLORS + NUM_COLORS,
        CMS_COLORS,          cms_colors,
        NULL);

    /* Create panel and set the colormap segment on the panel */
    panel = (Panel)xv_create(frame, PANEL,
        PANEL_LAYOUT,        PANEL_VERTICAL,
        WIN_CMS,             cms,
        NULL);

    /* Create panel items */
    objects = (Panel_item)xv_create(panel, PANEL_TOGGLE,
        PANEL_LABEL_STRING,      "Objects",
        PANEL_LAYOUT,            PANEL_HORIZONTAL,
        PANEL_CHOICE_STRINGS,    "Textsw", "Textsw View",
                                 "Panel", "Icon", NULL,

        NULL);

    panel_fg_bg = (Panel_item)xv_create(panel, PANEL_CHECK_BOX,
```

Example 20-3. The color_objs.c program (continued)

```
            PANEL_LABEL_STRING,    "Fg/Bg",
            PANEL_CHOOSE_ONE,      TRUE,
            PANEL_LAYOUT,          PANEL_HORIZONTAL,
            PANEL_CHOICE_STRINGS,  "Background", "Foreground", NULL,
            NULL);

    chip = (Server_image)xv_create(XV_NULL, SERVER_IMAGE,
        XV_WIDTH,          16,
        XV_HEIGHT,         16,
        SERVER_IMAGE_DEPTH, 1,
        SERVER_IMAGE_BITS,  black_bits,
        NULL);
    color_choices = (Panel_item)xv_create(panel, PANEL_CHOICE,
        PANEL_LAYOUT,          PANEL_HORIZONTAL,
        PANEL_LABEL_STRING,    "Colors",
        PANEL_CLIENT_DATA,     panel_fg_bg,
        XV_X,                  (int)xv_get(panel_fg_bg, XV_X),
        PANEL_NEXT_ROW,        15,
        PANEL_CHOICE_IMAGES,
            chip, chip, chip, chip, chip, chip, chip, chip, NULL,
        PANEL_CHOICE_COLOR,    0, CMS_CONTROL_COLORS + 0,
        PANEL_CHOICE_COLOR,    1, CMS_CONTROL_COLORS + 1,
        PANEL_CHOICE_COLOR,    2, CMS_CONTROL_COLORS + 2,
        PANEL_CHOICE_COLOR,    3, CMS_CONTROL_COLORS + 3,
        PANEL_CHOICE_COLOR,    4, CMS_CONTROL_COLORS + 4,
        PANEL_CHOICE_COLOR,    5, CMS_CONTROL_COLORS + 5,
        PANEL_CHOICE_COLOR,    6, CMS_CONTROL_COLORS + 6,
        PANEL_CHOICE_COLOR,    7, CMS_CONTROL_COLORS + 7,
        PANEL_NOTIFY_PROC,     color_notify,
        NULL);

    (void) xv_create(panel, PANEL_BUTTON,
        PANEL_LABEL_STRING,    "Quit",
        PANEL_NOTIFY_PROC,     exit,
        NULL);
    (void)window_fit_height(panel);

    /* create textsw and set the colormap segment for it */
    textsw = (Textsw)xv_create(frame, TEXTSW,
        WIN_CMS,               cms,
        WIN_BELOW,             panel,
        WIN_ROWS,              15,
        WIN_COLUMNS,           80,
        TEXTSW_FILE_CONTENTS, "/etc/motd",
        WIN_BACKGROUND_COLOR, CMS_CONTROL_COLORS + 0,
        NULL);

    /* adjust panel dimensions */
    (void)xv_set(panel, WIN_WIDTH, xv_get(textsw, WIN_WIDTH), NULL);

    icon_image = (Server_image)xv_create(NULL, SERVER_IMAGE,
        XV_WIDTH,          64,
        XV_HEIGHT,         64,
        SERVER_IMAGE_DEPTH, 1,
        SERVER_IMAGE_BITS,  icon_bits,
        NULL);
    /* associate icon with the base frame */
    icon = (Icon)xv_create(XV_NULL, ICON,
```

Example 20-3. The color_objs.c program (continued)

```
            ICON_IMAGE,              icon_image,
            WIN_CMS,                 cms,
            WIN_BACKGROUND_COLOR, CMS_CONTROL_COLORS + 0,
            NULL);
        xv_set(frame, FRAME_ICON, icon, NULL);

        window_fit(frame);

        xv_main_loop(frame);
}
/*
 * This routine gets called when a color selection is made.
 * Set the foreground or background on the currently selected object.
 * WIN_FOREGROUND_COLOR & WIN_BACKGROUND_COLOR allow the application
 * to specify indices into the colormap segment as the foreground
 * and background values.
 */
void
color_notify(panel_item, choice, event)
Panel_item      panel_item;
int             choice;
Event           *event;
{
    int cnt;
    Xv_opaque object, get_object();
    unsigned objs = (unsigned)xv_get(objects, PANEL_VALUE);
    int fg = (int)xv_get(xv_get(panel_item, PANEL_CLIENT_DATA),
                    PANEL_VALUE);

    /* the value of the objects panel item is a bit mask ... "on" bits
     * mean that the choice is selected.  Get the object associated
     * with the choice and set it's color.  "&" tests bits in a mask.
     */
    for (cnt = 0; objs; cnt++, objs >>= 1)
        if (objs & 1)
            if ((object = get_object(cnt)) != panel)
                xv_set(object,
                    fg? WIN_FOREGROUND_COLOR : WIN_BACKGROUND_COLOR,
                    CMS_CONTROL_COLORS + choice, NULL);
            else if (fg)
                PANEL_EACH_ITEM(panel, panel_item)
                    xv_set(panel_item,
                        PANEL_ITEM_COLOR, CMS_CONTROL_COLORS + choice,
                        NULL);
                PANEL_END_EACH
            else
                notice_prompt(panel, NULL,
                    NOTICE_FOCUS_XY, event_x(event), event_y(event),
                    NOTICE_MESSAGE_STRINGS,
                        "You can't set the color of a panel.", NULL,
                    NOTICE_BUTTON_YES, "Ok",
                    NULL);
}
/*
 *    Return the XView handle to nth object.
 */
```

Example 20-3. The color_objs.c program (continued)

```
Xv_opaque
get_object(n)
int n;
{
    switch (n) {
        case SELECT_TEXTSW:
            return textsw;
        case SELECT_TEXTSW_VIEW:
            return xv_get(textsw, OPENWIN_NTH_VIEW, 0);
        case SELECT_PANEL:
            return panel;
        case SELECT_ICON:
            return icon;
        default:
            return textsw;
    }
}
```

21

Error Recovery and Help

In This Chapter:

21
Error Recovery and Help

This chapter addresses two general-usage facilities that apply to all XView packages: Error Handling and Help. All XView packages, including extensions to existing packages or those you may write yourself, should address error handling to provide adequate feedback for the programmer. The help mechanism is available for the application programmer to register help information in response to user requests.

The chapter starts by addressing error handling and recovery. There are two different types of errors addressed: XView errors and Xlib protocol errors. The two are very different from one another; XView errors are generated by misusing the XView Toolkit in some way, while Xlib protocol errors result from calling Xlib functions incorrectly or using incorrect values to those functions. We'll start with XView errors since, as you may already know, it is easy to generate run-time errors when writing XView applications.

21.1 XView Errors

XView errors are caused by specifying invalid or unknown attributes, objects or values. Often, XView errors are generated by simply failing to terminate a list of values of attribute-value pairs. Whatever the reason, in the event of an error, the XView internals call the function `xv_error()`.

This function is the highest level interface into the XView error package. Like many of the other XView functions, `xv_error()` takes a `NULL`-terminated attribute-value list of parameters. These parameters, set by the calling function, describe the nature of the error encountered. `xv_error()` then calls either a programmer-supplied function or a default function that prints the nature of the error to `stderr`. Before discussing the details of these routines, let's first address the problem of when you need to use them and to what extent.

XView error handling is most useful during the early development of applications. If you want to force a core dump for debugging purposes or if you want to supress the standard error messages from being displayed on the controlling tty's `stderr`, then all you need to do is install a general error handling routine. If you are writing your own XView packages or wish to get detailed information about the nature of an XView error, Section 21.4, "Advanced Error Handling," addresses these issues.

First, we'll address the specific task of how to install an error handler for an XView application, then we'll move on to more advanced error handling methods.

21.1.1 Simple Error handling

An error handler is installed using the attribute, XV_ERROR_PROC in the call to xv_init().

```
xv_init(XV_INIT_ARGC_PTR_ARGV, &argc, argv,
    XV_ERROR_PROC,   my_error_proc,
    NULL);
```

Because xv_init() is called only once, the error routine cannot be changed or uninstalled. The routine must be installed at this time, and it remains installed for the life of the application.

The XView error handler is called whenever xv_error() is called. That is, when there is an internal error in XView, not if there is an X Protocol error or errors of any other kind.

The following call generates an XView error:

```
xv_set(NULL, PANEL_LABEL, "foo", NULL);
```

The reason for the error is that an invalid XView object was given to xv_set(). This may seem like a simplistic example because no one would ever intentionally pass NULL as an object. However, attempting to set attributes for uninitialized objects is not an uncommon error. A more common mistake made by the novice XView programmer is forgetting to use a NULL terminator at the end of the attribute-value list to xv_set() or xv_create(). This is also a more subtle error that may not always generate an error due to the undefined value of the missing parameter.*

When xv_error() is called, it in turn calls the registered error handling routine, which takes the following form:

```
error_proc(object, avlist)
    Xv_object        object;
    Attr_attribute   avlist[ATTR_STANDARD_SIZE];
```

Since XView errors are always generated in response to an internal XView package or routine, there is always an object associated with the error. This is passed as the object parameter. The avlist provides details about the nature of the error. Note that this is *not* an attribute-value list in the form of the other attribute-value lists used throughout most of the book. It is an array of attributes and values that have been constructed from a NULL-terminated attribute-value list. See Chapter 22, *XView Internals*, for more details.

---

*A fundamental understanding of variable argument lists shows that a missing parameter (the NULL parameter in this case) translates into an unpredictable value, which by many coincidences may turn out to be 0.

The following code fragment shows a sample error procedure that supports this interface.

```
error_proc(object, avlist)
Xv_object          object;
Attr_avlist        avlist;
{
    char buf[32];

    printf("%s\nDump core? ", xv_error_format(object, avlist));
    fflush(stdout);
    if (gets(buf) && (buf[0] == 'y' || buf[0] == 'Y'))
        abort(); /* may return if application is trapping SIGIOT */
    return XV_OK;
}
```

Using xv_error_format()

The above procedure makes use of the routine `xv_error_format()`. This function returns a pointer to a static `char *` describing the XView error that has occurred. It takes as parameters an XView object and an `Attr_avlist`. Because `xv_error_format()` returns a pointer to a static string, it should be copied into your own buffer if you wish to retain the value since repeated calls overwrite the contents.

Since the parameters to `xv_error_format()` are the same as those passed to the error function, they may be passed on to the format function without further processing. This function is useful if you don't want to parse the `Attr_avlist` yourself, but still wish to print the error message.

This is all very simple if you do not care to put a great deal of work into your error handling routine and parse the `avlist`. Note that we aren't even testing to see if the severity of the error was recoverable or not. If an error occurs, no matter how innocent, we want to trace it down to the offending function call.

21.1.2 X Error Handling

Catching errors that occur from Xlib or the X server should be done using the methods described in Volume One, *Xlib Programmer's Manual*. Here, you can write your own routine that handles Xlib errors as well as errors with the server.

To register an Xlib error handler, you may use `XSetErrorHandler()` or you can use the attribute `XV_X_ERROR_PROC` in the call to `xv_init()`.

```
int x_error_proc();

xv_init(XV_INIT_ARGC_PTR_ARGV, &argc, argv,
    XV_X_ERROR_PROC,  x_error_proc,
    NULL);
```

If an Xlib error occurs, your routine is called with the following parameters:

```
int
x_error_proc(dpy, event)
    Display     *dpy;
    XErrorEvent *event;
```

The routine should return XV_OK if you have handled the error to your satisfaction. In this case, XView will ignore the error and continue on with the execution of the program. If the routine returns XV_ERROR, then XView calls its default error handler, prints an error message to stderr and exits with a status of 1.

21.1.3 Advanced Error Handling

If you wish to examine in detail the nature of an XView error within your error handling procedure or are implementing your own XView package, the following sections may be useful. Each section addresses the error attributes and their associated values. Using the information described here along with Section 22.2, "Internal Attribute-Value Lists," in Chapter 22, *XView Internals*, we discuss how you can construct a call to xv_error() and parse an error list passed to your error handling function.

Error Types

The header file *<xview/xv_error.h>* contains the definitions of the types and functions used by the error package. These error types are used as parameters to xv_error() and from there to your error handling routine. The following list of attributes should be used if you are going to be calling xv_error() or if you wish to parse the Attr_avlist from the error handling routine.

ERROR_BAD_ATTR
> An attribute was specified that is not defined by XView. If the calling function forgets to terminate a list with a NULL, this is most likely the error value passed.

ERROR_BAD_VALUE
> A bad value was provided for an attribute. This includes out of range values, and so on. If you think the value given is correct, check its type. Passing floats when in fact they are read as doubles may cause this problem.

ERROR_CANNOT_GET
> xv_get() was used on an ungettable attribute.

ERROR_CANNOT_SET
> xv_set() was used on an unsettable attribute.

ERROR_CREATE_ONLY
> xv_set() was used to set an attribute that is only valid using xv_create().

ERROR_INVALID_OBJECT
> The object parameter to the routine is invalid. Either the object was uninitialized or the object had been (or is in the process of being) destroyed.

ERROR_LAYER

> The layer of software that detected the error. Possible error layers are the operating system, the X server, the XView Toolkit and the application.

ERROR_PKG

> The toolkit package that detected the error.

ERROR_SERVER_ERROR

> The error detected by the server; takes an XErrorEvent * as a value.

ERROR_SEVERITY

> The severity of the error detected. Its value is of type Error_severity. This is an enumerated type whose values may be ERROR_RECOVERABLE or ERROR_NON_RECOVERABLE. Unrecoverable errors should definitely cause the program to exit, whereas recoverable errors can cause an exit if you so desire.

ERROR_STRING

> Used by the calling function to xv_error() to give a description of the error if necessary. Trailing newlines are stripped.

21.1.4 Calling xv_error()

If you are trying to write your own XView package or add an extension to an existing package, you may need to call xv_error(). Calling it is similar to calling xv_set(); the first parameter is a handle to an XView object followed by a NULL-terminated attribute-value list consisting of the above attributes. It takes the form:

```
int
xv_error(object, attrs)
    Xv_object object;
```

object is the object for which the offending call had taken place. If the programmer called xv_set() on a frame object and the attributes passed were invalid, then you would call xv_error(), passing the frame as the object and a set of ERROR_-attribute-value pairs from the above list.

For example, the following call assumes the calling function tried to set an invalid attribute in the FRAME package. (Note that this is only an example, since the FRAME package does not do this.)

```
switch (attribute) {
    case FRAME_FOREGROUND :
        /* ... */
        break;
    case FRAME_OLD_RECT :
        xv_error(frame,
            ERROR_STRING,      "You cannot set this attribute.",
            ERROR_CANNOT_SET, attribute,
            ERROR_PKG,         FRAME,
            NULL);
        break;
    /* ... */
}
```

As you can see, unless you are implementing the internals of an XView package, `xv_error()` may be of limited use. However, this example demonstrates how `xv_error()` can be called internally by XView.

Error Severity

In the above example, the reason to call `xv_error()` is not a serious one; at least, not one that should terminate the program. By default, calling `xv_error()` is a recoverable error, so in order to specify a non-recoverable error, the call to `xv_error()` should pass the attribute, `ERROR_SEVERITY` and the value `ERROR_NON_RECOVERABLE`. Unrecoverable errors generally terminate using `exit()` with a non-zero exit status. However, `abort()` may be used instead to generate a core image used for debugging.

In any event, if the error handler is called, it should print a warning message and either continue or exit accordingly. If you install your own error routine, the choice is yours. Example 21-1 shows how the error severity can be evaluated and acted upon accordingly.

21.1.5 Revisiting the Error Handler

Advanced usage of the `ERROR` package provides us with the ability to scan the attribute list in search of the causes of the error. With this information, you can print out more useful error messages or display them in a manner other than printing to `stderr`.

Recall that there are two parameters passed to the function:

```
error_proc(object, avlist)
    Xv_object      object;
    Attr_avlist    avlist;
```

`object` is the object in which the `xv_*` call failed to operate. You can get the type of object by calling:

```
Xv_pkg *pkg = (Xv_pkg *)xv_get(object, XV_TYPE);
```

If the error itself pertains to the object, then getting the type of the object may generate another error. You should not attempt to get the package until you test the error code in the `Attr_avlist` to be sure the error is not with the `object` parameter. If the error is not due to the object itself, the package returned by `xv_get()` indicates to which XView package the object belongs. This value matches the same argument as the second parameter to `xv_create()`. For example, the package returned may be `MENU`, `CANVAS`, `PANEL_BUTTON`, `SERVER`, etc.

The `Attr_avlist` may be scanned for the attributes listed in the previous section. Example 21-1 shows how this is done. This is a very simplistic example and is for demonstration purposes only. A more complete example may be found in the function `xv_error_format()` in the XView source code.

Example 21-1. Example Error Parsing Function

```
int
my_error_handler(object, avlist)
Xv_object      object;
Attr_avlist  avlist;
{
    Attr_avlist  attrs;
    Error_layer  layer;
    Error_severity severity = ERROR_RECOVERABLE;
    int n = 0;
    char strs[64][7];

    for (attrs = avlist; *attrs && n < 5; attrs = attr_next(attrs)) {
        switch ((int) attrs[0]) {
            case ERROR_BAD_ATTR:
                sprintf(strs[n++], "bad attribute %s",
                    attr_name(attr[1]));
                break;
            case ERROR_BAD_VALUE:
                sprintf(strs[n++],
                    "bad value (0x%x) for attribute %s", attrs[1],
                    attr_name(attrs[2]));
                break;
            case ERROR_INVALID_OBJECT:
                sprintf(strs[n++], "invalid object (%s)",
                    (char *) attrs[1]);
                break;
            case ERROR_STRING:
                sprintf(strs[n++], "%s", (char *) attrs[1]);
                break;
            case ERROR_PKG:
                sprintf(strs[n++], "Package: %s",
                    ((Xv_pkg *)attrs[1])->name);
                break;
            case ERROR_SEVERITY:
                severity = attrs[1];
        }
    }
    strcpy(strs[n++], "Core dump?");
    strs[n] = 0;
    if (notice_prompt(base_frame, (Event *)NULL,
        NOTICE_MESSAGE_STRINGS_ARRAY_PTR, strs,
        NOTICE_BUTTON_YES,              "Yes",
        NOTICE_BUTTON_NO,               "No",
        NULL) == NOTICE_YES)
            abort();

    if (severity == ERROR_NON_RECOVERABLE)
        exit(1);
    return XV_OK;
}
```

This error handling routine sets a set of error messages in an array of buffers. A notice is used to display the messages and prompt the user to generate a core image of the program for debugging. Selecting "Yes" causes abort() to be called. Otherwise, the program exits if the severity is recoverable and continues if it is not.

One particular note of interest is the use of the routine `attr_name()`. This is a hypothetical routine that you would have to write to convert the actual enumerated attribute values into strings that make sense to read. If you write your own XView package with new attributes, you will have to write a routine equivalent to `attr_name()`. The routine should return a static `char *` describing the attribute. If the attribute has no corresponding string (e.g., it is an unknown attribute), it should return a string indicating the integer or hexadecimal value.

21.2 The Help Package

OPEN LOOK describes a help mechanism that enables the user to get help from anywhere in the user interface. The user requests the information via the Help key on the keyboard, or, if one does not exist, the F1 function key. When this key is used, the window under the pointer receives the `ACTION_HELP` event. In such cases, a *Help window* is displayed as shown in Figure 21-1.

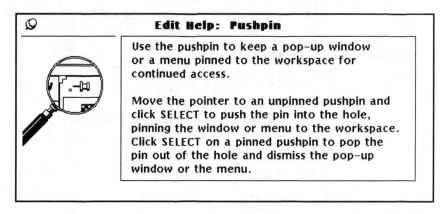

Figure 21-1. A sample Help window

21.2.1 Using XV_HELP_DATA

The attribute `XV_HELP_DATA` is used to provide XView with information about where to find the text for the help frame. The attribute's value is a string in the form of:

```
"filename:token"
```

The `filename` is found from a list of directories set in the `$HELPPATH` environment variable. The actual filename has the *.info* suffix appended to its base name. Thus, the complete path to the filename which contains the help information is:

```
$HELPPATH/filename.info
```

If `$HELPPATH` is not set, the directory `/usr/lib/help` is used. However, if `$HELP-PATH` *is* set, then that path is searched exclusively and `/usr/lib/help` is *not* searched unless it is explicitly listed in the variable's setting. Therefore, users should always have the default path in their environment setting. Since $HELPPATH may be set to any number of directories, a possible setting would be (for the C shell):

```
setenv HELPPATH /usr/lib/help:/path/to/other/help/directories:.
```

Or, for the Bourne shell:

```
HELPPATH=/usr/lib/help:/path/to/other/help/directories:.
export HELPPATH
```

The trailing "." indicates that the current directory is included.

Once the filename is found, the *token* is searched for within the file. The file must contain the string "*:token*" at the beginning of the line. All the text following the token is displayed in the scrolling text subwindow within the help frame. The text ends when a line is found that starts with a "#" or a ":".

21.2.2 Attaching Help Data

Let's say you have written a program called my_program. In this program, there is a panel with a button labeled "Save". The user wants to know exactly what this button will do if selected. The user can select the Help key over the panel item in order to obtain help associated with the item. To support this action, you must attach help data to the panel items in the following manner:

```
    . . .
    extern Frame frame;
    extern void save_it();
    Panel panel;

    panel = (Panel)xv_create(frame, PANEL, NULL);

    xv_create(panel, PANEL_BUTTON,
        XV_HELP_DATA,       "my_program:save",
        PANEL_LABEL_STRING,  "Save",
        PANEL_NOTIFY_PROC,   save_it,
        NULL);
    xv_create(panel, PANEL_TEXT,
        XV_HELP_DATA,       "my_program:target",
        PANEL_LABEL_STRING,  "Filename: ",
        NULL);
    . . .
```

The value for XV_HELP_DATA contains the name of the program as the "filename" to search for and the token is "*:save*". The filename was chosen based on the name of the application for easier administration of the help files. The next step is to create the file *my_program.info* and add the help text. The file might look like this:

```
This is the help file for "my_program".  Each token in this program
corresponds to a panel item.  These lines are considered comment lines
since they do not fall between two colons, or a colon and a "#".

:save
When selecting this panel item, all changes made
to the current document will be saved in the target
file.  To change the target file, type in a new
name at the "Filename:" text item.
#

:target
This filename represents the name of the file to use
to load a new file or to store editing changes.  Full
pathnames should be specified to insure that you get
the correct filename.
#
```

The "#" used to terminate help text makes the file more readable. Otherwise, it could be
omitted, in which case the text would terminate at the next ":*token*" or the end of the
file—whichever comes first.

21.2.3 Displaying Help Manually

If the window corresponds to an XView package that handles its own events, such as *Panels*
or *Menus*, then XView displays the help frame automatically. All you need to provide is the
data for the help message by using the attribute XV_HELP_DATA discussed in the next section.

If you are handling events (such as a canvas) in the window, then you are responsible for displaying the help frame as well as providing the help data. The function to accomplish this is
xv_help_show(). It takes the following form:

```
xv_help_show(window, help_data, event)
    Xv_Window       window;
    char            *help_data; /* "file:key" */
    Event           *event;
```

The window parameter is an XView window associated with an XView object. The
help_data parameter is a string identical to the value of XV_HELP_DATA discussed in the
next section. The event parameter represents the event that caused the need for the help
window to be displayed. This event structure may be modified upon return, so it should not
be referenced after use.

A canvas's event handler would have to track help key events, display the help frame and
provide the text to display in the frame. The following code fragments show how this might
be done.

```
    ...
canvas = xv_create(frame, CANVAS,
    ...
    WIN_CONSUME_EVENTS, ..., ACTION_HELP, ..., NULL,
    WIN_EVENT_PROC, my_event_handler,
    NULL);
```

```
      . . .
      my_event_handler(window, event)
      Xv_Window window;
      Event *event;
      {
          if (event_action(event) == ACTION_HELP) {
              xv_help_show(window, "canvas:help_info", event);
              return;
          }
          . . .
      }
```

The meaning of "canvas:help_info" is the same as the help data described earlier.

21.2.4 Helpfile Installation

Once the help file has been written, you should install it in */usr/lib/help* on your system. If you don't, then the user must set the $HELPPATH environment variable correctly to point to the path where the file actually resides. Otherwise, the user's request for help will result in a notice that help being posted cannot be found. Further, the file and the path to the file (including directories and links) must be readable and searchable.

If circumstances prevent you from installing the help file in the designated area, it is not reasonable to expect the user to know where the help file is. That is, do not expect that the user has set the $HELPPATH variable correctly. You should set the environment for the user. The path must be set to include at least two pathnames: */usr/lib/help* and the path to your help file. Both are needed because the user might request help from XView objects that provide their own help; these help files reside in the default directory and may be needed.

The following code fragment shows how $HELPPATH should be initialized to locate help files that do not reside in */usr/lib/help*.

```
      #include <stdio.h> /* for BUFSIZ */

      #define HELPPATHNAME "/help/directory" /* set this yourself */

      main(argc, argv)
      int argc;
      char *argv[];
      {
          extern char *getenv();
          char *helppath, buf[BUFSIZ];

          xv_init(XV_INIT_ARGC_PTR_ARGV, &argc, argv, NULL);

          /* ... */
          sprintf(buf, "HELPPATH=/usr/lib/help:%s:", HELPPATHNAME);
          if (helppath = getenv("HELPPATH"))
              strcat(buf, helppath);
          putenv(buf);

          /* ... */

          xv_main_loop(...);
      }
```

Notice that we are setting the value of $HELPPATH regardless of its previous value. We don't know if the previous value of $HELPPATH existed; if it did, we don't know if the necessary pathnames were already in it. It's not worth the effort writing code to parse the string to see if the path exists. Even if it does, we want to be sure it is at the beginning of the variable. This insures that the path is searched first. Since the same path can be set more than once, no harm is done by prefixing the variable with the desired pathnames.

Further, the use of putenv() requires that the char * buffer passed be valid throughout the life of the variable (e.g., until it is unset or reset later). In most cases, we would have to use malloc() and pass in new memory or use a static variable. However, since this putenv() is called from main, the variable space used by buf will not be corrupted until main() exits. So we don't bother with allocating memory.

Lastly, it should be mentioned that the effects of putenv() are temporary; the new path setting affects this process and application only. Each process has its own version of HELP-PATH, so setting it explicitly for our application does not affect other programs.

The way that XView defines and implements help is still under development and this interface is subject to change in future releases.

22

XView Internals

In This Chapter:

22
XView Internals

This chapter discusses the internal mechanisms that XView uses to implement the existing object classes. The information in this chapter should give you the ability to build your own objects that are "extensible" or are extensions of other existing classes. By writing extensions to XView classes, you can modify their appearance or functionality. By creating new classes, you can create objects that go beyond what the existing XView library provides.

However, you should be forewarned that building XView extensions is not intended to be a solution to every problem. You are strongly encouraged to implement the type of object or enhancements you need using the facilities provided by XView and the existing XView objects. Furthermore, this chapter should be used as an introductory resource. It does not contain enough information to fully explain how all the internal XView objects work, nor does it give you the ability to build an entire library of user interface objects.

If OPEN LOOK compliance is important in your applications, you should be sure that you fully understand the OPEN LOOK specifications before attempting to build new objects or modify existing ones. Because the XView internals do not enforce user interface policy, you could build non-OPEN LOOK-compliant user interface code. However, the existing XView objects were written to conform to OPEN LOOK as much as possible. While you are strongly encouraged to examine the XView source as a model, this chapter only acts as a guide to that model and may not address all issues involved with all XView packages.

In Chapter 2, *The XView Programmer's Model*, we introduced and discussed the hierarchy of XView objects and the use of the basic functions intrinsic to XView: `xv_create()`, `xv_set()`, `xv_get()`, `xv_find()` and `xv_destroy()`. We will now take a closer look at how that model is utilized by XView internals.

We are going to start with a general discussion of the concepts that XView uses as a framework. The methods described are intrinsic to all XView packages. After that, we examine how attributes and their associated "values" interact with XView and its packages. Once these issues have been addressed, we illustrate the how to write your own XView packages and extensions using these concepts.

The Logo package is a simple package that displays an X logo in the middle of a window. The Bitmap package is similar, but it allows the programmer to display an arbitrary bitmap in a window. Finally, the Image package is used to demonstrate how to write an extension to an existing XView package. In this case, it is an extension from the server image package found in Chapter 15, *Nonvisual Objects*.

22.1 Methods

The *intrinsics* layer of XView is the mechanism that defines and controls the class inheritance model; in other words, it establishes parent/child relationship among XView classes. The XView intrinsics handle the creation, modification, query and destruction of actual instances of object classes. Each object class contains a *method* (as it is called in object-oriented programming terminology) to respond to any XView-intrinsic request. A method is a function that is written and compiled into the executable program to perform the designated task.

For example, when the programmer calls `xv_create()` to create an instance of a particular class, the XView intrinsics invokes the *initialize method* from that class. For `xv_set()`, it invokes the *set method* and so on. The XView intrinsics define the methods while the actual classes provide the functions that perform them.

Each *class* is represented programmatically by declaring a data structure consisting of pointers to functions that correspond to each of the methods. When the programmer calls `xv_get()`, the intrinsics de-reference the pointer to the *get* method and call it as a function.

Static Subclassing

You recall from Chapter 2, *The XView Programmer's Model*, that XView classes are subclassed from one another starting from the *generic* class. This class contains basic information about the object such as its *x,y* position, its geometry specification, its reference count (how many other objects refer to it in some way), what server and display the object is associated with and so on. Most classes share this information and are therefore subclassed from the generic class.

From the generic class, new subclasses are created to describe more specifics about that particular class's appearance, functionality or other attributes. Subclassing causes each new class to inherit everything from its parent class, so the child class does not need to be redefined or reinitialized. New subclasses define their own methods so that the intrinsics can utilize the parts of new classes that differentiate them from their parent classes. When the programmer calls `xv_create()` to create an instance from a particular class, the intrinsics call the initialize method for each subclass in the hierarchy in succession.

To implement this using the C language, each class is physically defined by a data structure that contains pointers to functions previously written for that class. All this information must be compiled into the XView library (or at least linked with the rest of the object modules at compile time). Because the functions and data structures are pre-written, the subclasses are *static* — they cannot be changed during the execution of the program.* In sum, XView uses *static subclassing*.

22.1.1 Order of Methods

As discussed in Chapter 2, *The XView Programmer's Model*, whenever an object is created, the XView intrinsics initialize each class from top to bottom. Thus, the generic class is first instantiated by calling its initialize method, followed by the next subclass, all the way down until the class of the type requested is instantiated. When completed, an instance of the class has been created with all the default properties of the classes set.

However, the initialization sequence does not stop there. As Figure 22-1 shows, the initialization sequence consists of three phases.

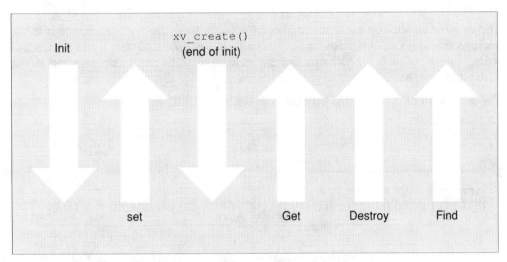

Figure 22-1. Calling directions for init, set, get, destroy and find

After the initialization methods are called for each of the packages, XView calls the *set* methods to handle any attribute-value pairs specified in the programmer's call to xv_ create(). This is done even if there were no attributes specified. This phase is executed in the *reverse order* of the initialize method, moving from the bottom up.

The final phase of the initialization sequence calls the *set* function again, but in the original order (e.g., from the top down). Here, the *set* method is called with only one attribute, XV_END_CREATE. This is the only time that the *set* method is called from the top down. This final phase indicates that the creation phase is over and that the class should resolve any unfinished work. Each phase of this operation is discussed in more detail in later sections.

---

*Limitations of the C language prevent the ability to do dynamic subclassing.

22.2 Internal Attribute-Value Lists

Each of the methods introduced above (with the exception of the destroy method) must deal with attributes and attribute-value lists. Before we begin to discuss the details of how the methods work, the fundamentals of attributes must be understood. This includes the nature of attributes, how their internal values are constructed, the nature of the values *associated* with attributes, package IDs and so on.

22.2.1 Attribute Values

The semantics of the term *value* can be confusing. There are two *values* that are used when referring to attributes. The type most commonly used is the value *associated* with the attribute. That is, "brown" is the value associated with the attribute PANEL_ITEM_COLOR. However, PANEL_ITEM_COLOR is declared as an enumerated type that has a "value" just as C variables have values.

The value of an attribute variable contains information about the type of attribute it is, the package it belongs to, how many "value" parameters are associated with it and the types of those "values". This is all accomplished by setting particular bits within segments of the 32-bit data type, Attr_attribute.

The breakdown of the bits in the attribute is shown in Figure 22-2.

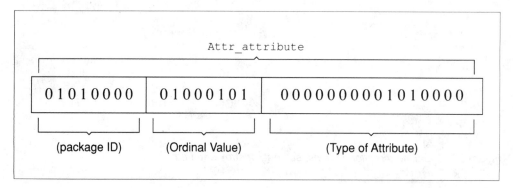

Figure 22-2. The bits in an attribute

All this is done via macros defined in <*xview/attrs.h*> along with a complete listing of all the different types of attributes that may be used.

Let's examine a real attribute, XV_RECT. This attribute can be used to set or get the bounding box of an XView object (e.g., x and y, width and height). The attribute is declared in <*xview/generic.h*> as:

```
XV_RECT = XV_ATTR(ATTR_RECT_PTR, 74)
```

The value of XV_RECT expands to a long value set by the macros XV_ATTR and ATTR_RECT_PTR. These are macros whose values are used as masks which can identify the attribute later. The value of 74 is a unique number with respect to the other attributes in the package.

Thus, when the internals of an XView procedure want to determine the value of XV_RECT, they know that the "value" that the programmer specified must be a Rect *. Furthermore, it is known that xv_get() should return the same type. This loose type checking is by no means enforced. It is used for various reasons including, the ability of the programmer to identify the type of value a particular attribute should take.

The attribute's "type" is also used to determine how many programmer-supplied "values" are associated with it. For example, the attribute PANEL_CHOICE_STRINGS indicates that the value associated with it is a NULL-terminated list of char pointers. We can check this by looking at the value of the attribute in *<xview/panel.h>*:

```
PANEL_CHOICE_STRINGS =
    PANEL_ATTR(ATTR_LIST_INLINE(ATTR_NULL, ATTR_STRING), 22)
```

Here, the use of PANEL_ATTR shows that the attribute is part of the PANEL package. The macro ATTR_LIST_INLINE shows that the value associated with the attribute is a NULL-terminated list. The macro ATTR_STRING shows that it is a list of strings, or char pointers.

The list of possible *types* of attributes is in *<xview/attr.h>*.

22.2.2 Creating Attribute Lists

When functions that take attribute-value lists are called, XView internally converts the entire list into an array of Attr_Attribute values. The size of the array can not exceed ATTR_STANDARD_SIZE. This array of attributes and values is assigned the type, Attr_avlist.

The array can be created using the function attr_make(), and the actual variable argument list of attributes and values is stored in the array via the function attr_create_list().

For example, xv_create() takes a variable argument list of attribute-value pairs, calls attr_make() to create the list, attr_create_list() to store the attributes in the new Attr_avlist array and then calls the initialize functions for the class hierarchy (see Section 22.4.4, "The Initialize Method").

Any function whose interface is called with a variable argument list has a corresponding (internal) function that takes the Attr_avlist parameter rather than the variable argument list. This is due to the fact that variable argument lists cannot be passed to subsequent functions reliably. XView overcomes this problem by converting the entire list of attributes and values into the Attr_attribute array and passing it around to functions.

Attribute Lists within Attribute Lists

Sometimes, the same attribute-value list is used in multiple calls to `xv_create()` or `xv_set()`. Specifying the same list all the time is wasteful since it requires the same processing for each call. In order to optimize and simplify this problem, XView provides an interface for both the XView programmer and the package implementor by introducing the attribute, `ATTR_LIST`.

The value to the `ATTR_LIST` attribute is an `Attr_avlist`, the same type returned by `attr_create_list()`. The following code fragment shows how this can be used:

```
    . . .
    Canvas canvas1, canvas2, canvas3;
    Attr_avlist attr_list;

    attr_list = attr_create_list(
        WIN_CMS,            cms,
        WIN_EVENT_PROC,     my_event_proc,
        XV_WIDTH,           100,
        NULL);

    canvas1 = xv_create(frame, CANVAS,
        ATTR_LIST,              attr_list,
        WIN_BACKGROUND_COLOR, 1,
        NULL);
    canvas2 = xv_create(frame, CANVAS,
        ATTR_LIST,              attr_list,
        WIN_BACKGROUND_COLOR, 2,
        NULL);
    canvas3 = xv_create(frame, CANVAS,
        ATTR_LIST,              attr_list,
        WIN_BACKGROUND_COLOR, 3,
        NULL);

    free(attr_list);
    . . .
```

The only restriction on the use of `ATTR_LIST` is that it must be the *first* attribute specified in the call to `xv_create()`, `xv_set()` or any other `xv_*` routine that accepts attribute-value lists.

Lastly, since `attr_create_list()` allocates memory, the list should be freed when it is no longer needed.

22.2.3 Interpreting Attributes

When a routine is passed an `Attr_avlist`, it needs to scan the list looking for attributes of interest. The function may not be interested in all the attributes, so when scanning the list, it needs to skip ahead to successive attributes for evaluation. To facilitate this task, XView provides the macro `attr_next()` to make scanning `Attr_avlist` easier. This macro looks at a particular attribute and, by the nature of the attribute itself, knows how many items to scan ahead for the next one. The macro returns a pointer to that next attribute.

The first thing to do when scanning the `Attr_avlist` is to set a pointer to the beginning of the list and then advance forward until you reach the `NULL` attribute indicating the end of the attribute-value pairs.

```
function(param1, param2, avlist)
Xv_opaque    param1;
Xv_opaque    param2;
Attr_avlist  avlist;
{
    Attr_avlist      attrs;
    for (attrs = avlist; attrs[0]; attrs = attr_next(attrs)) {
        switch ((int) attrs[0]) {
            ...
        }
    }
    ...
}
```

The `for()` loop initializes the `attrs` variable to the beginning of the list and tests for the `NULL` attribute. Upon each iteration of the loop, the variable is set to the next attribute in the list. For this to work, `attrs` should never be moved in either direction in the list. To look at the value of a particular index into the attribute list, you should index that position relative to the current value of `attrs`. This is precisely what is done in the `switch()` statement within the loop.

`attr_next()` looks at the "type" of the attribute to determine how many, if any, value parameters are associated with the attribute. For attributes that take *lists* such as `PANEL_CHOICE_STRINGS`, it knows to look ahead for the next `NULL`-valued index in the array. This is why lists may not contain the value `NULL` or 0 as elements in the list. Once a `NULL` or 0 is found, `attr_next()` returns the element following the terminating `NULL`.*

The `switch` looks at index 0 of the `attrs` pointer for the attribute to evaluate. Each `case` in the `switch` statement handles the value that pertains specifically to the package in question. For example, the *set* routine for the `CANVAS` package has the following code fragment:

```
Attr_avlist attr;
for (attr = avlist; attr[0]; attr = attr_next(avlist)) {
    switch ((int) attr[0]) {
        case CANVAS_WIDTH:
            if (canvas->width != (int) attr[1]) {
                width = (int) attr[1];
                new_paint_size = TRUE;
            }
            break;
        case CANVAS_HEIGHT:
            if (canvas->height != (int) attr[1]) {
                height = (int) attr[1];
                new_paint_size = TRUE;
            }
            break;
```

---

*For portability reasons, `NULL` should always be used rather than 0 to terminate a list.

```
        /* .... */
        default:
            *status = xv_check_bad_attr(&xv_canvas_pkg, attr);
    }
}
```

For each attribute, the `case` statement knows what to interpret as the value parameter in the attribute list. The `CANVAS_WIDTH` case sets the `width` variable to the value set in `attr[1]` and assumes it is an `int`.

22.2.4 Checking for Bad Attributes

When the attribute being evaluated in the `switch` statement falls to the default case, there may or may not be something wrong with the attribute. Since the `switch` statement should have had a case for all the known attributes to the package, it is assumed that the attribute that had fallen through probably belongs to another package.

To check for this, the function `xv_check_bad_attr()` is used. The form of the function is:

```
int
xv_check_bad_attr(pkg, attr)
    Xv_pkg          *pkg;
    Attr_attribute  attr;
```

The functions check to see if the attribute in the second parameter belongs to the package specified in the first parameter. If the attribute *does* belong to the package, then an error message is printed and the function returns `XV_OK`. Otherwise, the function does nothing and returns `XV_ERROR`. Yes, this is counter-intuitive, but this value is utilized more appropriately by the *get* method. Details are discussed in Section 22.7.3, "The Bitmap Get Method."

An unknown attribute does not indicate that an error has been made. Remember that packages can be subclassed from other packages, so an attribute may apply to another level of the class hierarchy and will be dealt with at another time by another function.

Searching for Specific Attributes

Rather than scanning the entire `Attr_avlist` looking for one particular attribute, XView provides the convenience function, `attr_find()`. This function takes an `Attr_avlist` and an `Attr_attribute` as parameters and returns the location within the list where the attribute was found.

Here is its implementation:

```
Attr_avlist
attr_find(attrs, attr)
register Attr_avlist attrs;
register Attr_attribute attr;
{
    for (; *attrs; attrs = attr_next(attrs)) {
      if (*attrs == (Xv_opaque) attr)
          break;
    }
    return (attrs);
}
```

22.2.5 Consuming Attributes

Once an attribute has been evaluated, it should be *consumed* so that no other functions may see it. Consuming attributes should not be done if multiple packages (or functions) care to examine the same attribute. The `attr_skip()` macro knows to skip over attributes (and their associated values) that have been consumed.

Attribute consumption is done with the `ATTR_CONSUME()` macro.*

22.3 XView Packages

Earlier, we introduced the concept of XView *methods* and how they are used to define the interaction between a particular class and the XView intrinsics. These methods, along with a set of attributes, macros, types and functions, collectively make up an XView *package*. The XView library is made up of statically subclassed (pre-built) packages representing user interface objects.

22.3.1 The Xv_pkg Type

Packages (and thus, classes) are declared by creating a global variable of type `Xv_pkg`. This package is defined in *<xview/pkg_public.h>* as:

```
typedef struct _xview_pkg {
    char                *name;
    Attr_attribute       attr_id;
    unsigned             size_of_object;
    struct _xview_pkg   *parent_pkg;
    int                 (*init)();
    Xv_opaque           (*set)();
    Xv_opaque           (*get)();
```

---

*While the pre-built XView packages *should* consume attributes, few of them actually do. This will change in later releases of XView.

```
        int                 (*destroy)();
        Xv_object           (*find)();
    } Xv_pkg;
```

The fields of the `Xv_pkg` type are declared and used as follows:

name
: The name of the package is a unique, descriptive string. This is useful for debugging the ERROR package, and it may also be used in the future to implement resource handling from the resource database. Therefore, it should not contain whitespace or dots (periods). Underscores and hyphens are allowed, but should be avoided for aesthetic reasons. A combination of upper and lower case letters should be used to imply multi-word names (e.g., "DigitalClock")

attr_id
: This is the ID of the package. It is set to a unique number and is used in attributes' values to associate them with the corresponding package. For XView extensions (packages you write), the value should lie between ATTR_PKG_UNUSED_FIRST and ATTR_PKG_UNUSED_LAST.

size_of_object
: This is the size of the public part of the object. XView objects are broken down into a public part and a private part. XView is responsible for allocating the public part, while the initialize method is responsible for allocating the private part. The value of the `size_of_object` field is used by the XView intrinsics to know how much space to allocate when creating a new instance of the public part from this class.

init
: This is the *initialize* method for the package. It is a pointer to a function that returns an error status (XV_OK or XV_ERROR) depending on whether the initialization process was successful in creating an instance of the object.

set
: This is the *set* method. This is a pointer to a function that is called when the programmer calls `xv_set()`. The function typically returns an error status (XV_OK or XV_ERROR) but may return an opaque data type if it chooses.

get
: This is the *get* method. This is a pointer to a function that is called when the programmer calls `xv_get()`. The function returns the value of the attribute specified in the call to `xv_get()`. A status value may be set indicating an error.

destroy
: This is the *destroy* method; it is a pointer to a function that is called when the object is destroyed via `xv_destroy()` or when the window manager invokes it in a "save yourself" operation (discussed later). When an object is being destroyed, the function frees any allocated fields of the private data structure. The function returns either XV_OK or XV_ERROR.

find
: The *find* method is a pointer to a function that returns a handle to an existing instance of the package specified to `xv_find()`. If no instances of the package with the specified attributes can be found, NULL is returned and XView may call the initialize routine depending on the value of XV_AUTO_CREATE.

Details about the form of the functions listed above are given later in Section 22.4.2, "The Implementation File."

22.3.2 Public and Private Data

In XView, the object that is made available to the programmer writing XView applications is a public data type defined in the public header file for the package. The only information this type contains is a handle to two data types: the object's parent-data type and the *private* data. The public data type is what xv_create() returns to the user. Its nature will become clear in the sample XView package we create later.

The parent data is the public data type of the parent package (the superclass). The private data type is used by the implementation of the XView class. In it, there is a pointer to an object that contains specific information about the object itself. This may include a window, boolean variables, other data structures and so on. It also contains a pointer back to the public data type.

The *initialize* routine allocates and initializes the fields within the private data type. The initialize routine is also responsible for setting the handles of the public and private data types to one another. Once this double-linking occurs, an instance of the class is complete and the XView intrinsics return a handle to the public type. This is discussed in detail later in Section 22.4.4, "The Initialize Method."

22.4 The Logo Package

This section presents an implementation for a simple package utilizing the concepts introduced so far. This example may help explain some of the more confusing concepts for those still unsure of the material presented.

The example package is called *logo*. All this object does is draw the X logo in the middle of a window. To do this, we require a window, the Pixmap containing the X logo and a GC to specify the colors to use when rendering the pixmap. Creating a window is a very complicated task; there's so much to worry about with colormaps, visuals, displays and screens. Since the XView WINDOW package already handles this, the logo class is subclassed from it to take advantage of the WINDOW package's capabilities. That package can handle all the window-related details without intervention from the logo package. More generic attributes such as the geometry, hand position of the object are handled by the GENERIC package.

The only thing the logo package needs to concern itself with is providing the data for the bitmap showing the X logo. Once we have that, all we need to do is render it to the window when repaint or Expose events take place.

22.4.1 Header Files

Packages usually contain two header files (or *include* files): one that is included by applications that intend to use the package, and another that is included by the source code that implements the package itself.

The Public Header File

The file *logo.h* is the public header file for the logo package.

```
/* logo.h -- public header file for the logo XView class. */
#include <xview/xview.h>
#include <xview/window.h>

extern Xv_pkg logo_pkg;

#define LOGO &logo_pkg

typedef Xv_opaque Logo;

typedef struct {
    Xv_window_struct    parent_data;
    Xv_opaque           private_data;
} Logo_public;
```

Since the logo package is subclassed from the WINDOW package, we must include *<xview/window.h>*. We can't include that file unless we include *<xview/xview.h>* first. You'll find that most packages include at least the basic XView header files.

Next, we declare the logo_pkg object as an external variable of type Xv_pkg *. This is a global variable that we must declare later in an implementation source file. The LOGO definition refers to the address of this global variable. The Logo type is a typedef of Xv_opaque. This is basically a convenience type for the benefit of the programmer and follows the style of the other XView packages.

With the #define of LOGO and the declaration of the Logo type, the necessary types are available to make it possible for the programmer to create an instance of the logo object:

```
Logo logo;

logo = xv_create(parent, LOGO, NULL);
```

For the simple logo package, this is all that is necessary to declare in the public header file. There are no attributes specific to the logo package. Had we wanted to provide attributes, their declarations would be here in the public header file. We'll add attributes to the logo package later in the chapter.

The parent parameter in the call to xv_create() for a logo object must be a Frame because the logo is subclassed from the WINDOW package. This is because the FRAME package is the only one that manages subwindow layout.

Finally, the last thing declared in the public header file is the public data type, Logo_ public. This is the actual object returned by xv_create(). Since the programmer has no need to reference fields in this data type, an *opaque* data type is sufficient. Therefore, the programmer uses the Logo type.

The `Logo_public` structure has the two fields discussed earlier: a handle to the parent object and a pointer to the private data. The parent handle is a public data type similar to the logo's public data type. In this case, the public data type for the parent object is `Xv_window_struct`. We use the real data type for this rather than the *opaque* type, `Xv_Window`, because XView needs to reference internal fields within it.

The `private_data` field is a pointer to the actual data structure used by the internals of the logo object. But in the spirit of true object oriented programming, this type is hidden from the programmer by declaring it to be `Xv_opaque`.

The Private Header File

The primary purpose of the private header file is to declare the private data structure mentioned above. This file is named with the *_impl.h* suffix implying that it is used by the code that *implements* the logo object methods. Here is the *logo_impl.h* file for the logo package:

```
/* logo_impl.h -- implementation-dependent header file for the
 * logo XView class.
 */
#include "logo.h"

typedef struct {
    Xv_object   public_self;    /* pointer back to self */
    GC          gc;             /* GC to render logo */
    Pixmap      bitmap;             /* xlogo bitmap */
} Logo_private;

#define LOGO_PUBLIC(item)       XV_PUBLIC(item)
#define LOGO_PRIVATE(item)      XV_PRIVATE(Logo_private, Logo_public, item)
```

The public header file is always included in the private header file since it has all the necessary declarations specific to the package and it includes other header files that may be needed.

The private logo structure is declared next. The first field in all private data structures is a handle back to the public data structure. Again, when the *initialize* routine for the package is called, an instance of the private data type of allocated and its `public_self` field is set to the public data type passed. This is shown in Section 22.4.4, "The Initialize Method."

The rest of the fields in the private data structure are those that are specific to the aspects of the logo package that vary from instance to instance. This includes a handle to a `Pixmap` (which is the X logo bitmap) and a `GC`. When multiple instances of the object are created, each instance uses a discrete pixmap and `GC` since each instance of the class may have different window attributes. That is, the programmer may create a logo on a color window and another logo for a monochrome window.

A general rule of thumb is that there should be few, if any, global variables in the implementation of a package. These variables should almost always be declared as fields within the private data type. Therefore, all variables that are needed by the package and that may have different values depending on the instance are declared as fields within the logo's private data structure.

The last two lines of the private header file are:

```
#define LOGO_PUBLIC(item)    XV_PUBLIC(item)
#define LOGO_PRIVATE(item) \
            XV_PRIVATE(Logo_private, Logo_public, item)
```

These macros are used to facilitate the task of cross referencing to and from the public and private data types. Because these types are declared as Xv_opaque, typecasting is necessary to coerce the type into a data type needed. They utilize the two XView macros, XV_PUBLIC and XV_PRIVATE. These macros are defined in *<xview/pkg.h>* as:

```
#define XV_PRIVATE(private_type, public_type, obj) \
    ((private_type *)((public_type *) (obj))->private_data)

#define XV_PUBLIC(obj) ((obj)->public_self)
```

These macros are used frequently in source files that implement an XView package.

22.4.2 The Implementation File

The next task is to declare the logo package and to implement all the methods. This may be done in one or more source files. For maintenance, it is much easier to declare as much as possible in one file and declare all functions as static. This is to insure that the functions used by the package are used *only* by the package. However, in the event that more than one file is used to contain all the functions necessary to implement a package, it is impossible to restrict the scope of a function in this manner. XView, therefore, introduces two reserved types that can be used to declare functions for either internal (private) use or public use.

The types Xv_public and Xv_private are both defined to be extern to indicate that they may be called from outside of the files they are declared in. However, the meaning of these types indicates the intended use of the function. Programmers should never call "private" functions whereas they are allowed to call the public ones. It is assumed that the private functions are those that aid in the implementation of the package. Again, functions should be declared as static whenever possible.

22.4.3 The Package Declaration

A package is declared by initializing a global variable of type Xv_pkg. All the fields of the data structure are initialized to identify the package. The logo package is declared by creating a logo_pkg variable of this type.*

```
Xv_pkg logo_pkg = {
    "Logo",                 /* package name */
    ATTR_PKG_UNUSED_FIRST,  /* package ID */
    sizeof(Logo_public),    /* size of the public struct */
```

---

*This declaration may be done in the file that contains the package implementation. However, for systems with shared libraries, it is advantageous to put this variable declaration and initialization in a file by itself so that the compiler can link it in with the shared libraries. You should consult your compiler and operating system documents for instructions on how to create shared libraries.

```
        WINDOW,                  /* subclassed from the WINDOW package */
        logo_init,
        logo_set,
        logo_get,
        logo_destroy,
        NULL                     /* disable the use of xv_find() */
    };
```

The package ID is set to ATTR_PKG_UNUSED_FIRST because it is assumed that this is the first unused package in the XView library. In short, a package ID only needs to be distinct from the IDs of parent and child packages. While this is the only *requirement* imposed by XView, it is still recommended that all packages have unique package IDs. The value of the package ID must fall within the range ATTR_PKG_UNUSED_FIRST through ATTR_PKG_UNUSED_LAST.

The size_of_public field of the logo_pkg is set to the size of the public structure using the C macro: sizeof(). The XView intrinsics initialize the public structure before calling the initialize method by allocating the number of bytes set by this field.

The parent package from which the logo package is subclassed is set in the parent_pkg field. This is the WINDOW package so this field is initialized to the WINDOW package. You may recall that this is a macro that refers to the address of the WINDOW package's global variable: xv_window_pkg (implying that the two are interchangeable).

The rest of the fields in the logo_pkg structure are initialized to the pointers to the appropriate functions. Notice, however, that the *find* method is disabled by having its field initialized to NULL. Any routine that does not apply to a particular package may be set to NULL; XView will not try to invoke NULL methods.

The xv_find() routine is unset for the logo package because it doesn't make sense to be able to reuse an instance of a logo object. That is, because the logo package is subclassed from the WINDOW package, it is impossible to render a window in more than one place on the screen at a time. It is only possible to create multiple instances of this type of object even though the package may display the same logo image.*

This is contrary to the way the font package works, for example. Fonts can be rendered anywhere and they do not contain windows, so referencing the same font instance is reasonable. However, the scope of availability for fonts is restricted to each server. Not all fonts may exist on all servers, and even if they do, they do not share the same XIDs. Thus, you cannot render a string using a font in a window that resides on a server other than the server from which the font was obtained.

Use of the *find* method is discussed in detail in Section 22.8, "The Find Method," later in this chapter.

_____

*It is possible to share the same logo *image*, if not the entire logo object. This can be accomplished using the *Bitmap* package discussed next.

22.4.4 The Initialize Method

The *initialize* method is responsible for allocating an instance of the `private_data` structure and linking the private and public structures together. Once the public and private structures have been initialized and linked, an instance of the class has been created. However, it
is incomplete because none of the attributes of the class have been set in the new instance.
This may be done in the initialize routine and in the set routine, called later.

The function takes the following form:

```
int
init_func(owner, package_public, avlist)
    Xv_opaque       owner;
    Xv_opaque       *package_public;
    Attr_avlist     avlist;
```

The `owner` parameter is the object passed as the owner to the call to `xv_create`. It is declared as `Xv_opaque` here because its actual type varies from package to package. However,
the type of the owner is also a public data type. For the logo package, the owner is a `Frame`
since frames are used to manage subwindow layout (and the logo package is subclassed from
the `WINDOW` package).

The `package_public` parameter is a pointer to the public data type declared in the public
header file. For the logo package, this type is `Logo_public`. The XView intrinsics have allocated this data type before calling the routine.

The `avlist` parameter contains the attribute-value pairs specified in the call to `xv_`
`create()`. These may or may not be evaluated from within the initialize routine depending
on the nature of the attribute. We'll get to this in a moment.

The function returns `XV_OK` or `XV_ERROR` depending on whether it was successful allocating
and initializing the necessary resources. If there is an error of any kind that should prevent
the object from being instantiated, all allocated resources should be freed and the function
should return `XV_ERROR`. If there is an error during any phase of the initialize method,
XView calls the *destroy* method for each package (except for the package whose initialize
routine actually returned `XV_ERROR`). The `op` parameter passed has the value `DESTROY_`
`CLEANUP`. See Section 22.4.7, "The Destroy Method," for details.

The following is a listing of the initialize function for the logo package:

```
static int
logo_init(owner, logo_public, avlist)
Xv_opaque       owner;
Logo_public     *logo_public;
Attr_avlist     avlist; /* ignored here */
{
    Logo_private *logo_private = xv_alloc(Logo_private);
    Display *dpy;
    Window win;

    if (!logo_private)
        return XV_ERROR;

    dpy = (Display *)xv_get(owner, XV_DISPLAY);
    win = (Window)xv_get(logo_public, XV_XID);

    /* link the public to the private and vice-versa */
    logo_public->private_data = (Xv_opaque)logo_private;
    logo_private->public_self = (Xv_opaque)logo_public;

    /* create the 1-bit deep pixmap of the X logo */
    if ((logo_private->bitmap = XCreatePixmapFromBitmapData(dpy, win,
        xlogo32_bits, xlogo32_width, xlogo32_height,
        1, 0, 1)) == NULL) {
        free(logo_private);
        return XV_ERROR;
    }
    /* set up event handlers to get resize and repaint events */
    xv_set(logo_public,
        WIN_NOTIFY_SAFE_EVENT_PROC,      logo_redraw,
        WIN_NOTIFY_IMMEDIATE_EVENT_PROC, logo_redraw,
        NULL);

    return XV_OK;
}
```

The first thing this function does is allocate the private data structure for the logo object using the `xv_alloc()` macro. This macro is defined to be:

```
#define xv_alloc(t) ((t *)xv_calloc((unsigned)1, (unsigned)sizeof(t)))
```

Because `xv_calloc()` is used, the entire private data structure is allocated and all the fields are initialized to NULL or 0 (thus the analogy to `calloc()`). The fields of the logo data structure that must be initialized are the `bitmap` and the GC.

The bitmap is the X logo, a `Pixmap` created by `XCreatePixmapFromBitmapData()`. In order to create the pixmap, `XCreatePixmapFromBitmapData()` requires a pointer to the `Display` and an X window, both of which can be obtained from the window part of the logo object. Since the initialize phase of XView initializes classes from the generic package down through subclasses, we know the logo's parent (the WINDOW package) has already been initialized and we can use its XID.

While we have initialized the logo's pixmap to use, we cannot initialize the GC for the logo because we do not know the ultimate foreground and background colors of the window. These pixel values are extracted from the window's colormap segment, and although the window for the logo has been created and initialized, its cms has not been assigned yet. This is not done until the window's *set* routine is called. Since the WINDOW package does not evaluate the WIN_CMS attribute in *its* initialize routine, the logo package cannot attempt to read it from the logo package's initialize routine. This must be done later, after the WINDOW package's set routine has had a chance to set the window's cms.

Providing a practical example, consider the following code fragment:

```
cms = xv_create(NULL, CMS,
    CMS_SIZE, 2,
    CMS_NAMED_COLORS, "blue", "red", NULL,
    NULL);

logo = xv_create(frame, LOGO,
    WIN_CMS,  cms,
    NULL);
```

Here, the programmer intended the logo to be rendered in red with a blue background. This is accomplished by creating a colormap segment with two colors: blue and red. During the *initialization* phase of object creation, the WINDOW package creates its window, but only assigns a default colormap segment. It is only during the *set* phase that the window is assigned the colormap segment from the WIN_CMS attribute. Since the set phase is done in reverse order (e.g., the logo's set routine is called before its parent's set routine), the logo package cannot query its window's colors until later. The only opportunity for the logo package to get the window's colors is during the extra call to the set routine in which XV_END_CREATE is passed. The set routine in this case is called in ascending order (top down) and the logo can now query its window's colormap segment.

It is true that if the programmer specifies attribute-value pairs in the call to xv_create(), those pairs are passed to the initialize function in the avlist parameter. However, since the logo package has no attributes of its own for the user to specify, the avlist is ignored in favor of allowing the other packages to deal with attributes. While we could have looked in this attribute list for a WIN_CMS attribute and captured the pixel values from it, a parent package can override or change its mind about which attributes it actually decides to use. Although this may be unlikely, the XView design allows for it to happen and, therefore, XView packages should be written with this possibility in mind.

A general rule of thumb is that packages should not test for attributes from other packages through the avlist. Instead, the preferred method is to use xv_get() to allow the package that is responsible for the attribute to return whatever value it deems appropriate. Note that this is not always true — there are some cases where packages not only look for attributes that don't belong to them, but they override them. The PANEL package, for example, does not allow the programmer to change the foreground and background colors on its window by intercepting or modifying certain color-related attributes. The PANEL package does this in order to prevent the programmer from violating OPEN LOOK.

On the other hand, let's suppose we wanted to restrict the colors used by the logo window to black and white. In this case, we would want to override the WIN_CMS specification if the programmer provided one. We would do this by *consuming* the WIN_CMS attribute (and presumably the WIN_CMS_NAME attribute) from the avlist using the ATTR_CONSUME() macro (Section 22.2.3, "Consuming Attributes"). The attribute may be consumed here in the initialize routine or later in the set routine. If the WINDOW package chose to consume these attributes, it could have done so before we got to them. However, by consuming them in the logo's initialize routine, we can prevent the WINDOW package from consuming them in its set routine called later. If an attribute that is consumed is just done to prevent another package from evaluating it, chances are that this attribute should not have been set by the programmer. In such a case, a warning should be dispatched via xv_error().

Finally, the last thing done in logo_initialize() is setting the event handlers for the window. This is not intended to track events generated by the user, but to track WIN_REPAINT (Expose) and WIN_RESIZE (ConfigureNotify) events for the logo's window. This is done to determine when and where the logo should be drawn.

The method used to track these events is by using the specified attributes:

```
xv_set(logo_public,
    WIN_NOTIFY_SAFE_EVENT_PROC,      logo_redraw,
    WIN_NOTIFY_IMMEDIATE_EVENT_PROC, logo_redraw,
    NULL);
```

These are *private attributes* (e.g., not for general programmer use) from the WINDOW package specifically for purpose of having the internals of XView packages be able to specify event handlers that do not conflict with or be overridden by the programmer. The programmer, as you may recall, uses the attribute, WIN_EVENT_PROC to handle events destined for the window. In fact, this attribute will continue to work as expected despite the use of the WIN_NOTIFY_* attributes listed above.

These two private attributes are similar to the Notifier's notify_set_event_func() function. The programmer can interpose on the logo's event function just as described in Chapter 19, *The Notifier*, as usual. In this case, the programmer's interposing functions are called ahead of the logo_redraw() function (by design).

The logo_redraw() Function

The logo_redraw() function itself does not have anything to do with XView internals or package implementation. However, it is described here so as to keep the continuity of the discussion.

This function simply renders the logo in the object's window. It uses XCopyPlane() to render the logo because the logo Pixmap is known to be 1-bit deep whereas the logo's window can be any depth. This is done for the last in a possible series of Expose events as shown:

```
logo_redraw(logo_public, event)
Logo_public    *logo_public;
Event          *event;
{
    Logo_private *logo_private = LOGO_PRIVATE(logo_public);
    XEvent *xevent = event_xevent(event);

    if (xevent->xany.type == Expose && xevent->xexpose.count == 0) {
        Display *dpy = (Display *)xv_get(logo_public, XV_DISPLAY);
        Window window = (Window)xv_get(logo_public, XV_XID);
        int width = (int)xv_get(logo_public, XV_WIDTH);
        int height = (int)xv_get(logo_public, XV_HEIGHT);
        int x = (width - xlogo32_width)/2;
        int y = (height - xlogo32_height)/2;

        XCopyPlane(dpy, logo_private->bitmap, window, logo_private->gc,
            0, 0, xlogo32_width, xlogo32_height, x, y, 1L);
```

```
    } else if (xevent->xany.type == ConfigureNotify)
        XClearArea(xv_get(logo_public, XV_DISPLAY),
            xv_get(logo_public, XV_XID), 0, 0,
            xevent->xconfigure.width, xevent->xconfigure.height, True);
}
```

The ConfigureNotify event is tested to see if the window resized. If it did, the window needs to be cleared and the logo redrawn in the new center of the window. The window is cleared using XClearArea() and passing True as the last parameter indicating that an Expose event should be generated. When the event is delivered, logo_redraw() is called again, and the logo is redrawn.

22.4.5 The Set Method

After the initialize routines for all the classes have been called, the *set* method is invoked in reverse order (from the bottom up). That is, the generic package's set routine is called last and the logo's set routine is called first.

The form of the set routine is:

```
Xv_opaque
set_func(pkg_public, avlist)
    Xv_opaque    *pkg_public;
    Attr_avlist  avlist;
```

The first parameter is a handle to the public data type representing the package. The avlist parameter is a list of the attributes and values that have not been consumed by the initialize routine or previously called set routines from other packages. In this routine, package-specific attributes are scanned and evaluated, modifying the private data type according to the attributes' values.

Most applications ignore the return value of xv_set(), so it is usually sufficient to return XV_OK. However, you can return anything you like. For example, your own package may wish to return the previous value of an attribute if xv_set() was used to change it. This may not be clearly defined, as xv_set() can be called to set many attributes.

Here is the set routine for the logo package:

```
logo_set(logo_public, avlist)
Logo_public *logo_public;
Attr_avlist avlist;
{
    Logo_private *logo_private = LOGO_PRIVATE(logo_public);
    Attr_attribute *attrs;

    for (attrs = avlist; *attrs; attrs = attr_next(attrs))
        switch ((int) attrs[0]) {
            case XV_END_CREATE : {
                /* this stuff *must* be here rather than in the "init"
                 * routine because the CMS is not loaded into the
                 * window object until the "set" routines are called.
                 */
                Cms cms = xv_get(logo_public, WIN_CMS);
                XGCValues gcvalues;
                Display *dpy =
```

```
                    (Display *)xv_get(logo_public, XV_DISPLAY);
                gcvalues.foreground =
                    x(unsigned long)v_get(cms, CMS_FOREGROUND_PIXEL);
                gcvalues.background =
                    (unsigned long)xv_get(cms, CMS_BACKGROUND_PIXEL);
                gcvalues.graphics_exposures = False;
                logo_private->gc = XCreateGC(dpy,
                    xv_get(logo_public, XV_XID),
                    GCForeground|GCBackground|GCGraphicsExposures,
                    &gcvalues);
            }
        default :
            xv_check_bad_attr(LOGO, attrs[0]);
            break;
        }
    return XV_OK;
}
```

A handle to the logo's private data structure is needed since the set routine changes the value of fields within that structure. The LOGO_PRIVATE() macro is used to get a pointer to the private data from the public object.

Since the logo package has no attributes, there is no need to scan for attributes specific to the logo package or any other package. Recall, however, that we still need to initialize the GC for the logo. Therefore, we scan for the XV_END_CREATE attribute.

NOTE

The set routine must return XV_OK when XV_END_CREATE is in the avlist. Any other return value causes XView to assume that there was an error in initialization.

At this point in time, the WINDOW package has initialized itself completely and we can therefore get the colors from the window's colormap segment. We use xv_get() and ask for its WIN_CMS.

The sample *Bitmap* package goes into more detail about the set routine.

22.4.6 The Get Method

The *get* method is simple: it basically returns the value of the attribute specified in the programmer's call to xv_get(). The form of the get function is:

```
Xv_opaque
get_func(pkg_public, status, attr, avlist)
    pkg_public      *pkg_public;
    int             *status;
    Attr_attribute  attr;
    Attr_avlist     avlist;
```

The `attr` parameter is the attribute for which the programmer wants the value.* However, there are some attributes used by `xv_get()` that take an additional parameter. For example, when using `CANVAS_NTH_VIEW`, an additional `int` parameter is required to indicate which view to return. For such cases, the additional parameter(s) is in the `avlist`.

The `status` parameter must be set by the get routine to either `XV_OK` or `XV_ERROR` depending on whether the attribute requested has been evaluated. If set to `XV_OK`, the XView internals assume that the value returned by the function is what is to be the return value for the original `xv_get()` call.

The calling sequence for the get method is from the bottom up — that is, the specific packages are called first followed by each parent up the chain to the generic object. Each class in the chain is called until one of them sets the `status` parameter to `XV_OK`.

If an unknown attribute is requested, `status` should be set to `XV_ERROR`, but the function should return `XV_OK`. This tells XView that the attribute requested does not belong to this package and that it should try the next package in the chain.

Here is the get function for the logo object:

```
logo_get(logo_public, status, attr, args)
Logo_public     *logo_public;
int             *status;
Attr_attribute  attr;
Attr_avlist     args;
{
    *status = xv_check_bad_attr(LOGO, attr);
    return (Xv_opaque)XV_OK;
}
```

Since the logo object has no attributes, it sets the `status` parameter and returns. As noted earlier, since there are no attributes specific to the logo package, this routine is unnecessary; we could have declared the function pointer as `NULL` in the `Xv_pkg` data structure causing the get method for this package to be unused.

A more detailed discussion of the get method, including a discussion on `xv_check_bad_attr()`, is given in the example *Bitmap* package.

22.4.7 The Destroy Method

When the programmer calls `xv_destroy()` or if XView decides to destroy objects or classes externally, the *destroy* method for the package is called. The calling sequence for the destroy method is from the bottom up, as it is for the get method.

The main task of the destroy routine is to free the private data type and any other cleanup that may accompany it. This includes freeing allocated data, closing open file descriptors, unlinking temp files and so on. However, this is not the only reason the destroy method is called; in fact, there are 4 different reasons or conditions in which the function may be invoked.

---

*Remember, `xv_get()` can only be used to get the value of one attribute only.

The form of the destroy function is:

```
int
destroy_func(pkg_public, status)
    Xv_opaque       *pkg_public;
    Destroy_status   status;
```

As with all the methods, the first parameter is a handle to the public data type for the package. The `status` parameter is of type `Destroy_status`. It describes the condition for which the function has been called. This is the same situation as the `destroy_func()` described in Section 19.9.5, "Modifying a Frame's Destruction," in Chapter 19, *The Notifier*.

For the logo object, we need to destroy the allocated pixmap and free the allocated GC. The logo's destroy function is:

```
logo_destroy(logo_public, status)
Logo_public      *logo_public;
Destroy_status    status;
{
    Logo_private *logo_private = LOGO_PRIVATE(logo_public);

    if (status == DESTROY_CLEANUP) {
        XFreePixmap(xv_get(logo_public, XV_DISPLAY),
            logo_private->bitmap);
        XFreeGC(xv_get(logo_public, XV_DISPLAY), logo_private->gc);
        free(logo_private);
    }

    return XV_OK;
}
```

Unless the status is `DESTROY_CLEANUP`, nothing is freed. This assures that the instance of the logo object remains in tact in case the destroy method was invoked for other reasons. Please consult Chapter 19, *The Notifier*, and Chapter 4, *Frames*, for details on how to handle the other conditions possible for the destroy function.

22.5 Example Program Listing

At this point, we have discussed everything necessary to implement the logo object except for a main application that creates an instance of a logo object.

Writing this application is really no different from the way it is done for any other XView package, as you can see from Example 22-1.

Example 22-1. The logo.c program

```
/* logo.c -- demonstrate the use of the logo package. */
#include <xview/xview.h>
#include <xview/cms.h>
#include "logo.h"

main(argc, argv)
char *argv[];
{
    Frame frame;
```

Example 22-1. The logo.c program (continued)

```
    Cms cms;
    Logo logo;

    xv_init(XV_INIT_ARGC_PTR_ARGV, &argc, argv, NULL);

    frame = (Frame)xv_create(NULL, FRAME, NULL);
    cms = xv_create(NULL, CMS,
        CMS_SIZE,        2,
        CMS_NAMED_COLORS, "blue", "red", NULL,
        NULL);
    logo = xv_create(frame, LOGO,
        XV_WIDTH,        100,
        XV_HEIGHT,       100,
        WIN_CMS,         cms,
        NULL);

    window_fit(frame);
    xv_main_loop(frame);
}
```

All the pieces are in play—the `logo` variable is of type `Logo`, the call to `xv_create()` has
`LOGO` as the package name and the owner of the logo is the frame object. The program allocates a colormap segment that has the colors red and blue to demonstrate that colors can be
assigned to the logo through the `WINDOW` package attributes. However, if this application is
run on a monochrome screen, the output is rendered in black and white, as in Figure 22-3.

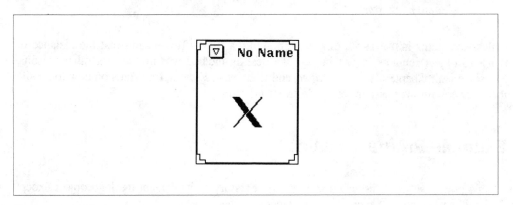

Figure 22-3. Output of logo.c

The frame may be resized by the user and the logo is always redrawn in the middle of its window. This is the task of the `logo_redraw()` routine registered by the logo object in its initialize routine.

The entire logo implementation module is listed in Appendix F, *Example Programs*.

22.6 Compiling an Implementation File

This is a brief overview of how to compile a file or set of files to implement an XView package. If the package is used only by a particular application that you are writing, you can add the source and object files to your own Makefile or Imakefile just as you would for the sources in your main application. However, if you want to build an XView object and add it to the base XView library for general use, then there are several steps you need to take. You should consult your system manuals for details specific to your system.

First, you should compile your program to generate an object file:

```
cc -c Logo.c
```

You may require additional compilation flags depending on your environment. The include files are presumed to be in the same directory as the source file. If you install them anywhere else, you should change the #include directives at the top of the source files to use a different syntax. If you installed the header files in the default XView location (e.g., */usr/include/xview*), the #include directives should say:

```
#include <xview/logo.h>
```

Anywhere else should have the line:

```
#include <logo.h>
```

If this is the case, your compile line options should include the -I parameter.

```
cc -c -I<include_path> Logo.c
```

Once *Logo.c* (the package implementation file) has been compiled, you may compile *logo.c* (the sample application) and link all of them with the default XView library:

```
% cc -c Logo.c
% cc -c logo.c
% cc logo.o Logo.o -lxview -lX11 -o logo
```

22.7 The Bitmap Package

The logo package is a very simplistic one since it does virtually nothing but render the X logo in the middle of its window. There are no attributes specific to the logo package to make the package configurable by the programmer. The next example package, the Bitmap package, demonstrates how attributes are defined and used in XView packages.

The Bitmap package is similar to the logo package in that it just displays a bitmap in the middle of a window. However, the Bitmap package provides the programmer with the ability to specify the file containing the bitmap: the create- and set-only attribute, BITMAP_FILE. To provide the programmer with the ability to get the pixmap, the attribute BITMAP_PIXMAP is available as a get-only attribute.

We cannot get `BITMAP_FILE` because the filename is not retained. Once the bitmap has been loaded, the programmer can get it with the `BITMAP_PIXMAP` attribute. Clearly, the code can easily be modified to support the ability to get the filename or to set the pixmap directly.

The first thing to do is declare these attribute types in the public header file, *bitmap.h*:

```
#include <xview/xview.h>
#include <xview/window.h>

extern Xv_pkg bitmap_pkg;

#define BITMAP &bitmap_pkg

typedef Xv_opaque Bitmap;

#define ATTR_PKG_BITMAP              ATTR_PKG_UNUSED_FIRST
#define BITMAP_ATTR(type, ordinal) ATTR(ATTR_PKG_BITMAP, type, ordinal)

typedef enum {
    BITMAP_FILE      = BITMAP_ATTR(ATTR_STRING, 1),
    BITMAP_PIXMAP    = BITMAP_ATTR(ATTR_OPAQUE, 2), /* get-only */
};

typedef struct {
    Xv_window_struct    parent_data;
    Xv_opaque           private_data;
} Bitmap_public;
```

There are several new aspects to the header file that are used to support the new attributes. First, we define a new macro, `BITMAP_ATTR()`. It is defined as:

```
#define BITMAP_ATTR(type, ordinal) \
    ATTR(ATTR_PKG_BITMAP, type, ordinal)
```

This macro aids in the initialization of the bitmap attribute values by setting the package ID portion of the attribute to be the bitmap package.

Following the macro definitions, the attributes for the bitmap package are defined in the enumerated type definition. `BITMAP_FILE` is declared with `ATTR_STRING` indicating that the programmer-specified value associated with the attribute is a string. The 1 is a unique number to the attributes within the bitmap package, so we start at 1 for the first attribute and increment this number by one for each new attribute.

The private data is declared for the bitmap object in the implementation-specific header file, *bitmap_impl.h*. As you can see, the only changes are new fields used to support the new method of specifying a bitmap filename:

```
#include "bitmap.h"

typedef struct {
    Xv_object    public_self;   /* pointer back to self */
    GC           gc;            /* GC to render logo */
    Pixmap       bitmap;
    int          width, height; /* ...of pixmap */
} Bitmap_private;

#define BITMAP_PUBLIC(item)  XV_PUBLIC(item)
#define BITMAP_PRIVATE(item) \
    XV_PRIVATE(Bitmap_private, Bitmap_public, item)
```

The width and height fields are introduced because these are needed to calculate how to center the bitmap on the window. These are fields rather than global variables because their values are unique on a per-instance basis. However, even though these are fields in the private data structure, this does not mean that there *have* to be corresponding attributes.

22.7.1 The Bitmap Initialize Method

The initialization routine does not initialize any fields of the private data since the set routine, which is eventually called, handles the attributes adequately. The basic initialize functionality of allocating the private data and linking the public and private structures together is still done:

```
bitmap_init(owner, bitmap_public, avlist)
Xv_opaque        owner;
Bitmap_public    *bitmap_public;
Attr_avlist      avlist; /* ignored here */
{
    Bitmap_private *bitmap_private = xv_alloc(Bitmap_private);

    if (!bitmap_private)
        return XV_ERROR;

    /* link the public to the private and vice-versa */
    bitmap_public->private_data = (Xv_opaque)bitmap_private;
    bitmap_private->public_self = (Xv_opaque)bitmap_public;

    /* set up event handlers to get resize and repaint events */
    xv_set(bitmap_public,
        WIN_NOTIFY_SAFE_EVENT_PROC,      bitmap_redraw,
        WIN_NOTIFY_IMMEDIATE_EVENT_PROC, bitmap_redraw,
        NULL);

    return XV_OK;
}
```

As you can see, the event handling function is declared and used the same way as for the logo object.

22.7.2 The Bitmap Set Method

The set method looks for the BITMAP_FILE attribute and, when given, reads in the corresponding bitmap file. Since the BITMAP_PIXMAP attribute is a get-only attribute, if given, the programmer is warned of the error via xv_error().

```
bitmap_set(bitmap_public, avlist)
Bitmap_public *bitmap_public;
Attr_avlist avlist;
{
    Bitmap_private *bitmap_private = BITMAP_PRIVATE(bitmap_public);
    Attr_attribute *attrs;

    for (attrs = avlist; *attrs; attrs = attr_next(attrs))
        switch ((int) attrs[0]) {
            case BITMAP_FILE : {
```

```
            int val, x, y;
            Display *dpy =
                (Display *)xv_get(bitmap_public, XV_DISPLAY);
            Window window =
                (Window)xv_get(bitmap_public, XV_XID);
            Pixmap old = bitmap_private->bitmap;
            if (XReadBitmapFile(dpy, window, attrs[1],
                &bitmap_private->width, &bitmap_private->height,
                &bitmap_private->bitmap, &x, &y) != BitmapSuccess)
            {
                xv_error(bitmap_public,
                    ERROR_STRING, "Unable to load bitmap file",
                    ERROR_PKG,      BITMAP,
                    NULL);
                bitmap_private->bitmap = old;
            }
            break;
        }
        case BITMAP_PIXMAP :
            xv_error(bitmap_public,
                ERROR_CANNOT_SET, attrs[0],
                ERROR_PKG,         BITMAP,
                NULL);
            break;
        case XV_END_CREATE : {
            /* this stuff *must* be here rather than in the "init"
             * routine because the CMS is not loaded into the
             * window object until the "set" routines are called.
             */
            Cms cms = xv_get(bitmap_public, WIN_CMS);
            XGCValues gcvalues;
            Display *dpy =
                (Display *)xv_get(bitmap_public, XV_DISPLAY);
            gcvalues.foreground =
                (unsigned long)xv_get(cms, CMS_FOREGROUND_PIXEL);
            gcvalues.background =
                (unsigned long)xv_get(cms, CMS_BACKGROUND_PIXEL);
            gcvalues.graphics_exposures = False;
            bitmap_private->gc =
                XCreateGC(dpy, xv_get(bitmap_public, XV_XID),
                    GCForeground|GCBackground|GCGraphicsExposures,
                    &gcvalues);
        }
        default :
            xv_check_bad_attr(BITMAP, attrs[0]);
            break;
        }
    }
    return XV_OK;
}
```

22.7.3 The Bitmap Get Method

The get method supports the `BITMAP_PIXMAP` attribute by returning a handle to the actual `Pixmap` used by the bitmap object. The `BITMAP_FILE` attribute cannot be gotten, but rather than producing an error message—we could do so—instead we just fall through to the default case and set the `status` parameter to the value returned by `xv_check_bad_attr()`.

```
bitmap_get(bitmap_public, status, attr, args)
Bitmap_public    *bitmap_public;
int              *status;
Attr_attribute   attr;
Attr_avlist      args;
{
    Bitmap_private *bitmap_private = BITMAP_PRIVATE(bitmap_public);

    switch ((int) attr) {
        case BITMAP_PIXMAP :
            return (Xv_opaque)bitmap_private->bitmap;
        case BITMAP_FILE : /* can't get this attribute */
        default :
            *status = xv_check_bad_attr(BITMAP, attr);
            return (Xv_opaque)XV_OK;
    }
}
```

As you may recall, `xv_check_bad_attr()` checks that the attribute given is part of the package specified in the first parameter. If so, `xv_error()` is called, warning that the attribute was not handled. This is an error because attribute *does* apply to the package and should have been evaluated appropriately. This happens to be the case in the above scenario; the `BITMAP_FILE` attribute belongs to the Bitmap package, but we have not handled the attribute. Thus, a warning is printed saying:

```
XView Warning: Bitmap attribute not allowed.
```

Since the bitmap package does not allow the programmer to use `xv_get()` for the `BITMAP_FILE` attribute, this is an appropriate warning.

The `status` variable is set to the return value of `xv_check_bad_attr()` because this is the same value needed by the internals to XView—that is, the function that called this get routine. Recall that the get routine for each package is called until one of them returns `XV_OK` in the `*status` parameter. This is the indicator that the attribute passed applies to that particular package and that the sequence of calling the packages' get functions should cease. Since `BITMAP_FILE` does apply to the Bitmap package, `*status` is set to `XV_OK`. Thus, when the function returns `XV_OK`, the get method stops and returns to the programmer.

As an opposite case, consider what happens when an attribute that does *not* apply to the Bitmap package is evaluated. Let's say the programmer called:

```
int width = (int)xv_get(bitmap, XV_WIDTH);
```

In this case, the `switch` would fall through to the default case and call `xv_check_bad_attr()`. This time, however, the attribute does not belong to the Bitmap package (it belongs to the generic package) and an error message is not printed. `xv_check_bad_attr()` returns `XV_ERROR` indicating that the get method should continue on to the next package in the class hierarchy. Thus, `*status` is set correctly.

Some Confusion

This interface for xv_check_bad_attr() may seem confusing, but if you follow a simple rule of thumb, it can be made easy. Always have the default case in a switch statement set the status variable to the return value of xv_check_bad_attr(), and always return XV_OK from the function itself.

There still exists one problem, but there is no way to overcome it in the current XView API. That is, if the program that called xv_get() ever passes a bad or invalid attribute, the function returns XV_OK and it is impossible to determine if that value is a legitimate return value. Fortunately, this type of error should be worked out before it ever gets to the end user, so application developers should pay close attention to the error messages printed to stderr.

22.7.4 Creating a Bitmap Instance

The rest of the implementation for the Bitmap package may be seen in Appendix F, *Example Programs*. The destroy method is the same as the logo's destroy method and there is no find method for the Bitmap package. In this section, we show a small example program that demonstrates how an application might create an instance from the bitmap package.

Example 22-2. The bitmap.c program

```
/* bitmap.c -- demonstrate the use of the Bitmap package. */
#include <xview/xview.h>
#include <xview/cms.h>
#include "bitmap.h"

main(argc, argv)
char *argv[];
{
    Frame frame;
    Cms cms;
    Bitmap bitmap;

    xv_init(XV_INIT_ARGC_PTR_ARGV, &argc, argv, NULL);

    if (argc <= 1)
     puts("Specify bitmap filename"), exit(1);

    frame = (Frame)xv_create(NULL, FRAME, NULL);
    cms = xv_create(NULL, CMS,
        CMS_SIZE,        2,
        CMS_NAMED_COLORS, "blue", "red", NULL,
        NULL);
    bitmap = xv_create(frame, BITMAP,
        XV_WIDTH,        100,
        XV_HEIGHT,       100,
        WIN_CMS,         cms,
     BITMAP_FILE,       argv[1],
        NULL);

    window_fit(frame);
    xv_main_loop(frame);
}
```

22.8 The Find Method

One aspect of the XView intrinsics that we have not yet addressed is the method for retrieving handles to objects of a particular class that already have been created. It is not appropriate to do this for the logo object because it is a window-based object. The need for a programmer to use `xv_find()` to retrieve an existing object stems from the ability to reuse the object in more than one instance.

Window-based objects cannot be rendered in more than one location on the screen, so the find method is not appropriate for packages subclassed from the `WINDOW` package. The most common example of objects that use a find method are those that have no windows associated with them. Fonts, for example, can be rendered anywhere as they are just handles to a type of information. Colormap segments can be shared by different windows, so it is possible to find existing colormap segments and reuse them.

To Find, or not to Find

When choosing whether or not you should provide a *find* method to a package that you are writing, you should consider whether or not it makes sense to be able to share the same instance of the object in multiple places. If your XView object is application-specific (i.e., it cannot be used in a general way by "any" application), then you should probably reconsider whether you should make an XView object or try to implement it using existing XView objects or other methods.

Allowing the programmer to use `xv_find()` for a package helps the application keep down its use of system resources, such as memory. It also aids in performance, since the objects are shared among the entire application.

22.8.1 Conceptual Implementation

When the programmer calls `xv_find()`, the *find* method for the package specified (second parameter) is called. The purpose of this function is to cycle through all the objects that have been created of the package's type and find the one that matches the attributes specified. Recall that `xv_find()` may work just like `xv_create()` (see Chapter 2, *The XView Programmer's Model*).

In order to cycle through a list of objects of a particular package, that list must be created and updated every time an object is created or destroyed. That is, each time an object is created, the new object is added to the list, whereas each time an object is destroyed, it is removed from the list. The next issue is where to store this list.

It cannot reside within the package's private data since each instance of the object would have to be updated every time a new instance is created or another destroyed. Instead, we must choose a central location where the list can be obtained directly by the find and initialize procedures. We could choose a global, but private, variable representing the head of the list, but this would cause problems for packages that must have separate lists according to various constraints.

With fonts, for example, each server has unique font IDs and font objects cannot be shared among different servers. So, a list of font objects that have been created could be attached to the server object associated with the font. For colormap segments, since they are dependent upon colormaps, there has to be a separate list of available colormap segments for each available screen on a server (a cms associated with a color screen won't work very well with a cms assigned to a monochrome screen).

For all the XView objects that currently exist and that support `xv_find()`, you may find a different choice of implementation. If you design an XView object that is not unique to each server, you may very well wish not to attach the data to the server object. On the other hand, if the object depends on the unique qualities of the screen within the server (for which there can be many), then you may wish to attach the list head to the screen object associated with a server. Still, your XView object may not even depend on any X or XView related information in which case you needn't attach the list to any XView object at all. It may very well be a global variable that you access directly.

If you decide to follow the methods that some of the existing XView packages use, you may wish to attach lists to XView objects directly. Chapter 7, *Panels*, describes these methods including `XV_KEY_DATA`. We can attach a list of objects from a particular package to another XView object (such as a `Xv_Server` object) using the attribute `XV_KEY_DATA` with the package *identifier* (ID) as the key* and the head of the list as the data type for the key.

Scope of List Availability

Wherever you decide to attach the list of your XView objects, remember that the list is restricted to the application. It is impossible for `xv_find()` to retrieve an instance of an XView object that was created on a separate application that happens to be running on the same machine. Also, note that while there is one server that may support many applications running concurrently, XView creates an instance of a *server* object on a per-application basis, so attaching lists to a server or screen object does not imply that the list is available outside your application's context.

22.8.2 Actual Implementation

When the programmer calls `xv_find()`, XView starts with the package specified and works its way to the GENERIC package until it calls that package's find procedure, if available. If a package returns an object, then XView terminates the calling sequence and returns the object found. If no object is actually returned, XView may automatically create the object by invoking the initialize method just as if the programmer called `xv_create()` rather than `xv_find()`. It will only do this if the attribute XV_AUTO_CREATE is TRUE (the default). If the programmer sets this attribute to FALSE, then `xv_find()` returns NULL and the programmer doesn't get an object.

---

*We don't have to use the package ID as the key, but since it tends to be distinct from the other package IDs, it is a good choice.

Because of the sequence that XView uses to call the find method for classes, package-specific attributes are considered first, followed by the more generic ones. If the programmer calls xv_find() and passes only one attribute-value pair, such as XV_WIDTH, 100 then if no objects of the package type requested is found, the more generic (parent) packages' find methods are called until one returns an object that happens to have a width of 100 pixels.

22.9 The Image Package

Server images (a front end for Pixmaps), like fonts, can be rendered anywhere on the screen (in windows, in other server images and so on), under certain constraints (e.g., window depth and so on). So it is possible to find and reuse instances of server images. However, the current implementation of the server image package does not support a find method. So, we are going to demonstrate how to implement the find method by creating an extension to the server image package that does nothing but support the call to xv_find(). The new package is called *Image* and does not have any package-specific attributes.

There are three routines that provide the functionality of the *find* method: the initialize routine, the destroy routine, and the find routine itself. The initialize routine is responsible for creating the list or, if it already exists, adding the newly created object to the list. The destroy routine is responsible for removing the instance of the object being destroyed from the list. Lastly, the find routine is responsible for checking the list for matching attribute-value pairs and returning the matching object.

The Public Image Header File

The public header file for the image package is fairly simple:

```
#include <xview/xview.h>
#include <xview/svrimage.h>

extern Xv_pkg image_pkg;

#define IMAGE &image_pkg

typedef Xv_opaque Image;

#define ATTR_PKG_IMAGE          ATTR_PKG_UNUSED_FIRST+1

typedef struct {
    Xv_server_image     parent_data;
    Xv_opaque           private_data;
} Image_public;
```

The parent_data field of the public image structure is Xv_server_image because the image package is subclassed from Server_image.

The Private Image Header File

The private header file is equally simple:

```
#include <stdio.h> /* for BUFSIZ */
#include "image.h"

typedef struct _image {
    Xv_object    public_self;                /* pointer back to self */
    char         *filename;          /* for get/find */
    Xv_Screen    screen;             /* need to retain for list */
    struct _image *next;         /* linked list for find */
} Image_private;

#define IMAGE_PUBLIC(item)    XV_PUBLIC(item)
#define IMAGE_PRIVATE(item)   XV_PRIVATE(Image_private, Image_public, item)
```

The private data structure contains several fields that enable the image package to allow the find method to work. The `filename` field is used to save the filename specified as the value to the `SERVER_IMAGE_BITMAP_FILE` attribute. Because the server image implementation does not save this data, the image package does. The `next` field is used to create a linked list of these objects to attach to the screen object set in the `screen` field. This is the list that the find method uses to find existing objects from a call to `xv_find()`.

The Image Package Declaration

The package is initialized in the following way:

```
Xv_pkg image_pkg = {
    "Image",                        /* package name */
    ATTR_PKG_IMAGE,                 /* package ID */
    sizeof(Image_public),           /* size of the public struct */
    SERVER_IMAGE,                   /* subclassed from the server image */
    image_init,
    image_set,
    image_get,
    image_destroy,
    image_find
};
```

22.9.1 The Image Initialize Method

The task of the initialize routine for the image class is primarily to initialize the private data of the image object and to create and/or add to the linked list of the private data types. The routine is defined as follows:

```
image_init(owner, image_public, avlist)
Xv_Screen       owner;
Image_public    *image_public;
Attr_avlist     avlist;                 /* ignored here */
{
    Attr_attribute *attrs;
    Image_private *image_private = xv_alloc(Image_private);
    Image_private *list; /* linked list of image instances */
```

```
            Xv_Screen screen = owner? owner : xv_default_screen;

            if (!image_private || !screen)
                return XV_ERROR;

            /* link the public to the private and vice-versa */
            image_public->private_data = (Xv_opaque)image_private;
            image_private->public_self = (Xv_opaque)image_public;

            for (attrs = avlist; *attrs; attrs = attr_next(attrs))
                if (attrs[0] == SERVER_IMAGE_BITMAP_FILE)
                    image_private->filename =
                        strcpy(malloc(strlen(attrs[1])+1), attrs[1]);

            image_private->next = (Image_private *)NULL;
            image_private->screen = screen;

            /* get the list of existing images from the screen */
            if (list = (Image_private *)xv_get(screen,
                            XV_KEY_DATA, ATTR_PKG_IMAGE)) {
                /* follow list till the end */
                while (list->next)
                    list = list->next;
                /* assign new image object to end of list */
                list->next = image_private;
            } else {
                /* no image objects on this screen -- create a new list */
                xv_set(screen,
                    XV_KEY_DATA, ATTR_PKG_IMAGE, image_private,
                    NULL);
            }
            return XV_OK;
        }
```

The owner for the image object is an Xv_Screen object just as with the Server_image object. Once the private data is allocated and the public and private structures are linked to one another, the fields are initialized. The avlist is scanned, checking for SERVER_IMAGE_BITMAP_FILE. If the programmer called xv_create() passing that attribute, then we need to find out what its value is so we can store it for later retrieval. Remember, we must do this because the Server_image package does not.

Next, the screen object is queried to see if there have been any other Image objects stored. The list returned, if any, is the actual linked list of objects. We need this list in order to append the new instance to the end of it. If the list does not exist, the instance created here is set as the head of the list and is stored in the screen object via XV_KEY_DATA. The package ID is used as the key identifier and the new instance is used as the head of the list.

22.9.2 The Image Set Method

The only purpose for the Image's set method is to test to see if the programmer is changing the image's pixmap. If so, that would invalidate the value for SERVER_IMAGE_ BITMAP_FILE, if set. If not set, then nothing is done.

```
    image_set(image_public, avlist)
    Image_public    *image_public;
    Attr_avlist      avlist;
```

```
{
    Attr_attribute *attrs;
    Image_private *image_private = IMAGE_PRIVATE(image_public);

    /* loop thru attrs looking for anything that would invalidate
     * the fact that the filename is set to a valid file.  If the
     * programmer is assigning a new pixmap or data to this server
     * image, the filename that was originally associated with the
     * object is no longer valid.  Disable for later get/find calls.
     */
    if (image_private->filename)
        for (attrs = avlist; *attrs; attrs = attr_next(attrs))
            if (attrs[0] == SERVER_IMAGE_PIXMAP ||
                attrs[0] == SERVER_IMAGE_BITS   ||
                attrs[0] == SERVER_IMAGE_X_BITS) {
                    free(image_private->filename);
                    image_private->filename = NULL;
            }

    return (Xv_opaque)XV_OK;
}
```

22.9.3 The Image Get Method

The get routine for the Image package provides the ability to return values for SERVER_
IMAGE_BITMAP_FILE and XV_SCREEN. The filename is stored in the Image's private data
structure, so we return this value, if set. The function is as follows:

```
image_get(image_public, status, attr, args)
Image_public  *image_public;
int           *status;
Attr_attribute attr;
Attr_avlist    args;
{
    Image_private *image_private = IMAGE_PRIVATE(image_public);

    switch ((int) attr) {
        case SERVER_IMAGE_BITMAP_FILE :
            return (Xv_opaque)image_private->filename;
        case XV_SCREEN :
            return (Xv_opaque)image_private->screen;
        default :
            *status = xv_check_bad_attr(IMAGE, attr);
            return (Xv_opaque)XV_OK;
    }
}
```

22.9.4 The Image Destroy Method

When an instance of the Image class is destroyed, the destroy procedure is called with the
status of DESTROY_CLEANUP. The first parameter to the destroy function is a handle to the
object being destroyed. The task of the destroy function for the Image package is to remove
the item from the list of items attached to the screen object and free it. Once the object has
been freed, all references to the object become invalid. And of course, once the object has
been removed from the screen's list, then xv_find() will fail to find it.

```
image_destroy(image_public, status)
Image_public     *image_public;
Destroy_status    status;
{
    Image_private *image_private = IMAGE_PRIVATE(image_public);
    Image_private *list; /* linked list of image instances */
    Xv_Screen screen = image_private->screen;

    if (status == DESTROY_CLEANUP) {
        /* get the list of existing images from the screen */
        list = (Image_private *)xv_get(screen,
                        XV_KEY_DATA, ATTR_PKG_IMAGE);
        if ((Image)XV_PUBLIC(list) == (Image)image_public)
            xv_set(screen,
                XV_KEY_DATA, ATTR_PKG_IMAGE, list->next,
                NULL);
        for ( ; list->next; list = list->next)
            if ((Image)XV_PUBLIC(list->next) == (Image)image_public) {
                list->next = list->next->next;
                break;
            }
        if (list->filename)
            free(list->filename);
        free(list);
    }

    return XV_OK;
}
```

22.9.5 The Image Find Method

The find procedure is the main purpose of the Image package. Its purpose is to find an existing Image object whose attributes match those specified to the programmer's call to
xv_find(). If there is more than one matching object, the find routine usually returns the
first one found because it is simpler to implement it that way. However, this is not required
and the object returned may be arbitrary provided that the specified attributes match.

```
image_find(owner, pkg, avlist)
Xv_Screen       owner;
Xv_pkg          *pkg;
Attr_avlist     avlist;                 /* ignored here */
{
    Image_private *list; /* linked list of image instances */
    /* this is what the server image package does */
```

```
Xv_Screen screen = owner? owner : xv_default_screen;
Attr_attribute *attrs;
/* consider all the attrs we allow "find" to match on */
int     width = -1, height = -1, depth = -1;
Pixmap  pixmap = (Pixmap)NULL;
char    *filename = NULL;

/* get the list of existing images from the screen */
list = (Image_private *)xv_get(screen,
              XV_KEY_DATA, ATTR_PKG_IMAGE);

if (!list)
   return NULL;

/* loop thru each attribute requested and save the value
 * associated with it.  Later, we'll loop thru the existing
 * objects looking for the object that has the same values.
 */
for (attrs = avlist; *attrs; attrs = attr_next(attrs))
    switch ((int)attrs[0]) {
        case XV_WIDTH :
            width = (int)attrs[1];
            break;
        case XV_HEIGHT :
            height = (int)attrs[1];
            break;
        case SERVER_IMAGE_DEPTH :
            depth = (int)attrs[1];
            break;
        case SERVER_IMAGE_PIXMAP :
            pixmap = (Pixmap)attrs[1];
            break;
        case SERVER_IMAGE_BITMAP_FILE :
            filename = (char *)attrs[1];
            break;
        case SERVER_IMAGE_BITS :
        case SERVER_IMAGE_X_BITS :
        case SERVER_IMAGE_COLORMAP :
        case SERVER_IMAGE_SAVE_PIXMAP :
        default :
            return NULL; /* you can't "find" for these attrs */
    }
/* Now loop thru each object looking for those whose
 * value that match those specified above.
 */
for ( ; list; list = list->next) {
    /* If it doesn't match, continue to the next object in
     * the list.  Repeat for each requested attribute.
     */
    if (width > -1 &&
        (width != (int)xv_get(XV_PUBLIC(list), XV_WIDTH)))
        continue;
    if (height > -1 &&
        (height != (int)xv_get(XV_PUBLIC(list), XV_HEIGHT)))
        continue;
    if (depth > -1 && (depth != (int)xv_get(XV_PUBLIC(list),
                            SERVER_IMAGE_DEPTH)))
        continue;
    if (pixmap && (pixmap != (Pixmap)xv_get(XV_PUBLIC(list),
```

```
                                    SERVER_IMAGE_PIXMAP)))
            continue;
        if (filename &&
            (!list->filename || strcmp(filename, list->filename)))
            continue;
        /* all matches seemed to be successful, return this object */
        return XV_PUBLIC(list);
    }
    /* nothing found */
    return NULL;
}
```

A find procedure can be implemented in many ways; the one provided above is just one way.

22.9.6 The Image.c Program

Example 22-3 demonstrates one way that the image package can be used. It creates a pixmap based on the bitmap filename given on the command line (a filename must be given). Then it uses xv_find() to find the same object first by the same bitmap filename and then again by using the Pixmap associated with the image.

While the program functionally does very little, it is only intended to demonstrate how multiple server images can be shared in an application via the new Image package.

Example 22-3. The image.c Program

```c
/* logo.c -- demonstrate the use of the logo package. */
#include <xview/xview.h>
#include "image.h"

main(argc, argv)
int argc;
char *argv[];
{
    Frame frame;
    Image image1, image2;
    Pixmap pixmap;

    xv_init(XV_INIT_ARGC_PTR_ARGV, &argc, argv, NULL);

    if (argc < 2)
     puts("specify filename"), exit(1);

    /* frame = (Frame)xv_create(NULL, FRAME, NULL); */
    if (!(image1 = xv_create(NULL, IMAGE,
        XV_WIDTH,                   100,
        XV_HEIGHT,                  100,
        SERVER_IMAGE_BITMAP_FILE,   argv[1],
        NULL)))
         puts("unsuccessfully created image1"), exit(1);
    if (!(image2 = xv_find(NULL, IMAGE,
        SERVER_IMAGE_BITMAP_FILE,   argv[1],
     NULL)))
         puts("unsuccessfully created image2"), exit(1);
    printf("image1 %s image2\n",
      (image2 != image1)? "matched" : "didn't match");
    pixmap = (Pixmap)xv_get(image1, SERVER_IMAGE_PIXMAP);
```

Example 22-3. The image.c Program (continued)

```
    if (!(image2 = xv_find(NULL, IMAGE,
        SERVER_IMAGE_PIXMAP,  pixmap,
    NULL)))
        puts("unsuccessfully created image2"), exit(1);
    printf("image1 %s image2\n",
     (image2 != image1)? "matched" : "didn't match");

    /* window_fit(frame); */
    /* xv_main_loop(frame); */
}
```

22.10 Chapter Summary

This chapter has addressed issues involved in the internals to the XView Toolkits. While you have been exposed to the methods used by the internals in order to develop your own XView packages or to build extensions on other packages, not everything has been covered. For example, it is currently not possible to create panel item packages or extensions from existing panel items.

XView is still under development and future versions of the toolkit may be able to provide missing functionality as well as further enhance and specify the API.

A
Attribute Summary

A
Attribute Summary

This appendix lists all XView attributes in alphabetical order. Each attribute is described briefly. Following its description is a list of the attribute's type, default value and associated procedures. For brevity, the procedures `xv_create`, `xv_find`, `xv_get` and `xv_set` exclude the `xv_` prefix.

ATTR_LIST

Specifies a `NULL`-terminated attribute-value list. It has no value type or default, but when used, it must be the first attribute in an attribute-value list. Usage is:

```
xv_create(object, pkg,
        ATTR_LIST, avlist,
        other_attrs, ..., 0);
```

CANVAS_AUTO_EXPAND

If `TRUE`, canvas width and height are never allowed to be less than the edges of the canvas window.

Type: Boolean
Default: TRUE
Procs: create, get, set

CANVAS_AUTO_SHRINK

If `TRUE`, canvas width and height are never allowed to be greater than the edges of the canvas window.

Type: Boolean
Default: TRUE
Procs: create, get, set

CANVAS_CMS_REPAINT

Specifies whether the canvas repaint procedure is called whenever a new colormap segment is set on the canvas, and/or the foreground and background colors of the canvas are changed.

Type: Boolean
Default: FALSE
Procs: create, get, set

CANVAS_FIXED_IMAGE

Sets the `BitGravity` for the canvas paint window to be `NorthWestGravity` when `TRUE` or `ForgetGravity` when `FALSE`.

Type: Boolean
Default: TRUE
Procs: create, get, set

CANVAS_HEIGHT

Specifies the height of the canvas paint window in pixels.

Type: int
Default: 0
Procs: create, get, set

CANVAS_MIN_PAINT_HEIGHT

If `CANVAS_AUTO_SHRINK` is `TRUE`, limits shrinking of canvas paint window height to specified value.

Type: int
Default: 0
Procs: create, get, set

CANVAS_MIN_PAINT_WIDTH

If `CANVAS_AUTO_SHRINK` is `TRUE`, limits shrinking of canvas paint window width to specified value.

Type: int
Default: 0
Procs: create, get, set

CANVAS_NO_CLIPPING
Ignores clip rects in pixwin (pw_*) calls during repaints in all the paint windows of the canvas. (Sunview compatibility only)

Type: Boolean
Default: FALSE
Procs: create, get, set

CANVAS_NTH_PAINT_WINDOW
Returns the paint window associated with the *n*th view, and takes an argument of the value of *n*. 0 is the index of the first view.

Type: Xv_opaque
Procs: get

CANVAS_PAINT_CANVAS_WINDOW
Gets the canvas from a canvas paint window.

Type: Xv_window
Procs: get

CANVAS_PAINTWINDOW_ATTRS
Distributes modifications across all paint windows in a given canvas. It takes an in-line attribute-value list of window attributes.

Type: A-V list
Procs: create, set

CANVAS_REPAINT_PROC
Names a procedure called when canvas paint window has been damaged and must be repaired. See canvas_repaint_proc() in Appendix B, *Summary of Procedures and Macros*.

Default: NULL
Procs: create, get, set

CANVAS_RESIZE_PROC
Names a procedure called when canvas width or height changes. See canvas_resize_proc() in Appendix B, *Summary of Procedures and Macros*.

Default: NULL
Procs: create, get, set

CANVAS_RETAINED
Specified whether the X server should attempt to retain backing store for the canvas (and paint windows). Note, this does not guarantee that window are retained; the server may not be able to comply.

Type: Boolean
Default: TRUE
Procs: create, get, set

CANVAS_VIEW_CANVAS_WINDOW
Gets the canvas from a canvas view window.

Type: Xv_opaque
Procs: get

CANVAS_VIEW_PAINT_WINDOW
Gets the paint window for the specified canvas view window.

Type: Xv_window
Procs: get

CANVAS_VIEWABLE_RECT
Gets the visible part of the specified paint window in the paint window's coordinates.

Type: Rect *
Procs: get

CANVAS_WIDTH
Specifies the width of the canvas paint window in pixels.

Type: int
Default: 0
Procs: create, get, set

CANVAS_X_PAINT_WINDOW
When TRUE, adds additional parameters to the canvas_repaint_proc(). See Appendix B, *Summary of Procedures and Macros*.

Type: Boolean
Default: FALSE
Procs: create, get, set

CMS_BACKGROUND_PIXEL
Returns the background pixel (index 0) in a colormap segment.

Type: unsigned long
Default: None
Procs: get

CMS_COLOR_COUNT
Returns the foreground pixel (index CMS_SIZE-1) in a colormap segment.

Type: unsigned long
Default: None
Procs: create, set

CMS_CONTROL_CMS

Indicates whether this colormap segment is a control colormap segment for use by panels.

Type: int
Default: FALSE
Procs: create, set, get

CMS_FOREGROUND_PIXEL

Returns the foreground pixel (index CMS_SIZE-1) in a colormap segment.

Type: unsigned long
Default: None
Procs: get

CMS_INDEX

Specifies the starting index to to CMS_COLOR_COUNT entries into the colormap.

Type: unsigned long
Default: 0 (If control cms, CMS_CONTROL_COLORS)
Procs: create, set

CMS_INDEX_TABLE

Used to translate the logical indices of the window's colormap segment into actual pixal values.

Type: unsigned long *
Default: N/A
Procs: get

CMS_NAME

Specifies the name of the colormap segment.

Type: char *
Default: Unique name generated internally
Procs: create, get, set

CMS_NAMED_COLORS

Specifies the names of the colors to be loaded into the colormap segment. The NULL-terminated list of color names is parsed by XParseColor().

Type: List of char *
Default: None
Procs: create, set

CMS_PIXEL

Translates the passed logical index into the actual colormap index.

```
index = xv_get(cms, CMS_PIXEL, 2);
```

Type: unsigned long
Default: None
Procs: get

CMS_SCREEN

Returns the screen with which the colormap segment is associated.

Type: Xv_opaque
Default: default screen
Procs: get

CMS_SIZE

Specifies the size of the colormap segment.

Type: int
Default: XV_DEFAULT_CMS_SIZE (if control cms, CMS_CONTROL_COLORS)
Procs: create, get

CMS_TYPE

Specifies the type of the colormap segment (XV_STATIC_CMS or XV_DYNAMIC_CMS).

Type: Cms_type
Default: XV_STATIC_CMS
Procs: create

CMS_X_COLORS

Specifies the colors to be loaded into the colormap segment. Colors are specified as an array of XColor.

Type: XColor *
Default: None
Procs: create, set, get

CURSOR_BACKGROUND_COLOR

Specifies the background color of a cursor as an RGB triplet.

Type: Xv_singlecolor *
Default: white (255, 255, 255)
Procs: create, get, set

CURSOR_FOREGROUND_COLOR

Specifies the foreground color of a cursor as an RGB triplet.

Type: Xv_singlecolor *
Default: black (0, 0, 0)
Procs: create, get, set

CURSOR_IMAGE

Specifies the cursor's image.

Type: Server_image
Default: 16 x 16 x 1
Procs: create, get, set

CURSOR_X_HOT
Specifies the x coordinate of the hotspot. Its value cannot be negative.

Type: int
Default: 0
Procs: create, get, set

CURSOR_Y_HOT
Specifies the y coordinate of the hotspot. Its value cannot be negative.

Type: int
Default: 0
Procs: create, get, set

FONT_CHAR_HEIGHT
Gets the font's character height in pixels including ascenders and descenders.

Type: int
Procs: get

FONT_CHAR_WIDTH
Returns the width (int) of a specified character (char).

Type: int
Procs: get

FONT_DEFAULT_CHAR_HEIGHT
Gets the character height for the default font. Does not take a valve.

Type: char
Procs: get

FONT_DEFAULT_CHAR_WIDTH
Gets the character width for the default font. Does not take a valve.

Type: int
Procs: get

FONT_INFO
Returns a point to the X structure XFont-Struct.

Type: XFontStruct *
Default: N/A
Procs: \&get

FONT_FAMILY
Specifies the name of a font family.

Type: char *
Default: none
Procs: create, find, get

FONT_RESCALE_OF
Given an existing font and a rescale factor, the returned font will be a similar font in the specified scale.

Type: Xv_Font, Window_rescale_
           state
Procs: create, find

FONT_SCALE
Specifies the relative scale of font with respect to other fonts within the same family and style.

Type: Window_rescale_state
Default: WIN_SCALE_MEDIUM
Procs: create, find, get

FONT_SIZE
Specifies the size of a font in pixels.

Type: int
Default: 12
Procs: create, find, get

FONT_SIZES_FOR_SCALE
Specifies a set of four integral sizes (measured in *points*) to which a font can be scaled.

Type: int, int, int, int
Default: 10, 12, 14, 19
Procs: create, find

FONT_STRING_DIMS
Given a string and the address of a Font_string_dims structure, xv_get() fills in and returns a pointer to the structure describing the pixel dimensions of the string.

Type: char *
Procs: get

FONT_STYLE
Specifies a font style.

Type: char *
Default: NULL (Roman)
Procs: create, find, get

FRAME_BACKGROUND_COLOR
Specifies the frame's background color. This does not affect the title bar of the frame, which is controlled by the window manager. Use with FRAME_INHERIT_COLORS to

propagate the specified colors to subwindows of the frame.

Type: Xv_singlecolor *
Default: 255,255,255
Procs: create,get

FRAME_BUSY
Sets label to gray and changes cursor to hour-glass.

Type: Boolean
Default: FALSE
Procs: create,get,set

FRAME_CLOSED
Sets or gets the frame's closed/iconified state.

Type: Boolean
Default: FALSE
Procs: create,get,set

FRAME_CLOSED_RECT
Sets the *size* of a closed frame base. Ignores x, y positioning.

Type: Rect *
Default: 64 x 64
Procs: create,get,set

FRAME_CMD_PANEL
Gets the default panel in the command frame.

Type: Panel
Procs: get

FRAME_CMD_PUSHPIN_IN
Indicates whether the pushpin is in or out.

Type: Boolean
Default: FALSE
Procs: create,get,set

FRAME_DEFAULT_DONE_PROC
The default procedure is to set the subframe to WIN_SHOW, FALSE.

Default: FRAME_DEFAULT_DONE_PROC
Procs: create,get,set

FRAME_DONE_PROC
Names a client's procedure to be called when user chooses Done from subframe's menu.

Default: FRAME_DEFAULT_DONE_PROC
Procs: create,get,set

FRAME_FOREGROUND_COLOR
Specifies the frame's foreground color. This does not affect the title bar which is controlled by the window manager. Use with FRAME_INHERIT_COLORS to propagate the specified colors to subwindows of the frame.

Type: Xv_singlecolor *
Default: 0,0,0
Procs: create,get

FRAME_ICON
Identifies the base frame's icon.

Type: Xv_opaque
Default: NULL
Procs: create,get,set

FRAME_INHERIT_COLORS
Makes child windows inherit the foreground and background colors of the frame. Windows do not inherit colors in the title bar set by the window manager.

Type: Boolean
Default: FALSE
Procs: create,get

FRAME_LABEL
Specifies the label used in the window manager's titlebar for the frame.

Type: char *
Default: NULL
Procs: create,get,set

FRAME_LEFT_FOOTER
Specifies the left-justified footer.

Type: char *
Default: NULL
Procs: create,get,set

FRAME_NO_CONFIRM
If TRUE, allows destruction of base frame without confirmation.

Type: Boolean
Default: TRUE
Procs: create,get,set

FRAME_NTH_SUBFRAME
Gets the frame's *n*th (from 0) subframe.

Type: int
Default: NULL
Procs: get

FRAME_NTH_SUBWINDOW
Gets the frame's *n*th (from 0) subwindow.

Type: int
Default: NULL
Procs: get

FRAME_RIGHT_FOOTER
Specifies the right-justified footer.

Type: char *
Default: NULL
Procs: create, get, set

FRAME_SHOW_FOOTER
Indicates whether the footer is visible.

Type: Boolean
Default: FALSE
Procs: create, get, set

FRAME_SHOW_HEADER
Indicates whether the header is visible.

Type: Boolean
Default: TRUE
Procs: create, get, set

FRAME_SHOW_LABEL
Indicates whether the frame's label is
displayed. This is equivalent to FRAME_
SHOW_HEADER.

Type: Boolean
Default: TRUE
Procs: create, get, set

FRAME_SHOW_RESIZE_CORNER
Determines whether a frame has a resize corner. This applies only to command frames
and property windows; not base frames.

Type: Boolean
Default: FALSE
Procs: create, get, set

FULLSCREEN_ALLOW_EVENTS
When in a fullscreen grab and the server has
"frozen," sets the release the grab according
to the Xlib grab conventions. See values
listed in <*X11/X.h*>.

Type: Xv_opaque, where the value is
any of the AllowEvents modes
in <*X11/X.h*>.
Procs: create, set

FULLSCREEN_ALLOW_SYNC_EVENT
When in a synchronous grab mode, specifies
that event processing should continue until
the next mouse button or keyboard event.

Type: none
Procs: create, set

FULLSCREEN_COLORMAP_WINDOW
Uses colormap of specified window;
xv_get identifies that window.

Type: Xv_window
Default: root window
Procs: create, get

FULLSCREEN_CURSOR_WINDOW
Restricts cursor to specified window;
xv_get identifies that window.

Type: Xv_window
Default: none
Procs: create, get

FULLSCREEN_GRAB_KEYBOARD
Controls the keyboard portion of a grab.

Type: Boolean
Default: TRUE
Procs: create, get, set

FULLSCREEN_GRAB_POINTER
Controls the pointer portion of a grab.

Type: Boolean
Default: TRUE
Procs: create, get, set

FULLSCREEN_GRAB_SERVER
Controls the server portion of a grab.

Type: Boolean
Default: TRUE
Procs: create, get, set

FULLSCREEN_INPUT_WINDOW
Specifies the window from which input is
read; xv_get identifies that window.

Type: Xv_window
Default: root window
Procs: create, get

FULLSCREEN_KEYBOARD_GRAB_KBD_MODE

Determines the grab mode for the keyboard when grabbing the keyboard.

Type: `Fullscreen_grab_mode`
Default: `FULLSCREEN_ASYNCHRONOUS`
Procs: `create, get, set`

FULLSCREEN_KEYBOARD_GRAB_PTR_MODE

Determines the grab mode for the pointer when grabbing the keyboard.

Type: `Fullscreen_grab_mode`
Default: `FULLSCREEN_ASYNCHRONOUS`
Procs: `create, get, set`

FULLSCREEN_OWNER_EVENTS

Determines whether events are reported normally (TRUE) or only with respect to the grab window (FALSE) if selected by the event mask.

Type: `Boolean`
Default: `FALSE`
Procs: `create, get, set`

FULLSCREEN_PAINT_WINDOW

Specifies or gets the canvas paint window.

Type: `Xv_opaque`
Default: root window
Procs: `create, get`

FULLSCREEN_POINTER_GRAB_KBD_MODE

Determines the grab mode for the keyboard when grabbing the pointer.

Type: `Fullscreen_grab_mode`
Default: `FULLSCREEN_ASYNCHRONOUS`
Procs: `create, get, set`

FULLSCREEN_POINTER_GRAB_PTR_MODE

Determines the grab mode for the pointer when grabbing the pointer.

Type: `Fullscreen_grab_mode`
Default: `FULLSCREEN_ASYNCHRONOUS`
Procs: `create, get, set`

FULLSCREEN_RECT

Returns a pointer to the rectangle containing the canvas paint window that is currently fullscreen.

Type: `Rect *`
Default: root window's bounding box
Procs: `create, get`

FULLSCREEN_SYNC

Specifies whether to grab in synchronous (TRUE) or asynchronous (FALSE) mode.

Type: `Boolean`
Default: `FALSE`
Procs: `create, get, set`

ICON_IMAGE

Sets or gets the remote image for icon's image.

Type: `Server_image`
Default: `NULL`
Procs: `create, get, set`

ICON_IMAGE_RECT

Sets or gets the bounding box (`rect`) for the icon's image.

Type: `Rect *`
Default: origin (0,0), width 64, height 64
Procs: `create, get, set`

ICON_LABEL_RECT

Sets or gets the bounding box for the icon's label. Relative to the icon, 0, 0 is upper-left corner of icon.

Type: `Rect *`
Default: bottom left-hand corner of icon
Procs: `create, get, set`

ICON_MASK_IMAGE

The icon's GC's clipmask is set to this bitmap.

Type: `Pixmap/Server_image`
Default: `FALSE`
Procs: `create, get, set`

ICON_TRANSPARENT

Sets the background color of the icon to be the same as the work space's background color.

Type: `int`
Default: `FALSE`
Procs: `create, get, set`

ICON_TRANSPARENT_LABEL

It draws the given string into an icon using the foregound only. It does not affect any other pixels in the bounding box for each character.

Type: `char *`
Default: `NULL`
Procs: `create, get, set`

MENU_ACTION_IMAGE

Provides a shortcut for creating or modifying an *image* menu item (i.e., a `Server_image`) and associating it with a notify procedure. It takes two values: a server-image and a notify procedure.

Type: `Server_image *,`
            `(void *)()`
Default: `N/A`
Procs: `create, set`

MENU_ACTION_ITEM

Provides a shortcut for creating or modifying a menu *item* and associating it with a notify procedure. It takes two values: a string and a notify procedure.

Type: `char *, (void *)()`
Default: `N/A`
Procs: `create, set`

MENU_APPEND_ITEM

Appends an item to end of menu.

Type: `Menu_item`
Default: `N/A`
Procs: `set`

MENU_CLASS

Gets an enumerated type that identifies the menu class, as set by the package. One of `MENU_CHOICE`, `MENU_COMMAND`, or `MENU_TOGGLE`.

Type: `Menu_class`
Default: defined by package
Procs: `get`

MENU_CLIENT_DATA

Specifies an arbitrary value to be attached to a menu.

Type: `caddr_t`
Default: None
Procs: `create, get, set`

MENU_COL_MAJOR

If `TRUE`, string items in the menu will be sorted in column-major order (like `1s (1)`) instead of row-major order. This attribute does not apply unless the menu uses multiple columns.

Type: `Boolean`
Default: `FALSE`
Procs: `create, get, set`

MENU_DEFAULT

Default menu item as a position.

Type: `int`
Default: `1`
Procs: `create, get, set`

MENU_DEFAULT_ITEM

Default menu item as opaque handle.

Type: `Menu_handle`
Default: handle of first item
Procs: `get, set, create`

MENU_DESCEND_FIRST

If this attribute is specified in `xv_find`, then the search will be done "depth first." If it is not specified, the search will be "deferred"; that is, it will be done horizontally through the menu structure.

Type: no value
Default: deferred
Procs: `find`

MENU_DONE_PROC

Specifies a callback procedure that is called when the menu group is dismissed. See `menu_done_proc()` in Appendix B, *Summary of Procedures and Macros.*

Default: `NULL`
Procs: `create, get, set`

MENU_FEEDBACK

If `FALSE`, item is never inverted and is not selectable.

Type: `Boolean`
Default: `TRUE`
Procs: `create, get, set`

MENU_FIRST_EVENT

Gets the event which was initially passed into `menu_show`. (The event's contents *can* be modified.)

Type: `Event *`
Procs: `get`

MENU_GEN_PIN_WINDOW

Creates a command window as the pin window based on the static (not dynamic) menu's contents. The `frame` is the parent frame; the `name` is the pin window's name.

All menu items *must* have notify procedures; `MENU_NOTIFY_PROC` for the menu itself is ignored.

Type: Frame, char *
Default: no pin window
Procs: create, set

MENU_GEN_PROC

Names a client-provided procedure that is called to generate a menu or menu item. See `menu_gen_proc()` in Appendix B, *Summary of Procedures and Macros*. This attribute takes two values: a string and a generate procedure.

Default: none
Procs: create, get, set

MENU_GEN_PROC_IMAGE

Defines the generate procedure and server image for a menu item.

Type: Server_image *,
           (* Menu) ()
Default: NULL
Procs: create, set

MENU_GEN_PROC_ITEM

Defines the generate procedure and text string for a menu item.

Type: char *, (* Menu) ()
Default: NULL
Procs: create, set

MENU_GEN_PULLRIGHT

Defines the generate procedure for the menu item's submenu.

Type: generate proc
Default: NULL
Procs: create, get, set

MENU_GEN_PULLRIGHT_IMAGE

Provides a shortcut for creating an image for a menu item (or a menu item's submenu) and associating it with a pullright-menu generate procedure.

Type: Server_image *,
           (* Menu) ()
Default: none
Procs: create, set

MENU_GEN_PULLRIGHT_ITEM

Provides a shortcut for creating a menu item (or a menu item's submenu) and associating

it with a pullright menu generate procedure. See `menu_gen_proc()` in Appendix B, *Summary of Procedures and Macros*.

Type: char *, (* Menu) ()
Default: none
Procs: create, set

MENU_IMAGE

Specifies the menu item's server image.

Type: Server_image
Default: NULL
Procs: create, get, set

MENU_IMAGE_ITEM

Creates an image menu item with value specified.

Type: Server_image
Default: none
Procs: create, get, set

MENU_IMAGES

Creates a menu item with multiple images.

Type: list of Server_image
Default: none
Procs: create, get, set

MENU_INACTIVE

If TRUE, item is grayed out and not selectable.

Type: Boolean
Default: FALSE
Procs: create, get, set

MENU_INSERT

Inserts new item after *n*th item in the menu.

Type: int, Menu_item
Default: N/A
Procs: create, get, set

MENU_INSERT_ITEM

Inserts the item given as the second value after the one given as the first value.

Type: Menu_item, Menu_item
Procs: create, set

MENU_INVERT

If TRUE, item's display is inverted.

Type: Boolean
Default: FALSE
Procs: create, get, set

Attribute Summary

MENU_ITEM

Allows you to create menu items *in-line* with the call to the `xv_create()` used to create your menu. Takes a *menu item*-specific attribute-value list that would otherwise be used in a separate call to `xv_create()` to create menu items with the `MENUITEM` package.

Type: A-V list
Procs: `create, set`

MENU_LAST_EVENT

Gets the last event read by the menu. (The event's contents can be modified.)

Type: `Event *`
Procs: `get`

MENU_NCOLS

Specifies the number of columns in a menu.

Type: `int`
Default: `1`
Procs: `create, get, set`

MENU_NITEMS

Returns the number of items in a menu.

Type: `int`
Procs: `get`

MENU_NOTIFY_PROC

Names a procedure called when the user selects a menu item. See `menu_notify_proc()` in Appendix B, *Summary of Procedures and Macros*.

Default: `NULL`
Procs: `create, get, set`

MENU_NOTIFY_STATUS

If the menu is attached to a menu button that is part of an unpinned pop-up window, then the window is dismissed if `MENU_NOTIFY_STATUS` is `XV_OK`. If `MENU_NOTIFY_STATUS` is set to `XV_ERROR`, then the window is not dismissed.

Type: `int`
Default: `XV_OK`
Procs: `create, get, set`

MENU_NROWS

Sets or gets the number of rows in a menu.

Type: `int`
Procs: `create, get, set`

MENU_NTH_ITEM

Gets the *n*th menu item. *n* starts at 1.

Type: `int`
Procs: `get`

MENU_PARENT

To be used with `xv_get()` on a `MENU` object. Returns the the `MENUITEM` parent if the menu is a pullright or `NULL` if the menu is the toplevel menu.

Type: `Menu_item`
Default: `NULL`
Procs: `get`

MENU_PIN

Determines whether the menu will have pushpin.

Type: `Boolean`
Default: `FALSE`
Procs: `create, get, set`

MENU_PIN_PROC

Names a procedure called if user chooses the pin menu item. The default procedure displays a window whose layout is similar to the menu it replaces. See `menu_pin_proc()` in Appendix B, *Summary of Procedures and Macros*.

Default: `menu_default_pin_proc()`
Procs: `create, get, set`

MENU_PIN_WINDOW

The handle of the command frame representing the pin window for the menu when pinned up. Use `MENU_GEN_PIN_WINDOW` to have XView manage this frame automatically.

Type: `Frame_cmd`
Default: `none`
Procs: `create, get, set`

MENU_PULLRIGHT

Item's pullright menu.

Type: `Menu`
Default: `NULL`
Procs: `create, get, set`

MENU_PULLRIGHT_IMAGE

Creates an image menu item with pullright submenu.

Type: `Server_image, Menu`
Default: N/A
Procs: `create, set`

MENU_PULLRIGHT_ITEM

Creates a string menu item with pullright submenu.

Type: `char *, Menu`
Default: N/A
Procs: `create, set`

MENU_RELEASE

Specifies that the item gets destroyed when its parent menu is destroyed (default for items created in-line).

Type: no value
Default: if in-line, destroy item; if `Append/Replace`, do *not* destroy item
Procs: `create, set`

MENU_RELEASE_IMAGE

Specifies that the string or `Server_image` associated with the item is freed when the item is destroyed.

Type: no value
Default: do not release text string or server image
Procs: `create, set`

MENU_REMOVE

Removes the *n*th item from the menu.

Type: `int`
Procs: `set`

MENU_REMOVE_ITEM

Removes the specified menu item.

Type: `Menu_item`
Procs: `set`

MENU_REPLACE

Replaces the *n*th item with specified item.

Type: `int, Menu_item`
Procs: `create, set`

MENU_REPLACE_ITEM

Replaces the item given as first value with the one given as the second value in the menu (the old item is not replaced in any other menus in which it may appear).

Type: `Menu_item, Menu_item`
Procs: `create, set`

MENU_SELECTED

If `TRUE`, the item is currently selected.

Type: `Boolean`
Default: `FALSE`
Procs: `create, get, set`

MENU_STRING

Sets or gets the menu item's string.

Type: `char *`
Default: `NULL`
Procs: `create, get, set`

MENU_STRING_ITEM

Defines the text string and value for a menu item.

Type: `char *, Xv_opaque`
Default: `NULL`
Procs: `create, set`

MENU_STRINGS

Sets the string for multiple menu items.

Type: list of `char *`
Procs: `create, set`

MENU_TITLE

Specifies that the item is the menu's title. Returns `TRUE` or `FALSE` on `get`.

Type: no value on `set`, `Boolean` on `get`
Default: menu item is *not* the menu title
Procs: `create, get, set`

MENU_TITLE_ITEM

Creates a string title item. Must be used with menus that do not originate from pullright items or pulldown menu buttons.

Type: `char *`
Default: no title
Procs: `create, set`

MENU_TYPE

Returns `MENU_MENU` or `MENU_ITEM`. Informs you whether you have a menu or a menu item.

Type: `Menu_attribute` (an enum)
Default: `MENU_MENU`
Procs: `get`

MENU_VALID_RESULT

If TRUE, then a zero return value represents a legitimate value.

Type: `Boolean`
Default: `FALSE`
Procs: `create, get, set`

MENU_VALUE

Sets or gets the item's value.

Type: `Xv_opaque`
Default: `NULL`
Procs: `create, get, set`

NOTICE_BUTTON

Specifies a string to be displayed in a button and a value to use if the button is selected. Value is returned by `notice_prompt()`.

Type: `char *, int`
Default: none
Procs: `notice_prompt`

NOTICE_BUTTON_NO

Specifies a string associated with the NO (cancel) button, which can also be triggered via a keyboard accelerator. The value returned if this button is selected is NOTICE_NO.

Type: `char *`
Default: none
Procs: `notice_prompt`

NOTICE_BUTTON_YES

Specifies a string to associate with the YES (confirm) button, which is also triggered via a keyboard accelerator. The value returned when this button is selected is NOTICE_YES.

Type: `char *`
Default: none
Procs: `notice_prompt`

NOTICE_FOCUS_XY

Describes the x, y position, relative to the specified client window, from which the notice shadow emanates.

Type: `int, int`
Default: mouse position
Procs: `notice_prompt`

NOTICE_FONT

Specifies the font to be used in the notice message(s).

Type: `Xv_Font`
Default: one size larger than that used by client frame
Procs: `notice_prompt`

NOTICE_MESSAGE_STRINGS

Specifies the text to print in a notice. Value is a NULL terminated list of strings.

Type: `list of char *`
Default: `NULL`
Procs: `notice_prompt`

NOTICE_MESSAGE_STRINGS_ARRAY_PTR

Specifies the text to print in a notice. The value is a variable pointing to a NULL-terminated array of strings.

Type: `char**`
Default: `NULL`
Procs: `notice_prompt`

NOTICE_NO_BEEPING

Allows a client to specify that no beeping should take place, regardless of defaults database setting. The default for this option is FALSE; that is, beep however many times specified in the database.

Type: `int`
Default: `TRUE`
Procs: `notice_prompt`

NOTICE_TRIGGER

Specifies an XView event that causes the notice to return. When this event occurs, the value returned is NOTICE_TRIGGERED. The event parameter to `notice_prompt` contains specifics about the event that triggered it.

Type: `int`
Default: N/A
Procs: `notice_prompt`

OPENWIN_ADJUST_FOR_HORIZONTAL_SCROLLBAR

Reserves space in openwin-class objects (e.g., canvas) for a horizontal scrollbar. On xv_set, adjusts (extends) the height of a subwindow that does *not* have a horizontal scrollbar to align properly with one that does.

Type: `Boolean`
Default: `TRUE`
Procs: `create, get, set`

OPENWIN_ADJUST_FOR_VERTICAL_SCROLLBAR

Reserves space in openwin-class objects (e.g., canvas) for a vertical scrollbar. On `xv_set`, adjusts (extends) the width of a subwindow that does *not* have a vertical scrollbar to align properly with one that does.

Type: `Boolean`
Default: `TRUE`
Procs: `create, get, set`

OPENWIN_AUTO_CLEAR

If `TRUE`, exposed areas of windows are cleared (i.e., painted the background color) before the repaint proc is called.

Type: `Boolean`
Default: `TRUE` unless subwindow's canvas is retained
Procs: `create, get, set`

OPENWIN_HORIZONTAL_SCROLLBAR

Returns the handle of the horizontal scrollbar associated with the specified view.

Type: `Xv_scrollbar`
Default: `none`
Procs: `get`

OPENWIN_NO_MARGIN

If `TRUE`, the view window's two pixel bottom and right margins are turned off.

Type: `Boolean`
Default: `FALSE`
Procs: `create, get, set`

OPENWIN_NTH_VIEW

Gets the handle of a specified openwin view window. Openwin view windows are numbered from 0.

Type: `int, Xv_window`
Procs: `get`

OPENWIN_NVIEWS

Gets the number of views contained in the open window.

Type: `int`
Default: `1`
Procs: `get`

OPENWIN_SELECTED_VIEW

Specifies the currently selected openwin view.

Type: `Xv_window`
Default: `none`
Procs: `create, get, set`

OPENWIN_SHOW_BORDERS

Displays openwin borders. This must remain on for openwin objects to have scrollbars attached to them.

Type: `Boolean`
Default: `TRUE` (`FALSE` for panels)
Procs: `create, get`

OPENWIN_SPLIT

Takes as its value a list of attribute-value pairs beginning with `OPENWIN_SPLIT_`.

Type: `A-V list`
Procs: `create, set`

OPENWIN_SPLIT_DESTROY_PROC

Names a procedure to call when a split openwin is destroyed. See `openwin_split_destroy_proc()` in Appendix B, *Summary of Procedures and Macros*.

Default: `NULL`
Procs: `create, get, set`

OPENWIN_SPLIT_DIRECTION

Sets the direction of the split either horizontally or vertically.

Type: `Openwin_split_direction`
Default: `OPENWIN_SPLIT_HORIZONTAL`
Procs: `create, set`

OPENWIN_SPLIT_INIT_PROC

Names a procedure to call when a split window is created. See `openwin_init_split()` in Appendix B, *Summary of Procedures and Macros*.

Default: `NULL`
Procs: `create, get, set`

OPENWIN_SPLIT_POSITION

Sets the position (in pixels) of the view.

Type: `int`
Default: `none`
Procs: `set, create`

OPENWIN_SPLIT_VIEW

Specifies which view to split. Its value is the handle of the view you want to split.

Type: `Xv_window`
Procs: `set`

OPENWIN_SPLIT_VIEW_START

Specifies which part of the data (measured in scrollbar-units) is displayed at the start of the view (*top* for vertical; *left* for horizontal).

Type: `int`
Default: continue from previous view
Procs: `set, create, get`

OPENWIN_VERTICAL_SCROLLBAR

Returns the handle of the vertical scrollbar associated with the specified view.

Type: `Scrollbar`
Default: none
Procs: `get`

OPENWIN_VIEW_ATTRS

Distributes modifications across all *views* in a given open window. It does not affect paintwindows.

Type: A-V list
Procs: `create, set`

PANEL_BACKGROUND_PROC

Names an event handling procedure called when an event falls on the background of the panel. See `panel_background_proc()` in Appendix B, *Summary of Procedures and Macros.*

Default: `panel_default_handle_event`
Procs: `create, get, set`

PANEL_CARET_ITEM

Specifies the text item that currently has the caret.

Type: `Panel_item`
Default: first text item
Procs: `create, get, set`

PANEL_CHOICE_IMAGE

Specifies the image for choice item indicated by the first argument.

Type: `int, server_image`
Default: none
Procs: `create, get, set`

PANEL_CHOICE_IMAGES

Specifies the image for each of several choices.

Type: list of `Server_image`
Default: `NULL`
Procs: `create, get, set`

PANEL_CHOICE_NROWS

Specifies the number of rows to use in the layout of panel choices.

Type: `int`
Default: 1 for horizontal layout (`PANEL_LAYOUT`)
Procs: `create, get, set`

PANEL_CHOICE_NCOLS

Specifies the number of columns to use in the layout of panel choices.

Type: `int`
Default: 1 for vertical layout (`PANEL_LAYOUT`)
Procs: `create, get, set`

PANEL_CHOICE_STRING

Sets the string for choice item specified by first argument.

Type: `int, char *`
Default: `NULL`
Procs: `create, get, set`

PANEL_CHOICE_STRINGS

Sets the string for each choice. You must specify at least one choice. The least you can specify is a single `NULL` string.

Type: list of `char *`
Default: `NULL`
Procs: `create, set`

PANEL_CHOICE_X

Second argument is left edge of choice specified by first argument.

Type: `int, int`
Default: determined by `PANEL_LAYOUT`
Procs: `create, get, set`

PANEL_CHOICE_XS

Left edge of each choice.

Type: list of `int`
Default: determined by `PANEL_LAYOUT`
Procs: `create, set`

PANEL_CHOICE_Y

Second argument is top edge of choice specified by first argument.

Type: `int, int`
Default: determined by `PANEL_LAYOUT`
Procs: `create, get, set`

PANEL_CHOICE_YS

Top edge of each set.

Type: list of `int`
Default: determined by `PANEL_LAYOUT`
Procs: `create, set`

PANEL_CHOOSE_NONE

Allows scrolling lists or choice items to have no currently selected item. Not applicable if `PANEL_CHOOSE_ONE` is `FALSE`.

Type: `Boolean`
Default: `TRUE`
Procs: `create, get, set`

PANEL_CHOOSE_ONE

If `TRUE`, creates an exclusive scrolling list. If `FALSE`, creates a non-exclusive scrolling list.

Type: `Boolean`
Default: `TRUE`
Procs: `create, get, set`

PANEL_CLIENT_DATA

Specifies an arbitrary value to be attached to a panel or to individual panel items.

Type: `caddr_t`
Default: None
Procs: `create, get, set`

PANEL_DEFAULT_ITEM

Sets the default item on a panel or gets the handle to the current default item. The system default is the first item created.

Type: `Panel_item`
Default: first item
Procs: `create, get, set`

PANEL_DEFAULT_VALUE

Identifies the default choice in `PANEL_CHOICE_STACK` items.

Type: `int` or `unsigned`
Default: first choice
Procs: `create, get, set`

PANEL_DIRECTION

Identifies the horizontal or vertical orientation of a slider or gague.

Type: `int`
Default: `PANEL_HORIZONTAL`
Procs: `create, get, set`

PANEL_DISPLAY_LEVEL

Specifies the number of choices to display. One of `PANEL_ALL`, `PANEL_CURRENT`, or `PANEL_NONE`.

Type: `char*`
Default: `PANEL_ALL`
Procs: `create, set`

PANEL_EXTRA_PAINT_HEIGHT

Defines the increment by which the panel grows in the y direction. It is used when `window_fit_height()` is called.

Type: `int`
Default: 1 pixel
Procs: `create, get, set`

PANEL_EXTRA_PAINT_WIDTH

Defines the increment by which the panel grows in the x direction. It is used when `window_fit_width()` is called.

Type: `int`
Default: 1 pixel
Procs: `create, get, set`

PANEL_FEEDBACK

Specifies feedback to give when an item is selected. If `PANEL_DISPLAY_LEVEL` is `PANEL_CURRENT`, the default is `PANEL_NONE`; otherwise, it is `PANEL_MARKED`.

Type: `Panel_setting`
Default: see description
Procs: `create, get, set`

PANEL_FIRST_ITEM

Gets the handle of the first item on a panel. The `PANEL_EACH_ITEM` macro (see Appendix B) can be used to iterate over each item in a panel, starting with this first item.

Type: `Panel_item`
Procs: `get`

PANEL_GAUGE_WIDTH

Sets the length of a panel gauge item regardless of its horizontal or vertical orientation.

Type: `Boolean`
Default: `FALSE`
Procs: `create, get, set`

PANEL_INACTIVE

If `TRUE`, panel button item cannot be selected. Inactive items are displayed with gray-out pattern.

Type: `Boolean`
Default: `FALSE`
Procs: `create, get, set`

PANEL_ITEM_CLASS

Gets the panel item *type* of the panel item specified.

Type: `Panel_item_type`
Procs: `get`

PANEL_ITEM_COLOR

Specifies the colormap index to use for the item. A value of −1 implies the foreground color for the panel window.

Type: `int`
Default: −1
Procs: `create, get, set`

PANEL_ITEM_MENU

Specifies the menu associated with the panel button item.

Type: `Menu`
Default: `NULL`
Procs: `create, get, set`

PANEL_ITEM_RECT

Gets the rectangle surrounding the panel item.

Type: `Rect *`
Procs: `get`

PANEL_ITEM_X

Specifies the x position (in pixels) where the last panel item was created. If no item was created, then it specifies the x position where the first item will be created.

Type: `int`
Procs: `create, get, set`

PANEL_ITEM_X_GAP

Specifies the number of x-coordinate pixels between items. Provides space between items appearing in the same row.

Type: `int`
Default: 10 pixels
Procs: `create, get, set`

PANEL_ITEM_Y

Specifies the y position (in pixels) where the last panel item was created. If no item was created, then it specifies the y position where the first item will be created.

Type: `int`
Default: none
Procs: `create, get, set`

PANEL_ITEM_Y_GAP

Specifies the number of y-coordinate pixels between items. Provides space between items appearing in the same column.

Type: `int`
Default: 13 pixels
Procs: `create, get, set`

PANEL_LABEL_BOLD

If `TRUE`, `PANEL_MESSAGE_ITEMS`'s label is rendered in bold.

Type: `Boolean`
Default: `FALSE`
Procs: `create, get, set`

PANEL_LABEL_IMAGE

Specifies the image for an item's label.

Type: `Server_image`
Default: `NULL`
Procs: `create, get, set`

PANEL_LABEL_STRING

Specifies the string for the item's label.

Type: `char *`
Default: `NULL`
Procs: `create, get, set`

PANEL_LABEL_WIDTH

Specifies the width of the panel label in pixels.

Type: `int`
Default: width of text string or server image
Procs: `create, get, set`

PANEL_LABEL_X

Specifies the x coordinate of the *label* portion of panel items that have *values* associated with them (e.g., text items). Intended to be used when `PANEL_VALUE_X` is specified.

Type: int (in pixels)
Default: PANEL_ITEM_X from parent
          panel.
Procs: create, get, set

PANEL_LABEL_Y

Specifies the y coordinate of the *label* portion of panel items that have *values* associated with them (e.g., text items). Intended to be used only if PANEL_VALUE_Y is specified.

Type: int (in pixels)
Default: PANEL_ITEM_Y from parent
          panel.
Procs: create, get, set

PANEL_LAYOUT

In a PANEL create call, this attribute controls the layout of panel items. When used in a create panel *item* call, this attribute controls the direction in which the item's *components* are laid out.

Type: Panel_setting
Default: PANEL_HORIZONTAL
Procs: create, get, set

PANEL_LIST_CLIENT_DATA

Sets or gets up to 32 bits of user-entered data from a row number on the list. This attribute takes two values: a row number, and a 32-bit data value.

Type: int, caddr_t
Default: NULL
Procs: create, get, set

PANEL_LIST_CLIENT_DATAS

Works much like its companion attribute, PANEL_LIST_CLIENT_DATA, except that it takes a NULL-terminated value list of client data as its value. Position in the value list determines the row to which the data will be associated.

Type: list
Default: NULL
Procs: create, set

PANEL_LIST_DELETE

Deletes a row from the scrolling list. The list is adjusted automatically after the deletion.

Type: int
Default: none
Procs: create, set

PANEL_LIST_DISPLAY_ROWS

Sets the number of rows in a list that will be displayed.

Type: int
Default: 5
Procs: create, get, set

PANEL_LIST_GLYPH

Takes a row and Server_image to let you assign a glyph or icon to a row. The height of the glyph may not exceed the height of scrolling list row. Also see PANEL_LIST_ROW_HEIGHT.

Value type: int, Server_image
Return type: Server_image
Default: NULL
Procs: create, get, set

PANEL_LIST_GLYPHS

Works the same as its companion attribute, PANEL_LIST_GLYPH, except that it takes a NULL-terminated value list as its value. The height of the glyph may not exceed the height of scrolling list row. Also see PANEL_LIST_ROW_HEIGHT.

Type: list of Server_image
Default: NULL
Procs: create, set

PANEL_LIST_INSERT

Inserts a list item at a specified row number. This attribute allocates space, attaches a row number to the list, and inserts an empty string. Clients must set PANEL_LIST_GLYPH and/or PANEL_LIST_STRING at this row number to set the glyph item and/or string.

Type: int
Procs: create, set

PANEL_LIST_NROWS

Gets the total number of rows in the scrolling list.

Type: int
Default: NULL
Procs: get

PANEL_LIST_ROW_HEIGHT

Specifies the height of each row in the scrolling list.

Type: `int`
Default: height of panel's font
Procs: `create, get`

PANEL_LIST_SELECT

Takes two values: a row number and a Boolean that lets you select (`TRUE`) or deselect (`FALSE`) the specified row.

Type: `int, Boolean`
Default: `FALSE`
Procs: `set, create`

PANEL_LIST_SELECTED

Returns whether the specified row number is selected (`TRUE`) or not (`FALSE`).

Value type: `int`
Return type: `Boolean`
Procs: `get`

PANEL_LIST_STRING

Sets (specifies) string to a specified row. xv_get returns the pointer to the character string assigned to the row.

Value type: `int, char *`
Return type: `char *`
Default: empty string
Procs: `create, get, set`

PANEL_LIST_STRINGS

Works the same as its companion attribute, `PANEL_LIST_STRING`, except that it takes a NULL-terminated list of strings as its value.

Type: `list, char *`
Default: empty string
Procs: `create, get, set`

PANEL_LIST_WIDTH

Sets or gets the width in pixels of the scrolling list. By default, the list will be just wide enough to accommodate the largest item on the list.

Type: `int`
Default: slightly larger than largest item on list
Procs: `create, get, set`

PANEL_MASK_CHAR

Specifies the character used to mask type-in characters. Use the space character for no

character echo (caret does not advance). Use the NULL character to disable masking.

Type: `char`
Default: `NULL`
Procs: `create, set, get`

PANEL_MAX_VALUE

Specifies the maximum value of the slider or numeric text item.

Type: `int`
Default: `100`
Procs: `create, get, set`

PANEL_MIN_VALUE

Specifies the minimum value of the slider or numeric text item.

Type: `int`
Default: `0`
Procs: `create, get, set`

PANEL_NCHOICES

Returns the number of choices available in a choice or toggle item.

Type: `int`
Default: `N/A`
Procs: `get`

PANEL_NEXT_COL

Specifies the amount of white space (in pixels) between the last column and the next (new) column. If you specify –1, the default gap (`PANEL_ITEM_X_GAP`) is used.

Type: `Panel_item`
Default: none
Procs: `create`

PANEL_NEXT_ITEM

Gets the handle of the next item on a panel. Usage is:

```
next_item = xv_get(this_item,
            PANEL_NEXT_ITEM);
```

Type: `Panel_item`
Procs: `get`

PANEL_NEXT_ROW

Specifies the amount of white space (in pixels) between the last row and the next (new) row. If you specify –1, the default gap (`PANEL_ITEM_Y_GAP`) will be used.

Type:	Panel_item
Default:	none
Procs:	create

PANEL_NOTIFY_LEVEL

Specifies when to call the notify function. Either PANEL_ALL, or PANEL_NONE.

Type:	Panel_setting
Default:	PANEL_SPECIFIED
Procs:	create, get, set

PANEL_NOTIFY_PROC

Procedure to call when a panel item is selected. See panel_notify_proc() in Appendix B, *Summary of Procedures and Macros.*

Default:	NULL
Procs:	create, get, set

PANEL_NOTIFY_STATUS

If the panel item is part of an unpinned pop-up window, then the window is dismissed if PANEL_NOTIFY_STATUS is XV_OK. If PANEL_NOTIFY_STATUS is set to XV_ERROR, then the window is not dismissed.

Type:	int
Default:	XV_OK
Procs:	create, get, set

PANEL_NOTIFY_STRING

String of characters that triggers notification when typed in a text item. Applies only when PANEL_NOTIFY_LEVEL is PANEL_SPECIFIED.

Type:	char *
Default:	\n \r \t (i.e., newline, carriage return, and tab)
Procs:	create, get, set

PANEL_PAINT

Controls the panel item's painting behavior in xv_set calls. Possible values are PANEL_ITEM_CLEAR, PANEL_ITEM_NO_CLEAR, or PANEL_ITEM_NONE.

Type:	Panel_setting
Default:	PANEL_CLEAR
Procs:	create, set

PANEL_PARENT_PANEL

Returns the panel that contains the item. Same as XV_OWNER.

Type:	Panel
Procs:	get

PANEL_READ_ONLY

For text and panel list items, if TRUE, editing is disabled; if FALSE, editing is enabled. xv_set applies to text items only.

Type:	Boolean
Default:	FALSE
Procs:	create, get, set

PANEL_REPAINT_PROC

Specifies the name of the client-supplied panel repaint procedure.

Default:	NULL
Procs:	create, get, set

PANEL_SHOW_RANGE

If TRUE, shows the minimum and maximum slider values.

Type:	Boolean
Default:	TRUE
Procs:	create, get, set

PANEL_SHOW_VALUE

If TRUE, shows the "value" part of items that have values.

Type:	Boolean
Default:	TRUE
Procs:	create, get, set

PANEL_TICKS

Specifies the number of evenly spaced tick marks to be displayed on slider or gauge panel items.

Type:	int
Default:	0
Procs:	create, get, set

PANEL_SLIDER_WIDTH

Specifies the length of the slider bar in pixels. The length is set whether the slider is horizontally or vertically oriented.

Type:	int
Default:	100
Procs:	create, get, set

PANEL_TOGGLE_VALUE

Specifies the value of a particular toggle choice. Second argument is value of choice specified by first argument.

Type:	int, int
Default:	NULL
Procs:	create, get, set

PANEL_VALUE

Indicates the current value of a panel item. Its type varies depending on the type of panel item specified. See Chapter for details.

Type:	Varies
Procs:	create, get, set

PANEL_VALUE_DISPLAY_LENGTH

Maximum number of characters to display in a text string. Note that the length of the value display may not be less than the combined width of the left and right "more text" buttons. In 12-point font, this is four characters.

Type:	int
Default:	80
Procs:	create, get, set

PANEL_VALUE_STORED_LENGTH

Maximum number of characters to store in the value string for text items.

Type:	int
Default:	80
Procs:	create, get, set

PANEL_VALUE_X

Specifies the x coordinate of the *value* portion of panel items that have separate *label* and *value* entities (e.g., text items). For use in conjunction with PANEL_LABEL_X.

Type:	int
Default:	(See Chapter 7, *Panels*.)
Procs:	create, get, set

PANEL_VALUE_Y

Specifies the top edge of value. This is the companion attribute to PANEL_VALUE_X.

Type:	int
Default:	(See Chapter 7, *Panels*.)
Procs:	create, get, set

SCREEN_NUMBER

Specifies the number of the screen associated with object.

Type:	int
Default:	0
Procs:	get

SCREEN_SERVER

Specifies the server associated with this screen.

Type:	Display *
Default:	value of DISPLAY environment variable
Procs:	get

SCROLLBAR_COMPUTE_SCROLL_PROC

Specifies a procedure to compute the elevator and proportional indicator values.

Default:	scrollbar_default_ compute_scroll_proc
Procs:	create, get, set

SCROLLBAR_DIRECTION

The orientation of the scrollbar as either SCROLLBAR_VERTICAL or SCROLLBAR_ HORIZONTAL.

Type:	Scrollbar_setting
Default:	none
Procs:	create, get

SCROLLBAR_LAST_VIEW_START

Specifies the offset of view into object prior to scroll.

Type:	int
Default:	0
Procs:	get

SCROLLBAR_MENU

Specifies a pointer to the scrollbar's menu. Clients can add items to the *default* menu but cannot remove items from it.

Type:	Menu
Default:	scrollbar creates a default menu
Procs:	get

SCROLLBAR_NORMALIZE_PROC

Specifies a procedure that does normalization (set the viewable area of the object that the scrollbar scrolls).

Default:	NULL
Procs:	create, get, set

SCROLLBAR_NOTIFY_CLIENT

Used by the Notifier. Indicates client that is notified when scrollbar is scrolled. See Chapter 10, *Scrollbars*.

Type: Xv_opaque
Default: subwindow scrollbar is attached to contents
Procs: create, get, set

SCROLLBAR_OBJECT_LENGTH
Specifies the length of scrollable object in scrollbar units. Value must be greater than or equal to zero.

Type: int
Default: 0
Procs: create, get, set

SCROLLBAR_PAGE_LENGTH
Specifies the length of a page in scrollbar units for page-scrolling purposes.

Type: int
Default: 0
Procs: create, get, set

SCROLLBAR_PIXELS_PER_UNIT
Specifies the number of pixels constituting a scrollbar unit. For example, when scrolling a list of icons, each unit might be 64 pixels.

Type: int
Default: 1
Procs: create, get, set

SCROLLBAR_SPLITTABLE
Indicates whether the object that contains the scrollbar is splittable.

Type: Boolean
Default: FALSE
Procs: create, get, set

SCROLLBAR_VIEW_LENGTH
Specifies the length of viewing window in scrollbar units.

Type: int
Default: 0
Procs: create, get, set

SCROLLBAR_VIEW_START
Specifies the current offset into scrollbar object in scrollbar units. The value must be greater than or equal to zero.

Type: int
Default: 0
Procs: create, get, set

SELN_REQ_BYTESIZE
Specifies the number of bytes in the selection.

Type: int
Default: none
Procs: selection_ask,
selection_init_request,
selection_query

SELN_REQ_COMMIT_PENDING_DELETE
Instructs the replier to delete any secondary selection made in pending delete mode.

Type: none
Default: none
Procs: selection_ask,
selection_init_request,
selection_query

SELN_REQ_CONTENTS_ASCII
Specifies a NULL-terminated list of 4-byte words containing the selection's ASCII contents. If the last word of the contents is not full (including NULL terminator for the string), it is NULL-padded.

Type: char *
Default: none
Procs: selection_ask,
selection_init_request,
selection_query

SELN_REQ_CONTENTS_PIECES
Specifies that the value is a NULL-terminated list of 4-byte words containing the selection's contents described in the textsw's piece-table format.

Type: char *
Default: none
Procs: selection_ask,
selection_init_request,
selection_query

SELN_REQ_DELETE
Instructs the holder of the selection to delete the contents of the selection from its window (used only by text subwindows).

Type: void
Default: none
Procs: selection_ask,
selection_init_request,
selection_query

SELN_REQ_END_REQUEST

Returns an error for failed or unrecognized requests.

Type: void
Default: none
Procs: selection_ask,
          selection_init_request,
          selection_query

SELN_REQ_FAKE_LEVEL

Gives a level to which the selection should be expanded before processing the remainder of this request. The original level should be maintained on the display, however, and restored as the true level on completion of the request.

Type: int
Default: none
Procs: selection_ask,
          selection_init_request,
          selection_query

SELN_REQ_FILE_NAME

Specifies a NULL-terminated list of 4-byte words. Contains the name of the file which holds the *shelf* selection.

Type: char *
Default: none
Procs: selection_ask,
          selection_init_request,
          selection_query

SELN_REQ_FIRST

Gives the number of bytes that precede the first byte of the selection.

Type: int
Default: none
Procs: selection_ask,
          selection_init_request,
          selection_query

SELN_REQ_FIRST_UNIT

Gives the number of units of the selection's current level (line, paragraph, etc.) which precede the first unit of the selection.

Type: int
Default: none
Procs: selection_ask,
          selection_init_request,
          selection_query

SELN_REQ_LAST

Gives the byte index of the last byte of the selection.

Type: int
Default: none
Procs: selection_ask,
          selection_init_request,
          selection_query

SELN_REQ_LAST_UNIT

Gives the unit index of the last unit of the selection at its current level.

Type: int
Default: none
Procs: selection_ask,
          selection_init_request,
          selection_query

SELN_REQ_LEVEL

Gives the current level of the selection.

Type: int
Default: none
Procs: selection_ask,
          selection_init_request,
          selection_query

SELN_REQ_RESTORE

Instructs the replier to restore the selection referred to in this request, if it has maintained sufficient information to do so.

Type: none
Default: none
Procs: selection_ask,
          selection_init_request,
          selection_query

SELN_REQ_SET_LEVEL

Gives a level to which the selection should be set. This request should affect the true level.

Type: int
Default: none
Procs: selection_ask,
          selection_init_request,
          selection_query

SELN_REQ_YIELD

Requests the holder of the selection to yield it. SELN_SUCCESS, SELN_DIDNT_HAVE, and SELN_WRONG_RANK are legitimate responses. The latter comes from a holder asked to yield the primary selection when it knows a function key is down.

Type: Seln_result
Default: none
Procs: selection_ask,
          selection_init_request,
          selection_query

SERVER_EXTENSION_PROC
Specifies the procedure used to handle event specifically created by extensions to the server.

Type: void (*)()
Default: NULL
Procs: create, get, set

SERVER_IMAGE_BITMAP_FILE
Specifies a file containing the X11 bitmap to be created.

Type: char *
Default: none
Procs: create

SERVER_IMAGE_BITS
Specifies the SunView pixrect image bits for the server image. Use SERVER_IMAGE_X_BITS for standard X11 bitmaps.

Type: short *.
Default: uninitialized
Procs: create, set

SERVER_IMAGE_DEPTH
Specifies the bit plane depth of the server image.

Type: int
Default: 1
Procs: create, get, set

SERVER_IMAGE_PIXMAP
Allows an existing pixmap to be associated with a server image. An xv_get using this attribute is equivalent to an xv_get of the XV_XID of the server image.

Type: Pixmap
Default: none
Procs: create, get, set

SERVER_IMAGE_SAVE_PIXMAP
Allows the application to specify that the old pixmap must not be destroyed if a new pixmap is created as the result of changing any server image attriutes or assigning a new pix-

map directly. You should retain a handle to old pixmap first.

Type: Boolean
Default: FALSE
Procs: get, set, create

SERVER_IMAGE_X_BITS
Specifies the bits to use in a server image. Bits are stored in an array of char.

Type: char *
Default: None
Procs: create, set

SERVER_NTH_SCREEN
Specifies the screen with given number.

Type: int, Screen
Default: N/A
Procs: create, get, set

SERVER_SYNC
Synchronizes with the server once. Does not set synchronous mode.

Type: Boolean
Default: N/A
Procs: set

SERVER_SYNC_AND_PROCESS_EVENTS
Synchronizes with the server and processes any already delivered events.

Type: no value
Default: none
Procs: create, set

TEXTSW_AGAIN_RECORDING
If FALSE, changes to the textsw are not repeated when the user invokes AGAIN. Disabling reduces memory overhead.

Type: Boolean
Default: TRUE
Procs: create, get, set

TEXTSW_AUTO_INDENT
If TRUE, automatically indents a new line to match the previous line.

Type: Boolean
Default: FALSE
Procs: create, get, set

TEXTSW_AUTO_SCROLL_BY
Specifies the number of lines to scroll when type-in moves insert point below the view.

Type: int
Default: 1
Procs: create, get, set

TEXTSW_BLINK_CARET
Determines whether the caret blinks (don't blink for better performance).

Type: Boolean
Default: FALSE
Procs: create, get, set

TEXTSW_BROWSING
If TRUE, prevents editing of displayed text. If another file is loaded in, browsing stays on.

Type: Boolean
Default: FALSE
Procs: create, get, set

TEXTSW_CHECKPOINT_FREQUENCY
Specifies the number of edits between checkpoints. Set to 0 to disable checkpointing.

Type: int
Default: 0
Procs: create, get, set

TEXTSW_CLIENT_DATA
Specifies the pointer to arbitrary client data.

Type: Xv_opaque
Default: NULL
Procs: create, get, set

TEXTSW_CONFIRM_OVERWRITE
Specifies confirmation of any request to write to an existing file.

Type: Boolean
Default: TRUE
Procs: create, get, set

TEXTSW_CONTENTS
Specifies the text for a subwindow. xv_get needs additional parameters (see Chapter 8, *Text Subwindows*).

Type: char *
Default: NULL
Procs: create, get, set

TEXTSW_CONTROL_CHARS_USE_FONT
If FALSE, control characters always display as an up arrow followed by a character instead of whatever glyph is in the current font.

Type: Boolean
Default: FALSE
Procs: create, get, set

TEXTSW_DISABLE_CD
Stops textsw from changing current working directory and grays out associated items in the menu.

Type: Boolean
Default: FALSE
Procs: create, get, set

TEXTSW_DISABLE_LOAD
Prevents files from being loaded into the textsw and grays out the associated items in the menu.

Type: Boolean
Default: FALSE
Procs: create, get, set

TEXTSW_EDIT_COUNT
Monotonically increments count of the number of edits made to the textsw.

Type: int
Procs: get

TEXTSW_FILE
For xv_create and xv_set, specifies the name of the file to load; for xv_get, returns the name of the file loaded or NULL if no file was loaded.

Type: char *
Default: NULL
Procs: create, get, set

TEXTSW_FILE_CONTENTS
Initializes the text subwindow contents from a file, yet still edits the contents in memory as if specified using TEXT_FILE_CONTENTS.

Type: char *
Default: NULL
Procs: create, set

TEXTSW_FIRST
Specifies the zero-based index of first displayed character.

Type: int
Procs: get

TEXTSW_FIRST_LINE
Specifies the zero-based index of first displayed line.

Type: int
Procs: get

TEXTSW_FONT
Specifies the font to use in a text subwindow.

Type: Xv_Font
Procs: create, get, set

TEXTSW_HISTORY_LIMIT
Specifies the number of user action sequences that can be undone.

Type: int
Default: 50
Procs: create, get, set

TEXTSW_IGNORE_LIMIT
Specifies the number of edits textsw allows before vetoing destroy. Valid values are 0, which means the destroy will be vetoed if there have been any edits, and TEXTSW_INFINITY, which means the destroy will never be vetoed.

Type: int
Default: 0
Procs: create, get, set

TEXTSW_INSERT_FROM_FILE
Inserts the contents of a file into a text subwindow at the current insertion point.

Type: char *
Default: none
Procs: set, create

TEXTSW_INSERT_MAKES_VISIBLE
Controls whether insertion causes repositioning to make inserted text visible. Possible values are TEXTSW_ALWAYS or TEXTSW_IF_AUTO_SCROLL.

Type: Textsw_enum
Default: TEXTSW_ALWAYS
Procs: create, get, set

TEXTSW_INSERTION_POINT
Specifies the index of the current insertion point.

Type: Textsw_index
Default: none
Procs: create, get, set

TEXTSW_LENGTH
Specifies the length of the textsw's contents.

Type: int
Procs: get

TEXTSW_LINE_BREAK_ACTION
Determines how the textsw treats file lines too big to fit on one display line. Possible values are TEXTSW_CLIP, TEXTSW_WRAP_AT_CHAR, or TEXTSW_WRAP_AT_WORD.

Type: Textsw_enum
Default: TEXTSW_WRAP_AT_CHAR
Procs: create, get, set

TEXTSW_LOWER_CONTEXT
Specifies the minimum number of lines to maintain between insertion point and bottom of view. A value of –1 turns auto scrolling off.

Type: int
Default: 0
Procs: create, get, set

TEXTSW_MEMORY_MAXIMUM
Specifies how much memory to use when not editing files (e.g., editing in memory). This attribute only takes effect at create time or after the window is reset with textsw_reset. The lower bound is 1K bytes, which is silently enforced.

Type: int
Default: 20000
Procs: create, get, set

TEXTSW_MODIFIED
Specifies whether the textsw has been modified.

Type: Boolean
Procs: get

TEXTSW_MULTI_CLICK_SPACE
Specifies the maximum number of pixels between successive mouse clicks to still have the clicks considered a multi-click.

Type: `int`
Default: `4`
Procs: `create, get, set`

TEXTSW_MULTI_CLICK_TIMEOUT

Specifies the maximum number of milliseconds between successive mouse clicks to still have the clicks considered a multi-click.

Type: `int`
Default: `390`
Procs: `create, get, set`

TEXTSW_NOTIFY_PROC

Names a notify procedure. See `textsw_notify_proc` in Appendix B, *Summary of Procedures and Macros*.

Default: `NULL`
Procs: `create, set`

TEXTSW_READ_ONLY

If `TRUE`, prevents editing of the displayed text. If another file is loaded in, read-only status is turned off again.

Type: `Boolean`
Default: `FALSE`
Procs: `create, get, set`

TEXTSW_STATUS

If set, specifies the address of a variable of type `Textsw_status`. A value that reflects what happened during the call to `xv_create` is then written into it.

Type: `Textsw_status *`
Default: `none`
Procs: `create`

TEXTSW_STORE_CHANGES_FILE

Controls whether the *target* filename given to `textsw_store()` to save the current contents to a file changes the name of the file being edited (`TEXTSW_FILE`).

Type: `Boolean`
Default: `TRUE`
Procs: `create, set`

TEXTSW_SUBMENU_EDIT

Returns the submenu associated with the `Edit` panel button.

Type: `Menu`
Procs: `get`

TEXTSW_SUBMENU_FILE

Returns the submenu associated with the `File` panel button.

Type: `Menu`
Procs: `get`

TEXTSW_SUBMENU_FIND

Returns the submenu associated with the `Find` panel button.

Type: `Menu`
Procs: `get`

TEXTSW_SUBMENU_VIEW

Returns the submenu associated with the `View` panel button.

Type: `Menu`
Procs: `get`

TEXTSW_UPPER_CONTEXT

Specifies the minimum number of lines to maintain between the start of the selection and top of view. A value of –1 means defeat the normal actions.

Type: `int`
Default: `2`
Procs: `create, get, set`

TTY_ARGV

The command, specified as an argument vector, that the tty subwindow executes.

Type: `char**`
Default: `none`
Procs: `create, set`

TTY_ARGV_DO_NOT_FORK

Lets a user start a tty subwindow without forking off a shell.

Type: `char**`
Default: `none`
Procs: `create`

TTY_CONSOLE

If `TRUE`, tty subwindow grabs console output.

Type: `Boolean`
Default: `FALSE`
Procs: `set, create`

TTY_PAGE_MODE

If TRUE, output will stop after each page.

Type: Boolean
Default: FALSE
Procs: create,get,set

TTY_PID

The process ID of the program being run in the tty subwindow.

Type: int
Default: none
Procs: create,get,set

TTY_QUIT_ON_CHILD_DEATH

If TRUE, window_done is called on the parent frame of the tty window when its child terminates.

Type: Boolean
Default: FALSE
Procs: set,create

TTY_TTY_FD

Gets the file descriptor of the pseudo-tty associated with the tty subwindow.

Type: int
Procs: get

WIN_ALARM

Rings the bell for that window.

Type: no value
Default: off
Procs: set,create

WIN_ALARM_DATA

Gets the number of flashes and number of beeps used as alarm. (Currently always returns the same value.)

Type: Xv_opaque
Default: 1 beep, 1 flash
Procs: get

WIN_BACKGROUND_COLOR

Specifies the background color of a window as an index into the colormap segment associated with the window.

Type: int
Default: 0
Procs: create,get,set

WIN_BELOW

Causes the window to be positioned below the sibling window given as the value.

Restricted to windows with the same immediate parent (i.e., subwindows). Does not affect the xv_x of the window.

Type: Xv_Window
Default: varies
Procs: set,create

WIN_BIT_GRAVITY

Sets the Xlib-specific "bit gravity" property on the underlying X window associated with the object. See *<X11/X.h>* for list of legal values.

Type: int
Default: NorthWestGravity
Procs: set,create,get,set

WIN_CLIENT_DATA

Specifies an arbitrary value to be attached to a window.

Type: caddr_t
Default: None
Procs: create,get,set

WIN_CMD_LINE

Lets an application set its *specify command line* resource. When a user invokes *Save Workspace* from an OPEN LOOK window manager, the string is written to *̃ .openwin-init*. The handle for xv_set should be the base frame.

Type: string
Default: none
Procs: create,get,set

WIN_CMS_DATA

Specifies the data for the colormap segment associated with the window. The data is written into the currently allocated colormap segment. If a new segment is desired, set it using WIN_CMS_NAME first.

Type: Xv_cmsdata *
Default: none
Procs: create,get,set

WIN_CMS_NAME

Specifies the colormap segment to be associated with the window.

Type: char *
Default: none
Procs: create,get,set

WIN_COLLAPSE_EXPOSURES

Collapses multiple `Exposure` (and `GraphicsExpose`) events destined for the same window.

Type: `Boolean`
Default: `TRUE`
Procs: `create, get, set`

WIN_COLUMNS

Specifies the window's width (including left and right margins) in columns relative to the width of the window's font.

Type: `int`
Default: varies
Procs: `create, get, set`

WIN_CONSUME_EVENT

Specifies that the window will accept an event of type specified.

Type: event code
Default: none
Procs: `create, get, set`

WIN_CONSUME_EVENTS

Specifies a `NULL`-terminated list of event types that this window accepts.

Type: list XView Events.
Default: Varies from package to package.
Procs: `create, set`

WIN_CONSUME_X_EVENT_MASK

The input mask is specified using X event masks found in <X11/X.h>.

Type: `unsigned long`
Default: Varies from package to package.
Procs: `create, get, set`

WIN_CURSOR

Specifies the window's cursor.

Type: `Xv_Cursor`
Default: default cursor
Procs: `create, get, set`

WIN_DEPTH

Specifies the pixel depth of the window.

Type: `int`
Default: function of the screen
Procs: `create, get`

WIN_DESIRED_HEIGHT

Specifies the desired height of the window in pixels. This is subtly different from using

`XV_HEIGHT`.

Type: `int`
Default: none
Procs: `create, get, set`

WIN_DESIRED_WIDTH

Specifies the desired width of the window in pixels. This is subtly different from using `XV_WIDTH`.

Type: `int`
Default: none
Procs: `create, get, set`

WIN_DYNAMIC_VISUAL

Specifies the type of colormap segment to be used with the window. This attribute needs to be set on the actual drawing window of an object that uses dynamic colors. (SunView-compatible `pw_putcolormap` and `pw_setcmsname` routines must set this attribute to `TRUE` during creation.)

Type: `Boolean`
Default: `FALSE`
Procs: `create`

WIN_EVENT_PROC

Used by canvas and panel. Be sure to set `WIN_EVENT_PROC` and `WIN_CONSUME_EVENTS` on the *canvas paint window*, not on the canvas or the canvas view window.

Type: `int`
Default: none
Procs: `create, get, set`

WIN_FIT_HEIGHT

Causes the window to shrink or expand its height according to the window's contents leaving a margin specified by the value given. Typically used with panels to fit panel items.

Type: `int`
Default: depends on window size
Procs: `get`

WIN_FIT_WIDTH

Causes the window to shrink or expand its width according to the window's contents leaving a margin specified by the value given.

Type: int
Default: depends on window size
Procs: get

WIN_FOREGROUND_COLOR
Specifies the foreground color of a window as an index into the colormap segment associated with the window.

Type: int
Default: size –1 (where size is the number of colors in the colormap segment associated with the window)
Procs: create, get, set

WIN_FRAME
Specifies the window's frame.

Type: Frame
Default: NULL
Procs: get

WIN_GRAB_ALL_INPUT
Specifies that the window will get all events regardless of location of the pointer.

Type: Boolean
Default: FALSE
Procs: set, create

WIN_HORIZONTAL_SCROLLBAR
A handle to the horizontal scrollbar for that window.

Type: Scrollbar
Default: NULL
Procs: create, get, set

WIN_IGNORE_EVENT
Specifies that the window will not receive this event. (Certain events cannot be ignored.)

Type: XView event code
Default: none
Procs: set, create

WIN_IGNORE_EVENTS
Specifies a NULL-terminated list of events that this window will not receive. (Certain events cannot be ignored.)

Type: list of event codes
Default: none
Procs: set, create

WIN_INPUT_MASK
Specifies the window's input mask.

Type: Inputmask *
Default: Varies from package to package.
Procs: create, get, set

WIN_INPUT_ONLY
Specifies that a window can receive input only; although it has other window properties, it cannot be drawn into.

Type: none
Default: not transparent
Procs: create

WIN_IS_CLIENT_PANE
When used with xv_create(), the attribute has no value; using the attribute sets it to TRUE. When used, the window is considered to be an OPEN LOOK GUI application-specific pane which can override resources, such as fonts. Currently, the only packages that support this are text and tty/term.

Type: Boolean
Default: FALSE
Procs: create, get

WIN_KBD_FOCUS
Indicates whether the window has the keyboard focus.

Type: Boolean
Default: FALSE
Procs: create, get, set

WIN_MAP
Indicates whether to map or unmap the window. This does not imply *raised* (to the top of the window tree).

Type: Boolean
Default: FALSE
Procs: create, get, set

WIN_MENU
Specifies the window's menu, if applicable. (Scrollbars and text subwindows, but not canvases or panels.)

Type: Menu
Default: none
Procs: create, get, set

WIN_MOUSE_XY
Specifies the mouse's position within the window. Returns a static Rect * on get.

Type: int, int
Default: current mouse position
Procs: create, get, set

WIN_NOTIFY_IMMEDIATE_EVENT_PROC
Used to specify a notify interpose function, as in:

```
notify_interpose_event_func
(window, func,
 NOTIFY_IMMEDIATE)
```

See   window_interpose_func()   in Appendix B, *Summary of Procedures and Macros.*

Default: NULL
Procs: create, get, set

WIN_NOTIFY_SAFE_EVENT_PROC
Used to specify a notify interpose function, as in:

```
notify_interpose_event_func
(window, func,
 NOTIFY_SAFE)
```

See   window_interpose_func()   in Appendix B, *Summary of Procedures and Macros.*

WIN_NO_CLIPPING
Ignores clip rects in pixwin (pw_*) calls during repaints in all paint windows of the window. SunView compatibility only.

Type: Boolean
Default: FALSE
Procs: create, get, set

WIN_NO_DECORATIONS
Establishes that this window is not controlled by the window manager. (Override-Redirect is set to TRUE.)

Type: Boolean
Default: FALSE
Procs: set, create

WIN_PARENT
Specifies the window's parent in the window tree. Same as XV_OWNER.

Type: Xv_Window
Default: none
Procs: create, get, set

WIN_PERCENT_HEIGHT
Sets a subwindow's height as a percentage of the frame's height.

Type: int
Default: 0
Procs: create, get, set

WIN_PERCENT_WIDTH
Sets a subwindow's width as a percentage of the frame's width.

Type: int
Default: 0
Procs: create, get, set

WIN_RECT
Specifies the bounding box of a window.

Type: Rect *
Default: NULL
Procs: create, get, set

WIN_RETAINED
Hints the server to keep a backing store for this window. The server may ignore this request.

Type: Boolean
Default: FALSE
Procs: create, get, set

WIN_RIGHT_OF
Causes a sibling window to be laid out just to the right of the window given as the value. Restricted to windows that share the same immediate parent. Does not set XV_Y.

Type: Xv_Window
Default: arbitrary
Procs: set, create

WIN_ROW_GAP
Specifies the gap between rows in the window.

Type: int
Default: 0
Procs: create, get, set

WIN_ROW_HEIGHT
Specifies the height of a row in the window.

Type: int
Default: font's default height
Procs: create, get, set

WIN_ROWS
Specifies the window's height (including top and bottom margins) in rows.

Type: int
Default: 34
Procs: create, get, set

WIN_SAVE_UNDER
Provides hints to the server about whether or not the screen area beneath a window should be saved while a window, such as a pop-up menu, is in place. This is not the same as WIN_RETAINED.

Type: Boolean
Default: FALSE
Procs: set

WIN_SCREEN_RECT
Returns the bounding box of the screen containing the window. Data points to per-process static storage.

Type: Rect *
Default: screen dependent
Procs: get

WIN_SET_FOCUS
Gets the input from the window, if possible.

Type: no value
Default: none
Procs: set, create

WIN_TOP_LEVEL
Establishes whether the window is the child of another window or is a frame.

Type: Boolean
Default: varies
Procs: get

WIN_TRANSPARENT
Specifies that the window's background pixmap should be transparent.

Type: none
Default: not transparent
Procs: create

WIN_VERTICAL_SCROLLBAR
Specifies that scrollbar orientation is vertical.

Type: Scrollbar
Default: none
Procs: create, get, set

WIN_WINDOW_GRAVITY
Window gravity lets you define how the window should be repositioned if its parent is resized.

Type: int
Default: NorthWestGravity
Procs: set, create, get, set

WIN_X_COLOR_INDICES
Translates the logical indices of the window's colormap segment (from 0 to size-1) into the actual indices into the colormap used by the window.

Type: unsigned long *
Procs: get

WIN_X_EVENT_MASK
Expects an X event mask. Acts in the same manner as WIN_CONSUME_X_EVENT_MASK, but instead of appending to the current input mask, replaces it with a new mask.

Type: unsigned long
Default: none
Procs: create, get, set

XV_AUTO_CREATE
Specifies whether to create an object not found by xv_find().

Type: Boolean
Default: TRUE
Procs: find

XV_BOTTOM_MARGIN
Specifies the margin at the bottom of an object.

Type: int
Default: varies with object
Procs: create, get, set

XV_ERROR_PROC
The application's *XView* error handler. This function should return XV_OK if the error is to be ignored by XView. Return XV_ERROR if XView is to process the X error and exit. This is different from XV_X_ERROR_PROC.

Type: int (*)()
Default: None
Procs: xv_init

XV_FONT
Specifies an object's font.

Type: Xv_Font
Default: lucida medium
Procs: create, get, set

XV_HEIGHT
Specifies the height of an object in pixels.

Type: int
Default: N/A
Procs: create, get, set

XV_HELP_DATA
Specifies the help string used by the help package to display on-line help. The text string has the form file:keyword. The help package looks for the key keyword in the file *$HELPDIR/file.info*.

Type: char *
Default: no help available
Procs: create, get, set

XV_INIT_ARGC_PTR_ARGV
Interprets command line args. Strips −W command-line frame arguments out of argv, and decrements argc accordingly.

Type: int *, char **
Default: none
Procs: create

XV_INIT_ARGS
Interprets command line arguments. Does not strip −W command-line frame arguments out of argv.

Type: int, char **
Default: none
Procs: create

XV_KEY_DATA
Stores a 32-bit data value on an object. You may set multiple XV_KEY_DATA values on objects by using different keys.

Type: int, XV_opaque
Default: none
Procs: create, get, set

XV_LABEL
Specifies a frame's header or an icon's label.

Type: char *
Default: NULL
Procs: create, get, set

XV_LEFT_MARGIN
Specifies the margin at the left of the object.

Type: int
Default: Varies with object
Procs: create, get, set

XV_MARGIN
Specifies the offset from the border of this object.

Type: int
Default: varies with object
Procs: create, get, set

XV_NAME
Specifies an optional name for an object. In some cases, this attribute is used internally by packages (e.g., the SERVER package sets the display connection name using this attribute).

Type: char *
Default: varies with object
Procs: create, get, set

XV_OWNER
Specifies the object's owner. The object returned varies among packages.

Type: Xv_opaque
Procs: get

XV_RECT
Specifies the object's bounding box; that is, the smallest rectangle that contains the object.

Type: Rect *
Default: none
Procs: create, get, set

XV_RIGHT_MARGIN
Specifies the margin at the right of the object.

Type: int
Default: varies with object
Procs: create, get, set

XV_ROOT
Specifies the root window for an object. (Object must contain a window.)

Type: Xv_object
Default: root window for default screen
Procs: get

XV_SHOW

Causes the object to be displayed or undisplayed. If object is a window, bring object to the top.

Type: `Boolean`
Default: varies
Procs: `create, get, set`

XV_TOP_MARGIN

Specifies the margin at the top of the object.

Type: `int`
Default: varies with object
Procs: `create, get, set`

XV_TYPE

Returns the package that belongs to an object.

Type: `Xv_pkg *`
Default: varies with object
Procs: `get`

XV_WIDTH

Specifies the width of the object in pixels.

Type: `int`
Default: none
Procs: `create, get, set`

XV_X

Specifies the x position of the object relative to its parent.

Type: `int`
Default: varies with object
Procs: `create, get, set`

XV_X_ERROR_PROC

Specifies the application's Xlib error handler (different from `XV_ERROR_PROC`). May alternatively use `XSetErrorHandler()`.

Type: `int (*) ()`
Default: None
Procs: `xv_init`

XV_XID

Gets the XID of the specified object such as the pixmap associated with a `Server_image` or the X Window associated with a canvas paint window.

Type: `int`
Default: varies with object
Procs: `get`

XV_Y

Specifies the y position of the object relative to its parent.

Type: `int`
Default: varies with object
Procs: `create, get, set`

B
Summary of Procedures and Macros

B

Summary of Procedures and Macros

This appendix lists the XView procedures and macros in alphabetical order and describes each of them briefly. The description includes the call that uses the procedure or macro.

attr_create_list()

Takes an attribute value list and converts them into an array of `Attr_attri-butes`, also known as an `Attr_avlist`.

```
Attr_avlist
attr_create_list(attrs)
```

The return value is used as the value for the attribute `ATTR_LIST`.

CANVAS_EACH_PAINT_WINDOW()

Macro providing built-in support for iteration across all the paint windows contained in a given canvas. Allows you to perform operations on multiple paint windows for which there are no canvas attributes.

CANVAS_END_EACH

Closes the loop started by `CANVAS_EACH_PAINT_WINDOW()`. These two macros are meant to be used together.

canvas_paint_window()

Returns the paint window associated with the first view in the canvas. If the canvas is not split, first view is the only view.

```
Xv_window
canvas_paint_window(canvas)
        Canvas          canvas;
```

This is defined to be

```
xv_get(canvas, CANVAS_NTH_PAINT_WINDOW, 0);
```

canvas_repaint_proc()

Client-supplied callback procedure called when getting a WIN_REPAINT event. Function is attached to a canvas by setting CANVAS_REPAINT_PROC on the canvas' *paint windows*.

```
void
canvas_repaint_proc(canvas, paint_window, repaint_area)
        Canvas          canvas;
        Xv_Window       paint_window;
        Rectlist        *repaint_area;
```

If CANVAS_X_PAINT_WINDOW is TRUE, the repaint callback is called with the following parameters:

```
void
canvas_repaint_proc(canvas, paint_window, display, xid,
                    xrectlist)
        Canvas          canvas;
        Xv_Window       paint_window;
        Display         *display;
        Window          xid;
        Xv_xrectlist    *xrects;
```

display is the display handle to the X11 server connection. xid is the X11 window identifier for the canvas paint window. The Xv_xrectlist structure contains an array of XRectangles and a count that specifies the repaint area for the canvas paint window.

canvas_resize_proc()

Procedure called when canvas width or height changes. This function is installed using the attribute CANVAS_RESIZE_PROC.

```
void
canvas_resize_proc(canvas, width, height)
        Canvas          canvas;
        int             width;
        int             height;
```

cursor_copy()

Creates and returns a copy of src_cursor.

```
Xv_Cursor
cursor_copy(src_cursor)
        Xv_Cursor       src_cursor;
```

frame_get_rect()

Gets the rect of the frame. x, y is the upper-left corner of the window coordinate space. Width and height include the window manager decoration.

```
void
frame_get_rect(frame, rect)
        Frame           frame;
        Rect            *rect;
```

frame_set_rect()

Sets the rect of the frame. `x, y` is the upper-left corner of the window coordinate space. Width and height include the window manager decoration.

```
void
frame_set_rect(frame, rect)
        Frame           frame;
        Rect            *rect;
```

menu_action_proc()

See `menu_notify_proc()` below.

menu_done_proc()

The procedure called whenever a menu group is dismissed by the user. Installed by `MENU_DONE_PROC`.

```
void
menu_done_proc(menu, result)
        menu            menu;
        Xv_opaque       result;
```

`menu` is the base (top) level menu, as specified in `menu_show()`. `result` is the value of the item selected, unless the user specifies `menu_return_item`. You can get notification that any menu in a menu group is done by attaching `MENU_DONE_PROC` to each menu. However, you will get better results with `menu_item` notify procedures.

menu_gen_proc()

This menu generating procedure is called whenever a menu item that has the `MENU_GEN_PROC` attribute set and the menu needs to be displayed or traversed. It should return a handle to a menu that has either been dynamically created or statically stored.

```
Menu
menu_gen_proc(m, op)
        Menu            m;
        Menu_generate   op;
```

MENUITEM_SPACE

Used to create a blank menu item.

menu_notify_proc()

The notify procedure is attached to menus and menu items using `MENU_NO-TIFY_PROC`. This function is called whenever the user selects a menu item.

```
void
menu_notify_proc(menu, menu_item)
        Menu            menu;
        Menu_item       menu_item;
```

The `menu` identifies which menu the `menu_item` belongs to.

Procedures and Macros

menu_pin_proc()

This client supplied procedure is called whenever the user attempts to pin up a menu. Attached to menus using the attribute, MENU_PIN_PROC.

```
void
menu_pin_proc(menu, x, y)
        Menu          menu;
        int           x, y;
```

x, y are the fullscreen coordinates of the upper-left corner of the pin window.

menu_return_item()

Predefined notify procedure which, if given as the value for MENU_ NOTIFY_PROC, causes the menu_done_proc() (if any) to return the selected item rather than its value.

```
Menu_item
menu_return_item(menu, menu_item)
        Menu          menu;
        Menu_item     menu_item;
```

menu_return_value()

Predefined notify procedure which, if given as the value for MENU_ NOTIFY_PROC, causes the menu_done_proc() (if any) to return the value of the selected item rather than the item itself.

```
void
menu_return_value(menu, menu_item)
        Menu          menu;
        Menu_item     menu_item;
```

menu_show()

Displays menu and gets a selection from the user.

```
void
menu_show(menu, window, event, NULL)
        Menu          menu;
        Xv_Window     window;
        Event         *event;
```

window is the handle of the window over which the menu is displayed. event is the event which causes the menu to come up. The final NULL is required for public (non-XView internal) usage.

notice_prompt()

Displays notice and does not return until the user pushes a button or until its trigger or the default has been seen. It returns a value of NOTICE_FAILED if notice_prompt() fails for any reason; otherwise, it is equivalent to the ordinal value of the button which caused the return (i.e., button actually selected or default button if default action triggered return). The client_window should be the window for which the notice has been generated. This is important for fonts and positioning information. For the correct positioning of the notice, clients should specify `NOTICE_FOCUS_XY`. The event will be completely filled in at the time the `notice_prompt()` returns. The possible status values that may be returned from this function are:

- The `int()` value passed with every `NOTICE_BUTTON` attribute.

- `NOTICE_YES` if a confirm button or trigger was pushed.

- `NOTICE_NO` if a cancel button or trigger was pushed.

- `NOTICE_FAILED` if the notice failed to pop up.

```
int
notice_prompt(window, event, attributes)
        XV_Window              window;
        Event                  *event;
        attribute-list         attributes;
```

OPENWIN_EACH_VIEW()

Macro providing built-in support for iteration across all the views contained in a given openwin. Allows you to perform operations on multiple views for which there are no openwin attributes.

OPENWIN_END_EACH

Closes the loop started by `OPENWIN_EACH_VIEW()`. These macros are meant to be used together, as in the following example:

```
OPENWIN_EACH_VIEW(openwin, view)
        Openwin                openwin;
        Openwin_item           item;
        xv_set(openwin, attributes, 0);
OPENWIN_END_EACH;
```

openwin_init_split()

Procedure installed by applications using `OPENWIN_SPLIT_INIT_PROC`. This function is called when the user *splits* two views. The attributes passed are handles to the openwin and the new view.

```
openwin_init_split(openwin, view)
        Openwin                openwin;
        Xv_Window              view;
```

openwin_split_destroy_proc()

Procedure installed by applications using `OPENWIN_SPLIT_DESTROY_PROC`. This function is called when the user *joins* two views.

```
openwin_split_destroy_proc(openwin)
        Openwin                openwin;
```

panel_advance_caret()

Advances the caret to the next text item. If on the last text item, rotate back to the first. Returns the new caret item or NULL if there are no text items.

```
Panel_item
panel_advance_caret(panel)
    Panel       panel;
```

panel_background_proc()

Event handling procedure called when an event falls on the background of the panel (e.g., not on any panel items). This is installed by the client using PANEL_BACKGROUND_PROC.

```
void
panel_background_proc(panel, event)
    Panel       panel
    Event       *event
```

panel_backup_caret()

Backs the caret up to the previous text item. If already on the first text item, rotate back to the last. Returns the new caret item, or NULL if there are no text items.

```
Panel_item
panel_backup_caret(panel)
    Panel       panel;
```

PANEL_CHECK_BOX

Macro for "PANEL_TOGGLE, PANEL_FEEDBACK, PANEL_MARK." Creates non-exclusive choice item(s) with check_boxes instead of boxes.

```
xv_create(panel, PANEL_CHECK_BOX, NULL);
```

PANEL_CHOICE_STACK

Macro for "PANEL_CHOICE, PANEL_DISPLAY_LEVEL, PANEL_CURRENT." Creates an OPEN LOOK abbreviated menu button.

```
xv_create(panel, PANEL_CHOICE_STACK, NULL);
```

panel_default_handle_event()

Default event procedure for panel items PANEL_EVENT_PROC and for the panel's background (PANEL_BACKGROUND_PROC). Implements the standard event-to-action mapping for the item types.

```
panel_default_handle_event(panel_object, event)
    Xv_object   panel_object;
    Event       *event;
```

Note that panel_object may be a PANEL or PANEL_ITEM.

PANEL_EACH_ITEM()

Macro to iterate over each item in a panel. The corresponding macro
`panel_end_each` closes the loop opened by `PANEL_EACH_ITEM()`.

```
PANEL_EACH_ITEM(panel, item)
        Panel           panel;
        Panel_item      item;
```

PANEL_END_EACH

Closes the loop started by `PANEL_EACH_ITEM()`. Same usage as
`OPENWIN_EACH_VIEW()`.

panel_event_proc()

Client specified event handling procedure for handling events on panel items.
This procedure is installed using `PANEL_EVENT_PROC`.

```
void
panel_event_proc(item, event)
        Panel_item      item
        Event           *event
```

panel_notify_proc()

Client specified callback routine invoked when the user *activates* panel items
(accepts preview). The form for button, text, and numeric text items is:

```
notify_proc(item, event)
        Panel_item      item;
        Event           *event;
```

For buttons, the return value of `notify_proc` is of type `int` and is either
`XV_OK` or `XV_ERROR`. For text and numeric text items, the return value type is
`Panel_setting` and is one of `PANEL_INSERT`, `PANEL_NEXT`, `PANEL_NONE`, or
`PANEL_PREVIOUS`.

Choice and slider items have an additional parameter that specifies the current
value:

```
notify_proc(item, value, event)
        Panel_item      item;
        int             value;
        Event           *event;
```

For nonexclusive items, the value parameter is of type `unsigned int` because
it represents a *mask* of choices that are selected (e.g., if the first and third items
are selected, then the first and third bits in the `value` parameter are on—this
value happens to be five). For slider, choice, and toggle (nonexclusive settings)
items, `panel_notify_proc` is of type `void`; that is, it does not return a value.

The form for panel list items is:

```
int
notify_proc(item, op, event)
        Panel_item              item;
        Panel_list_op           op;
        Event                   *event;
```

Procedures and
Macros

For panel list items, op indicates a select, validate, or delete operation. Of these, only `PANEL_LIST_OP_VALIDATE` requires a return value: `XV_OK` to validate a change or `XV_ERROR` to invalidate a change.

panel_paint()

Paints an item or an entire panel. `paint_behavior` can be either `PANEL_CLEAR`, which causes the area occupied by the panel or item to be cleared prior to painting, or `PANEL_NO_CLEAR`.

```
int
panel_paint(panel_object, paint_behavior)
        Xv_object            panel_object;
        Panel_setting        paint_behavior;
```

Note that `panel_object` may be a `PANEL` or `PANEL_ITEM`.

panel_text_notify()

Default notify procedure for panel text items. Causes caret to advance on Return or Tab, caret to back up on Shift-Return or Shift-Tab, printable characters to be inserted into item's value, and all other characters to be discarded.

```
Panel_setting
panel_text_notify(item, event)
        Panel_item           item
        Event                *event
```

PANEL_TOGGLE

Macro for "`PANEL_CHOICE, PANEL_CHOOSE_ONE, FALSE.`" Used to create non-exclusive choice item(s).

```
xv_create(panel, PANEL_TOGGLE, NULL);
```

SCROLLABLE_PANEL

Used to create a scrollbar panel. To add a scrollbar after creating the panel, create a scrollbar with the panel as its parent. Example:

```
panel = xv_create(frame, SCROLLABLE_PANEL, NULL);
xv_create(panel, SCROLLBAR, NULL);
```

Note: scrollable panels are not OPEN LOOK-compliant.

scrollbar_default_compute_scroll_proc()

Computes default scrolling based on scroll position. `pos` is the position from the start of the cable event. `length` is the length of the cable. `offset` and `object_length` are output parameters. The offset is given in client units to scroll by. The object length is in client units.

```
void
scrollbar_default_compute_scroll_proc(
        scroll_public, pos, available_cable, motion,
        offset, object_length)
                Scrollbar                scroll_public
                Scrollbar                scroll_public
                int                      pos;
                int                      available_cable;
                Scroll_motion            motion;
                unsigned long            *offset;
                unsigned long            *object_length;
```

scrollbar_paint()

Repaints all portions of the scrollbar.

```
void
scrollbar_paint(scrollbar)
        Scrollbar               scrollbar;
```

selection_acquire()

Acquires the selection of a specified rank. This is typically used internally by
XView packages. It is not used to *inquire* about the current selection.

```
Seln_rank
selection_acquire(server, client, asked)
        Xv_Server       server;
        Seln_client     client;
        Seln_rank       asked;
```

client is the opaque handle returned from selection_create(). The client
uses this call to become the new holder of the selection of rank asked. asked
should be one of SELN_CARET, SELN_PRIMARY, SELN_SECONDARY,
SELN_SHELF, or SELN_UNSPECIFIED. If successful, the rank actually acquired
is returned.

If asked is SELN_UNSPECIFIED, the client indicates it wants whichever of the
primary or secondary selections is appropriate given the current state of the
function keys; the one acquired can be determined from the return value.

selection_ask()

selection_ask() is a simplified form of selection_request() that looks
and acts very much like seln_query(). The only difference is that it does not
use a callback proc and so cannot handle replies that require more than a single
buffer (e.g., long text selections). If it receives a reply consisting of more than
one buffer, it returns the first buffer and discards the rest. The return value is a
pointer to a static buffer; in case of error, this will be a valid pointer to a NULL
buffer:

```
buffer->status = SELN_FAILED
```

The call looks like this:

```
Seln_request *
selection_ask(server, holder, attributes, ..., NULL)
        Xv_Server      server;
        Seln_holder   *holder;
        Attr_union     attributes;
```

selection_clear_functions()

The server is told to forget about any function keys it thinks are down, resetting
its state to all-up. If it knows of a current secondary selection, the server will tell
its holder to yield.

```
void
selection_clear_functions()
```

selection_create()

The server is initialized for this client. `Client_data` is a 32-bit opaque client
value which the server will pass back in callback procedures, as described
above. The first two arguments are addresses of client procedures which will be
called from the selection functions when client processing is required. These oc-
casions occur when the server sees a function-key transition which may interest
this client and when another process wishes to make a request concerning the selection this client holds.

```
Seln_client
selection_create(
        server, function_proc, request_proc, client_data)
                Xv_Server,       server;
                void            (*function_proc) ();
                Seln_result     (*request_proc) ();
                Xv_opaque        client_data;
```

selection_destroy()

A client created by `selection_create` is destroyed—any selection it may
hold is released, and various pieces of data associated with the selection mechanism are freed. If this is the last client in this process using the Selection Service, the RPC socket is closed and its notification removed.

```
void
selection_destroy(server, client)
        Xv_Server      server;
        Seln_client    client;
```

selection_done()

Client indicates it is no longer the holder of the selection of the indicated rank.
The only cause of failure is absence of the server. It is not necessary for a client
to call this procedure when it has been asked by the server to yield a selection.

```
Seln_result
selection_done(server, client, rank)
        Xv_Server      server;
        Seln_client    client;
        Seln_rank      rank;
```

selection_figure_response()

Procedure to determine the correct response according to the standard user interface when `seln_inform()` returns `*buffer` or the client's `function_procs` called with it. The `addressee_rank` field in `Seln_function_buffer` will be modified to indicate the selection which should be affected by this client; `holder` will be set to point to the element of `*buffer` which should be contacted in the ensuing action, and the return value indicates what that action should be. Possible return values are SELN_DELETE, SELN_FIND, SELN_IGNORE, SELN_REQUEST, and SELN_SHELVE.

```
Seln_response
selection_figure_response(server, buffer, holder)
    Xv_Server                   server;
    Seln_function_buffer        *buffer;
    Seln_holder                 *holder;
```

selection_hold_file()

The server is requested to act as the holder of the specified rank, whose ASCII contents have been written to the file indicated by path. This allows a selection to persist longer than the application which made it can maintain it. Most commonly, this will be done by a process which holds the shelf when it is about to terminate.

```
Seln_result
selection_hold_file(server, rank, path)
    Xv_Server       server;
    Seln_rank       rank;
    char            *path;
```

selection_inform()

Low-level, policy-independent procedure for informing the server that a function key has changed state. Most clients will prefer to use the higher-level procedure `seln_report_event`, which handles much of the standard interpretation required.

```
Seln_function_buffer
selection_inform(server, client, which, down)
    Xv_Server       server;
    Seln_client     client;
    Seln_function   which;
    int             down;
```

selection_init_request()

Procedure used to initialize a buffer before calling `selection_request`. (It is also called internally by `selection_ask` and `seln_query`.) It takes a pointer to a request buffer, a pointer to a `struct` referring to the selection holder to which the request is to be addressed, and a list of attributes which constitute the request to be sent. The attributes are copied into `buffer->data`, and the corresponding size is stored into `buffer->buf_size`. Both elements of `reques-ter_data` are zeroed; if the caller wants to handle long requests, consumer-proc and context pointers must be entered in these elements after `selec-tion_init_request` returns.

```
void
selection_init_request(
        server, buffer, holder, attributes, ..., NULL)
                Xv_Server               server;
                Selection_request       *buffer;
                Seln_holder             *holder;
                char                    *attributes;
```

selection_inquire()

Returns a `Seln_holder` structure containing information which enables the holder of the indicated selection to be contacted. If the `rank` argument is `SELN_UNSPECIFIED`, the server will return access information for either the primary or the secondary selection holder, as warranted by the state of the function keys it knows about. The `rank` element in the returned struct will indicate which is being returned.

This procedure may be called without `selection_create()` having been called first.

```
Seln_holder
selection_inquire(server, rank)
        Xv_Server       server;
        Seln_rank       rank;
```

selection_inquire_all()

Returns a `Seln_holders_all` struct from the Selection Service; it consists of a `Seln_holder` struct for each of the four ranks.

```
Seln_holders_all
selection_inquire_all()
```

selection_query()

Transmits a request to the selection holder indicated by the `holder` argument. `consume` and `context` are used to interpret the response and are described below. The remainder of the arguments to `selection_query` constitute an attribute-value list which is the request. (The last argument should be a 0 to terminate the list.) The procedure pointed to by `reader` will be called repeatedly with a pointer to each buffer of the reply. The value of the `context` argument will be available in `buffer->requester_data.context` for each buffer. This item is not used by the selection library; it is provided for the convenience

of the client. When the reply has been completely processed (or when the consume proc returns something other than SELN_SUCCESS), selection_query
returns.

```
Selection_result
selection_query(
        server, holder, reader, context, attributes, ...,
        NULL)
                Xv_Server        server;
                Seln_holder      *holder;
                Seln_result      (*reader)();
                char *            *context;
                A-V list          attributes;
```

selection_report_event()

High-level procedure for informing the server of a function key transition which
may affect the selection. It incorporates some of the policy of the standard user
interface and provides a more convenient interface to selection_inform.

Seln_client_node is the client handle returned from selection_create; it
may be 0 if the client guarantees it will not need to respond to the function transition.

Event is a pointer to the struct inputevent which reports the transition
seln_report_event. selection_report_event generates a corresponding call to seln_inform and, if the returned struct is not null, passes it to the
client's function_proc callback procedure.

```
void
selection_report_event(server, client, event)
        Xv_Server        server;
        Seln_client_node *client;
        Event            *event;
```

selection_request()

Low-level, policy-independent mechanism for retrieving information about a
selection from the server. Most clients will access it only indirectly, through
selection_ask or selection_query.

selection_request takes a pointer to a holder (as returned by
seln_inquire) and a request constructed in *buffer. The request is trans-
mitted to the indicated selection holder, and the buffer rewritten with its
response. Failures in the RPC mechanism will cause a SELN_FAILED return; if
the process of the addressed holder is no longer active, the return value will be
SELN_NON_EXIST. Clients which call selection_request directly will find
it most convenient to initialize the buffer by a call to selec-
tion_init_request.

Request attributes which are not recognized by the selection holder will be
returned as the value of the attribute SELN_UNRECOGNIZED. Responses should
be provided in the order requests were encountered.

```
Seln_result
selection_request(server, holder, buffer)
        Xv_Server      server
        Seln_holder    *holder;
        Seln_request   *buffer;
```

selection_yield_all()

Procedure that queries the holders of all selections and, for each which is held by a client in the calling process, sends a yield request to that client and a Done to the server. It should be called by applications which are about to exit or to undertake lengthy computations during which they will be unable to respond to requests concerning selections they hold.

```
void
selection_yield_all()
```

textsw_add_mark()

Adds a new mark at position. flags can be either TEXTSW_MARK_ DEFAULTS or TEXTSW_MARK_MOVE_AT_INSERT.

```
Textsw_mark
textsw_add_mark(textsw, position, flags)
        Textsw             textsw;
        Textsw_index       position;
        unsigned           flags;
```

textsw_append_file_name()

Returns 0 if textsw is editing a file and, if so, appends the name of the file at the end of name.

```
int
textsw_append_file_name(textsw, name)
        Textsw             textsw;
        char               *name;
```

textsw_delete()

Returns 0 if the operation fails. Removes the span of characters beginning with first and ending one before last_plus_one.

```
Textsw_index
textsw_delete(textsw, first, last_plus_one)
        Textsw                 textsw;
        Textsw_index           first, last_plus_one;
```

textsw_edit()

Returns 0 if the operation fails. Erases a character, word or line, depending on whether unit is SELN_LEVEL_FIRST or SELN_LEVEL_LINE. If direction is 0, characters after the insertion point are affected; otherwise, characters before the insertion point are affected. The operation will be done count times.

```
Textsw_index
textsw_edit(textsw, unit, count, direction)
        Textsw          textsw;
        unsigned        unit, count, direction;
```

textsw_erase()

Returns 0 if the operation fails. Equivalent to `textsw_delete()` but does not affect the global shelf.

```
Textsw_index
textsw_erase(textsw, first, last_plus_one)
        Textsw                  textsw;
        Textsw_index            first, last_plus_one;
```

textsw_file_lines_visible()

Fills in `top` and `bottom` with the file line indices of the first and last file lines being displayed in `textsw`.

```
void
textsw_file_lines_visible(textsw, top, bottom)
        Textsw          textsw;
        int             *top, *bottom;
```

textsw_find_bytes()

Beginning at the position addressed by `first`, searches for the pattern specified by `buf` of length `buf_len`. Searches forward if flags is 0, else searches backward. Returns −1 if no match, else matching span placed in indices addressed by `first` and `last_plus_one`.

```
int
textsw_find_bytes(
        textsw, first, last_plus_one, buf, buf_len, flags)
        Textsw          textsw;
        Textsw_index *first, *last_plus_one;
        char            *buf;
        unsigned        buf_len, flags;
```

textsw_find_mark()

Returns the current position of `mark`. If this operation fails, it will return `TEXTSW_INFINITY`.

```
Textsw_index
textsw_find_mark(textsw, mark)
        Textsw                  textsw;
        Textsw_mark             mark;
```

textsw_first()

Returns the first `textsw` view.

```
Textsw
textsw_first(textsw)
        Textsw          textsw;
```

textsw_index_for_file_line()

Returns the character index for the first character in the line given by line. If this operation fails, it will return TEXTSW_CANNOT_SET.

```
Textsw_index
textsw_index_for_file_line(textsw, line)
        Textsw          textsw;
        int             line;
```

textsw_insert()

Inserts characters in buf into textsw at the current insertion point. The number of characters actually inserted is returned. This will equal buf_len unless there was a memory allocation failure. If there was a failure, it will return 0.

```
Textsw_index
textsw_insert(textsw, buf, buf_len)
        Textsw          textsw;
        char            *buf;
        int             buf_len;
```

textsw_match_bytes()

Searches for a block of text in the textsw's contents; ends with characters matching end_sym. This function places the starting index of the matching block in first and its ending index in last.

```
int
textsw_match_bytes(
        textsw, first, last_plus_one, start_sym,
        start_sym_len, end_sym, end_sym_len, field_flag)
                Textsw          textsw;
                Textsw_index *first, *last_plus_one;
                char            *start_sym, *end_sym;
                int             start_sym_len, end_sym_len;
                unsigned        field_flag;
```

textsw_next()

Returns the next view in the set of textsw views.

```
Textsw
textsw_next(textsw)
        Textsw          textsw;
```

textsw_normalize_view()

Repositions the text so that the character at position is visible and at the top of the subwindow.

```
void
textsw_normalize_view(textsw, position)
        Textsw          textsw;
        Textsw_index    position;
```

textsw_notify_proc()

Notify procedure installed by application using `TEXTSW_NOTIFY_PROC`.

```
void
notify_proc(textsw, avlist)
        Textsw      textsw
        Attr_avlist avlist
```

textsw_possibly_normalize()

If the character at `position` is already visible, this function does nothing. If it is not visible, it repositions the text so that it is visible and at the top of the subwindow.

```
void
textsw_possibly_normalize(textsw, position)
        Textsw          textsw;
        Textsw_index    position;
```

textsw_remove_mark()

Removes an existing mark from `textsw`.

```
void
textsw_remove_mark(textsw, mark)
        Textsw        textsw;
        Textsw_mark   mark;
```

textsw_replace_bytes()

Replaces the character span from `first` to `last_plus_one` with the characters in `buf`. The return value is the number of bytes inserted or deleted. The number is positive if bytes are inserted, negative if bytes are deleted. (The number is also negative if the original string is longer than the one that replaces it.) If this operation fails, it will return a value of 0.

```
Textsw_index
textsw_replace_bytes(
        textsw, first, last_plus_onebuf, buf_len)
            Textsw          textsw;
            Textsw_index    first;
            Textsw_index    last_plus_one;
            char            *buf;
            unsigned        buf_len;
```

textsw_reset()

Discards edits performed on the contents of `textsw`. If needed, a message box will be displayed at `x, y`.

```
void
textsw_reset(textsw, x, y)
        Textsw    textsw;
        int       x, y;
```

textsw_save()

Saves any edits made to the file currently loaded into textsw. If needed, a message box will be displayed at x, y.

```
unsigned
textsw_save(textsw, x, y)
        Textsw          textsw;
        int             x, y;
```

textsw_screen_line_count()

Returns the number of screen lines in textsw.

```
int
textsw_screen_line_count(textsw)
        Textsw          textsw;
```

textsw_scroll_lines()

Moves the text up or down by count lines. If count is positive, then the text is scrolled up on the screen. If negative, the text is scrolled down (backward in the file).

```
void
textsw_scroll_lines(textsw, count)
        Textsw          textsw;
        int             count;
```

textsw_set_selection()

Sets the selection to begin at first and includes all characters up to last_plus_one. A type value of 1 indicates primary selection, 2 indicates secondary selection.

```
void
textsw_set_selection(textsw, first, last_plus_one, type)
        Textsw          textsw;
        Textsw_index    first, last_plus_one;
        unsigned        type;
```

textsw_store_file()

Stores the contents of textsw to the file named by filename. If needed, a message box will be displayed at x, y.

```
unsigned
textsw_store_file(textsw, filename, x, y)
        Textsw          textsw;
        char            *filename;
        int             x, y;
```

ttysw_input()

Appends `len` number of characters from `buf` onto `tty`'s input queue. It returns the number of characters accepted.

```
int
ttysw_input(tty, buf, len)
        Tty     tty;
        char    *buf;
        int     len;
```

ttysw_output()

Appends `len` number of characters from `buf` onto `tty`'s output queue; it sends them through the terminal emulator to the TTY. It returns the number of characters accepted.

```
int
ttysw_output(tty, buf, len)
        Tty     tty;
        char    *buf;
        int     len;
```

window_done()

Destroys the entire hierarchy to which `win` belongs.

```
int
window_done(win)
        Xv_Window       win;
```

window_fit()

Causes `win` to fit its contents in the dimensions specified with `WIN_FIT_HEIGHT` and `WIN_FIT_WIDTH`. The macro is defined as:

```
xv_set(win, WIN_FIT_HEIGHT, WIN_FIT_WIDTH, 0, 0)
```

window_fit_height()

Causes `win` to fit its contents in the height specified with `WIN_FIT_HEIGHT`. The macro is defined as:

```
xv_set(win, WIN_FIT_HEIGHT, 0, NULL)
```

window_fit_width()

Causes `win` to fit its contents in the width specified with `WIN_FIT_WIDTH`. The macro is defined as:

```
xv_set(win, WIN_FIT_WIDTH, 0, NULL)
```

Procedures and Macros

window_read_event()

Reads the next input event for `window`. In case of error, sets the global variable `errno` and returns −1.

```
int
window_read_event(window, event)
        Xv_window      window;
        Event          *event;
```

WIN_NOTIFY_EVENT_PROC

`#defined` to be `WIN_NOTIFY_SAFE_EVENT_PROC`.

window_interpose_func()

Client function specified by using:

```
xv_set(window,
    WIN_NOTIFY_EVENT_PROC, window_interpose_function,
    NULL);
```

or by using:

```
notify_interpose_event_func(window,
    window_interpose_func, how);
```

`how` is either `NOTIFY_SAFE` or `NOTIFY_IMMEDIATE`. The `window_interpose_func()` takes the following parameters when called:

```
Notify_value
window_interpose_func(window, event, arg)
        Xv_Window      window;
        Event          *event;
        Xv_opaque      arg;
```

wmgr_bottom()

Sets stackmode to `Below` in `XConfigureWindow`.

```
void
wmgr_bottom(frame)
        Frame          frame;
```

wmgr_changelevel()

Sets stackmode in `XConfigureWindow`.

```
void
wmgr_changelevel(window,parent,top)
        Xv_Window      window;
        int            parent;
        int            top;
```

wmgr_close()

Sets `wmhints.initial_state` to `ICONICSTATE`.

```
void
wmgr_close(frame)
        Frame          frame;
```

wmgr_completechangerect()

        Calls `XConfigureWindow` with a new rect.

```
void
wmgr_completechangerect(window, rectnew, rectoriginal,
      parentprleft, parentprtop)
            Xv_window      window;
            Rect           *rectnew, *rectoriginal;
            int            parentprleft, parentprtop;
```

wmgr_open()

        Sets `wmhints.initial_state` to NORMALSTATE.

```
void
wmgr_open(frame)
      Frame          frame;
```

wmgr_refreshwindow()

        Calls `XConfigureWindow` repeatedly.

```
void
wmgr_refreshwindow(window)
      Xv_window      window;
```

wmgr_top() Sets stackmode to `Above` in `XConfigureWindow`.

```
void
wmgr_top(frame)
      Frame          frame;
```

xv_col() Returns an integer representing the number of pixels, excluding the left margin of the window.

```
int
xv_col(window, column)
      Xv_Window      window
      int            column;
```

xv_cols() Returns an integer representing the number of pixels, including the left margin of the window.

```
int
xv_cols(window, columns)
      Xv_Window      window
      int            columns;
```

xv_create() To create *any* XView object, call the generic procedure `xv_create`. This procedure will return a handle to some XView object. It takes as parameters the owner of the object being created, the type of object to create, and a list of attributes. The attribute list must terminate with a NULL. In specifying the type, you must use the name of some XView package. That name must be in all capital letters to distinguish it from the corresponding data type. The package is the name of the package to which the object you wish to create belongs.

The procedure `xv_create()` returns either the handle for the new object or `XV_NULL` if the attempt at object creation fails.

```
Xv_opaque
xv_create(owner, package, attributes)
        Xv_object       owner;
        Xv_pkg          *package;
        attribute-list  attributes;
```

xv_destroy()

To destroy an XView object and any subframes owned by that object, use the procedure `xv_destroy()`. It will return either `XV_ERROR` or `XV_OK`.

```
int
xv_destroy(object)
        Xv_object       object;
```

XV_DISPLAY_FROM_WINDOW()

Macro to get at the handle to the display object from a window object.

```
Xv_opaque
XV_DISPLAY_FROM_WINDOW(window)
        Xv_Window       window;
```

xv_find()

To find any XView object, use the procedure `xv_find()`. If the object is not found, `xv_find` will automatically attempt to create it.

```
Xv_opaque
xv_find(owner, package, attributes)
        Xv_object       owner;
        Xv_pkg          *package;
        attribute-list  attributes;
```

xv_get()

To get the value of any single attribute of *any* XView object, use the procedure `xv_get()`.

```
Xv_opaque
xv_get(object, attribute)
        Xv_object       object;
        attribute-list  attributes;
```

The procedure returns 0 for failure. As a result, you cannot detect errors when retrieving the values of attributes which might return 0 as a valid value. Note that, although you can supply `XV_NULL` as the owner when you create a new object with `xv_create`, you *must* give the object when asking for the value of an attribute.

For example, you cannot just ask for:

```
xv_get(XV_NULL, XV_FONT)
```

to determine the default font, but you can ask for the font associated with a particular screen, as in:

```
xv_get(Screen1, XV_FONT)
```

Some attributes require a screen or server to be supplied to `xv_get()`. For such attributes, you should ask any window you think should be on the same screen what to identify as its screen or server, using the attributes XV_SCREEN and XV_SERVER.

If you know your application only runs on a single screen, you can use the global values `xv_default_server` and `xv_default_screen` or you can ask the defaults database what the server is.

xv_init()   To initialize the Notifier, use the procedure `xv_init()`. It reads any passed attributes and the *~/.Xdefaults* Database as well as initializing the Defaults/Resource-Manager Database and loading the Server Resource-Manager Database.

```
int
main(argc, argv)
        int     argc;
        char    **argv:
{
/* initialization/declarations */
        .
        .
        .
    (void)xv_init(XV_INIT_ARGC_PTR_ARGV, &argc, argv, 0);
    frame = xv_create(NULL, FRAME, FRAME_LABEL, "foo", 0);
}
```

xv_row()   Returns an integer representing the number of pixels, excluding the top margin of the window.

```
int
xv_row(window, row)
        Xv_Window       window
        int             row;
```

xv_rows()   Returns an integer representing the number of pixels, including the top margin of the window.

```
int
xv_rows(window, rows)
        Xv_Window       window
        int             rows;
```

XV_SCREEN_FROM_WINDOW()

Macro to return the handle to the screen object from the window object.

```
XV_SCREEN_FROM_WINDOW(window)
        Xv_Window       window;
```

xv_send_message()

Lets two separate processes communicate with each other. You can specify the `addressee` field either with one of the constants XV_POINTER_WINDOW or XV_FOCUS_WINDOW or with the window's XID, if known. If the `addressee` is XV_POINTER, then the message is sent to the window that the pointer is in. If

Procedures and Macros

the addressee is XV_FOCUS_WINDOW, then the message is sent to the window that currently has the focus, regardless of the pointer position. If the addressee is a windows XID, then the message is sent to the window with the corresponding ID.

```
void
xv_send_message(
        window, addressee, msg_type, format, data, len)
                Xv_object       window;
                Xv_opaque       addressee;
                char            *msg_type;
                int             format;
                Xv_opaque       *data;
                int             len;
```

XV_SERVER_FROM_WINDOW()

Macro to get at the handle to the server object from a window object.

```
Xv_opaque
XV_SERVER_FROM_WINDOW(window)
        Xv_Window       window;
```

xv_set()   To set the value of one or more attributes of *any* XView object, call the procedure xv_set with the handle to the object whose attributes you wish to set and a list of attribute-value pairs terminating in a zero.

```
Xv_object
Xv_set(owner, type, attributes)
        Xv_object            owner;
        vu type              *type;
        attribute-list       attributes;
```

The procedure xv_set() returns XV_OK if it succeeds; otherwise, it returns an error code indicating that the attribute on which it ran encountered problems.

C
Data Types

C
Data Types

The following is a list of XView data types and their descriptions.

Canvas	Handle to an opaque structure that describes a canvas.
Canvas_attribute	One of the canvas attributes (CANVAS_*).
Xv_Cursor	Handle to an opaque structure that describes a cursor.
Xv_Cursor_attribute	One of the cursor attributes (CURSOR_*).
Destroy_status	Enumeration: DESTROY_PROCESS_DEATH DESTROY_CHECKING DESTROY_CLEANUP DESTROY_SAVE_YOURSELF
Event	The structure that describes an input event. Use macros for access.
Xv_Font	Pointer to an opaque structure that describes a font.
Xv_Font_attribute	One of the font attributes (FONT_*).
Frame	Pointer to an opaque structure that describes a frame.
Frame_att	One of the frame attributes (FRAME_*).
Window_scale_state	Enumeration: WIN_SCALE_SMALL WIN_SCALE_MEDIUM WIN_SCALE_LARGE WIN_RESCALE_EXTRALARGE
Fullscreen	Handle to an opaque structure that describes a fullscreen.
Fullscreen_attribute	One of the fullscreen attributes (FULLSCREEN_*).
Icon	Handle to an opaque structure that describes a icon.
Icon_attribute	One of the icon attributes (ICON_*).
Inputmask	Mask specifying which input events a window will receive.

Menu	Pointer to an opaque structure that describes a menu.
Menu_attribute	One of the menu attributes (MENU_*).
Menu_generate	Enumerated type for the operation parameter passed to generate procs.
Menu_item	Pointer to an opaque structure that describes a menu item.
Notice_attribute	One of the notice attributes (NOTICE_*).
Notify_arg	Opaque client optional argument.

Notify_destroy	Enumeration:
	    NOTIFY_SAFE
	    NOTIFY_IMMEDIATE

Notify_event	Opaque client event.

Notify_event_type	Enumeration of errors for notifier functions:
	    NOTIFY_SAFE
	    NOTIFY_IMMEDIATE

Notify_func	Notifier function.

Notify_signal_mode	Enumeration:
	    NOTIFY_SYNC
	    NOTIFY_ASYNC

Notify_value	Enumeration of possible return values for client notify procs:
	    NOTIFY_DONE
	    NOTIFY_IGNORED
	    NOTIFY_UNEXPECTED

Openwin_split_direction	Enumeration:
	    OPENWIN_SPLIT_HORIZONTAL
	    OPENWIN_SPLIT_VERTICAL

Panel	Pointer to an opaque structure that describes a panel.
Panel_attr	One of the panel attributes (PANEL_*).
Panel_item	Pointer to an opaque structure that describes a panel item.

Panel_item_type	Enumerated type:
	    PANEL_BUTTON_ITEM
	    PANEL_ITEM
	    PANEL_LIST_ITEM
	    PANEL_MESSAGE_ITEM
	    PANEL_NUMERIC_TEXT
	    PANEL_SLIDER_ITEM
	    PANEL_TEXT_ITEM
	    PANEL_TOGGLE_ITEM

Panel_list_op

Enumerated type:

    PANEL_LIST_OP_DELETE
    PANEL_LIST_OP_DESELECT
    PANEL_LIST_OP_SELECT
    PANEL_LIST_OP_VALIDATE

Panel_setting

Enumerated type:

    PANEL_CLEAR
    PANEL_NO_CLEAR
    PANEL_NONE
    PANEL_ALL
    PANEL_NON_PRINTABLE
    PANEL_SPECIFIED
    PANEL_CURRENT
    PANEL_DONE
    PANEL_MARKED
    PANEL_VERTICAL
    PANEL_HORIZONTAL
    PANEL_INVERTED
    PANEL_INSERT
    PANEL_NEXT
    PANEL_PREVIOUS
    PANEL_NONE_DOWN
    PANEL_LEFT_DOWN
    PANEL_MIDDLE_DOWN
    PANEL_RIGHT_DOWN
    PANEL_CHORD_DOWN

Rect

The structure describing a rectangle:

```
typedef struct rect {
        short r_left;
        short r_top;
        short r_width;
        short r_height;
} Rect;
```

Rectlist

A list of rectangles:

```
typedef struct rectlist {
        short rl_x, rl_y;
        Rectnode *rl_head;
        Rectnode *rl_tail;
        Rect rl_bound;
} Rectlist;
```

Rectnode

One of the individual rectangles in a rectlist:

```
typedef struct rectnode {
        Rectnode *rn_next;
        Rect      rn_rect;
} Rectnode;
```

Data Types

`Xv_Screen`	Pointer to an opaque structure that describes a screen.
`Xv_Screen_attr`	One of the screen attributes (`SCREEN_*`).
`Scrollbar`	The opaque handle for a scrollbar.
`Scrollbar_attr`	One of the scrollbar attributes (`SCROLL_*`).

`Scrollbar_motion`   Enumeration:
    `SCROLL_ABSOLUTE`
    `SCROLL_POINT_TO_MIN`
    `SCROLL_PAGE_FORWARD`
    `SCROLL_LINE_FORWARD`
    `SCROLL_MIN_TO_POINT`
    `SCROLL_PAGE_BACKWARD`
    `SCROLL_LINE_BACKWARD`
    `SCROLL_TO_END`
    `SCROLL_TO_START`
    `SCROLL_NONE`

`Scrollbar_setting`   Enumeration:
    `SCROLL_VERTICAL`
    `SCROLL_HORIZONTAL`

`Seln_attribute`	One of the seln attributes.
`Xv_Server`	Pointer to an opaque structure that describes a server.
`Server_attr`	One of the server attributes.
`Server_image`	Pointer to an opaque structure that describes a server image.

`Server_image_attribute`
    One of the Server_image attributes:
      `SERVER_IMAGE_DEPTH`
      `SERVER_IMAGE_BITS`

`Textsw`   Pointer to an opaque structure that describes a text subwindow.

`Textsw_action`   Enumeration of actions defined for client provided
`notify_proc`:
    `TEXTSW_ACTION_CAPS_LOCK`
    `TEXTSW_ACTION_CAPS_LOCK`
    `TEXTSW_ACTION_EDITED_FILE`
    `TEXTSW_ACTION_EDITED_MEMORY`
    `TEXTSW_ACTION_FILE_IS_READONLY`
    `TEXTSW_ACTION_LOADED_FILE`
    `TEXTSW_ACTION_SAVING_FILE`
    `TEXTSW_ACTION_STORING_FILE`
    `TEXTSW_ACTION_USING_MEMORY`
    `TEXTSW_ACTION_WRITE_FAILED`
    `TEXTSW_ACTION_REPLACED`
    `TEXTSW_ACTION_PAINTED`
    `TEXTSW_ACTION_SCROLLED`

```
                              TEXTSW_ACTION_DESTROY_VIEW
                              TEXTSW_ACTION_SPLIT_VIEW
```

Textsw_attribute   One of the textsw attributes.

Textsw_enum   Enumeration:
```
                              TEXTSW_NEVER
                              TEXTSW_ALWAYS
                              TEXTSW_ONLY
                              TEXTSW_IF_AUTO_SCROLL
                              TEXTSW_CLIP
                              TEXTSW_WRAP_AT_CHAR
                              TEXTSW_WRAP_AT_WORD
                              TEXTSW_WRAP_AT_LINE
```

Textsw_index   An index for a character within a text subwindow's text stream.

Textsw_view   Pointer to an opaque structure that describes a text subwindow view.

Textsw_expand_status   Enumeration describe expand status of text subwindow operations:
```
                              TEXTSW_FULL_BUF
                              TEXTSW_EXPAND_OK
                              TEXTSW_EXPAND_OTHER_ERROR
```

Textsw_status   Enumeration describing the status of text subwindow operations:

Tty   Pointer to an opaque structure that describes a `TTY` subwindow.

Xv_Window   Pointer to an opaque structure that describes a window.

Window_attr   One of the window attributes (`WIN_*`).

Window_scale_state   Enumeration:
```
                              WIN_SCALE_SMALL
                              WIN_SCALE_MEDIUM
                              WIN_SCALE_LARGE
                              WIN_SCALE_EXTRALARGE
```

Xv_error_action   Enumeration:
```
                              XV_ERROR_CONTINUE
                              XV_ERROR_RETRY
                              XV_ERROR_ABORT
```

Xv_error_attr   Enumeration:
```
                              XV_ERROR_SYSTEM
                              XV_ERROR_BAD_VALUE
                              XV_ERROR_CREATE_ONLY
                              XV_ERROR_CANNOT_SET
                              XV_BERROR_CANNOT_GET
                              XV_ERROR_SERVER
                              XV_ERROR_STRING
```

```
                         XV_ERROR_INVALID_OBJ
                         XV_ERROR_INTERNAL
```

`Xv_error_severity`	Enumeration:
	`XV_ERROR_RECOVERABLE`
	`XV_ERROR_NON_RECOVERABLE`

`Xv_object`	Pointer to an opaque structure that describes an XView object.
`Xv_opaque`	Pointer to an opaque structure.
`Xv_Xrectlist`	A list of rectangles returned by XView in X/11 rectangle list format.

D

Event Codes

D
Event Codes

Table D-1 lists the predefined event codes and their values:

Table D-1. Event Codes

Value	Event Code	Description
0	ASCII_FIRST	Marks beginning of ASCII range
127	ASCII_LAST	Marks end of ASCII range
128	META_FIRST	Marks beginning of META range
255	META_LAST	Marks end of META range
31744	ACTION_NULL_EVENT	Event is *not* translated into an action
31745	ACTION_ERASE_CHAR_BACKWARD	Erase char to the left of caret
31746	ACTION_ERASE_CHAR_FORWARD	Erase char to the right of caret
31747	ACTION_ERASE_WORD_BACKWARD	Erase word to the left of caret
31748	ACTION_ERASE_WORD_FORWARD	Erase word to the right of caret
31749	ACTION_ERASE_LINE_BACKWARD	Erase to the beginning of the line
31750	ACTION_ERASE_LINE_END	Erase to the end of the line
31752	ACTION_GO_CHAR_BACKWARD	Move the caret one character to the left
31753	ACTION_GO_CHAR_FORWARD	Move the caret one character to the right
31754	ACTION_GO_WORD_BACKWARD	Move the caret one word to the left
31755	ACTION_GO_WORD_FORWARD	Move the caret one word to the right
31756	ACTION_GO_WORD_END	Move the caret to the end of the word
31757	ACTION_GO_LINE_BACKWARD	Move the caret to the start of the line
31758	ACTION_GO_LINE_FORWARD	Move the caret to the start of the next line
31759	ACTION_GO_LINE_END	Move the caret to the end of the line
31760	ACTION_GO_LINE_START	Move the caret to the beginning of the line
31761	ACTION_GO_COLUMN_BACKWARD	Move the caret up one line, maintaining column position
31762	ACTION_GO_COLUMN_FORWARD	Move the caret down one line, maintaining column position
31763	ACTION_GO_DOCUMENT_START	Move the caret to the beginning of the text
31764	ACTION_GO_DOCUMENT_END	Move the caret to the end of the text
31765	ACTION_GO_PAGE_FORWARD	Move the caret to the next page
31766	ACTION_GO_PAGE_BACKWARD	Move the caret to the previous page

Value	Event Code	Description
31767	ACTION_STOP	Stop the operation
31768	ACTION_AGAIN	Repeat previous operation
31769	ACTION_PROPS	Show property sheet window
31770	ACTION_UNDO	Undo previous operation
31771	ACTION_REDO	Repeat previous operation
31772	ACTION_FRONT	Bring window to the front of the desktop
31773	ACTION_BACK	Put the window at the back of the desktop
31774	ACTION_COPY	Copy the selection to the clipboard
31775	ACTION_OPEN	Open a window from its icon form (or close if already open)
31776	ACTION_CLOSE	Close a window to an icon
31777	ACTION_PASTE	Copy clipboard contents to the insertion point
31778	ACTION_FIND_BACKWARD	Find the text selection to the left of the caret
31779	ACTION_FIND_FORWARD	Find the text selection to the right of the caret
31780	ACTION_REPLACE	Show find and replace window
31781	ACTION_CUT	Delete the selection and put on clipboard
31782	ACTION_SELECT_FIELD_BACKWARD	Select the previous delimited field
31783	ACTION_SELECT_FIELD_FORWARD	Select the next delimited field
31784	ACTION_COPY_THEN_PASTE	Copy, then paste, text
31785	ACTION_STORE	Store the specified selection as a new file
31786	ACTION_LOAD	Load the specified selection as a new file
31787	ACTION_INCLUDE_FILE	Includes the file
31788	ACTION_GET_FILENAME	Get the selected filename
31789	ACTION_SET_DIRECTORY	Set the directory to the selection
31790	ACTION_DO_IT	Do the appropriate default action
31791	ACTION_HELP	Set the directory to the selection
31792	ACTION_INSERT	"INSERT" key*
31796	ACTION_CAPS_LOCK	Toggle caps-lock state
31799	ACTION_SELECT	Left mouse button down or up
31800	ACTION_ADJUST	Middle mouse button down or up
31801	ACTION_MENU	Right mouse button down or up
31802	ACTION_DRAG_MOVE	For moving text
31803	ACTION_DRAG_COPY	Attempting to drag copy
31803	ACTION_SPLIT_HORIZONTAL	Split pane horizontally
31804	ACTION_DRAG_LOAD	Attempting to drag load
31806	ACTION_SPLIT_VERTICAL	Split pane vertically
31807	ACTION_SPLIT_INIT	Initialize a split pane
31808	ACTION_SPLIT_DESTROY	Destroy a split of a pane
31809	ACTION_RESCALE	Rescale a pane
31810	ACTION_PININ	Pop up's OPEN LOOK pushpin in window header is in
31811	ACTION_PINOUT	Pop up's OPEN LOOK pushpin in window header is out
31812	ACTION_DISMISS	OPEN LOOK "dismiss" of pop-up window

Value	Event Code	Description
31815	ACTION_TAKE_FOCUS	Take the input focus
31818	KBD_MAP	KeymapNotify
31819	WIN_GRAPHICS_EXPOSE	GraphicsExpose
31820	WIN_NO_EXPOSE	NoExpose
31821	WIN_VISIBILITY_NOTIFY	VisibilityNotify
31822	WIN_CREATE_NOTIFY	CreateNotify
31823	WIN_DESTROY_NOTIFY	DestroyNotify
31824	WIN_MAP_REQUEST	MapRequest
31825	WIN_REPARENT_NOTIFY	ReparentNotify
31826	WIN_GRAVITY_NOTIFY	GravityNotify
31827	WIN_RESIZE_REQUEST	ResizeRequest
31828	WIN_CONFIGURE_REQUEST	ConfigureRequest
31829	WIN_CIRCULATE_REQUEST	CirculateRequest
31830	WIN_CIRCULATE_NOTIFY	CirculateNotify
31831	WIN_PROPERTY_NOTIFY	PropertyNotify
31835	WIN_COLORMAP_NOTIFY	ColormapNotify
31836	MAPPING_NOTIFY	MappingNotify
31895	ACTION_MATCH_DELIMITER	Select text up to a matching delimiter
31897	ACTION_QUOTE	Cause next event in the input stream to pass untranslated by the keymapping system
31898	ACTION_EMPTY	Empty out the object or window.
32000	PANEL_EVENT_CANCEL	The panel or panel item is no longer "current"
32001	PANEL_EVENT_MOVE_IN	The pointer enters panel or panel item with no mouse buttons down
32002	PANEL_EVENT_DRAG_IN	The pointer enters panel or panel item with one or more mouse buttons down
32256	SCROLLBAR_REQUEST	Request the scrollbar client to scroll paint window to a new view start
32512	LOC_MOVE	Pointer moves
32513	LOC_WINENTER	Pointer enters window
32514	LOC_WINEXIT	Pointer exits window
32515	LOC_DRAG	Pointer moves while a button was down
32516	WIN_REPAINT	Some portion of window requires repainting
32517	WIN_RESIZE	Window has been resized
32518	WIN_MAP_NOTIFY	Notification of window being mapped
32519	WIN_UNMAP_NOTIFY	Notification of window being unmapped
32520	KBD_USE	Window is now the focus of keyboard input
32521	KBD_DONE	Window is no longer the focus of keyboard input
32522	WIN_CLIENT_MESSAGE	A message from another client
32563+i-1	BUT(i)	Press pointer buttons 1–10
32563	MS_LEFT	Press left mouse button
32564	MS_MIDDLE	Press middle mouse button
32565	MS_RIGHT	Press right mouse button
32573+i-1	KEY_LEFT(i)	Press left function keys 1–15

Table D-1. Event Codes (continued)

Value	Event Code	Description
32589+i-1	KEY_RIGHT(i)	Press right function keys 1–15
32605+i-1	KEY_TOP(i)	Press top function keys 1–15
32621+i-1	KEY_BOTTOM(i)	"BOTTOM" keys*
32621	KEY_BOTTOMLEFT	
32621	KEY_BOTTOMFIRST	
32622	KEY_BOTTOMRIGHT	
32636	KEY_BOTTOMLAST	

* May not be available on all keyboards.

E

Command Line Arguments

E
Command Line Arguments

In XView, each property can be set in one of three ways:

1. By specifying the short flag name plus its value (if any) on the command line.

2. By specifying the long flag name plus its value (if any) on the command line.

3. By editing the corresponding default or defaults in your ⁊.*Xdefaults* file.

In the absence of any of these actions, the default action is taken. Methods 1 and 2 each take precedence over method 3.

Naturally, an application can override defaults through the use of XView attributes, but a well-behaved application will always override application defaults with the command line arguments.

Arguments are all set in *italics*. Those arguments in parentheses describe the value or values. Arguments not in parentheses indicate a list from which you must choose.

Table E-1. XView Command Line Arguments

Short Flag	Long Flag	Default Argument(s)	Value	Example
-Wx	-scale	*medium*	small medium large extra_large	-Wx large
-Wt	-font	*(fontname-size)*	lucidasans-12	-Wt screen-14
-Ww	-width	*(columns)*	80	-Ww 120
-Wh	-height	*(rows)*	34	-Wh 24
-Ws	-size	*(pixels pixels)*	80 columns by 34 rows	-Ws 500 400
-Wp	-position	*(x y)*	from top left to bottom right of screen	-Wp 237 625

Short Flag	Long Flag	Default Argument(s)	Value	Example
-WP	-icon_position	*(x y)*	along edge of screen	-WP 500 0
-Wl	-label	*(header_string)*	none	-Wl "My tool"
-Wi	-iconic		open	-Wi
-Wf	-foreground_color	*(red green blue)*	black	-Wf 0 0 0
-Wb	-background_color	*(red green blue)*	white	-Wb 255 255 255
-Wg	-set_default_color		no	-Wg
-WI	-icon_image	*(pixmap_pathname)*	blank	-WI mytool.icon
-WL	-icon_label	*(footer_string)*	none	-WL "Idle"
-WT	-icon_font	*(fontname-size)*	lucidasans-12	-WT screen-10
-Wr	-display	*(hostname:display)*	DISPLAY environment variable	-Wr myhost:0
-Wdr	-disable_retained		enable retained windows on monochrome displays	-Wdr
	-disable_screen_saver	*0*	XSetScreenSaver not called	-disable_ screen_ saver 1
		1	XSetScreenSaver called	--disable_ screen_ saver 0
	-sync	*0*	run asynchronously	-sync 0
		1	run synchronously	-sync 1
-WH	-help			
-Wdxio	-disable_xio_error_handler		-Wdxio	

Table E-2. Resource Names of Command Line Arguments

Short Flag	Resource Name(s)
-Wx	window.scale
-Wt	font.name
-Ww	window.columns
-Wh	window.rows
-Ws	window.width
	window.height
-Wp	window.x
	window.y
-WP	icon.x
	icon.y
-Wl	window.header
-Wi	window.iconic
-Wf	window.color.foreground
-Wb	window.color.background
-Wg	window.inheritcolor
-WI	icon.pixmap
-WL	icon.footer
-WT	icon.font.name
-Wr	server.name
-Wdr	window.mono.disableRetained 0
-WH	(Prints out a list of generic command line arguments.)
-Wdxio	(Disables the I/O error handler installed by xv_init().)

F

OPEN LOOK
User Interface Compliance

In This Appendix:

OPEN LOOK User Interface Compliance

This appendix lists the ways that the XView Toolkit is not compliant with the *OPEN LOOK Graphical User Interface Functional Specification*. It is not a complete list of the ways that OpenWindows 1.0 is not an OPEN LOOK UI-compliant environment. OPEN LOOK UI compliance has two components: toolkit compliance and environment compliance.

An OPEN LOOK UI-compliant toolkit allows a developer to write an application that will be OPEN LOOK UI-compliant if run with an OPEN LOOK UI window manager. The toolkit might also support the application running successfully with, for example, a MOTIF™ window manager, but in such a configuration, the application would not be OPEN LOOK UI-compliant. An OPEN LOOK UI-compliant environment consists of an OPEN LOOK UI window manager, file manager, workspace properties window, and other such utility programs. To guarantee an OPEN LOOK UI application, the developer must write the application with an OPEN LOOK UI-compliant toolkit *and* run the application in an OPEN LOOK UI-compliant environment.

This list is in three parts. The first part consists of those features missing from XView 1.0 that are specified as Level 1 OPEN LOOK UI features. The second part lists some of the Level 2 OPEN LOOK UI features supported by XView 1.0. The third part lists the rest of the Level 2 OPEN LOOK UI features, which are not supported by XView 1.0.

Level 1 Features Not Supported in XView 1.0

The Level 1 features listed on the following pages are not supported in XView 1.0.

Keyboard and Mouse Customization

XView 1.0 hard-codes the bindings for function keys, mouse buttons, and mouse modifiers that OPEN LOOK UI says the user should be able to customize.

An OPEN LOOK UI toolkit should allow the user to specify the keys used for `CUT`, `COPY`, `PASTE`, `PROPERTIES`, `UNDO`, `CANCEL`, `DEFAULTACTION`, `NEXTFIELD`, and `PREVFIELD`.

- In XView 1.0, these key bindings are hard-coded to L10, L6, L8, L3, L4, L1, Return, Tab, and Shift-Tab.

An OPEN LOOK UI toolkit should allow the user to change the mouse buttons used for SELECT, ADJUST, and MENU; the specified default mouse button bindings are LEFT, MIDDLE, and RIGHT.

- In XView 1.0, the specified default mouse button bindings are hard-coded.

An OPEN LOOK UI toolkit should allow the user to change the mouse modifiers used for SETMENUDEFAULT, DUPLICATE, PAN, and CONSTRAIN. The specified default modified mouse actions are Control-RIGHT for SETMENUDEFAULT, Control-LEFT for DUPLI-CATE, Meta-LEFT for PAN, and LEFT-and-MIDDLE-chorded for CONSTRAIN.

- In XView 1.0, the specified defaults for SETMENUDEFAULT and DUPLICATE are hard-coded, and PAN and CONSTRAIN are not supported.

In an OPEN LOOK UI toolkit, clicking ADJUST when there is no selection will set an initial insert point (the same as clicking SELECT).

- In XView 1.0, this selects a single character.

In an OPEN LOOK UI toolkit, the user can bind a modified mouse action to selecting a single character, but the default binding is NONE.

- In XView 1.0, selecting a single character is hard-coded to clicking ADJUST when there is no selection.

Input Focus Feedback

In an OPEN LOOK UI toolkit, only one text area (that is, text field or text pane) within a window may have a caret, whether active or inactive.

- XView 1.0 allows multiple inactive carets to be displayed in a single window (but only one active caret). As a result, if you use the *follow-mouse* input focus model instead of the *click-to-type* model, you may believe that an inactive caret is not being properly activated. In fact, that inactive caret should not have been displayed.

Menu Default Setting

In an OPEN LOOK UI toolkit, the user can press or release the SETMENUDEFAULT mouse modifier either before or after pressing MENU to change the menu default setting, thus allowing the user to change the menu default and invoke the new default in a single menu action.

- In XView 1.0, the user must press SETMENUDEFAULT before pressing MENU to change the menu default.

Default Buttons in Pop Ups

In an OPEN LOOK UI toolkit, notices, command windows, and property windows must always have a "default button," even when there is only one button, and that the DEFAULTACTION keyboard accelerator always invokes the default button.

* XView 1.0 does not provide this automatically, but applications can implement this feature using XView primitives.

Help

In an OPEN LOOK UI toolkit, help text can have bold text, italic text, and glyphs (small pictures).

* XView 1.0 does not support this.

In an OPEN LOOK UI toolkit, applications can add a More button to the help window.

* XView 1.0 does not allow this.

Window Background

In an OPEN LOOK UI toolkit, window backgrounds are used to access the Window menu, to select a window, and to move it by dragging.

* XView 1.0 does not support this.

Notices

In an OPEN LOOK UI toolkit, notices do not freeze the screen; input to other applications is always possible.

* In XView 1.0, notices block input to all applications.

In an OPEN LOOK UI toolkit, each window of an application displays the standard busy pattern in the header when a notice is displayed.

* XView 1.0 does not give the window manager enough information for this to work.

Text Functions

In an OPEN LOOK UI toolkit, an UNDO after an UNDO reverses the effect of the UNDO, restoring the original state.

* In XView 1.0, the second UNDO undoes the next-previous edit. There is no way in XView 1.0 to reverse the effect of an UNDO.

Control Items

In an OPEN LOOK UI toolkit, an abbreviated menu button can have a text field to the right of the menu button. The text field is used to add items to the menu.

- XView 1.0 does not have this feature.

In an OPEN LOOK UI toolkit, menu buttons (and abbreviated menu buttons) highlight on MENU down, and change to the standard busy pattern on MENU-up in stay-up mode.

- XView 1.0 does not provide this.

In an OPEN LOOK UI toolkit, a default setting for exclusive and non-exclusive settings is only displayed when the controls are used on a menu.

- XView 1.0 indicates a default setting for exclusive and non-exclusive settings even when the controls are used in command and property windows.

In an OPEN LOOK UI toolkit, a slider can be shown with a read-only current value.

- XView 1.0 does not support this.

In an OPEN LOOK UI toolkit, the user can click SELECT to the left or right of a slider drag box on the slider bar to decrement or increment respectively, the setting by one unit. The pointer jumps as needed to allow repeated clicks.

- XView 1.0 does not support this.

In an OPEN LOOK UI toolkit, some exclusive settings can have no choice selected; the user clicks SELECT on the current choice to cause it to be deselected, yielding a value of "none."

- XView 1.0 requires exclusive settings to have one choice selected.

In an OPEN LOOK UI toolkit, an indeterminate state is defined on exclusive and non-exclusive settings.

- XView 1.0 does not support this.

In an OPEN LOOK UI toolkit, the bold border width on exclusive and non-exclusive settings is adjusted (to either 2 or 3 pixels) depending on the display resolution.

- XView 1.0 does not provide this.

Scrolling Lists

In an OPEN LOOK UI toolkit, scrolling lists can be put into an editable mode, and in that mode, the item selected for editing is inverted.

- XView 1.0 does not allow scrolling lists to be edited; they can only be changed by the application.

In an OPEN LOOK UI toolkit, scrolling lists can support no current choice (display or edit only), one current choice (exclusive list), or zero or more current choices (non-exclusive list).

- XView 1.0 only provides non-exclusive lists.

In an OPEN LOOK UI toolkit, a current choice in a non-exclusive list can be "deselected" by clicking on it.

- XView 1.0 does not support this.

Property Windows

In an OPEN LOOK UI toolkit, there is a required Settings pop-up menu for a property window.

- XView 1.0 does not provide this automatically, but applications can implement this menu themselves.

In an OPEN LOOK UI toolkit, property windows have two required buttons, `Apply` and `Reset`, and an optional button, `Set Default`.

- Again, XView 1.0 does not provide this automatically, but applications can implement this feature using XView primitives.

In an OPEN LOOK UI toolkit, there is a way to have two active selections when using property windows.

- XView 1.0 does not support this.

In an OPEN LOOK UI toolkit, when there are two active selections, the `Apply` button becomes a menu button with `Original Selection` and `New Selection` items.

- XView 1.0 does not support this.

Inactive Controls

In an OPEN LOOK UI toolkit, the scrollbar up or down arrow is dimmed when the scroll elevator is at the beginning or end of the document, respectively. When there is no data in the document, both arrows are dimmed.

- XView 1.0 does not support this.

In an OPEN LOOK UI toolkit, a menu's pushpin is dimmed if the menu has already been pinned.

- XView 1.0 does not support this.

Level 2 Features Supported in XView 1.0

The following Level 2 features are supported in XView 1.0.

- Abbreviated buttons

- Nonstandard basic windows

- Numeric text fields with increment/decrement buttons

- Some keyboard accelerators

- Splittable panes

    - *Missing*: Dimming the pane's border or its contents to indicate that the pane is about to disappear when removing a split pane using cable anchors.

- Split View and Join Views items on Scrollbar menu

- Dragging text to move/copy

    - *Missing*: Text duplicate and text move pointers should use a more-arrow instead of an ellipsis ...

- Quick Move and Quick Duplicate on (most) text

- Some Level 2 Workspace Properties

Level 2 Features Not Supported in XView 1.0

The following Level 2 features are not supported in XView 1.0.

- Blocking pop-up windows

- Change bars in property windows

- Color

    - Window manager provides color in headers and footers

    - Color backgrounds are supported in notices (only)

    - *Missing*: Color backgrounds in control areas and menus

    - *Missing*: Grayscale/color glyphs for "3-D" appearance

- Multi-line text areas

- Edit menu for text fields

- Read-only gauges

- Menus containing more than one type of control

- Resizable panes

- Selectable panes

- Minimum scrollbar
- View must be updated while scrollbar elevator is dragged
- Page-oriented scrollbar
- Automatic scrolling
- Panning
- Glyphs in scrolling lists
- Hierarchical scrolling lists
- Sliders with end-boxes and tickmarks
- Vertical sliders
- Soft function keys
- Window scaling

G

Example Programs

In This Chapter:

G
Example Programs

This appendix contains nine example programs that supplement the programs in the chapters:

- *item_move.c*
- *xv_termsw.c*
- *scroll_cells2.c*
- *menu_dir2.c*
- *type_font.c*
- *fonts.c*
- *seln.c*
- *seln_line.c*
- *x_draw.c*
- *Logo.c*
- *Bitmap.c*

Some of these programs are extensions to programs presented earlier in this book; they are listed here to demonstrate extended usage. Other programs in this appendix attempt to integrate features from unrelated XView packages that exceeded the scope of a particular chapter.

item_move.c

The first program demonstrates how you can use an event handler within a panel to allow the user to create panel items, move them around within the panel, and delete them. Chapter 7, *Panels*, discusses specifics about how panels work. Chapter 5, *Canvases and Openwin*, discusses the canvas and openwin issues, since the panel is subclassed from those packages.

Example G-1. The item_move.c program

```
/*
 * item_move.c
 *    Move items around in a panel using an event handler specific
 * to the panel.  Two panels are created -- the left panel contains
 * panel buttons that allow you to create certain types of items that
 * are put in the second panel.  Use the ADJUST mouse button to move
 * items around in the second panel.
 */
#include <stdio.h>
#include <xview/xview.h>
#include <xview/panel.h>

/* we need handles to the base frame and a panel -- instead of using
 * global variables, we're going to attach the objects to the objects
 * which need to reference them.  Attach using XV_KEY_DATA --
 * here are the keys.
 */
#define PACKAGE_KEY     100
#define FRAME_KEY       101
#define PANEL_KEY       102

main(argc, argv)
int argc;
char *argv[];
{
    Frame       frame;
    Panel       panel;
    Panel_item  create_text, item;
    void        quit(), my_event_proc();
    int         selected(), create_item();

    xv_init(XV_INIT_ARGC_PTR_ARGV, &argc, argv, NULL);

    frame = (Frame)xv_create(XV_NULL, FRAME,
        FRAME_LABEL,            "Use Middle Button To Move Items",
        FRAME_SHOW_FOOTER,      TRUE,
        NULL);
    /*
     * Create panel for known panel items.  Layout panel vertically.
     */
    panel = (Panel)xv_create(frame, PANEL,
        PANEL_LAYOUT,           PANEL_VERTICAL,
        NULL);

    /*
     * Create the standard "Quit" button to exit program.
     */
    (void) xv_create(panel, PANEL_BUTTON,
        PANEL_LABEL_STRING,     "Quit",
```

```
                PANEL_NOTIFY_PROC,         quit,
                XV_KEY_DATA,               FRAME_KEY,         frame,
                NULL);
    /*
     * create text panel item, attach the frame as client data for
     * use by the notify procedure create_item().  Text items inherit
     * the layout of "label" and "value" from its parent panel.
     * override for the text item by setting PANEL_LAYOUT explicitly.
     */
    create_text = (Panel_item)xv_create(panel, PANEL_TEXT,
        PANEL_LABEL_STRING,        "Create Button:",
        PANEL_NOTIFY_PROC,         create_item,
        PANEL_LAYOUT,              PANEL_HORIZONTAL,
        PANEL_VALUE_DISPLAY_LENGTH,     10,
        NULL);

    /*
     * panel button determines which type of button to create -- a
     * button or a message item.  See create_item().
     */
    item = (Panel_item)xv_create(panel, PANEL_CHOICE,
        PANEL_DISPLAY_LEVEL,       PANEL_CURRENT,
        PANEL_LAYOUT,              PANEL_HORIZONTAL,
        PANEL_LABEL_STRING,        "Item type",
        PANEL_CHOICE_STRINGS,      "Button", "Message", "Text", NULL,
        NULL);
    window_fit(panel);

    /* Create a new panel to be used for panel creation.  The panel
     * from above is no longer referenced.  The panel created here
     * is the panel used throughout the rest of this program.  The
     * panel referenced in WIN_RIGHT_OF and XV_HEIGHT is the old one
     * since the new one isn't created yet.
     */
    panel = (Panel)xv_create(frame, PANEL,
        WIN_RIGHT_OF,              canvas_paint_window(panel),
        XV_WIDTH,                  300,
        XV_HEIGHT,                 xv_get(panel, XV_HEIGHT),
        OPENWIN_SHOW_BORDERS,      TRUE,
        NULL);

    /* Install event handling routine for the panel */
    xv_set(canvas_paint_window(panel),
        WIN_EVENT_PROC,            my_event_proc,
        XV_KEY_DATA,               PANEL_KEY,         panel,
        NULL);
    /* attach various items to the text item for text_select() */
    xv_set(create_text,
        XV_KEY_DATA,               FRAME_KEY,         frame,
        XV_KEY_DATA,               PACKAGE_KEY,       item,
        XV_KEY_DATA,               PANEL_KEY,         panel,
        NULL);
    window_fit(frame);
    xv_main_loop(frame);
}
/*
```

```
 * Process events for the panel's subwindow.  This routine gets -all-
 * events that occur in the panel subwindow and does not interfere
 * with the normal processing of events dispatched to panels items.
 * my_event_proc is only interested in ADJUST button events that
 * happen on top of panel items.  When the user clicks and _drags_ the
 * ADJUST button on a panel item, the item is moved to where the mouse
 * moves to.
 */
void
my_event_proc(window, event)
Xv_Window window;
Event *event;
{
    static Panel_item   item;
    static int  x_offset, y_offset;
    Panel       panel = (Panel)xv_get(window, XV_KEY_DATA, PANEL_KEY);
    Frame       frame = (Frame)xv_get(panel, XV_OWNER);
    Rect        *rect, *item_rect;
    char        buf[64];

    /*
     * If the mouse is dragging an item, reset its new location.
     */
    if (event_action(event) == LOC_DRAG && item) {
        Panel_item pi;
        Rect r;
        /*
         * Get the rect of item, then *copy* it -- never change data
         * returned by xv_get().  Modify the copied rect reflecting
         * new X,Y position of panel item and check to see if it
         * intersects with any existing panel items.
         */
        rect = (Rect *)xv_get(item, XV_RECT);
        rect_construct(&r, /* see <xview/rect.h> for macros */
            rect->r_left, rect->r_top, rect->r_width, rect->r_height);
        r.r_left = event->ie_locx - x_offset;
        r.r_top = event->ie_locy - y_offset;
        PANEL_EACH_ITEM(panel, pi)
            if (pi == item)
                continue;
            /* don't let panel items overlap */
            item_rect = (Rect *)xv_get(pi, XV_RECT);
            if (rect_intersectsrect(item_rect, &r))
                return;
        PANEL_END_EACH
        /* no overlap -- move panel item. */
        xv_set(item,
            PANEL_ITEM_X, r.r_left,
            PANEL_ITEM_Y, r.r_top,
            NULL);
    }
    /* If it's not the ADJUST button, we're not interested */
    if (event_action(event) != ACTION_ADJUST)
        return;
    /*
     * next two cases is ADJUST button just-down or just-released
```

```
        */
    if (event_is_down(event)) {
        /* Middle button down on an item -- determine panel item */
        PANEL_EACH_ITEM(panel, item)
            rect = (Rect *)xv_get(item, XV_RECT);
            if (rect_includespoint(rect,
                event->ie_locx, event->ie_locy)) {
                x_offset = event->ie_locx - rect->r_left;
                y_offset = event->ie_locy - rect->r_top;
                break;
            }
        PANEL_END_EACH
        if (item)
            sprintf(buf, "Moving item: '%s'",
                (char *)xv_get(item, PANEL_LABEL_STRING));
        else
            buf[0] = 0;
    } else if (item) {
        char *name = (char *)xv_get(item, PANEL_LABEL_STRING);

        /* test if item is inside panel by comparing XV_RECTs */
        rect = (Rect *)xv_get(panel, XV_RECT);
        if (!rect_includespoint(rect,
            event->ie_locx + rect->r_left,
            event->ie_locy + rect->r_top)) {
            /* item is outside the panel -- remove item */
            xv_destroy(item);
            sprintf(buf, "Removed '%s' from panel", name);
        } else
            sprintf(buf, "'%s' moved to %d %d", name,
                (int)xv_get(item, XV_X), (int)xv_get(item, XV_Y));
        /* set "item" to null so that new drag
         * events don't attempt to move old item.
         */
        item = NULL;
    }
    xv_set(frame, FRAME_LEFT_FOOTER, buf, NULL);
}

/*
 * Callback routine for all panel buttons except "Quit".
 * If the panel item is the text item, determine the name of the new
 * panel button the user wishes to create.  Loop through all the
 * existing panel items looking for one with the same label.  If so,
 * return PANEL_NONE and set the frame's footer with an error message.
 * Otherwise, create a new panel item with the label, reset the text
 * item value and return PANEL_NEXT.
 */
int
create_item(item, event)
Panel_item item;
Event *event;
{
    Xv_pkg      *pkg;
    Panel       panel = (Panel)xv_get(item, XV_KEY_DATA, PANEL_KEY);
    Frame       frame = (Frame)xv_get(item, XV_KEY_DATA, FRAME_KEY);
    Panel_item  pi, pkg_item;
```

```
        char          buf[64];

        pkg_item = (Panel_item)xv_get(item, XV_KEY_DATA, PACKAGE_KEY);
        (void) strncpy(buf, xv_get(item, PANEL_VALUE), sizeof buf);
        if (!buf[0])
            return PANEL_NONE;
        switch((int)xv_get(pkg_item, PANEL_VALUE)) {
            case 1: pkg = PANEL_MESSAGE; break;
            case 2: pkg = PANEL_TEXT; break;
            default: pkg = PANEL_BUTTON;
        }
        /* loop thru all panel items and check for item with same name */
        PANEL_EACH_ITEM(panel, pi)
            if (!strcmp(buf, xv_get(pi, PANEL_LABEL_STRING))) {
                xv_set(frame, FRAME_LEFT_FOOTER, "Label Taken", NULL);
                return PANEL_NONE;
            }
        PANEL_END_EACH
        (void) xv_create(panel, pkg,
            PANEL_LABEL_STRING,       buf,
            PANEL_NOTIFY_PROC,        selected,
            XV_KEY_DATA,              FRAME_KEY,        frame,
            /* only for text items, but doesn't affect other items */
            PANEL_VALUE_DISPLAY_LENGTH, 10,
            PANEL_LAYOUT,             PANEL_HORIZONTAL,
            NULL);
        xv_set(item, PANEL_VALUE, "", NULL);
        return PANEL_NEXT;
    }

    /*
     * For panel buttons. return XV_OK or XV_ERROR if the item was
     * selected using the left mouse button or not.
     */
    int
    selected(item, event)
    Panel_item item;
    Event *event;
    {
        Frame         frame = (Frame)xv_get(item, XV_KEY_DATA, FRAME_KEY);
        char          buf[64];

        if (event_action(event) == ACTION_SELECT) {
            sprintf(buf, "'%s' selected", xv_get(item, PANEL_LABEL_STRING));
            xv_set(frame, FRAME_RIGHT_FOOTER, buf, NULL);
            return XV_OK;
        }
        return XV_ERROR;
    }

    /*
     * callback for the "Quit" item.  Destroy the frame, which
     * causes xv_main_loop() to return.
     */
    void
    quit(item, event)
    Panel_item item;
```

Example G-1. The item_move.c program (continued)

```
Event *event;
{
    Frame frame = (Frame)xv_get(item, XV_KEY_DATA, FRAME_KEY);
    if (event_action(event) == ACTION_SELECT)
        xv_destroy_safe(frame);
}
```

xv_termsw.c

This book has never discussed the *term* subwindow. Basically, it is a tty subwindow that can be edited like a text subwindow. It may also contain a scrollbar. *xv_termsw.c* shows you how to create a *term* subwindow.

Example G-2. The xv_termsw.c program

```
/*
 * xv_termsw.c
 * Demonstrate incorporation of a Term subwindow in an application;
 * keyboard input to the termsw can come either directly to the
 * termsw or from an adjoining panel text item.
 */
#include <stdio.h>
#include <xview/xview.h>
#include <xview/panel.h>
/* #include <xview/tty.h> */
#include <xview/termsw.h>

Termsw          term;
Panel_item      text_item;

main(argc,argv)
int     argc;
char    *argv[];
{
    Frame       frame;
    Panel       panel;
    int         notify_proc();

    xv_init(XV_INIT_ARGS, argc, argv, NULL);

    frame = (Frame)xv_create(NULL, FRAME, NULL);
    panel = (Panel)xv_create(frame, PANEL, NULL);
    text_item = (Panel_item)xv_create(panel, PANEL_TEXT,
        PANEL_LABEL_STRING,         "Command:",
        PANEL_NOTIFY_PROC,          notify_proc,
        PANEL_VALUE_DISPLAY_LENGTH, 20,
        NULL);
    (void) xv_create(panel, PANEL_BUTTON,
        PANEL_LABEL_STRING,     "Apply",
        PANEL_NOTIFY_PROC,      notify_proc,
        NULL);
    window_fit_height(panel);

    term = (Termsw)xv_create(frame, TERMSW, NULL);

    window_fit(frame);
    xv_main_loop(frame);
}

/*
 * This procedure is called when the user this return on the
 * panel text item or clicking on the <apply> button.
 * Use ttysw_input() to feed the string to the terminal window.
 */
int
notify_proc(item,event)
```

```
Panel_item        item;
Event     *event;
{
    char          str[81];

    sprintf(str, "%.81s\n", (char *)xv_get(text_item, PANEL_VALUE));
    ttysw_input(term, str, strlen(str));
    xv_set(text_item, PANEL_VALUE, "", NULL);
    return XV_OK;
}
```

scroll_cells2.c

This program is based heavily on *scroll_cells.c*, which is found in Chapter 10, *Scrollbars*. This version of the program deals with resize events. When a resize occurs, the `object`, `view`, and `page` length attributes are set to correctly reflect the size of the scrollbar with respect to the object it scrolls.

Example G-3. The scroll_cells2.c program

```
/*
 * scroll_cells2.c -- scroll a bitmap of cells around in a canvas.
 * This is a simplified version of scroll_cells.c graphically. That
 * is, it does not display icons, just rows and columns of cells.
 * The difference with this version is that it attempts to accommodate
 * resize events not addressed in the scroll_cells.c.
 * This new function is at the end of the file.
 */
#include <stdio.h>
#include <X11/X.h>
#include <X11/Xlib.h>      /* Using Xlib graphics */
#include <xview/xview.h>
#include <xview/canvas.h>
#include <xview/scrollbar.h>
#include <xview/xv_xrect.h>

#define CELL_WIDTH           64
#define CELL_HEIGHT          64
#define CELLS_PER_HOR_PAGE   5 /* when paging w/scrollbar */
#define CELLS_PER_VER_PAGE   5 /* when paging w/scrollbar */
#define CELLS_PER_ROW        16
#define CELLS_PER_COL        16

Pixmap          cell_map;         /* pixmap copied onto canvas window */
Scrollbar       horiz_scrollbar;
Scrollbar       vert_scrollbar;
GC              gc;               /* General usage GC */

main(argc, argv)
int argc;
char *argv[];
{
    Frame       frame;
    Canvas      canvas;
    void        repaint_proc(), resize_proc();

    /* Initialize, create frame and canvas... */
    xv_init(XV_INIT_ARGC_PTR_ARGV, &argc, argv, NULL);

    frame = xv_create(XV_NULL, FRAME,
        FRAME_LABEL,            argv[0],
        FRAME_SHOW_FOOTER,      TRUE,
        NULL);

    canvas = xv_create(frame, CANVAS,
        /* make subwindow the size of a "page" */
        XV_WIDTH,               CELL_WIDTH * CELLS_PER_HOR_PAGE,
        XV_HEIGHT,              CELL_HEIGHT * CELLS_PER_VER_PAGE,
        /* canvas is same size as window */
```

```
        CANVAS_WIDTH,               CELL_WIDTH * CELLS_PER_HOR_PAGE,
        CANVAS_HEIGHT,              CELL_HEIGHT * CELLS_PER_VER_PAGE,
        /* don't retain window -- we'll repaint it all the time */
        CANVAS_RETAINED,            FALSE,
        /* We're using Xlib graphics calls in repaint_proc() */
        CANVAS_X_PAINT_WINDOW,      TRUE,
        CANVAS_REPAINT_PROC,        repaint_proc,
        CANVAS_RESIZE_PROC,         resize_proc,
        OPENWIN_AUTO_CLEAR,         FALSE,
        NULL);
    /*
     * Create scrollbars attached to the canvas. When user clicks
     * on cable, page by the page size (PAGE_LENGTH). Scrolling
     * should move cell by cell, not by one pixel (PIXELS_PER_UNIT).
     */
    vert_scrollbar = xv_create(canvas, SCROLLBAR,
        SCROLLBAR_DIRECTION,             SCROLLBAR_VERTICAL,
        SCROLLBAR_PIXELS_PER_UNIT,       CELL_HEIGHT,
        NULL);
    horiz_scrollbar = xv_create(canvas, SCROLLBAR,
        SCROLLBAR_DIRECTION,             SCROLLBAR_HORIZONTAL,
        SCROLLBAR_PIXELS_PER_UNIT,       CELL_WIDTH,
        NULL);

    /*
     * create pixmap and draw cells into it.  This portion of the
     * program could use XCopyArea to render real bitmaps whose sizes
     * do not exceed whatever CELL_WIDTH and CELL_HEIGHT are defined
     * to be.  The cell_map will be copied into the window via
     * XCopyPlane in the repaint procedure.
     */
    {
        short           x, y, pt = 0;
        XPoint          points[256];
        XGCValues       gcvalues;
        Display *dpy = (Display *)xv_get(canvas, XV_DISPLAY);

        cell_map = XCreatePixmap(dpy, DefaultRootWindow(dpy),
            CELLS_PER_ROW * CELL_WIDTH + 1,
            CELLS_PER_COL * CELL_HEIGHT + 1,
            1); /* We only need a 1-bit deep pixmap */

        /* Create the gc for the cell_map -- since it is 1-bit deep,
         * use 0 and 1 for fg/bg values.  Also, limit number of
         * events generated by setting graphics exposures to False.
         */
        gcvalues.graphics_exposures = False;
        gcvalues.background = 0;
        gcvalues.foreground = 1;
        gc = XCreateGC(dpy, cell_map,
            GCForeground|GCBackground|GCGraphicsExposures, &gcvalues);

        /* dot every other pixel */
        for (x = 0; x <= CELL_WIDTH * CELLS_PER_ROW; x += 2)
            for (y = 0; y <= CELL_HEIGHT * CELLS_PER_COL; y += 2) {
                if (x % CELL_WIDTH != 0 && y % CELL_HEIGHT != 0)
                    continue;
```

Example Programs

```
                    points[pt].x = x, points[pt].y = y;
                    if (++pt == sizeof points / sizeof points[0]) {
                        XDrawPoints(dpy, cell_map, gc,
                            points, pt, CoordModeOrigin);
                        pt = 0;
                    }
                }
            if (pt != sizeof points) /* flush out the remaining points */
                XDrawPoints(dpy, cell_map, gc,
                            points, pt, CoordModeOrigin);
            /* label each cell indicating the its coordinates */
            for (x = 0; x < CELLS_PER_ROW; x++)
                for (y = 0; y < CELLS_PER_COL; y++) {
                    char buf[8];
                    sprintf(buf, "%d,%d", x+1, y+1);
                    XDrawString(dpy, cell_map, gc,
                        x * CELL_WIDTH + 5, y * CELL_HEIGHT + 25,
                        buf, strlen(buf));
                }
            /* we're now done with the cell_map, so free gc and
             * create a new one based on the window that will use it.
             */
            XFreeGC(dpy, gc);
            gcvalues.background = WhitePixel(dpy, DefaultScreen(dpy));
            gcvalues.foreground = BlackPixel(dpy, DefaultScreen(dpy));
            gcvalues.plane_mask = 1L;
            gc = XCreateGC(dpy, DefaultRootWindow(dpy),
                GCForeground|GCBackground|GCGraphicsExposures, &gcvalues);
        }

    /* shrink frame to minimal size and start notifier */
    window_fit(frame);
    xv_main_loop(frame);
}

/*
 * The repaint procedure is called whenever repainting is needed in
 * a paint window.  Since the canvas is not retained, this routine
 * is going to be called any time the user scrolls the canvas.  The
 * canvas will handle repainting the portion of the canvas that
 * was in view and has scrolled onto another viewable portion of
 * the window.  The xrects parameter will cover the new areas that
 * were not in view before and have just scrolled into view.  If
 * the window resizes or if the window is exposed by other windows
 * disappearing or cycling thru the window tree, then the number
 * of xrects will be more than one and we'll have to copy the new
 * areas one by one.  Clipping isn't necessary since the areas to
 * be rendered are set by the xrects value.
 */
void
repaint_proc(canvas, paint_window, dpy, win, xrects)
Canvas          canvas;
Xv_Window       paint_window;
Display         *dpy;
Window          win;
Xv_xrectlist    *xrects;
{
```

```
    int x, y;

    x = (int)xv_get(horiz_scrollbar, SCROLLBAR_VIEW_START);
    y = (int)xv_get(vert_scrollbar, SCROLLBAR_VIEW_START);

    for (xrects->count--; xrects->count >= 0; xrects->count--) {
        printf("top-left cell = %d, %d -- %d,%d %d,%d\n", x+1, y+1,
            xrects->rect_array[xrects->count].x,
            xrects->rect_array[xrects->count].y,
            xrects->rect_array[xrects->count].width,
            xrects->rect_array[xrects->count].height);

        XCopyPlane(dpy, cell_map, win, gc,
            x * CELL_WIDTH,
            y * CELL_HEIGHT,
            xv_get(paint_window, XV_WIDTH),
            xv_get(paint_window, XV_HEIGHT),
            0, 0, 1L);
    }
}

/*
 * If the application is resized, then we may wish to reset the
 * paging and viewing parameters for the scrollbars.
 */
void
resize_proc(canvas, new_width, new_height)
Canvas canvas;
int new_width, new_height;
{
    int page_w = (int)(new_width/CELL_WIDTH);
    int page_h = (int)(new_height/CELL_HEIGHT);

    if (!vert_scrollbar || !horiz_scrollbar)
        return;

    printf("new width/height in cells: w = %d, h = %d\n",
        page_w, page_h);

    xv_set(horiz_scrollbar,
        SCROLLBAR_OBJECT_LENGTH,         CELLS_PER_ROW,
        SCROLLBAR_PAGE_LENGTH,           page_w,
        SCROLLBAR_VIEW_LENGTH,           page_w,
        NULL);
    xv_set(vert_scrollbar,
        SCROLLBAR_OBJECT_LENGTH,         CELLS_PER_COL,
        SCROLLBAR_PAGE_LENGTH,           page_h,
        SCROLLBAR_VIEW_LENGTH,           page_h,
        NULL);
}
```

menu_dir2.c

In Chapter 11, *Menus*, the program *menu_dir.c* demonstrates the use of an XView menu in a canvas subwindow. A menu is brought up with the MENU mouse button and displays menu choices representing the files in the directory. The problem with *menu_dir.c* is that the entire menu cascade is created for all the subdirectories at the very beginning of the program. If the directory stack is very deep, it could take a very long time to build. You could also run out of memory in the process. Further, if the contents of the directory tree is dynamic, the menu entries could become invalid over time.

These problems are solved in *menu_dir2.c* because it creates only the top-level menu. For each directory entry under the top-level, rather than creating an associated pullright menu, a MENU_GEN_PULLRIGHT procedure is specified. This routine creates that menu only at the time it is needed. So, when the user invokes the menu and tries to descend into a submenu representing a subdirectory in the directory tree, only then is the directory entry searched and a new submenu created. When the user backs out of the menu, the menu is destroyed—attempting to re-enter the submenu causes the process to be repeated.

An exercise for the ambitious programmer would be to modify this program so that the submenus are not destroyed until the entire menu cascade has been dismissed. This enhancement would optimize the perceived performance of the program for the user because, once a directory subpath has been searched and a menu created, the menu is cached so that re-entry into the same submenu would be instantaneous.

Example G-4. The menu_dir2.c program

```
/*
 * menu_dir2.c -
 * Demonstrate the use of an XView menu in a canvas subwindow.
 * A menu is brought up with the MENU mouse button and displays
 * menu choices representing the files in the directory.  If a
 * directory entry is found, a new pullright item is created with
 * that subdir as the pullright menu's contents.  This implementation
 * creates directories on an as-needed basis.  Thus, we provide a
 * MENU_GEN_PULLRIGHT procedure.
 *
 * argv[1] indicates which directory to start from.
 */
#include <xview/xview.h>
#include <xview/canvas.h>
#include <sys/stat.h>
#include <sys/dir.h>
#include <X11/Xos.h>
#ifndef MAXPATHLEN
#include <sys/param.h>
#endif /* MAXPATHLEN */

Frame     frame;

main(argc,argv)
int       argc;
char      *argv[];
{
    Canvas        canvas;
```

```
    extern void exit();
    void        my_event_proc();
    Menu        menu;
    Menu_item   mi, add_path_to_menu();

    xv_init(XV_INIT_ARGC_PTR_ARGV, &argc, argv, NULL);

    frame = (Frame)xv_create(NULL, FRAME,
        FRAME_LABEL,                argv[1]? argv[1] : "cwd",
        FRAME_SHOW_FOOTER,          TRUE,
        NULL);
    canvas = (Canvas)xv_create(frame, CANVAS,
        FRAME_LABEL,      argv[0],
        XV_WIDTH,         400,
        XV_HEIGHT,        100,
        NULL);

    mi = add_path_to_menu(argc > 1? argv[1] : ".");
    menu = (Menu)xv_get(mi, MENU_PULLRIGHT);
    /* We no longer need the item since we have the menu from it */
    xv_destroy(mi);

    /* associate the menu to the canvas win for easy etreival */
    xv_set(canvas_paint_window(canvas),
        WIN_CONSUME_EVENTS,       WIN_MOUSE_BUTTONS, NULL,
        WIN_EVENT_PROC,           my_event_proc,
        WIN_CLIENT_DATA,          menu,
        NULL);

    window_fit(frame);
    window_main_loop(frame);
}

/*
 * my_action_proc - display the selected item in the frame footer.
 */
void
my_action_proc(menu, menu_item)
Menu    menu;
Menu_item        menu_item;
{
    xv_set(frame,
        FRAME_LEFT_FOOTER,        xv_get(menu_item, MENU_STRING),
        NULL);
}

/*
 * Call menu_show() to display menu on right mouse button push.
 */
void
my_event_proc(canvas, event)
Canvas  canvas;
Event *event;
{
    if ((event_id(event) == MS_RIGHT) && event_is_down(event)) {
        Menu menu = (Menu)xv_get(canvas, WIN_CLIENT_DATA);
        menu_show(menu, canvas, event, NULL);
    }
}
```

```
/*
 * return an allocated char * that points to the last item in a path.
 */
char *
getfilename(path)
char *path;
{
    char *p;

    if (p = rindex(path, '/'))
        p++;
    else
        p = path;
    return strcpy(malloc(strlen(p)+1), p);
}

/* gen_pullright() is called in the following order:
 *    Pullright menu needs to be displayed. (MENU_PULLRIGHT)
 *    Menu is about to be dismissed (MENU_DISPLAY_DONE)
 *        User made a selection (before menu notify function)
 *        After the notify routine has been called.
 * The above order is done whether or not the user makes a
 * menu selection.
 */
Menu
gen_pullright(mi, op)
Menu_item mi;
Menu_generate op;
{
    Menu menu;
    Menu_item new, old = mi;
    char buf[MAXPATHLEN];

    if (op == MENU_DISPLAY) {
        menu = (Menu)xv_get(mi, XV_OWNER);
        sprintf(buf, "%s/%s",
            xv_get(menu, MENU_CLIENT_DATA), xv_get(mi, MENU_STRING));
        /* get old menu and free it -- we're going to build another */
        if (menu = (Menu)xv_get(mi, MENU_PULLRIGHT)) {
            free(xv_get(menu, MENU_CLIENT_DATA));
            xv_destroy(menu);
        }
        if (new = add_path_to_menu(buf)) {
            menu = (Menu)xv_get(new, MENU_PULLRIGHT);
            xv_destroy(new);
            return menu;
        }
    }
    if (!(menu = (Menu)xv_get(mi, MENU_PULLRIGHT)))
            menu = (Menu)xv_create(NULL, MENU,
                MENU_STRINGS, "Couldn't build a menu.", NULL,
                NULL);
    return menu;
}

/*
 * The path passed in is scanned via readdir().  For each file in the
```

```
 * path, a menu item is created and inserted into a new menu.  That
 * new menu is made the PULLRIGHT_MENU of a newly created panel item
 * for the path item originally passed it.  Since this routine is
 * recursive, a new menu is created for each subdirectory under the
 * original path.
 */
Menu_item
add_path_to_menu(path)
char *path;
{
    DIR                 *dirp;
    struct direct       *dp;
    struct stat         s_buf;
    Menu_item           mi;
    Menu                next_menu;
    char                buf[MAXPATHLEN];
    static int          recursion;

    /* don't add a folder to the list if user can't read it */
    if (stat(path, &s_buf) == -1 || !(s_buf.st_mode & S_IREAD))
        return NULL;
    if (s_buf.st_mode & S_IFDIR) {
        int cnt = 0;
        if (!(dirp = opendir(path)))
            /* don't bother adding to list if we can't scan it */
            return NULL;
        if (recursion)
            return (Menu_item)-1;
        recursion++;
        next_menu = (Menu)xv_create(XV_NULL, MENU, NULL);
        while (dp = readdir(dirp))
            if (strcmp(dp->d_name, ".") && strcmp(dp->d_name, "..")) {
                (void) sprintf(buf, "%s/%s", path, dp->d_name);
                mi = add_path_to_menu(buf);
                if (!mi || mi == (Menu_item)-1) {
                    int do_gen_pullright = (mi == (Menu_item)-1);
                    /* unreadable file or dir - deactivate item */
                    mi = (Menu_item)xv_create(XV_NULL, MENUITEM,
                        MENU_STRING,   getfilename(dp->d_name),
                        MENU_RELEASE,
                        MENU_RELEASE_IMAGE,
                        NULL);
                    if (do_gen_pullright)
                        xv_set(mi,
                            MENU_GEN_PULLRIGHT, gen_pullright,
                            NULL);
                    else
                        xv_set(mi, MENU_INACTIVE, TRUE, NULL);
                }
                xv_set(next_menu, MENU_APPEND_ITEM, mi, NULL);
                cnt++;
            }
        closedir(dirp);
        mi = (Menu_item)xv_create(XV_NULL, MENUITEM,
            MENU_STRING,           getfilename(path),
            MENU_RELEASE,
```

```
                MENU_RELEASE_IMAGE,
                MENU_NOTIFY_PROC,     my_action_proc,
                NULL);
        if (!cnt) {
            xv_destroy(next_menu);
            /* An empty or unsearchable directory - deactivate item */
            xv_set(mi, MENU_INACTIVE, TRUE, NULL);
        } else {
            xv_set(next_menu,
                MENU_TITLE_ITEM, strcpy(malloc(strlen(path)+1), path),
                MENU_CLIENT_DATA, strcpy(malloc(strlen(path)+1), path),
                NULL);
            xv_set(mi, MENU_PULLRIGHT, next_menu, NULL);
        }
        recursion--;
        return mi;
    }
    return (Menu_item)xv_create(NULL, MENUITEM,
        MENU_STRING,             getfilename(path),
        MENU_RELEASE,
        MENU_RELEASE_IMAGE,
        MENU_NOTIFY_PROC,        my_action_proc,
        NULL);
}
```

type_font.c

This very simple program captures keyboard events in a canvas and uses XDrawString() to render what the user types. It also looks for backspacing. This is not intended to replace the text subwindow in any way, but rather to demonstrate how some text rendering functions can be implemented. See Chapter 16, *Fonts*, for more information about fonts.

Example G-5. The type_font.c program

```
/*
 * simple_font.c -- very simple program showing how to render text
 * using fonts loaded by XView.
 */
#include <ctype.h>
#include <X11/X.h>
#include <X11/Xlib.h>
#include <xview/xview.h>
#include <xview/panel.h>
#include <xview/font.h>

Display *dpy;
GC      gc;
XFontStruct *font_info;

main(argc, argv)
int     argc;
char    *argv[];
{
    Frame       frame;
    Panel       panel;
    Canvas      canvas;
    XGCValues   gcvalues;
    Xv_Font     font;
    void        my_event_proc();
    extern void exit();

    xv_init(XV_INIT_ARGC_PTR_ARGV, &argc, argv, NULL);

    frame = (Frame)xv_create(XV_NULL, FRAME,
        FRAME_LABEL,            argv[0],
        NULL);

    panel = (Panel)xv_create(frame, PANEL,
        PANEL_LAYOUT,           PANEL_VERTICAL,
        NULL);
    xv_create(panel, PANEL_BUTTON,
        PANEL_LABEL_STRING,     "Quit",
        PANEL_NOTIFY_PROC,      exit,
        NULL);
    window_fit(panel);

    canvas = (Canvas)xv_create(frame, CANVAS,
        XV_WIDTH,               400,
        XV_HEIGHT,              200,
        CANVAS_X_PAINT_WINDOW,  TRUE,
        NULL);
    xv_set(canvas_paint_window(canvas),
        WIN_EVENT_PROC,         my_event_proc,
```

```
        NULL);

    window_fit(frame);

    dpy = (Display *)xv_get(frame, XV_DISPLAY);
    font = (Xv_Font)xv_get(frame, XV_FONT);
    font_info = (XFontStruct *)xv_get(font, FONT_INFO);

    gcvalues.font = (Font)xv_get(font, XV_XID);
    gcvalues.foreground = BlackPixel(dpy, DefaultScreen(dpy));
    gcvalues.background = WhitePixel(dpy, DefaultScreen(dpy));
    gcvalues.graphics_exposures = False;
    gc = XCreateGC(dpy, RootWindow(dpy, DefaultScreen(dpy)),
        GCForeground | GCBackground | GCFont | GCGraphicsExposures, &gcvalues);

    xv_main_loop(frame);
}

void
my_event_proc(win, event)
Xv_Window win;
Event *event;
{
    static int x = 10, y = 10;
    Window xwin = (Window)xv_get(win, XV_XID);
    char c;

    if (event_is_up(event))
        return;

    if (event_is_ascii(event)) {
        c = (char)event_id(event);
        if (c == '\n' || c == '
            y += font_info->max_bounds.ascent +
                        font_info->max_bounds.descent;
            x = 10;
        } else if (c == 7 || c == 127) { /* backspace or delete */
            if (x > 10)
                x -= XTextWidth(font_info, "m", 1);
            /* use XDrawImageString to overwrite previous text */
            XDrawImageString(dpy, xwin, gc, x, y, "  ", 2);
        } else {
            XDrawString(dpy, xwin, gc, x, y, &c, 1);
            x += XTextWidth(font_info, &c, 1);
        }
    } else if (event_action(event) == ACTION_SELECT) {
        x = event_x(event);
        y = event_y(event);
    }
}
```

fonts.c

This program is similar to *type_font.c* above. However, *fonts.c* provides an interface for the user to pick and choose from a subset of the font families and styles available on the X server. If a font "name" is specified, then the family, style and size choices are ignored. Using the SELECT button on the canvas window positions the current typing location at the *x,y* coordinates of the button-down event. The characters typed are printed in the current font.

Example G-6. The fonts.c program

```
/*
 * fonts.c -- provide an interface for the user to pick and choose
 * between font families and styles known to XView.  The program
 * provides several panel buttons to choose between font types, and
 * a canvas window in which the user can type.  The characters typed
 * are printed in the current font.  If a font "name" is specified,
 * then the family, style and size are ignored.  Using the SELECT
 * button on the canvas window positions the current typing location
 * at the x,y coordinates of the button-down event.
 */
#include <ctype.h>
#include <X11/X.h>
#include <X11/Xlib.h>
#include <xview/xview.h>
#include <xview/panel.h>
#include <xview/font.h>

Display *dpy;
GC       gc;
XFontStruct *cur_font;
Panel_item family_item, style_item, scale_item, name_item;
int canvas_width;

main(argc, argv)
int      argc;
char     *argv[];
{
    Frame       frame;
    Panel       panel;
    Canvas      canvas;
    XGCValues   gcvalues;
    Xv_Font     font;
    void        change_font();
    void        my_event_proc(), my_resize_proc();
    int         change_font_by_name();
    extern void exit();

    xv_init(XV_INIT_ARGC_PTR_ARGV, &argc, argv, NULL);

    frame = (Frame)xv_create(XV_NULL, FRAME,
        FRAME_LABEL,            argv[0],
        FRAME_SHOW_FOOTER,      TRUE,
        NULL);

    panel = (Panel)xv_create(frame, PANEL,
        PANEL_LAYOUT,           PANEL_VERTICAL,
```

```
            NULL);
    (void) xv_create(panel, PANEL_BUTTON,
        PANEL_LABEL_STRING,     "Quit",
        PANEL_NOTIFY_PROC,      exit,
        NULL);
    family_item = (Panel_item)xv_create(panel, PANEL_CHOICE,
        PANEL_LABEL_STRING,     "Family",
        PANEL_LAYOUT,           PANEL_HORIZONTAL,
        PANEL_DISPLAY_LEVEL,    PANEL_CURRENT,
        PANEL_CHOICE_STRINGS,
            FONT_FAMILY_DEFAULT, FONT_FAMILY_DEFAULT_FIXEDWIDTH,
            FONT_FAMILY_LUCIDA, FONT_FAMILY_LUCIDA_FIXEDWIDTH,
            FONT_FAMILY_ROMAN, FONT_FAMILY_SERIF, FONT_FAMILY_COUR,
            FONT_FAMILY_CMR, FONT_FAMILY_GALLENT,
            FONT_FAMILY_OLGLYPH, FONT_FAMILY_OLCURSOR, NULL,
        PANEL_NOTIFY_PROC,      change_font,
        NULL);
    style_item = (Panel_item)xv_create(panel, PANEL_CHOICE,
        PANEL_LABEL_STRING,     "Style",
        PANEL_LAYOUT,           PANEL_HORIZONTAL,
        PANEL_DISPLAY_LEVEL,    PANEL_CURRENT,
        PANEL_CHOICE_STRINGS,
            FONT_STYLE_DEFAULT, FONT_STYLE_NORMAL, FONT_STYLE_BOLD,
            FONT_STYLE_ITALIC, FONT_STYLE_BOLD_ITALIC, NULL,
        PANEL_NOTIFY_PROC,      change_font,
        NULL);
    scale_item = (Panel_item)xv_create(panel, PANEL_CHOICE,
        PANEL_LABEL_STRING,     "Scale",
        PANEL_LAYOUT,           PANEL_HORIZONTAL,
        PANEL_DISPLAY_LEVEL,    PANEL_CURRENT,
        PANEL_CHOICE_STRINGS,
            "Small", "Medium", "Large", "X-Large", NULL,
        PANEL_NOTIFY_PROC,      change_font,
        NULL);
    name_item = (Panel_item)xv_create(panel, PANEL_TEXT,
        PANEL_LABEL_STRING,     "Font Name:",
        PANEL_LAYOUT,           PANEL_HORIZONTAL,
        PANEL_VALUE_DISPLAY_LENGTH, 20,
        PANEL_NOTIFY_PROC,      change_font_by_name,
        NULL);
    window_fit(panel);

    canvas = (Canvas)xv_create(frame, CANVAS,
        XV_WIDTH,               400,
        XV_HEIGHT,              200,
        CANVAS_X_PAINT_WINDOW,  TRUE,
        CANVAS_RESIZE_PROC,     my_resize_proc,
        NULL);
    xv_set(canvas_paint_window(canvas),
        WIN_EVENT_PROC,         my_event_proc,
        WIN_CONSUME_EVENT,      LOC_WINENTER,
        NULL);

    window_fit(frame);

    dpy = (Display *)xv_get(frame, XV_DISPLAY);
    font = (Xv_Font)xv_get(frame, XV_FONT);
```

```
    cur_font = (XFontStruct *)xv_get(font, FONT_INFO);
    xv_set(frame, FRAME_LEFT_FOOTER, xv_get(font, FONT_NAME), NULL);

    gcvalues.font = cur_font->fid;
    gcvalues.foreground = BlackPixel(dpy, DefaultScreen(dpy));
    gcvalues.background = WhitePixel(dpy, DefaultScreen(dpy));
    gcvalues.graphics_exposures = False;
    gc = XCreateGC(dpy, RootWindow(dpy, DefaultScreen(dpy)),
        GCForeground | GCBackground | GCFont | GCGraphicsExposures,
        &gcvalues);

    xv_main_loop(frame);
}

void
my_event_proc(win, event)
Xv_Window win;
Event *event;
{
    static int x = 10, y = 10;
    Window xwin = (Window)xv_get(win, XV_XID);
    char c;

    if (event_is_up(event))
        return;

    if (event_is_ascii(event)) {
        c = (char)event_action(event);
        XDrawString(dpy, xwin, gc, x, y, &c, 1);
        /* advance x to next position.  If over edge, linewrap */
        if ((x += XTextWidth(cur_font, &c, 1)) >= canvas_width) {
            y += cur_font->max_bounds.ascent +
                    cur_font->max_bounds.descent;
            x = 10;
        }
    } else if (event_action(event) == ACTION_SELECT) {
        x = event_x(event);
        y = event_y(event);
    } else if (event_action(event) == LOC_WINENTER)
        win_set_kbd_focus(win, xwin);
}

/*
 * check resizing so we know how wide to allow the user to type.
 */
void
my_resize_proc(canvas, width, height)
Canvas canvas;
int width, height;
{
    canvas_width = width;
}

void
change_font(item, value, event)
Panel_item    item;
Event         *event;
{
    static int  family, style, scale;
```

```
    char            buf[128];
    Frame           frame;
    char            *family_name;
    char            *style_name;
    int             scale_value;
    Xv_Font         font;

    frame = (Frame)xv_get(xv_get(item, PANEL_PARENT_PANEL), XV_OWNER);
    family_name = (char *)xv_get(family_item, PANEL_CHOICE_STRING,
                                    xv_get(family_item, PANEL_VALUE));
    style_name = (char *)xv_get(style_item, PANEL_CHOICE_STRING,
                                    xv_get(style_item, PANEL_VALUE));
    scale_value = (int) xv_get(scale_item, PANEL_VALUE);
    xv_set(frame, FRAME_BUSY, TRUE, NULL);
    font = (Xv_Font)xv_find(frame, FONT,
        FONT_FAMILY,     family_name,
        FONT_STYLE,      style_name,
        /* scale_value happens to coincide with Window_rescale_state */
        FONT_SCALE,      scale_value,
        /*
         * If run on a server that cannot rescale fonts, only font
         * sizes that exist should be passed
         */
        FONT_SIZES_FOR_SCALE, 12, 14, 16, 22,
        NULL);
    xv_set(frame, FRAME_BUSY, FALSE, NULL);

    if (!font) {
        if (item == family_item) {
            sprintf(buf, "cannot load '%s'", family_name);
            xv_set(family_item, PANEL_VALUE, family, NULL);
        } else if (item == style_item) {
            sprintf(buf, "cannot load '%s'", style_name);
            xv_set(style_item, PANEL_VALUE, style, NULL);
        } else {
            sprintf(buf, "Not available in %s scale.",
                xv_get(scale_item, PANEL_CHOICE_STRING, scale));
            xv_set(scale_item, PANEL_VALUE, scale, NULL);
        }
        xv_set(frame, FRAME_RIGHT_FOOTER, buf, NULL);
        return;
    }
    if (item == family_item)
        family = value;
    else if (item == style_item)
        style = value;
    else
        scale = value;
    cur_font = (XFontStruct *)xv_get(font, FONT_INFO);
    XSetFont(dpy, gc, cur_font->fid);
    sprintf(buf, "Current font: %s", xv_get(font, FONT_NAME));
    xv_set(frame, FRAME_LEFT_FOOTER, buf, NULL);
}

change_font_by_name(item, event)
Panel_item item;
Event *event;
```

```
{
    char buf[128];
    char *name = (char *)xv_get(item, PANEL_VALUE);
    Frame frame = (Frame)xv_get(xv_get(item, XV_OWNER), XV_OWNER);
    Xv_Font font;

    xv_set(frame, FRAME_BUSY, TRUE, NULL);
    font = (Xv_Font)font = (Xv_Font)xv_find(frame, FONT,
        FONT_NAME,          name,
        NULL);
    xv_set(frame, FRAME_BUSY, FALSE, NULL);

    if (!font) {
        sprintf(buf, "cannot load '%s'", name);
        xv_set(frame, FRAME_RIGHT_FOOTER, buf, NULL);
        return PANEL_NONE;
    }
    cur_font = (XFontStruct *)xv_get(font, FONT_INFO);
    XSetFont(dpy, gc, cur_font->fid);
    sprintf(buf, "Current font: %s", xv_get(font, FONT_NAME));
    xv_set(frame, FRAME_LEFT_FOOTER, buf, NULL);
    return PANEL_NONE;
}
```

seln.c

seln.c is a simple program demonstrating some uses of the selection service. See Chapter 18, *The Selection Service*, for more information.

Example G-7. The seln.c program

```
/*
 * seln.c -- print the primary selection from the server.  If the
 * selection is in a text subwindow, then print information about
 * the line number(s) the selection spans and the indexes of the
 * bytes within the textsw's text stream.  This simple program
 * may not be sufficient for general usage -- see comments in
 * get_selection() comments below.
 */
#include <stdio.h>
#include <xview/xview.h>
#include <xview/textsw.h>
#include <xview/panel.h>
#include <xview/server.h>
#include <xview/seln.h>

Xv_Server       server;
Textsw          textsw;

char *get_selection();

main(argc, argv)
char *argv[];
{
    Frame       frame;
    Panel       panel;
    void        print_seln(), exit();

    xv_init(XV_INIT_ARGC_PTR_ARGV, &argc, argv, NULL);

    frame = (Frame) xv_create(NULL, FRAME,
        FRAME_LABEL,            argv[0],
        NULL);
    panel = (Panel) xv_create(frame, PANEL,
        WIN_WIDTH,              WIN_EXTEND_TO_EDGE,
        NULL);
    (void) xv_create(panel, PANEL_BUTTON,
        PANEL_LABEL_STRING,     "Quit",
        PANEL_NOTIFY_PROC,      exit,
        NULL);
    (void) xv_create(panel, PANEL_BUTTON,
        PANEL_LABEL_STRING,     "Get Selection",
        PANEL_NOTIFY_PROC,      print_seln,
        NULL);
    window_fit(panel);

    textsw = (Textsw)xv_create(frame, TEXTSW,
        WIN_X,                  0,
        WIN_BELOW,              panel,
        WIN_ROWS,               10,
        WIN_COLUMNS,            80,
        TEXTSW_FILE_CONTENTS,   "/etc/passwd",
        NULL);
```

```
    window_fit(frame);

    server = (Xv_Server)xv_get(xv_get(frame, XV_SCREEN), SCREEN_SERVER);

    xv_main_loop(frame);
}

void
print_seln()
{
    char *text = get_selection();

    if (text)
        printf("---selection---\n%s\n---end seln---0, text);
}

/*
 * Get the selection using selection_ask().  Note that if the
 * selection is bigger than about 2K, the whole selection will
 * not be gotten with one call, thus this method of getting the
 * selection may not be sufficient.
 */
char *
get_selection()
{
    long            sel_lin_num, lines_selected;
    Textsw_index    first, last;
    Seln_holder     holder;
    Seln_result     result;
    int             len;
    Seln_request    *request;
    static char     selection_buf[BUFSIZ];
    register char   *ptr;

    /* get the holder of the primary selection */
    holder = selection_inquire(server, SELN_PRIMARY);

    /* If the selection occurs in the text subwindow, print lots
     * of info about the selection.
     */
    if (seln_holder_same_client(&holder, textsw)) {
        /* ask for information from the selection service */
        request = selection_ask(server, &holder,
            /* get the index of the first and last chars in seln */
            SELN_REQ_FIRST,              NULL,
            SELN_REQ_LAST,              NULL,
            /* get the actual selection bytes */
            SELN_REQ_CONTENTS_ASCII,    NULL,
            /* fool the textsw to think entire lines are selected */
            SELN_REQ_FAKE_LEVEL,        SELN_LEVEL_LINE,
            /* line numbers of beginning and ending of the seln */
            SELN_REQ_FIRST_UNIT,        NULL,
            SELN_REQ_LAST_UNIT,         NULL,
            NULL);
        /* set the ptr to beginning of data -- SELN_REQ_FIRST */
        ptr = request->data;
        /* "first" is data succeeding SELN_REQ_FIRST -- skip attr */
        first = *(Textsw_index *)(ptr += sizeof(SELN_REQ_FIRST));
        ptr += sizeof(Textsw_index); /* skip over value of "first" */
```

Example Programs

```
            /* "last" is data succeeding SELN_REQ_LAST -- skip attr */
            last  = *(Textsw_index *)(ptr += sizeof(SELN_REQ_LAST));
            ptr += sizeof(Textsw_index); /* skip over value of "last" */

            /* advance pointer past SELN_REQ_CONTENTS_ASCII */
            ptr += sizeof(SELN_REQ_CONTENTS_ASCII);
            len = strlen(ptr); /* length of string in request */
            (void) strcpy(selection_buf, ptr);
            /*
             * advance pointer past length of string.  If the string
             * length isn't aligned to a 4-byte boundary, add the
             * difference in bytes -- then advance pointer passed "value".
             */
            if (len % 4)
                len = len + (4 - (len % 4));
            ptr += len + sizeof(Seln_attribute); /* skip over "value" */

            /* advance past SELN_REQ_FAKE_LEVEL, SELN_LEVEL_LINE */
            ptr += sizeof(SELN_REQ_FAKE_LEVEL) + sizeof(SELN_LEVEL_LINE);

            sel_lin_num = *(long *)(ptr += sizeof(SELN_REQ_FIRST_UNIT));
            ptr += sizeof(long);
            lines_selected = *(long *)(ptr += sizeof(SELN_REQ_LAST_UNIT));
            ptr += sizeof(long);

            /* hack to workaround bug with SELN_REQ_LAST_UNIT always
             * returning -1.  We have to count the line numbers ourselves.
             */
            if (lines_selected < 0) {
                register char *p;
                lines_selected++;
                for (p = selection_buf; *p; p++)
                    if (*p == '\n')
                        lines_selected++;
            }
            printf("index in textsw: %d-%d, line number(s) = %d-%d\n",
                first+1, last+1, sel_lin_num+1,
                sel_lin_num+lines_selected+1);
    } else {
        /* the selection is not in the text subwindow */
        request = selection_ask(server, &holder,
            SELN_REQ_CONTENTS_ASCII, NULL,
            NULL);
        if (request->status != SELN_SUCCESS) {
            printf("selection_ask() returns %d\n", request->status);
            return "";
        }
        (void) strcpy(selection_buf,
            request->data + sizeof(SELN_REQ_CONTENTS_ASCII));
    }
    return selection_buf;
}
```

seln_line.c

seln_line.c demonstrates another use of the selection service. See Chapter 18, *The Selection Service*, for more information.

Example G-8. The seln_line.c program

```c
/*
 * seln_line.c -- demonstrate how to use the selection service to get
 * the line number of the primary selection in a textsw.
 */
#include <stdio.h>
#include <xview/xview.h>
#include <xview/textsw.h>
#include <xview/panel.h>
#include <xview/seln.h>

Textsw  textsw;

main(argc, argv)
char *argv[];
{
    Frame        frame;
    Panel        panel;
    void         exit();
    int          seln_proc();

    xv_init(XV_INIT_ARGC_PTR_ARGV, &argc, argv, NULL);

    frame = (Frame)xv_create(NULL, FRAME,
        FRAME_SHOW_FOOTER,       TRUE,
        NULL);

    panel = (Panel)xv_create(frame, PANEL,
        WIN_WIDTH,               WIN_EXTEND_TO_EDGE,
        NULL);

    (void) xv_create(panel, PANEL_BUTTON,
        PANEL_LABEL_STRING,      "Quit",
        PANEL_NOTIFY_PROC,       exit,
        NULL);
    (void) xv_create(panel, PANEL_BUTTON,
        PANEL_LABEL_STRING,      "Get Selection",
        PANEL_NOTIFY_PROC,       seln_proc,
        PANEL_CLIENT_DATA,       frame,
        NULL);
    (void) xv_create(panel, PANEL_TEXT,
        PANEL_LABEL_STRING,              "No-op:",
        PANEL_VALUE_DISPLAY_LENGTH,      30,
        NULL);

    window_fit(panel);

    textsw = (Textsw)xv_create(frame, TEXTSW,
        WIN_X,                   0,
        WIN_BELOW,               panel,
        WIN_ROWS,                10,
        WIN_COLUMNS,             80,
        TEXTSW_FILE_CONTENTS,    "/etc/passwd",
```

```
        NULL);
    window_fit(frame);
    xv_main_loop(frame);
}

int
seln_proc(item, event)
Panel_item item;
Event *event; /* unused */
{
    Frame           frame = (Frame)xv_get(item, PANEL_CLIENT_DATA);
    Seln_holder     holder;
    Seln_request   *buffer;
    int             line_number;
    char           *msg[32];

    /*
     * get primary selection
     */
    holder = seln_inquire(SELN_PRIMARY);
    /*
     * ask for the data containing line number of the first
     * character of the selection
     */
    buffer = seln_ask(&holder,
        SELN_REQ_FAKE_LEVEL, SELN_LEVEL_LINE,
        SELN_REQ_FIRST_UNIT, 0,
        NULL);
    /*
     * determine the window that contains the selection
     */
    if (seln_holder_same_client(&holder, textsw)) {
        xv_set(frame,
            FRAME_LEFT_FOOTER, "selection in textsw",
            NULL);
        /*
         * convert data into the line number
         */
        sprintf(msg, "Selection: line %ld",
            *(long *)(buffer->data + 3 * sizeof(Seln_attribute)));
        xv_set(frame,
            FRAME_RIGHT_FOOTER, msg,
            NULL);
    } else
        xv_set(frame,
            FRAME_LEFT_FOOTER, "selection elsewhere",
            NULL);

    return XV_OK;
}
```

x_draw.c

This program uses several Xlib drawing functions to draw various types of geometric objects. We integrate the XView color model (see Chapter 20, *Color*) to render each object in a different color.

Example G-9. The x_draw.c program

```c
/*
 * x_draw.c -- demonstrates the use of Xlib drawing functions
 * inside an XView canvas.  Color is used, but not required.
 */
#include <xview/xview.h>
#include <xview/canvas.h>
#include <xview/cms.h>
#include <xview/xv_xrect.h>

/* indices into color table renders specified colors. */
#define WHITE    0
#define RED      1
#define GREEN    2
#define BLUE     3
#define ORANGE   4
#define AQUA     5
#define PINK     6
#define BLACK    7

GC gc;                  /* GC used for Xlib drawing */
unsigned long *colors;  /* the color table */

/*
 * initialize cms data to support colors specified above.  Assign
 * data to new cms -- use either static or dynamic cms depending
 * on -dynamic command line switch.
 */
main(argc, argv)
int     argc;
char    *argv[];
{
    static char stipple_bits[] = {0xAA, 0xAA, 0x55, 0x55};
    static Xv_singlecolor cms_colors[] = {
        { 255, 255, 255 },
        { 255, 0, 0 },
        { 0, 255, 0 },
        { 0, 0, 255 },
        { 250, 130, 80 },
        { 30, 230, 250 },
        { 230, 30, 250 },
    };
    Cms            cms;
    Frame          frame;
    Canvas         canvas;
    XFontStruct    *font;
    Display        *display;
    XGCValues      gc_val;
    XID            xid;
    void           canvas_repaint();
```

```
    Xv_cmsdata   cms_data;
    int          use_dynamic = FALSE;

    /* Create windows */
    xv_init(XV_INIT_ARGC_PTR_ARGV, &argc, argv, NULL);
    if (*++argv && !strcmp(*argv, "-dynamic"))
        use_dynamic = TRUE;

    frame = xv_create(NULL, FRAME,
        FRAME_LABEL,     "xv_canvas_x_draw",
        XV_WIDTH,        400,
        XV_HEIGHT,       300,
        NULL);

    cms = xv_create(NULL, CMS,
        CMS_SIZE,        7,
        CMS_TYPE,        use_dynamic? XV_DYNAMIC_CMS : XV_STATIC_CMS,
        CMS_COLORS,      cms_colors,
        NULL);

    canvas = xv_create(frame, CANVAS,
        CANVAS_REPAINT_PROC,     canvas_repaint,
        CANVAS_X_PAINT_WINDOW,   TRUE,
        WIN_DYNAMIC_VISUAL,      use_dynamic,
        WIN_CMS,                 cms,
        NULL);

    /* Get display and xid */
    display = (Display *)xv_get(frame, XV_DISPLAY);
    xid = (XID)xv_get(canvas_paint_window(canvas), XV_XID);

    if (!(font = XLoadQueryFont(display, "fixed"))) {
        puts("cannot load fixed font");
        exit(1);
    }

    /* Create and initialize GC */
    gc_val.font = font->fid;
    gc_val.stipple =
        XCreateBitmapFromData(display, xid, stipple_bits, 16, 2);
    gc = XCreateGC(display, xid, GCFont | GCStipple, &gc_val);

    /* get the colormap from the canvas now that
     * the cms has been installed
     */
    colors = (unsigned long *)xv_get(canvas, WIN_X_COLOR_INDICES);

    /* Start event loop */
    xv_main_loop(frame);
}

/*
 * Draws onto the canvas using Xlib drawing functions.
 */
void
canvas_repaint(canvas, pw, display, xid, xrects)
    Canvas          canvas;
    Xv_Window       pw;
    Display         *display;
    Window          xid;
```

```
Xv_xrectlist      *xrects;
{
    static XPoint box[] = {
        {0,0}, {100,100}, {0,-100}, {-100,100}, {0,-100}
    };
    static XPoint points[] = {
        {0,0}, /* this point to be overwritten below */
        {25,0}, {25,0}, {25,0}, {25,0}, {-100,25},
        {25,0}, {25,0}, {25,0}, {25,0}, {-100,25},
        {25,0}, {25,0}, {25,0}, {25,0}, {-100,25},
        {25,0}, {25,0}, {25,0}, {25,0}, {-100,25},
        {25,0}, {25,0}, {25,0}, {25,0}, {-100,25},
    };

    XSetForeground(display, gc, colors[RED]);
    XDrawString(display, xid, gc, 30, 20, "XFillRectangle", 14);
    XFillRectangle(display, xid, gc, 25, 25, 100, 100);
    XSetFunction(display, gc, GXinvert);
    XFillRectangle(display, xid, gc, 50, 50, 50, 50);
    XSetFunction(display, gc, GXcopy);

    XSetForeground(display, gc, colors[BLACK]);
    XDrawString(display, xid, gc, 155, 20, "XFillRect - stipple", 19);
    XSetFillStyle(display, gc, FillStippled);
    XFillRectangle(display, xid, gc, 150, 25, 100, 100);
    XSetFillStyle(display, gc, FillSolid);

    XSetForeground(display, gc, colors[BLUE]);
    XDrawString(display, xid, gc, 280, 20, "XDrawPoints", 11);
    points[0].x = 275; points[0].y = 25;
    XDrawPoints(display, xid, gc, points,
        sizeof(points)/sizeof(XPoint), CoordModePrevious);

    XSetForeground(display, gc, colors[ORANGE]);
    XDrawString(display, xid, gc, 30, 145, "XDrawLine - solid", 17);
    XDrawLine(display, xid, gc, 25, 150, 125, 250);
    XDrawLine(display, xid, gc, 25, 250, 125, 150);

    XSetForeground(display, gc, colors[AQUA]);
    XDrawString(display, xid, gc, 155, 145, "XDrawLine - dashed", 18);
    XSetLineAttributes(display, gc, 5,
        LineDoubleDash, CapButt, JoinMiter);
    XDrawLine(display, xid, gc, 150, 150, 250, 250);
    XDrawLine(display, xid, gc, 150, 250, 250, 150);
    XSetLineAttributes(display, gc, 0, LineSolid, CapButt, JoinMiter);

    XSetForeground(display, gc, colors[PINK]);
    XDrawString(display, xid, gc, 280, 145, "XDrawLines", 10);
    box[0].x = 275; box[0].y = 150;
    XDrawLines(display, xid, gc, box, 5, CoordModePrevious);

    XSetForeground(display, gc, colors[GREEN]);
    XDrawRectangle(display, xid, gc,
        5, 5, xv_get(pw, XV_WIDTH)-10, xv_get(pw, XV_HEIGHT)-10);
    XDrawRectangle(display, xid, gc,
        7, 7, xv_get(pw, XV_WIDTH)-14, xv_get(pw, XV_HEIGHT)-14);
}
```

Example Programs

The Logo.c Module

In Chapter 22, *XView Internals*, the methods for writing XView extensions is discussed. Example G-10 contains all the functions outlined in the chapter. The chapter also contains listings of the header files required by this module.

Example G-10. The Logo.c Module

```
/*
 * Logo.c -- a XView object class that paints an X logo in a window.
 * This object is subclassed from the window object to take advantage
 * of the window it creates.  This object has no attributes, so the
 * set and get functions are virtually empty.  The only internal
 * fields used by this object are a GC and a Pixmap.  The GC is used
 * to paint the Pixmap into the window.  The window object has no GC
 * associated with it or we would have inherited it.  This will
 * probably go away in the next version of XView.
 */
#include "logo_impl.h"
#include <xview/notify.h>
#include <xview/cms.h>
#include <X11/bitmaps/xlogo32>

/* declare the "methods" used by the logo class. */
static int logo_init(), logo_destroy();
static Xv_opaque logo_set(), logo_get();
static void logo_repaint();

Xv_pkg logo_pkg = {
    "Logo",                     /* package name */
    ATTR_PKG_UNUSED_FIRST,      /* package ID */
    sizeof(Logo_public),        /* size of the public struct */
    WINDOW,                     /* subclassed from the window package */
    logo_init,
    logo_set,
    logo_get,
    logo_destroy,
    NULL                        /* disable the use of xv_find() */
};

/* the only thing this object does is paint an X into its own window.
 * This is the event handling routine that is used to check for
 * Expose or Configure event requests.  the configure event clears
 * the window and the "expose" event causes a repaint of the X image.
 * The GC has its foreground and background colros set from the
 * CMS of the window from which this logo object is subclassed.
 */
static void
logo_redraw(logo_public, event)
Logo_public     *logo_public;
Event           *event;
{
    Logo_private *logo_private = LOGO_PRIVATE(logo_public);
    XEvent *xevent = event_xevent(event);

    if (xevent->xany.type == Expose && xevent->xexpose.count == 0) {
        Display *dpy = (Display *)xv_get(logo_public, XV_DISPLAY);
        Window window = (Window)xv_get(logo_public, XV_XID);
```

```
        int width = (int)xv_get(logo_public, XV_WIDTH);
        int height = (int)xv_get(logo_public, XV_HEIGHT);
        int x = (width - xlogo32_width)/2;
        int y = (height - xlogo32_height)/2;

        XCopyPlane(dpy, logo_private->bitmap, window, logo_private->gc,
            0, 0, xlogo32_width, xlogo32_height, x, y, 1L);
    } else if (xevent->xany.type == ConfigureNotify)
        XClearArea(xv_get(logo_public, XV_DISPLAY),
            xv_get(logo_public, XV_XID), 0, 0,
            xevent->xconfigure.width, xevent->xconfigure.height, True);

}

/* initialize the logo object -- create (alloc) an instance of it.
 * There are two parts to an object class: a public part and a private
 * part.  Each contains a pointer to the other, so link the two
 * together and initialize the remaining fields of the logo data
 * structure.  This includes creating the Xlogo pixmap.  However,
 * we do no initialize the logo's GC because it is dependent on its
 * window's cms and that isn't assigned to the window till the "set"
 * method.  See logo_set() below.
 */
static int
logo_init(owner, logo_public, avlist)
Xv_opaque       owner;
Logo_public     *logo_public;
Attr_avlist     avlist; /* ignored here */
{
    Logo_private *logo_private = xv_alloc(Logo_private);
    Display *dpy;
    Window win;

    if (!logo_private)
        return XV_ERROR;

    dpy = (Display *)xv_get(owner, XV_DISPLAY);
    win = (Window)xv_get(logo_public, XV_XID);

    /* link the public to the private and vice-versa */
    logo_public->private_data = (Xv_opaque)logo_private;
    logo_private->public_self = (Xv_opaque)logo_public;

    /* create the 1-bit deep pixmap of the X logo */
    if ((logo_private->bitmap = XCreatePixmapFromBitmapData(dpy, win,
        xlogo32_bits, xlogo32_width, xlogo32_height,
        1, 0, 1)) == NULL) {
        free(logo_private);
        return XV_ERROR;
    }
    /* set up event handlers to get resize and repaint events */
    xv_set(logo_public,
        WIN_NOTIFY_SAFE_EVENT_PROC,      logo_redraw,
        WIN_NOTIFY_IMMEDIATE_EVENT_PROC, logo_redraw,
        NULL);

    return XV_OK;
}

/* logo_set() -- the function called to set attributes in a logo
```

```
 * object.  This function is called when a logo is created after
 * the init routine as well as when the programmer calls xv_set.
 */
static Xv_opaque
logo_set(logo_public, avlist)
Logo_public *logo_public;
Attr_avlist avlist;
{
    Logo_private *logo_private = LOGO_PRIVATE(logo_public);
    Attr_attribute *attrs;

    for (attrs = avlist; *attrs; attrs = attr_next(attrs))
        switch ((int) attrs[0]) {
            case XV_END_CREATE : {
                /* this stuff *must* be here rather than in the "init"
                 * routine because the CMS is not loaded into the
                 * window object until the "set" routines are called.
                 */
                Cms cms = xv_get(logo_public, WIN_CMS);
                XGCValues gcvalues;
                Display *dpy =
                    (Display *)xv_get(logo_public, XV_DISPLAY);
                gcvalues.foreground =
                    x(unsigned long)v_get(cms, CMS_FOREGROUND_PIXEL);
                gcvalues.background =
                    (unsigned long)xv_get(cms, CMS_BACKGROUND_PIXEL);
                gcvalues.graphics_exposures = False;
                logo_private->gc = XCreateGC(dpy,
                    xv_get(logo_public, XV_XID),
                    GCForeground|GCBackground|GCGraphicsExposures,
                    &gcvalues);
            }
            default :
                xv_check_bad_attr(LOGO, attrs[0]);
                break;
        }

    return XV_OK;
}

/* logo_get() -- There are no logo attributes to get, so just return */
static Xv_opaque
logo_get(logo_public, status, attr, args)
Logo_public     *logo_public;
int             *status;
Attr_attribute  attr;
Attr_avlist     args;
{
    *status = xv_check_bad_attr(LOGO, attr);
    return (Xv_opaque)XV_OK;
}

/* destroy method: free the pixmap and the GC before freeing the object */
static int
logo_destroy(logo_public, status)
Logo_public     *logo_public;
Destroy_status  status;
```

Example G-10. The Logo.c Module (continued)

```
{
    Logo_private *logo_private = LOGO_PRIVATE(logo_public);

    if (status == DESTROY_CLEANUP) {
        XFreePixmap(xv_get(logo_public, XV_DISPLAY),
            logo_private->bitmap);
        XFreeGC(xv_get(logo_public, XV_DISPLAY), logo_private->gc);
        free(logo_private);
    }

    return XV_OK;
}
```

The Bitmap.c Module

In Chapter 22, *XView Internals*, the Bitmap package was introduced, but not fully listed. The following listing contains the entire Bitmap package implementation except for its header files (which are listed in the chapter).

Example G-11. The Bitmap.c Module

```
/*
 * Bitmap.c -- an XView object class that displays an arbitrary
 * pixmap.  This is similar to the Logo object, but the programmer
 * may specify the bitmap to use via the BITMAP_FILE attribute.
 */
#include "bitmap_impl.h"
#include <xview/notify.h>
#include <xview/cms.h>
#include <X11/Xutil.h>

/* declare the "methods" used by the bitmap class. */
static int bitmap_init(), bitmap_destroy();
static Xv_opaque bitmap_set(), bitmap_get();
static void bitmap_repaint();

Xv_pkg bitmap_pkg = {
    "Bitmap2",               /* package name */
    ATTR_PKG_BITMAP,         /* package ID */
    sizeof(Bitmap_public),   /* size of the public struct */
    WINDOW,                  /* subclassed from the window package */
    bitmap_init,
    bitmap_set,
    bitmap_get,
    bitmap_destroy,
    NULL                     /* disable the use of xv_find() */
};

static void
bitmap_redraw(bitmap_public, event)
Bitmap_public      *bitmap_public;
Event              *event;
{
    Bitmap_private *bitmap_private = BITMAP_PRIVATE(bitmap_public);
    XEvent *xevent = event_xevent(event);

    if (bitmap_private->bitmap &&
        xevent->xany.type == Expose && xevent->xexpose.count == 0) {
        Display *dpy = (Display *)xv_get(bitmap_public, XV_DISPLAY);
        Window window = (Window)xv_get(bitmap_public, XV_XID);
        int width = (int)xv_get(bitmap_public, XV_WIDTH);
        int height = (int)xv_get(bitmap_public, XV_HEIGHT);
        int x = (width - bitmap_private->width)/2;
        int y = (height - bitmap_private->height)/2;

        XCopyPlane(dpy, bitmap_private->bitmap, window,
            bitmap_private->gc, 0, 0, bitmap_private->width,
            bitmap_private->height, x, y, 1L);
    } else if (xevent->xany.type == ConfigureNotify)
        XClearArea(xv_get(bitmap_public, XV_DISPLAY),
            xv_get(bitmap_public, XV_XID), 0, 0,
```

```
                xevent->xconfigure.width, xevent->xconfigure.height,
                True);
}

/* initialize the bitmap object by creating (alloc) an instance
 * of it.  There are two parts to an object class: a public part
 * and a private part.  Each contains a pointer to the other, so
 * link the two together and initialize the remaining fields of
 * the bitmap data structure.  Do no initialize the bitmap's GC
 * because it is dependent on its window's cms and that isn't
 * assigned to the window till the "set" method.  Also, wait till
 * till the "set" method to initialize the bitmap file specified.
 */
static int
bitmap_init(owner, bitmap_public, avlist)
Xv_opaque       owner;
Bitmap_public    *bitmap_public;
Attr_avlist      avlist; /* ignored here */
{
    Bitmap_private *bitmap_private = xv_alloc(Bitmap_private);

    if (!bitmap_private)
        return XV_ERROR;

    /* link the public to the private and vice-versa */
    bitmap_public->private_data = (Xv_opaque)bitmap_private;
    bitmap_private->public_self = (Xv_opaque)bitmap_public;

    /* set up event handlers to get resize and repaint events */
    xv_set(bitmap_public,
        WIN_NOTIFY_SAFE_EVENT_PROC,      bitmap_redraw,
        WIN_NOTIFY_IMMEDIATE_EVENT_PROC, bitmap_redraw,
        NULL);

    return XV_OK;
}

/* bitmap_set() -- the function called to set attributes in a bitmap
 * object.  This function is called when a bitmap is created after
 * the init routine as well as when the programmer calls xv_set.
 */
static Xv_opaque
bitmap_set(bitmap_public, avlist)
Bitmap_public *bitmap_public;
Attr_avlist avlist;
{
    Bitmap_private *bitmap_private = BITMAP_PRIVATE(bitmap_public);
    Attr_attribute *attrs;

    for (attrs = avlist; *attrs; attrs = attr_next(attrs))
        switch ((int) attrs[0]) {
            case BITMAP_FILE : {
                int val, x, y;
                Display *dpy =
                    (Display *)xv_get(bitmap_public, XV_DISPLAY);
                Window window =
                    (Window)xv_get(bitmap_public, XV_XID);
                Pixmap old = bitmap_private->bitmap;
                if (XReadBitmapFile(dpy, window, attrs[1],
```

```
                            &bitmap_private->width, &bitmap_private->height,
                            &bitmap_private->bitmap, &x, &y) != BitmapSuccess)
                    {
                        xv_error(bitmap_public,
                            ERROR_STRING, "Unable to load bitmap file",
                            ERROR_PKG,     BITMAP,
                            NULL);
                        bitmap_private->bitmap = old;
                    }
                    break;
                }
            case BITMAP_PIXMAP :
                xv_error(bitmap_public,
                    ERROR_CANNOT_SET, attrs[0],
                    ERROR_PKG,         BITMAP,
                    NULL);
                break;
            case XV_END_CREATE : {
                /* this stuff *must* be here rather than in the "init"
                 * routine because the CMS is not loaded into the
                 * window object until the "set" routines are called.
                 */
                Cms cms = xv_get(bitmap_public, WIN_CMS);
                XGCValues gcvalues;
                Display *dpy =
                    (Display *)xv_get(bitmap_public, XV_DISPLAY);
                gcvalues.foreground =
                    (unsigned long)xv_get(cms, CMS_FOREGROUND_PIXEL);
                gcvalues.background =
                    (unsigned long)xv_get(cms, CMS_BACKGROUND_PIXEL);
                gcvalues.graphics_exposures = False;
                bitmap_private->gc =
                    XCreateGC(dpy, xv_get(bitmap_public, XV_XID),
                        GCForeground|GCBackground|GCGraphicsExposures,
                        &gcvalues);
            }
            default :
                xv_check_bad_attr(BITMAP, attrs[0]);
                break;
        }
    return XV_OK;
}

static Xv_opaque
bitmap_get(bitmap_public, status, attr, args)
Bitmap_public    *bitmap_public;
int              *status;
Attr_attribute   attr;
Attr_avlist      args;
{
    Bitmap_private *bitmap_private = BITMAP_PRIVATE(bitmap_public);

    switch ((int) attr) {
        case BITMAP_PIXMAP :
            return (Xv_opaque)bitmap_private->bitmap;
        case BITMAP_FILE : /* can't get this attribute */
        default :
```

```
                *status = xv_check_bad_attr(BITMAP, attr);
                return (Xv_opaque)XV_OK;
        }
}

/* destroy method: free the pixmap and the GC before freeing object */
static int
bitmap_destroy(bitmap_public, status)
Bitmap_public       *bitmap_public;
Destroy_status      status;
{
    Bitmap_private *bitmap_private = BITMAP_PRIVATE(bitmap_public);

    if (status == DESTROY_CLEANUP) {
        if (bitmap_private->bitmap)
            XFreePixmap(xv_get(bitmap_public, XV_DISPLAY),
                bitmap_private->bitmap);
        XFreeGC(xv_get(bitmap_public, XV_DISPLAY),
            bitmap_private->gc);
        free(bitmap_private);
    }
    return XV_OK;
}
```

Index

CURSOR_X_HOT attribute 486
CURSOR_Y_HOT attribute 486

D

DefaultColormap macro 407
defaults.h header file 334
defaults (See also resources) 331
  package 331 - 339
defaults_get_boolean procedure 335
defaults_get_character procedure 336
defaults_get_enum procedure 337
defaults_get_integer procedure 336
defaults_get_string procedure 337
defaults_init procedure 334
defaults_load_db procedure 334
defaults_set_boolean procedure 335
defaults_set_character procedure 336
defaults_set_integer procedure 336
defaults_set_string procedure 337
defaults_store_db procedure 334
delayed binding 241, 294
destroying frames 73
DESTROY_CHECKING 381, 394
DESTROY_CLEANUP 394
DESTROY_PROCESS_DEATH 381, 394
DESTROY_SAVE_YOURSELF Destroy_status 395
Destroy_status 394
  DESTROY_SAVE_YOURSELF 395
destruction of objects 394
  safe 381
dispatching by Notifier, explicit 397
  implicit 397
dispatching, explicit 399
Display structure 301
display, distinguished from screen 6
displaying frames 66
distributed processing, about 6
drag and drop operation 121
draw programs 80
drawing in a canvas 79
dup2 system call 385

E

edit log 192
editing (See text subwindow)
enum, ITIMER_REAL 372
  ITIMER_VIRTUAL 372
  NOTIFY_ASYNC 370
  NOTIFY_SYNC 370

enumerated resources 337
enumerated type, ERROR_NON_RECOVERABLE 431
  ERROR_RECOVERABLE 431
environment variable, HELPPATH 434, 437
error handling, advanced usage 430
  Xlib errors 429
errors, advanced usage 430
  at run time 427
  recovery 427
  types 430
  Xlib 429
ERROR_BAD_ATTR attribute 430
ERROR_BAD_VALUE attribute 430
ERROR_CANNOT_GET attribute 430
ERROR_CANNOT_SET attribute 430
ERROR_CREATE_ONLY attribute 430
ERROR_INVALID_OBJECT attribute 430
ERROR_LAYER attribute 431
ERROR_NON_RECOVERABLE enumerated type 431
ERROR_PKG attribute 431
error_proc procedure 428
ERROR_RECOVERABLE enumerated type 431
ERROR_SERVER_ERROR attribute 431
ERROR_SEVERITY attribute 431
ERROR_STRING attribute 431
escape sequences, sending to TTY subwindows 211
event handling, in CANVAS package 96
event-driven input handling 366
event, ACTION_DRAG_COPY 122
  ACTION_DRAG_MOVE 122
  ACTION_MENU 242
  ACTION_SELECT 117, 155
  Expose 82
  GraphicsExpose 82
  KBD_DONE 113
  KBD_USE 113, 120
  LOC_DRAG 96, 112
  LOC_MOVE 96, 112
  LOC_WINENTER 96, 112, 120
  LOC_WINEXIT 96, 112
  MapNotify 53
  MS_LEFT 117
  realize 53
  SCROLLBAR_REQUEST 232
  WIN_ASCII_EVENTS 96, 113
  WIN_CIRCULATE_NOTIFY 115
  WIN_COLORMAP_NOTIFY 112
  WIN_CREATE_NOTIFY 115
  WIN_DESTROY_NOTIFY 115
  WIN_GRAPHICS_EXPOSE 114
  WIN_GRAVITY_NOTIFY 115
  WIN_LEFT_KEYS 113

XView Programming Manual

getting coordinate position 286
motion events 112
position 116
mouse; button events; registering interest in 111
MS_LEFT event 117

N

nonexclusive choice 152
nonvisual objects 301 - 313
about 33
NOTICE package 271 - 280
use of FULLSCREEN package 309
notice.h header file 272
notice, about 27, 271
creating 272
displaying 272
implementation 271
origin 273
responses 274
suppressing beep 277
triggers 275
NOTICE_BUTTON attribute 275, 494
NOTICE_BUTTON_NO attribute 274, 494
NOTICE_BUTTON_YES attribute 274, 494
NOTICE_FOCUS_XY attribute 273, 494
NOTICE_FONT attribute 494
NOTICE_MESSAGE_STRINGS attribute 275, 494
NOTICE_MESSAGE_STRINGS_ARRAY_PTR attribute
    433, 494
NOTICE_NO attribute 396
NOTICE_NO_BEEPING attribute 277, 494
notice_prompt procedure 272
notice_prompt procedure 522
NOTICE_TRIGGER attribute 494
NOTICE_YES attribute 396
notification procedures, in a text subwindow
    203
notification, menus 256
Notifier procedures, notify_default_wait3 377
notify_do_dispatch 397
notify_interpose_destroy_func 393
notify_interpose_event_func 391
notify_next_event_func 392
notify_post_destroy 381
notify_post_event 382
notify_post_event_and_arg 380
notify_set_destroy_func 369
notify_set_exception_func 370
notify_set_input_func 370, 383
notify_set_itimer_func 367, 372
notify_set_output_func 370, 383

notify_set_signal_func 370 - 371
notify_set_wait3_func 369, 377
notify_veto_destroy 394
Notifier 38, 365 - 402
about 10, 365
base event handler 390
client events 378
client 368
control 396
definition 367
destroy event delivery time 381
error codes 400
explicit dispatching 397, 399
file descriptors 382
flow of control in Notifier-based programs 35
handling X events 52
implicit dispatching 397
interposing on frame open/close 391
interposing on resize events 393
interposition 390
miscellaneous issues 402
operation 366
overview 35
pipes 385
posting client events 379
posting destroy events 381
posting events with an argument 380
posting events 382
procedures of 366
prohibited signals 369
reading 383
role of xv_main_loop procedure 52
safe destruction 381
signal handling 369
SIGTERM handling 376
timers 372
notify procedure 35
notify.h header file 368
Notify_arg 380, 382
NOTIFY_ASYNC enum 370
NOTIFY_BADF 400
NOTIFY_BAD_ITIMER 400
NOTIFY_BAD_SIGNAL 400
Notify_client 382
Notify_copy 380
NOTIFY_COPY_NULL 380
notify_default_wait3 procedure 377
NOTIFY_DESTROY_VETOED 381, 400
notify_dispatch procedure 397
NOTIFY_DONE 377, 382
notify_do_dispatch procedure 397

Index

Z

NAME _____

COMPANY _____

ADDRESS _____

CITY _____ STATE ____ ZIP _____

BUSINESS REPLY MAIL

FIRST CLASS MAIL PERMIT NO. 80 SEBASTOPOL, CA

POSTAGE WILL BE PAID BY ADDRESSEE

O'Reilly & Associates, Inc.

632 Petaluma Avenue
Sebastopol, CA 95472-9902

NAME _____

COMPANY _____

ADDRESS _____

CITY _____ STATE ____ ZIP _____

BUSINESS REPLY MAIL

FIRST CLASS MAIL PERMIT NO. 80 SEBASTOPOL, CA

POSTAGE WILL BE PAID BY ADDRESSEE

O'Reilly & Associates, Inc.

632 Petaluma Avenue
Sebastopol, CA 95472-9902

O'Reilly & Associates, Inc.

Creators and Publishers of Nutshell Handbooks,
concise, down-to-earth guides on selected UNIX topics

The X Window System series:

Vol. 0   *X Protocol Reference Manual*
Vol. 1   *Xlib Programming Manual*
Vol. 2   *Xlib Reference Manual*
Vol. 3   *X Window User's Guide*
Vol. 4   *X Toolkit Intrinsics Progamming Manual*
Vol. 5   *X Toolkit Intrinsics Reference Manual*
Vol. 7   *XView Programming Manual*

and   *The X Window System in a Nutshell,*
a quick reference

Send me more information on:

❑ O'Reilly catalog and newsletter
❑ Placing a standing order for new titles
❑ Retail sales
❑ Corporate sales
❑ Bookstore locations
❑ Overseas distributors
❑ Upcoming books on the subject:

_____

_____

❑ Writing a Nutshell Handbook

O'Reilly & Associates, Inc.

Creators and Publishers of Nutshell Handbooks,
concise, down-to-earth guides on selected UNIX topics

The X Window System series:

Vol. 0   *X Protocol Reference Manual*
Vol. 1   *Xlib Programming Manual*
Vol. 2   *Xlib Reference Manual*
Vol. 3   *X Window User's Guide*
Vol. 4   *X Toolkit Intrinsics Progamming Manual*
Vol. 5   *X Toolkit Intrinsics Reference Manual*
Vol. 7   *XView Programming Manual*

and   *The X Window System in a Nutshell,*
a quick reference

Send me more information on:

❑ O'Reilly catalog and newsletter
❑ Placing a standing order for new titles
❑ Retail sales
❑ Corporate sales
❑ Bookstore locations
❑ Overseas distributors
❑ Upcoming books on the subject:

_____

_____

❑ Writing a Nutshell Handbook